P9-EDU-871

Directory of Unpublished
Experimental Mental Measures

VOLUME 7

BERT A. GOLDMAN, EDD
Professor of Education
University of North Carolina at Greensboro

DAVID F. MITCHELL, PHD
Assistant Professor of Sociology
University of North Carolina at Greensboro

PAULA E. EGELSON, EDD
Senior Research Specialist
SouthEastern Regional Vision for Education
University of North Carolina at Greensboro

Series Editors: Bert A. Goldman and David F. Mitchell

American Psychological Association, Washington, DC

Copyright © 1997 by the American Psychological Association.
All rights reserved. Except as permitted under the United States
Copyright Act of 1976, no part of this publication may be reproduced or
distributed in any form or by any means, or stored in a database or retrieval system, without the prior written permission of the publisher.

Published by
American Psychological Association
750 First Street, NE
Washington, DC 20002

Copies may be ordered from
APA Order Department
P.O. Box 92984
Washington, DC 20090-2984

In the UK and Europe, copies may be ordered from
American Psychological Association
3 Henrietta Street
Covent Garden, London
WC2E 8LU England

Compositor: Jennie Ruby, EDTEC Editorial Technologies,
Arlington, VA

Printer: United Book Press, Baltimore, MD

Cover and Text Designer: Minker Design, Bethesda, MD

ISBN: 1-55798-449-2

Printed in the United States of America
First Edition

Contents

AUGUSTANA UNIVERSITY COLLEGE
LIBRARY

iii

...

Preface

Purpose: This *Directory of Unpublished Experimental Mental Measures*, Volume 7, marks the seventh in a series of publications designed to fill a need for reference tools in behavioral and social science research. The authors believe there is an ongoing need for a directory such as this to enable researchers to determine what types of noncommercial experimental test instruments are currently in use. This reference provides researchers with ready access to information about recently developed or recently used experimental measurement scales. The instruments are not evaluated, but the information given about each test should make it possible for researchers to make a preliminary judgment of its usefulness. It does not provide all necessary information for researchers contemplating the use of a particular instrument. It does describe basic test properties and in most cases identifies additional sources from which technical information concerning an instrument can be obtained.

Development: Thirty-seven relevant professional journals available to the authors were examined. The following list includes those journals which, in the judgment of the authors, contained instruments of value to researchers in education, psychology, and sociology. Foreign journals were not surveyed for use in this directory. Measures identified in dissertations were excluded as a matter of expediency and because the microfilm abstracts generally contain minimal information.

American Journal of Sociology
Brain and Language
Career Development Quarterly
Child Development
Child Study Journal
Educational and Psychological Measurement
Educational Research Quarterly
Gifted Child Quarterly
Journal of Applied Psychology
Journal of College Student Development
Journal of Consulting and Clinical Psychology
Journal of Counseling Psychology
Journal of Creative Behavior
Journal of Educational Psychology
Journal of Educational Research
Journal of Experimental Education
Journal of General Psychology
Journal of Marriage and the Family
Journal of Occupational Psychology
Journal of Personality Assessment
Journal of Psychopathology and Behavioral Assessment

Journal of Research and Development in Education
Journal of Research in Personality
Journal of School Psychology
Journal of Social Psychology
Journal of Vocational Behavior
Measurement and Evaluation in Counseling and Development
Perceptual and Motor Skills
Personnel Psychology
Psychological Reports
Research in Higher Education
School Counselor
Social Psychology Quarterly
Sociology of Education
Sociology and Social Research
Vocational Guidance Quarterly

Volume 7 lists tests described in the 1991-1995 issues of the previously cited journals. An attempt was made to omit commercially published standardized tests, task-type activities such as memory word lists used in serial learning research, and achievement tests developed for a single, isolated course of study. The reader should not assume that the instruments described herein form a representative sample of the universe of unpublished experimental mental measures.

Organization: Following is a brief description of each of the 24 categories under which the authors grouped the measures of Volume 7.

Achievement: Measure learning and/or comprehension in specific areas. Also includes tests of memory and tests of spatial ability.

Adjustment—Educational: Measure academic satisfaction. Also includes tests of school anxiety.

Adjustment—Psychological: Evaluate conditions and levels of adjustment along the psychological dimension, including, for example, tests of mood, fear of death, anxiety, depression, etc.

Adjustment—Social: Evaluate aspects of interactions with others. Also includes tests of alienation, conformity, need for social approval, social desirability, instruments for assessing interpersonal attraction and sensitivity.

Adjustment—Vocational: Identify burnout, vocational maturity, job-related stress, job frustration, job satisfaction, etc.

Aptitude: Predict success in given activities.

Attitude: Measure reaction to a variety of experiences and objects.

Behavior: Measure general and specific types of activities such as classroom behavior, drug-use behavior, abusive and violent behavior.

Communication: Evaluate information exchange. Also includes tests of self-disclosure and counselor/client interaction.

Concept Meaning: Measure one's understanding of words and other concepts. Also includes tests of conceptual structure and style, and information processing.

Creativity: Measure ability to reorganize data or information into unique configurations. Also includes tests of divergent thinking.

Development: Measure emerging characteristics, primarily for preschool ages. Also includes tests of identity, cognitive, and moral development.

Family: Measure intrafamily relations. Also includes tests of marital satisfaction, nurturance, parental interest, and warmth.

Institutional Information: Evaluate institutions and their functioning, community and involvement satisfaction, and organizational climate.

Motivation: Measure goal strength. Also includes measures of curiosity and need to achieve.

Perception: Determine how one sees self and other objects. Also includes tests dealing with empathy, imagery, locus of control, self-concept, self-esteem, and time.

Personality: Measure general personal attributes. Also includes biographical information, defense mechanisms, and temperament.

Preference: Identify choices. Also includes tests of preference for objects, taste preference, and sex-role preference.

Problem-Solving and Reasoning: Measure general ability to reason through a number of alternative solutions, to generate such solutions to problems, etc.

Status: Identify a hierarchy of acceptability.

Trait Measurement: Identify and evaluate unitary traits. Also includes tests of anger, anxiety, authoritarianism, blame, cheating, and narcissism.

Values: Measure worth one ascribes to an object or activity. Includes tests of moral, philosophical, political, and religious values.

Vocational Evaluation: Evaluate a person for a specific position.

Vocational Interest: Measure interest in specific occupations and vocations as well as interest in general categories of activity.

The choice of the category under which each test was grouped was determined by the purpose of the test and/or its apparent content. The authors attempted to include basic facts for each test. Three facts are always listed. They are test name, purpose, and source. In addition, at least four of the following facts (starred in the list below) had to be present in the source in order for the test to be listed in the *Directory:* number of items, time required, format, reliability, validity, or related research. Readers should note that if no information was given for any one of the starred facts, the heading was not included in the entry. For example, if no information about validity was given in the source, validity was not listed in the test entry.

Test Name

The name of the test listed in the *Directory* was usually given by the author of the paper in which it was found. When a name was not given in the source, one was created for it by the authors of the *Directory.*

Purpose

The general purpose of each scale was usually stated in the source, or was suggested by its name. When available, additional detail about the test's purpose is given.

Description

Number of items: The number of items in a scale as stated in the source.

Time required: Few scales are administered under a time constraint. When they are, the time requirements are specified here.

Format: The descriptions of the formats of the scales varied widely in the sources. The authors of the *Directory* have presented the essential characteristics of the format such as general type (Likert, true-false, checklist, and semantic differential). Less common formats are briefly described in additional detail as needed.

Statistics

Reliability: When available, reliabilities and the Ns on which they were based are reported. Commonly reported reliabilities are Alpha, split-half, item-total, and KR-20.

Validity: When available, validity data were reported. The authors of the *Directory* have also included correlations with other tests and group difference information that help define the characteristic being measured by the test.

Source

Author

Title

Journal (Includes date of publication, volume, and page number)

*Related Research

The purpose of this section is to provide additional information about the test. In some cases the original source of the test is given. If an existing test was revised for use with a special population, the original version may be cited. In other cases, a publication that offered additional technical information is listed.

Readers should note that the numbers within the indexes refer to test numbers, not page numbers. As a convenience to readers, the authors have incorporated the indexes from the six previous volumes into the subject index and in doing so have converted all page numbers in Volume 1 to test numbers. Thus, numbers 1 through 339 refer to tests in Volume 1, numbers 340 through 1034 refer to tests in Volume 2, numbers 1035 through 1595 refer to tests in Volume 3, numbers 1596 through 2369 refer to tests in Volume 4, numbers 2370 through 3665 refer to tests in Volume 5, and numbers 3666 through 5363 refer to tests in Volume 6. Numbers 5364 through 7441 refer to tests in Volume 7.

The authors thank Julia Capone and Deetra Thompson for typing the manuscript. Special appreciation is expressed to Richard Allen for doing the complex and time-consuming final sorting and processing of the entries included in this volume. Their efforts made it

∎ ∎ ∎

possible to finish the manuscript on schedule. Further, the authors wish to thank the American Psychological Association for continuing the publication of the *Directories*.

Bert Arthur Goldman

David F. Mitchell

Paula Egelson

CHAPTER 1
Achievement

5364

Test Name: ADOLESCENT AIDS SURVEY

Purpose: To measure AIDS knowledge.

Number of Items: 21

Format: Correct responses determined scores.

Reliability: Alpha was .42.

Authors: Toennies, L. M., and Zagumny, M. J.

Article: Association of demographic characteristics, knowledge, and worry about HIV infection with occupational and non-occupational behaviors of medical students.

Journal: *Psychological Reports*, April 1994, *74*(2), 587–593.

Related Research: Tesch, B., et al. (1989). Knowledge of AIDS among healthcare students. *Wisconsin Medical Journal, 88*, 16–18.

■■■

5365

Test Name: AIDS KNOWLEDGE TEST

Purpose: To determine knowledge about HIV transmission.

Number of Items: 30

Format: Responses are made on true–false–don't-know format.

Reliability: Standardized alpha coefficient was .76.

Authors: Kauth, M. R., et al.

Article: HIV sexual risk reduction among college women: Applying a peer influence model.

Journal: *Journal of College Student Development*, September 1993, *34*(4), 346–351.

Related Research: DiClemente, R. J., et al. (1986). Adolescents and AIDS: A survey of knowledge, attitudes and beliefs about AIDS in San Francisco. *American Journal of Public Health, 76*, 1443–1445.

■■■

5366

Test Name: AIDS KNOWLEDGE QUESTIONNAIRE

Purpose: To measure AIDS knowledge.

Number of Items: 18

Format: True–false–don't-know format. All items are presented.

Reliability: Alpha was .76.

Validity: Correlations with other variables ranged from .21 to .22.

Authors: Kyes, K. B., and Tumbelaka, L.

Article: Comparison of Indonesian and American college students' attitudes toward homosexuality.

Journal: *Psychological Reports*, February 1994, *74*(1), 227–237.

■■■

5367

Test Name: AIDS PREVENTION SURVEY

Purpose: To assess knowledge and attitudes about AIDS among ethnically varied college students.

Format: Likert format.

Reliability: Alphas ranged from .61 to .84.

Validity: Beta coefficients were –.36 (reality distortion) and .14 (hallucinations and delusions).

Author: Bassman, L.

Article: Reality testing and self-reported AIDS self-care behavior.

Journal: *Psychological Reports*, February 1992, *70*(1), 59–65.

Related Research: Thomas, S. B. (1987). Minority health research laboratories AIDS prevention survey. Unpublished manuscript, University of Maryland.

■■■

5368

Test Name: AIDS RISK KNOWLEDGE TEST

Purpose: To assess practical knowledge of AIDS risk behavior.

Number of Items: 24

Format: Responses are made using a true–false format.

Reliability: Cronbach's alpha was .68.

Author: St. Lawrence, J. S.

Article: African-American adolescents' knowledge, health-related attitudes, sexual behavior and contraceptive decisions: implications for the prevention of adolescent HIV infection.

Journal: *Journal of Consulting and Clinical Psychology*, February 1993, *61*(1), 104–112.

Related Research: Kelly, J. A., et al. (1990). Psychological factors that predict AIDS high-risk versus AIDS precautionary behavior. *Journal of Consulting and Clinical Psychology, 58*, 117–120.

5369

Test Name: AUTHOR RECOGNITION TEST

Purpose: To measure amount of exposure to print in children.

Number of Items: 40

Format: Includes 25 children's authors and 15 foil names. All items are presented.

Reliability: Split-half (odd/even) corrected reliability was .86. Cronbach's alpha was .81.

Validity: Correlations with other variables ranged from -.27 to .70.

Authors: Allen, L., et al.

Article: Multiple indicators of children's reading habits and attitudes: Construct validity and cognitive correlates.

Journal: *Journal of Educational Psychology*, December 1992, *84*(4), 489–503.

Related Research: Cunningham, A. E., & Stanovich, K. E. (1991). Tracking the unique effects of print exposure in children: Associations with vocabulary, general knowledge, and spelling. *Journal of Educational Psychology*, *83*, 264–274.

■ ■ ■

5370

Test Name: BASEBALL KNOWLEDGE TEST

Purpose: To measure knowledge of baseball.

Number of Items: 39

Format: Multiple-choice items.

Reliability: KR-20 reliability was .81.

Validity: Correlations with other variables ranged from -.27 to .53.

Authors: Benton, S. L., et al.

Article: Knowledge, interest, and narrative writing.

Journal: *Journal of Educational Psychology*, March 1995, *87*(1), 66–79.

Related Research: Recht, D.R., & Leslie, L. (1988). Effect of prior knowledge on good and poor readers' memory of text. *Journal of Educational Psychology*, *80*, 16–20.

■ ■ ■

5371

Test Name: COGNITIVE ACHIEVEMENT BATTERY ON SCIENTIFIC LITERACY

Purpose: To measure knowledge of science, application of science, and integration of science.

Number of Items: 60

Format: Multiple-choice. Sample items are presented.

Reliability: Reliability was .89.

Author: Reynolds, A. J.

Article: Note on adolescents' time-use and scientific literacy.

Journal: *Psychological Reports*, February 1991, *68*(1), 63–70.

Related Research: Miller, J. D., et al. (1990). Longitudinal study of American youth: Base year (1987–1988) and second year (1988–1989) user's manual and codebook: Student, parent and teacher data. DeKalb: Northern Illinois University, Public Opinion Laboratory.

■ ■ ■

5372

Test Name: COGNITIVE SKILLS INVENTORY

Purpose: To measure cognitive skills.

Number of Items: 40

Format: Includes four factors: integration, repetition, monitoring, and coping. There is a Spanish version. Twenty-eight of the items are presented.

Reliability: Reliability coefficients for the Spanish version ranged from .55 to .84.

Authors: Moreno, V., and DiVesta, F. J.

Article: Cross-cultural comparisons of study habits.

Journal: *Journal of Educational Psychology*, June 1991, *83*(2), 231–239.

Related Research: DiVesta, F. J., & Moreno, V. (1990). *Development of the Cognitive Skills Inventory* (CSI). Unpublished manuscript.

■ ■ ■

5373

Test Name: CULTURAL KNOWLEDGE CHECKLIST

Purpose: To determine familiarity with some historical events and individuals that shaped modern society.

Number of Items: 144

Format: Half of the items are correct and half are foil items. Subjects check those items they know. All items are presented.

Reliability: Split-half corrected reliability was .85.

Validity: Correlations with other variables ranged from -.20 to .88.

Authors: Stanovich, K. E., and Cunningham, A. E.

Article: Where does knowledge come from? Specific associations between print exposure and information acquisition.

Journal: *Journal of Educational Psychology*, June 1993, *85*(2), 211–229.

■ ■ ■

5374

Test Name: "FEELING GOOD" BOOKLET TEST

Purpose: To test for

comprehension on the information presented in the booklet "Feeling Good."

Number of Items: 58

Format: Responses are made using a true–false format.

Reliability: Split-half reliability coefficient was .81. Coefficient alpha was .84.

Authors: Jamison, C., and Scogin, F.

Article: The outcome of cognitive bibliotherapy with depressed adults.

Journal: *Journal of Consulting and Clinical Psychology*, August 1995, *63*(4), 624–635.

Related Research: Jamison, C., & Scogin, F. (1989, March). *Cognitive bibliotherapy test.* Paper presented at the 35th annual meeting of the Southeastern Psychological Association, Washington, DC.

■ ■ ■

5375

Test Name: GENERAL PSYCHOLOGY COMPETENCY EXAMINATION

Purpose: To assess one's knowledge of general psychology.

Number of Items: 30

Format: Multiple-choice.

Validity: Correlation with final grades was .42.

Authors: Fehrmann, M. L., et al.

Article: The Angoff cutoff score method: The impact of frame-of-reference rater training.

Journal: *Educational and Psychological Measurement*, Winter 1991, *51*(4), 857–874.

Related Research: Fehrmann, M. L. (1989). *Standard setting: Frame of reference training, generalizability training, and the Angoff method.* Unpublished

master's thesis, Texas A&M University, Department of Psychology, College Station, TX.

■ ■ ■

5376

Test Name: HIV DISEASE KNOWLEDGE QUESTIONNAIRE

Purpose: To measure knowledge of HIV disease.

Number of Items: 13

Format: Open-ended questioning format. All items presented, along with scoring rules.

Reliability: Test–retest ranged from .53 to .78 for periods from 1 to 6 months among normal, retarded, and psychiatric-patient participants.

Validity: Scores increased following 4 hours of instruction about HIV disease ($p < .05$).

Authors: McCown, W., and Johnson, J.

Article: The Basic HIV Disease Knowledge Questionnaire: A Rasch-scale instrument to measure essential HIV knowledge.

Journal: *Psychological Reports*, October 1991, *69*(2), 543–549.

■ ■ ■

5377

Test Name: KNOWLEDGE OF DEPRESSION TEST

Purpose: To test patients' spouses' knowledge about depression.

Number of Items: 30

Format: True–false format. Sample items are presented.

Reliability: Alpha was .98.

Validity: Correlation with years of education was .45.

Authors: Bauserman, S. A. K., et al.

Article: Marital attributions in

spouses of depressed patients.

Journal: *Journal of Psychopathology and Behavioral Assessment*, September 1995, *17*(3), 231–249

■ ■ ■

5378

Test Name: KNOWLEDGE OF DEVELOPMENT SCALE

Purpose: To assess knowledge of normal development and developmental disabilities.

Number of Items: 27

Format: Forced-choice questionnaire.

Validity: Correlations with other variables ranged from -.33 to .70.

Author: Bailey, W. T.

Article: Fathers' knowledge of development and involvement with preschool children.

Journal: *Perceptual and Motor Skills*, December 1993, *77*(3) Part 1, 1032–1034.

Related Research: Shea, V., & Fowler, M. G. (1983). Parental and pediatric trainee knowledge of development. *Development and Behavioral Pediatrics, 4*, 21–25.

■ ■ ■

5379

Test Name: MAGAZINE RECOGNITION TEST

Purpose: To identify magazine recognition.

Number of Items: 80

Format: Includes the names of 40 magazines and 40 foils. Examples are given.

Reliability: Split-half, corrected reliability was .86.

Validity: Correlations with other variables ranged from -.12 to .87.

Authors: Stanovich, K. E., and Cunningham, A. E.

Article: Where does knowledge come from? Specific associations between print exposure and information acquisition.

Journal: *Journal of Educational Psychology*, June 1993, *85*(2), 211–229.

■ ■ ■

5380

Test Name: MATHEMATICS ACHIEVEMENT TEST

Purpose: To measure algebra achievement of Grade 12.

Number of Items: 40

Format: Cognitive levels include identification of concepts, computation, comprehension of concepts, and application and problem solving. Content areas include number and set of numbers, powers and radicals, polynomials, solving equations and inequalities, systems of equations and functions, graphs, and variation.

Reliability: Cronbach's alpha was .77.

Validity: Correlations with other variables ranged from .18 to .65.

Authors: Randhawa, B. S., et al.

Article: Role of mathematics self-efficacy in the structural model of mathematics achievement.

Journal: *Journal of Educational Psychology*, March 1993, *85*(1), 41–48.

■ ■ ■

5381

Test Name: MATH PROBLEMS PERFORMANCE SCALE

Purpose: To assess math performance.

Number of Items: 18

Format: Multiple-choice format.

Reliability: KR-20 was .86.

Authors: Pajares, F., and Miller, M. D.

Article: Mathematics self-efficacy and mathematics performances: The need for specificity of assessment.

Journal: *Journal of Counseling Psychology*, April 1995, *42*(2), 190–198.

Related Research: Dawling, D. M. (1978). *The development of a mathematics confidence scale and its application in the study of confidence in women college students.* Unpublished doctoral dissertation, Ohio State University, Columbus.

■ ■ ■

5382

Test Name: NEWSPAPER RECOGNITION CHECKLIST

Purpose: To identify newspaper recognition.

Number of Items: 24

Format: Includes the names of 12 magazines and 12 foils.

Reliability: Split-half, corrected reliability was .68.

Validity: Correlations with other variables ranged from -.15 to .84.

Authors: Stanovich, K. E., and Cunningham, A. E.

Article: Where does knowledge come from? Specific associations between print exposure and information acquisition.

Journal: *Journal of Educational Psychology*, June 1993, *85*(2), 211–229.

■ ■ ■

5383

Test Name: PLAYGROUND SKILLS TEST

Purpose: To measure playground skill.

Number of Items: 6

Format: Includes items involving speed, negotiating horizontal rungs, and risk taking.

Validity: Correlations with other variables ranged from -.06 to .46.

Author: Butcher, J.

Article: Socialization of children's playground skill.

Journal: *Perceptual and Motor Skills*, December 1993, *77*(3) Part 1, 731–738.

Related Research: Butcher, J. (1991). Development of a playground skills test. *Perceptual and Motor Skills*, *72*, 259–266.

■ ■ ■

5384

Test Name: PRACTICAL KNOWLEDGE TEST

Purpose: To measure knowledge directly relevant to daily living in a complex technological society.

Number of Items: 19

Time Required: 13 minutes.

Format: Items are open-ended questions. Examples are presented.

Reliability: Split-half corrected reliability was .73.

Validity: Correlations with other variables ranged from -.27 to .71.

Authors: Stanovich, K. E., and Cunningham, A. E.

Article: Where does knowledge come from? Specific associations between print exposure and information acquisition.

Journal: *Journal of Educational Psychology*, June 1993, *85*(2), 211–229.

■ ■ ■

5385

Test Name: QUARTERLY PROFILE EXAMINATION

Purpose: To measure knowledge of

basic and clinical sciences of medicine.

Number of Items: 400

Format: Multiple-choice items.

Validity: Correlations with Parts I and II of the National Board of Medical Examiners' examinations ranged from .70 to .80.

Authors: Arnold, L., and Willoughby, T. L.

Article: Curricular integration at the University of Missouri-Kansas City School of Medicine.

Journal: *Perceptual and Motor Skills*, February 1993, *76*(1), 35–40.

Related Research: Willoughby, T. L., & Bixby, A. R. (1991). Measuring educational progress with a longitudinal testing system. In A. J. M. Luijten (Ed.), *Issues in public examinations* (pp. 161–174). The Hauge, Netherlands: CG Konninklijke Bibliotheek.

■ ■ ■

5386

Test Name: REVISED CRAIG LIPREADING INVENTORY

Purpose: To evaluate lipreading ability.

Number of Items: 27

Format: Includes 2 subtests: word and sentence.

Reliability: Reliability coefficients ranged from .70 to .80.

Authors: Updike, C. D., et al.

Article: Revised Craig Lipreading Inventory.

Journal: *Perceptual and Motor Skills*, February 1992, *74*(1), 267–277.

Related Research: Craig, W. M. (1964). Effects of preschool training on the development of reading and lipreading skills of deaf children. *American Annals of Deaf, 109*, 280–296.

5387

Test Name: SCREENING ABILITY SCALE

Purpose: To measure screening ability.

Number of Items: 7

Format: Responses are made on a 7-point scale ranging from 1 (*disagree strongly*) to 7 (*agree strongly*). All items are presented.

Reliability: Alpha coefficients were .59 and .69.

Validity: Correlations with other variables ranged from -.05 to -.43.

Authors: Fried, Y., and Tiegs, R. B.

Article: Supervisors' role conflict and role ambiguity differential relations with performance ratings of subordinates and the moderating effect of screening ability.

Journal: *Journal of Applied Psychology*, June 1995, *80*(3), 282–291.

Related Research: Mehrabian, A. (1977). A questionnaire measure of individual differences in stimulus screening and associated differences in arousability. *Environmental Psychology and Nonverbal Behavior, 1*, 89–113.

■ ■ ■

5388

Test Name: SEK TEST

Purpose: To provide a visual measure of figure–ground.

Number of Items: 16

Time Required: 12 minutes.

Format: One of five colored forms is chosen for each item.

Reliability: Alpha coefficients ranged from .49 to .91.

Validity: Correlation with the Eysenck Personality Inventory was .15.

Authors: Dunn, A., and Eliot, J.

Article: Extroversion–introversion and spatial intelligence.

Journal: *Perceptual and Motor Skills*, August 1993, *77*(1), 19–24.

Related Research: Eliot, J. (Ed.). (1988). *The MICA study: The relationship between spatial abilities and art achievement.* College Park: University of Maryland.

■ ■ ■

5389

Test Name: SKINNER'S RADICAL BEHAVIORISM TEST

Purpose: To assess knowledge Skinner's behaviorism.

Number of Items: 32

Format: Yes–no format. All items presented.

Reliability: Split-half reliability was .77.

Validity: Students who have taken courses in behavior theory and behavior modification scored higher than students who did not have the courses ($t = 10.17$ and 2.98, respectively).

Author: Yousef, J. M.

Article: Arabic students' understanding of Skinner's radical behaviorism.

Journal: *Psychological Reports*, August 1992, *71*(1), 51–56.

■ ■ ■

5390

Test Name: STATISTICAL KNOWLEDGE TEST

Purpose: To measure statistical knowledge.

Number of Items: 31

Format: Includes 5 categories: calculations, propositions (words), propositions (symbols), conceptual understandings (words), and conceptual understandings (symbols). Items are multiple choice with 3, 4, or 5 answer choices. Examples are presented.

Reliability: Reliability coefficients ranged from .09 to .73.

Authors: Huberty, C. J., et al.

Article: Relations among dimensions of statistical knowledge.

Journal: *Educational and Psychological Measurement*, Summer 1993, *53*(2), 523–532.

Related Research: Hiebert, J., & Leferre, P. (1986). Conceptual and procedural knowledge in mathematics: An introductory analysis. In J. Hiebert (Ed.), *Conceptual and procedural knowledge: The case of mathematics* (pp. 1–27). Hillsdale, NJ: Erlbaum.

• • •

5391

Test Name: TEACHER RATING SCALE

Purpose: To provide teachers' ratings of children's academic competence.

Number of Items: 8

Format: Includes three aspects of school-related competence: academic, motivation, and independence. Responses are made on a 4-point scale. Examples are presented.

Reliability: Internal consistency was .92.

Validity: Correlations with other variables ranged from -.05 to .64.

Authors: Grolnick, W. S., et al.

Article: Inner resources for school achievement: Motivational mediators of children's perceptions of their parents.

Journal: *Journal of Educational*

Psychology, December 1991, *83*(4), 508–517.

• • •

5392

Test Name: TITLE RECOGNITION SCALE

Purpose: To provide a measure of children's exposure to print.

Number of Items: 39

Format: Includes 25 children's book titles and 14 foils for book names. All items are presented.

Reliability: Cronbach's alpha was .82.

Authors: Cunningham, A. E., and Stanovich, K. E.

Article: Tracking the unique effects of print exposure in children: Associations with vocabulary, general knowledge, and spelling.

Journal: *Journal of Educational Psychology*, June 1991, *83*(2), 264–274.

Related Research: Cunningham, A. E., & Stanovich, K. E. (1990). Assessing print exposure and orthograph processing skill in children: A quick measure of reading experience. *Journal of Educational Psychology*, *82*, 733–740.

• • •

5393

Test Name: TITLE RECOGNITION TEST—FORM 1

Purpose: To assess amount of exposure to print in children.

Number of Items: 40

Format: Includes actual children's book titles and 15 foils for book names. All items are presented.

Reliability: Split-half (odd/even) corrected reliability was .84. Cronbach's alpha was .80.

Validity: Correlations with other variables ranged from -.22 to .70.

Authors: Allen, L., et al.

Article: Multiple indicators of children's reading habits and attitudes: Construct validity and cognitive correlates.

Journal: *Journal of Educational Psychology*, December 1992, *84*(4), 489–503.

Related Research: Cunningham, A. E., & Stanovich, K. E. (1991). Tracking the unique effects of print exposure in children: Associations with vocabulary, general knowledge, and spelling. *Journal of Educational Psychology*, *83*, 264–274.

• • •

5394

Test Name: TITLE RECOGNITION TEST—FORM 2

Purpose: To assess amount of exposure to print in children.

Number of Items: 41

Format: Includes 25 actual book titles and 16 foils. All items are presented.

Reliability: Split-half (odd/even) corrected reliability was .82. Cronbach's alpha was .78.

Validity: Correlations with other variables ranged from -.19 to .65.

Authors: Allen, L., et al.

Article: Multiple indicators of children's reading habits and attitudes: Construct validity and cognitive correlates.

Journal: *Journal of Educational Psychology*, December 1992, *84*(4), 489–503.

Related Research: Cunningham, A. E., & Stanovich, K. E. (1991). Tracking the unique effects of print exposure in children: Associations with vocabulary, general knowledge, and spelling. *Journal of Educational Psychology*, *83*, 264–274.

5395

Test Name: TRAINING SCALE

Purpose: To measure training.

Number of Items: 8

Format: Includes 3 dimensions: technical, interpersonal, and academic. Responses are made on a 7-point Likert-type scale ranging from 1 (*strongly disagree*) to 7 (*strongly agree*). Examples are presented.

Reliability: Coefficient alpha was .75.

Validity: Correlations with other variables ranged from -.29 to .48.

Author: Saks, A. M.

Article: Longitudinal field investigation of the moderating and mediating effects of self-efficacy on the relationship between training and newcomer adjustment.

Journal: *Journal of Applied Psychology*, April 1995, *80*(2), 211–225.

■ ■ ■

5396

Test Name: VISUAL ARTS ACHIEVEMENT TEST

Purpose: To assess third-graders' visual arts learning.

Number of Items: 38

Format: Includes 4 factors.

Reliability: Alpha coefficients ranged from .75 to .85. Test–retest reliability was .85 (*N*= 22).

Author: Bezruczko, N.

Article: Validation of a multiple choice visual arts achievement test.

Journal: *Educational and Psychological Measurement*, August 1995, *55*(4), 664–674.

Related Research: Bezruczko, N. (1994). *Development and evaluation of a visual arts achievement test.* Unpublished report. (ERIC Document Reproduction No. ED 359 255)

■ ■ ■

5397

Test Name: VISUAL MEMORY TEST

Purpose: To measure visual memory malingering.

Number of Items: 15

Time Required: 10 seconds.

Format: Respondents reproduce from memory figures on one page.

Validity: Correlations with other variables ranged from -.29 to .60.

Authors: Hays, J.R., et al.

Article: Psychiatric norms for the Rey 15-Item Visual Memory Test.

Journal: *Perceptual and Motor Skills*, June 1993, *76*(3) Part 2, 1331–1334.

Related Research: Rey, A. (1964). *L'examen clinique en psychologie.* Paris: Presses Universitaires de France.

■ ■ ■

5398

Test Name: WORD ANALYSIS TEST

Purpose: To assess student's ability to delete phonemes from words.

Number of Items: 33

Format: Children are asked to pronounce words after a particular sound is deleted.

Validity: Correlations with other variables ranged from -.02 to .67.

Author: Spector, J. E.

Article: Predicting progress in beginning reading: Dynamic assessment of phonemic awareness.

Journal: *Journal of Educational Psychology*, September 1992, *84*(3), 353–363.

Related Research: Bruce, D. J. (1964). An analysis of word sounds by young children. *British Journal of Educational Psychology, 34*, 158–170.

CHAPTER 2
Adjustment—Educational

5399

Test Name: ACADEMIC ATTRIBUTION SCALE

Purpose: To identify students' attributions for successes and failure in various school situations.

Number of Items: 18

Format: For each item the student circles one of 5 attributions: effort, ability, task difficulty, luck, and strategy. An example is given.

Reliability: Guttman lower bound reliability was .88.

Authors: Howard-Rose, D., and Winne, P. H.

Article: Measuring component and sets of cognitive processes in self-regulated learning.

Journal: *Journal of Educational Psychology*, December 1993, *85*(4), 591–604.

Related Research: Corno, L., et al. (1982). Where there's a way there's a will: Self-regulating the low achieving student. (ERIC Document Reproduction Service No. ED 222499)

. . .

5400

Test Name: ACADEMIC AUTONOMY SCALE

Purpose: To assess behaviors and attitudes that indicate skills and independence in being able to fulfill educational goals and academic requirements.

Number of Items: 10

Format: Responses are made using a true–false format.

Reliability: Coefficient alpha was .70. Test–retest was .79.

Author: Cornelius, A.

Article: The relationship between athletic identity, peer and faculty socialization, and college student development.

Journal: *Journal of College Student Development*, November 1995, *36*(6), 560–573.

Related Research: Winston, R. B., Jr. (1990). The Student Development Task and Lifestyle Inventory: An approach to measuring students' psychosocial development. *Journal of Counseling and Human Development*, *31*, 108–120.

. . .

5401

Test Name: ACADEMIC PROCRASTINATION SCALE

Purpose: To measure academic procrastination.

Number of Items: 5

Format: Responses are made on a 5-point scale ranging from 1 (*never procrastinate*) to 5 (*always procrastinate*).

Reliability: Coefficient alpha was .80.

Validity: Correlations with other variables ranged from -.48 to .61.

Author: Wesley, J. C.

Article: Effects of ability, high school achievement, and procrastinatory behavior on college performance.

Journal: *Educational and Psychological Measurement*, Summer 1994, *54*(2), 404–408.

Related Research: Soloman, L. J., and Rothblum, E. D. (1984). Academic procrastination: Frequency and cognitive-behavioral correlates. *Journal of Counseling Psychology*, *31*, 503–509.

. . .

5402

Test Name: ACADEMIC PROCRASTINATION SCALE

Purpose: To assess to what extent students delay academic activity and to what extent delay results in guilt or anxiety.

Number of Items: 10

Format: 7-point Likert format. A sample item is presented.

Reliability: Alpha was .88.

Validity: Correlations with other variables ranged from -.28 to .49.

Authors: Senecal, C., et al.

Article: Self-regulation and academic procrastination.

Journal: *The Journal of Social Psychology*, October 1995, *135*(5), 607–619.

Related Research: Soloman, L. J., & Rothblum, E. D. (1984). Academic procrastination: Frequency and cognitive-behavioral correlates. *Journal of Counseling Psychology*, *31*, 503–509.

5403

Test Name: ADJUSTMENT TO COLLEGE LIFE MEASURE

Purpose: To measure academic adjustment to college.

Number of Items: 24

Format: Responses are made on a 9-point scale ranging from 1 (*applies very closely to me*) to 9 (*doesn't apply to me at all*).

Reliability: Internal consistency reliabilities ranged form .82 to .89.

Validity: Correlations with other variables ranged from -.05 to .21 (*N* = 119).

Author: Camp, C. C., and Chartrand, J. M.

Article: A comparison and evaluation of interest congruence indices.

Journal: *Journal of Vocational Behavior*, October 1992, *41*(2), 162-182.

Related Research: Baker, W., & Syrik, B. (1984). Measuring adjustment to college. *Journal of Counseling Psychology*, *31*, 179-189.

■ ■ ■

5404

Test Name: ATTACHMENT Q-SET

Purpose: To assess children's relationship with their primary teacher.

Number of Items: 65

Format: Items are sorted into nine piles ranging from 1 (*least characteristic*) to 9 (*most characteristic*).

Reliability: Interobserver reliability ranged from .83 to .95.

Authors: Howes, C., and Hamilton, C. E.

Article: Children's relationships with caregivers: Mothers and child care teachers.

Journal: *Child Development*, August 1992, *63*(4), 859–866.

Related Research: Waters, E., & Deanne, K. E. (1985). Defining and assessing individual differences in attachment relationships: Q-methodology and the organization of behavior in infancy and early childhood. In I. Bretherton and E. Waters (Eds.), *Growing points of attachment theory and research* (pp. 41–65). *Monographs of the Society for Research in Child Development*, *50* (1, Serial No. 209).

■ ■ ■

5405

Test Name: BAMED TEACHER RATING FORM

Purpose: To provide contemporary instructional and clinical estimates of Danish adolescents' academic progress and psychological adaptation.

Number of Items: 106

Format: Includes 23 scales. Responses are made on a 5-point scale ranging from 1 (*well below average*) to 5 (*well above average*). All items are included.

Reliability: Alpha coefficients ranged from .72 to .95.

Authors: Baker, R. L., et al.

Article: Utility of scales derived from teacher judgments of adolescent academic performance and psychosocial behavior.

Journal: *Educational and Psychological Measurement*, Summer 1991, *51*(2), 271–286.

Related Research: Hoge, R. D., & Coladarci, T. (1989). Teacher-based judgments of achievement. *Review of Educational Research*, *59*, 297–313.

5406

Test Name: CLASS INVOLVEMENT MEASURE

Purpose: To measure involvement in postsecondary classes.

Number of Items: 11

Format: 7-point response categories. Sample items described.

Reliability: Alpha was .84.

Validity: Correlations with other variables ranged from -.23 (*number of absences*) to .28 (*achievement*).

Authors: Farrell, G. M., and Mudrack, P. E.

Article: Academic involvement and the nontraditional student.

Journal: *Psychological Reports*, December 1992, *71*(3) Part I, 707–713.

Related Research: Kanungo, R. N. (1982). Measurement of job and work involvement. *Journal of Applied Psychology*, *67*, 341–349.

■ ■ ■

5407

Test Name: COLLEGE PERFORMANCE QUESTIONNAIRE

Purpose: To measure opportunity, capacity, and willingness among college students in relation to academic work.

Number of Items: 39

Format: 5-point Likert format. All items are presented.

Reliability: Alphas ranged from .70 to .82 across subscales.

Validity: Correlations with grades ranged from .15 to .57. Interscale correlations ranged from .13 to .38.

Author: Pringle, C. D.

Article: An initial test of a theory of individual performance.

Journal: *Psychological Reports*, June 1994, *74*(3) Part I, 963–973.

▪ ▪ ▪

5408

Test Name: COLLEGE STUDENTS' INVENTORY OF RECENT LIFE EXPERIENCES

Purpose: To assess hassles peculiar to the college experience.

Number of Items: 49

Format: 4-point frequency scales. Sample items are presented.

Reliability: Alpha was .88. Subscale alphas ranged from .59 to .75.

Author: Lai, J. C. L.

Article: The moderating effect of optimism on the relation between hassles and somatic complaints.

Journal: *Psychological Reports*, June 1995, *76*(3) Part I, 883–894.

Related Research: Kohn, P. M., et al. (1990). The Inventory of College Students' Life Experiences: A decontaminated hassles scale for a special population. *Journal of Behavioral Medicine*, *13*, 619–630.

▪ ▪ ▪

5409

Test Name: EXTRACURRICULAR INVOLVEMENT INVENTORY

Purpose: To measure the intensity of involvement in organized student activities.

Number of Items: Varies according to number of extracurricular activities participated in during last 4 weeks.

Format: Quality dimension assessed by responses made on a 4-point scale (*very often* to *never*). Quantity dimensions assessed by

how much time students report extending in organization's activity.

Reliability: Test–retest correlation was .55.

Authors: Hunt, S., and Rentz, A. L.

Article: Greek-letter social group members' involvement and psychosocial development.

Journal: *Journal of College Student Development*, July 1994, *35*(4), 289–295.

Related Research: Winston, R. B., & Massaro, A. V. (1987). Extracurricular Involvement Inventory: An instrument for assessing intensity of student involvement. *Journal of College Student Personnel*, *28*, 169–175.

▪ ▪ ▪

5410

Test Name: FIRST-YEAR STUDENT QUESTIONNAIRE

Purpose: To measure social and academic integration and commitment to use in discriminating between freshman year persisters and voluntary dropouts.

Number of Items: 30

Format: Responses are made on a 5-point Likert scale (*strongly disagree* to *strongly agree*).

Reliability: Alpha reliabilities among the scales ranged from .71 to .84.

Author: Wolfe, J. S.

Article: Institutional integration, academic success, and persistence of first-year commuter and resident students.

Journal: *Journal of College Student Development*, September 1993, *34*(5), 321–326.

Related Research: Pascarella, E. T., & Terenzini, P. T. (1980). Predicting freshmen persistence

and voluntary dropout decisions from a theoretical model. *Journal of Higher Education, 51*, 60–75.

▪ ▪ ▪

5411

Test Name: GRADUATE STRESS INVENTORY—REVISED

Purpose: To measure the degree to which graduate students perceive situations in their lives to be stressful.

Number of Items: 21

Format: Includes 3 factors: environmental stress, academic stress, and family/monetary stress. All items are presented.

Reliability: Test–retest (1 week) reliability ranged from .80 to .85 (*N* = 63). Alpha coefficients ranged from .30 to .74.

Author: Rocha-Singh, I. A.

Article: Perceived stress among graduate students: Development and validation of the Graduate Stress Inventory.

Journal: *Educational and Psychological Measurement*, Fall 1994, *54*(3), 714–727.

Related Research: Rocha-Singh, I. A. (1990). *Doctoral students' perceptions of stress and social support: Implications for the retention of targeted students of color.* Unpublished doctoral dissertation, University of California, Santa Barbara.

▪ ▪ ▪

5412

Test Name: INDIVIDUAL STUDENT AFFECTIVE PERFORMANCE MEASURE

Purpose: To assess individual students' educational outcomes.

Number of Items: 37

Format: Includes the following: self-concept, attitudes toward peers, attitudes toward school, attitudes toward teachers, self-efficacy of learning, feeling of homework overload, and intention to drop out. Responses are made on a 5-point scale. Examples are presented.

Reliability: Coefficient alphas ranged from .74 to .77.

Author: Cheng, Y. C.

Article: Classroom environment and student affective performance: An effective profile.

Journal: *Journal of Experimental Education*, Spring 1994, *62*(3), 221–239.

Related Research: Cheng, Y. C. (1993, January). *Principal leadership as a critical factor for school performance: Evidence from multi-levels of primary schools.* Paper presented at the International Congress for School Effectiveness and Improvement, Norrkoping, Sweden.

• • •

5413

Test Name: LEARNING INTERDEPENDENCE SCALES

Purpose: To assess cooperation, perceptions of joint outcomes, sharing resources, fairness of grading, teacher support, intrinsic learning, and satisfaction.

Number of Items: 33

Format: 5-point Likert format.

Reliability: Alphas ranged from .81 to .87.

Authors: Archer-Kath, J., et al.

Article: Individual versus group feedback in cooperative groups.

Journal: *The Journal of Social Psychology*, October 1994, *133*(5), 681–694.

Related Research: Johnson, D. W., et al. (1983). Social interdependence and classroom climate. *Journal of Psychology, 114*, 135–142.

5414

Test Name: LEARNING ORIENTATION/GRADE ORIENTATION SCALE

Purpose: To measure students' learning versus grade orientation.

Number of Items: 20

Format: Responses are either *agree* or *disagree.*

Validity: Correlations with other variables ranged from -.02 to .13.

Authors: Roig, M., and Neaman, M. A. W.

Article: Alienation, learning or grade orientation, and achievement as correlates of attitudes toward cheating.

Journal: *Perceptual and Motor Skills*, June 1994, *78*(3) Part 2, 1096–1098.

Related Research: Eison, J. A. (1981). A new instrument for assessing students' orientations towards grades and learning. *Psychological Reports, 48*, 919–924.

• • •

5415

Test Name: LIEBERT-MORRIS WORRY-EMOTIONALITY SCALE

Purpose: To measure test anxiety.

Number of Items: 10

Format: Responses are made on a 5-point scale ranging from 1 (*not at all*) to 5 (*very strongly*).

Reliability: Alpha coefficients were .79 and .88.

Author: Naveh-Benjamin, M.

Article: A comparison of training programs intended for different types of test-anxious students: Further support for an information-processing model.

Journal: *Journal of Educational*

Psychology, March 1991, *83*(1), 134–139.

Related Research: Morris, L. W., et al. (1981). Cognitive and emotional components of anxiety: Literature review and a revised worry-emotionality scale. *Journal of Educational Psychology, 73*, 541–555.

• • •

5416

Test Name: MATHEMATICS ANXIETY SCALE

Purpose: To measure mathematics anxiety.

Number of Items: 10

Format: Responses to each item are made on a 5-point Likert-type scale ranging from 1 (*strongly agree*) to 5 (*strongly disagree*).

Reliability: Split-half reliability was .92.

Validity: Correlations with other variables ranged from -.06 to -.47.

Authors: Cooper, S. E., and Robinson, D. A. G.

Article: The relationship of mathematics self-efficacy beliefs to mathematics anxiety and performance.

Journal: *Measurement and Evaluation in Counseling and Development.* April 1991, *24*(1), 4–11.

Related Research: Betz, N. E., & Hackett, G. (1983). The relationship of mathematics self-efficacy expectations to perceived career options in college women and men. *Journal of Vocational Behavior, 23*, 329–345.

• • •

5417

Test Name: PERCEIVED ACADEMIC SUCCESS SCALE

Purpose: To determine the respondents' perceived chances of success in graduate school.

Number of Items: 6

Format: Responses are made on a 6-point Likert scale (*strongly disagree* to *strongly agree*).

Reliability: Cronbach's alpha was .85.

Authors: Hodgson, C. S., and Simon, J. M.

Article: Graduate student academic and psychological functioning.

Journal: *Journal of College Student Development*, May/June 1995, *36*(3), 244–259.

Related Research: Zung, W. W. K. (1965). A self-rating depression scale. *Archives of General Psychiatry, 12,* 63–70.

■ ■ ■

5418

Test Name: PERCEIVED TEACHER SUPPORT OF QUESTIONING SCALE

Purpose: To measure students' perception of teacher's encouragement for students to ask questions.

Number of Items: 12

Format: Includes 6 content categories: Specific Instructions, Emotional Response to Questions, Informative Response, Value of Questions, Reward, and Opportunity. Responses are made on a 5-point scale ranging from 1 (*not at all*) to 5 (*very true*). All items are presented.

Reliability: Alpha coefficients were .82 and .84.

Validity: Correlations with other variables ranged from -.31 to .30.

Authors: Karabenick, S. A., and Sharma, R.

Article: Perceived teacher support of student questioning in the college classroom: Its relation to student characteristics and role in the classroom questioning process.

Journal: *Journal of Educational Psychology*, March 1994, *86*(1), 90–103.

■ ■ ■

5419

Test Name: PSYCHOLOGICAL DISTRESS INVENTORY

Purpose: To assess college students' distress symptoms.

Number of Items: 50

Format: Responses are made on a 5-point Likert-type scale.

Reliability: Test–retest coefficients ranged from .72 to .83. Cronbach's alphas for the scales ranged from .87 to .83.

Validity: Coefficients for the scales ranged from .65 to .74.

Authors: Long, B. E., et al.

Article: Differences in student development reflected by the career decisions of college seniors.

Journal: *Journal of College Student Development*, January/February 1995, *36*(1), 47–52.

Related Research: Lustman, P. J., et al. (1984). Factors influencing college student health: Development of the Psychological Distress Inventory. *Journal of Counseling Psychology, 31,* 28–35.

■ ■ ■

5420

Test Name: PSYCHOLOGICAL SENSE OF SCHOOL MEMBERSHIP SCALE

Purpose: To assess school belonging.

Number of Items: 18

Format: Items involve perceived liking, personal acceptance, inclusion, respect, and encouragement for participation. Responses are made on a 5-point Likert-type format ranging from 1 (*not at all true*) to 5 (*completely true*). Examples are given.

Reliability: Alpha was .80.

Validity: Correlations with other variables ranged from .12 to .55.

Authors: Goodenow, C., and Grady, K. E.

Article: The relationship of school belonging and friends' values to academic motivation among urban adolescent students.

Journal: *Journal of Experimental Education*, Fall 1993, *62*(1), 60–71.

Related Research: Goodenow, C. (1993). The psychological sense of school membership among adolescents: Scale development and educational correlates. *Psychology in the Schools, 30,* 79–90.

■ ■ ■

5421

Test Name: PSYCHOLOGICAL SEPARATION INVENTORY

Purpose: To measure four aspects (functional independence, attitudinal independence, emotional independence, and conflictual independence) of college adjustment.

Number of Items: 138

Format: Responses are made on a 5-point Likert scale (*not at all true of me* to *very true of me*).

Reliability: Internal consistency reliability across the subscales ranged from .84 to .92. Test–retest reliability ranged from .69 to .96.

Authors: Kenny, M. E., and Donaldson, G. A.

Article: The relationship of parental attachment and

psychological separation to the adjustment of first-year college women.

Journal: *Journal of College Student Development*, September 1992, *33*(5), 422–430.

Related Research: Hoffman, J. (1984). Psychological separation of late adolescents from their parents. *Journal of Counseling Psychology, 34*, 157–163.

■ ■ ■

5422

Test Name: REACTION AND ADAPTATION TO COLLEGE TEST

Purpose: To measure anxiety factors, study strategies, students' beliefs concerning success, and motivation.

Number of Items: 60

Time Required: Untimed (but takes approximately 20 minutes to complete).

Format: Responses are made on a 7-point Likert scale ranging from 1 (*never*) to 7 (*always*).

Reliability: Scales have an internal consistency ranging from .63 to .95.

Authors: Larose, S., and Roy, R.

Article: The role of prior academic performance and non-academic attributes in the prediction of the success of high-risk college students.

Journal: *Journal of College Student Development*, March 1991, *32*, 171–180.

Related Research: Falardeau, I., et al. (1989). *Test de Reactions et d'Adapation au Collegial (TRAC)*. Ste-Foy, Quebec, Canada: Cegep de Sainte-Foy.

■ ■ ■

5423

Test Name: REACTIONS TO TESTS

Purpose: To measure test anxiety.

Number of Items: 40

Format: Includes 4 subscales: Tension, Worry, Test-Irrelevant Thinking, and Bodily Symptoms. Responses are made on a 4-point Likert-type scale.

Reliability: Alpha coefficients ranged from .86 to .93.

Validity: Correlations with other variables ranged form -.36 to .35.

Authors: Roedel, T. D., et al.

Article: Validation of a measure of learning and performance goal orientations.

Journal: *Educational and Psychological Measurement*, Winter 1994, *54*(4), 1013–1021.

Related Research: Sarason, I .G. (1984). Stress, anxiety, and cognitive interference: Reactions to tests. *Journal of Personality and Social Psychology, 46*(4), 929–938.

■ ■ ■

5424

Test Name: SCALE OF THOUGHTS IN ORAL EXAMINATIONS

Purpose: To measure thoughts people have before or during oral examinations.

Number of Items: 36

Format: Checklist format. Participants check 12 positive, 12 neutral, and 12 negative thoughts. Sample items are presented.

Reliability: Alphas ranged from .64 to .83 across subscales.

Authors: Glass, C. R., et al.

Article: Cognition, anxiety and performance on a career-related oral examination.

Journal: *Journal of Counseling Psychology*, January 1995, *42*(1), 47–54.

Related Research: Arnkoff, D. B., et al. (1992). Cognitive processes, anxiety, and performance on doctoral dissertation oral examinations. *Journal of Counseling Psychology, 39*, 382–388.

■ ■ ■

5425

Test Name: SCHOOL FAILURE TOLERANCE SCALE

Purpose: To measure school-failure tolerance.

Number of Items: 36

Format: Includes 3 subscales: Feelings About Failure, Action Following Failure, and Preferred Difficulty. Examples are presented.

Reliability: Alpha coefficients ranged from .71 to .88.

Authors: Clifford, M. M., et al.

Article: Academic risk taking, development, and external constraint.

Journal: *Journal of Experimental Education*, Fall 1990, *59*(1), 45-64.

Related Research: Clifford, M. M. (1988). Failure tolerance and academic risk-taking in ten- to twelve-year-old students. *British Journal of Educational Psychology, 58*, 15-27.

■ ■ ■

5426

Test Name: SCHOOL-RELATED ATTITUDES SCALE

Purpose: To measure affective and cognitive attitudes toward school.

Number of Items: 35

Format: 5-point Likert format. Sample items presented.

Reliability: Theta reliabilities exceeded .75.

Author: Majoribanks, K.

Article: Relationship of children's ethnicity, gender, and social status to their family environment and school-related outcomes.

Journal: *The Journal of Social Psychology*, February 1991, *131*(1), 83–91.

Related Research: Dillon, W. R., & Kumar, A. (1985). Attitude organization and the attitude-behavior relation: A critique of Bagozzi and Burnkrants' reanalysis of Fishbein and Ajzen. *Journal of Personality and Social Psychology*, *49*, 33–46.

■ ■ ■

5427

Test Name: SCIENCE ANXIETY QUESTIONNAIRE

Purpose: To measure college students' science anxiety.

Number of Items: 28

Format: Includes 3 factors: Anxiety Towards Being Observed, Anxiety Towards Practical Applications, and Anxiety Towards Taking Tests. All items are presented.

Reliability: Reliability estimates ranged from .88 to .92.

Authors: Roth, W. M., & Roychoudhury, A.

Article: Nonmetric multidimensional item analysis in the construction of an anxiety attitude survey.

Journal: *Educational and Psychological Measurement*, Winter 1991, *51*(4), 931–942.

Related Research: Hermes, J. G. (1985). The comparative effectiveness of a science anxiety group and stress management program in the treatment of science anxious college students. *Dissertation Abstracts International*, *46*(6), 2064.

5428

Test Name: STATE TEST ANXIETY REPORT

Purpose: To measure multiple-choice test anxiety.

Number of Items: 15

Format: Includes three subscales: Worry, Emotionality, and Task-Generated Interference scales.

Reliability: Alpha reliabilities ranged from .73 to .88.

Author: Register, A. C.

Article: Stress inoculation bibliotheraphy in the treatment of test anxiety.

Journal: *Journal of Counseling Psychology*, April 1991, *38*(2), 115–119.

Related Research: Deffenbacher, J. L., & Hazaleus, S. L. (1985). Cognitive, emotional, and physiological components of test anxiety. *Cognitive Therapy and Research*, *9*, 169–180.

■ ■ ■

5429

Test Name: STATISTICS ANXIETY SCALE

Purpose: To measure statistics anxiety.

Number of Items: 10

Format: Responses are made on a 5-point Likert scale ranging from 1 (*strongly agree*) to 5 (*strongly disagree*).

Reliability: Alpha coefficient was .90. Test–retest (3 months) reliability was .75 (N= 196).

Authors: Pretorius, T. B., and Norman, A. M.

Article: Psychometric data on the Statistics Anxiety Scale for a sample of South African students.

Journal: *Educational and Psychological Measurement*, Winter 1992, *52*(4), 933–937.

Related Research: Betz, N. E. (1978). Prevalence, distribution and correlates of math anxiety in college students. *Journal of Counseling Psychology*, *25*, 441–448.

■ ■ ■

5430

Test Name: STRAIN SCALE

Purpose: To assess students' perceptions of the extent experienced stress interfered with academic performance.

Number of Items: 5

Format: Responses are made on a 5-point scale ranging from 1 (*not at all*) to 5 (*extremely*). An example is presented.

Reliability: Internal consistency was .87.

Validity: Correlations with other variables ranged from -.40 to .63.

Authors: Hackett, G., et al.

Article: Gender, ethnicity, and social cognitive factors predicting the academic achievement of students in engineering.

Journal: *Journal of Counseling Psychology*, October 1992, *39*(4), 527–538.

Related Research: Mendozo, P. (1981). Stress and coping behavior of Anglo and Mexican American university students. In T. H. Escobedo (Ed.), *Education and Chicanos: Issues and research* [Monograph No. 8] (pp. 89–111). Los Angeles: University of California, Spanish Speaking Mental Health Research Center.

■ ■ ■

5431

Test Name: STUDENT ADAPTATION TO COLLEGE QUESTIONNAIRE

Purpose: To measure college adjustment (academic adjustment, social adjustment, personal–emotional adjustment).

Number of Items: 67

Format: Responses are made on a 9-point Likert scale.

Reliability: Cronbach alphas for the subscales ranged from .73 to .90.

Authors: Rice, K. G., and Whaley, T. J.

Article: A short-term longitudinal study of within-semester stability and change in attachment and college student adjustment.

Journal: *Journal of College Student Development*, September 1994, *35*(5), 324–330.

Related Research: Baker, R. W., & Siryk, B. (1984). Measuring adjustment to college. *Journal of Counseling Psychology, 33*, 31–38.

■ ■ ■

5432

Test Name: STUDENT ADJUSTMENT QUESTIONNAIRE

Purpose: To assess student adjustment at college.

Number of Items: 36

Format: 4-point rating scales range from 1 (*does not apply to me at all*) to 4 (*applies very much to me*). Sample items are presented.

Reliability: Alpha was .90.

Authors: Jou, Y. H., and Fukada, H.

Article: Effects of social support on adjustment of Chinese students in Japan.

Journal: *The Journal of Social Psychology*, February 1995, *135*(1), 39–47.

Related Research: Baker, R. W. (1981). *Freshman Transition Questionnaire*. Unpublished manual, Clark University.

Uehara, A. (1988). Cross-cultural adjustment for foreign students. In *Theoretical and practical studies on language acquisition and cross-cultural adjustment*. Hiroshima, Japan: Hiroshima University, Faculty of Education (in Japanese).

■ ■ ■

5433

Test Name: STUDENT RESISTANCE TO SCHOOLING INVENTORY

Purpose: To measure high school students' resistance to schooling.

Number of Items: 25

Format: Includes three dimensions: cognitive, affective, and behavioral. Responses are made on a 4-point scale ranging from 1 (*disagree*) to 4 (*strongly agree*). All items are presented.

Reliability: Alpha coefficients ranged from .80 to .85.

Author: Sun, A.

Article: Development and factor analysis of the student resistance to schooling inventory.

Journal: *Educational and Psychological Measurement*, October 1995, *55*(5), 841–849.

Related Research: Mickelson, R. (1990). The attitude-achievement paradox among Black adolescents. *Sociology of Education, 63*(1), 44–61.

■ ■ ■

5434

Test Name: STUDENT SATISFACTION SCALE

Purpose: To measure student satisfaction with a gifted school program.

Number of Items: 7

Format: Likert format. Items are described.

Reliability: Alpha was .82.

Corrected item-total correlations ranged from .29 to .82.

Validity: Correlations with other variables ranged from -.33 to .58.

Authors: Cornell, D. G., et al.

Article: Socioemotional adjustment of adolescent girls enrolled in a residential acceleration program.

Journal: *Gifted Child Quarterly*, Spring 1991, *35*(2), 58–66.

■ ■ ■

5435

Test Name: STUDENTS CONFLICT STRESS SCALE

Purpose: To measure students' conflict stress.

Number of Items: 10

Format: Responses are made on a 5-point scale ranging from 1 (*strongly disagree*) to 5 (*strongly agree*). Examples are presented.

Reliability: Coefficient alpha was .84.

Validity: Correlations with other variables ranged from -.31 to .61.

Authors: Koeske, G. F., and Koeske, R. D.

Article: Student "burnout" as a mediator of the stress-outcome relationship.

Journal: *Research in Higher Education*, August 1991, *32*(4), 415–431.

■ ■ ■

5436

Test Name: STUDENTS' EVENTS STRESS SCALE

Purpose: To measure stress of events for students.

Number of Items: 48

Format: Student indicates general frequency of events stress for students during the past 3 months. Examples are given.

Reliability: Coefficient alpha was .84.

Validity: Correlations with other variables ranged from -.21 to .45.

Authors: Koeske, G. F., and Koeske, R. D.

Article: Student "burnout" as a mediator of the stress-outcome relationship.

Journal: *Research in Higher Education*, August 1991, *32*(4), 415–431.

Related Research: Koeske, G. F., & Koeske, R. D. (1990). The buffering effect of social support on negative consequences of parenting stress. *American Journal of Orthopsychiatry*, *60*, 440–451.

■ ■ ■

5437

Test Name: STUDENT STRESS INVENTORY

Purpose: To measure four types of stressors and reactions to stress.

Number of Items: 51

Format: 5-point rating scales (*never* to *most of the time*). All items are presented.

Reliability: Alphas ranged from .57 to .92. Test–retest (within 3 weeks) ranged from .57 to .92.

Validity: Male–female differences on subscales were all statistically significant, with women reporting higher stress than men.

Author: Gadzella, B. M.

Article: Student-Life Stress Inventory: Identification of and reactions to stress.

Journal: *Psychological Reports*, April 1994, *74*(2), 395–402.

■ ■ ■

5438

Test Name: SURVEY OF STUDENT NEEDS

Purpose: To assess the needs of college students.

Number of Items: 42

Format: Responses are made on a 4-point Likert scale (*high need* to *no need*).

Reliability: Test–retest reliability coefficient was .94.

Authors: Gallagher, R. P., et al.

Article: The personal, career, and learning skill needs of college students.

Journal: *Journal of College Student Development*, July 1992, *33*(4), 301–309.

Related Research: Gallagher, R. P., & Scheuring, S. B. (1978). *Survey of student needs at the University of Pittsburgh.* Unpublished manuscript.

■ ■ ■

5439

Test Name: SYDNEY ATTRIBUTION SCALE

Purpose: To measure students' self-attribution in failed and in successful academic situations.

Number of Items: 7

Format: Includes 12 scales. Also includes 24 scenarios depicting academic success or failure situations into which students imagine themselves.

Reliability: Alpha coefficients ranged from .74 to .90.

Authors: Craven, R. G., et al.

Article: Effects of internally focused feedback and attributional feedback on enhancement of academic self-concept.

Journal: *Journal of Educational Psychology*, March 1991, *83*(1), 17–27.

Related Research: Marsh, H. W. (1984). Relationships among dimensions of self-attribution, dimensions of self-concept, and academic achievements. *Journal of Educational Psychology*, *76*, 1291–1380.

■ ■ ■

5440

Test Name: TEST AND CLASS ANXIETY RATING SCALE

Purpose: To assess anxiety in settings involving the academic study of statistics.

Number of Items: 8

Format: 5-point Likert format.

Reliability: Alpha was .91. Item point-biserial correlations ranged from .66 to .85. Test–retest reliability (5 weeks) was .83.

Validity: Correlations with Mathematics Test Anxiety factor was .76.

Authors: Onwuegbuzie, A. J., and Seaman, M. A.

Article: The effect of time constraints and statistics test anxiety on test performance in a statistics course.

Journal: *Journal of Experimental Education*, Winter 1995, *63*(2), 115–124.

Related Research: Cruise, R. J., & Wilkins, E. M. (1980). *STARS: Statistical Anxiety Rating Scale.* Unpublished manuscript, Andrews University, Berrien Springs, Michigan.

■ ■ ■

5441

Test Name: TEST ANXIETY SCALE FOR CHILDREN

Purpose: To assess test anxiety.

Number of Items: 30

Format: Respondents either agree or disagree with each item.

Reliability: Split-half reliability was .88. Alpha coefficients were .88 and .89.

Validity: Convergent validity between the instrument and a questionnaire measure of school anxiety was .82.

Authors: Ludlow, L. H., and Guida, F. V.

Article: The Test Anxiety Scale for children as a generalized measure of academic anxiety.

Journal: *Educational and Psychological Measurement*, Winter 1991, *51*(4), 1013–1021.

Related Research: Sarason, S. B., et al. (1960). *Anxiety in elementary school children*. New York: Wiley.

■ ■ ■

5442

Test Name: TEST ANXIETY SCALE—HEBREW VERSION

Purpose: To measure test anxiety.

Number of Items: 37

Format: 2-point agree/disagree scales.

Reliability: Alpha was .86.

Authors: Milgram, N. A., et al.

Article: Situational and personal determinants of academic procrastination.

Journal: *The Journal of General Psychology*, April 1994, *119*(2), 123–133.

Related Research: Sarason, I. G.

(1972). Experimental approaches to test anxiety. In C. D. Spielberger (Ed.), *Anxiety: Current trends in theory and research, Vol. 2*. New York: Academic Press.

■ ■ ■

5443

Test Name: UNIVERSITY ALIENATION SCALE

Purpose: To measure components of alienation in college students on campus.

Number of Items: 25

Format: Responses are made on a 5-point Likert scale.

Reliability: Corrected reliability for the total scale was .92. Split-half coefficients for powerlessness, normlessness, and social engagement subscales were .79, .89, and .72.

Authors: Steward, R. J., et al.

Article: Alienation and interactional style: A study of successful Anglo, Asian, and Hispanic university students.

Journal: *Journal of College Student Development*, March 1992, *33*(2), 149–156.

Related Research: Burbach, H. J., & Thompson, M. A. (1972). Development of a contextual measure of alienation. *Pacific Sociological Review, 15*, 224–234.

5444

Test Name: WITHDRAWAL BEHAVIOR SCALE

Purpose: To measure five constructs of withdrawal behavior.

Number of Items: 27

Format: Includes 5 constructs: Academic Integration, Social Integration, Ending Institutional Commitment, Ending Goal Commitment, and Financial Attitudes.

Reliability: Alpha coefficients ranged from .36 to .82.

Authors: Mallette, B. I., and Oabrera, A. F.

Article: Determinants of withdrawal behavior: An exploratory study.

Journal: *Research in Higher Education*, April 1991, *32*(2), 179–194.

Related Research: Pascarella, E. T., & Tarenzini, P. T. (1980). Predicting freshman persistence and voluntary dropout decisions from a theoretical model. *Journal of Higher Education, 51*(1), 60–75.

Nettles, M. T., et al. (1985). *The causes and consequences of college students' performance: A focus on Black and White students' attrition rates, progression rates, and grade point averages* (Report No. CB 50-CCCSP 385). Tennessee Higher Education Commission.

CHAPTER 3
Adjustment—Psychological

5445

Test Name: ABILITY TO COPE SCALE

Purpose: To measure ability to cope.

Number of Items: 5

Format: Includes handling on-the-job problems, determining what to do to accomplish one's work, and being sure of how to do one's work. Responses are made on a 7-point Likert-type scale ranging from 1 (*strongly disagree*) to 7 (*strongly agree*). Sample items are presented.

Reliability: Coefficient alpha was .87.

Validity: Correlations with other variables ranged from -.29 to .53.

Author: Saks, A. M.

Article: Longitudinal field investigation of the moderating and mediating effects of self-efficacy on the relationship between training and newcomer adjustment.

Journal: *Journal of Applied Psychology*, April 1995, *80*(2), 211–225.

■ ■ ■

5446

Test Name: ACADEMIC PRESSURE SCALE FOR ADOLESCENTS

Purpose: To measure stress.

Number of Items: 35

Format: 5-point Likert format.

Reliability: Test–retest was .78. Sample items presented.

Author: Jones, R. W.

Article: Gender-specific differences in the perceived antecedents of academic stress.

Journal: *Psychological Reports*, June 1993, *72*(3) Part I, 739–743.

Related Research: West, C. K., & Wood, E. S. (1970). Academic pressures on public school students. *Educational Leadership*, *3*, 585–589.

■ ■ ■

5447

Test Name: ACTIVATION-DEACTIVATION ADJECTIVE CHECKLIST, SHORT FORM

Purpose: To measure four mood states: energetic, tense, tired, and calm.

Number of Items: 20

Format: 4-point scales.

Reliability: Reliability ranged from .57 to .87 on repeated adjectives.

Validity: Correlations with arousal measures ranged from .46 to .68.

Author: Dillon, K. M.

Article: Popping sealed air-capsules to reduce stress.

Journal: *Psychological Reports*, August 1992, *71*(1), 243–246.

Related Research: Thayer, R. E. (1989). *The biopsychology of mood and arousal*. New York: Oxford University Press.

■ ■ ■

5448

Test Name: ADAPTABILITY TO CHANGE QUESTIONNAIRE

Purpose: To assess the capacity to adapt to life changes.

Number of Items: 30

Format: Responses are made on a 4-point Likert-type scale. Consists of the following areas: bodily changes, changes to one's external environment, new situations, major accomplishments, and changes in the lives of significant others.

Reliability: Coefficient alpha was .84.

Authors: Holmbeck, G. N., and Wandrei, M. L.

Article: Individual and relational predictors of adjustment in first-year college students.

Journal: *Journal of Counseling Psychology*, January 1993, *40*(1), 73–78.

Related Research: Holmbeck, G. N. (1989). *A measure of adaptability to change* [unpublished measure]. Chicago: Loyola University.

■ ■ ■

5449

Test Name: ADJECTIVE CHECKLIST

Purpose: To measure one's performance satisfaction.

Number of Items: 16

Format: Responses are made on 7-point scales anchored by opposite adjective pairs. Examples are presented.

Reliability: Coefficients alpha was .97.

Validity: Correlations with other variables ranged from -.46 to .63.

Authors: Thomas, K. M., and Mathieu, J. E.

Article: Role of causal attributions in dynamic self-regulation and goal processes.

Journal: *Journal of Applied Psychology*, December 1994, *79*(6), 812–818.

Related Research: Weiner, B. (1986). *An attributional theory of achievement motivation and emotion.* New York: Springer-Verlag.

• • •

5450

Test Name: ADOLESCENT PERCEIVED EVENTS SCALE

Purpose: To assess the occurrence and impact of stressful events.

Number of Items: 210

Format: Responses are made on a 9-point scale ranging from *extremely undesirable* to *extremely desirable*.

Reliability: Test–retest for ratings of event occurrence was 89%.

Validity: Concurrent validity was 82% agreement.

Authors: Brooks, J. H., and DuBois, D. L.

Article: Individual and environmental predictors of adjustment during the first year of college.

Journal: *Journal of College Student Development*, July 1995, *36*(4), 347–360.

Related Research: Compas, B. E., et al. (1987). Assessment of major and daily stressful events during adolescence: The Adolescent Perceived Events Scale. *Journal of Consulting and Clinical Psychology, 55,* 534–541.

5451

Test Name: AFFECT ADJECTIVE CHECKLIST

Purpose: To measure the respondent's level of distress.

Number of Items: 21

Format: Respondents check adjectives that describe how they feel.

Reliability: Internal reliability coefficient was .85.

Authors: Schneider, W. J., and Nevid, J. S.

Article: Overcoming math anxiety: A comparison of stress inoculation training and systematic desensitization.

Journal: *Journal of College Student Development*, July 1993, *34*(4), 283–288.

Related Research: Zuckerman, M. (1960). The development of an affect adjective checklist for the measurement of anxiety. *Journal of Counseling Psychology, 24,* 457–462.

• • •

5452

Test Name: AFFECT BALANCE SCALE

Purpose: To measure positive and negative affect.

Number of Items: 10

Format: 4-point Likert format. Sample items described.

Reliability: Alphas ranged from .70 to .79 across subscales and gender.

Authors: Paden, S. L., and Buehler, C.

Article: Coping with the dual-income lifestyle.

Journal: *Journal of Marriage and the Family*, February 1995, *57*(1), 101–110.

Related Research: Bradburn, N.

M. (1969). *The structure of psychological well-being.* Chicago: Aldine.

• • •

5453

Test Name: AFFECT INTENSITY MEASURES

Purpose: To measure the strength with which people experience emotion.

Number of Items: 40

Format: 6-point Likert format.

Reliability: Subscale reliabilities ranged from .69 to .90.

Validity: Factor intercorrelations ranged from -.37 to .51. Goodness-of-fit of various measurement models is discussed.

Author: Wienfurt, K. P., et al.

Article: The factor structure of the Affect Intensity Measure: In search of a measurement model.

Journal: *Journal of Research in Personality*, September 1994, *28*(3), 314–331.

Related Research: Larsen, R. J. (1984). Theory and measurement of affective intensity as an individual difference characteristic. *Dissertation Abstracts International, 85,* 2297B. (University Microfilms No. 84-22112)

• • •

5454

Test Name: AFFECTIVE COMMITMENT SCALE

Purpose: To measure affective commitment.

Number of Items: 7

Format: Responses are made on a 5-point scale ranging from 1 (*strongly disagree*) to 5 (*strongly agree*). An example is presented.

Reliability: Coefficient alpha was .87 ($N = 193$).

Validity: Correlations with other variables ranged from -.49 to .68 ($N = 193$).

Authors: Bauer, T. N., and Green, S. G.

Article: Effect of newcomer involvement in work-related activities: A longitudinal study of socialization.

Journal: *Journal of Applied Psychology*, April 1994, *79*(2), 211–223.

Related Research: McGee, G. W., & Ford, R. C. (1987). Two (or more?) dimensions of organizational commitment: Reexamination of the affective and continuance commitment scales. *Journal of Applied Psychology*, *72*, 638–641.

■ ■ ■

5455

Test Name: AFFECTIVE COMMITMENT SCALE— REVISED

Purpose: To assess affective commitment.

Number of Items: 8

Reliability: Internal consistency was .85.

Validity: Correlations with other variables ranged from .02 to .93 ($N = 732$).

Author: Greenberg, J.

Article: Using socially fair treatment to promote acceptance of a work site smoking ban.

Journal: *Journal of Applied Psychology*, April 1994, *79*(2), 288–297.

Related Research: Meyer, J. P., & Allen, N. J. (1984). Testing the "side-bet theory" of organizational commitment: Some methodological considerations. *Journal of Applied Psychology*, *69*, 372–378.

5456

Test Name: AFFECTIVE DISPOSITION SCALE

Purpose: To measure affective disposition.

Number of Items: 25

Format: Responses are made on a trichotomous response scale ranging from 1 (*dissatisfy*) to 3 (*satisfied*). All items are presented.

Reliability: Coefficient alpha was .78.

Validity: Correlations with other variables ranged from -.10 to .54.

Author: Judge, T. A.

Article: Does affective disposition moderate the relationships between job satisfaction and voluntary turnover?

Journal: *Journal of Applied Psychology*, June 1993, *78*(3), 395–401.

Related Research: Weitz, J. (1952). A neglected concept in the study of job satisfaction. *Personnel Psychology*, *5*, 201–205.

■ ■ ■

5457

Test Name: ANXIETY MEASURE

Purpose: To measure cognitive and somatic anxiety.

Number of Items: 14

Format: Includes two subscales: cognitive anxiety and somatic anxiety.

Reliability: Alpha coefficients were .86 (cognitive) and .80 (somatic).

Author: Barton, J.

Article: Choosing to work at night: A moderating influence on individual tolerance to shift work.

Journal: *Journal of Applied Psychology*, June 1994, *79*(3), 449–454.

Related Research: Schwartz, G. E., et al. (1987). Patterning of cognitive and somatic processes in the self-regulation of anxiety: Effects of meditation versus exercise. *Psychosomatic Medicine*, *40*, 321–328.

■ ■ ■

5458

Test Name: ANXIETY SCALE

Purpose: To measure anxiety.

Number of Items: 9

Format: 9-point frequency scales.

Reliability: Split-half was .70. Test–retest was .72.

Authors: Whiteman, V. L., and Shorkey, C. T.

Article: Reliability and validity of the Ego and Discomfort Anxiety Inventory.

Journal: *Psychological Reports*, August 1994, *75*(1) Part II, 384–386.

Related Research: Costello, C. G., & Comrey, A. L. (1967). Scales for measuring depression and anxiety. *Journal of Psychology*, *66*, 303–313.

■ ■ ■

5459

Test Name: ANXIETY SENSITIVITY INDEX

Purpose: To measure concern about the consequences of anxiety.

Number of Items: 16

Format: 5-point agreement scales.

Reliability: Test–retest reliability (2 weeks) was .75.

Authors: Hoffart, A., et al.

Article: Assessment of fear of fear among agoraphobic patients: The Agoraphobic Cognitions Scale.

Journal: *Journal of Psychopathology and Behavioral*

Assessment, June 1992, *14*(2), 175–187.

Related Research: Reiss, S., et al. (1986). Anxiety sensitivity, anxiety frequency and the prediction of fearfulness. *Behavior Research and Therapy*, *24*, 1–8.

• • •

5460

Test Name: ANXIETY STRAIN SCALE

Purpose: To measure anxiety strain.

Number of Items: 8

Format: Responses are made on a 5-point Likert-type scale. An example is presented.

Reliability: Alpha coefficients ranged from .77 to .83.

Validity: Correlations with other variables ranged from -.22 to .57.

Authors: Newton, T., and Keenan, T.

Article: Further analyses of the dispositional argument in organizational behavior.

Journal: *Journal of Applied Psychology*, December 1991, *76*(6), 781–787.

Related Research: Keenan, A., & McBain, G. D. M. (1979). Effects of Type A behavior, intolerance of ambiguity, and locus of control on the relationship between role stress and work-related outcomes. *Journal of Occupational Psychology*, *52*, 1–9.

• • •

5461

Test Name: ANXIOUS ROMANTIC ATTACHMENT SCALE

Purpose: To measure anxious attachment in a romantic context.

Number of Items: 33

Format: 9-point Likert format. Sample items are presented.

Reliability: Alphas ranged from .89 to .94.

Validity: Correlation with Adult Attachment Scale was .44.

Authors: Sperling, M. B., and Boraro, S.

Article: Attachment anxiety and reciprocity as moderators of interpersonal attraction.

Journal: *Psychological Reports*, February 1995, *76*(1), 323–335.

Related Research: Hindy, C. G., & Schwartz, J. C. (1984). *Individual differences in the tendency toward anxious romantic attachment.* Paper presented at the Second International Conference on Personal Relationships, Madison, Wisconsin.

• • •

5462

Test Name: ARABIC CHILDREN'S DEPRESSION INVENTORY

Purpose: To measure depression in children.

Number of Items: 27

Format: 3-point frequency scales (*rarely*, *sometimes*, *often*).

Reliability: Alphas ranged from .86 to .88.

Validity: Correlations with Kovac's Depression Inventory was .53.

Author: Abdullatif, H. I.

Article: Prevalence of depression among middle school Kuwaiti students following the Iraqi invasion.

Journal: *Psychological Reports*, October 1995, *77*(2), 643–649.

Related Research: Abdel-Khalek, A. M. (1993). The construction and validation of the Arabic Children's Depression Inventory. *European Journal of Psychological Assessment*, *9*, 41–50.

• • •

5463

Test Name: AUTOMATIC THOUGHTS QUESTIONNAIRE

Purpose: To assess frequency of negative automatic thoughts associated with depression.

Number of Items: 30

Format: Responses are made on a 5-point Likert scale. Examples are presented.

Reliability: Split-half reliability was .97. Coefficient alpha was .96.

Author: Lightsey, O. R., Jr.

Article: "Thinking positive" as a stress buffer: The role of positive automatic cognitions in depression and happiness.

Journal: *Journal of Counseling Psychology*, July 1994, *41*(3), 325-334.

Related Research: Hollon, S. D., & Kendall, P. C. (1980). Cognitive self-statements in depression: Development of an Automatic Thoughts Questionnaire. *Cognitive Therapy and Research*, *4*, 383–395.

• • •

5464

Test Name: AUTOMATED THOUGHTS QUESTIONNAIRE—POSITIVE

Purpose: To measure positive automatic thoughts.

Number of Items: 30

Format: Responses are made on a 5-point scale ranging from 1 (*not at all*) to 5 (*all the time*). Includes 4 factors: Positive Daily

Functioning, Positive Self-Evaluation, Others' Evaluations of the Self, and Positive Future Expectations. Examples are presented.

Reliability: Coefficient alpha was .94. Split-half reliability was .95.

Author: Lightsey, O. R., Jr.

Article: "Thinking positive" as a stress buffer: The role of positive automatic cognitions in depression and happiness.

Journal: *Journal of Counseling Psychology*, July 1994, *41*(3), 325-334.

Related Research: Ingram, R. E., & Wisnicki, K. S. (1988). Assessment of positive automatic cognition. *Journal of Consulting and Clinical Psychology*, *56*, 898–902.

■ ■ ■

5465

Test Name: AVOIDANCE OF ONTOLOGICAL CONFRONTATION WITH DEATH SCALE

Purpose: To measure avoidance of activities that could arouse anxiety about death.

Number of Items: 20

Format: True–false format.

Reliability: Test–retest reliabilities ranged from .76 to .91.

Authors: Lefcourt, H. M., and Shepherd, R. S.

Article: Organ donation, authoritarianism and perspective-taking humor.

Journal: *Journal of Research in Personality*, March 1995, *29*(1), 121–128.

Related Research: Thauberger, P. C., et al. (1979). The avoidance of ontological confrontation of death: A psychometric research scale. *Essence*, *3*, 9–12.

5466

Test Name: BECK ANXIETY INVENTORY

Purpose: To measure the severity of anxiety.

Number of Items: 21

Format: 4-point scales range from 0 (*not at all*), to 3 (*severely, I can hardly stand it*).

Reliability: Alphas ranged from .58 to .92.

Validity: Correlations with other variables ranged from -.05 to .71.

Authors: Osman, A., et al.

Article: The Beck Anxiety Inventory: Psychometric properties in a community population.

Journal: *Journal of Psychopathology and Behavioral Assessment*, December 1993, *15*(4), 287–297.

Related Research: Beck, A. T., et al. (1988). An inventory for measuring clinical anxiety: Psychometric properties. *Journal of Consulting and Clinical Psychology*, *56*, 893–897.

■ ■ ■

5467

Test Name: BEHAVIOR AND SYMPTOM IDENTIFICATION SCALE (BASIS-32)

Purpose: To measure symptom and problem difficulty of psychiatric patients.

Number of Items: 32

Time Required: 15–30 minutes.

Format: 5-point scales.

Reliability: Alphas ranged from .63 to .80 across subscales. Full scale alpha was .89.

Author: Eisen, S. V.

Article: Assessment of subjective distress by patients' self-report versus structured interview.

Journal: *Psychological Reports*, February 1995, *76*(1), 35–39.

Related Research: Eisen, S. V., et al. (1994). Reliability and validity of a brief patient-report instrument for psychiatric outcome evaluation. *Hospital and Community Psychiatry*, *45*, 242–247.

■ ■ ■

5468

Test Name: BELL GLOBAL PSYCHOPATHOLOGY SCALE

Purpose: To measure psychopathology.

Number of Items: 36

Format: Includes 6 subscales: Depression, Anxiety, Phobias, Obsessive–Compulsiveness, Serious Psychopathology, and Alcohol/Drug Abuse. A 5-point Likert scale is used.

Reliability: Internal consistency and test–retest were both greater than .80.

Validity: Correlations with other variables ranged from -.58 to .64.

Author: Zamostny, K. P., et al.

Article: Narcissistic injury and its relationship to early trauma, early resources, and adjustment to college.

Journal: *Journal of Counseling Psychology*, October 1993, *40*(4), 501–510.

Related Research: Schwab, J. J., et al. (1979). *Social order and mental health*. New York: Brunner/Mazel.

■ ■ ■

5469

Test Name: BOREDOM PRONENESS SCALE

Purpose: To measure boredom.

Number of Items: 28

Format: True–false format.

Reliability: Internal reliabilities ranged from .79 to .84.

Validity: Correlations with other variables ranged from -.42 (life satisfaction) to .67 (self-reported boredom.)

Author: Watt, J. D.

Article: Effect of boredom proneness on time perception.

Journal: *Psychological Reports*, August 1991, *69*(1), 323-327.

Related Research: Farmer, R. F., & Sundberg, N. D. (1986). Boredom proneness—the development and correlates of a new scale. *Journal of Personality Assessment, 50*, 4–17.

Vodanovich, S. J., & Verner, K. M. (1991). Boredom proneness: Its relationship to positive and negative affect. *Psychological Reports, 69*, 1139–1146.

Watt, J. D., & Vodanovich, S. J. (1992). Relationship between boredom proneness and impulsivity. *Psychological Reports, 70*, 688–690.

■ ■ ■

5470

Test Name: BRAINSTORMING STRESS SCALE

Purpose: To measure brainstorming stress.

Number of Items: 10

Format: Responses are made on 7-point scales. All items are presented.

Reliability: Coefficient alpha was .92.

Validity: Correlations with other variables ranged form -.55 to .16.

Authors: Aiello, J. R., and Kolb, K. J.

Article: Electronic performance monitoring and social context: Impact on productivity and stress.

Journal: *Journal of Applied*

Psychology, June 1995, *80*(3), 339–353.

■ ■ ■

5471

Test Name: BRIEF REASONS FOR LIVING INVENTORY

Purpose: To distinguish suicidal from nonsuicidal prison inmates.

Number of Items: 12

Format: All items are presented.

Reliability: Alpha was .86.

Validity: Correlations with the long version of the scale ranged from .58 to .94 across subscales. Correlations with suicide ideation were significant after control variables were introduced.

Authors: Ivanoff, A., et al.

Article: Fewer reasons for staying alive when you are thinking of killing yourself: The Brief Reasons for Living Inventory.

Journal: *Journal of Psychopathology and Behavioral Assessment*, March 1994, *16*(1), 1–13.

Related Research: Linehan, M. M., et al. (1983). Reasons for staying alive when you are thinking of killing yourself: The Reasons for Living Inventory. *Journal of Consulting and Clinical Psychology, 51*, 276–286.

■ ■ ■

5472

Test Name: BRIEF SYMPTOM INVENTORY

Purpose: To assess symptomatology by self-report.

Number of Items: 53

Time Required: 10 minutes.

Format: Respondents rate experience with each symptom in last 7 days on a 5-point scale ranging from 0 (*not at all*), to 4 (*extremely*).

Reliability: Alphas ranged from .71 to .85 across subscales. Test–retest reliabilities ranged form .68 to .91.

Validity: Correlations between symptom dimensions ranged from .92 to .98.

Authors: Piersma, H. L., et al.

Article: Unidimensionality of the Brief Symptom Inventory (BSI) in adult and adolescent inpatients.

Journal: *Journal of Personality Assessment*, October 1994, *63*(2), 338-344.

Related Research: Derogatis, L. R., & Melisaratos, N. (1983). The Brief Symptom Inventory: An introductory report. *Psychological Medicine, 13*, 595–605.

■ ■ ■

5473

Test Name: CATASTROPHIC COGNITIONS QUESTIONNAIRE—MODIFIED

Purpose: To assess catastrophic cognitions in relation to anxiety disorder.

Number of Items: 21

Format: 5-point rating scales. All items are presented.

Reliability: Alphas ranged from .83 to .91. Test–retest reliabilities (2 weeks) ranged from .58 to .71.

Validity: Correlations with other variables ranged from .10 to .91.

Authors: Khawaja, N. G., et al.

Article: Modification of the Catastrophic Cognitions Questionnaire (CCQ-M) for normals and patients: Exploratory and LISREL analysis.

Journal: *Journal of Psychopathology and Behavioral Assessment*, December 1994, *16*(4), 325–342.

Related Research: Khawaja, N. G., & Oei, T. P. S. (1989).

Development of a catastrophic cognitions questionnaire. *Journal of Anxiety Disorders, 6,* 305–318.

■ ■ ■

5474

Test Name: CENTER FOR EPIDEMIOLOGICAL STUDIES DEPRESSION SCALE

Purpose: To indicate depressive symptomatology.

Number of Items: 4

Format: All items are presented.

Reliability: Coefficient alpha was .81.

Validity: Correlations with the Basic Personality Inventory ranged from -.02 to .47.

Authors: Melchior, L. A., et al.

Article: A short depression index for women.

Journal: *Educational and Psychological Measurements,* Winter 1993, *53*(4), 1117–1125.

Related Research: Radloff, L. A. (1977). The CES-D Scales: A self-report depression scale for research in the general population. *Applied Psychological Measurement, 1,* 385–401.

■ ■ ■

5475

Test Name: CENTER FOR EPIDEMIOLOGICAL STUDIES DEPRESSION SCALE

Purpose: To indicate depressive symptomatology.

Number of Items: 8

Format: All items are presented.

Reliability: Coefficient alpha was .86.

Validity: Correlations with the Basic Personality Inventory ranged from -.00 to .54 (*N* = 83).

Authors: Melchior, L. A., et al.

Article: A short depression index for women.

Journal: *Educational and Psychological Measurement,* Winter 1993, *53*(4), 1117–1125.

Related Research: Radloff, L. S. (1977). The CES-D Scales: A self-report depression scale for research in the general population. *Applied Psychological Measurement, 1,* 385–401.

■ ■ ■

5476

Test Name: CENTER FOR EPIDEMIOLOGIC STUDIES DEPRESSION SCALE

Purpose: To assess depression.

Number of Items: 16

Format: Responses are made on a 4-point scale ranging from *rarely* or *none of the time* (less than 1 day) to most or all of the time (5–7 days).

Reliability: Alpha coefficients were .87 and .88.

Authors: Brody, G. H., et al.

Article: Financial resources, parent psychological functioning, parent co-caregiving, and early adolescent competence in rural two-parent African-American families.

Journal: *Child Development,* April 1994, *65*(2), 590–605.

Related Research: Radloff, L. S. (1977). The CES-D Scale: A self-report depression scale for research in the general population. *Applied Psychological Measurement, 1,* 385–401.

■ ■ ■

5477

Test Name: CENTER FOR EPIDEMIOLOGIC STUDIES DEPRESSION SCALE

Purpose: To assess depression.

Number of Items: 20

Format: Includes such dimensions as depressed mood, feelings of guilt and worthlessness, feeling of helplessness and hopelessness, psychomotor retardation, loss of appetite, and sleep disturbance. Responses are made on a 4-point scale.

Reliability: Coefficient alpha was .87.

Validity: Correlations with other variables ranged from -.09 to .48.

Authors: Frone M. R., et al.

Article: Antecedents and outcomes of work-family conflict: Testing a model of the work-family interface.

Journal: *Journal of Applied Psychology,* February 1992, *77*(1), 65–78.

Related Research: Radloff, L. S. (1977). The CES-D scale: A self-report depression scale for research in the general population. *Applied Psychological Measurement, 1,* 385–501.

■ ■ ■

5478

Test Name: CHILDHOOD DEPRESSION INVENTORY

Purpose: To assess children's feelings of depression.

Number of Items: 27

Format: Items are scored on a 0-to-2 scale.

Reliability: Coefficient alpha was .84.

Authors: McHale, S. M., and Pawletko, T. M.

Article: Differential treatment of siblings in two female contexts.

Journal: *Child Development,* February 1992, *63*(1), 68–81.

Related Research: Kovacs, M.

(1981). Rating scales to assess depression in school-aged children. *Acta Paedopsychiatric*, *46*, 305–310.

• • •

5479

Test Name: CHILDREN'S DEPRESSION SCALE

Purpose: To measure depression in children aged 9–16.

Number of Items: 66

Format: 5-point response scales.

Reliability: Cronbach's alpha was .90.

Validity: Correlations with Offer Self Image Scales ranged from .26 to .67.

Author: Patton, W.

Article: Relationship Between Self-Image and Depression in Adolescents.

Journal: *Psychological Reports*, June 1991, *68*(3) Part I, 867–870.

Related Research: Lang, M., & Tisher, M. (1978). *Children's Depression Scale—Research Edition*. Hawthorn, Victoria, Australia: Australian Council for Educational Research.

• • •

5480

Test Name: CHILDREN'S SOMATIZATION INVENTORY

Purpose: To assess children's physical complaints.

Number of Items: 35

Format: Responses are made on a 5-point scale from 0 (*not at all*) to 4 (*a whole lot*).

Reliability: Test–retest Pearson reliability was .50 for well patients. Test–retest Pearson reliability was .66 for patients with recurrent abdominal pain. Coefficient alpha was .90.

Author: Walker, L. S.

Article: Somatic complaints in pediatric patients: A prospective study of the role of negative life events, child social and academic competence, and parental somatic symptoms.

Journal: *Journal of Consulting and Clinical Psychology*, December 1994, *62*(6), 1213–1221.

Related Research: Garber, J., et al. (1991). Somatization symptoms in a community sample of children and adolescents: Further validation of the children's somatization inventory. *Psychological Assessment*, *3*, 588–595.

• • •

5481

Test Name: CHRONIC SELF-DESTRUCTIVENESS SCALE

Purpose: To assess the tendency to act in ways to increase the probability of negative consequences and to decrease the probability of positive consequences.

Number of Items: 52

Format: 5-point Likert format.

Reliability: Alphas ranged from .73 to .97 across populations. Test–retest reliabilities (1 month) ranged from .90 to .98.

Validity: Correlations with other variables ranged from -.69 to .38.

Authors: Sharp, M., and Schill, T.

Article: Chronic self-destructiveness and the self-defeating personality: Similarities and differences.

Journal: *Journal of Personality Assessment*, April 1995, *64*(2), 270–278.

Related Research: Kelley, K., et al. (1985). Chronic self-destructiveness: Conceptualization, measurement, and initial validation of the

construct. *Motivation and Emotion*, *19*, 135–151.

• • •

5482

Test Name: CLAUSTROPHOBIA GENERAL COGNITIONS QUESTIONNAIRE

Purpose: To measure cognitions if subjects were to enter claustrophobic situations in which they were fearful.

Number of Items: 26

Format: 5-point scales. All items are presented.

Reliability: Alphas ranged from .84 to .88 across subscales.

Validity: Correlations with claustrophobic anxiety and avoidance ranged form .22 to .84.

Authors: Febbraro, G. A. R., and Clum, G. A.

Article: A dimensional analysis of claustrophobia.

Journal: *Journal of Psychopathology and Behavioral Assessment*, December 1995, *17*(4), 335–351.

• • •

5483

Test Name: CLAUSTROPHOBIA SITUATIONS QUESTIONNAIRE

Purpose: To assess claustrophobic anxiety and avoidance.

Number of Items: 42 (anxiety); 40 (avoidance).

Format: 5-point scales. All items are presented.

Reliability: Alphas ranged from .87 to .94 across subscales.

Validity: Correlations with claustrophobia cognitions ranged from .22 to .84.

Authors: Febbraro, G. A. R., and Clum, G. A.

Article: A dimensional analysis of claustrophobia.

Journal: *Journal of Psychopathology and Behavioral Assessment*, December 1995, *17*(4), 335–351.

• • •

5484

Test Name: CLINICAL ANXIETY SCALE (FRENCH)

Purpose: To assess the frequency and intensity of anxious feelings.

Number of Items: 5

Format: 5-point frequency scales.

Reliability: Alpha was .86.

Authors: Senecal, C., et al.

Article: Self-regulation and academic procrastination.

Journal: *The Journal of Social Psychology*, October 1995, *135*(5), 607–619.

Related Research: Weisthuis, D., & Thyer, B. A. (1989). Development and validation of the Clinical Anxiety Scale: A rapid assessment instrument for empirical practice. *Educational and Psychological Measurement*, *49*, 153–163.

• • •

5485

Test Name: COGNITIVE ANXIETY INVENTORY— STATE

Purpose: To measure cognitive anxiety—state.

Number of Items: 6

Format: Responses are made on a 5-point scale ranging from 1 (*fits me not at all*) to 5 (*fits me extremely well*). All items are presented.

Reliability: Coefficient alpha was .92.

Authors: Weinstein, M., and Smith, J. C.

Article: Isometric squeeze relaxation (progressive relaxation) vs. meditation: Absorption and focusing as predictors of state effects.

Journal: *Perceptual and Motor Skills*, December 1992, *75*(3) Part 2, 1263–1271.

Related Research: Weinstein, M., & Smith, J. C. (1987). *Development of the Cognitive Anxiety Inventory*. Unpublished manuscript, Roosevelt University, Chicago.

• • •

5486

Test Name: COGNITION CHECKLIST

Purpose: To distinguish between the cognitive symptoms of anxiety and depression.

Number of Items: 26

Format: 5-point scales (*never* to *always*). All items are presented.

Reliability: Alphas ranged from .71 to .89.

Validity: Correlations with other variables ranged from .25 to .65 (partial correlations ranged from .05 to .39).

Authors: Osman, A., et al.

Article: Systematic evaluation of the psychometric properties of the Cognition Checklist with college students.

Journal: *Psychological Reports*, April 1995, *76*(2), 523–528.

Related Research: Beck, A.T., et al. (1987). Differentiating anxiety and depression: A test of the cognitive content-specificity hypothesis. *Journal of Abnormal Psychology*, *96*, 179–183.

• • •

5487

Test Name: COGNITIVE INTERFERENCE QUESTIONNAIRE

Purpose: To measure the frequency of intrusive thoughts.

Number of Items: 22

Format: 5-point scales.

Reliability: Alphas ranged from .78 to .90 across subscales.

Validity: Correlations with other variables ranged from .07 to .51.

Author: Comunin, A. L.

Article: Anxiety, cognitive interference and school performance of Italian children.

Journal: *Psychological Reports*, December 1993, *73*(3) Part I, 747–754.

Related Research: Sarason, I. G. (1984). Stress, anxiety, and cognitive interference: Reactions to tests. *Journal of Personality and Social Psychology*, *46*, 929–938.

• • •

5488

Test Name: COGNITIVE TRIAD INVENTORY

Purpose: To measure cognitions associated with depression.

Format: 6-point agreement scales.

Reliability: Alphas ranged from .81 to .93 across subscales.

Validity: Correlations with other variables ranged from .44 to .55.

Authors: Schill, T., and Sharp, M.

Article: Self-defeating personality and depression: A closer look.

Journal: *Psychological Reports*, June 1995, *76*(3) Part II, 1167–1170.

Related Research: Beckham, E. E., et al. (1986). Development of an instrument to measure Beck's cognitive triad: The Cognitive Triad Inventory. *Journal of Consulting and Clinical Psychology*, *54*, 566–567.

5489

Test Name: COLLEGE STUDENT LIFE EVENTS SCHEDULE

Purpose: To assess stress.

Number of Items: 112

Format: Each item is an event to which the respondent indicates the time period in which an event occurred. The participant then rates impact of all items that occurred during the past year.

Reliability: Test–retest reliability was .92 ($N = 68$).

Validity: Correlation with the Life Experience Scale was .62; correlations with other variables ranged from -.38 to .14.

Authors: Wohlgemuth, E., and Betz, N. E.

Article: Gender as a moderator of the relationships of stress and social support to physical health in college students.

Journal: *Journal of Counseling Psychology*, July 1991, *38*(3), 367–374.

Related Research: Sandler, I. N., & Lakey, B. (1982). Locus of control as a stress moderator: The role of control perceptions and social support. *American Journal of Community Psychology, 10*, 65–80.

■ ■ ■

5490

Test Name: COMPETITIVE SPORT ANXIETY INVENTORY

Purpose: To measure cognitive anxiety, somatic anxiety, and confidence.

Number of Items: 27

Format: A Likert format is employed. An example is given.

Reliability: Alpha coefficients ranged from .91 to .94.

Validity: Correlations with other variables ranged from -.50 to .70.

Authors: Jambor, E. A., et al.

Article: Association among fitness components, anxiety, and confidence following aerobic training in aquarunning.

Journal: *Perceptual and Motor Skills*, April 1994, *78*(2), 595–602.

Related Research: Martens, R., et al. (1982). *Cognitive and somatic dimensions of competitive anxiety*. Paper presented at the annual meeting of the North American Society for the Psychology of Sport and Physical Activity, University of Maryland, College Park.

■ ■ ■

5491

Test Name: COMPETITIVE STATE ANXIETY INVENTORY—2

Purpose: To measure precompetition state anxiety.

Number of Items: 27

Format: Includes 3 subscales: Cognitive Anxiety, Somatic Anxiety, and Self-Confidence. Responses are made on a 4-point scale ranging from 1 (*not at all*) to 4 (*very much so*). An example is presented.

Validity: Correlations with the Profile of Mood States ranged from -.43 to .39.

Authors: Terry, P. C., and Slade, A.

Article: Discriminant effectiveness of psychological state measures in predicting performance outcome in karate competition.

Journal: *Perceptual and Motor Skills*, August 1995, *81*(1), 275–286.

Related Research: Martens, R., et al. (1990). The Competitive State Anxiety Inventory—2 (CSAI—2). In R. Martens et al. (Eds.), *Competitive anxiety in sport* (pp.

117–190). Champaign, IL: Herman Kinetics.

■ ■ ■

5492

Test Name: COPE

Purpose: To assess coping.

Number of Items: 60

Format: 4-point scales ranging from 1 (*I usually don't do this at all*) to 4 (*I usually do this a lot*).

Reliability: Alphas ranged from .65 to .91 across subscales.

Validity: Correlations with other variables ranged from -.25 to .89.

Authors: Clark, K. K., et al.

Article: Validation evidence for three coping measures.

Journal: *Journal of Personality Assessment*, December 1995, *65*(3), 434–455.

Related Research: Carver, C. S., et al. (1989). Assessing coping strategies: A theoretically based approach. *Journal of Personality and Social Psychology, 45*, 267–283.

■ ■ ■

5493

Test Name: COPING HUMOR SCALE

Purpose: To assess role of humor in coping with problems.

Number of Items: 7

Format: 4-point Likert format. All items presented.

Reliability: Alpha was .56.

Authors: Thorson, J. A., and Powell, F. C.

Article: Measurement of sense of humor.

Journal: *Psychological Reports*, October 1991, *69*(2), 691-702.

Related Research: Martin, R. A., & Lefcourt, H. M. (1983). Sense of humor as a moderator of the relation between stressors and mood. *Journal of Personality and Social Psychology, 45*, 1313–1324.

■■■

5494

Test Name: COPING INVENTORY FOR STRESSFUL SITUATIONS

Purpose: To assess stable coping styles.

Number of Items: 48

Format: 5-point Likert format ranges from 1 (*not at all*) to 5 (*very much*).

Reliability: Alphas ranged from .83 to .90. Test–retest reliabilities (6 weeks) ranged from .51 to .73.

Authors: Heppner, P. P., et al.

Article: Progress in resolving problems: A problem-focused style of coping.

Journal: *Journal of Counseling Psychology*, July 1995, *42*(3), 279–293.

Related Research: Endler, N. S., & Parker, J. D. A. (1994). Assessment of multidimensional coping, task, emotion, and avoidance strategies. *Psychological Assessment, 6*, 50–60.

■■■

5495

Test Name: COPING RESPONSES SCALE

Purpose: To assess ways of coping in stressful situations.

Number of Items: 19

Format: Responses are made on a yes–no format.

Reliability: Internal consistency was .62. Test–retest reliability was .75.

Authors: Ludwick-Rosenthal, R., and Neufeld, R. W. J.

Article: Preparation for undergoing invasive medical procedure: Interacting effects of information and coping style.

Journal: *Journal of Consulting and Clinical Psychology*, February 1993, *61*(1), 156–164.

Related Research: Billings, A. G., & Moos, R. H. (1981). The role of coping responses and social resources in attenuating the stress of life events. *Journal of Behavioral Medicine, 4*, 139–157.

■■■

5496

Test Name: COPING SCALE

Purpose: To assess the control and escape dimensions of coping.

Number of Items: 8

Format: 5-point scales range from *hardly ever* to *almost always*. Sample items are presented.

Reliability: Alphas ranged from .58 to .70.

Authors: Rush, M. C., et al.

Article: Psychological resiliency in the public sector: "Hardiness" and pressure for change.

Journal: *Journal of Vocational Behavior*, February 1995, *46*(1), 17–39.

Related Research: Latack, J. C. (1986). Coping with job stress: Measures and future directions for scale development. *Journal of Applied Psychology, 71*, 377–385.

■■■

5497

Test Name: COPING STRATEGIES INVENTORY

Purpose: To measure situation-specific coping.

Number of Items: 72

Format: 5-point frequency scales range from 1 (*not at all*) to 5 (*very much*).

Reliability: Internal consistency ranged from 75 to .94. Test–retest reliability (2 weeks) ranged from .67 to .83.

Authors: Heppner, P. P., et al.

Article: Progress in resolving problems: A problem-focused style of coping.

Journal: *Journal of Counseling Psychology*, July 1995, *42*(3), 279–293.

Related Research: Tobin, D. L., et al. (1989). The hierarchical factor structure of the coping strategies inventory. *Cognitive Therapy and Research, 13*, 343–361.

■■■

5498

Test Name: COPING STRATEGIES SCALE

Purpose: To measure the importance of planning, seeking support, cognitive restructuring, and limiting job responsibilities.

Number of Items: 19

Format: Sample items described.

Reliability: Alphas ranged from .66 to .82.

Authors: Paden, S. L., and Buehler, C.

Article: Coping with dual-income lifestyle.

Journal: *Journal of Marriage and the Family*, February 1995, *57*(1), 101–110.

Related Research: Elman, M. R., & Gilbert, L. A. (1984). Coping strategies for role conflict in married professional women with children. *Family Relations, 33*, 317–327.

Schnittger, M. H., et al. (1990). Coping among dual-career men and women across the life cycle. *Family Relations, 39*, 199–205.

5499

Test Name: COPING STRATEGY INDICATOR

Purpose: To measure three modes of coping: problem solving, social-support seeking, and avoidance.

Number of Items: 33

Format: Respondents describe a recent (last 6 months) stressful event and then rate it on 33 items.

Reliability: Test–retest reliability was .56.

Authors: Amirkan, J. H.

Article: Criterion validity of a coping measure.

Journal: *Journal of Personality Assessment*, April 1994, *62*(2), 242–261.

Related Research: Amirkan, J. H. (1990). A factor analytically derived measure of coping: The Coping Strategy Indicator. *Journal of Personality and Social Psychology*, *59*, 1066–1076.

Clark, K. K., et al. (1995). Validation evidence for three coping measures. *Journal of Personality Assessment*, *65*, 434–455.

• • •

5500

Test Name: DAILY ASSESSMENT FORUM

Purpose: To measure symptom patterns of late luteal-phase disphoric disorder.

Number of Items: 33

Format: Checklist format.

Reliability: Test–retest correlations (25 days) ranged from .45 to .66.

Authors: Rivera-Tovar, A. D., et al.

Article: Symptom patterns in late luteal-phase dysphoric disorder.

Journal: *Journal of Psychopathology and Behavioral*

Assessment, June 1992, *14*(2), 189–199.

Related Research: Halbreich, U., & Endicott, J. (1982). Classification of premenstrual syndrome. In R. C. Friedman (Ed.), *Behavior and the menstrual cycle* (pp. 243–265). New York: Marcel Dekker.

• • •

5501

Test Name: DAILY HASSLES QUESTIONNAIRE

Purpose: To assess temporally limited life events.

Number of Items: 81

Format: A 4-point scale ranging from 1 (*not at all a hassle*) to 4 (*a very big hassle*).

Reliability: Coefficient alpha was .95.

Validity: Correlations with other variables ranged from -.38 to .58.

Authors: DuBois, D. L., et al.

Article: A prospective study of life stress, social support, and adaptation in early adolescence.

Journal: *Child Development*, June 1992, *63*(3), 542–557.

Related Research: Rowlinson, R. T., & Felner, R. D. (1988). Major life events, hassles, and adaptation in adolescence: Confounding in the conceptualization and measurement of life stress and adjustment revisited. *Journal of Personality and Social Psychology*, *55*, 432–444.

• • •

5502

Test Name: DAILY HASSLES SCALE

Purpose: To identify kind and degree of daily hassles.

Number of Items: 118

Format: The degree of severity of each daily hassle experienced is indicated on a 3-point scale. Hassles ranged from minor annoyances to fairly major pressures.

Validity: Correlations with other variables ranged from -.16 to .25 (*N* = 222).

Authors: Cantanzaro, S. J., and Greenwood, G.

Article: Expectancies for negative mood regulation, coping, and dysphoria among college students.

Journal: *Journal of Counseling Psychology*, January 1994, *41*(1), 34–44.

Related Research: Kanner, A. D., et al. (1981). Comparisons of two modes of stress measurement: Daily hassles and uplift versus major life events. *Journal of Behavioral Medicine*, *4*, 1–39.

• • •

5503

Test Name: DEATH ANXIETY SCALE

Purpose: To assess thoughts, feelings, and behaviors toward death.

Number of Items: 15

Format: True–false format.

Reliability: Test–retest ranged from .80 to .85.

Authors: Lefcourt, H. M., and Shepherd, R. S.

Article: Organ donation, authoritarianism and perspective-taking humor.

Journal: *Journal of Research in Personality*, March 1995, *29*(1), 121–128.

Related Research: Templar, D. I. (1970). The construction and validation of a death anxiety scale. *Journal of General Psychology*, *82*, 165–177.

5504

Test Name: DEATH BEHAVIOR QUESTIONNAIRE

Purpose: To assess willingness to confront death-salient situations.

Number of Items: 12

Format: Fill-in-the-blank format using a 5-point *won't* to *will* scale.

Reliability: Alpha was .74.

Validity: Correlations with other variables ranged from -.35 to .26.

Authors: Lefcourt, H. M., and Shepherd, R. S.

Article: Organ donation, authoritarianism and perspective-taking humor.

Journal: *Journal of Research in Personality*, March 1995, *29*(1), 121–128.

■ ■ ■

5505

Test Name: DEPRESSION–HAPPINESS SCALE

Purpose: To measure continuous negative to positive affect.

Number of Items: 25

Format: 4-point rating scale.

Reliability: Alpha was .91.

Validity: Correlations with other variables ranged from .43 to .62.

Authors: Lewis, C. A., and Joseph, S.

Article: Convergent validity of the Depression-Happiness Scale with measures of happiness and satisfaction with life.

Journal: *Psychological Reports*, June 1995, *76*(3) Part I, 876–878.

Related Research: McGreal, R., & Joseph, S. (1993). The Depression-Happiness Scale. *Psychological Reports*, *73*, 1279–1282.

5506

Test Name: DEPRESSION INDEX

Purpose: To measure depression.

Number of Items: 10

Reliability: Coefficient alpha was .80.

Validity: Correlations with other variables ranged from -.39 to .55.

Authors: Jex, S. M., et al.

Article: The measuring of occupational stress items to survey respondents.

Journal: *Journal of Applied Psychology*, October 1992, *77*(5), 623–628.

Related Research: Quinn, R. P., & Shepard, L. J. (1974). *Quality of Employment Survey*. Ann Arbor: University of Michigan, Institute for Social Research.

Zung, W. W. K. (1965). A self-rating depression scale. *Archives of General Psychiatry*, *12*, 63–70.

■ ■ ■

5507

Test Name: DEPRESSION-PRONENESS RATING SCALE

Purpose: To identify depression-prone individuals irrespective of their present affective state.

Number of Items: 3

Format: 9-point rating scales. All items presented.

Reliability: Alphas ranged from .76 to .83. Test–retest reliabilities ranged from .72 to .90.

Author: Cooley, E. L.

Article: Family expressiveness and proneness to depression among college women.

Journal: *Journal of Research in Personality*, September 1992, *26*(3), 281–287.

Related Research: Zemore, R.

(1983). Development of a self-report measure of depression-proneness. *Psychological Reports*, *52*, 211–216.

■ ■ ■

5508

Test Name: DEPRESSION SCALE

Purpose: To measure depression.

Number of Items: 3

Reliability: Reliability was .85.

Validity: Correlations with other variables ranged from -.35 to .58 (*N* = 398).

Authors: Thomas, L. T., and Ganster, D. L.

Article: Impact of family-supportive work variables on work-family conflict and strain: A control perspective.

Journal: *Journal of Applied Psychology*, February 1995, *80*(1), 6–15.

Related Research: Ware, J. E., et al. (1979). Conceptualization and measurement of health for adults in the Health Insurance Study: Vol. 3, Mental Health. Santa Monica, CA: Rand.

■ ■ ■

5509

Test Name: DEPRESSION SCALE

Purpose: To identify emotions experienced while thinking about work.

Number of Items: 8

Format: Responses are made on a 7-point scale ranging from 1 (*not at all*) to 7 (*very strong*). Examples are presented.

Reliability: Coefficient alpha was .90.

Validity: Correlations with other variables ranged from .16 to .58.

Authors: Buunk, B. P., and Janssen, P. P. M.

Article: Relative deprivation, career issues, and mental health among men in midlife.

Journal: *Journal of Vocational Behavior*, June 1992, *40*(3), 338–350.

■ ■ ■

5510

Test Name: DEPRESSION SCALE

Purpose: To provide a depression index.

Number of Items: 10

Format: Responses are made on a 4-point Likert format.

Reliability: Coefficient alpha was .82.

Validity: Correlations with other variables ranged from -.08 to .80.

Authors: Schaubroeck, J., et al.

Article: Dispositional affect and work-related stress.

Journal: *Journal of Applied Psychology*, June 1992, *77*(3), 322–335.

Related Research: Quinn, R. P., & Shepard, L. J. (1974). *Quality of Employment Survey*. Ann Arbor, MI: Institute for Social Research.

■ ■ ■

5511

Test Name: DEPRESSIVE EXPERIENCES QUESTIONNAIRE— ADOLESCENT VERSION

Purpose: To assess experiences associated with depression but not usually considered as symptoms of depression.

Number of Items: 66

Format: All items are presented.

Reliability: Test–retest reliabilities

(10 days to 1 year) ranged from .52 to .86.

Validity: Correlations with other variables ranged from -.43 to .83.

Authors: Blatt, S. J., et al.

Article: Psychometric properties of the Depressive Experiences Questionnaire for Adolescents.

Journal: *Journal of Personality Assessment*, August 1992, *59*(1), 82–98.

Related Research: Blatt, S. J., et al. (1976). Experiences of depression in normal young adults. *Journal of Abnormal Psychology, 85*, 383–389.

Blatt, S. J., et al. (1994). Subscales within the dependency factor of the Depressive Experiences Questionnaire. *Journal of Personality Assessment, 64*, 319–339.

■ ■ ■

5512

Test Name: DEPRESSIVE SYMPTOMS MEASURE

Purpose: To assess depressive symptoms.

Number of Items: 18

Format: 5-point frequency scales range from 0 (*never*) to 5 (*fairly often*).

Reliability: Alpha was .86.

Authors: Catanzaro, S. J., et al.

Article: Hassles, coping, and depressive symptoms in an elderly community sample: The role of mood regulation expectancies.

Journal: *Journal of Counseling Psychology*, July 1995, *42*(3), 259–265.

Related Research: Moos, R. H., et al. (1983). *Health and Daily Living Form Manual.* (Available from Social Ecology Laboratory, Department of Psychiatry and Behavioral Sciences, Stanford

University School of Medicine, Stanford, CA 94305)

■ ■ ■

5513

Test Name: DEPRESSIVE SYMPTOMS SCALE (FRENCH)

Purpose: To measure depression.

Number of Items: 6

Format: 5-point frequency scales.

Reliability: Alpha was .78.

Authors: Senecal, C., et al.

Article: Self-regulation and academic procrastination.

Journal: *The Journal of Social Psychology*, October 1995, *135*(5), 607–619.

Related Research: Derogatis, L. R., et al. (1974). The Hopkins Symptom Checklist (HSCL): A self-report symptom inventory. *Behavioral Science, 19*, 1–15.

■ ■ ■

5514

Test Name: DIABETES QUALITY OF LIFE

Purpose: To measure quality of life among people with diabetes.

Number of Items: 46

Format: 5-point satisfaction scales.

Reliability: Alphas ranged from .66 to .92. Test–retest ranged from .78 to .92.

Authors: Rankin, S. H., et al.

Article: Reliability and validity for a Chinese translation of the Center for Epidemiology Studies— Depression.

Journal: *Psychological Reports*, December 1993, *73*(3) Part II, 1291–1298.

Related Research: Jacobson, A., et al. (1988). Reliability and validity of a diabetes quality of life measure for the Diabetes Control and Complications Trial (DCCT). *Diabetes Care, 11,* 725–732.

■ ■ ■

5515

Test Name: DISCOMFORT ANXIETY INVENTORY

Purpose: To measure ego anxiety and discomfort anxiety.

Number of Items: 10

Format: Guttman format. All items are presented.

Reliability: Reproducibility ranged from .91 to .94. Scalability ranged from .83 to .84. Alphas ranged from .75 to .87.

Validity: Correlations with other variables ranged from .37 to .45.

Authors: Shorkey, C. T., and Whiteman, V. L.

Article: Development of the Ego and Discomfort Anxiety Inventory: Initial reliability and validity.

Journal: *Psychological Reports,* August 1993, *73*(1), 83–95.

■ ■ ■

5516

Test Name: DUKE HEALTH PROFILE

Purpose: To measure mental activity and attitude toward self.

Number of Items: 15

Format: Responses are made on a 6-point scale. Includes 4 factors.

Validity: Correlations with other variables ranged from -.15 to .22.

Authors: Delin, C. R., and Delin, P. S.

Article: Mental activity, health, and life satisfaction.

Journal: *Perceptual and Motor Skills,* December 1995, *81*(3) Part 1, 944–946.

Related Research: Parkerson, G. R., et al. (1990). The Duke

Health Profile: A 17-item measure of health and dysfunction. *Medical Care, 28*(11), 1056–1070.

■ ■ ■

5517

Test Name: DYSFUNCTIONAL ATTITUDE SCALE

Purpose: To measure the underlying assumptions that maintain depression.

Number of Items: 100

Format: 7-point Likert format.

Reliability: Correlations between parallel forms ranged from .79 to .92. Alphas ranged from .88 to .97.

Validity: Reliabilities were similar in depressed and nondepressed patients.

Authors: Nelson, L. D., et al.

Article: The Dysfunctional Attitude Scale: How well can it measure depressive thinking?

Journal: *Journal of Psychopathology and Behavioral Assessment,* September 1992, *14*(3), 217–223.

Related Research: Weissman, A., & Beck, A. (1978). *Development and validation of the Dysfunctional Attitude Scale.* Paper presented at the meeting of the Association for Advancement of Behavior Therapy, Chicago, Illinois.

■ ■ ■

5518

Test Name: DYSFUNCTIONAL ATTITUDE SCALE—FORM A

Purpose: To assess depressogenic attitudes and beliefs that reflect an individual's predisposition to depression.

Number of Items: 40

Format: Responses are made on a 7-point Likert scale ranging from 1

(*totally agree*) to 7 (*totally disagree*).

Reliability: Alpha coefficients were .90 (males) and .88 (females).

Validity: Correlations with other variables ranged from -.29 to .78.

Author: Moilanen, D. L.

Article: Depressive information processing among nonclinic, nonreferred college students.

Journal: *Journal of Counseling Psychology,* July 1993, *40*(3), 340–347.

Related Research: Weissman, A. N., & Beck, A. T. (1978, March). *Development and validation of the Dysfunctional Attitude Scale: A preliminary investigation.* Paper presented at the annual meeting of the American Educational Research Association, Toronto, Ontario, Canada.

■ ■ ■

5519

Test Name: EARLY TRAUMA CHECKLIST

Purpose: To provide a checklist of traumas relating to psychological damage, in general, and more specifically to development of the self.

Number of Items: 18

Format: Includes 4 factors: loss, abuse, chaos, and parental dysfunction.

Validity: Correlations with other variables ranged from -.29 to .43.

Authors: Zamostny, K. P., et al.

Article: Narcissistic injury and its relationship to early trauma, early resources, and adjustment to college.

Journal: *Journal of Counseling Psychology,* October 1993, *40*(4), 501–510.

Related Research: Zamostny, K. P., et al. (1991). *Early Resources*

Checklist. Unpublished instrument.

■ ■ ■

5520

Test Name: ECONOMIC HARDSHIP SCALE

Purpose: To measure perceived economic hardship.

Number of Items: 6

Format: 5-point frequency scales. Sample items presented.

Reliability: Alpha was .89.

Author: Amato, P. R.

Article: Psychological distress and the recall of childhood family characteristics.

Journal: *Journal of Marriage and the Family*, November 1991, *53*(4), 1011–1019.

Related Research: Pearlin, L., & Schoaler, C. (1978). The structure of coping. *Journal of Health and Social Behavior, 19,* 2–21.

■ ■ ■

5521

Test Name: EGO AND DISCOMFORT ANXIETY INVENTORY

Purpose: To measure anxiety of fear of negative ratings by others and fear of pain.

Number of Items: 10

Format: 6-point agreement scales.

Reliability: Test–retest ranged from .53 to .82.

Validity: Correlations with other variables ranged from .34 to .68.

Authors: Whiteman, V. L., and Shorkey, C. T.

Article: Reliability and validity of the Ego and Discomfort Anxiety Inventory.

Journal: *Psychological Reports,*

August 1994, *75*(1) Part II, 384–386.

Related Research: Shorkey, C. T., & Whiteman, V. L. (1993). Development of the Ego and Discomfort Anxiety Inventory: Initial validity and reliability. *Psychological Reports,* 73, 83–95.

■ ■ ■

5522

Test Name: EMOTIONAL STRESS SCALE

Purpose: To assess stress experienced in professional, marital, and parental roles.

Number of Items: 12

Format: 7-point frequency scales.

Reliability: Alphas ranged from .85 to .89 for women and from .88 to .92 for men.

Authors: Guelzow, M. G., et al.

Article: An exploratory path analysis of the stress process for dual-career men and women.

Journal: *Journal of Marriage and the Family*, February 1991, *53*(1), 131–164.

Related Research: Gilbert, L. A., et al. (1981). Coping with conflict between professional and maternal roles. *Family Relations, 30,* 419–426.

■ ■ ■

5523

Test Name: EXISTENTIONAL ANXIETY SCALE

Purpose: To measure concern about death, freedom, choice, meaning of life, and isolation.

Number of Items: 28

Format: 5-point Likert format.

Reliability: Alpha was .74.

Authors: Bylski, N. C., and Westman, A. S.

Article: Relationships among

defense style, existential anxiety and religiosity.

Journal: *Psychological Reports,* June 1991, *68*(3) Part II, 1389–1390.

Related Research: May, R., & Yalom, I. (1989). Existential psychotherapy. In R. J. Corsini & D. Wedding (Eds.), *Current psychotherapies* (pp. 362–402). Itasca, IL: F. E. Peacock.

■ ■ ■

5524

Test Name: FEAR OF NEGATIVE EVALUATION SCALE

Purpose: To measure fear of negative evaluation.

Number of Items: 30

Format: True–false format.

Reliability: KR-20 was .94.

Validity: Correlations with other variables ranged from -.58 to .77.

Authors: Whiteman, V. L., and Shorkey, C. T.

Article: Reliability and validity of the Ego and Discomfort Anxiety Inventory.

Journal: *Psychological Reports,* August 1994, *75*(1) Part II, 384–386.

Related Research: Watson, D., & Friend, R. (1969). Measurement of social-evaluative anxiety. *Journal of Consulting and Clinical Psychology, 33,* 448–457.

■ ■ ■

5525

Test Name: FEAR OF POWERLESSNESS SCALE

Purpose: To measure degree to which people fear the loss of power.

Number of Items: 36

Format: True–false format.

Reliability: KR-20 was .86.

Validity: Correlations with other variables ranged from -.19 to .52.

Author: Comunian, A. L.

Article: Anger, curiosity and optimism.

Journal: *Psychological Reports*, December 1994, *75*(3) Part II, 1523–1528.

Related Research: Good, L. R., et al. (1973). An objective measure of the motive to avoid powerlessness. *Psychological Reports*, *33*, 616–618.

■■■

5526

Test Name: FEAR OF SUCCESS SCALE

Purpose: To measure the benefits of success, the cost of success, and the relative value of success in relation to alternatives.

Number of Items: 27

Format: 7-point Likert format. All items presented.

Reliability: Internal consistency ranged from .69 to .73.

Author: Fried-Buchalter, S.

Article: Fear of success, fear of failure, and the impostor phenomenon: A factor analytic approach to convergent and discriminant validity.

Journal: *Journal of Personality Assessment*, April 1992, *58*(2), 368–379.

Related Research: Zuckerman, M., & Allison, S. N. (1976). An objective measure of fear of success: Construction and validation. *Journal of Personality Assessment*, *40*, 422–431.

■■■

5527

Test Name: FEAR QUESTIONNAIRE

Purpose: To measure the severity and change of phobic symptoms in phobic patients.

Number of Items: 24

Format: 9-point avoidance scales.

Reliability: Alphas ranged from .71 to .86 across subscales.

Validity: Correlations with other variables ranged from -.34 to .51.

Authors: Osman, A., et al.

Article: Further psychometric evaluation of the Fear Questionnaire: Responses of college students.

Journal: *Psychological Reports*, December 1993, *73*(3) Part II, 1363–1377.

Related Research: Marks, I. M., & Mathews, A. M. (1979). Brief self-rating for phobic patients. *Behavior Research and Therapy*, *17*, 265–267.

■■■

5528

Test Name: FEAR SURVEY SCHEDULE FOR CHILDREN

Purpose: To determine level of fear in children.

Number of Items: 80

Format: Responses are made on a 3-point scale ranging from *none* to *a lot*.

Reliability: Alpha was .95. Test–retest reliability was .55 after a 3-month interval.

Authors: Yang, B., et al.

Article: Only children and children with siblings in People's Republic of China: Levels of fear, anxiety, and depression.

Journal: *Child Development*, October 1995, *66*(5), 1301–1311.

Related Research: Ollendick, T. H. (1983). Reliability and validity of the revised Fear Survey

Schedule for Children (FSSC—R). *Behavior Research and Therapy*, *21*, 685–692.

■■■

5529

Test Name: FEELINGS AND CONCERNS SURVEY

Purpose: To assess feelings and concerns related to depression.

Number of Items: 18

Format: 5-point Likert format.

Reliability: Alpha was .87. Test–retest reliability (2–4 weeks) was .79.

Authors: Heppner, P. P., et al.

Article: Progress in resolving problems: A problem-focused style of coping.

Journal: *Journal of Counseling Psychology*, July 1995, *42*(3), 279–293.

Related Research: Nelson, E. (1981). *Feelings and concerns survey*. Unpublished manuscript.

■■■

5530

Test Name: FINANCIAL CONCERNS SCALE—REVISED

Purpose: To assess financial concerns.

Number of Items: 8

Format: Responses are made on a 5-point scale ranging from 1 (*seldom*) to 5 (*almost constantly*).

Reliability: Alpha coefficients were .83 and .92.

Validity: Correlations with other variables ranged from -.41 to .62.

Authors: Mallinckrodt, B., and Bennett, J.

Article: Social support and the impact of job loss in dislocated blue-collar workers.

Journal: *Journal of Counseling*

Psychology, October 1992, *39*(4), 482–489.

Related Research: Mallinckrodt, B., & Fretz, B. R. (1988). Social support and the impact of job loss and older professionals. *Journal of Counseling Psychology, 35,* 281–286.

● ● ●

5531

Test Name: FRUSTRATION STRAIN SCALE

Purpose: To measure feelings of frustration.

Number of Items: 4

Format: Responses are made on a 5-point Likert-type scale. A sample item is presented.

Reliability: Alpha coefficients were .80 and .84.

Validity: Correlations with other variables ranged from -.36 to .59.

Authors: Newton, T., and Keenan, T.

Article: Further analyses of the dispositional argument in organizational behavior.

Journal: *Journal of Applied Psychology*, December 1991, *76*(6), 781–787.

Related Research: Keenan, A., & Newton, T. J. (1984). Frustration in organizations: Relationships to role stress, climate and psychological strain. *Journal of Occupational Psychology, 57,* 57–65.

● ● ●

5532

Test Name: GENERAL HEALTH SURVEY

Purpose: To measure health-related quality of life.

Number of Items: 20 (one item taken as an overall indicator).

Format: 5-point rating scale (*excellent* to *poor*). Sample item presented.

Reliability: Correlations with the MOS multi-item inventory ranged from .52 to .82. Alphas of subscales in the total MOS ranged from .80 to .91. Test–retest was .82 ($p < .001$) for the single item.

Author: Kempen, G. I. J. M.

Article: The MOS Short-Form General Health Survey: Single item vs. multiple measures of health related quality of life: Some nuances.

Journal: *Psychological Reports*, April 1992, *70*(2), 608–610.

Related Research: Stewart, A. L., et al. (1988). The MOS Short-Form General Health Survey: Reliability and validity in a patient population. *Medical Care, 26,* 724–735.

● ● ●

5533

Test Name: GENERAL WELL-BEING QUESTIONNAIRE

Purpose: To measure suboptimal health over past 6 months.

Number of Items: 24

Format: 5-point frequency scales.

Reliability: Alphas ranged from .71 to .75.

Author: Ferguson, E.

Article: Rotter's Locus of Control Scale: A ten-item two factor model.

Journal: *Psychological Reports*, December 1993, *73*(3) Part II, 1267–1278.

Related Research: Cox, T., et al. (1983). The nature and assessment of general well-being. *Journal of Psychosomatic Research, 27,* 353–360.

5534

Test Name: GERIATRIC DEPRESSION SCALE

Purpose: To screen for depression in the elderly.

Number of Items: 30

Format: Yes–no format.

Reliability: Alpha was .94. Test–retest reliability was .85.

Validity: Correlations with other variables ranged from .73 to .91.

Authors: Kogan, E. S., et al.

Article: Clinical cutoffs for the Beck Depression Inventory and the Geriatric Depression Scale with older adult psychiatric outpatients.

Journal: *Journal of Psychopathology and Behavioral Assessment*, September 1994, *16*(3), 233–242.

Related Research: Yesavage, J. A., et al. (1983). Development and validation of a geriatric depression screening scale: A preliminary report. *Journal of Psychiatric Research, 17,* 37–49.

● ● ●

5535

Test Name: GERIATRIC HOPELESSNESS SCALE

Purpose: To assess loss of physical and cognitive ability, loss of personal worth, spiritual failure, hopelessness about recovering, lost nurturance, and respect.

Number of Items: 30

Format: True–false format.

Reliability: Alpha was .69.

Validity: Correlations with other variables ranged from -.40 to .25.

Authors: Hayslip, B., Jr., et al.

Article: Hopelessness in community-residing aged persons: A viable construct?

Journal: *Journal of Personality Assessment*, December 1995, 57(3), 498–505.

Related Research: Fry, P. S. (1984). Assessment of pessimism and despair in the elderly: A geriatric scale of hopelessness. In T. L. Brink (Ed.), *Clinical gerontology* (pp. 193–204). New York: Haworth.

■ ■ ■

5536

Test Name: GLOBAL ASSESSMENT SCALE

Purpose: To measure psychological adjustment.

Number of Items: 1

Format: Subjects are rated on a 100-point scale. Ten descriptive paragraphs are used to indicate 10-point intervals on the scale.

Reliability: The interrater reliability was .73 (median was .72).

Validity: Correlations with other variables ranged from -.64 to .10.

Authors: Kuhlman, T., et al.

Article: A team format for the Global Assessment Scale: Reliability and validity on an inpatient unit.

Journal: *Journal of Personality Assessment*, April 1991, 56(2), 335–347.

Related Research: Endicott, J., et al. (1976). The Global Assessment Scale: A procedure for measuring overall severity of psychiatric disturbance. *Archives of General Psychiatry, 33,* 766–771.

■ ■ ■

5537

Test Name: HAPPINESS MEASURES

Purpose: To provide a self-report measure of emotional well-being.

Number of Items: 2

Format: Includes a measure of happiness using an 11-point scale ranging from 0 (*extremely unhappy*) to 10 (*extremely happy*) and an estimate of the percentages of time spent happy, unhappy, and neutral.

Reliability: Test–retest coefficients ranged from .98 (over 2 days) to .86 or .88 (over 2 weeks) to .81 (over 1 month).

Author: Lightsey, O. R., Jr.

Article: "Thinking positive" as a stress buffer: The role of positive automatic cognitions in depression and happiness.

Journal: *Journal of Counseling Psychology*, July 1994, 41(3), 325–334.

Related Research: Fordyce, M. W. (1988). A review of research on the Happiness Measures: A sixty second index of happiness and mental health. *Social Indicators Research, 20,* 355–381.

■ ■ ■

5538

Test Name: HASSLES AND UPLIFTS SCALE

Purpose: To assess to what extent daily activities are hassles and uplifts.

Number of Items: 53

Format: 4-point scales ranged from 0 (*none or not applicable*), to 3 (*a great deal*).

Validity: Correlations with other variables ranged from -.23 to .63.

Authors: Clark, K. K., et al.

Article: Validation evidence for three coping measures.

Journal: *Journal of Personality Assessment*, December 1995, 65(3), 434–455.

Related Research: Delongis, A., et al. (1988). The impact of daily stress on health and mood: Psychological and social resources as mediators. *Journal of Personality and Social Psychology, 54,* 486–495.

■ ■ ■

5539

Test Name: HASSLES SCALE

Purpose: To assess the frustrating demands of everyday transactions.

Number of Items: 117

Format: Each item that has occurred during the past week is rated on a 3-point Likert scale ranging from 1 (*somewhat severe*) to 3 (*extremely severe*). Severity, Frequency, and Intensity ratings are obtained.

Reliability: Test–retest (1 month) reliability coefficients ranged from .48 to .79.

Validity: Correlations with other variables ranged from -.09 to .75.

Authors: Dixon, W. A., et al.

Article: Use of different sources of stress to predict hopelessness and suicide ideation in a college population.

Journal: *Journal of Counseling Psychology*, July 1992, 39(3), 342–349.

Related Research: Kanner, A. D., et al. (1981). Comparison of two modes of stress measurement: Daily hassles and uplifts versus major life events. *Journal of Behavioral Medicine, 4,* 1–39.

■ ■ ■

5540

Test Name: HASSLES SCALE FOR CHILDREN

Purpose: To determine the type and degree of "hassles" in children's daily lives.

Number of Items: 49

Format: Responses are made on a

3-point scale ranging from *a little* to *a lot*.

Reliability: Cronbach's alpha was .88 and test–retest was .74.

Authors: Carson, D. K., et al.

Article: Stress and coping as predictors of young children's development and psychological adjustment.

Journal: *Child Study Journal*, December 1992, *22*(4), 273–302.

Related Research: Parfenoff, S. H., & Jose, P. E. (1989, April). *Measuring daily hassles in children.* Paper presented at the biennial meeting of the Society for Research in Child Development, Kansas City, Missouri.

■ ■ ■

5541

Test Name: HEALTH AND DAILY LIVING FORM— REVISED VERSION

Purpose: To assess use of coping styles.

Number of Items: 32

Format: 4-point frequency scales.

Reliability: Reliability ranged from .60 to .74.

Authors: Klebanov, P. K., et al.

Article: Does neighborhood and family poverty affect mothers' parenting, mental health, and social support?

Journal: *Journal of Marriage and the Family*, May 1994, *56*(2), 441–455.

Related Research: Moos, R. H., et al. (1986). *Health and daily living form manual.* Palo Alto, CA: Veterans Administration and Stanford University Medical Centers.

■ ■ ■

5542

Test Name: HEALTH COMPLAINTS SCALE

Purpose: To assess health complaints.

Number of Items: 6

Format: Responses are made on a 4-point scale ranging from 1 (*never*) to 4 (*very often*).

Reliability: Coefficient alpha was .53.

Validity: Correlations with other variables ranged from -.03 to .30.

Authors: Buunk, B. P., and Janssen, P. P. M.

Articles: Relative deprivation, career issues, and mental health among men in midlife.

Journal: *Journal of Vocational Behavior*, June 1992, *40*(3), 338–350.

Related Research: Van Dykhuizen, N. (1980). *From stressors to strains.* Lisse, The Netherlands: Swetz and Zeitlinger.

■ ■ ■

5543

Test Name: HEALTH COMPLAINTS SCALE

Purpose: To measure the frequency of individuals' experience with various illness and symptoms in the past year.

Number of Items: 22

Format: 5-point rating scales.

Reliability: Alphas ranged from .82 to .83.

Authors: Spence, J. T., et al.

Article: Workaholism: Definition, measurement and preliminary results.

Journal: *Journal of Personality Assessment*, February 1992, *58*(1), 160–178.

Related Research: Spence, J. T., et al. (1987). Impatience versus achievement strivings in the Type A pattern: Differential effects on students' health and academic achievement. *Journal of Applied Psychology*, 75, 522–528.

■ ■ ■

5544

Test Name: HEALTH CONCERNS QUESTIONNAIRE

Purpose: To identify health concerns of the elderly.

Number of Items: 55

Format: Produces 2 scores: Total Distress and Unweighted Symptom Count.

Reliability: Alpha coefficients ranged from .70 to .91.

Validity: Correlations with the MMPI ranged from -.44 to .49.

Authors: Nation, P. C., and Dush, D. M.

Article: Factor structure of the Health Concerns Questionnaire in elderly chronic pain patients.

Journal: *Perceptual and Motor Skills*, April 1994, *78*(2), 652–654.

Related Research: Spoth, R. L., & Dush, D. M. (1988). The Adult Health Concerns Questionnaire: A psychiatric symptom checklist. *Innovations in Clinical Practice*, 7, 289–297.

■ ■ ■

5545

Test Name: HEALTH CONDITION SCALE

Purpose: To assess the health condition of respondents.

Number of Items: 21

Format: Responses are in a yes–no format.

Reliability: Coefficient alpha was .71.

Author: Hanisch, K. A.

Article: Reasons people retire and their relations to attitudinal and behavioral correlates in retirement.

Journal: *Journal of Vocational Behavior*, August 1994, *45*(1), 1–16.

Related Research: Hanisch, K. A. (1992, November). *The development of a health condition scale and its relation to health and retirement satisfaction.* Paper presented at the American Psychological Association/National Institute for Occupational Safety and Health Conference, Washington, DC.

▪▪▪

5546

Test Name: HEALTH/FITNESS STATUS

Purpose: To provide a self-report of health/fitness status.

Number of Items: 4

Format: Responses are made on 5-point scales. All items are presented.

Reliability: Coefficient alpha was .83.

Validity: Correlations with other variables ranged from -.22 to .36.

Authors: Woodruff, S. I., and Conway, T. L.

Article: A longitudinal assessment of the impact of health/fitness status and health behavior on perceived quality of life.

Journal: *Perceptual and Motor Skills*, August 1992, *75*(1), 3–14.

▪▪▪

5547

Test Name: HEALTH OPINION SURVEY

Purpose: To measure psychological functioning.

Number of Items: 45

Format: 5-point and 3-point rating scales.

Reliability: Alphas ranged from .85 to .95 across subscales.

Authors: Uba, L., and Chung, R.

Article: The relationship between trauma and financial and physical well-being among Cambodians in the United States.

Journal: *The Journal of General Psychology*, July 1991, *118*(3), 215–225.

Related Research: Leighton, D. C., et al. (1963). *The character of danger.* New York: Basic Books.

▪▪▪

5548

Test Name: HEALTH-PROMOTING LIFESTYLE PROFILE

Purpose: To measure six dimensions of wellness: self-actualization, health responsibility, exercise, nutrition, interpersonal support, and stress management.

Number of Items: 48

Reliability: Total alpha was .92. Subscale alphas ranged from .70 to .90. Test–retest ranged from .81 to .90 on subscales. Total test–retest was .93.

Validity: Validity demonstrated by first- and second-order factor analysis.

Authors: Oleckno, W. A., and Blacconiere, M. J.

Article: Relationship of religiosity to wellness and other health-related behaviors and outcomes.

Journal: *Psychological Reports*, June 1991, *68*(3) Part I, 819–826.

Related Research: Walker, S. N., et al. (1987). The Health-Promoting Lifestyle Profile: Development and psychometric properties. *Nursing Research, 36,* 76–81.

▪▪▪

5549

Test Name: HIV SYMPTOMS SCALE

Purpose: To assess symptoms of HIV.

Number of Items: 18

Format: 5-point frequency scales ranging from *never* to *two or more times a week*.

Reliability: Alpha was .93.

Validity: Correlations with other variables ranged from .27 (*depression*) to .21 (*coping*).

Authors: DeGenova, M. K., et al.

Article: Ways of coping among HIV-infected individuals.

Journal: *The Journal of Social Psychology*, October 1994, *133*(5), 655–663.

▪▪▪

5550

Test Name: HOPELESSNESS SCALE

Purpose: To assess the degree to which one's cognitive schemata are characterized by pessimistic expectation.

Number of Items: 20

Format: True–false items. Examples are presented.

Reliability: Internal consistency was .93.

Validity: Correlations with clinical ratings was .74 and with other variables ranged from .45 to .70 ($N = 217$).

Authors: Dixon, W. A., et al.

Article: Problem-solving appraisal, hopelessness, and suicide ideation: Evidence for a mediational model.

Journal: *Journal of Counseling Psychology*, January 1994, *41*(1), 91–98.

Related Research: Beck, A. J., et al. (1974). The measure of pessimism: The Hopelessness Scale. *Journal of Consulting and Clinical Psychology, 42,* 861–865.

5551

Test Name: HOPELESSNESS SCALE FOR CHILDREN

Purpose: To measure hopelessness in children.

Number of Items: 17

Format: Responses are made using a true–false format.

Reliability: Coefficient alpha was .45 for young children and .62 for older children.

Authors: Guerra, N. G., et al.

Article: Stressful events and individual beliefs as correlates of economic disadvantage and aggression among urban children.

Journal: *Journal of Consulting and Clinical Psychology*, August 1995, *63*(4), 518–528.

Related Research: Kazlin, A. E., et al. (1983). Hopelessness, depression, and suicidal intent among psychiatrically disturbed inpatient children. *Journal of Consulting and Clinical Psychology*, *51*, 504–510.

■ ■ ■

5552

Test Name: HOPE SCALE

Purpose: To assess cognitive dispositional attributes of goal attainment and meeting goals.

Number of Items: 8

Format: 4-point Likert format ranges from 1 (*definitely false*) to 4 (*definitely true*).

Reliability: Internal consistency ranged from .60 to .80.

Validity: Correlations with other variables ranged from -.60 to .58.

Authors: Multon, K. D., et al.

Article: An empirical derivation of career decision subtypes in a high school sample.

Journal: *Journal of Vocational Behavior*, August 1995, *47*(1), 76–92.

Related Research: Snyder, C. R., et al. (1991). The will and the ways: Development and validation of an individual-differences measure of hope. *Journal of Personality and Social Psychology*, *60*, 570–585.

■ ■ ■

5553

Test Name: HOPE SCALE

Purpose: To provide an individual-differences measure of hope.

Number of Items: 12

Format: Items measure agency and pathways. Sample items are presented.

Reliability: Internal consistency coefficients ranged from .63 to .84. Test–retest (3 weeks) reliability was .85; for 8 weeks test–retest reliability was .76, and for 10 weeks test–retest reliability was .82.

Validity: Correlations with other variables ranged from -.04 to .36.

Authors: Heppner, M. J., et al.

Article: Assessing psychological resources during career change: Development of the Career Transition Inventory.

Journal: *Journal of Vocational Behavior*, February 1994, *44*(1), 55–74.

Related Research: Snyder, C. R., et al. (1991). The will and the ways: Development and validation of an individual differences measure of hope. *Journal of Personality and Social Psychology*, *60*, 570–585.

■ ■ ■

5554

Test Name: HOPKINS SYMPTOM CHECKLIST—25, HMONG VERSION

Purpose: To assess clinical symptoms over time.

Number of Items: 25

Format: 4-point scales range from *not at all* to *extremely*.

Reliability: Alphas ranged from .82 to .89.

Authors: Mouanoutoua, V. L., and Brown, L. G.

Article: Hopkins Symptom Checklist—25, Hmong Version: A screening instrument for psychological distress.

Journal: *Journal of Personality Assessment*, April 1995, *64*(2), 376–383.

Related Research: Mattsson, N. B., et al. (1969). Dimensions of symptom distress in anxious neurotic outpatients. *Psychopharmacology Bulletin*, *5*, 19–32.

■ ■ ■

5555

Test Name: HOPKINS SYMPTOM CHECKLIST

Purpose: To assess psychological functioning.

Number of Items: 58

Format: Includes 5 scales: somatization, obsessive–compulsive, interpersonal sensitivity, anxiety, and depression. Responses indicating frequency for each symptom are made on a 4-point scale ranging from 0 (*not at all*) to 3 (*very frequently, much of the time*).

Reliability: Alpha coefficients ranged from .84 to .87; Test–retest (1 week) reliabilities ranged from .75 to .84.

Validity: Correlations with other variables ranged from -.33 to .37.

Authors: Kenny, M. E., and Donaldson, G. A.

Article: Contributions of parental

attachment and family structure to the social and psychological functioning of first-year college students.

Journal: *Journal of Counseling Psychology*, April 1991, *38*(4), 479–486.

Related Research: Derogatis, L., et al. (1974). The Hopkins Symptom Checklist (HSCL): A self-report symptom inventory. *Behavioral Science, 19*, 1–15.

■ ■ ■

5556

Test Name: ILLNESS EFFECTS QUESTIONNAIRE

Purpose: To measure quality of life by appraising illness in terms of biological, psychological, and interpersonal disruption.

Number of Items: 20

Format: 8-point rating scales.

Reliability: Alpha was .93. Test–retest (1 day) ranged from .93 to .99.

Authors: Wagner, M. K., et al.

Article: Cognitive determinants of quality of life after cancer.

Journal: *Psychological Reports*, August 1995, *77*(1), 147–154.

Related Research: Greenberg, G. D., et al. (1989). *Manual for Illness Effects Questionnaire.* Philadelphia: Author.

■ ■ ■

5557

Test Name: IMPACT OF EVENT SCALE

Purpose: To measure reactions to a traumatic event.

Number of Items: 15

Format: All items are presented.

Reliability: Alphas ranged from .92 to .93.

Authors: Hendrix, C. C., et al.

Article: Validation of the Impact of Event Scale on a sample of American Vietnam veterans.

Journal: *Psychological Reports*, August 1994, *75*(1) Part I, 321–322.

Related Research: Horowitz, M., et al. (1979). Impact of Event Scale: A measure of subjective stress. *Psychosomatic Medicine, 41*, 209–218.

■ ■ ■

5558

Test Name: INDEX OF LIFE STRESS

Purpose: To assess stressful life events experienced by foreign students from Asia.

Number of Items: 31

Format: 4-point rating scales range from 0 (*never*) to 3 (*often*). All items are presented.

Reliability: Test–retest reliability (1 month) was .87. KR-20 reliability was .86.

Validity: Correlations with other variables ranged form -.47 to .51.

Authors: Yang, B., and Clum, G. A.

Article: Measures of life stress and social support specific to an Asian student population.

Journal: *Journal of Psychopathology and Behavioral Assessment*, March 1991, *17*(1), 51–67.

■ ■ ■

5559

Test Name: INVENTORY OF BELIEFS RELATED TO OBSESSION SCALE

Purpose: To measure intrusive or obsessional thoughts.

Number of Items: 20

Format: 6-point scales range from

1 (*I firmly believe this statement is false*) to 6 (*I firmly believe this statement is true*).

Reliability: Alphas ranged from .76 to .82. Test–retest reliability was .74.

Validity: Correlations with other variables ranged from -.05 to .90.

Authors: Freeston, M. H., et al.

Article: Beliefs about obsessional thoughts.

Journal: *Journal of Psychopathology and Behavioral Assessment*, March 1993, *15*(1), 1–21

■ ■ ■

5560

Test Name: INVENTORY OF PHYSICAL SYMPTOMS

Purpose: To assess physical symptoms of an obvious psychological nature.

Number of Items: 37

Format: 4-point rating scales ranged from 0 (*not at all*) to 3 (*quite a bit*).

Reliability: Alpha was .87.

Authors: Santor, D. A., and Zuroff, D. C.

Article: Depressive symptoms: Effects of negative affectivity and failing to accept the past.

Journal: *Journal of Personality Assessment*, October 1994, *63*(2), 294–312.

Related Research: Cohen, S., & Hokerman, H. M. (1983). Positive events as buffers of life change stress. *Journal of Applied and Social Psychology, 13*, 99–125.

■ ■ ■

5561

Test Name: INVENTORY TO DIAGNOSE DEPRESSION

Purpose: To assess and diagnose

major depression.

Number of Items: 25

Reliability: Alpha was .89.

Validity: Correlations with other variables ranged from .67 to .70.

Authors: Haaga, A. F., et al.

Article: Discriminant validity of the Inventory to Diagnose Depression.

Journal: *Journal of Personality Assessment*, April 1993, *60*(2), 285–289.

Related Research: Zimmerman, M., et al. (1986). A self-report scale to diagnose major depressive disorder. *Archives of General Psychiatry, 43*, 1076–1081.

■ ■ ■

5562

Test Name: ITCHING SCALE

Purpose: To assess patients' cognitions concerning itching.

Number of Items: 20 (2 scales)

Format: Responses are made on a 5-point Likert scale ranging from 0 (*never*) to 4 (*always*).

Reliability: One scale has a Cronbach's alpha of .90. The other scale has a Cronbach's alpha of .80.

Authors: Ehlers, A., et al.

Article: Treatment of atopic dermatitis: A comparison of psychological and dermatological approaches to relapse prevention.

Journal: *Journal of Consulting and Clinical Psychology*, August 1995, *63*(4), 624–635.

Related Research: Ehlers, A., et al. (1993). Kognitive faktoren bein juckeriz: Enwicklung and validierung eines fragebogens [Cognitive factors in itching: Development and validation of a questionnaire]. *Verhaltenstherapie, 3*, 112–119.

5563

Test Name: JOB AFFECT SCALE

Purpose: To measure four mood states.

Number of Items: 12

Format: The mood states include nervousness, relaxation, enthusiasm, and fatigue. Responses are made on a 5-point scale ranging from 1(*very slightly or not at all*) to 5 (*extremely*). All items are presented.

Reliability: Alpha coefficients ranged from .66 to .91.

Validity: Correlations with other variables ranged from -.26 to .33. Test–retest (4 weeks) correlations ranged from .39 to .48.

Authors: Oldham, G. R., et al.

Article: Listen while you work? Quasi-experimental relations between personal stereo-headset use and employee work responses.

Journal: *Journal of Applied Psychology*, October 1995, *80*(5), 547–564.

Related Research: Brief, A. P., et al. (1988). Should negative affectivity remain on unmeasured variable in the study of job stress? *Journal of Applied Psychology, 73*, 193–198.

■ ■ ■

5564

Test Name: LEISURE SATISFACTION MEASUREMENT

Purpose: To measure leisure time satisfaction.

Number of Items: 24

Format: Responses are made on a 5-point Likert-type scale ranging from *almost never true* to *almost always true*.

Reliability: Alpha reliability coefficient was .94.

Authors: Ragheb, M. G., and McKinney, J.

Article: Campus recreation and perceived academic stress.

Journal: *Journal of College Student Development*, January 1993, *34*(1), 5–10.

Related Research: Beard, J. G., & Ragheb, M. G. (1980). Measuring leisure satisfaction. *Journal of Leisure Research, 12*, 20–33.

■ ■ ■

5565

Test Name: LIFE EVENTS CHECKLIST

Purpose: To measure the occurrence of major life events.

Number of Items: 46

Format: Checklist uses a 4-point scale ranging from 1 (*no effect*) to 4 (*great effect*).

Validity: Correlations with other variables ranged from -.21 to .35.

Authors: DuBois, D. L., et al.

Article: A prospective study of life stress, social support, and adaptation in early adolescence.

Journal: *Child Development*, June 1992, *63*(3), 542–557.

Related Research: Johnson, J. H., & McCutcheon, S. M. (1980). Assessing life stress in older children and adolescents: Preliminary findings with the Life Events Checklist. In I. G. Sarason & C. D. Spielberger (Eds.), *Stress anxiety* (Vol. 7; pp. 111–125). Washington, DC: Hemisphere.

■ ■ ■

5566

Test Name: LIFE EVENTS SURVEY FOR COLLEGIATE ATHLETICS

Purpose: To measure life stress for student athletes.

Number of Items: 69

Format: Responses are made on an 8-point Likert scale (*extremely negative* to *extremely positive*).

Reliability: Test–retest reliabilities ranged from .76 to .84.

Author: Petrie, T. A.

Article: Racial differences in the prediction of college football players' academic performances.

Journal: *Journal of College Student Development*, November 1993, *34*(5), 418–421.

Related Research: Petrie, T. A. (1992). Psychosocial antecedents of athletic injury: The effects of life stress and social support on women collegiate gymnasts. *Behavioral Medicine, 18*, 1–16.

■■■

5567

Test Name: LIFE EXPERIENCES SURVEY

Purpose: To rate life events in the past 6 months as to positive or negative impact.

Number of Items: 30

Format: Checklist and 7-point rating scales. All items are presented.

Validity: Correlations with other variables ranged from -.15 to .14.

Authors: Bartelstone, J. H., and Trull, T. J.

Article: Personality, life events and depression.

Journal: *Journal of Personality Assessment*, April 1995, *64*(2), 279–294.

Related Research: Sarason, I. G., et al. (1978). Assessing the impact of life changes: Development of the Life Experiences Survey. *Journal of Consulting and Clinical Psychology, 101*, 26–36.

5568

Test Name: LIFE EXPERIENCES SURVEY

Purpose: To measure events that occurred in the past year.

Number of Items: 47

Format: Yes–no and 7-point rating scales for each item.

Reliability: Alphas ranged from .56 to .88.

Authors: McKenry, P. C., et al.

Article: Toward a biopsychosocial model of domestic violence.

Journal: *Journal of Marriage and the Family*, May 1995, *57*(2), 307–320.

Related Research: Sarason, I., et al. (1978). Assessing the impact of life changes: Development of the life experiences survey. *Journal of Consulting and Clinical Psychology, 64*, 932–946.

■■■

5569

Test Name: LIFE EXPERIENCES SURVEY

Purpose: To measure life stress.

Number of Items: 57

Format: Responses are made on a 7-point anchored scale ranging from -3 to 3.

Reliability: Test–retest reliability was .63.

Authors: Rudd, M. D., et al.

Article: Help negation after acute suicidal crisis.

Journal: *Journal of Consulting and Clinical Psychology*, June 1995, *63*(3), 499–503.

Related Research: Sarason, I., et al. (1978). Assessing the impact of life changes: Development of the Life Experiences Survey. *Journal of Consulting and Clinical Psychology, 46*, 932–946.

5570

Test Name: LIFE EXPERIENCES SURVEY

Purpose: To measure life stress by assessing the incidences of various important life change events that have occurred during the past 6 months or 1 year.

Number of Items: 64

Format: Severity for each event is determined by rating on a 7-point Likert scale ranging from -3 (*extremely negative*) to +3 (*extremely positive*). Severity, Frequency, and Intensity ratings can be obtained.

Reliability: Test–retest (6 weeks) reliability ranged from .63 to .64.

Validity: Correlations with other variables ranged from -.11 to .75.

Authors: Dixon, W. A., et al.

Article: Use of different sources of stress to predict hopelessness and suicide ideation in a college population.

Journal: *Journal of Counseling Psychology*, July 1992, *39*(3), 342–349.

Related Research: Sarason, I., et al. (1975). Assessing the impact of life changes: Development of the Life Experiences Survey. *Journal of Consulting and Clinical Psychology, 46*, 932–946.

■■■

5571

Test Name: LIFE ORIENTATION TEST

Purpose: To measure dispositional optimism.

Number of Items: 4

Format: 5-point agree–disagree format.

Reliability: Alpha was .77.

Authors: Strutton, D., and Lumpkin, J.

Article: Relationship between

optimism and coping strategies in the work environment.

Journal: *Psychological Reports*, December 1992, *71*(3) Part II, 1179–1186.

Related Research: Scheier, M., & Caruer, C.S. (1987). Dispositional optimism and physical well-being: The influence of generalized outcome expectancies on health. *Journal of Personality*, *55*, 169–210.

■ ■ ■

5572

Test Name: LIFE ORIENTATION TEST

Purpose: To measure optimism and pessimism.

Number of Items: 8

Format: 5-point agreement scales. Sample items presented.

Reliability: Alpha was .76. Test–retest (4 weeks) was .79.

Authors: Carver, C. S., et al.

Article: The possible selves of optimists and pessimists.

Journal: *Journal of Research in Personality*, June 1994, *28*(2), 133–141.

Related Research: Scheier, M., & Carver, C. S. (1985). Optimism, coping and health: Assessment and implications of generalized outcome expectancies. *Health Psychology*, *4*, 219–247.

■ ■ ■

5573

Test Name: LIFE ORIENTATION TEST

Purpose: To measure dispositional optimism.

Number of Items: 10

Format: Responses are made on a 5-point scale ranging from 0 (*strongly disagree*) to 4 (*strongly agree*).

Reliability: Coefficient alpha was .77.

Authors: Fontaine, K. R., and Shaw, D. F.

Article: Effects of self-efficacy and dispositional optimism on adherence to step aerobic exercise classes.

Journal: *Perceptual and Motor Skills*, August 1995, *81*(1), 251–255.

Related Research: Scheier, M. F., et al. (1994). Distinguishing optimism from neuroticism (and trait anxiety, self-mastery, and self-esteem): A re-evaluation of the Life Orientation Test. *Journal of Personality and Social Psychology*, *67*, 1063–1078.

■ ■ ■

5574

Test Name: LIFE ORIENTATION TEST

Purpose: To measure dispositional optimism.

Number of Items: 12

Format: Responses are made on a 5-point scale ranging from 1 (*strongly agree*) to 5 (*strongly disagree*). Examples are presented.

Reliability: Coefficient alpha was .76. Test–retest (4 weeks) reliability was .79.

Authors: Cross, S. E., and Markus, H. R.

Article: Self-schemas, possible selves, and competent performance.

Journal: *Journal of Educational Psychology*, September 1994, *86*(3), 423–438.

Related Research: Scheier, M. F., & Carver, C. S. (1985). Optimism, coping, and health: Assessment and implications of generalized outcome expectancies.

Health Psychology, *4*, 219–247.

■ ■ ■

5575

Test Name: LIFE SATISFACTION INDEX— FORM A

Purpose: To measure the presence or absence of feelings of happiness.

Number of Items: 11

Format: Items refer to the presence or feelings of happiness, life satisfaction, and zest for life.

Validity: Correlations with other variables ranged from .09 to .70.

Authors: Robbins, S. B., et al.

Article: Goal continuity as a mediator of early retirement adjustment: Testing a multidimensional model.

Journal: *Journal of Counseling Psychology*, January 1994, *41*(1), 18–26.

Related Research: Liang, J., et al. (1980). Social interaction and morale: A reexamination. *Journal of Gerontology*, *35*, 109–125.

■ ■ ■

5576

Test Name: LIFE SATISFACTION INDEX— GREEK VERSION

Purpose: To measure adults' feelings of satisfaction with their lives.

Number of Items: 20

Reliability: Alpha was .78.

Validity: Correlations with other variables ranged from -.51 to -.37.

Authors: Malikiosi-Loizos, M., and Anderson, L. R.

Article: Reliability of a Greek translation of the Life Satisfaction Index.

Journal: *Psychological Reports*,

June 1994, *74*(3) Part II, 1319–1322.

Related Research: Neugarten, B. L., et al. (1961). The measurement of life satisfaction. *Journal of Gerontology*, *31*, 134–143.

* * *

5577

Test Name: LIFE SATISFACTION QUESTIONNAIRE

Purpose: To assess satisfaction with work, spouse (partner), and family relationships and life in general.

Number of Items: 17

Format: 7-point satisfaction scales. All items described.

Reliability: Alphas ranged from .71 to .87 across subscales.

Validity: Correlations between scales ranged from .23 to .61.

Authors: Bunker, B. B., et al.

Article: Quality of life in dual career families: Commuting versus single-residence couples.

Journal: *Journal of Marriage and the Family*, May 1992, *54*(2), 399–407.

* * *

5578

Test Name: LIFE SATISFACTION SCALE

Purpose: To measure life satisfaction.

Number of Items: 4

Format: Responses are made on a 5-point Likert scale ranging from 1 (*very satisfied*) to 5 (*very satisfied*).

Reliability: Coefficient alpha was .67.

Validity: Correlations with other variables ranged from -.32 to .42.

Authors: Prussia, G. E., et al.

Article: Psychological and behavioral consequences of job loss: A covariance structure analysis using Wiener's (1985) Attribution Model.

Journal: *Journal of Applied Psychology*, June 1993, *78*(3), 382–394.

Related Research: Kinicki, A. V., & Latack, J. C. (1990). Explication of the construct of coping with involuntary job loss. *Journal of Vocational Behavior*, *36*, 339–360.

* * *

5579

Test Name: LIFE SATISFACTION SCALE

Purpose: To measure life satisfaction.

Number of Items: 5

Format: 7-point agreement scales. Sample item presented.

Reliability: Alphas ranged from .71 to .82.

Authors: Kurdek, L. A., and Fine, M. A.

Article: Cognitive correlates of satisfaction for mothers and stepfathers in stepfather families.

Journal: *Journal of Marriage and the Family*, August 1971, *53*(3), 565–572.

Related Research: Diever, E. R., et al. (1985). The Satisfaction with Life Scale. *Journal of Personality Assessment*, *49*, 71–75.

* * *

5580

Test Name: LIFE SATISFACTION SCALE

Purpose: To assess overall life satisfaction.

Number of Items: 12

Format: Includes 10 bipolar objectives with responses made on a 7-point scale and two general questions. Examples are presented.

Reliability: Coefficient alpha was .89.

Validity: Correlations with other variables ranged from -.08 to .41.

Authors: Judge, T. A., and Watanabe, S.

Article: Another look at the job satisfaction–life satisfaction relationship.

Journal: *Journal of Applied Psychology*, December 1993, *78*(6), 939–948.

* * *

5581

Test Name: LIFE SATISFACTION SCALE

Purpose: To rate satisfaction with aspects of living.

Number of Items: 20

Format: Responses are made on a 7-point Likert scale.

Reliability: Alpha was .87.

Author: Healy, C.

Article: Exploring a path linking anxiety, career maturity, grade point average, and life satisfaction in a community college population.

Journal: *Journal of College Student Development*, May 1991, *32*, 207–211.

Related Research: Sorenson, A. G. (1986, April). *A life satisfaction scale assessing 15 areas identified by John Flanagan as important to life.* Paper presented at the 1986 American Educational Research Association Convention, Washington, DC.

* * *

5582

Test Name: LIFE SUCCESS MEASURES SCALE

Purpose: To measure the dimensions of life success.

Number of Items: 42

Format: 5-point Likert format ranges from 5 (*always important*) to 1 (*never important*).

Reliability: Alphas ranged from .58 to .89.

Authors: Chusmir, L. H., and Parker, B.

Article: Success strivings and their relationship to affective work behaviors: Gender differences.

Journal: *The Journal of Social Psychology*, February 1992, *132*(1), 87–99.

Related Research: Parker, B., & Chusmir, L. H. (1991). *Development and validation of the life success measures scale.* Unpublished manuscript, Florida Atlantic University, Ft. Lauderdale, Florida.

■ ■ ■

5583

Test Name: LOSS QUESTIONNAIRE

Purpose: To measure symptoms commonly associated with love loss.

Number of Items: 20

Format: Items are rated on a 4-point scale.

Reliability: Cronbach's alpha was .79 (*N* = 64)

Validity: Correlations with other variables were .70 and .52.

Authors: Ogles, B. M., et al.

Article: Comparison of self-help books for coping with loss: Expectations and attributions.

Journal: *Journal of Counseling Psychology*, October 1991, *38*(4), 387–393.

5584

Test Name: MALAISE INVENTORY

Purpose: To screen for a wide range of adult emotional disorders.

Number of Items: 24

Format: Responses are made using a yes–no format.

Reliability: Alpha reliability was .78. Test–retest in one sample of women was .91.

Authors: Chase-Lansdale, P. L., et al.

Article: The long-term effects of parental divorce on the mental health of young adults: A developmental perspective.

Journal: *Child Development*, December 1995, *66*(6), 1614–1634.

Related Research: Rutter, M., et al. (Eds.). (1970). *Education, health, and behavior.* London: Longman.

■ ■ ■

5585

Test Name: MANIFEST ANXIETY SCALE

Purpose: To measure manifest anxiety.

Number of Items: 50

Reliability: Spearman-Brown values were .78 (men) and .88 (women).

Validity: Correlations with other variables ranged from .52 to .83.

Authors: Payne, R. B., and Corly, T. J.

Article: Motivational effects of anxiety or psychomotor performance.

Journal: *Perceptual and Motor Skills*, December 1994, *79*(3) Part 2, 1507–1521.

Related Research: Taylor, J. A.

(1953). A personality scale of manifest anxiety. *Journal of Abnormal and Social Psychology*, *48*, 285–290.

■ ■ ■

5586

Test Name: MATERNAL RISK FOR DEPRESSIVE SYMPTOMOTOLOGY— QUESTIONNAIRE FORM

Purpose: To identify the context placing a mother at risk for depression.

Number of Items: 37

Format: Includes 4 subscales. Likert-style response is used.

Reliability: Alpha coefficients for the 3 subscales used ranged from .65 to .72.

Authors: Hock, E., and Schirtzinger, M. B.

Article: Maternal separation anxiety: Its developmental course and relation to maternal mental health.

Journal: *Child Development*, February 1992, *63*(1), 93–102.

Related Research: Schirtzinger, M. B., & Hock, E. (1990). *Maternal depression: Measurement and characteristics.* Unpublished manuscript, Ohio State University, Columbus.

■ ■ ■

5587

Test Name: MENTAL HEALTH INVENTORY

Purpose: To measure affective states.

Number of Items: 38

Format: 5- and 6-point Likert scales.

Reliability: Alpha was .96.

Authors: Florian, V., and Dangoor, N.

Article: Personal familial adaptation of women with severe physical disabilities: A further validation of the ABCX model.

Journal: *Journal of Marriage and the Family*, August 1994, *56*(3), 735–746.

Related Research: Viet, C. T., & Ware, J. E. (1983). The structure of psychological distress and well-being in the general population. *Journal of Consulting and Clinical Psychology*, *51*, 730–742.

•••

5588

Test Name: MENTAL, PHYSICAL, AND SPIRITUAL WELL-BEING SCALE

Purpose: To measure positive aspects of health.

Number of Items: 30

Format: All items presented.

Reliability: Alphas ranged from .75 to .85 across subscales. Test–retest reliability (1 month) ranged from .87 to .97.

Validity: Correlations with the General Health Questionnaire ranged from -.10 to -.39.

Authors: Vella-Broderick, D. A., and Allen, F. C.

Article: Development and psychometric validation of the Mental, Physical, and Spiritual Well-Being Scale.

Journal: *Psychological Reports*, October 1995, *77*(2), 659–674.

•••

5589

Test Name: META-REGULATION AND EVALUATION SCALES

Purpose: To measure thoughts about mood (such as "I shouldn't feel this way") in two dimensions: evaluation and regulation.

Number of Items: 39

Format: 5-point rating scales. All items presented.

Reliability: Alphas ranged from .75 to .87. Correlations between scales ranged from -.32 to .54.

Validity: Correlations with criterion scales ranged from -.43 to .50.

Authors: Mayer, J. D., and Stevens, A. A.

Article: An emerging understanding of the reflective (meta-) experience of mood.

Journal: *Journal of Research in Personality*, September 1994, *28*(3), 351–373.

•••

5590

Test Name: MINI-MENTAL STATE TEST

Purpose: To evaluate mental status.

Number of Items: 5–10 minutes.

Format: Includes sheet of paper for scoring, pencil, knife, tape, button, and watch.

Reliability: Test–retest reliability was .89.

Validity: Concurrent validity with WAIS-Verbal was .78 and with WAIS-Performance was .66.

Authors: Fuller, G. B., and Doan, G. H.

Article: Differentiation of Alzheimer and cerebrovascular patients with the Minnesota Percepto-Diagnostic Test—Revised.

Journal: *Perceptual and Motor Skills*, December 1992, *75*(3) Part 1, 715–721.

Related Research: Folstein, M. E., et al. (1975). Mini-Mental State: A practical method for grading the cognitive state of patients for the clinician. *Journal of Psychiatric Research*, *12*, 189–198.

5591

Test Name: MODIFIED SCALE FOR SUICIDAL IDEATION

Purpose: To assess the intensity, pervasiveness, and characteristics of suicidal ideation.

Number of Items: 18

Reliability: Internal consistency was .94.

Validity: Correlations with other variables ranged from .32 to .47 ($N = 217$).

Authors: Dixon, W. A., et al.

Article: Problem-solving appraisal, hopelessness, and suicide ideation: Evidence for a mediational model.

Journal: *Journal of Counseling Psychology*, January 1994, *41*(1), 91–98.

Related Research: Miller, I. W., et al. (1986). The modified scale for suicidal ideation: Reliability and validity. *Journal of Consulting and Clinical Psychology*, *54*, 724–725.

Beck, A. T., et al. (1979). Assessment of suicidal intention: The Scale for Suicidal Ideation. *Journal of Consulting and Clinical Psychology*, *47*, 343–352.

•••

5592

Test Name: MOOD SURVEY

Purpose: To measure happy and sad moods.

Number of Items: 9

Format: Participants indicate their agreement with each item. An example is presented.

Reliability: Alpha coefficients were .91 and .92.

Validity: Correlations with other variables ranged from -.70 to .83.

Authors: Judge, T. A., and Locke, E. A.

Article: Effect of dysfunctional thought processes on subjective well-being and job satisfaction.

Journal: *Journal of Applied Psychology*, June 1993, *78*(3), 475–490.

Related Research: Underwood, B., & Froming, W. J. (1980). The mood survey: A personality measure of happy and sad moods. *Journal of Personality Assessment, 44,* 404–414.

■ ■ ■

5593

Test Name: MOTOR ACTIVITY ANXIETY TEST

Purpose: To assess one's willingness to face threatening motor requirements.

Number of Items: 16

Format: Each item is a picture to be rated on a 1 to 5 scale indicating degree of willingness to do what is depicted. Includes 4 factors.

Reliability: Coefficient alpha was .84.

Validity: Correlations with other variables ranged from .27 to .49.

Authors: Bortoli, L., and Robazza, C.

Article: Relationships between scores on the Motor Activity Anxiety Test and the Fear Survey Schedule.

Journal: *Perceptual and Motor Skills*, December 1995, *81*(3) Part 2, 1192–1194.

Related Research: Bortoli, L., & Robazza, C. (1994). The Motor Activity Anxiety Test. *Perceptual and Motor Skills, 79,* 299–305.

■ ■ ■

5594

Test Name: MULTIDIMENSIONAL SEXUALITY QUESTIONNAIRE

Purpose: To measure 12 psychosexual tendencies: depression, anxiety, preoccupation, fear, internal control, external control, internal awareness, image control, motivation, assertiveness, esteem, and satisfaction.

Number of Items: 60

Format: 5-point Likert format.

Reliability: Alphas ranged from .62 to .90 across subscales.

Validity: Correlations with other variables ranged from -.37 to .43.

Author: Dupras, A.

Article: Internalized homophobia and psychosexual adjustment among gay men.

Journal: *Psychological Reports*, August 1994, *75*(1) Part I, 23–28.

Related Research: Snell, W. E., et al. (1993). The Multidimensional Sexuality Questionnaire: An objective measure of psychological tendencies associated with human sexuality. *Annals of Sex Research, 6,* 27–55.

■ ■ ■

5595

Test Name: MULTIPLE ROLE STRESS SCALE

Purpose: To measure stress resulting from constantly shifting from one role to another.

Number of Items: 8

Format: Responses are made on a 5-point scale ranging from 1 (*strongly disagree*) to 5 (*strongly agree*). A sample item is presented.

Reliability: Coefficient alpha was .89.

Validity: Correlations with other variables ranged from .00 to .33.

Author: Peluchette, J. V. E.

Article: Subjective career success: The influence of individual difference, family, and organizational variables.

Journal: *Journal of Vocational Behavior*, October 1993, *43*(2), 198–208.

Related Research: Kopelman, R., et al. (1983). A model of work, family, and interrole conflict: A construct validation study. *Organizational Behavior and Human Performance, 32,* 198–215.

■ ■ ■

5596

Test Name: MULTI-TASK BEHAVIORAL AVOIDANCE TASK

Purpose: To assess behavioral avoidance in agoraphobia.

Number of Items: 6

Format: Participants are required to try to complete three tasks and to rate anxiety by self-report. Tasks are described.

Reliability: Alpha ranged from .81 to .84.

Validity: Correlations with other variables ranged from -.71 to .22.

Authors: de Beurs, E., et al.

Article: Behavioral assessment of avoidance in agoraphobia.

Journal: *Journal of Psychopathology and Behavioral Assessment*, December 1991, *13*(4), 285–300.

■ ■ ■

5597

Test Name: NEGATIVE AFFECTIVITY SCALE

Purpose: To identify negative feeling states.

Number of Items: 10

Format: Responses are made on a 5-point scale ranging from 1 (*very slightly* or *not at all*) to 5 (*extremely*).

Reliability: Reliability was .90.

Validity: Correlations with other variables ranged from -.24 to .48.

Authors: Begley, T. M., and Czajka, J. M.

Article: Panel analysis of the moderating effects of commitment on job satisfaction, intent to quit, and health following organizational change.

Journal: *Journal of Applied Psychology*, August 1993, *78*(4), 552–556.

Related Research: Watson, D., et al. (1938). Development and validation of brief measures of positive and negative affect: The PANAS scales. *Journal of Personality and Social Psychology*, *54*, 1063–1070.

■ ■ ■

5598

Test Name: NEGATIVE MOOD INDEX

Purpose: To measure negative mood.

Number of Items: 6

Format: 4-point rating scales.

Reliability: Alpha was .93.

Authors: MacEwen, K. E., and Bailing, J.

Article: Effects of maternal employment experiences on children's behavior via mood, cognitive difficulties and parenting behavior.

Journal: *Journal of Marriage and the Family*, August 1991, *53*(3), 635–644.

Related Research: Nowlis, V. (1965). Research with the Mood Adjective Checklist. In S. S. Tompkins & C. E. Izard (Eds.), *Affect, cognition and personality* (pp. 352–389). New York: Springer.

5599

Test Name: NEGATIVE MOOD REGULATION SCALE

Purpose: To measure generalized expectancies for negative mood regulation.

Number of Items: 30

Format: Responses are made on a 5-point scale ranging from 1 (*strongly disagree*) to 5 (*strongly agree*). Examples are presented.

Reliability: Alpha coefficients ranged from .86 to .92. Test–retest (4 weeks) correlations ranged from .73 to .74. Test–retest (6–8 weeks) correlations ranged from .67 to .78.

Validity: Correlations with other variables ranged from -.48 to -.46 (*N* = 222).

Authors: Cantanzaro, S. J., and Greenwood, G.

Article: Expectancies for negative mood regulation, coping, and dysphoria among college students.

Journal: *Journal of Counseling Psychology*, January 1994, *41*(1), 34–44.

Related Research: Catanzaro, S. J., & Mearns, J. (1990). Measuring generalized expectancies for negative mood regulation: Initial scale development and implications. *Journal of Personality Assessment*, *54*, 546–563.

■ ■ ■

5600

Test Name: NEUTRAL OBJECTS SATISFACTION QUESTIONNAIRE

Purpose: To measure individual satisfaction with everyday life events.

Number of Items: 24

Format: Responses are made on a 3-point scale ranging from *satisfied* through *neutral* to *dissatisfied*.

Reliability: Coefficient alpha for the general happiness and disposition scales were .80 and .78.

Authors: Hanisch, K. A.

Article: Reasons people retire and their relations to attitudinal and behavioral correlates in retirement.

Journal: *Journal of Vocational Behavior*, August 1994, *45*(1), 1–16.

Related Research: Weitz, J. (1952). A neglected concept in the study of job satisfaction. *Personnel Psychology*, *5*, 201–205.

■ ■ ■

5601

Test Name: NEUTRAL OBJECTS SATISFACTION QUESTIONNAIRE

Purpose: To measure affective disposition.

Number of Items: 25

Format: Respondents indicate their feeling about each item by circling 1 (*dissatisfied*), 2 (*neutral*), or 3 (*satisfied*). All items are presented.

Reliability: Split-half reliability was .75.

Authors: Judge, T. A., and Bretz, R. D., Jr.

Article: Report on an alternative measure of affective disposition.

Journal: *Educational and Psychological Measurement*, Winter 1993, *53*(4), 1095–1104.

Related Research: Weitz, J. (1952). A neglected concept in the study of job satisfaction. *Personnel Psychology*, *5*, 201-205.

■ ■ ■

5602

Test Name: OBJECT RELATIONS AND REALITY TESTING INVENTORY

Purpose: To assess reality testing with several subscales: hallucination and delusions, reality distortion, and uncertainty of perception.

Number of Items: 90

Format: True–false format. Sample item presented.

Reliability: Alphas ranged from .79 to .90 across subscales.

Author: Bassman, L.

Article: Reality testing and self-reported AIDS self-care behavior.

Journal: *Psychological Reports*, February 1992, *70*(1), 59–65.

Related Research: Bell, M. (1988). *An introduction to the Bell Object Relations and Reality Testing Inventory.* Unpublished manuscript, VA Medical Center, Psychology Service 116B, West Haven, CT 06512.

■ ■ ■

5603

Test Name: OBJECT RELATIONS INVENTORY

Purpose: To discriminate borderline personality from schizophrenia.

Number of Items: 45

Format: True–false format.

Reliability: Alpha was .79 or higher across subscales.

Authors: Little, T., et al.

Article: Narcissism and object relations.

Journal: *Psychological Reports*, December 1992, *71*(3) Part I, 799–808.

Related Research: Bell, M., et al. (1986). A scale for the assessment of object relations: Reliability, validity and factorial invariance. *Journal of Clinical Psychology*, *42*, 733–741.

5604

Test Name: OBSESSIVE THOUGHTS QUESTIONNAIRE

Purpose: To assess obsessive thoughts.

Number of Items: 29

Format: 5-point rating scales range from 0 (*this does not trouble me at all*) to 4 (*this thought troubles me constantly*).

Reliability: Alpha was .91.

Validity: Correlations with the Yale–Brown Scale ranged from .00 to .69.

Authors: Frost, R. O., et al.

Article: The relationship of the Yale-Brown Obsessive Compulsive Scale (YBOCS) to other measures of compulsive symptoms in a nonclinical population.

Journal: *Journal of Personality Assessment*, August 1995, *65*(1), 158–168.

Related Research: Bouvard, M., et al. (1984). Etude preliminaire d'une linte de pensees obsedantes. *L'Ecephale*, *XV*, 351–354.

■ ■ ■

5605

Test Name: OCCUPATIONAL LIFE ASSESSMENT (JAPANESE)

Purpose: To assess life strain.

Number of Items: 46

Format: 5-point scales ranging from 1 (*not at all applicable*) to 5 (*highly applicable*).

Reliability: Alpha was .90.

Validity: Correlations with other variables ranged from -.27 to .47.

Authors: Matusi, T., et al.

Article: Work-family conflict and stress-buffering effects of husband support and coping behavior among Japanese married working women.

Journal: *Journal of Vocational Behavior*, October 1995, *47*(2), 172–198.

Related Research: Tanaka, K., et al. (1993). The development of a Japanese version of the Occupational Stress Inventory: Basic analysis of theoretical applicability. *Bulletin of Faculty of Education, No 93*, Okayama University.

■ ■ ■

5606

Test Name: ORIENTATION TO LIFE QUESTIONNAIRE

Purpose: To measure the comprehensibility, manageability, and meaningfulness of life.

Number of Items: 29

Format: 7-point Likert format.

Reliability: Alpha was .90.

Authors: Florian, V., and Dangoor, N.

Article: Personal familial adaptation of women with severe physical disabilities: A further validation of the ABCX model.

Journal: *Journal of Marriage and the Family*, August 1994, *56*(3), 735–746.

Related Research: Antonovsky, A. (1987). *Unraveling the mystery of health: How people manage stress and stay well.* San Francisco: Jossey-Bass.

■ ■ ■

5607

Test Name: OUTCOME QUESTIONNAIRE

Purpose: To evaluate progress in therapy by assessing symptoms and distress.

Number of Items: 45

Time Required: 7 minutes.

Reliability: Alpha was .93.

Authors: Nebeker, R. S., et al.

Article: Ethnic Differences on the Outcome Questionnaire.

Journal: *Psychological Reports*, December 1995, *77*(3) Part I, 875–879.

Related Research: Lambert, M. J., et al. (1994*). Administration and scoring manual for the Outcome Questionnaire* (OQ–45.11). Salt Lake City, UT: IHC Center for Behavioral Healthcare Efficacy.

■ ■ ■

5608

Test Name: OVERALL QUALITY OF LIFE

Purpose: To assess life satisfaction/positive affect in a variety of areas.

Number of Items: 14

Format: Responses are made on a 7-point scale ranging from 1 (*terrible*) to 7 (*delighted*). All items are presented.

Reliability: Coefficient alpha was .91.

Validity: Correlations with other variables ranged from -.23 to .35.

Authors: Woodruff, S. I., and Conway, T. L.

Article: A longitudinal assessment of the impact of health/fitness status and health behavior on perceived quality of life.

Journal: *Perceptual and Motor Skills*, August 1992, *75*(1), 3–14.

Related Research: Caplan, R. D., et al. (1984). *Tranquilizer use and well-being: A longitudinal study of social and psychological effects.* Ann Arbor, MI: Institute for Social Research.

■ ■ ■

5609

Test Name: PARAGRAPHS ABOUT LEISURE

Purpose: To assess the psychological benefits of leisure.

Number of Items: 44

Format: Each item is a paragraph that describes a psychological need. Participants respond to each item on a 5-point scale ranging from 1 (*not true*) to 5 (*definitely true*).

Reliability: Spearman-Brown split-half reliability ranged from .88 to .99.

Validity: Omega-squared values ranged from .08 to .56 for various subscales across different leisure activities.

Authors: Tinsley, E. A., and Eldredge, B. D.

Article: Psychological benefits of leisure participation: A taxonomy of leisure activities based on their need-gratifying properties.

Journal: *Journal of Counseling Psychology*, April 1995, *42*(2), 123–132.

Related Research: Tinsley, E. A., & Kass, R. A. (1980). The construct validity of the Leisure Activities Scales and the Paragraphs About Leisure. *Educational and Psychological Measurement, 40*, 219–226.

■ ■ ■

5610

Test Name: PARANOIA SCALE

Purpose: To measure paranoia.

Number of Items: 24

Format: 5-point scale.

Reliability: Alpha was .80.

Authors: Christofferson, D., and Stamp, C.

Article: Examining the relationship between Machiavellianism and paranoia.

Journal: *Psychological Reports*, February 1995, *76*(1), 67–70.

Related Research: Fenigstein, A., & Vanable, P. A. (1992). Paranoia and self-consciousness.

Journal of Personality and Social Psychology, 62, 129–138.

■ ■ ■

5611

Test Name: PARENT SOMATIC COMPLAINTS

Purpose: To assess the extent of parent physical symptoms.

Number of Items: 12

Format: Responses are made on a 5-point scale (respondents indicate the extent to which they had experienced each symptom in the previous year).

Reliability: Coefficient alpha was .83 for mothers and .81 for fathers.

Author: Walker, L. S.

Article: Somatic complaints in pediatric patients: A prospective study of the role of negative life events, child social and academic competence, and parental somatic symptoms.

Journal: *Journal of Consulting and Clinical Psychology*, December 1994, *62*(6), 1213–1221.

Related Research: Derogatis, L. R., et al. (1973). SCL-90: An outpatient psychiatric rating scale—preliminary report. *Psychopharmacology Bulletin, 9*, 13–28.

■ ■ ■

5612

Test Name: PATIENTS' COPING STRATEGIES AFTER SURGERY SCALE

Purpose: To examine patients' pain coping strategies employed during the first 3 days following dental surgery.

Number of Items: 13

Format: Responses are made on a 5-point scale ranging from *not used at all* to *used most of the time.* Includes 2 factors: Avoidance and Attention.

Reliability: Coefficient alpha was .82.

Validity: Correlations with other variables ranged from -.26 to .64.

Authors: Baume, R. R., et al.

Article: Pain perception, coping strategies, and stress management among periodontal patients with repeated surgeries.

Journal: *Perceptual and Motor Skills*, February 1995, *80*(1), 307–319.

■ ■ ■

5613

Test Name: PATIENT STRESS BEHAVIOR INDEX

Purpose: To assess patients' stress-related behavior during periodontal surgical procedure.

Number of Items: 5

Format: Periodontist rates patients on a 5-point scale.

Reliability: Coefficient alpha was .87.

Validity: Correlations with other variables ranged from .01 to .52.

Authors: Baume, R. M., et al.

Article: Pain perception, coping strategies, and stress management among periodontal patients with repeated surgeries.

Journal: *Perceptual and Motor Skills*, February 1995, *80*(1), 307–319.

■ ■ ■

5614

Test Name: PERCEIVED CLIENT SENSITIVITY TO LOSS SCALE

Purpose: To assess client vulnerability to feelings of loss during counseling termination.

Number of Items: 4

Format: Responses are made on a 5-point Likert-type scale ranging

from 1 (*not at all*) to 5 (*a great deal*).

Reliability: Coefficient alpha was .66.

Validity: Correlations with other variables ranged from -.26 to .44.

Authors: Boyer, S. P., and Hoffman, M. A.

Article: Counselor affective reactions to termination: Impact of counselor loss history and perceived client sensitivity to loss.

Journal: *Journal of Counseling Psychology*, July 1993, *40*(3), 271–277.

Related Research: Marx, J. A., & Gelso, C. J. (1987). Termination of individual counseling in a university center. *Journal of Counseling Psychology*, *34*, 3–9.

Gould, R. P. (1978). Students' experience with the termination phase of individual treatment. *Smith College Studies in Social Work*, *48*, 235–269.

■ ■ ■

5615

Test Name: PERCEIVED LIFE SATISFACTION SCALE

Purpose: To provide an index of a young person's life satisfaction.

Number of Items: 19

Format: Responses are made on a 6-point Likert scale.

Reliability: Internal consistency ranged from .70 to .80.

Authors: Dow, T., and Huebner, E. S.

Article: Adolescents' perceived quality of life: An exploratory investigation.

Journal: *Journal of School Psychology*, Summer 1994, *32*(2), 185–199.

Related Research: Smith, D. C., Adelman, H. S., et al. (1987). Students' perceptions of control at

school and problem behavior and attitudes. *Journal of School Psychology*, *25*, 167–176.

■ ■ ■

5616

Test Name: PERCEIVED STRESS SCALE

Purpose: To measure perceived stress.

Number of Items: 14

Format: 5-point Likert format. Sample items are presented.

Reliability: Alphas ranged from .81 to .86.

Authors: Chwalisz, K., and Kisler, V.

Article: Perceived stress: A better measure of caregiver burden.

Journal: *Measurement and Evaluation in Counseling and Development*, April 1995, *28*(1), 88–98.

Related Research: Cohen, S. (1986). Contrasting the Hassles Scale and the Perceived Stress Scale: Who's really measuring perceived stress? *Health Psychology*, *7*(3), 269–297.

■ ■ ■

5617

Test Name: PERSONAL COPING SCALE

Purpose: To assess personal coping with conflicting role demands.

Number of Items: 8

Format: 5-point scales. Sample items are presented.

Reliability: Alphas ranged from .74 to .76.

Validity: Correlations with other variables ranged from -.20 to .38.

Authors: Cohen, A., and Kirchmeyer, C.

Article: A multidimensional

approach to the relation between organizational commitment and nonwork participation.

Journal: *Journal of Vocational Behavior*, April 1995, *46*(2), 189–202.

Related Research: Kirchmeyer, C. (1993). Nonwork to work spillover: A more balanced view of the experiences and coping of professional women and men. *Sex Roles*, *20*, 1–22.

∎∎∎

5618

Test Name: PERSONALITY ADJUSTMENT QUESTIONNAIRE

Purpose: To measure psychological adjustment.

Number of Items: 42

Format: 4-point Likert format. Sample items presented.

Reliability: Total alpha was .70. Subscale alphas ranged from .42 to .61.

Authors: Rohner, R. P., et al.

Article: Effects of corporal punishment, perceived caretaker warmth and cultural beliefs on the psychological adjustment of children in St. Kitts, West Indies.

Journal: *Journal of Marriage and the Family*, August 1991, *53*(3), 681–693.

Related Research: Rohner, R. P. (1986). *The warmth dimension: Foundations of parental acceptance rejection theory.* Newbury Park, CA: Sage Publications.

∎∎∎

5619

Test Name: PERSONAL PROBLEMS INVENTORY— MODIFIED

Purpose: To identify problem

concerns and willingness to seek help.

Number of Items: 22

Format: Includes three areas: academic, interpersonal, and substance abuse.

Reliability: Alpha coefficients ranged from .62 to .94.

Authors: Solberg, V. S., et al.

Article: Asian-American students' severity of problems and willingness to seek help from university counseling centers: Role of previous counseling experience, gender, and ethnicity.

Journal: *Journal of Counseling Psychology*, July 1994, *41*(3), 275–279.

Related Research: Cash, T. F., et al. (1975). When counselors are heard but not seen: Initial impact of physical attractiveness. *Journal of Counseling Psychology*, *22*, 273–279.

∎∎∎

5620

Test Name: PERSONAL STYLE INVENTORY—REVISED

Purpose: To assess vulnerability to depression.

Number of Items: 48

Format: 6-point Likert format. All items are presented.

Reliability: Alphas ranged from .70 to .88.

Validity: Correlations with other variables ranged from -.24 to .86.

Authors: Robins, C. J., et al.

Article: The Personal Style Inventory: Preliminary validation studies of new measures of sociotropy and autonomy.

Journal: *Journal of Psychopathology and Behavioral Assessment*, December 1994, *16*(4), 277–300.

∎∎∎

5621

Test Name: PERSONAL STYLES SCALE

Purpose: To measure derivatives of psychodynamic conflict.

Number of Items: 25

Format: Respondents check if items describe them. All items presented.

Reliability: KR-20 reliability was .88. Test–retest reliability (2 weeks) was .81.

Validity: Correlations with 94-item revision was .92. Correlations with other variables ranged from -.47 to .73. Other validity data are presented.

Authors: Conte, H. R., et al.

Article: Development of a self-report conflict scale.

Journal: *Journal of Personality Assessment*, February 1995, *64*(1), 168–184.

∎∎∎

5622

Test Name: PERSONAL VIEWS SURVEY

Purpose: To measure hardiness as commitment, control, and challenge.

Number of Items: 45

Time Required: 10 minutes.

Reliability: Internal consistencies ranged from .68 to .89.

Validity: Correlations with other variables ranged from -.54 to .54. Subscale correlations ranged from .42 to .68.

Authors: Maddi, S. R., and Khoshaba, D. M.

Articles: Hardiness and mental health.

Journal: *Journal of Personality Assessment*, October 1994, *63*(2), 265–274.

Related Research: Bartone, P. T. (1991, June). *Development and validation of a short hardiness measure.* Poster presented at the convention of the American Psychological Society, Washington, DC.

■ ■ ■

5623

Test Name: PERSONAL VIEWS SURVEY

Purpose: To measure views about life in terms of control, commitment, and challenge.

Number of Items: 50

Format: 4-point scales range from 0 (*not at all true*) to 3 (*completely true*).

Reliability: Alphas ranged from .70 to .84.

Validity: Correlations with other variables ranged from -.16 to .49.

Authors: Niles, S. G., and Sowa, C. J.

Articles: Mapping the nomalogical network of career self-efficacy.

Journal: *The Career Development Quarterly*, September 1992, *41*(1), 13–21.

Related Research: Hardiness Institute. (1987). *Fact sheet for third generation hardiness test.* Unpublished manuscript.

■ ■ ■

5624

Test Name: PHYSICAL HEALTH COMPLAINTS

Purpose: To identify physical health complaints.

Number of Items: 10

Format: Responses are either *never*, *once or twice*, or *three or more times*.

Reliability: Reliabilities were .74 and .70.

Validity: Correlations with other variables ranged from -.28 to .21.

Authors: Begley, T. M., and Czjka, J. M.

Article: Panel analysis of the moderating effects of commitment on job satisfaction, intent to quit, and health following organizational change.

Journal: *Journal of Applied Psychology*, August 1993, *78*(4), 552–556.

Related Research: Caplan, R. D., et al. (1975). *Job demands and worker health.* Washington, DC: U.S. Department of Health, Education, and Welfare.

■ ■ ■

5625

Test Name: PHYSICAL SYMPTOMATOLOGY SCALE

Purpose: To measure physical symptomatology.

Number of Items: 17

Format: Participants are asked the frequency with which they have experienced a list of physical symptoms. An example is presented.

Reliability: Coefficient alpha was .87.

Validity: Correlations with other variables ranged from -.21 to .55.

Authors: Schaubroeck, J., et al.

Article: Dispositional affect and work-related stress.

Journal: *Journal of Applied Psychology*, June 1992, *77*(3), 322–335.

Related Research: Caplan, R. D., et al. (1975). *Job demands and worker health* (Department of Health, Education and Welfare Publication No. 75-160). Washington, DC: U.S. Department of Health, Education and Welfare.

5626

Test Name: PHYSICAL SYMPTOMS CHECKLIST

Purpose: To measure symptoms of ill health such as headache, cough, and upset stomach.

Number of Items: 35

Format: 4-point frequency scales.

Reliability: Alpha was .86.

Author: Lai, J. C. L.

Article: The moderating effect of optimism on the relation between hassles and somatic complaints.

Journal: *Psychological Reports*, June 1995, *76*(3) Part I, 883–894.

Related Research: Cohen, S., & Hoberman, H. (1983). Positive events and social supports as buffers of life change stress. *Journal of Applied Social Science*, *13*, 99–125.

■ ■ ■

5627

Test Name: PHYSICAL SYMPTOMS INVENTORY

Purpose: To identify physical symptoms experienced by participants.

Number of Items: 42

Format: Responses are made on a Likert-type scale.

Reliability: Coefficient alpha was .90.

Authors: Holmbeck, G. N., and Wandrei, M. L.

Article: Individual and relational predictors of adjustment in first-year college students.

Journal: *Journal of Counseling Psychology*, January 1993, *40*(1), 73–78.

Related Research: Wahler, H. J. (1969). The Physical Symptoms Inventory: Measuring levels of somatic complaining behavior.

Journal of Clinical Psychology, 24, 207–211.

■ ■ ■

5628

Test Name: PHYSICAL SYMPTOMS SURVEY

Purpose: To measure somatic complaints.

Number of Items: 25

Format: 6-point frequency scales and 5-point intensity scales.

Reliability: Test–retest reliabilities ranged from .81 (2 weeks) to .73 (4 weeks).

Authors: Gannon, L., et al.

Article: A two-domain model of well-being: Everyday events, social support, and gender-related personality factors.

Journal: *Journal of Research in Personality,* September 1992, *26*(3), 288–301.

Related Research: Cuevas, J., & Vaux, A. (1982, May). *The Physical Symptoms Survey: Descriptive, reliability and validity data from college and alcoholic samples.* Paper presented at the Annual Midwestern Psychological Association.

■ ■ ■

5629

Test Name: POSITIVE AFFECTIVITY SCALE

Purpose: To measure positive affectivity.

Number of Items: 10

Format: Responses are made on a 5-point Likert-type scale. An example is presented.

Reliability: Coefficient alpha was .88.

Authors: Lee, C., and Bobko, P.

Article: Self-efficacy beliefs: Comparison of five measures.

Journal: *Journal of Applied Psychology,* June 1994, *79*(3), 364–369.

Related Research: Watson, D., et al. (1988). Development and validation of brief measures of positive and negative affect: The PANAS scales. *Journal of Personality and Social Psychology, 54,* 1063–1070.

■ ■ ■

5630

Test Name: POSITIVE AND NEGATIVE AFFECT SCALE

Purpose: To measure positive and negative affect.

Number of Items: 10

Format: 5-point rating scales.

Reliability: Alphas ranged from .84 to .90. Test–retest reliabilities ranged from .39 to .47.

Authors: Leon, G. R., et al.

Article: Interrelationships of personality and coping in a challenging extreme situation.

Journal: *Journal of Research in Personality,* December 1991, *25*(4), 357–371.

Related Research: Watson, D., et al. (1988). Development and validation of brief measures of positive and negative affect: The PANAS scales. *Journal of Personality and Social Psychology, 54,* 1063–1070.

■ ■ ■

5631

Test Name: POSITIVE AND NEGATIVE AFFECT SCHEDULE

Purpose: To determine children's dispositional negative affectivity.

Number of Items: 12

Format: Responses are made on a 5-point scale ranging from *very slightly* to *extremely.*

Reliability: Alphas for negative affect were .90, .87, and .88 for teachers, mothers, and fathers, respectively.

Author: Eisenberg, N.

Article: The role of emotionality and regulation in children's social functioning: A longitudinal study.

Journal: *Child Development,* October 1995, *66*(5), 1360–1384.

Related Research: Watson, D., et al. (1988). Development and validation of brief measures of positive and negative affect: The PANAS Scales. *Journal of Personality and Social Psychology, 54,* 1063–1070.

■ ■ ■

5632

Test Name: POSITIVE AND NEGATIVE AFFECT SCHEDULE SCALES

Purpose: To assess positive and negative affects.

Number of Items: 20

Format: Addresses both positive and negative emotions. Examples are given.

Reliability: Reliability coefficients were .87 (positive affect) and .89 (negative affect).

Validity: Correlations with other variables ranged from -.80 to .57.

Authors: Judge, T. A., and Locke, E. A.

Article: Effect of dysfunctional thought processes on subjective well-being and job satisfaction.

Journal: *Journal of Applied Psychology,* June 1993, *78*(3), 475–490.

Related Research: Watson, D., et al. (1988). Development and validation of brief measures of positive and negative affect: The PANAS scales. *Journal of Personality and Social Psychology, 54,* 1063–1070.

5633

Test Name: POSITIVE LIFE ORIENTATION TEST

Purpose: To measure dispositional optimism.

Number of Items: 4

Format: 5-point Likert format. All items are presented.

Reliability: Alpha was .71. Test–retest was .71 (3 weeks).

Author: Lai, J. C. L.

Article: The Moderating effect of optimism on the relation between hassles and somatic complaints.

Journal: *Psychological Reports*, June 1995, *76*(3) Part I, 883–894.

Related Research: Scheier, M. F., & Carver, C. S. (1985). Optimism, coping, and health: Assessment and implications of generalized outcome expectancies. *Health Psychology*, 4, 219–247.

• • •

5634

Test Name: PRERACE QUESTIONNAIRE—MODIFIED.

Purpose: To measure antecedents of anxiety.

Number of Items: 21

Format: Items are grouped into three sections: Preparation, Last Race, and Forthcoming Race. Cycling-form and cycle-course items were added. Responses are made on a 9-point scale. Examples are presented.

Reliability: Internal consistency ranged from .63 to .78.

Authors: Lane, A., et al.

Article: Antecedents of multidimensional competitive state anxiety and self-confidence in duathletes.

Journal: *Perceptual and Motor Skills*, June 1995, *80*(3) Part 1, 911–919.

Related Research: Jones, J. G., et al. (1990). Antecedents of multidimensional competitive state anxiety and self-confidence in elite intercollegiate middle-distance runners. *The Sport Psychologist*, 4, 107–118.

• • •

5635

Test Name: PRIMARY APPRAISAL SCALE

Purpose: To measure stressors.

Number of Items: 13

Format: 5-point rating scales.

Reliability: Alphas ranged from .61 to .74 across subscales.

Authors: MacNair, R. A., and Elliott, T. R.

Article: Self-perceived problem-solving ability, stress appraisal and coping over time.

Journal: *Journal of Research in Personality*, June 1992, *26*(2), 150–164.

Related Research: Folkman, S., et al. (1986). Appraisal, coping, health status and psychological symptoms. *Journal of Personality and Social Psychology*, 50, 571–579.

• • •

5636

Test Name: PROBLEM CHECKLIST

Purpose: To measure the frequency of current problems.

Number of Items: 15

Format: Responses are made on a 7-point Likert-type scale ranging from 1 (*not frequent*) to 7 (*very frequent*).

Reliability: Test–retest reliability was .62.

Authors: Brack, G., et al.

Article: The relationship of problem solving and reframing to

stress and depression in female college students.

Journal: *Journal of College Student Development*, March 1992, *33*(2), 124–131.

Related Research: Nezu, A. M. (1985). Differences in psychological distress between affective and ineffective problem solvers. *Journal of Counseling Psychology*, *32*(1), 135-138.

• • •

5637

Test Name: PROBLEM-FOCUSED STYLE OF COPING SCALE

Purpose: To measure stable coping styles.

Number of Items: 18

Format: 5-point Likert format ranges from 1 (*almost never*) to 5 (*almost all the time*). All items are presented.

Reliability: Alphas ranged from .73 to .77 across subscales. Test–retest reliabilities (3 weeks) ranged from .65 to .71.

Validity: Correlations with other variables ranged from -.66 to .50.

Authors: Heppner, P. P., et al.

Article: Progress in resolving problems: A problem-focused style of coping.

Journal: *Journal of Counseling Psychology*, July 1995, *42*(3), 279–293.

• • •

5638

Test Name: PSYCHAP INVENTORY

Purpose: To measure an individual's level of happiness.

Number of Items: 80

Format: Responses are made on forced-choice polarized statement options.

Reliability: (Interform) averages were approximately .92 for same-day to 3-day intervals, and .74 for longer-term interform reliability averages.

Authors: Booth, R., et al.

Article: An examination of the relationship between happiness, loneliness, and shyness in college students.

Journal: *Journal of College Student Development*, March 1992, *33*(2), 157–162.

Related Research: Fordyce, M. (1986). The Psychap Inventory: A multi-scale test to measure happiness and its concomitants. *Social Indicators Research*, *18*, 1–33.

■ ■ ■

5639

Test Name: PSYCHIATRIC EPIDEMIOLOGY RESEARCH INSTRUMENT

Purpose: To measure symptoms of psychological distress.

Number of Items: 25

Format: 3-point frequency scales.

Reliability: Alpha was .89.

Authors: Rook, K., et al.

Article: Stress transmission: The effects of husbands' job stressors on the emotional health of their wives.

Journal: *Journal of Marriage and the Family*, February 1991, *53*(1), 165–177.

Related Research: Dohrenwend, B. P., et al. (1980). Non-specific psychological distress and other dimensions of psychopathology. *Archives of General Psychiatry*, *37*, 1229–1236.

■ ■ ■

5640

Test Name: PSYCHOLOGICAL BIRTH ORDER INVENTORY

Purpose: To assess the psychological birth order of an individual.

Number of Items: 40

Format: Yes–no format. Sample items presented.

Reliability: Test–retest ranged from .70 to .87.

Authors: White, J., et al.

Article: Associations of scores on the White-Campbell Psychological Birth Order Inventory and the Kern Lifestyle Scale.

Journal: *Psychological Reports*, December 1995, *77*(3), 1187–1196.

Related Research: Campbell, L., et al. (1991). The relationship of psychological birth order to actual birth order. *Individual Psychology*, *47*, 381–391.

■ ■ ■

5641

Test Name: PSYCHOLOGICAL DISTRESS INDEX

Purpose: To measure psychological distress: depression, anger, anxiety, cognitive problems, and romantization.

Number of Items: 29

Format: All items are presented.

Reliability: Alphas ranged from .74 to .93.

Validity: Odds ratios for severe and nonsevere distress represented for sex, age, income, education, and other variables.

Authors: Préville, M., et al.

Article: The structure of psychological distress.

Journal: *Psychological Reports*, August 1996, *77*(1), 275–293.

■ ■ ■

5642

Test Name: PSYCHOLOGICAL DISTRESS SCALE

Purpose: To assess depressive symptomatology.

Number of Items: 7

Format: 4-point frequency scales.

Reliability: Alpha was .78.

Authors: Frone, M. R., et al.

Article: Relationship of work-family conflict to substance use among employed mothers: The role of negative affect.

Journal: *Journal of Marriage and the Family*, November 1994, *56*(4), 1019–1030.

Related Research: Nehemkis, A., et al. (1978). Drug abuse instrument handbook: Selected items for psychosocial drug research (OHEW Publication No. ADM 79-394). Washington, DC: U.S. Government Printing Office.

■ ■ ■

5643

Test Name: PSYCHOLOGICAL SCREENING INVENTORY

Purpose: To assess the domain of psychopathology.

Number of Items: 36

Reliability: Alphas ranged from .70 to .87 across subscales.

Validity: Subscale correlations with subscales of the NEO Five Factor Inventory ranged from -.40 to .61.

Author: Holden, R. R.

Article: Associations between the Holden Psychological Screening Inventory and the NEO Five-Factor Inventory in a non-clinical sample.

Journal: *Psychological Reports*, December 1992, *71*(3) Part II, 1039–1042.

Related Research: Holden, R. R. (1991). *Psychometric properties of the Holden Psychological Screening Inventory (HPSI)*.

Unpublished paper presented at the Canadian Psychological Association Convention, Calgary, Alberta.

• • •

5644

Test Name: PSYCHOLOGICAL SEPARATION INVENTORY

Purpose: To measure psychological separation.

Number of Items: 138

Format: Includes four dimensions of psychological separation: functional independence, emotional independence, conflictual independence, and attitudinal independence. Items are rated for accuracy from 1 (*not at all true of me*) to 5 (*very true of me*).

Reliability: Internal consistency estimates ranged from .88 to .92 and test–retest reliabilities ranged from .49 to .96.

Authors: Blustein, D. L., et al.

Article: Contributions of psychological separation and parental attachment to the career development process.

Journal: *Journal of Counseling Psychology*, January 1991, *38*(1), 39–50.

Related Research: Hoffman, J. (1984). Psychological separation of late adolescents from their parents. *Journal of Counseling Psychology*, *31*, 170–178.

• • •

5645

Test Name: PSYCHOLOGICAL WELL-BEING SCALE.

Purpose: To measure psychological well-being.

Number of Items: 14

Format: 7-point rating scales. Sample item presented.

Reliability: Alpha was .92. Test–retest (1 year) was .63.

Author: Barnett, R. C., et al.

Article: Adult daughter-parent relationships and their associations with daughters' subjective well-being and psychological stress.

Journal: *Journal of Marriage and the Family*, February 1991, *53*(1), 29–42.

Related Research: Davies, A. R., et al. (1985). *Scoring manual: Adult health status and satisfaction measures used in Rand's health insurance experiment* (WD-2742-HHS). Washington, DC: U.S. Department of Health and Human Services.

• • •

5646

Test Name: PSYCHOLOGICAL WELL-BEING SCALE

Purpose: To assess autonomy, environment mastery, personal growth, purpose in life, self-acceptance, and positive relations with others.

Number of Items: 84

Format: 6-point Likert format.

Reliability: Total alpha was .95. Alphas ranged from .70 to .87 across subscales.

Authors: Cooper, H., et al.

Article: Situation and personality correlates of psychological well-being: Social activity and personal control.

Journal: *Journal of Research in Personality*, December 1995, *29*(4), 395–417.

Related Research: Ryff, C. D. (1989). Happiness is everything or is it? Explorations on the meaning of psychological well-being. *Journal of Personality and Social Psychology*, *57*, 1069–1081.

5647

Test Name: PSYCHOSOCIAL STRESS SCALE

Purpose: To measure psychosocial stress.

Number of Items: 29

Format: Checklist format.

Reliability: Alphas ranged from .64 to .83 across subscales.

Authors: Jones-Johnson, G., and Johnson, W. R.

Article: Subjective underemployment and psychosocial stress: The role of perceived social and supervisor support.

Journal: *The Journal of Social Psychology*, February 1992, *132*(1), 11–21.

Related Research: Gurin, G., et al. (1960). *Americans view their mental health.* New York: Basic Books.

• • •

5648

Test Name: QUESTIONNAIRE ON STRESS IN DIABETIC PATIENTS

Purpose: To assess stress associated with living with diabetes.

Number of Items: 90

Format: 5-point stress rating scales.

Reliability: Alphas ranged from .63 to .88 across subscales.

Validity: Correlations with other variables ranged from -.42 to .48. The questionnaire discriminated between insulin users and nonusers, long-term and short-term sufferers, those with acute complications and those without acute complications, and those who had and had not experienced hypoglycemic shock.

Authors: Duran, G., et al.

Article: Assessing daily problems with diabetes: A subject-oriented approach to compliance.

Journal: *Psychological Reports*, April 1995, *76*(1), 495–503.

• • •

5649

Test Name: REASONS FOR LIVING INVENTORY

Purpose: To assess suicidal behavior.

Number of Items: 48

Format: 6-point importance alternatives.

Reliability: Alphas ranged from .80 to .91 across subscales. Total alpha was .70. Test–retest ranged from .75 to .85 across subscales and for the total scales was .83.

Authors: Osman, A., et al.

Article: The Reasons for Living Inventory: Psychometric properties.

Journal: *Psychological Reports*, August 1991, *69*(1), 271–278.

Related Research: Linehan, M. M., et al. (1983). Reasons for staying alive when you are thinking about killing yourself: The Reasons for Living Inventory. *Journal of Consulting and Clinical Psychology*, 51, 276–286.

Osman, A., et al. (1992). Factor structure and reliability of the Reasons for Living Inventory. *Psychological Reports, 70*, 107–112.

• • •

5650

Test Name: REGRESSIVE COPING CHECKLIST

Purpose: To measure attempts to deny, minimize, or avoid stressful situations.

Number of Items: 8 (or 14).

Format: Checklist format.

Reliability: Alphas ranged from .57 to .74 for the 14-item version.

Authors: Pierce, C. M. B., and Molloy, G. N.

Article: A modified regressive coping checklist: Some Australian data.

Journal: *Psychological Reports*, June 1991, *70*(3) Part I, 1007–1009.

Related Research: Kobasa, S. C. (1982). Commitment and coping in stress resistance among lawyers. *Journal of Personality and Social Psychology, 42*, 707–717.

• • •

5651

Test Name: RETIREMENT EXPERIENCES AND PLANNING SCALES

Purpose: To measure well-being, financial satisfaction, and activities related to retirement.

Number of Items: 80

Format: Several formats are used. Sample items are presented.

Reliability: Alphas ranged from .62 to .90.

Authors: MacEwen, K. E., et al.

Article: Predicting retirement anxiety: The roles of parental socialization and personal planning.

Journal: *The Journal of Social Psychology*, April 1995, *135*(2), 203–213.

Related Research: Smith, P. C., et al. (1969). *The measurement of satisfaction in work and retirement: A strategy for the study of attitudes.* Chicago: Rand McNally.

5652

Test Name: REVISED CHILDREN'S MANIFEST ANXIETY SCALE

Purpose: To assess the presence of a variety of anxiety-related symptoms.

Number of Items: 37

Format: Responses are made using a yes–no format.

Reliability: Alpha was .78. Test–retest was .68 after a 9-month interval.

Authors: Yang, B., et al.

Article: Only children and children with siblings in People's Republic of China: Levels of fear, anxiety, and depression.

Journal: *Child Development*, October 1995, *66*(5), 1301–1311.

Related Research: Reynolds, C. R., & Richmond, B. O. (1978). What I think and feel: A revised measure of children's manifest anxiety. *Journal of Abnormal Child Psychology, 6*, 271–280.

• • •

5653

Test Name: SATISFACTION WITH ILLNESS SCALE

Purpose: To measure the extent to which chronic and acute illness has a positive consequence for patients.

Number of Items: 5

Format: 7-point agree–disagree format. All items presented.

Reliability: Alpha was .82.

Validity: Correlations with Satisfaction With Life Scale ranged from .20 to .45.

Authors: Hyland, M. E., and Kenyon, C. A. P.

Article: A measure of positive health-related quality of life: The

Satisfaction With Illness Scale.

Journal: *Psychological Reports,* December 1992, *71*(3) Part II, 1137–1138.

Related Research: Diener, E., et al. (1985). The Satisfaction With Life Scale. *Journal of Personality Assessment, 49,* 71–75.

■ ■ ■

5654

Test Name: SATISFACTION WITH LIFE SCALE

Purpose: To measure the perception of general subjective well-being.

Number of Items: 5

Format: 5-point Likert format.

Reliability: Alpha was .87.

Validity: Correlations with other variables ranged from .12 to .55.

Authors: Clark, K. K., et al.

Article: Validation evidence for three coping measures.

Journal: *Journal of Personality Assessment,* December, 1995, *65*(3), 434–455.

Related Research: Diener, E., et al. (1985). The Satisfaction With Life Scale. *Journal of Personality Assessment, 49,* 71–75.

■ ■ ■

5655

Test Name: SCALE FOR SUICIDE IDEATION

Purpose: To measure the intensity, pervasiveness, and characteristics of suicidal intent.

Number of Items: 19

Format: Responses are made on a 3-point Likert scale. Sample items are presented.

Reliability: Internal consistency was .89; interrater reliability was .83.

Validity: Correlations with other variables ranged from -.19 to .22.

Authors: Dixon, W. A., et al.

Article: Use of different sources of stress to predict hopelessness and suicide ideation in a college population.

Journal: *Journal of Counseling Psychology,* July 1992, *39*(3), 342–349.

Related Research: Beck, A. T., et al. (1979). Assessment of suicidal intention: The Scale for Suicide Ideation. *Journal of Consulting and Clinical Psychology, 47,* 343–352.

■ ■ ■

5656

Test Name: SELF-ASSESSMENT QUESTIONNAIRE—NIJMEGEN

Purpose: To assess how people behave and feel in general.

Number of Items: 98

Format: 4-point frequency scales.

Reliability: Alphas ranged from .59 to .92 across subscales.

Authors: Bleiker, E. M. A., et al.

Article: Personality traits of women with breast cancer: Before and after diagnosis.

Journal: *Psychological Reports,* June 1995, *76*(3) Part II, 1139–1146.

Related Research: Ploeg, H. M. vander, et al. (1989). Rationality and antiemotionality as risk factors for cancer: Concept differentiation. *Journal of Psychosomatic Research, 33,* 217–225.

■ ■ ■

5657

Test Name: SELF-RATING DEPRESSION SCALE

Purpose: To assess level of depression.

Number of Items: 20

Format: Respondents rate the frequency with which each symptom is experienced on a 4-point scale from 1 (*a little of the time*) to 4 (*most of the time*).

Reliability: Cronbach's alpha was .83.

Authors: Kelly, A. E., et al.

Article: Effects of counselor as audience on internalization of depressed and nondepressed self-presentations.

Journal: *Journal of Counseling Psychology,* January 1991, *38*(1), 126–132.

Related Research: Zung, W. W. K. (1965). A self-rating depression scale. *Archives of General Psychiatry, 12,* 63–70.

■ ■ ■

5658

Test Name: SELF-RATING DEPRESSION SCALE

Purpose: To determine the degree of psychological distress.

Number of Items: 20

Format: Responses are made on a 6-point Likert scale.

Reliability: Internal consistency ranged from .88 to .93.

Authors: Hodgson, C. S., and Simon, J. M.

Article: Graduate student academic and psychological functioning.

Journal: *Journal of College Student Development,* May/June 1995, *36*(3), 244–259

Related Research: Zung, W. W. K. (1965). A self-rating depression scale. *Archives of General Psychiatry, 12,* 63–70.

5659

Test Name: SELF-RATING SCALE

Purpose: To measure the executive functions of the frontal lobes.

Number of Items: 16

Format: 4-point true–false scales. All items are presented.

Reliability: Alpha was .72.

Validity: Head-injury patients scored significantly different from individuals in a control group on over-all executive dysfunction and on the Decision-Making Difficulties subscales.

Authors: Coolidge, F. L., and Griego, J. A.

Article: Executive functions of the frontal lobes: Psychometric properties of a self-rating scale.

Journal: *Psychological Reports*, August 1995, *77*(1), 24–26.

Related Research: Coolidge, F. L., & Merwin, M. M. (1992). Reliability and validity of the Coolidge Axis II Inventory: A new inventory for the assessment of personality disorders. *Journal of Personality Assessment, 59*, 223–238.

■ ■ ■

5660

Test Name: SELF-REPORTED SYMPTOM SURVEY

Purpose: To identify physical symptoms experienced by the participant during previous 5 weeks.

Number of Items: 15

Format: Responses are made on a 5-point scale ranging from 1 (*not at all*) to 5 (*about every day*).

Validity: Correlations with other variables ranged from -.38 to .37.

Authors: Wohlgemuth, E., and Betz, N. E.

Article: Gender as a moderator of the relationships of stress and social support to physical health in college students.

Journal: *Journal of Counseling Psychology*, July 1991, *38*(3), 367–374.

Related Research: Thoresen, C. E., & Eagleston, J. R. (1985). Counseling for health. *The Counseling Psychologist, 13*(1), 15–88.

■ ■ ■

5661

Test Name: SELF-REPORT HEALTH SCALE

Purpose: To assess overall health among old persons.

Number of Items: 4

Reliability: Internal reliability was .76. Test–retest (3 weeks) was .92.

Validity: Correlations with other variables ranged from .63 to .67.

Author: Hoskins, C. N.

Article: Adjustment to breast cancer in couples.

Journal: *Psychological Reports*, October 1995, *77*(2), 435–454.

Related Research: Lawton, M. P., et al. (1982). A research and service oriented multilevel assessment instrument. *Journal of Gerontology, 37*, 91–99.

■ ■ ■

5662

Test Name: SENSE OF HUMOR QUESTIONNAIRE

Purpose: To assess three elements of humor: metamessage sensitivity, personal liking of humor, and emotional permissiveness.

Number of Items: 21

Reliability: Internal consistency ranged from .00 to .65 across subscales.

Validity: Correlations with other humor scales ranged from .22 to .56.

Authors: Deaner, S. I., and McConatha, J. T.

Article: The relation of humor to depression and personality.

Journal: *Psychological Reports*, June 1993, *72*(3) Part I, 755–763.

Related Research: Svebak, S. (1974). Revised questionnaire on the sense of humor. *Scandinavian Journal of Psychology, 15*, 99–107.

Martin, R. A., & Lefcourt, H. M. (1984). Situational Humor Response Questionnaire: Quantitative measurement of sense of humor. *Journal of Personality and Social Psychology, 47*, 145–155.

■ ■ ■

5663

Test Name: SENTENCES COMPLETION TEST

Purpose: To evaluate the quality of active coping by the patient.

Number of Items: 40

Format: Completing uncompleted sentence stems.

Reliability: Interrater reliability was .88. Test–retest was .60.

Authors: Shefler, G., et al.

Article: A randomized controlled outcome and follow-up study of Mann's time-limited psychotherapy.

Journal: *Journal of Consulting and Clinical Psychology*, August 1995, *63*(4), 585–593.

Related Research: Shanan, J. (1967). The tendency for active coping, a basic element in mental health (in Hebrew). *Meganot, 15*, 188–195.

5664

Test Name: SERIOUSNESS OF ILLNESS SCALE

Purpose: To measure the seriousness of illness.

Number of Items: 30

Format: Participants indicate if they experienced the symptom in the past 2 years. Severity scores are based on physicians' ratings.

Reliability: Alpha was .73.

Validity: Correlations with other variables ranged from .10 to .59.

Authors: Clark, K. K., et al.

Article: Validation evidence for three coping measures.

Journal: *Journal of Personality Assessment*, December 1995, *65*(3), 434–455.

Related Research: Wyler, A. R., et al. (1968). Seriousness of illness rating scale. *Journal of Psychosomatic Research, 11,* 363–374.

• • •

5665

Test Name: SEXUAL DESIRE CONFLICT SCALE FOR WOMEN

Purpose: To measure women's experiences of subjective discomfort and conflict in relation to sexual desire.

Number of Items: 33

Format: 5-point Likert format. All items presented.

Reliability: Cronbach's alpha was .93. Average interitem correlation was .29.

Validity: Correlations with other related variables ranged from .38 to .50.

Authors: Kaplan, L., and Harder, D. W.

Article: The Sexual Desire Conflict Scale for Women: Construction,

internal consistency and two initial validity tests.

Journal: *Psychological Reports*, June 1991, *68*(3) Part II, 1275–1282.

• • •

5666

Test Name: SEXUALITY SCALES

Purpose: To measure esteem, depression, and preoccupations associated with sexuality.

Number of Items: 30 (and 15-item short form)

Format: 5-point agreement scales. All items presented.

Reliability: Item reliabilities ranged from .13 to .93 (long form). Short-form internal reliabilities ranged from .89 to .96.

Validity: Correlations with other variables ranged from -.21 to .38.

Authors: Wiederman, M. W., and Allgeier, E. R.

Article: The measurement of sexual-esteem: Investigation of Snell and Papini's (1989) Sexuality Scale.

Journal: *Journal of Research in Personality*, March 1993, *27*(1), 88–102.

Related Research: Snell, W. E., & Papini, D. R. (1989). The Sexuality Scale: An instrument to measure sexual-esteem, sexual-depression, and sexual preoccupation. *The Journal of Sex Research, 26,* 256–263.

• • •

5667

Test Name: SHAME-PRONENESS QUESTIONNAIRE

Purpose: To assess proneness to feelings of shame.

Number of Items: 30

Format: Employs a 6-point Likert scale.

Validity: Correlations with other variables ranged from -.50 to .34.

Authors: Wright, D. M., and Heppner, P. P.

Article: Coping among non-clinical college-age children of alcoholics.

Journal: *Journal of Counseling Psychology*, October 1991, *38*(4), 465–472.

Related Research: Shreve, B. W., & Patton, M. J. (1987). *Construction of the Shame-Proneness Scale.* Unpublished manuscript.

Kerr, A. E., et al. (August, 1991). *Interpersonal correlates of narcissism in a group of adolescents.* Paper presented at the 99th Annual Convention of the American Psychological Association, San Francisco.

• • •

5668

Test Name: SITUATIONAL CHARACTERISTICS QUESTIONNAIRE

Purpose: To assess panic disorder and vestibular dysfunction.

Number of Items: 36

Format: 3-point Likert format and scoring of items is described. All items are presented.

Reliability: Test–retest reliabilities ranged from .66 to .87. Alphas ranged from .67 to .88.

Validity: Correlations with other variables ranged from .27 to .71.

Authors: Jacob, R. G., et al.

Article: Discomfort with space and motion: A possible marker of vestibular dysfunction assessed by the Situational Characteristics Questionnaire.

Journal: *Journal of Psychopathology and Behavioral Assessment*, December 1993, *15*(4), 299–324.

5669

Test Name: SITUATION HUMOR RESPONSE SCALE

Purpose: To assess humor and amusability in situations that vary in potential for eliciting humor.

Number of Items: 21

Format: 5-point scales range from *I would laugh heartily* to *I would not be amused*.

Reliability: Alphas ranged from .70 to .85.

Authors: Lefcourt, H. M., and Shepherd, R. S.

Article: Organ donation, authoritarianism and perspective-taking humor.

Journal: *Journal of Research in Personality*, March 1995, *29*(1), 121–128.

Related Research: Martin, R. A., & Lefcourt, H. M. (1984). The Situational Humor Response Questionnaire: A quantitative measure of the sense of humor. *Journal of Personality and Social Psychology*, *47*, 145–155.

■ ■ ■

5670

Test Name: SOCIAL COPING QUESTIONNAIRE FOR GIFTED STUDENTS

Purpose: To measure coping among gifted students.

Number of Items: 35

Format: Response scales range from 1 (*strongly false*) to 7 (*strongly true*). All items are presented.

Reliability: Alphas ranged from .54 to .79 across subscales.

Validity: Group difference data are presented.

Author: Swiatek, M. A.

Article: An empirical investigation

of social coping strategies used by gifted adolescents.

Journal: *Gifted Child Quarterly*, Summer 1995, *39*(3), 154–161.

■ ■ ■

5671

Test Name: SOMATIC COMPLAINTS INDEX

Purpose: To assess frequency of health symptoms (backaches, headaches, sleeping trouble).

Number of Items: 10

Format: Respondents determine number of times they experienced listed health symptoms.

Reliability: Alpha was .82.

Authors: Harrison, D. A., and Liska, L. Z.

Article: Promoting regular exercise in organizational fitness programs: Health-related differences in motivational building blocks.

Journal: *Personnel Psychology*, Spring 1994, *47*(1), 47–71.

Related Research: Caplan, R. D., et al. (1980). *Job demands and worker health*. Ann Arbor, MI: Institute for Social Research.

■ ■ ■

5672

Test Name: SOMATIC COMPLAINTS INVENTORY

Purpose: To measure frequency of somatic complaints.

Number of Items: 11

Format: Often/Sometimes/Rarely response categories. A sample item is presented.

Reliability: Reliabilities ranged from .79 to .89.

Validity: Correlations with other variables ranged from -.46 to .61.

Authors: Meir, E. I., et al.

Article: The benefits of congruence.

Journal: *The Career Development Quarterly*, March 1995, *43*(3), 257–266.

Related Research: Caplan, R. D., et al. (1975). *Job demands and worker health: Main effects and occupational differences* (HEW Publication No. NIOSH 75-160). Washington, DC: National Institute for Occupational Safety and Health.

■ ■ ■

5673

Test Name: SOMATIC RESPONSE SURVEY

Purpose: To measure perception of normal physical sensations during stressful situations.

Number of Items: 28

Format: 5-point response alternatives (*never* to *always*) follow each stressful event (such as "stomach feels upset").

Reliability: Alphas ranged from .49 to .89 across subscales.

Validity: Sex difference test reported.

Authors: McCroskery, J. H., and Reihman, J.

Article: Development of the Somatic Response Inventory.

Journal: *Psychological Reports*, June 1991, *68*(3) Part II, 1097–1098.

Related Research: Landy, F. J., & Stern, R. M. (1971). Factor analysis of Somatic Perception Questionnaire. *Journal of Psychometric Research*, *15*, 179–181.

■ ■ ■

5674

Test Name: SOMATIC TENSION SCALE

Purpose: To identify possible physical symptom outcomes of stress.

Number of Items: 5

Reliability: Coefficient alpha was .72.

Validity: Correlations with other variables ranged from -.32 to .61.

Author: Macan, T. H.

Article: Time management: Test of a process model.

Journal: *Journal of Applied Psychology*, June 1994, *79*(3), 381–391.

Related Research: House, R. J., & Rizzo, J. R. (1972). Role conflict and ambiguity as critical variables in a model of organizational behavior. *Organizational Behavior and Human Performance*, 7, 467–505.

• • •

5675

Test Name: STRAIN SCALE

Purpose: To measure strain.

Number of Items: 20

Format: Includes 4 scales: Vocational, Interpersonal, Psychological, and Physical Strain. Responses are made on a 5-point scale ranging from 1 (*not at all true*) to 5 (*highly true*). Sample items are presented.

Reliability: Alpha coefficients ranged from .73 to .88.

Validity: Correlations with other variables ranged from -.21 to .62.

Authors: Matsui, T., and Onglatco, M.-L.

Article: Career self-efficacy as a moderator of the relations between occupational stress and strain.

Journal: *Journal of Vocational Behavior*, August 1992, *41*(1), 79–88.

Related Research: Osipow, S. H., & Spokane, A. R. (1983). *Manual for measures of occupational stress, strain, and*

coping. Columbus, OH: Marathon Consulting Press.

• • •

5676

Test Name: STRESSFUL TRANSACTION SCALE

Purpose: To assess each stage of a stressful transaction.

Number of Items: 16

Format: Includes 4 subscales: Threat, Challenge, Harm, and Benefit. Responses are made on a 7-point scale ranging from 0 (*not at all*) to 6 (*a great deal*).

Reliability: Alpha coefficients ranged from .81 to .90.

Authors: Scherer, R. F., et al.

Article: Assessment of cognitive appraisal and coping linkages using two forms of canonical correlation.

Journal: *Perceptual and Motor Skills*, August 1994, *79*(1) Part 1, 259–264.

Related Research: Folkman, S., & Lazarus, R. S. (1985). If it changes, it must be a process: Study of emotion and coping during three stages of a college examination. *Journal of Personality and Social Psychology*, *48*, 150–170.

• • •

5677

Test Name: STRESSORS INVENTORY

Purpose: To identify the degree of stress caused by common experiences.

Number of Items: 19

Format: Responses are made on a 5-point scale ranging from 1 (*not at all stressful*) to 5 (*extremely stressful*). Examples are presented.

Reliability: Internal consistency

reliability was .86.

Validity: Correlations with other variables ranged from -.34 to .63.

Authors: Hackett, G., et al.

Article: Gender, ethnicity, and social cognitive factors predicting the academic achievement of students in engineering.

Journal: *Journal of Counseling Psychology*, October 1992, *39*(4), 527–538.

Related Research: Mendozo, P. (1981). Stress and coping behavior of Anglo and Mexican American university students. In T. H. Escobedo (Ed.), *Education and Chicanos: Issues and research* [Monograph No. 8] (pp. 89–111). Los Angeles: University of California, Spanish Speaking Mental Health Research Center.

• • •

5678

Test Name: STRESS QUESTIONNAIRE

Purpose: To determine sources of stress that might be present in the work or personal life of the respondents.

Number of Items: 61

Format: Responses are made on a 5-point Likert scale ranging from a low of 1 to a high of 5.

Reliability: Internal consistency ranged from .85 to .93 across subscales.

Author: Scott, N.

Article: Chief student affairs officers: Stressors and strategies.

Journal: *Journal of College Student Development*, March 1992, *33*(2), 108–116.

Related Research: Adams, J. D. (1978). Improving stress management. *Social Change*, *8*(4), 1–4.

5679

Test Name: STRESS REACTION SCALE

Purpose: To measure trait negative affectivity.

Number of Items: 14

Format: True–false format.

Reliability: Alpha was .82. Test–retest reliability (12 weeks) was .72.

Validity: Correlations with perceived stress was .44.

Authors: Bowman, G. D., and Stern, M.

Article: Adjustment to occupational stress: The relationship of perceived control to effectiveness of coping strategies.

Journal: *Journal of Counseling Psychology*, July 1995, *42*(3), 294–303.

Related Research: Watson, D., & Pennebaker, J. W. (1989). Health complaints, stress and distress: Exploring the central role of negative affectivity. *Psychological Review, 96*, 234–254.

■ ■ ■

5680

Test Name: STRESS REACTIONS CHECKLIST

Purpose: To measure stress reactions.

Number of Items: 18

Format: 4-point scales (*not at all* to *always*).

Reliability: Alpha was .89.

Author: Torki, M. A.

Article: Associations between personality and stress reactions during and after invasion of Kuwait.

Journal: *Psychological Reports*, April 1994, *74*(2), 667–673.

Related Research: Vocational Instructional Material Laboratory. (1983). *Managing stress before it manages you.* Columbus: Ohio State University.

■ ■ ■

5681

Test Name: STRESS-RELATED SYMPTOMS CHECKLIST

Purpose: To identify stress-related symptoms.

Number of Items: 25

Format: Responses are made on a 5-point scale ranging from 0 to 4. An example is presented.

Validity: Correlation with the Arousal Predisposition Scale was .48.

Authors: Hicks, R. A., et al.

Article: Arousability and stress-related physical symptoms: A validation study of Coren's Arousal Predisposition Scale.

Journal: *Perceptual and Motor Skills*, April 1992, *74*(2), 659–662.

Related Research: Daville, D. M., et al. (1990). Type AB behavior and self-reported health problems. *Psychological Reports, 67*, 960–962.

■ ■ ■

5682

Test Name: STRESS SCALE

Purpose: To measure psychological and psychophysiological stress.

Number of Items: 8

Format: 3-point scales.

Reliability: Alpha was .73.

Author: Atkinson, A. M.

Article: Stress levels of family day care providers, mothers employed outside the home, and mothers at home.

Journal: *Journal of Marriage and the Family*, May 1992, *54*(2), 379–386.

Related Research: Johnson, D. R., & Meile, R. L. (1981). Does dimensionality bias in Langner's 22-item index affect the validity of social status comparisons? An empirical investigation. *Journal of Health and Social Behavior, 22*, 415–433.

■ ■ ■

5683

Test Name: STRESS SCALE

Purpose: To measure stress.

Number of Items: 13

Format: Includes 6 categories of job stressors: aspect of job, structure–climate–information flow, career development, relationships at work, aspects of role, and extra organizational variables. Responses are made on a 4-point scale ranging from 1 (*definitely disagree*) to 4 (*definitely agree*).

Reliability: Coefficient alpha was .91.

Validity: Correlations with other variables ranged from -.47 to .52.

Authors: Morrow, P. C., et al.

Article: Sexual harassment behaviors and work related perceptions and attitudes.

Journal: *Journal of Vocational Behavior*, December 1994, *45*(3), 295–309.

Related Research: Parker, D. F., & DeCotiis, T. A. (1983). Organizational determinants of job stress. *Organizational Behavior and Human Performance, 32*, 160–177.

■ ■ ■

5684

Test Name: STUDENTS' LIFE SATISFACTION SCALE

Purpose: To measure the global

life satisfaction of children as young as third grade.

Number of Items: 7

Format: A self-report scale ranging from 1 (*never*) to 4 (*almost always*).

Reliability: Coefficient alpha was .82.

Authors: Dow, T., and Huebner, E. S.

Article: Adolescent's perceived quality of life: An exploratory investigation.

Journal: *Journal of School Psychology*, Summer 1994, *32*(2), 185–199.

Related Research: Huebner, E. S. (1991a). Initial development of the students' life satisfaction scale. *School Psychology International*, *12*, 231–240.

• • •

5685

Test Name: SUBJECTIVE UNIT OF DISCOMFORT INDICATOR

Purpose: To assess anxiety.

Number of Items: 1

Format: Subject rates his or her anxiety at the moment on a 100-point scale.

Validity: Correlations with other anxiety measures ranged from .46 to .72.

Authors: Kaplan, D. M., et al.

Article: A validity study of the Subjective Unit of Discomfort (SUD) score.

Journal: *Measurement and evaluation in counseling and development*, January 1995, *27*(1), 195–199.

Related Research: Wolpe, J. (1969). *The practice of behavior therapy* (1st ed.). New York: Pergamon.

5686

Test Name: SYMPTOM CHECKLIST

Purpose: To measure global psychological distress.

Number of Items: 10

Format: Includes three factors: depression, somatization, and phobic anxiety. Several items are presented.

Reliability: Coefficient alpha for the French Canadian version was .84.

Validity: Correlations with the Psychiatric Symptom Inventory was .81. Correlations with other variables ranged from -.31 to .33.

Authors: Sabourin, S., and Coallier, J. C.

Article: The relationship between response style and reports of career indecision.

Journal: *Measurement and Evaluation in Counseling and Development*, July 1991, *24*(2), 69–79.

Related Research: Nguyen, T. D., et al. (1983). Assessment of patient satisfaction: Development and refinement of a service evaluation questionnaire. *Evaluation and Program Planning*, *6*, 299–314.

• • •

5687

Test Name: SYMPTOM CHECKLIST-90—REVISED

Purpose: To assess psychological symptoms over nine dimensions.

Number of Items: 90

Format: Responses are made on a 5-point scale.

Validity: Coefficients across the dimensions ranged from .50 to .75.

Authors: Bradford, E., and Lyddon, W. J.

Article: Current parental attachment: Its relation to perceived psychological distress and relationship satisfaction in college students.

Journal: *Journal of College Student Development*, July 1993, *34*(4), 256–260.

Related Research: Derogatis, L. R., et al. (1973). SCL-90: An outpatient psychiatric scale preliminary report. *Psychopharmacology Bulletin*, *9*, 13–28.

• • •

5688

Test Name: SYMPTOMS OF STRESS INVENTORY

Purpose: To assess the physiological, behavioral, and cognitive components of the stress response.

Number of Items: 94

Reliability: Alphas ranged from .71 to .97.

Validity: Correlations with other variables ranged from .29 to .35. Correlations between subscales ranged from .35 to .89.

Authors: DeBerard, M. S., and Kleinknecht, R. A.

Article: Loneliness, duration of loneliness, and reported stress symptomatology.

Journal: *Psychological Reports*, June 1995, *76*(3) Part II, 1363–1369.

Related Research: Thompson, E., et al. (1978). *The symptoms of stress inventory*. Seattle: Department of Psychosocial Nursing, University of Washington.

• • •

5689

Test Name: TARGET COMPLAINTS SCALE

Purpose: To specify complaints in patients.

Number of Items: 3

Format: Patients specify 3 main complaints in order of severity.

Reliability: Test–retest was .68.

Authors: Shefler, G., et al.

Article: A randomized controlled outcome and follow-up study of Mann's time-limited psychotherapy.

Journal: *Journal of Consulting and Clinical Psychology*, August 1995, *63*(4), 585–593.

Related Research: Battle, C., et al. (1966). Target complaints as criteria of improvement. *American Journal of Psychotherapy*, *20*, 184–192.

■ ■ ■

5690

Test Name: TEDIUM SCALE

Purpose: To assess being tired and anxious.

Number of Items: 20

Format: 5-point frequency scales range from *never* to *always*.

Reliability: Alphas ranged from .82 to .85 across subscales.

Author: Knoop, R.

Article: Relieving stress through value-rich work.

Journal: *The Journal of Social Psychology*, December 1994, *133*(6), 829–836.

Related Research: Pines, A., et al. (1981). *Burnout—From tedium to personal growth*. New York: Free Press.

■ ■ ■

5691

Test Name: TEMPLAR DEATH ANXIETY SCALE

Purpose: To measure affective

arousal associated with death awareness.

Number of Items: 15

Format: True–false format. Sample item presented.

Reliability: KR-20 was .73. Test–retest was .83.

Authors: Schumaker, J. F., et al.

Article: Death anxiety in Japan and Australia.

Journal: *The Journal of Social Psychology*, August 1991, *131*(4), 511–518.

Related Research: Templar, D. I. (1970). The construction and validation of a death anxiety scale. *Journal of General Psychology*, *82*, 165–177.

■ ■ ■

5692

Test Name: THOUGHT OCCURRENCE QUESTIONNAIRE

Purpose: To measure tendency to experience intrusive thought.

Number of Items: 28

Format: 5-point scales.

Reliability: Alphas ranged from .65 to .82 across subscales.

Validity: Correlations with other variables ranged from .07 to .44.

Author: Comunin, A. L.

Article: Anxiety, cognitive interference and school performance of Italian children.

Journal: *Psychological Reports*, December 1993, *73*(3) Part I, 747–754.

Related Research: Sarason, I. G., et al. (1986). Cognitive interference: Situational determinants and trait-like characteristics. *Journal of Personality and Social Psychology*, *51*, 1–12.

5693

Test Name: TIME URGENCY SCALE

Purpose: To measure time urgency.

Number of Items: 33

Format: Includes five factors: competitiveness, eating behavior, general hurry, task-related hurry, and speech pattern. Employs a Likert-type format.

Reliability: Alpha coefficients ranged from .60 to .89.

Authors: Landy, F. J., et al.

Article: Time urgency: The constant and its measurement.

Journal: *Journal of Applied Psychology*, October 1991, *76*(5), 644–657.

Related Research: Edwards, J. R., et al. (1990). Examining relationships among self-report measures of Type A behavior pattern: The effects of measurement error, and differences in underlying constructs. *Journal of Applied Psychology*, *75*, 440–454.

■ ■ ■

5694

Test Name: TRAUMA REACTION INDEX

Purpose: To measure posttraumatic stress disorder following airline crashes, combat, natural disasters, battering, and personal injury.

Number of Items: 20

Format: 5-point frequency scales.

Reliability: Alpha was .90.

Author: Violanti, J. M.

Article: Survivors' trauma and departmental response following deaths of police officers.

Journal: *Psychological Reports*, October 1995, *77*(2), 611–615.

Related Research: Frederick, C. J. (1985). Selected foci in the spectrum of posttraumatic stress disorder. In J. Laube & S. Murphy (Eds.), *Perspectives on disaster recovery* (pp. 110–130). Norwalk, NJ: Appleton-Century.

• • •

5695

Test Name: VULNERABILITY SCALE

Purpose: To measure frequency of experiences associated with feeling vulnerable.

Number of Items: 21

Format: 7-point rating scales (*never* to *always*). Sample items presented.

Reliability: Internal consistency was .88. Test–retest reliability (4 weeks) was .81.

Authors: Glover, H., et al.

Article: Vulnerability Scale scores in female inpatients diagnosed with self-injurious behavior, dissociative identity disorder, and major depression.

Journal: *Psychological Reports*, December 1995, *77*(3) Part I, 987–993.

Related Research: Glover, H., et al. (1994). Vulnerability scale: A preliminary report of psychometric properties. *Psychological Reports*, *75*, 1651–1668.

• • •

5696

Test Name: WAYS OF COPING CHECKLIST

Purpose: To assess coping strategies.

Number of Items: 43

Format: Checklist format. All items presented.

Reliability: Alphas ranged from .61 to .79 across subscales.

Authors: Strutton, D., and Lumpkin, J.

Article: Relationship between optimism and coping strategies in the work environment.

Journal: *Psychological Reports*, December 1992, *71*(3) Part II, 1179–1186.

Related Research: Folkman, S., & Lazarus, R. S. (1985). If it changes, it must be process: A study of emotion and coping during three stages of a college examination. *Journal of Personality and Social Psychology*, *48*, 150–170.

• • •

5697

Test Name: WAYS OF COPING CHECKLIST

Purpose: To measure coping.

Number of Items: 65

Format: Yes–no format. All items are presented.

Reliability: Alphas ranged from .59 to .74 cross subscales.

Authors: Haghighatgou, H., and Peterson, C.

Article: Coping and depressive symptoms among Iranian students.

Journal: *The Journal of Social Psychology*, April 1995, *135*(2), 175–180.

Related Research: Aldwin, C., et al. (1980). *Ways of Coping Checklist: A process measure.* Paper presented at the 88th Annual Meeting of the American Psychological Association, Montreal, Quebec, Canada.

• • •

5698

Test Name: WAYS OF COPING CHECKLIST—REVISED

Purpose: To assess coping strategies.

Number of Items: 36

Format: Includes two factors: disengagement coping and engagement coping.

Validity: Correlations with other variables ranged from -.25 to .52.

Authors: Long, B. C., et al.

Article: Casual model of stress and coping: Women in management.

Journal: *Journal of Counseling Psychology*, April 1992, *39*(2), 227–239.

Related Research: Long, B. C. (1990). Relation between coping strategies sex-typed traits, and environmental characteristics: A comparison of male and female managers. *Journal of Counseling Psychology*, *37*, 185–194.

• • •

5699

Test Name: WAYS OF COPING INVENTORY

Purpose: To measure coping strategies.

Number of Items: 41

Format: Responses are made on a 7-point Likert scale (*never* to *always*).

Reliability: Alpha coefficients among the eight identified factors ranged from .81 to .47.

Authors: Stith, S. M., et al.

Article: A typology of college students who use violence in their dating relationships.

Journal: *Journal of College Student Development*, September 1992, *33*(5), 411–421.

Related Research: Falkman, S., et al. (1986). The dynamics of a stressful encounter: Cognitive appraisal, coping and encounter outcomes. *Journal of Personality and Social Psychology*, *50*, 992–1003.

5700

Test Name: WAYS OF COPING—REVISED

Purpose: To assess eight coping strategies.

Number of Items: 66

Format: 4-point scales range from 0 (*not used*) to 3 (*used a great deal*).

Reliability: Alphas ranged from .36 to .83.

Validity: Correlations with other variables ranged from -.14 to .95.

Authors: Clark, K. K., et al.

Article: Validation evidence for three coping measures.

Journal: *Journal of Personality Assessment*, December 1995, *65*(3), 434–455.

Related Research: Folkman, S., & Lazarus, R. S. (1985). If it changes it must be a process: A study of emotion and coping during three stages of a college examination. *Journal of Personality and Social Psychology*, *48*, 150–170.

■ ■ ■

5701

Test Name: WEIGHT-LOSS QUESTIONNAIRE

Purpose: To measure the sociopsychological variables that influence weight-loss behavior.

Number of Items: 48

Format: 4-point Likert format.

Reliability: Alphas ranged from .89 to .99 across subscales.

Authors: Pratt, C. A., et al.

Article: A multivariate analysis of weight-loss behavior.

Journal: *Psychological Reports*, December 1992, *71*(3) Part II, 1075–1084.

Related Research: Pratt, C. A. (1989). Development of a screening questionnaire to study attrition in weight control programs. *Psychological Reports*, *64*, 1007–1013.

CHAPTER 4
Adjustment—Social

5702

Test Name: ACCEPTABILITY TO OTHERS SCALE

Purpose: To assess perceived acceptance by the group.

Number of Items: 5

Format: Responses are made on a 5-point scale ranging from 1 (*almost always*) to 5 (*very rarely*). Sample items are presented.

Reliability: Coefficient alpha was .79 (N = 193).

Validity: Correlations with other variables ranged from -.35 to .48 (N = 193).

Authors: Bauer, T. N., and Green, S. G.

Article: Effect of newcomer involvement in work-related activities: A longitudinal study of socialization.

Journal: *Journal of Applied Psychology*, April 1994, *79*(2), 211–223.

Related Research: Robinson, J. P., et al. (1991). *Measures of personality and social psychological attitudes.* San Diego, CA: Academic Press.

···

5703

Test Name: ACCULTURATION ATTITUDES SCALE

Purpose: To measure four modes of acculturation: assimilation, integration, separation and marginalization.

Number of Items: 56

Format: 5-point Likert format

ranges from 1 (*strongly disagree*) to 5 (*strongly agree*).

Reliability: Alphas ranged from .71 to .76.

Validity: Correlations with other variables ranged from .40 to .54.

Authors: Leong, F. T. L., et al.

Article: Group counseling expectations among Asian American students: The role of culture-specific factors.

Journal: *Journal of Counseling Psychology*, April 1995, *42*(2), 217–222.

Related Research: Kim, U., & Berry, J. W. (1985). Acculturation attitudes of Korean immigrants to Toronto. In I. R. Lagunes & Y. H. Poortinga (Eds.), *From a different perspective: Studies of behavior across cultures* (pp. 93–105). Lisse, Canada: Suets and Zeitlinger.

···

5704

Test Name: ACCULTURATION RATING SCALE FOR MEXICAN AMERICANS

Purpose: To provide a general measure of acculturation in psychiatric as well as normal Mexican American populations.

Number of Items: 20

Format: The scale differentiates five types of Mexican Americans: Very Mexican, Mexican-Oriented Bicultural, True Bicultural, Anglo-Oriented Bicultural, and Very Anglicized.

Reliability: Test–retest reliability

correlations were .80 (1 month) and .72 (6 weeks).

Validity: Correlations with staff ratings was .75.

Authors: Hess, R. S. and Street, E. M.

Article: The effect of acculturation on the relationship of counselor ethnicity and client ratings.

Journal: *Journal of Counseling Psychology*, January 1991, *38*(1), 71–75.

Related Research: Cuellar, I., et al. (1980). An Acculturation Rating Scale for Mexican-American normal and clinical populations. *Hispanic Journal of Behavioral Sciences, 2*, 199–217.

···

5705

Test Name: ACCULTURATIVE STRESS SCALE

Purpose: To measure the acculturative stress of international students including perceived discrimination, homesickness, fear, quiet, perceived hatred, and culture shock.

Number of Items: 36

Format: Likert format. All items are presented.

Validity: Seven factors that accounted for 71% of explained variance were extracted.

Authors: Sandhu, D. S., and Asrabadi, B. R.

Article: Development of an Acculturative Stress Scale for

AUGUSTANA UNIVERSITY COLLEGE
LIBRARY

international students: Preliminary findings.

Journal: *Psychological Reports*, August 1994, *75*(1) Part II, 435–448.

■ ■ ■

5706

Test Name: ADAPTED PARENTS AND FRIENDS SCALE

Purpose: To determine social support from parents and friends.

Number of Items: 22

Format: Responses are made on a 5-point Likert scale.

Reliability: Cronbach alpha coefficient for the parent support scale was .91 and friend support scale was .78.

Authors: Zimmerman, M. A., et al.

Article: Family structure and psychosocial correlates among urban African-American adolescent males.

Journal: *Child Development*, December 1995, *66*(6), 1598–1613.

Related Research: Procidano, M. E., & Heller, K. (1983). Measures of perceived social support from friends and from family: Three validation studies. *American Journal of Community Psychology*, *11*, 1–24.

■ ■ ■

5707

Test Name: ADAPTIVE SOCIAL BEHAVIOR INVENTORY

Purpose: To assess social competence in children.

Number of Items: 30

Format: Responses are made on a 3-point scale ranging from *rarely* to *almost always*.

Reliability: Cronbach alpha was .84.

Author: Smith, M. C.

Article: Child-rearing practices associated with better developmental outcomes in preschool-age foster children.

Journal: *Child Study Journal*, December 1994, *24*(4), 299–326.

Related Research: Hogan, A. E., et al. (1992). The Adaptive Social Behavior Inventory (ASBI): A new assessment of social competence in high risk three-year-olds. *Journal of Psychoeducational Assessment*, *10*, 230–239.

■ ■ ■

5708

Test Name: ADJUSTMENT INVENTORY

Purpose: To measure social and emotional adjustment based on levels of distress and restraint.

Number of Items: 84

Format: 5-point Likert format. A sample item is presented.

Reliability: Alphas ranged from .86 to .95 over subscales. Test–retest reliabilities (2 weeks to 7 months) ranged from .84 to .73.

Validity: Correlations with other variables ranged from -.69 to .63.

Authors: Sharp, M., and Schill, T.

Article: Chronic self-destructiveness and the self-defeating personality: Similarities and differences.

Journal: *Journal of Personality Assessment*, April 1995, *64*(2), 270–278.

Related Research: Weinberger, D. A. (1991). *Social-emotional adjustment in older children and adults: I. Psychometric properties of the Weinberger Adjustment Inventory*. Unpublished manuscript, Case Western Reserve University, Cleveland, Ohio.

5709

Test Name: ADULT ATTACHMENT SCALE

Purpose: To assess comfort with intimacy and emotional closeness.

Number of Items: 18

Format: 5-point scales range from 1 (*not at all characteristic of me*) to 5 (*very characteristic of me*).

Reliability: Alpha and test–retest reliabilities exceeded .58.

Authors: Mallinckrodt, B., et al.

Article: Attachment patterns in the psychotherapy relationship: Development of the Client Attachment to Therapist Scale.

Journal: *Journal of Counseling Psychology*, July 1995, *42*(3), 307–317.

Related Research: Collins, N. L., & Read, S. J. (1990). Adult attachment, working models, and relationship quality in dating couples. *Journal of Personality and Social Psychology*, *58*, 644–663.

■ ■ ■

5710

Test Name: AFFILIATION SCALE

Purpose: To assess the degree to which the participants experienced a self-directed group setting.

Number of Items: 10

Format: Uses a yes–no format.

Reliability: Internal consistency was .74.

Authors: Robbins, S. B., et al.

Article: Efficacy of leader-led and self-directed career workshops for middle-aged and older adults.

Journal: *Journal of Counseling Psychology*, January 1994, *41*(1), 83–90.

Related Research: Trickett, E. J.,

& Moos, A. H. (1973). Social environment of junior high and high school classrooms. *Journal of Educational Psychology*, *65*, 93–102.

...

5711

Test Name: AIDS PSYCHOSOCIAL SCALE

Purpose: To measure psychosocial variables relevant to sexuality and AIDS.

Number of Items: 28

Format: 5-point Likert format. All items presented.

Reliability: Alphas ranged from .53 to .74 across subscales.

Author: Perkel, A. K.

Article: Development and testing of the AIDS Psychosocial Scale.

Journal: *Psychological Reports*, December 1992, *71*(3), 767–778.

Related Research: Martin, J. L., & Vance, C. S. (1984). Behavioral and psychological factors in AIDS: Methodological and substantive issues. *American Psychologist*, *39*, 1303–1308.

...

5712

Test Name: ALIENATION SCALE

Purpose: To measure alienation in three dimensions: powerlessness, normlessness, and isolation.

Number of Items: 24

Format: 5-point Likert format.

Reliability: Total reliability was .78.

Validity: Correlations with other variables ranged from -.38 to .19.

Authors: Grandbois, G. H., and Schadt, D.

Article: Indian identification and alienation in an urban community.

Journal: *Psychological Reports*, February 1994, *74*(1), 211–216.

Related Research: Dean, D. G. (1961). Alienation: Its meaning and measurement. *American Sociological Review*, *26*, 753–758.

...

5713

Test Name: ALIENATION TEST

Purpose: To provide an inverse measure of S. Maddi et al.'s concept of hardiness.

Number of Items: 60

Format: Includes 4 subscales.

Reliability: Stability estimates range from .59 to .78.

Authors: Kush, K., and Cochran, L.

Article: Enhancing a sense of agency through career planning.

Journal: *Journal of Counseling Psychology*, October 1993, *40*(4), 434–439.

Related Research: Maddi, S., et al. (1979). An alienation test. *Journal of Humanistic Psychology*, *19*, 73–76.

...

5714

Test Name: AMERICAN– INTERNATIONAL RELATIONS SCALE

Purpose: To measure the acculturation of international students, scholars, and academicians to the White-dominant society.

Number of Items: 34

Format: Includes 3 subscales: Perceived Prejudice, Acculturation, and Language Usage. Examples are presented.

Reliability: Alpha coefficients ranged from .79 to .89.

Authors: Sodowsky, G. R., and Plake, B. S.

Article: Psychometric properties of the American-International Relations Scale.

Journal: *Educational and Psychological Measurement*, Spring 1991, *51*(2), 207–215.

Related Research: Berry, J. H. W. (1983). Acculturation: A comparative analysis of alternative forms. In R. J. Samuda & S. L. Woods (Eds.), *Perspectives in immigrant and minority education* (pp. 65–78). Lanham, MD: University Press.

...

5715

Test Name: ANTI-BLACK RACISM SCALE

Purpose: To assess anti-Black sentiment.

Number of Items: 10

Format: 7-point agreement scales. Sample items are presented.

Reliability: Alpha was .76.

Validity: Correlation with authoritarianism was .60.

Authors: Duckitt, J., and Farre, B.

Article: Right-wing authoritarianism and political intolerance among Whites in the future majority-rule South Africa.

Journal: *The Journal of Social Psychology*, December 1994, *133*(6), 735–741.

Related Research: Duckitt, J. H. (1991). The development and validation of a subtle racism scale in South Africa. *South African Journal of Psychology*, *21*, 233–239.

...

5716

Test Name: ANTI-SEMITISM SCALE

Purpose: To measure anti-Semitism.

Number of Items: 11

Format: Likert format.

Reliability: Alpha was .94.

Validity: Correlations with other variables ranged from -.03 to .28.

Author: Dunbar, E.

Article: The prejudiced personality, racism, and anti-semitism: The PR Scale forty years later.

Journal: *Journal of Personality Assessment*, October 1995, *65*(2), 270–277.

Related Research: Selznick, G. J., & Steinberg, S. (1969). *The tenacity of prejudice.* New York: Harper & Row.

■ ■ ■

5717

Test Name: ANTI-WHITE RACISM SCALE

Purpose: To assess anti-White sentiment.

Number of Items: 10

Format: 7-point agreement scales. Sample items are presented.

Reliability: Alpha was .79.

Validity: Correlation with authoritarianism was -.32.

Authors: Duckitt, J., and Farre, B.

Article: Right-wing authoritarianism and political intolerance among Whites in the future majority-rule South Africa.

Journal: *The Journal of Social Psychology*, December 1994, *133*(6), 735–741.

■ ■ ■

5718

Test Name: ATTACHMENT SCALE

Purpose: To assess emotional dependence in interpersonal relationships.

Number of Items: 9

Format: 7-point agreement response options.

Reliability: Alphas ranged from .86 to .90.

Validity: Correlations with other variables ranged from -.29 to .60.

Authors: Smith, L. M., et al.

Article: Identity strivings within the mother-daughter relationship.

Journal: *Psychological Reports*, April 1995, *76*(2), 495–503.

Related Research: Thompson, L., & Walker, A. J. (1984). Mothers and daughters: Aid patterns and attachments. *Journal of Marriage and the Family*, *46*, 313–322.

■ ■ ■

5719

Test Name: ATTRACTION TO GROUP SCALE

Purpose: To measure participants' attitudes toward their group experience.

Number of Items: 18

Format: Responses are made on a 7-point scale ranging from 1 (*strongly disagree*) to 7 (*strongly agree*).

Reliability: Internal consistency reliability was .87 (N = 75).

Authors: Robinson, F. F., and Hardt, D. A.

Article: Effects of cognitive and behavioral structure and discussion of corrective feedback outcomes on counseling group development.

Journal: *Journal of Counseling Psychology*, October 1992, *39*(4), 473–481.

Related Research: Hulse, D. (1981). *The effects of cognitive-behavioral pretraining on attraction to feedback and attraction to the group.*

Unpublished doctoral dissertation, Indiana University, Bloomington.

■ ■ ■

5720

Test Name: AUTONOMY AND RELATEDNESS INVENTORY

Purpose: To assess the quality of the man's relationship with his female partner.

Number of Items: 32

Format: 5-point rating scales. Sample items described.

Reliability: Alpha was .71.

Authors: McKenry, P. C., et al.

Article: Toward a biopsychosocial model of domestic violence.

Journal: *Journal of Marriage and the Family*, May 1995, *57*(2), 307–320.

Related Research: Schaefer, E. S., & Edgerton, S. M. (1982). *Autonomy and Relatedness Inventory (ARI).* Unpublished manuscript, University of North Carolina at Chapel Hill, School of Public Health.

■ ■ ■

5721

Test Name: BALANCED INVENTORY OF DESIRABLE RESPONDING

Purpose: To measure social desirability.

Number of Items: 40

Format: Includes two dimensions: self-deception and impression management. Responses are made on a 7-point scale ranging from 1 (*not true*) to 7 (*very true*).

Reliability: Alpha coefficients ranged from .70 to .82.

Validity: Correlations with other variables ranged from -.28 to .52.

Authors: King, W. C., Jr., and Miles, E. W.

Article: A quasi-experimental assessment of the effect of computerizing noncognitive paper-and-pencil measurements: A test of measurement equivalence.

Journal: *Journal of Applied Psychology*, December 1995, *80*(6), 643–651.

Related Research: Paulhus, D. L. (1991). Measurement and control of response bias. In J. P. Robinson, P. R. Shaver, & L. S. Wrightsman (Eds.), *Measures of personality and social psychological attitudes* (pp. 17–59). San Diego, CA: Academic Press.

■ ■ ■

5722

Test Name: BEHAVIORAL ACCULTURATION SCALE—VIETNAMESE

Purpose: To measure behavioral acculturation.

Number of Items: 21

Format: 5-point scales. All items presented.

Reliability: Alpha was .72.

Authors: Celano, M. P., and Tyler, F. B.

Article: Behavioral acculturation among Vietnamese refugees in the United States.

Journal: *The Journal of Social Psychology*, June 1991, *133*(3), 373–385.

Related Research: Szapocznik, J., et al. (1978). Theory and measurement of acculturation. *Interamerican Journal of Psychology*, *12*, 113–130.

■ ■ ■

5723

Test Name: BELONGINGNESS SCALES

Purpose: To measure social connectedness and social

assurance.

Number of Items: 16

Format: 6-point Likert format ranges from 1 (*strongly agree*) to 6 (*strongly disagree*). All items are presented.

Reliability: Alpha was .91 for Connectedness. Alphas ranged from .77 to .82 for Assurance. Test–retest reliabilities ranged from .84 to .96.

Validity: The correlation between Connectedness and Assurance was .34.

Authors: Lee, R. M., and Robbins, S. B.

Article: Measuring belongingness: The Social Connectedness and Social Assurance Scales.

Journal: *Journal of Counseling Psychology*, April 1995, *42*(2), 232–241.

■ ■ ■

5724

Test Name: BICULTURAL INVOLVEMENT QUESTIONNAIRE—MODIFIED

Purpose: To measure biculturalism for Latinos.

Number of Items: 42

Format: Responses are made on a 5-point scale.

Reliability: Cronbach alpha coefficients ranged from .89 to .94.

Validity: Correlations with biculturalism scores reported by junior high school students' teachers was .42.

Authors: Gomez, M. J., and Fassinger, R. E.

Article: An initial model of Latino achievement: Acculturation, biculturalism, and achieving styles.

Journal: *Journal of Counseling Psychology*, April 1994, *41*(2),

205–215.

Related Research: Birman, D. (1991). *Biculturalism, sex-role attitudes, and adjustment of Latino immigrant adolescents.* Unpublished doctoral dissertation, University of Maryland, College Park.

■ ■ ■

5725

Test Name: BLACK IDENTIFICATION SCALE

Purpose: To measure a Black person's sense of belonging to the Black race and his or her concern for Black issues and causes.

Number of Items: 13

Format: All items presented. Agreement scales are implied but not specified.

Reliability: Alpha ranged from .71 to .82 across subscales.

Validity: Correlations with other related measures ranged from .13 to .44.

Authors: Whittler, T. E., et al.

Article: Strength of ethnic affiliation: Examining Black identification with Black culture.

Journal: *The Journal of Social Psychology*, August 1991, *131*(4), 461–467.

■ ■ ■

5726

Test Name: BLACK RACIAL IDENTITY ATTITUDE SCALE

Purpose: To measure racial identity attitudes of Black students corresponding to the four stages of Pre-encounter, Encounter, Immersion/Emmersion, and Internalization.

Number of Items: 50

Format: Responses are made on a 5-point Likert scale ranging from *strongly disagree* to *strongly agree*.

Reliability: Coefficient alpha reliabilities among the four subscales ranged from .51 to .80.

Authors: Taub, D. J., and McEwen, M. K.

Article: The relationship of racial identity attitudes to autonomy and mature interpersonal relationships in Black and White undergraduate women.

Journal: *Journal of College Student Development*, September 1992, *33*(5), 439–446.

Related Research: Parham, T. A., & Helms, J. E. (1981). The influence of Black students' racial identity attitudes on preferences for counselor's race. *Journal of Counseling Psychology, 26*, 250–257.

■ ■ ■

5727

Test Name: BLACK RACIAL IDENTITY ATTITUDE SCALE— FORM B

Purpose: To measure Black racial identity attitude.

Number of Items: 30

Format: Includes 4 subscales: Preencounter, Encounter, Immersion/Emersion, and Internalization. Responses are made on a 5-point Likert-type scale ranging from *strongly agree* to *strongly disagree.*

Reliability: Internal consistency coefficients ranged from .50 to .79.

Authors: Yanico, B. J., et al.

Article: A psychometric investigation of the Black Racial Identity Attitude Scale—Form B.

Journal: *Journal of Vocational Behavior*, April 1994, *44*(2), 218–234.

Related Research: Helms, J. E. (Ed.). (1990). *Black and White racial identity: Theory, research,*

and practice. Westport, CT: Greenwood.

■ ■ ■

5728

Test Name: BURDEN ASSESSMENT SCALE

Purpose: To measure perceived burdens of taking care of mentally ill relatives.

Number of Items: 19

Format: Varies. Includes 4-point frequency scales.

Reliability: Alphas ranged from .86 to .90.

Authors: Reinhard, S. C., and Horwitz, A. V.

Article: Caregiver burden: Differentiating the content and consequences of family caregiving.

Journal: *Journal of Marriage and the Family*, August 1995, *57*(3), 741–750.

Related Research: Reinhard, S. C., et al. (1994). Burden assessment scale for families of the seriously mentally ill. *Evaluation and Program Planning, 17*, 261–269.

■ ■ ■

5729

Test Name: BURDEN SCALE— BRIEF VERSION

Purpose: To measure the burden of being a caregiver.

Number of Items: 10

Format: 4-point Likert format. Sample items are presented.

Reliability: Alpha was .88.

Validity: Correlations with other variables ranged from -.27 to .26.

Authors: Chwalisz, K., and Kisler, V.

Article: Perceived stress: A better measure of caregiver burden

Journal: *Measurement and*

Evaluation in Counseling and Development, June 1995, *28*(2), 88–98.

Related Research: Russell, D. W., & Cutrona, C. E. (1987). *A longitudinal study of caretakers of Alzheimer's patients.* NIMH Grant No. NIH/PO1AGO7094-04.

■ ■ ■

5730

Test Name: CAREGIVER DISLOCATIONS SCALE

Purpose: To assess caregiver burden.

Number of Items: 16

Format: Responses are made on a 4-point scale.

Reliability: Alpha was .91.

Authors: Folkman, S., et al.

Article: Caregiver burden in HIV-positive and HIV-negative partners of men with AIDS.

Journal: *Journal of Consulting and Clinical Psychology*, August 1994, *62*(4), 746–756.

Related Research: Gottlieb, B. H., & Chrisjohn, R. C. (1988, May). *Perceived support and reactance as mediators of the impact of the dislocations of caregiving on depressed mood.* Paper presented at the Consortium for Research on Stress Processes, Toronto, Ontario, Canada.

■ ■ ■

5731

Test Name: CELEBRITY APPEAL QUESTIONNAIRE

Purpose: To measure the nature of parasocial interaction or audience–celebrity attraction.

Number of Items: 26

Format: 5-point rating scales. All items are presented.

Reliability: Total alpha was .95. Alphas ranged from .66 to .92

across subscales (Sex Appeal, Hero/Role model, Mystique, and Entertainer).

Validity: Multiple correlation with a fan rating scale was .80. Sex appeal accounted for 62% of explained variance.

Author: Stever, G. S.

Article: The Celebrity Appeal Questionnaire.

Journal: *Psychological Reports*, June 1991, *68*(3) Part I, 859–866.

■ ■ ■

5732

Test Name: CHECKLIST OF INTERPERSONAL TRANSACTIONS—REVISED

Purpose: To measure interpersonal behavior.

Number of Items: 96

Reliability: Internal consistency coefficients ranged from .43 to .81.

Validity: Correlations with other variables ranged from -.45 to .40.

Authors: Robbins, S. B., and Dupont, P.

Article: Narcissistic needs of the self and perceptions of interpersonal behavior.

Journal: *Journal of Counseling Psychology*, October 1992, *39*(4), 462–467.

Related Research: Kiesler, D., et al. (1990). Interpersonal behavior profiles of eight cases of *DSM–III* personality disorders. *Journal of Clinical Psychology*, *46*, 440–453.

■ ■ ■

5733

Test Name: CHILDREN'S FRIENDSHIP EXPECTANCY INVENTORY

Purpose: To determine friendship expectations in children.

Number of Items: 28

Format: Responses are made on a 5-point Likert scale ranging from *not important* to *very important*.

Reliability: Cronbach alpha coefficients ranged from .63 to .74 for the four subscales.

Authors: Clark, M. L., and Bittle, M. L.

Article: Friendship expectations and the evaluation of present friendships in middle childhood and early adolescence.

Journal: *Child Study Journal*, June 1992, *22*(2), 115–135.

Related Research: LaGaipa, J., & Wood, H. (1973, May). *The perception of friendship by socially accepted and rejected children.* Paper presented at the meeting of the Eastern Psychological Association, Washington, DC.

■ ■ ■

5734

Test Name: CHILDREN'S SOCIAL DESIRABILITY QUESTIONNAIRE

Purpose: To measure need for social approval.

Number of Items: 30

Format: Maximum score is 30.

Reliability: Alphas ranged from .82 to .95.

Author: Kalliopuska, M.

Article: Social desirability related to children's age, sex, and willingness to help.

Journal: *Psychological Reports*, April 1992, *70*(2), 479–482.

Related Research: Crandall, V. C., et al. (1965). A children's social desirability questionnaire. *Journal of Consulting Psychology*, *29*, 27–36.

5735

Test Name: CLOSE FRIENDSHIP SCALE

Purpose: To describe characteristics of the close friendship experience of adults.

Number of Items: 88

Format: Responses are made on a 6-point Likert-type scale.

Reliability: Odd–even reliability coefficients for the subscales ranged from .87 to .98. Intercorrelations of the subscales ranged from .49 to .74. Cronbach's alpha coefficients for the subscales ranged from .88 to .95. The coefficient for the total close friendship scale was .98.

Authors: Busse, W. M. O., et al.

Article: The effects of self-disclosure and competitiveness on friendship for male graduate students over 35.

Journal: *Journal of College Student Development*, March 1993, *34*(2), 169–174.

Related Research: Frum, J. (1979). *Development of the Close Friendship Scale and examination of the characteristics of friendship related to a person's sex.* Unpublished doctoral dissertation, University of Maryland, College Park.

■ ■ ■

5736

Test Name: COMPANION ANIMAL SEMANTIC DIFFERENTIAL

Purpose: To measure pet liking and bonding.

Number of Items: 18

Format: Items are scored from 1 (*high liking*) to 6 (*low liking*).

Reliability: Theta was .93.

Author: Loyer-Carlson, V.

Article: Pets and perceived family life quality.

Journal: *Psychological Reports*, June 1991, *70*(3) Part I, 947–952.

Related Research: Poresky, R. H., et al. (1988). The Companion Animal Semantic Differential: Long and short form reliability and validity. *Educational and Psychological Measurement, 48*, 255–260.

■ ■ ■

5737

Test Name: COMPREHENSION OF CONSENT/COERCION MEASURE

Purpose: To assess the ability to recognize situations in which a person is coerced or consents to engage in sex.

Number of Items: 10

Format: 6-point Likert format. A sample item is presented. Participants respond to five items for each of two scenarios.

Reliability: Internal consistency ranged from .75 to .79. Test–retest reliability (5 weeks to 5 months) ranged from .60 to .50.

Validity: Correlations with other variables ranged from -.46 to .28.

Authors: Heppner, M. J., et al.

Article: The differential effects of rape prevention programming on attitudes, behavior, and knowledge.

Journal: *Journal of Counseling Psychology*, October 1995, *42*(4), 508–518.

Related Research: Gibson, D. B., & Humphrey, C. F. (1993). *Educating in regards to sexual violence: An interactional dramatic acquaintance rape intervention.* Unpublished manuscript, University of Minnesota, Sexual Violence Program, Minneapolis.

5738

Test Name: COOPERATIVENESS AND COMPETITIVENESS SCALE—ITALIAN VERSION

Purpose: To measure cooperative and competitive activity.

Number of Items: 18 (9 cooperative and 9 competitive items).

Format: Respondents rank 10 activities according to importance. All items presented.

Reliability: Test–retest (4 weeks) yielded a *rho* of .55 (*p* < .01).

Author: DeMoja, C. A.

Article: Cooperativeness and competitiveness among pupils in Southern Italy.

Journal: *Psychological Reports*, February 1992, *70*(1), 99-105.

Related Research: Schwalb, D. W., & Schawlb, B. J. (1985). Japanese cooperative and competitive attitudes: Age and gender effects. *International Journal of Behavioral Development, 8*, 313–328.

■ ■ ■

5739

Test Name: CULTURAL MISTRUST INVENTORY

Purpose: To assess the extent to which Blacks mistrust Whites.

Number of Items: 48

Format: Responses are made on a 7-point Likert-type scale ranging from 1 (*strongly disagree*) to 7 (*strongly agree*). Examples are presented.

Reliability: Test–retest (2 weeks) reliability was .82. Cronbach's alpha was .89.

Validity: Correlations with other variables ranged from -.30 to .34.

Authors: Nickerson, K. J., et al.

Article: Cultural mistrust, opinions about mental illness, and Black students' attitudes toward seeking psychological help from White counselors.

Journal: *Journal of Counseling Psychology*, July 1994, *41*(3), 378–385.

Related Research: Terrell, F., & Terrell, S. L. (1981). An inventory to measure cultural mistrust among Blacks. *Western Journal of Black Studies, 3*, 180–185.

■ ■ ■

5740

Test Name: CYNICAL DISTRUST SCALE

Purpose: To measure the extent to which people see others as dishonest, ugly, mean, and unsocial.

Number of Items: 9

Format: All items presented. Items are adapted from the MMPI.

Reliability: Reliability was .75.

Authors: Greenglass, E. R., and Julkunen, J.

Article: Cook-Medley Hostility, anger and the Type A behavior pattern in Finland.

Journal: *Psychological Reports*, June 1991, *68*(3) Part II, 1059–1066.

Related Research: Greenglass, E. R., & Julkunen, J. (1989). Construct validity and sex differences in Cook-Medley Hostility. *Personality and Individual Differences, 10*, 209–218.

■ ■ ■

5741

Test Name: DATING COMPETENCE SCALE

Purpose: To assess dating competence.

Number of Items: 9

Format: 4-point scales ranging from 1 (*never*) to 4 (*always*). Sample items are presented.

Reliability: Alpha was .72.

Authors: Newcomb, M. D., and Rickards, S.

Article: Parent drug-use problems and adult intimate relations: Associations among community samples of young adult women and men.

Journal: *Journal of Counseling Psychology*, April 1995, *42*(2), 141–154.

Related Research: Levenson, R. W., & Gottman, J. M. (1978). Toward the assessment of social competence. *Journal of Consulting and Clinical Psychology*, 46, 353–462.

▪ ▪ ▪

5742

Test Name: DATING CONFLICT SCALE

Purpose: To measure conflict among college daters.

Number of Items: 10

Format: 5-point frequency scales. All items are presented.

Reliability: Omega was .87.

Author: Stets, J. E.

Article: Modeling control in relationships.

Journal: *Journal of Marriage and the Family*, May 1994, *57*(2), 489–501.

Related Research: Stets, J. E. (1993). Control in dating relationships. *Journal of Marriage and the Family*, 55, 673–685.

▪ ▪ ▪

5743

Test Name: PARENTING CONTROL SCALE

~ose: To measure successful

control in dating relationships.

Number of Items: 10

Format: 5-point frequency scales. All items presented.

Reliability: Omega reliability was .85.

Validity: Correlations with other variables ranged from -.18 to .41.

Author: Stets, J. E.

Article: Control in Dating Relationships.

Journal: *Journal of Marriage and the Family*, August 1993, *55*(3), 673–685.

Related Research: Stets, J. E. (1992). Interactive processes in dating aggression: A national study. *Journal of Marriage and the Family*, 54, 165–177.

Stets, J. E. Modeling control in relationships. *Journal of Marriage and the Family*, 57, 489–501.

▪ ▪ ▪

5744

Test Name: DATING INTERACTION SCALES

Purpose: To assess conflict, role-taking and interpersonal control in dating relationships.

Number of Items: 22

Format: 5-point frequency scales. All items presented.

Reliability: Omega reliabilities ranged from .75 to .86 across subscales.

Validity: Correlations between subscales ranged from -.21 to .44.

Author: Stets, J. E.

Article: Interactive processes in dating aggression: A national study.

Journal: *Journal of Marriage and the Family*, February 1992, *54*(1), 165–177.

5745

Test Name: DENIAL OF DISTRESS SCALE

Purpose: To measure the failure to admit to the negative consensual judgments of others.

Number of Items: 11

Format: 5-point true–false format. Sample item presented.

Reliability: Alphas ranged from .75 to .84. Test–retest (7 months) was .77.

Authors: Koenig, L. J., et al.

Article: Sex differences in adolescent depression and loneliness: Why are boys lonelier if girls are more depressed?

Journal: *Journal of Research in Personality*, March 1994, *28*(1), 27–43.

Related Research: Weinberger, D. A. (1991). *Social-emotional adjustment in older children and adults: I. Psychometric properties of the Weinberger Adjustment Inventory.* Unpublished manuscript, Case Western Reserve University, Cleveland, OH.

▪ ▪ ▪

5746

Test Name: DESPERATE LOVE SCALE

Purpose: To assess the intensity of a person's experience of desperate love in terms of desire for reciprocation, intensity of feelings, and fear of rejection.

Number of Items: 12

Format: 9-point Likert format.

Reliability: Test–retest reliability was .92. Alpha was .93.

Authors: Sperling, M. B., and Berman, W. H.

Article: An attachment classification of desperate love.

Journal: *Journal of Personality*

Assessment, February 1991, *56*(1), 45–55.

Related Research: Sperling, M. B. (1985). Discriminant measures for desperate love. *Journal of Personality Assessment, 49,* 324–328.

■ ■ ■

5747

Test Name: DIFFERENTIAL LONELINESS SCALE

Purpose: To measure quality of, quantity of, and satisfaction with current human relationships.

Number of Items: 60

Format: Yes–no format.

Reliability: Test–retest (1 month) was .85 for women and .97 for men. Alpha for Finnish version was .92.

Validity: Correlation with UCLA Loneliness-Scale was .70.

Authors: Kalliopuska, M., and Laitinen, M.

Article: Loneliness related to self-concept.

Journal: *Psychological Reports*, August 1991, *69*(1), 27–34.

Related Research: Schmidt, N., & Sermat, W. (1983). Measuring loneliness in different relationships. *Journal of Personality and Social Psychology, 44,* 1038–1047.

■ ■ ■

5748

Test Name: DIMENSIONS OF SOCIAL SUPPORT SCALE

Purpose: To measure the extent to which respondents were receiving informational and emotional support from a variety of sources.

Number of Items: 20

Format: Responses are made on a 5-point Likert scale (*not at all* to *extremely*) using the same 9-item set of questions for the four

support sources—mother, father, friend, and significant adult.

Reliability: Cronbach's alphas ranged from .95 to .85.

Author: Rodney, H. E.

Article: A profile of collegiate Black children of alcoholics.

Journal: *Journal of College Student Development*, May/June 1995, *36*(3), 228–235.

Related Research: Cohen, F. (1977). *Dimensions of Social Support Scale.* Unpublished document, Stanford University, School of Medicine, San Francisco.

■ ■ ■

5749

Test Name: EARLY RESOURCES CHECKLIST

Purpose: To provide a checklist of support sources to buffer the effects of early trauma.

Number of Items: 10

Format: Includes three factors: Interpersonal Relationships, Achievements, and Play.

Validity: Correlations with other variables ranged from -.25 to .25.

Authors: Zamostny, K. P., et al.

Article: Narcissistic injury and its relationship to early trauma, early resources, and adjustment to college.

Journal: *Journal of Counseling Psychology*, October 1993, *40*(4), 501–510.

Related Research: Zamostny, K. P., et al. (1991). *Early Resources Checklist.* Unpublished instrument.

■ ■ ■

5750

Test Name: ENRICHMENT AND RESOURCE DEPLETION FROM NONWORK SCALES

Purpose: To assess enrichment from and costs of hobbies, family, friends, and community associations.

Number of Items: 8

Format: Sample items are presented. 5-point scales.

Reliability: Alphas ranged from .74 (costs) to .76 (enrichment).

Validity: Correlations with other variables ranged from -.20 to .38.

Authors: Cohen, A., and Kirchmeyer, C.

Article: A multidimensional approach to the relation between organizational commitment and nonwork participation.

Journal: *Journal of Vocational Behavior*, April 1995, *46*(2), 189–202.

Related Research: Kirchmeyer, C. (1992). Nonwork participation and work attitudes: A test of scarcity vs. expansion models of personal resources. *Human Relations, 45,* 775–795.

Kirchmeyer, C. (1993). Nonwork to work spillover: A more balanced view of the experiences and coping of professional women and men. *Sex Roles, 28,* 1–22.

■ ■ ■

5751

Test Name: EQUITY SENSITIVITY INSTRUMENT

Purpose: To measure sensitivity to distribution of outcomes.

Number of Items: 4

Format: To respond to each item, 10 points indicating agreement are distributed between two statements.

Reliability: Alpha coefficients were .74 and .68.

Validity: Correlations with other variables ranged from -.23 to .24.

Authors: King, W. C., Jr., and Miles, E. W.

Article: A quasi-experimental assessment of effect of computerizing noncognitive paper-and-pencil measurements: A test of measurement equivalence.

Journal: *Journal of Applied Psychology*, December 1995, *80*(6), 643–651.

Related Research: King, W. C., & Miles, E. W. (1994). The measurement of equity sensitivity. *Journal of Occupational and Organizational Psychology*, *67*, 133–142.

■ ■ ■

5752

Test Name: ETHNIC ACCULTURATION SCALE

Purpose: To measure acculturation.

Number of Items: 4

Format: 5-point frequency scales. All items are described.

Reliability: Alpha was .90.

Authors: Booth-Kewleys, S., et al.

Article: Turnover among Hispanic and Non-Hispanic blue-collar workers in the US Navy's civilian workforce.

Journal: *The Journal of Social Psychology*, December 1993, *133*(6), 761–768.

Related Research: Kuvlesky, W. P., & Patella, V. M. (1971). Degree of ethnicity and aspirations for upward social mobility among Mexican American youth. *Journal of Vocational Behavior*, *I*, 231–244.

■ ■ ■

5753

Test Name: ETHNIC IDENTITY SCALES

Purpose: To measure Armenian,

Turkish, and global human identity.

Number of Items: 24

Format: 6-point Likert format. Sample items are presented.

Reliability: Alphas ranged from .60 to .83.

Authors: Der-Karabetian, A., and Balian, N.

Article: Ingroup, outgroup and global-human identities of Turkish Armenians.

Journal: *The Journal of Social Psychology*, August 1992, *132*(4), 497–504.

Related Research: Der-Karabetian, A. (1980). Relation of two cultural identities of Armenian Americans. *Psychological Reports*, *47*, 123–128.

■ ■ ■

5754

Test Name: EXCHANGE ORIENTATION SCALE

Purpose: To measure orientation to interpersonal social exchange.

Number of Items: 9

Format: 5-point scales (*definitely does not sound like me* to *definitely sounds like me*). Sample items presented.

Reliability: Alphas ranged from .62 to .68.

Authors: Vanyperen, N. W., and Buunk, B. P.

Article: Equity theory and exchange and communal orientation from a cross-national perspective.

Journal: *The Journal of Social Psychology*, February 1991, *131*(1), 5–20.

Related Research: Clark, M. S., et al. (1987). Recipients' mood, relationship type, and helping.

Journal of Personality and Social Psychology, *53*, 93–103.

■ ■ ■

5755

Test Name: FEAR OF INTIMACY SCALE

Purpose: To measure anxiety about close dating relationships.

Number of Items: 35

Format: 5-point rating scales range from 1 (*not at all characteristic of me*) to 5 (*extremely characteristic of me*).

Reliability: Internal consistency was .93. Test–retest (1 month) was .89.

Authors: Good, G. E., et al.

Article: Male gender role conflict: Psychometric issues and relations to psychological distress.

Journal: *Journal of Counseling Psychology*, January 1995, *42*(1), 3–10.

Related Research: Descutner, C. J., & Thelen, M. H. (1991). Development and validation of a fear of intimacy measure. *Psychological Assessment: A Journal of Clinical and Consulting Psychology*, *5*, 377–383.

■ ■ ■

5756

Test Name: FEAR OF NEGATIVE EVALUATION SCALE—BRIEF VERSION

Purpose: To assess a participant's apprehensions about others' evaluations and distress over negative evaluations.

Number of Items: 12

Format: 5-point Likert format.

Reliability: Alpha was .93.

Authors: Kolligian, J., Jr., and Sternberg, R. J.

Article: Perceived fraudulence in

young adults: Is there an "impostor syndrome?"

Journal: *Journal of Personality Assessment*, April 1991, *56*(2), 308–326.

Related Research: Leary, M. R. (1983). A brief version of the Fear of Negative Evaluation Scale. *Personality and Social Psychology Bulletin*, *9*, 371–375.

■ ■ ■

5757

Test Name: FUNDAMENTAL INTERPERSONAL RELATIONS ORIENTATION–BEHAVIOR QUESTIONNAIRE.

Purpose: To measure what behavior individuals express towards others and how individuals want others to behave towards them.

Number of Items: 54

Format: Six 9-item scales.

Reliability: Alphas averaged .94. Test–retest (10 weeks) was .69.

Validity: Correlations with other variables ranged from -.23 to .33.

Author: Hurley, J. R.

Article: FIRO-B's dissociation from two central dimensions of interpersonal behavior.

Journal: *Psychological Reports*, February 1991, *68*(1), 243–254.

Related Research: Schutz, W. C. (1958). *FIRO: A three-dimensional theory of interpersonal behavior.* New York: Wiley.

■ ■ ■

5758

Test Name: GENERAL ALIENATION SCALE

Purpose: To measure alienation.

Number of Items: 20

Format: Responses are made on a 5-point scale.

Validity: Correlations with other variables ranged from -.35 to .13.

Authors: Roig, M., and Neaman, M. A. W.

Article: Alienation, learning or grade orientation, and achievement as correlates of attitudes toward cheating.

Journal: *Perceptual and Motor Skills*, June 1994, *78*(3) Part 2, 1096–1098.

Related Research: Ray, J. J. (1982). Toward a definitive alienation scale. *The Journal of Psychology*, *112*, 67–70.

■ ■ ■

5759

Test Name: GROUP CLIMATE QUESTIONNAIRE—SHORT FORM

Purpose: To measure a participant's perception of the group atmosphere.

Number of Items: 12

Format: Items are rated on a 6-point Likert scale ranging from 1 (*not at all*) to 6 (*extremely*). Includes 3 dimensions: engaged, avoiding, and conflict.

Reliability: Alpha coefficients ranged from .88 to .94.

Authors: Kivlighan, D. M., Jr., and Angelone, E. O.

Article: Interpersonal problems: Variables influencing participants' perception of group climate.

Journal: *Journal of Counseling Psychology*, October 1992, *39*(4), 468–472.

Related Research: MacKenzie, K. R. (1983). The clinical application of a group climate measure. In R. R. Dies & K. R. MacKenzie (Eds.), *Advances in group therapy: Integrating research and practice* (pp. 159–170). Madison, CT: International Universities Press.

5760

Test Name: GROUP-INTERACTION MEASURE

Purpose: To measure positive group interaction.

Number of Items: 8

Format: Responses are made on a 5-point Likert-type scale ranging from 1 (*very little extent*) to 5 (*a very great extent*). All items are presented.

Reliability: Alpha coefficients ranged from .33 to .98.

Authors: Watson, W., et al.

Article: Member competence, group interaction, and group decision making: A longitudinal study.

Journal: *Journal of Applied Psychology*, December 1991, *76*(6), 803–809.

Related Research: Yalom, I. D. (1975). *The theory and practice of group psychotherapy.* New York: Basic Books.

■ ■ ■

5761

Test Name: HAWAIIAN ACCULTURATION SCALE

Purpose: To measure how culturally Hawaiian a person is by contemporary Hawaiian standards.

Number of Items: 21

Format: Yes–no and open-ended formats. All items presented.

Validity: Items discriminate between Hawaiians and Japanese and Hawaiians and Whites.

Author: Rezentes, W. C., III

Article: *Nă Mea Hawai'i*: A Hawaiian Acculturation Scale.

Journal: *Psychological Reports*, October 1993, *73*(2), 383–393.

Related Research: Cuellar, I., et al. (1980). An acculturation scale for Mexican-American normal and clinical populations. *Hispanic Journal of Behavioral Sciences, 2,* 199–217.

• • •

5762

Test Name: HOW GROUPS WORK SCALE

Purpose: To measure elements of group experience that contribute to learning and change.

Number of Items: 14

Format: 4-point scales range from *did not apply to learning in my group* to *one of the two most important experiences.*

Reliability: Hoyt reliability was .86.

Authors: Mawson, D. L., and Kahn, S. E.

Article: Group processes in a women's career intervention.

Journal: *The Career Development Quarterly,* March 1993, *41*(3), 238–245.

Related Research: Kivlighan, D., et al. (1987). Participants' perception of therapeutic factors in group counseling: The role of interpersonal style and stage of group development. *Small Group Behavior, 19,* 452–468.

• • •

5763

Test Name: IDENTIFICATION WITH A PSYCHOLOGICAL GROUP SCALE

Purpose: To measure identification with a psychological group.

Number of Items: 10

Format: Includes two components: Shared Experiences and Shared Characteristics. All items are presented.

Reliability: Alpha coefficient was .76.

Validity: Correlations with other variables ranged from -.02 to .83.

Authors: Mael, F. A., and Tetrick, L. E.

Article: Identifying organizational identification.

Journal: *Educational and Psychological Measurement,* Winter 1992, *52*(4), 813–824.

• • •

5764

Test Name: IMPORTANCE TO IDENTITY SCALE

Purpose: To measure the importance of nationality to self-identity.

Number of Items: 4

Format: Responses are made on a 5-point Likert-type scale ranging from 1 (*strongly disagree*) to 5 (*strongly agree*). An example is presented.

Reliability: Coefficient alpha was .79.

Validity: Correlations with other variables ranged from -.22 to .25.

Authors: Thomas, D. C., and Ravlin, E. C.

Article: Responses of employees to cultural adaptation by a foreign manager.

Journal: *Journal of Applied Psychology,* February 1995, *80*(1), 133–146.

Related Research: Luhtanen, R., & Crocker, J. (1991). Self-esteem and intergroup comparisons: Toward a theory of collective self-esteem. In J. Suls & T. A. Wills (Eds.), *Social cognition: Contemporary theory and research* (pp. 211–221). Hillsdale, NJ: Erlbaum.

• • •

5765

Test Name: INDIVIDUALISM–COLLECTIVISM SCALE

Purpose: To measure individualism and collectivism.

Number of Items: 29

Format: Includes 3 factors: Self-reliance with competition, low concerns for in-groups, and distance from in-groups.

Reliability: Alpha was .74.

Authors: Tata, S. P., and Leong, F. T. L.

Article: Individualism-collectivism, social-network orientation, and acculturation as predictors of attitudes toward seeking professional psychological help among Chinese Americans.

Journal: *Journal of Counseling Psychology,* July 1994, *41*(3), 280–287.

Related Research: Triandis, H. C., et al. (1988). Individualism and collectivism: Cross-cultural perspectives on self-in-group relationships. *Journal of Personality and Social Psychology, 54,* 323–338.

• • •

5766

Test Name: INTERACTION ANXIOUSNESS SCALE

Purpose: To measure dispositional social anxiety.

Number of Items: 15

Reliability: Alphas ranged from .88 to .89 across samples. Test–retest (8 weeks) was .80.

Validity: Correlations with other variables ranged from -.47 to .71.

Authors: Leary, M. R., and Kowalski, R. M.

Article: The Interaction Anxiousness Scale: Construct and criterion-related validity.

Journal: *Journal of Personality Assessment,* August 1993, *61*(1), 136–146.

Related Research: Leary, M. R.

(1983). Social anxiousness: The construct and its measurement. *Journal of Personality Assessment*, *47*, 66–75.

■ ■ ■

5767

Test Name: INTERPERSONAL ADJECTIVE SCALE—REVISED

Purpose: To assess the quality of interpersonal transactions.

Number of Items: 64

Format: Adjective rating scales range over four points.

Reliability: Alphas ranged from .74 to .85 across subscales.

Authors: Sharp, M., and Schill, T.

Article: Chronic self-destructiveness and the self-defeating personality: Similarities and differences.

Journal: *Journal of Personality Assessment*, April 1995, *64*(2), 270–278.

Related Research: Wiggins, J., et al. (1988). Psychometric and geometric characteristics of the revised Interpersonal Adjective Scales (IAS-R). *Multivariate Behavioral Research*, *23*, 517–530.

■ ■ ■

5768

Test Name: INTERPERSONAL CHECKLIST

Purpose: To provide a categorization of a person's predominant interpersonal style.

Number of Items: 128

Format: Includes two major factors: Control (dominant–submissive) and Affiliation (love–hate).

Reliability: Average test–retest reliability was .78.

Authors: Kivlighan, D. M., Jr., and Goldfine, D. C.

Article: Endorsement of therapeutic factors as a function of stage of group development and participant interpersonal attitudes.

Journal: *Journal of Counseling Psychology*, April 1991, *38*(2), 150–158.

Related Research: Leary, T. (1957). *Interpersonal diagnosis of personality*. New York: Ronald.

■ ■ ■

5769

Test Name: INTERPERSONAL CONFLICT SCALE

Purpose: To assess interpersonal conflict on the job.

Number of Items: 4

Format: Responses are made on a 5-point scale ranging from *never* to *extremely often*.

Reliability: Internal consistency was .66.

Validity: Correlations with other variables ranged from .12 to .46.

Authors: Chen, P. Y., and Spector, P. E.

Article: Negative affectivity as the underlying cause of correlations between stressors and strains.

Journal: *Journal of Applied Psychology*, June 1991, *76*(3), 398–407.

Related Research: Spector, P. E. (1987). Interactive effects of perceived control and job stressors on affective reactions and health outcomes for clerical workers. *Work and Stress*, *1*, 155–162.

■ ■ ■

5770

Test Name: INTERPERSONAL DEPENDENCE INVENTORY

Purpose: To measure interpersonal dependence.

Number of Items: 48

Format: 4-point scales range from 1 (*disagree*) to 4 (*agree*).

Reliability: Test–retest reliabilities (16 to 60 weeks) ranged from .41 to .68.

Validity: Correlations with Rorschach Oral Dependency scores ranged from -.35 to .37.

Authors: Boorstein, R. F., et al.

Article: Retest reliability scores on objective and projective measures of dependency: Relationship to life events and interest interval.

Journal: *Journal of Personality Assessment*, April 1994, *62*(3), 398–415.

Related Research: Hirschfeld, R. M., et al. (1977). A measure of interpersonal dependency. *Journal of Personality Assessment*, *41*, 610–618.

■ ■ ■

5771

Test Name: INTERPERSONAL DEPENDENCY INVENTORY

Purpose: To assess interpersonal dependency relative to emotional reliance on another person, lack of social self-confidence, and assertion of autonomy.

Number of Items: 48

Format: Responses are made on a 7-point scale ranging from 1 (*very characteristic of me*) to 7 (*not characteristic of me*). Sample items are presented.

Reliability: Split-half reliabilities ranged from .76 to .91.

Validity: Correlations with other variables ranged from -.46 to .70.

Authors: Cooper, A., and McCormack, W. A.

Article: Short-term group treatment for adult children of alcoholics.

Journal: *Journal of Counseling Psychology*, July 1992, *39*(3), 350–355.

Related Research: Hirschfeld, R. M. A., et al. (1977). A measure of interpersonal dependency. *Journal of Personality Assessment, 41*, 610–618.

■ ■ ■

5772

Test Name: INTERPERSONAL RATING SCALE

Purpose: To measure the acceptance and rejection of self and of others.

Number of Items: 9

Format: Semantic differential format. All adjective pairs presented.

Reliability: Alphas ranged from .77 to .93.

Author: May, B. A.

Article: The interaction between ratings of self, peers' perceptions, and reflexive self-ratings.

Journal: *The Journal of Social Psychology*, August 1991, *133*(4), 483–493.

Related Research: Hurley, J. R. (1989). Self-acceptance and other-acceptance scales for small groups. *Genetic, Social and General Psychology Monographs, 115*, 485–505.

■ ■ ■

5773

Test Name: INTERPERSONAL REACTIVITY INDEX

Purpose: To measure perspective-taking, empathic concern, personal distress, and fantasy.

Number of Items: 28

Format: 5-point Likert format.

Reliability: Internal consistency ranged from .71 to .77. Test–

retest reliability ranged from .62 to .71.

Authors: Brems, C., et al.

Article: Group modification of empathic verbalizations and self-disclosure.

Journal: *The Journal of Social Psychology*, April 1992, *132*(2), 189–200.

Related Research: Davis, M. H. (1980). A multidimensional approach to individual differences in empathy. *JSAS Catalog of Selected Documents in Psychology, 10*, 85.

■ ■ ■

5774

Test Name: INTERPERSONAL RELATIONSHIP ASSESSMENT TECHNIQUE

Purpose: To measure peer acceptance.

Number of Items: 8

Format: Guttman format.

Reliability: Reproducibility was .92. Scalability was .72.

Authors: Eshel, Y., and Dicker, R.

Article: Congruence and incongruence in perceived ethnic acceptance among Israeli students.

Journal: *The Journal of Social Psychology*, April 1995, *135*(2), 251–262.

Related Research: Schwartzwald, J., & Cohen, S. (1982). The relationship between academic tracking and the degree of interethnic acceptance. *Journal of Educational Psychology, 74*, 588–597.

■ ■ ■

5775

Test Name: INTERPERSONAL RELATIONSHIP SCALE

Purpose: To measure trust and

intimacy in interpersonal relationships.

Number of Items: 52

Format: 5-point response alternatives (*strongly agree* to *strongly disagree*).

Reliability: Test–retest (2 months) was .92.

Authors: Greenglass, E. R., and Julkunen, J.

Article: Cook-Medley hostility, anger, and the Type A behavior pattern in Finland

Journal: *Psychological Reports*, June 1991, *68*(3) Part II, 1059–1066.

Related Research: Schlein, S. P., et al. (1977). The Interpersonal Relationship Scale (IRS). In B. G. Gurney, Jr. (Ed.), *Relationship Enhancement* (pp. 349–354). San Francisco: Jossey-Bass.

■ ■ ■

5776

Test Name: INTERPERSONAL RELATIONS SCALE

Purpose: To measure the benefit from group participation.

Number of Items: 66

Format: Responses are made on a 5-point scale ranging from 1 (*less than once every 6 months*) to 5 (*at least one a day*).

Reliability: Alpha reliability was .96 and .93. Test–retest (3 weeks) reliability was .78.

Validity: Correlations with other variables ranged from .10 to .80.

Authors: Kivlighan, D. M., Jr., et al.

Article: Training group members to set session agendas: Effects on in-session behavior and member outcome.

Journal: *Journal of Counseling Psychology*, April 1993, *40*(2), 182–187.

Related Research: Shadish, W. R. (1984). Intimate behaviors and the assessment of benefits in clinical groups. *Small Group Behavior, 15,* 204–221.

■ ■ ■

5777

Test Name: INTERPERSONAL RELATIONS SCALE CHECKLIST

Purpose: To assess intimacy.

Number of Items: 66

Format: Items represent the following areas: discusses self and relationship to others, requests feedback, expresses positive feelings, accepts/likes self, communicates directly and effectively with others, takes risks by revealing feelings, expresses change of attitude, expresses closeness to others, expresses negative feelings, discusses others' feelings, and understands what happens between others.

Reliability: Interrater reliabilities ranged from .85 to .99.

Validity: Correlations with other variables ranged from .10 to .69.

Authors: Kivlighan, D. M., Jr., et al.

Article: Training group members to set session agendas: Effects on in-session behavior and member outcome.

Journal: *Journal of Counseling Psychology,* April 1993, *40*(2), 182–187.

Related Research: Shadish, W. R. (1984). Intimate behaviors and the assessment of benefits in clinical groups. *Small Group Behavior, 15,* 204–221.

■ ■ ■

5778

Test Name: INTERPERSONAL RELATIONS SCALE SEMANTIC DIFFERENTIAL

Purpose: To measure group outcome.

Number of Items: 11

Format: Responses are made on a scale from 1 (*bad, weak,* or *passive*) to 5 (*good, strong* or *active*).

Reliability: Alpha coefficients ranged from .90 to .96.

Validity: Correlations with other variables ranged from .10 to .75.

Authors: Kivlighan, D. M., Jr., et al.

Article: Training group members to set session agendas: Effects on in-session behavior and member outcome.

Journal: *Journal of Counseling Psychology,* April 1993, *40*(2), 182–187.

Related Research: Shadish, W. R. (1984). Intimate behaviors and the assessment of benefits in clinical groups. *Small Group Behavior, 15,* 204–221.

■ ■ ■

5779

Test Name: INTERPERSONAL SUPPORT EVALUATION LIST

Purpose: To measure perceived social support.

Number of Items: 30

Format: Includes 3 subscales: Belonging, Tangible, and Appraisal. Examples are presented.

Reliability: Alpha coefficients ranged from .88 to .90. Test–retest (2 weeks) reliability ranged from .74 to .87.

Validity: Correlations with other variables ranged from -.01 to .50.

Authors: Robbins, S. B., et al.

Article: Goal continuity as a mediator of early retirement

adjustment: Testing a multidimensional model.

Journal: *Journal of Counseling Psychology,* January 1994, *41*(1), 18–26.

Related Research: Cohen, S., et al. (1985). Measuring the functional component of social support. In I. Sarason & B. Sarason (Eds.), *Social support: Theory, research and practice* (pp. 73–94). Dordrecht, the Netherlands: Martinus Nijhoff.

■ ■ ■

5780

Test Name: INTERPERSONAL SUPPORT EVALUATION LIST

Purpose: To measure perceived availability of support.

Number of Items: 40

Format: Includes four subscales: Tangible Support, Appraisal, Self-Esteem, and Belonging. Responses to each item are either *probably true* or *probably false.*

Reliability: Alpha coefficients ranged from .62 to .90. Estimates of test–retest reliability were .87 (2 days), .70 (6 weeks), and .74 (6 months).

Validity: Correlations with other variables ranged from .31 to .74.

Authors: Wright, D. M., and Heppner, P. P.

Article: Examining the well-being of nonclinical college students: Is knowledge of the presence of parental alcoholism useful?

Journal: *Journal of Counseling Psychology,* July 1993, *40*(3), 324–334.

Related Research: Cohen, S., et al. (1985). Measuring the functional components of social support. In I. G. Sarason & B. R. Sarason (Eds.), *Social support: Theory, research, and applications* (pp. 73–94). Dordrecht, The Netherlands: Martinus Nijhoff.

5781

Test Name: INTERPERSONAL SUPPORT EVALUATION LIST

Purpose: To assess the availability of sources of social support.

Number of Items: 48

Format: Sample items are presented.

Reliability: Total alpha was .90. Subscale alphas ranged from .61 to .69.

Authors: Rhodewalt, F., and Morf, C. C.

Article: Self and interpersonal correlates of the Narcissistic Personality Inventory: A review and new findings.

Journal: *Journal of Research in Personality*, March 1995, *29*(1), 1–23.

Related Research: Cohen, S., & Hoberman, H. M. (1983). Positive events and social supports as buffers of life change stress. *Journal of Applied Social Psychology*, *13*, 99–125.

■ ■ ■

5782

Test Name: INTERPERSONAL TRUST SCALE

Purpose: To provide a self-report measure of trustworthiness.

Number of Items: 99

Format: Responses are made on a scale ranging from 1 (*strongly agree*) to 5 (*strongly disagree*).

Reliability: Split-half reliability was .76.

Authors: Howard, G. S., et al.

Article: In stories we trust: Studies of the reliability of autobiographies.

Journal: *Journal of Counseling Psychology*, July 1992, *39*(3), 398–405.

Related Research: Rotter, J. B.

(1967). A new scale for the measurement of interpersonal trust. *Journal of Personality, 35*, 651–665.

■ ■ ■

5783

Test Name: INTRAGROUP CONFLICT SCALE

Purpose: To assess intragroup conflict.

Number of Items: 7

Format: Responses are made on 5-point Likert scale ranging from 1 (*strongly disagree*) to 5 (*strongly agree*). All items are presented.

Reliability: Coefficient alpha was .92.

Validity: Correlations with other variables ranged from -.01 to -.48.

Authors: Saavedra, R., et al.

Article: Complex interdependence in task-performing groups.

Journal: *Journal of Applied Psychology*, February 1993, *78*(1), 61–72.

Related Research: Lee, C., et al. (1991). Relations of goal setting and goal sharing to performance and conflict for interdependent tasks. *British Journal of Management, 2*, 33–39.

■ ■ ■

5784

Test Name: INVENTORY OF INTERPERSONAL PROBLEMS

Purpose: To identify interpersonal problems.

Number of Items: 127

Format: Responses are made on a 5-point Likert Scale. Sample items are presented.

Reliability: Alpha coefficients ranged from .84 to .92.

Authors: Kivlighan, D. M., Jr., et al.

Article: Projection in group counseling: The relationship between members' interpersonal problems and their perception of the group leader.

Journal: *Journal of Counseling Psychology,* January 1994, *41*(1), 99–104.

Related Research: Horowitz, L. M., et al. (1988). Inventory of interpersonal problems: Psychometric properties and clinical application. *Journal of Consulting and Clinical Psychology, 56,* 885–892.

■ ■ ■

5785

Test Name: INVENTORY OF SOCIALLY SUPPORTIVE BEHAVIORS

Purpose: To assess the number of functional perceived social-supportive behaviors experienced in the participant's lives.

Number of Items: 40

Format: Responses are made on a 5-point scale ranging from 1 (*not at all*) to 5 (*about every day*). The instrument assessed the following four types of social support: emotional support, tangible assistance, cognitive information, and guidance.

Reliability: Test–retest reliability was .88 ($N = 69$); alpha coefficients were .93 and .94.

Validity: Correlation with others variables ranged from .00 to .40.

Authors: Wohlgemuth, E., and Betz, N. E.

Article: Gender as a moderator of the relationships of stress and social support to physical health in college students.

Journal: *Journal of Counseling Psychology*, July 1991, *38*(3), 367–374.

Related Research: Barrera, M., Jr., et al. (1981). Preliminary development of a scale of social support: Studies on college students. *American Journal of Community Psychology, 9,* 435–447.

■ ■ ■

5786

Test Name: JEALOUS RESPONSES SCALE

Purpose: To measure partner enhancing and partner attacking in jealousy-evoking situations.

Number of Items: 14

Format: 9-point rating scales.

Reliability: Alphas ranged from .85 to .87 across the two subscales.

Validity: Correlations with other measures of jealousy ranged from .07 to .42.

Author: Rich, J.

Article: A two-factor measure of jealous responses.

Journal: *Psychological Reports,* June 1991, *68*(3) Part I, 999–1007.

Related Research: White, G. L. (1989). *Jealousy: Theory, research, and clinical strategies.* New York: Guilford.

■ ■ ■

5787

Test Name: JIRITSU SCALE

Purpose: To measure the integrated dependence and independence dimensions of *jiritsu.*

Number of Items: 49

Format: 4-point rating scales. All items presented in English.

Reliability: Test–retest (1 month) ranged from .75 to .83 across subscales.

Author: Kamitani, Y.

Article: The structure of *jiritsu*

(socially sensitive independence) in young Japanese women.

Journal: *Psychological Reports,* June 1993, *72*(3) Part I, 855–866.

Related Research: Kato, T., & Takagi, H. (1980). [The development of sense of independence and the self-concept in adolescence.] *Japanese Journal of Educational Psychology, 28,* 336–340.

■ ■ ■

5788

Test Name: KINSHIP SCALE-REVISED

Purpose: To measure the construct of psychological kinship, the "as-if-family" relationships between genetically unrelated individuals.

Number of Items: 20

Format: All items are presented with a brief description of instructions given to participants.

Validity: Correlations with other variables ranged from .15 to .72.

Authors: Nava, G. R., and Bailey, K. G.

Article: Measuring psychological kinship: Scale refinement and validation.

Journal: *Psychological Reports,* February 1991, *68*(1), 215–227.

Related Research: Bailey, K. G., & Nava, G. R. (1989). Psychological kinship, love and liking: Preliminary validity data. *Journal of Clinical Psychology, 45,* 587–594.

■ ■ ■

5789

Test Name: LEXINGTON ATTACHMENT TO PETS SCALE

Purpose: To assess human–animal attachment among dog and cat owners.

Number of Items: 23

Format: 4-point rating scales.

Reliability: Alpha was .93.

Authors: Singer, R. S., et al.

Article: Dilemmas associated with rehousing homeless people who have companion animals.

Journal: *Psychological Reports,* December 1995, *77*(3) Part I, 851–857.

Related Research: Johnson, T. P., et al. (1991). Psychometric evaluation of the Lexington Attachment to Pets Scale (LAPS). *Anthrozoos, 5,* 160–175.

■ ■ ■

5790

Test Name: LONELINESS AND SOCIAL DISSATISFACTION SCALE

Purpose: To assess children's feelings of loneliness.

Number of Items: 24

Format: Responses are made on a scale ranging from 1 (*that is always true about me*) to 5 (*that's not true at all about me*).

Validity: Correlations with other variables ranged from -.48 to .48.

Authors: Renshaw, P. D., and Brown, P. J.

Article: Loneliness in middle childhood: Concurrent and longitudinal predictors.

Journal: *Child Development,* August 1993, *64*(4), 1271–1284.

Related Research: Asher, S. R., & Wheeler, V. A. (1985). Children's loneliness: A comparison of rejected and neglected peer status. *Journal of Consulting and Clinical Psychology, 53,* 500–505.

■ ■ ■

5791

Test Name: LONELINESS INVENTORY

Purpose: To measure loneliness.

Number of Items: 75

Format: 6-point frequency scales.

Reliability: Alpha was .96. Test–retest was .97.

Validity: Correlation with UCLA Loneliness Scale was .87.

Authors: Medora, N. P., and Woodward, J. C.

Article: Factors associated with loneliness among alcoholics in rehabilitation centers.

Journal: *The Journal of Social Psychology*, December 1991, *131*(6), 769–779.

Related Research: Woodward, J. C. (1988). *The solitude of loneliness.* Lexington, MA: DC Heath & Company, Lexington Books.

■ ■ ■

5792

Test Name: LONELINESS RATING SCALE

Purpose: To measure four affective dimensions of loneliness: depletion, isolation, agitation, and dejection.

Number of Items: 40

Format: Responses are made on a 5-point Likert scale (*never occurs* to *always occurs*).

Reliability: Test–retest reliability coefficients ranged from .61 to .71.

Validity: Coefficients with other variables ranged from .25 to .46.

Authors: Ginter, E. J., and Dwinell, P. L.

Article: The importance of perceived duration: Loneliness and its relationship to self-esteem and academic performance.

Journal: *Journal of College Student Development*, November 1994, *35*(6), 456–460.

Related Research: Scalise, J. J., et al. (1984). A multidimensional

loneliness measure: The Loneliness Rating Scale (LRS). *Journal of Personality Assessment*, *48*, 525–530.

■ ■ ■

5793

Test Name: LONELINESS SCALE

Purpose: To measure the intensity of loneliness.

Number of Items: 11

Format: Yes–no format. Sample items presented.

Reliability: KR-20 ranged from .78 to .85. Loevingers H ranged from .40 to .42.

Authors: van Tilburg, T., et al.

Article: The measurement of reciprocity in ego-centered networks of personal relationships: A comparison of various indices.

Journal: *Social Psychology Quarterly*, March 1991, *54*(1), 54–66.

Related Research: deJong-Gierveld, J., & Kamphuis, F. (1985). The development of a Rosch-type loneliness scale. *Applied Psychological Measurement*, *9*, 289–299.

■ ■ ■

5794

Test Name: LOSS OF FACE SCALE

Purpose: To measure attitudes toward losing face in public and behavioral attempts to maintain face.

Number of Items: 21

Format: 7-point Likert format ranges from 1 (*strongly disagree*) to 7 (*strongly agree*). Sample items are presented.

Reliability: Alpha was .83.

Validity: Correlations with other variables ranged from .20 to .57.

Authors: Leong, F. T. L., et al.

Article: Group counseling expectations among Asian American students: The role of culture-specific factors.

Journal: *Journal of Counseling Psychology*, April 1995, *42*(2), 217–222.

Related Research: Zane, N. (1991). *An empirical examination of loss of face among Asian Americans.* Unpublished manuscript. Graduate School of Education, University of California, Santa Barbara.

■ ■ ■

5795

Test Name: MARLOWE-CROWN SOCIAL DESIRABILITY SCALE—SHORT FORM

Purpose: To measure the social desirability response.

Number of Items: 13

Reliability: Alpha was .70.

Validity: Nine of the 13 items have been isolated by 2 of 3 studies of the original pool of 33 items in the full scale.

Author: Ballard, R.

Article: Short forms of the Marlowe-Crown Social Desirability Scale.

Journal: *Psychological Reports*, December 1992, *71*(3) Part II, 1155–1160.

Related Research: Crowne, D. P., & Marlowe, D. (1960). A new scale of social desirability independent of psychopathology. *Journal of Consulting Psychology*, *24*, 349–354.

■ ■ ■

5796

Test Name: MEDICAL SOCIAL DESIRABILITY SCALE

Purpose: To measure social

desirability among medical personnel.

Number of Items: 7

Format: 7-point Likert format. All items presented.

Reliability: Alpha was .62.

Validity: Correlation with a generic measure of social desirability (Marlowe-Crown) was .37.

Authors: Merrill, J. M., et al.

Article: Measuring social desirability among senior medical students.

Journal: *Psychological Reports*, December 1995, *77*(3) Part I, 859–864.

■■■

5797

Test Name: MEMBER LIKING OF THE LEADER SCALE

Purpose: To measure member liking of the leader.

Number of Items: 2

Format: Responses are made on a 7-point scale ranging from 1 (*strongly disagree*) to 7 (*strongly agree*). Both items are presented.

Reliability: Coefficient alpha was .86.

Authors: Liden, R .C., et al.

Article: A longitudinal study on the early development of leader-member exchanges.

Journal: *Journal of Applied Psychology*, August 1993, *78*(4), 662–674.

Related Research: Wayne, S. J., & Ferris, G. R. (1990). Influence tactics, affect, and exchange quality in supervisor-subordinate interactions: A laboratory experiment and field study. *Journal of Applied Psychology*, *75*, 487–499.

5798

Test Name: MILLER SOCIAL INTIMACY SCALE

Purpose: To measure the maximum level of intimacy currently experienced in a relationship.

Number of Items: 17

Format: Responses to each item are made on a 10-point scale.

Reliability: Alphas were .91 and .86 (*N* = 45); Test–retest reliabilities were .96 (2 months) and .84 (1 month).

Validity: Correlations with other variables ranged from -.02 to -.42.

Authors: Sharpe, M. J., and Heppner, P. P.

Article: Gender role, gender-role conflict, and psychological well-being in men.

Journal: *Journal of Counseling Psychology*, July 1991, *38*(3), 323–330.

Related Research: Miller, R. S., & Lefcourt, H. M. (1982). The assessment of social intimacy. *Journal of Personality Assessment*, *46*, 514–518.

■■■

5799

Test Name: MINES-JENSEN INTERPERSONAL RELATIONSHIPS INVENTORY

Purpose: To determine development in interpersonal relationships.

Number of Items: 42

Format: Responses are made on a 4-point Likert scale.

Reliability: Internal consistency coefficients on the two scales were .65 (tolerance) and .68 (quality of relationships).

Author: Taub, D.

Article: Relationship of selected

factors to traditional-age undergraduate women's development autonomy.

Journal: *Journal of College Student Development*, March/ April 1995, *36*(2), 141–151.

Related Research: Mines, R. A. (1977). *Development and validation of the Mines-Jensen Interpersonal Relationships Inventory.* (Iowa Student Development Project Technical Report #6). Unpublished manuscript, University of Iowa, Iowa City.

■■■

5800

Test Name: MODERN RACISM SCALE

Purpose: To assess racism.

Number of Items: 6

Format: 5-point Likert format. A sample item is presented.

Reliability: Test–retest reliability was .93.

Authors: Gold, B. T., and Ziegler, M.

Article: Measuring environmental/ biological attribution: A fundamental dimension.

Journal: *The Journal of Social Psychology*, December 1994, *133*(6), 837–845.

Related Research: McConahay, J. B., et al. (1981). Has racism declined in America? *Journal of Conflict Resolution*, *25*, 563–579.

■■■

5801

Test Name: MODIFIED INTERPERSONAL RELATIONSHIP SCALE

Purpose: To assess the overall quality of relations with one other person.

Number of Items: 49

Format: 5-point Likert format. All items presented.

Reliability: Alpha was .95.

Validity: Correlations with other variables ranged from -.51 to .63.

Authors: Garthoeffner, J. L., et al.

Article: The Modified Interpersonal Relationship Scale: Reliability and validity.

Journal: *Psychological Reports*, December 1993, *73*(3) Part I, 995–1004.

Related Research: Schlein, S., et al. (1990). The Interpersonal Relationship Scale. In J. Touliatos et al. (Eds.), *Handbook of family measurement techniques* (p. 248). Newbury Park, CA: Sage.

• • •

5802

Test Name: MULTIDIMENSIONAL RACIAL IDENTITY SCALE

Purpose: To measure racial identity.

Number of Items: 25

Format: 5-point Likert format. All items are presented.

Reliability: Total alpha was .88. Alphas ranged from .62 to .86 across subscales. Test–retest reliabilities (3 weeks) ranged from 89 to .96.

Validity: Correlations between scales ranged from .15 to .59.

Authors: Thompson, V. L. S.

Article: The multidimensional structure of racial identification.

Journal: *Journal of Research in Personality*, June 1995, *29*(2), 208–222.

Related Research: Sanders, V. L. (1988). *A multi-faceted approach to racial identification.* Unpublished doctoral dissertation, Duke University, Durham, NC.

5803

Test Name: MULTIDIMENSIONAL SOCIAL DECENTERING SCALE

Purpose: To assess an individual's attempt to understand, respond to, or make sense of the feelings, thoughts and perceptions of another.

Number of Items: 36

Format: 5-point Likert format. All items are presented.

Reliability: Test–retest reliabilities ranged from .71 to .86 across subscales.

Validity: Correlations with other variables ranged from .11 to .64. Correlations of scores with knowledgeable raters ranged from -.05 to .56.

Author: Redmon, M. V.

Article: A multidimensional theory and measure of social decentering.

Journal: *Journal of Research in Personality*, March 1995, *29*(1), 35–58.

• • •

5804

Test Name: MULTIDIMENSIONAL SUPPORT SCALE

Purpose: To assess availability and adequacy of social support.

Number of Items: 19

Format: 4-point frequency scales and 3-point satisfaction scales are used. All items are presented.

Reliability: Alphas ranged from .81 to .90 across subscales.

Authors: Winefield, H. R., et al.

Article: Social support and psychological well-being in young adults: The Multidimensional Support Scale.

Journal: *Journal of Personality*

Assessment, February 1992, *58*(1), 198–210.

Related Research: Winefield, A. H., et al. (1988). Psychological concomitants of a satisfactory employment and unemployment in young people. *Social Psychiatry and Psychiatric Epidemiology*, *23*, 149–157.

• • •

5805

Test Name: MULTIGROUP ETHNIC IDENTITY MEASURE

Purpose: To measure ethnic identity.

Number of Items: 14

Format: 4-point Likert format. Sample items presented.

Reliability: Reliability was .81.

Authors: Phinney, J. S., et al.

Article: The effect of ethnic threat on ethnic self-concept and own-group ratings.

Journal: *The Journal of Social Psychology*, August 1993, *133*(4), 469–478.

Related Research: Phinney, J. (1992). The Multigroup Ethnic Identity Measure: A new scale for use with diverse groups. *Journal of Adolescent Research*, *7*, 156–176.

• • •

5806

Test Name: MULTIGROUP ETHNIC IDENTITY MEASURE

Purpose: To measure racial/ethnic identity.

Number of Items: 20

Format: Responses are made on a 4-point Likert scale.

Reliability: Internal consistency reliabilities on the two scales were .90 (Ethnic Identity) and .74 for Other-Group Orientation.

Author: Taub, D.

Article: Relationship of selected factors to traditional-age undergraduate women's development of autonomy.

Journal: *Journal of College Student Development*, March/April 1995, *36*(2), 141–151.

Related Research: Phinney, J. S. (1992). The Multigroup Ethnic Identity Measure: A new scale for use with adolescents and young adults from diverse groups. *Journal of Adolescent Research, 7,* 156–176.

● ● ●

5807

Test Name: NETWORK ORIENTATION SCALE

Purpose: To measure the propensity to use social support networks in time of need.

Number of Items: 20

Format: 4-point agreement scales. All items presented.

Reliability: Alphas ranged from .73 to .74. Item total ranged from .04 to .48.

Validity: Correlations with other variables ranged from -.53 to -.09.

Author: Pretorious, T. B.

Article: Willingness to use social support: Use of the Network Orientation Scale with Black South African students.

Journal: *Psychological Reports*, December 1993, *73*(3) Part I, 1011–1017.

Related Research: Vaux, A. et al. (1986). Orientation toward utilization of support resources. *Journal of Community Psychology, 14,* 159–170.

● ● ●

5808

Test Name: NEW RACISM SCALE

Purpose: To measure White racism toward Blacks.

Number of Items: 7

Format: Multiple-choice format.

Reliability: Alpha coefficients ranged from .60 to .70.

Validity: Correlation with the Quick Discrimination Index ranged from .30 to .44 (*N* = 50).

Authors: Ponterotto, J. G., et al.

Article: Development and initial validation of the Quick Discrimination Index (QDI).

Journal: *Educational and Psychological Measurement*, December 1995, *55*(6), 1016–1031.

Related Research: Jacobson, C. R. (1985). Resistance to affirmative action: Self–interest or racism. *Journal of Conflict Resolution, 29,* 306–329.

● ● ●

5809

Test Name: OBJECT RELATIONS INVENTORY

Purpose: To measure interpersonal functions that are distinct from psychiatric symptomatology.

Number of Items: 45

Format: True–false format.

Reliability: Alphas ranged from .60 to .73.

Validity: Correlations with other variables ranged from .21 to .63.

Authors: Kurtz, J. E., et al.

Article: The concurrent validity of three self-report measures of borderline personality.

Journal: *Journal of Psychopathology and Behavioral Assessment*, September 1993, *15*(3), 255–266.

Related Research: Bell, M., et al. (1986). A scale for the assessment of object relations: Reliability,

validity and factorial invariance. *Journal of Clinical Psychology, 42,* 733–741.

● ● ●

5810

Test Name: ORGANIZATIONAL CONFLICT INVENTORY

Purpose: To measure styles of handling interpersonal conflict: integrating, obliging, dominating, avoiding, and compromising.

Number of Items: 28

Format: 5-point Likert format.

Validity: Items were significantly loaded on its specified factor (*t* ratios ranged from 11.6 to 25.98). For all 10 pairs of factors goodness of fit of the proposed model was less than for the constrained model (*p* < .001).

Authors: Rahim, M. A., and Wagner, N. R.

Article: Convergent and discriminant validity of the Rahim Organizational Conflict Scale—II.

Journal: *Psychological Reports*, February 1994, *74*(1), 35–38.

Related Research: Rahim, M. A. (1992). *Managing conflict in organizations* (2nd ed.). Westport, CT: Praeger.

● ● ●

5811

Test Name: PARTEN'S SOCIAL PARTICIPATION SCALE

Purpose: To measure social behavior in children.

Time Required: 2 minutes.

Format: Social behavior in children is recorded and placed in one of four areas—withdrawal, solitary, parallel, and interactive play.

Reliability: Cohen's kappa for interobserver agreement between two observers calculated each month ranged from .85 to .88.

Authors: Provost, M., and Lafreniere, P. J.

Article: Social participation and peer competence in preschool children: Evidence for discriminant and convergent validity.

Journal: *Child Study Journal*, March 1991, *21*(1), 57–72.

Related Research: Parten, M. B. (1932). Social participation among preschool children. *Journal of Abnormal and Social Psychology*, *27*, 243–269.

● ● ●

5812

Test Name: PASSIONATE LOVE SCALE

Purpose: To assess passionate feelings toward another person with whom the participant is in love.

Number of Items: 30

Format: 9-point Likert format. Sample items are presented.

Reliability: Alpha was .94.

Validity: Correlation with social desirability was .09.

Authors: Wang, A. Y., and Nguyen, H. T.

Article: Passionate love and anxiety: A cross-generational study.

Journal: *The Journal of Social Psychology*, August 1995, *135*(4), 459–470.

Related Research: Hatfield, E., & Sprecher, S. (1986). Measuring passionate love in intimate relationships. *Journal of Adolescence*, *9*, 383–410.

● ● ●

5813

Test Name: PEER ADJUSTMENT INDEX

Purpose: To measure attachments

between peers.

Number of Items: 6

Format: Peer nomination and 5-point rating formats are used. A sample item is presented.

Reliability: Alpha was .78. Item-total correlations ranged from .63 to .88.

Validity: Correlations with other variables ranged from -.16 to .42.

Authors: Cornell, D. G., et al.

Article: Socioemotional adjustment of adolescent girls enrolled in a residential acceleration program.

Journal: *Gifted Child Quarterly*, Spring 1991, *35*(2), 58–66.

Related Research: Asher, S. R., & Hymel, S. (1981). Children's social competence in peer relations: Sociometric and behavioral assessment. In J. D. Wine & M. D. Smye (Eds.), *Social competence* (pp. 125–157). New York: Guilford Press.

● ● ●

5814

Test Name: PERCEIVED DECODING ABILITY SCALE— FORM 1

Purpose: To measure social perception.

Number of Items: 16

Format: Responses are made on a 7-point scale ranging from -3 (*disagree*) to +3 (*agree*). An example is presented.

Reliability: Test–retest (3 weeks) reliability was .79. Armor's theta internal consistency was .72.

Authors: Wong, C-M. T., et al.

Article: A multitrait, multimethod study of academic and social intelligence in college students.

Journal: *Journal of Educational Psychology*, March 1995, *87*(1), 117–133.

Related Research: Zuckerman, M., & Larrance, D. T. (1979). Individual differences in perceived encoding and decoding abilities. In R. Rosenthal (Ed.), *Skill in non-verbal communication: Individual differences* (pp. 170–195). Cambridge, MA: Oegeschlager, Gunn & Hain.

● ● ●

5815

Test Name: PERCEIVED SOCIAL SUPPORT SCALE

Purpose: To measure perceived levels of social support received from family and friends.

Number of Items: 40

Format: Includes two subscales: Family and Friends. Examples are presented. A third was added: Teachers and Other School Personnel.

Reliability: Alpha coefficients ranged from .87 to .90.

Validity: Correlation with other variables ranged from -.63 to .36.

Authors: DuBois, D. L., et al.

Article: A prospective study of life stress, social support, and adaptation in early adolescence.

Journal: *Child Development*, June 1992, *63*(3), 542–557.

Related Research: Procidano, M. E., & Heller, K. (1983). Measures of perceived social support from friends and from family: Three validation studies. *American Journal of Community Psychology*, *11*, 1–24.

● ● ●

5816

Test Name: PERCEPTION OF TEASING SCALE

Purpose: To assess frequency and degree of upset associated with teasing related to weight and competence.

Number of Items: 11

Format: 5-point scales for frequency and impact. All items are presented.

Reliability: Alphas ranged from .75 to .88.

Validity: Correlations with other variables ranged from -.27 to .48.

Authors: Thompson, J. K., et al.

Article: The Perception of Teasing Scale (POTS): A revision and extension of the Physical Appearance Related Teasing Scale (PARTS).

Journal: *Journal of Personality Assessment*, August 1995, *65*(1), 146–157.

Related Research: Thompson, J. K., et al. (1991). Development and validation of the Physical Appearance Related Teasing Scale (PARTS). *Journal of Personality Assessment*, *56*, 513–521.

■ ■ ■

5817

Test Name: PERCEPTIONS OF DISCRIMINATION AGAINST BLACKS SCALE

Purpose: To measure one's perception of discrimination against Blacks.

Number of Items: 21

Format: Responses are made on a 5-point Likert scale.

Reliability: Coefficient alpha was .90.

Validity: Correlations with other variables ranged from -.04 to .62.

Authors: Evans, K. M., and Herr, E. L.

Article: The influence of racial identity and the perception of discrimination on the career aspirations of African American men and women.

Journal: *Journal of Vocational*

Behavior, April 1994, *44*(2), 173–184.

Related Research: Turner, B. F., & Turner, C. B. (1975). Race, sex, and perception of the opportunity structure among college students. *The Social Science Quarterly*, *16*, 345–360.

■ ■ ■

5818

Test Name: PERCEPTIONS OF DISCRIMINATION AGAINST WOMEN SCALE

Purpose: To measure one's perception of discrimination against women.

Number of Items: 21

Format: Responses are made on a 5-point Likert scale.

Reliability: Coefficient alpha was .83.

Validity: Correlations with other variables ranged from -.04 to .71.

Authors: Evans, K. M., and Herr, E. L.

Article: The influence of racial identity and the perception of discrimination on the career aspirations of African American men and women.

Journal: *Journal of Vocational Behavior*, April 1994, *44*(2), 173–184.

Related Research: Turner, B. F., & Turner, C. B. (1975). Race, sex, and perception of the opportunity structure among college students. *The Social Science Quarterly*, *16*, 345–360.

■ ■ ■

5819

Test Name: PERSONAL SUPPORT SCALE

Purpose: To assess the perceived degree of support and encouragement students receive from various sources.

Number of Items: 11

Format: Responses are made on a scale ranging from 1 (*little or no support*) to 5 (*a lot of support*).

Reliability: Internal consistency was .88.

Validity: Correlations with other variables ranged from -.12 to .16.

Authors: Hackett, G., et al.

Article: Gender, ethnicity, and social cognitive factors predicting the academic achievement of students in engineering.

Journal: *Journal of Counseling Psychology*, October 1992, *39*(4), 527–538.

■ ■ ■

5820

Test Name: PERSPECTIVE-TAKING SCALE

Purpose: To assess taking the perspective of the other in a dating relationship.

Number of Items: 4

Format: 5-point frequency scales. All items presented.

Reliability: Omega was .73.

Author: Stets, J. E.

Article: Modeling control in relationships.

Journal: *Journal of Marriage and the Family*, May 1995, *57*(2), 489–501.

Related Research: Stets, J. E. (1993). Control in dating relationships. *Journal of Marriage and the Family*, *55*, 673–685.

■ ■ ■

5821

Test Name: PHYSICAL ACTIVITY SOCIALIZATION INVENTORY

Purpose: To measure physical activity socialization.

Number of Items: 14

Format: Responses are "yes," "don't know," or "no."

Reliability: Test–retest reliability was .87.

Validity: Correlations with other variables ranged from .07 to .41.

Author: Merriman, W. J.

Article: Relationship among socialization, attitude, and placement with participation in physical activity of students with emotional disorders.

Journal: *Perceptual and Motor Skills*, February 1993, *76*(1), 287–292.

Related Research: Kennedy, M. (1980). *Sport role socialization and attitudes toward physical activity of wheelchair athletes.* Unpublished master's thesis, University of Oregon, Eugene.

■ ■ ■

5822

Test Name: PHYSICAL APPEARANCE RELATED TEASING SCALE

Purpose: To assess the amount of teasing individuals received as children because of their physical appearance.

Number of Items: 18

Format: 5-point frequency scales range from *never* to *frequently*. All items are presented.

Reliability: Alphas ranged from .71 to .91 across subscales. Test–retest reliability ranged from .86 to .87.

Validity: Correlations with other variables ranged from -.14 to .40.

Authors: Thompson, J. K., et al.

Article: Development and validation of the Physical Appearance Related Teasing Scale.

Journal: *Journal of Personality*

Assessment, June 1991, *56*(2), 513–521.

Related Research: Thompson, J. K., et al. (1994). The Perception of Teasing Scale (POTS): A revision and extension of the Physical Appearance Related Teasing Scales (PARTS). *Journal of Personality Assessment, 65,* 146–157.

■ ■ ■

5823

Test Name: POLITICAL TOLERANCE SCALE

Purpose: To assess political tolerance in South Africa.

Number of Items: 6

Format: 7-point agreement scales. All items are presented.

Reliability: Alpha was .74.

Validity: Correlation with authoritarianism was -.42.

Authors: Duckitt, J., and Farre, B.

Article: Right-wing authoritarianism and political intolerance among Whites in the future majority-rule South Africa.

Journal: *The Journal of Social Psychology*, December 1994, *133*(6), 735–741.

■ ■ ■

5824

Test Name: PRIVACY QUESTIONNAIRE—TURKISH VERSION

Purpose: To measure privacy.

Number of Items: 30

Format: 5-point frequency scales. All items are presented.

Validity: Factor analysis confirmed the 6-dimension model of privacy found by Pederson.

Authors: Rustemli, A., and Kokdemir, D.

Article: Privacy dimensions and preferences among Turkish students.

Journal: *The Journal of Social Psychology*, December 1993, *133*(6), 807–814.

Related Research: Pederson, D. M. (1987). Sex differences in privacy preferences. *Perceptual and Motor Skills, 64,* 1239–1242.

■ ■ ■

5825

Test Name: PRIVATE COLLECTIVE SELF-ESTEEM SCALE

Purpose: To assess feelings about one's own ethnic group membership.

Number of Items: 4

Format: 4-point rating scales. Sample items are presented.

Reliability: Alphas ranged from .74 to .82.

Authors: Phinney, J. S., et al.

Article: The effect of ethnic threat on ethnic self-concept and own-group ratings.

Journal: *The Journal of Social Psychology*, August 1993, *133*(4), 469–478.

Related Research: Luhtanen, R., & Crocker, J. (1990). *A collective self-esteem scale: Self-evaluation of one's own social identity.* Unpublished manuscript.

■ ■ ■

5826

Test Name: PROVISION OF SOCIAL RELATIONS SCALE

Purpose: To assess social involvement.

Number of Items: 15

Reliability: Internal consistency coefficients ranged from .75 to .89.

Validity: Correlations with the

Social Activities Scale were .54 and .56.

Authors: Souliére, M. D., et al.

Article: Concurrent and predictive validity of Prediger's two work-task preference dimensions.

Journal: *Journal of Vocational Behavior*, October 1991, *39*(2), 226–240.

Related Research: Turner, R. J., et al. (1983). Social support: Conceptualization, measurement, and implications for mental health. *Research in Community and Mental Health*, *3*, 67–111.

■ ■ ■

5827

Test Name: PSYCHOLOGICAL MALTREATMENT INVENTORY

Purpose: To measure maltreatment experienced by adults when they were children.

Number of Items: 25

Format: 6-point rating scales. All items are presented.

Reliability: Alpha was .81. Test–retest ranged from .75 to .78.

Validity: Interscale correlations ranged from .60 to .70. Correlations with other variables ranged from -.88 to .71.

Authors: Engles, M., and Moisan, D.

Article: The Psychological Maltreatment Inventory: Development of a measure of psychological maltreatment in childhood for use in adult clinical settings.

Journal: *Psychological Reports*, April 1994, *74*(2), 595–604.

■ ■ ■

5828

Test Name: PSYCHOLOGICAL SIZE AND DISTANCE SCALE

Purpose: To assess the extent to

which interpersonal status and positive and negative affect influence relationships.

Number of Items: 22

Format: Varied formats. Sample items are presented.

Reliability: Alphas ranged from .86 to .94.

Validity: Subscale correlations ranged from -.50 to .72.

Authors: Grasha, A. F., and Homan, M.

Article: Psychological size and distance in the relationships of adult children of alcoholics with their parents.

Journal: *Psychological Reports*, April 1995, *76*(2), 595–606.

Related Research: Grasha, A. F., & Ichiyama, M. (1989). *Grasha-Ichiymama Psychological Size and Distance Scale.* Cincinnati, OH: Communication and Education Associates.

■ ■ ■

5829

Test Name: QUALITY OF SAME-SEX RELATIONSHIPS QUESTIONNAIRE

Purpose: To measure relationship satisfaction, agreement, affirmation, and lack of tension in same-sex relationships.

Number of Items: 27

Format: Sample items presented.

Reliability: Alphas ranged from .60 to .85 across subscales.

Validity: Correlations between subscales ranged from .32 to .69.

Author: O'Brien, K.

Article: Primary relationships affect the psychological health of homosexual men at risk for AIDS.

Journal: *Psychological Reports*, August 1992, *71*(1), 147–153.

5830

Test Name: RACIAL IDENTITY ATTITUDE SCALE

Purpose: To determine racial identity attitudes.

Number of Items: 30

Format: Responses are made on a 5-point Likert scale ranging from 1 (*strongly disagree*) to 5 (*strongly agree*).

Reliability: Internal consistency reliability coefficients for the four subscales: Pre-encounter = .67; Encounter = .72; Immersion–Emersion = .66; Internalization = .71.

Authors: Mitchell, S. L., and Dell, D. M.

Article: The relationships between Black students' racial identity attitude and participation in campus organizations.

Journal: *Journal of College Student Development*, January 1992, *33*(1), 39–43.

Related Research: Parham, T. A., & Helms, J. E. (1981). The influence of Black students' racial identity attitudes on preference for counselor race. *Journal of Counseling Psychology*, *28*, 250–257.

■ ■ ■

5831

Test Name: RACISM(S) SCALE

Purpose: To measure three dimensions of racism: aversive, biological, and symbolic.

Number of Items: 11 (14)

Format: Nine-point rating scales. All items presented.

Reliability: Alphas ranged from .72 to .82. A 14-item Guttman version yielded a *rho* of .66 and a Loevinger coefficient of .55.

Validity: Correlations between subscales ranged from .45 to .67.

Authors: Kleinpenning, G., and Hagedoorn, L.

Article: Forms of racism and the cumulative dimension of ethnic attitudes.

Journal: *Social Psychology Quarterly*, March 1993, *56*(1), 21–36.

• • •

5832

Test Name: RATING OF ALTER COMPETENCE SCALE

Purpose: To evaluate other persons' social skills.

Number of Items: 27

Reliability: Alpha coefficients ranged from .88 to .91.

Validity: Correlations with rejection ranged from -.60 to -.71.

Author: Segrin, C.

Article: Effects of dysphoria and loneliness on social perceptual skills.

Journal: *Perceptual and Motor Skills*, December 1993, *77*(3) Part 2, 1315-1329.

Related Research: Cupach, W. R., & Spitzberg, B. H. (1981). *Relational competence: Measurement and validation.* Unpublished manuscript, Illinois State University, Department of Communication.

• • •

5833

Test Name: RELATIONAL INTERACTION SATISFACTION SCALE

Purpose: To measure satisfaction with a partner.

Number of Items: 8

Format: 5-point response categories (*never* to *very often*). Sample items presented.

Reliability: Alphas ranged from .87 to .88.

Authors: Vanyperen, N. W., and Buunk, B. P.

Article: Equity theory and exchange and communal orientation from a cross-national perspective.

Journal: *The Journal of Social Psychology*, February 1991, *131*(1), 5–20.

Related Research: Buunk, B. P. (1990). Relational Interaction Satisfaction Scale. In J. Touliatos et al. (Eds.), *Handbook of family measurement techniques* (pp. 106–107). Newbury Park, CA: Sage.

• • •

5834

Test Name: RELATIONS AND REALITY TESTING INVENTORY

Purpose: To assess object relations in four dimensions: alienation, insecure attachment, egocentricity and social incompetence.

Number of Items: 90

Format: True–false.

Reliability: Alphas ranged from .79 to .90.

Author: Bassman, L. E.

Article: Object relations and self-reported AIDS self-care behavior.

Journal: *Psychological Reports*, June 1991, *68*(3) Part I, 915–923.

Related Research: Bell, M., et al. (1985). A scale for the assessment of object relations: Reliability, validity, and factorial invariance. *Journal of Clinical Psychology*, *42*, 733–741.

• • •

5835

Test Name: RELATIONSHIP BELIEFS SCALE

Purpose: To measure beliefs about

what constitutes a successful relationship.

Number of Items: 54

Format: 6-point scales. All items presented.

Reliability: Alphas ranged from .51 to .87 across subscales. Test–retest (3 weeks) ranged from .64 to .89.

Validity: Correlations with other variables ranged from -.24 to .68. Correlations with relationship behavior ranged from -.01 to .75.

Authors: Fletcher, G. J. O., and Kininmonth, L. A.

Article: Measuring relationship beliefs: An individual differences scale.

Journal: *Journal of Research in Personality*, December 1992, *26*(4), 371–397.

• • •

5836

Test Name: RELATIONSHIP SATISFACTION SCALE

Purpose: To assess satisfaction in the relationship with a partner.

Number of Items: 8

Format: 5-point frequency scales. Sample items presented.

Reliability: Alpha was .86.

Authors: Van Yperen, N. W., & Buunk, B. P.

Article: Sex-role attitudes, social comparison, and satisfaction with relationships.

Journal: *Social Psychology Quarterly*, June 1991, *54*(2), 169–180.

Related Research: Buunk, B. P. (1990). Relational interaction satisfaction scale. In J. Touliatos et al. (Eds.), *Handbook of family measurement techniques* (pp. 106–107). Newbury Park, CA: Sage.

5837

Test Name: RESTRAINT SCALE

Purpose: To measure impulse control, consideration of others, suppression of aggression, and responsibility.

Number of Items: 36

Reliability: Alpha was .91.

Validity: Correlations with other variables ranged from -.29 to .63.

Authors: King, L. A., et al.

Article: The structure of inhibition.

Journal: *Journal of Research in Personality*, March 1992, *26*(1), 85–102.

Related Research: Weinberger, D. A., & Schwartz, G. E. (1990). Distress and restraint as superordinate dimensions of self-reported adjustment: A typological perspective. *Journal of Personality, 58,* 381–417.

■ ■ ■

5838

Test Name: ROMANTIC ATTRACTION SCALE

Purpose: To assess romantic attraction.

Number of Items: 8

Format: 7-point agreement scales. All items presented.

Reliability: Alpha was .88.

Authors: Williams, G. P., and Kleinke, C. L.

Article: Effects of mutual gaze and touch on attraction, mood, and cardiovascular activity.

Journal: *Journal of Research in Personality*, June 1993, *27*(2), 170–183.

Related Research: Hatfield, E., & Sprecher, S. (1986). Measuring passionate love in intimate relationships. *Journal of Adolescence, 9,* 383–410.

5839

Test Name: ROMANTICISM SCALE

Purpose: To measure feelings of romanticism.

Number of Items: 32

Format: 5-point Likert format.

Reliability: Split-half reliability was .90.

Authors: Medora, N. P., et al.

Article: Romanticism and self-esteem among pregnant adolescents, adolescent mothers, and nonpregnant, nonparenting teens.

Journal: *The Journal of Social Psychology*, October 1994, *133*(5), 581–591.

Related Research: Dean, D. G. (1961). Romanticism and emotional maturity: A preliminary study. *Marriage and Family Living, 23,* 44–45.

■ ■ ■

5840

Test Name: ROMANTIC LOVE SCALE—KOREAN VERSION

Purpose: To measure romantic love.

Number of Items: 29 (English version)

Format: 5-point Likert format.

Reliability: Alpha was .83.

Author: Brown, R. A.

Article: Romantic love and spouse selection criteria of male and female Korean college students.

Journal: *The Journal of Social Psychology*, April 1994, *133*(2), 183–189.

Related Research: Knox, D. H., & Sporakowski, M. J. (1968). Attitudes of college students toward love. *Journal of Marriage and the Family, 30,* 638–642.

5841

Test Name: SAMPLE PROFILE

Purpose: To measure love styles: storgic, agapic, manic, pragmatic, ludic, and erotic.

Number of Items: 50

Format: True–false format.

Validity: Correlations with other variables ranged from -.30 to .21.

Authors: Yancy, G., and Berglass, S.

Article: Love styles and life satisfaction

Journal: *Psychological Reports*, June 1991, *68*(3) Part I, 883–890.

Related Research: Lasswell, T. E., & Lasswell, M. E. (1976). I love you, but I'm not in love with you. *Journal of Marriage and Family Counseling, 38,* 211–224.

■ ■ ■

5842

Test Name: SATISFACTION WITH COMMUNICATION IN DATING RELATIONSHIPS QUESTIONNAIRE

Purpose: To measure satisfaction with communication and dating relationships.

Number of Items: 19

Reliability: Coefficient alpha was .88.

Validity: Correlations with communicative adaptability ranged from .19 to .46.

Author: Prisbell, M.

Article: Perceptions of satisfaction with communication and self-rated competence in dating relationships.

Journal: *Perceptual and Motor Skills*, August 1994, *79*(1) Part 2, 529–530.

Related Research: Hecht, M. L. (1978). The conceptualization and measurement of interpersonal communication satisfaction. *Human Communication Research, 4,* 350–368.

Rubin, R. B., & Rubin, A. M. (1989). Communication apprehension and satisfaction in interpersonal relationships. *Communication Research Reports, 6,* 15–22.

• • •

5843

Test Name: SELF–OTHERS SCALES

Purpose: To measure the extent to which individuals focus on their own thoughts, feelings, and behaviors, or on those of others with whom they interact.

Number of Items: 14

Format: 7-point rating scales. Sample items presented.

Reliability: Alphas ranged from .72 to .73 across subscales.

Authors: Green, V. A., and Wildermuth, N. L.

Article: Self-focus, other focus, and interpersonal needs as correlates of loneliness.

Journal: *Psychological Reports,* December 1993, *73*(3), 843–850.

Related Research: Goswick, R. A., & Jones, W. H. (1981). Loneliness, self-concept, and adjustment. *Journal of Psychology, 107,* 237–240.

• • •

5844

Test Name: SENSE OF COMMUNITY SCALE—CITY SUBSCALE

Purpose: To measure feelings of belongingness, integration of needs, reciprocal influence, and a shared history.

Number of Items: 5

Reliability: Alpha was .77.

Validity: Correlations between City Subscale and Total Sense of Community Scale scores ranged from .80 to .87.

Authors: Davidson, W. B., et al.

Article: Social predispositions for the development of sense of community.

Journal: *Psychological Reports,* June 1991, *68*(3) Part I, 817–818.

Related Research: Davidson, W., & Cotter, P. (1986). Measurement of sense of community within the sphere of city. *Journal of Applied Social Psychology, 16,* 608–619.

• • •

5845

Test Name: SEXUAL SOCIALIZATION SCALE

Purpose: To measure the extent to which the individual perceives he or she has been exposed to values emphasizing the importance of sexual conquest for self-esteem.

Number of Items: 20

Format: Responses are made on a 5-point Likert scale (*strongly disagree* to *strongly agree*).

Reliability: Cronbach's alpha was .67.

Authors: Bell, S. T., et al.

Article: Rape callousness in college freshmen: An empirical investigation of the sociocultural model of aggression towards women.

Journal: *Journal of College Student Development,* September 1992, *33*(5), 454–461.

Related Research: Kuriloff, P. J., et al. (1986). *Sexual Socialization Scale.* Unpublished scale, Graduate School of Education, University of Pennsylvania, Philadelphia.

5846

Test Name: SOCIAL ACTIVITIES SCALE

Purpose: To measure social activities.

Number of Items: 14

Reliability: Alpha coefficients were .74 and .77.

Validity: Correlations with other variables ranged from .29 to .56.

Authors: Souliére, M. D., et al.

Article: Concurrent and predictive validity of Prediger's two work-task preference dimensions.

Journal: *Journal of Vocational Behavior,* October 1991, *39*(2), 226–240.

Related Research: Labrosse, D. (1988). *Adjustment in vocational rehabilitation.* Unpublished honor's (BA) thesis, University of Ottawa, School of Psychology, Ottawa, Ontario, Canada.

• • •

5847

Test Name: SOCIAL ACTIVITY MEASURE

Purpose: To assess satisfaction and frequency of activity with parents, relatives, friends and organizations.

Number of Items: 14

Format: Format varies by item. All items are presented.

Validity: Correlations with other variables ranged from .00 to .30.

Authors: Cooper, H., et al.

Article: Situation and personality correlates of psychological well-being: Social activity and personal control.

Journal: *Journal of Research in Personality,* December 1995, *29*(4), 395–417.

Related Research: Cooper, H., et al. (1992). Social activity and subjective well-being. *Personality and Individual Differences*, *13*, 573–583.

•••

5848

Test Name: SOCIAL ANHEDONIA SCALE

Purpose: To assess the extent to which individuals have difficulty experiencing pleasure.

Number of Items: 40

Format: True–false format.

Reliability: Internal and temporal stabilities were in the high .70s and .80s.

Validity: Correlations with other variables ranged from -.66 to .62.

Author: Leak, G. K.

Article: An examination of the construct validity of the social anhedonia Scale.

Journal: *Journal of Personality Assessment*, February 1991, *56*(1), 84–95.

Related Research: Chapman, L. J., et al. (1976). Scales for physical and social anhedonia. *Journal of Abnormal Psychology*, *85*, 374–382.

•••

5849

Test Name: SOCIAL ASSESSMENT SCALE— SELF-REPORT

Purpose: To assess role performance in the past 2 weeks in various typical settings.

Number of Items: 54

Format: 5-point rating scales. Sample items are presented.

Reliability: Internal consistency was .74. Test–retest reliability was .80.

Authors: Funtowicz, M. N., and Widiger, T. A.

Article: Sex bias in the diagnosis of personality disorders: A different approach.

Journal: *Journal of Psychopathology and Behavioral Assessment*, June 1995, *17*(2), 145–165.

Related Research: Weissman, M., et al. (1978). Social adjustment by self-report in a community sample and in psychiatric outpatients. *Journal of Nervous and Mental Disease*, *166*, 317–326.

•••

5850

Test Name: SOCIAL DESIRABILITY SCALE

Purpose: To measure social desirability.

Number of Items: 11

Format: Two versions: English and Spanish. Responses are made on a 5-point Likert-type scale ranging from *strongly agree* to *strongly disagree*. All items are presented.

Reliability: Alpha coefficients ranged from .34 to .80.

Authors: Shultz, K. S., and Chávez, D. V.

Article: The reliability and factor structure of a social desirability scale in English and Spanish.

Journal: *Educational and Psychological Measurement*, Winter 1994, *54*(4), 935–940.

Related Research: Crowne, D. P., & Marlowe, D. (1960). A scale of social desirability independent of psychopathology. *Journal of Counseling Psychology*, *24*, 349–354.

•••

5851

Test Name: SOCIAL DESIRABILITY SCALE

Purpose: To measure one's need to

gain approval in a culturally acceptable manner.

Number of Items: 33

Format: True–false format.

Reliability: Internal consistency was .88. Test–retest reliability was .89.

Validity: Correlation with the Quick Discrimination Index ranged from -.04 to -.19 (*N* = 44).

Authors: Ponterrotto, J. G., et al.

Article: Development and initial validation of the Quick Discrimination Index (QDI).

Journal: *Educational and Psychological Measurement*, December 1995, *55*(6), 1016–1031.

Related Research: Crowne, D. P., & Marlowe, D. (1960). A new scale of social desirability independent of psychopathology. *Journal of Counseling Psychology*, *24*, 349–354.

•••

5852

Test Name: SOCIAL DESIRABILITY SCALE— REVISED

Purpose: To measure social desirability.

Number of Items: 31

Reliability: Reliability was .68.

Validity: Correlation with the Preference for Numerical Information Scale was .00.

Author: Viswanathan, M.

Article: Measurement of individual difference in preference for numerical information.

Journal: *Journal of Applied Psychology*, October 1993, *78*(5), 741–752.

Related Research: Crowne, D. P., & Marlowe, D. (1964). *The approval motive.* New York: Wiley.

5853

Test Name: SOCIAL DOMINANCE SCALE

Purpose: To measure desire for superiority and dominance of an in group over other social groups.

Number of Items: 10

Format: 5-point Likert format. All items presented.

Reliability: Alpha was .83.

Validity: Correlations with other variables ranged from .32 to .56.

Authors: Sidanius, J., and Liu, J. H.

Article: The Gulf War and the Rodney King Beating: Implications of the general conservatism and social dominance perspectives.

Journal: *The Journal of Social Psychology*, December 1992, *132*(6), 685–700.

● ● ●

5854

Test Name: SOCIAL DOMINANCE SCALE

Purpose: To measure social dominance orientation.

Number of Items: 20

Format: 7-point Likert format. All items are presented.

Reliability: Alpha was .84.

Authors: Sidenius, J., et al.

Article: In-group identification, social dominance orientation and differential intergroup social allocation.

Journal: *The Journal of Social Psychology*, April 1994, *133*(2), 151–167.

Related Research: Pratto, F., et al. (1994). Social dominance orientation: A personality variable predicting social and political attitudes. *Journal of Personality and Social Psychology*, *67*, 741–763.

5855

Test Name: SOCIAL INSIGHT SCALE

Purpose: To measure social insight.

Number of Items: 18

Format: Responses are made on a 7-point scale ranging from 1 (*never or almost never true*) to 7 (*always or almost always true*). Examples are presented.

Reliability: Coefficient alpha was .81.

Validity: Correlations with other variables ranged from .00 to .55.

Authors: Wong, C-M. T., et al.

Article: A multitrait-multimethod study of academic and social intelligence in college students.

Journal: *Journal of Educational Psychology*, March 1995, *87*(1), 117–133.

● ● ●

5856

Test Name: SOCIAL INTEGRATION SCALE

Purpose: To measure social integration.

Number of Items: 7

Format: Responses are made on a 5-point scale ranging from 1 (*strongly disagree*) to 5 (*strongly agree*). Examples are presented.

Validity: Correlations with other variables ranged from -.13 to .26.

Author: Morrison, E. W.

Article: Longitudinal study of the effects of information seeking on newcomer socialization.

Journal: *Journal of Applied Psychology*, April 1993, *78*(2), 173–183.

Related Research: Price, J. L., & Mueller, C. W. (1986). *Absenteeism and turnover of*

hospital employees. Greenwich, CT: JAI Press.

● ● ●

5857

Test Name: SOCIAL INTERACTION SELF-STATEMENT TEST

Purpose: To measure frequency of 15 positive and 15 negative self-statements in heterosocial situations.

Number of Items: 30

Format: 5-point frequency response categories.

Reliability: Alphas ranged from .89 to .91 across subscales.

Validity: Correlations with measure of anxiety ranged from -.32 to .46.

Authors: Osman, A., et al.

Article: Psychometric properties of the Social Interacton Self-Statement Test in a college sample.

Journal: *Psychological Reports*, December 1992, *71*(3) Part II, 1171–1177.

Related Research: Glass, C. R., et al. (1982). Cognitive assessment of social anxiety: Development and validation of a self-statement questionnaire. *Cognitive Therapy and Research*, *6*, 37–55.

● ● ●

5858

Test Name: SOCIAL INTIMACY SCALE

Purpose: To measure level of intimacy in a relationship.

Number of Items: 17

Format: Ten-point scales.

Reliability: Alphas ranged from .86 to .91. Test–retest (1–2 months) reliabilities ranged from .84 to .96.

Authors: Cournoyer, R. J., and Mahalik, J. R.

Article: Cross-sectional study of gender role conflict examining college-aged and middle-aged men.

Journal: *Journal of Counseling Psychology*, January 1995, *42*(1), 11–19.

Related Research: Miller, R. S., & Lefcourt, H. M. (1982). The assessment of social intimacy. *The Journal of Personality Assessment*, *46*, 514–518.

■ ■ ■

5859

Test Name: SOCIALLY DESIRABLE RESPONSE SET—5

Purpose: To measure socially desirable response sets.

Number of Items: 5

Format: 5-point Likert format ranges from 1 (*definitely true*) to 5 (*definitely false*).

Reliability: Alpha was .68. Test–retest reliability (1 month) was .75.

Validity: Correlations with the Marlowe-Crowne scale was .79.

Authors: Heppner, M. J., et al.

Article: The differential effects of rape prevention programming on attitudes, behavior, and knowledge.

Journal: *Journal of Counseling Psychology*, October 1995, *42*(4), 508–518.

Related Research: Hays, R. D., et al. (1989). A five item measure of socially desirable response set. *Educational and Psychological Measurement*, *49*, 629–636.

■ ■ ■

5860

Test Name: SOCIAL PROBLEM-SOLVING INVENTORY FOR ADOLESCENTS

Purpose: To measure automatic process, problem orientation, and problem-solving skills.

Number of Items: 64

Format: 5-point Likert format. Sample items are presented.

Reliability: Alphas ranged from .78 to .95 across subscales. Total alpha was .93. Test–retest reliabilities ranged from .64 to .83.

Validity: Correlations between scale and subscale scores ranged from .00 to .86. Correlations with other variables ranged from -.59 to .82.

Authors: Frauenknecht, M., and Black, D. R.

Article: Social Problem-Solving Inventory for Adolescents (SPSI-A): Development and preliminary psychometric evaluation.

Journal: *Journal of Personality Assessment*, June 1995, *64*(3), 522–539.

Related Research: D'Zurilla, T., & Nezu, A. (1990). Development and preliminary evaluation of the social problem-solving inventory. *Psychological Assessment: A Journal of Consulting and Clinical Psychology*, *2*, 156–163.

■ ■ ■

5861

Test Name: SOCIAL PROVISIONS SCALE

Purpose: To measure perceived satisfaction with social support.

Number of Items: 24

Format: Includes 6 subscales. Responses are made on a 4-point Likert-type scale ranging from 1 (*strongly disagree*) to 4 (*strongly agree*).

Reliability: Test–retest reliability was .59.

Validity: Correlations with other variables ranged from -.42 to .62.

Author: Mallinckrodt, B.

Article: Childhood emotional bonds with parents, development of adult social competencies, and availability of social support.

Journal: *Journal of Counseling Psychology*, October 1992, *39*(4), 453–461

Related Research: Cutrona, C. E, & Russell, D. W. (1987). The provisions of social relationships and adaptation to stress. In W. H. Jones & D. Perlman (Eds.), *Advances in personal relationships* (Vol. 1, pp. 37–67). Greenwich, CT: JAI Press.

■ ■ ■

5862

Test Name: SOCIAL REACTIONS INVENTORY

Purpose: To measure if a person perceives events as contingent upon his or her behavior or characteristics.

Number of Items: 23

Format: Forced-choice format.

Reliability: Test-retest was .72. KR internal consistency was .72.

Validity: Discriminant validity ranged from -.23 to -.70.

Authors: Wege, J. W., and Moeller, A. T.

Article: Effectiveness of a problem-solving training program.

Journal: *Psychological Reports*, April 1995, *76*(2), 495–503.

Related Research: Lefcourt, H. M. (1982). *Locus of control: Current trends in theory and research* (2nd ed.). Hillsdale, NJ: Erlbaum.

■ ■ ■

5863

Test Name: SOCIAL RELATIONS SURVEY

Purpose: To assess social skills such as assertiveness, directiveness, defense of rights, confidence, and empathy.

Number of Items: 128

Format: True–false format. Sample items are presented.

Reliability: Test–retest reliabilities (2 weeks) ranged from .75 to .91. KR-21 reliabilities exceeded .80.

Validity: Correlations with other variables ranged from -.71 to .66.

Authors: Lorr, M., et al.

Article: An inventory of social skills.

Journal: *Journal of Personality Assessment*, December 1991, *57*(3), 506–520.

• • •

5864

Test Name: SOCIAL SCENARIOS SCALE

Purpose: To measure students' willingness to condone, ignore, or confront discriminatory situations involving Blacks.

Number of Items: 16

Format: Responses are made on a 3-point Likert scale.

Reliability: Coefficient alpha was .72.

Authors: Neville, H., and Furlong, M.

Article: The impact of participation in a cultural awareness program on the racial attitudes and social behaviors of first-year college students.

Journal: *Journal of College Student Development*, September 1994, *35*(5), 371–377.

Related Research: Byrnes, D. A., & Kiger, G. (1988). Contemporary measures of attitudes toward Blacks. *Educational and Psychological Measurement*, *48*, 117–118.

• • •

5865

Test Name: SOCIAL SUPPORT APPRAISALS SCALE

Purpose: To assess the child's appraisals of peer, family, and teacher support.

Number of Items: 31

Format: Responses are made on a 5-point scale ranging from 1 (*always*) to 5 (*never*). Sample items are presented.

Reliability: Alpha coefficients ranged form .78 to .88. Test–retest reliability was .75.

Validity: Correlations with other variables ranged from -.28 to .23.

Authors: Dubow, E. F., et al.

Article: A two-year longitudinal study of stressful life events, social support, and social problem-solving skills: Contributions to children's behavioral and academic adjustment.

Journal: *Child Development*, June 1991, *62*(3), 583–599.

Related Research: Dubow, E. F., & Ullman, D. G. (1989). Assessing social support in elementary school children: The survey of children's social support. *Journal of Clinical and Child Psychology*, *18*, 52–64.

• • •

5866

Test Name: SOCIAL SUPPORT APPRAISALS SCALE—REVISED

Purpose: To assess the child's appraisal of peer, family, and teacher support.

Number of Items: 41

Format: Responses are made on a 5-point scale ranging from 1 (*always*) to 5 (*never*).

Reliability: Alpha coefficients ranged from .86 to .93.

Validity: Correlations with other variables ranged from -.30 to .38.

Authors: Dubow, E. F., et al.

Article: A two-year longitudinal

study of stressful life events, social support, and social problem-solving skills: Contributions to children's behavioral and academic adjustment.

Journal: *Child Development*, June 1991, *62*(3), 583–599.

Related Research: Dubow, E. F., & Ullman, D. G. (1989). Assessing social support in elementary school children: The survey of children's social support. *Journal of Clinical and Child Psychology*, *18*, 52–64.

• • •

5867

Test Name: SOCIAL SUPPORT BEHAVIOR SCALE

Purpose: To measure specific intentional efforts to help a person.

Number of Items: 45

Format: Responses are made on a 4-point scale ranging from *would not* to *would certainly*. All items are presented.

Validity: Correlations with other variables ranged from .06 to .54.

Author: Caruso, G.-A. L.

Article: The development of three scales to measure the supportiveness of relationships between parents and child care providers.

Journal: *Educational and Psychological Measurement*, Spring 1992, *52*(1), 149–160.

Related Research: Vaux, A., et al. (1987). Modes of social support: The social support behaviors (SS-B) scale. *American Journal of Community Psychology*, *15*, 209–237.

• • •

5868

Test Name: SOCIAL SUPPORT INDEX

Purpose: To measure all sources of extrafamilial social support, from extended family and institutional.

Number of Items: 18

Format: 5-point frequency scales.

Reliability: Alphas ranged from .36 to .68.

Authors: Ahmeduzzman, M., and Roopnarne, J. L.

Article: Sociodemographic factors, functioning style, social support, and fathers' involvement with preschoolers in African-American families.

Journal: *Journal of Marriage and the Family*, August 1992, *54*(3), 699–707.

Related Research: Trivette, C., & Dunst, C. (1988). Inventory of Social Support. In C. Dunst et al. (Eds.), *Enabling and empowering families: Principles and guidelines for practice* (pp. 159–163). Cambridge, MA: Brookline.

● ● ●

5869

Test Name: SOCIAL SUPPORT IN RESPONSE TO DEPRESSION SCALE

Purpose: To measure social support behavior.

Number of Items: 5

Format: 4-point frequency scales. All items are presented.

Reliability: Alpha was .76.

Authors: Koenig, L. J., et al.

Article: Sex differences in adolescent depression and loneliness: Why are boys lonelier if girls are more depressed?

Journal: *Journal of Research in Personality*, March 1994, *28*(1), 27–43.

Related Research: Nolen-Hoeksema, S., et al. (1983). Response styles and the duration of episodes of depressed mood.

Journal of Abnormal Psychology, *102*, 20–28.

● ● ●

5870

Test Name: SOCIAL SUPPORT INVENTORY

Purpose: To determine athletes' levels of satisfaction with support/help they have received over the past month.

Number of Items: 39

Format: Responses are made on a 7-point Likert scale ranging from *not at all satisfied* to *very satisfied*.

Reliability: Split-half and internal consistency (Cronbach's alpha) reliability coefficients were .94 and .96.

Author: Petrie, T. A.

Article: Racial differences in the prediction of college football players' academic performances.

Journal: *Journal of College Student Development*, November 1993, *34*(5), 418–421.

Related Research: Brown, S., et al. (1988). Perceived social support among college students: Factor structure of the Social Support Inventory. *Journal of Counseling Psychology*, *35*, 472–478.

● ● ●

5871

Test Name: SOCIAL SUPPORT MEASURE

Purpose: To measure social support.

Number of Items: 5

Format: The overall measure of support is the sum of the positively scored items.

Reliability: Interim correlations ranged from .06 to .30. Correlations of Individuals items with the overall support score ranged from .47 to .66.

Validity: Correlations of overall support with other variables ranged from -.14 to .58.

Authors: Reynolds, S., and Gilbert, P.

Article: Psychological impact of unemployment: Interactive effect of vulnerability and protective factors on depression.

Journal: *Journal of Counseling Psychology*, January 1991, *38*(1), 76–84.

Related Research: Ullah, P., et al. (1985). Social support, social pressures and psychological distress during unemployment. *Psychological Medicine, 15*, 283–295.

● ● ●

5872

Test Name: SOCIAL SUPPORT QUESTIONNAIRE

Purpose: To measure feedback and unconditional and emotional social support from others.

Number of Items: 11

Format: 7-point scales.

Reliability: Internal consistency was .75.

Authors: Rabinowitz, S., et al.

Article: Teaching interpersonal skills to occupational and environmental health professionals.

Journal: *Psychological Reports*, June 1994, *74*(3) Part II, 1299–1306.

Related Research: Ezion, D. (1984). Moderating effects of social support on the stress burnout relationship. *Journal of Applied Psychology*, *69*, 615–622.

● ● ●

5873

Test Name: SOCIAL SUPPORT QUESTIONNAIRE

Purpose: To assess the number of persons perceived as being supportive and the amount of satisfaction the individual feels about the support that is being received.

Number of Items: 27

Format: A sample item is presented. Responses to each item range from 0 to 9 indicating the number of supportive people who fill the role identified in each item.

Validity: Correlations with other variables ranged from -.08 to .82.

Authors: Wohlgemuth, E., and Betz, N. E.

Article: Gender as a moderator of the relationships of stress and social support to physical health in college students.

Journal: *Journal of Counseling Psychology*, July 1991, *38*(3), 367–374.

Related Research: Sarason, I. G., et al. (1983). Assessing social support: The Social Support Questionnaire. *Journal of Personality and Social Psychology, 44,* 127–139.

■ ■ ■

5874

Test Name: SOCIAL SUPPORT QUESTIONNAIRE—SHORT REPORT

Purpose: To identify one's perception of his or her social support.

Number of Items: 6

Format: Includes two scales: (a) the number of available others one feels he or she can consult in specific time of need and (b) an assessment of the person's satisfaction with the perceived available support at those specific times of need. A 6-point scale ranging from 1 (*very dissatisfied*) to 6 (*very satisfied*) is used.

Reliability: Internal reliabilities ranged from .90 to .93.

Validity: Conditions with other variables ranged from -.40 to .32.

Authors: Kashubeck, S., and Christensen, S. A.

Article: Differences in distress among adult children of alcoholics.

Journal: *Journal of Counseling Psychology*, July 1992, *39*(3), 356–362.

Related Research: Sarason, I. G., et al. (1987). A brief measure of social support: Practical and theoretical implications. *Journal of Social and Personal Relationships, 4,* 497–510.

■ ■ ■

5875

Test Name: SOCIAL SUPPORT SCALE

Purpose: To measure an individual's perception of support from spouse/partner, relatives, coworkers, and friends.

Number of Items: 4

Format: 5-point responses range from 5 (*a great deal*) to 1 (*not at all*).

Reliability: Alpha was .77.

Authors: Jones-Johnson, G., and Johnson, W. G.

Article: Subjective underemployment and psychosocial stress: The role of perceived social and supervisor support.

Journal: *The Journal of Social Psychology*, February 1992, *132*(1), 11–21.

Related Research: Kasl, S., & Cobb, S. (1979). Some mental health consequences of plant closings and job loss. In Ferman, L. A. & Gordus, J. P. (Eds.), *Mental health and the economy* (pp. 255–300). Kalamazoo, MI:

Upjohn Institute of Employment Research.

■ ■ ■

5876

Test Name: SOCIAL SUPPORT SCALE

Purpose: To measure supportive and negative social interaction in maintaining health.

Number of Items: 8

Format: 5-point scales (*not at all* to *very much*). All items presented.

Reliability: Alphas were .89 (support) and .61 (negative interaction).

Authors: Sharpe, P. A., et al.

Article: Measurement of social interaction in change of health behavior.

Journal: *Psychological Reports*, December 1995, *77*(3) Part I, 867–871.

Related Research: Marcoux, B. C., et al. (1990). Social networks and social support in weight loss. *Patient Education and Counseling, 15,* 229–238.

■ ■ ■

5877

Test Name: SOCIAL SUPPORT SCALE FOR CHINESE STUDENTS IN JAPAN

Purpose: To measure social support.

Number of Items: 29

Format: 4-point rating scales range from 1 (*not at all*) to 4 (*very much*). Sample items are presented.

Reliability: Alphas ranged from .95 to .96.

Authors: Jou, Y. H., and Fukada, H.

Article: Effects of social support on adjustment of Chinese students in Japan.

Journal: *The Journal of Social Psychology*, February 1995, *135*(1), 39–47.

Related Research: Jou, Y. H. (1994). An attempt to construct a social support scale for Chinese students in Japan. *Research in Social Psychology*, *8*, 235–245.

■ ■ ■

5878

Test Name: SOCIAL SYSTEM SCALE

Purpose: To measure intra- and intergroup contact in formal and informal social systems.

Number of Items: 16

Format: 5-point rating scales. All items are presented.

Reliability: Alpha was .96.

Authors: Ramirez, A., and Soriano, F. I.

Article: Differential patterns of intra- and interethnic interaction in social power systems.

Journal: *The Journal of Social Psychology*, June 1993, *133*(3), 307–316.

Related Research: Ramirez, A. (1988). Racism toward Hispanics: The culturally monolithic society. In P. A. Katz & D. A. Taylor (Eds.), *Eliminating racism: Profiles in controversy* (pp. 137–157). New York: Plenum Press.

■ ■ ■

5879

Test Name: SPORT INTEREST INVENTORY

Purpose: To measure sport socialization.

Number of Items: 46

Format: Responses are made on a scale ranging from 1 to 5.

Reliability: Reliability coefficients ranged from .85 to 98.

Authors: Lugo, A. M., et al.

Article: Use of Sport Socialization Inventory with cerebral palsied youth.

Journal: *Perceptual and Motor Skills*, February 1992, *74*(1), 203–208.

Related Research: Greendorfer, S. L., et al. (1986). Gender differences in Brazilian children's socialization into sport. *International Review for the Sociology of Sport*, *21*, 53–63.

■ ■ ■

5880

Test Name: SUINN-LEW ASIAN SELF-IDENTITY ACCULTURATION SCALE

Purpose: To measure multiple dimensions of acculturation relevant to Asian cultures.

Number of Items: 21

Format: Responses are made on a 5-point scale ranging from 1 (*nearly all*) to 5 (*none at all*). An example is presented.

Reliability: Internal reliability coefficients were .88 and .68.

Validity: Correlations with other variables ranged from -.25 to .18 ($N = 39$).

Authors: Lese, K. P., and Robbins, S. B.

Article: Relationship between goal attributes and the academic achievement of Southeast Asian adolescent refugees.

Journal: *Journal of Counseling Psychology*, January 1994, *41*(1), 45–52.

Related Research: Suinn, R., et al. (1987). The Suinn-Lew Asian Self-Identity Acculturation Scale: An initial report. *Educational and Psychological Measurement*, *47*, 401–407.

5881

Test Name: SUPPORT SCALE

Purpose: To assess the degree to which participants experienced an interpersonally supportive group setting.

Number of Items: 10

Format: Uses a yes–no format.

Reliability: Internal consistency was .84.

Authors: Robbins, S. B., et al.

Article: Efficacy of leader-led and self-directed career workshops for middle-aged and older adults.

Journal: *Journal of Counseling Psychology*, January 1994, *41*(1), 83–90.

Related Research: Trickett, E. J., & Moos, A. H. (1973). Social environment of junior high and high school classrooms. *Journal of Educational Psychology*, *65*, 93–102.

■ ■ ■

5882

Test Name: THE JOINERS' SCALE

Purpose: To measure the extent to which people join and maintain relationships in diverse groups.

Number of Items: 7

Format: 9-point Likert format. All items are presented.

Reliability: Alphas ranged from .81 to .90. Test–retest was .85.

Validity: Correlations with other variables ranged from -.35 to .48.

Authors: Winn, D. L., and Hamlet, M. A.

Article: The Joiners' Scale: Validation of a measure of social-complexity.

Journal: *Psychological Reports*, June 1994, *74*(3) Part I, 1027–1034.

5883

Test Name: TOUCH AVOIDANCE MEASURE

Purpose: To measure same- and opposite-sex touch avoidance.

Number of Items: 16

Format: Employs a 5-point scale.

Reliability: Reliability coefficients were .82 and .88.

Author: Crawford, C. B.

Article: Effects of sex and sex roles on avoidance of same- and opposite-sex touch.

Journal: *Perceptual and Motor Skills*, August 1994, *79*(1) Part 1, 107–112.

Related Research: Anderson, P. A., & Leibowitz, K. (1978). The development and nature of the construct Touch Avoidance. *Environmental Psychology and Nonverbal Behavior, 3*, 89–106.

■ ■ ■

5884

Test Name: TOUCH OK SCALE

Purpose: To assess acceptability of three types of touching behavior from father to child.

Number of Items:

Format: 4-point Likert format.

Reliability: Alpha was .85.

Validity: Correlation with son's age was -.28.

Author: Salt, R. E.

Article: Affectionate touch between fathers and preadolescent sons.

Journal: *Journal of Marriage and the Family*, August 1991, *53*(3), 545–554.

Related Research: Salt, R. (1985). *Touch OK Scale*. West Lafayette, IN: Purdue University.

5885

Test Name: UCLA LONELINESS SCALE

Purpose: To assess loneliness.

Number of Items: 11

Format: 4-point frequency scales range from *never* to *always*.

Reliability: Alpha was .88.

Author: Mullins, L. C.

Article: Loneliness: Its effects on older persons in congregate housing.

Journal: *Sociology and Social Research*, April 1991, *75*(3), 170-177.

Related Research: Russell, D., et al. (1980). The Revised UCLA Loneliness Scale: Concurrent and discriminate validity evidence. *Journal of Personality and Social Psychology, 39*, 472–480.

■ ■ ■

5886

Test Name: UCLA LONELINESS SCALE—REVISED

Purpose: To measure loneliness.

Number of Items: 39

Format: Includes negativity and positively keyed items. Examples are presented.

Reliability: Alpha coefficients ranged from .80 to .96.

Authors: Miller, T. R., and Cleary, T. A.

Article: Directions of wording effects in balanced scales.

Journal: *Educational and Psychological Measurement*, Spring 1993, *53*(1), 51–60.

Related Research: Russell, D., et al. (1980). The Revised UCLA Loneliness Scale: Concurrent and discriminant validity evidence. *Journal of Personality and Social Psychology, 39*, 472–480.

5887

Test Name: UCLA LONELINESS SCALE(S)

Purpose: To measure loneliness.

Number of Items: 20 (8) (4)

Format: 4-point frequency scales range from *often feel this way* to *never*. All items are presented.

Reliability: Alphas ranged from .71 to .74 for the 20-item scale, .56 to .60 for the 8-item scale, and from .31 to .45 for the 4-item scale.

Validity: Correlations between the three scale versions ranged from .59 to .87.

Authors: Wilson, D., et al.

Article: Psychometric properties of the revised UCLA Loneliness Scale and two short-form measures of loneliness in Zimbabwe.

Journal: *Journal of Personality Assessment*, August 1992, *59*(1), 72–81.

Related Research: Russell, D., et al. (1980). The revised UCLA Loneliness Scale: Concurrent and discriminant validity evidence. *Journal of Personality and Social Psychology, 39*, 472–480.

Hartshorne, T. S. (1993). Psychometric properties and confirmatory factor analysis of the UCLA Loneliness Scale. *Journal of Personality Assessment, 61*, 182–193.

■ ■ ■

5888

Test Name: UCLA LONELINESS SCALE—SHORT VERSION

Purpose: To measure loneliness.

Number of Items: 8

Format: 4-point frequency scale (*never* to *often*). All items presented.

Reliability: Alphas ranged from .78 to .79. 12-month stability ranged from .42 to .48.

Validity: Correlations with related constructs ranged from -.55 to .50.

Authors: Roberts, R. E., et al.

Article: A brief measure of loneliness suitable for use with adolescents.

Journal: *Psychological Reports*, June 1993, *72*(3) Part II, 1379–1391.

Related Research: Russell, D. (1982). The measurement of loneliness. In L. A. Peplau & D. Perlman (Eds.), *Loneliness: A sourcebook of current theory, research and therapy* (pp. 84–104). New York: Wiley.

• • •

5889

Test Name: UCLA LONELINESS SCALE—VERSION 2

Purpose: To detect variations in loneliness in every day life.

Number of Items: 20

Format: Responses are made on a scale ranging from 1 (*never*) to 4 (*often*). Examples are presented.

Reliability: Coefficient alpha was .94. Test–retest (2 months) reliability ranged from .62 to .73.

Validity: Correlations with other variables ranged from -.46 to .31.

Authors: Cooper, A., and McCormack, W. A.

Article: Short-term group treatment for adult children of alcoholics.

Journal: *Journal of Counseling Psychology*, July 1992, *39*(3) 350–355.

Related Research: Russell, D., et al. (1980). The Revised UCLA Loneliness Scale: Concurrent and discriminant validity evidence. *Journal of Personality and Social Psychology*, *39*, 472–480.

5890

Test Name: UNIVERSITY ALIENATION SCALE

Purpose: To measure university alienation.

Number of Items: 15

Format: Includes three subscales: Meaningless, Powerlessness, and Social Estrangement. An example is presented.

Reliability: Alpha coefficients ranged from .60 to .83.

Validity: Correlations with other variables (13 items) ranged from -.17 to .30 (*N* = 121).

Author: Cooke, D. K.

Article: The factor structure and predictive validity of Burbach's University Alienation Scale.

Journal: *Educational and Psychological Measurement*, Winter 1994, *54*(4), 973–982.

Related Research: Burbach, H. J. (1972). The development of a contextual measure of alienation. *Pacific Sociological Review*, *15*, 225–234.

• • •

5891

Test Name: VIETNAMESE CULTURAL IDENTIFICATION SCALE

Purpose: To assess Vietnamese Americans' degree of identification with Vietnamese culture.

Number of Items: 17

Format: Various formats. All items presented.

Reliability: Alpha was .79.

Validity: Correlation with depressive symptoms was .29 (*p* < .05).

Authors: Nguyen, L., and Peterson, C.

Article: Depressive symptoms among Vietnamese-American college students.

Journal: *The Journal of Social Psychology*, February 1993, *133*(1), 65–71.

• • •

5892

Test Name: WHITE RACIAL IDENTITY ATTITUDE SCALE

Purpose: To measure attitudes of White racial identity development.

Number of Items: 50

Format: Responses are made on a 5-point Likert-type scale ranging from 1 (*strongly disagree*) to 5 (*strongly agree*). Includes: Contact, Disintegration, Reintegration, Pseudo-Independence, and Autonomy scales.

Reliability: Alpha coefficients ranged from .53 to .86.

Authors: Carter, R. T., and Gushue, G. V.

Article: White racial identity development and work values.

Journal: *Journal of Vocational Behavior*, April 1994, *44*(2), 185–197.

Related Research: Helms, J. E. (1984). Toward a theoretical explanation of the effects of race on counseling: A Black and White model. *The Counseling Psychologist*, *13*, 695–710.

• • •

5893

Test Name: WILLINGNESS TO ENGAGE IN FUTURE INTERACTION SCALE

Purpose: To measure interpersonal rejection.

Number of Items: 11

Format: Responses are made on a 5-point Likert-type scale.

Reliability: Alpha coefficients ranged from .91 to .95.

Author: Segrin, C.

Article: Effects of dysphoria and loneliness on social perceptual skills.

Journal: *Perceptual and Motor Skills*, December 1993, *77*(3) Part 2, 1315–1329.

Related Research: Coyne, J. C. (1976). Depression and the response of others. *Journal of Abnormal Psychology*, *85*, 186–193.

CHAPTER 5
Adjustment—Vocational

5894

Test Name: ACADEMIC BARRIERS QUESTIONNAIRE

Purpose: To measure barriers to success in the academy among women: personal security, work priorities, sense of belonging, scholarly accomplishment.

Format: 5-point Likert format.

Reliability: Alphas ranged from .75 to .85 across subscales.

Validity: Senior faculty reported higher barrier scores than junior faculty on several individual items, but on only one subscale— Personal Security.

Authors: Johnsrud, L. K., and Wunsch, M.

Article: Junior and senior faculty women: Commonalities and difference in perceptions of academic life.

Journal: *Psychological Reports*, December 1991, *69*(3) Part I, 879–886.

• • •

5895

Test Name: ATTRIBUTIONS FOR SUCCESS SCALE

Purpose: To assess the importance of various reasons for success in a profession.

Number of Items: 8

Format: 4-point importance scales. All items presented.

Reliability: Alphas ranged from .58 (*internal*) to .82 (*external*).

Validity: Correlations between pairs of items ranged from -.13 to

.70. Two factors were extracted (*internal* and *external*).

Authors: Fox, M. F., and Ferri, V. C.

Article: Women, men and their attributions for success in academe.

Journal: *Social Psychology Quarterly*, September 1992, *55*(3), 257–271.

• • •

5896

Test Name: BEHAVIORAL INTENTIONS SCALE

Purpose: To assess turnover and smoking ban compliance intentions.

Number of Items: 4

Format: Topic of each item is presented.

Reliability: Internal consistency was .85.

Validity: Correlations with other variables ranged from .03 to .93 (*N*= 732).

Author: Greenberg, J.

Article: Using socially fair treatment to promote acceptance of a work site smoking ban.

Journal: *Journal of Applied Psychology*, April 1994, *79*(2), 288–297.

Related Research: Mobley, W. H., et al. (1978). An evaluation of precursors of hospital employee turnover. *Journal of Applied Psychology*, *63*, 408–414.

Mowday, R. T., et al. (1984). The psychology to the withdrawal

process: A cross-validational test of Mobley's intermediate linkage model of turnover in two samples. *Academy of Management Journal*, *27*, 79–94.

• • •

5897

Test Name: BURNOUT INVENTORY

Purpose: To measure burnout.

Number of Items: 20

Format: Responses are made on a 7-point scale.

Reliability: Reliability coefficients were .91 and .92.

Validity: Correlations with other variables ranged from -.65 to .70 (*N*= 120).

Authors: Meir, E. I., et al.

Article: The benefits of congruence.

Journal: *The Career Development Quarterly*, March 1995, *43*(3), 257–266.

Related Research: Pines, A., et al. (1981). *Burnout: From tedium to personal growth*. New York: The Free Press.

• • •

5898

Test Name: CAREER CHOICE ANXIETY

Purpose: To measure career choice anxiety.

Number of Items: 11

Format: Responses are made on a 5-point scale ranging from 1 (*not at all applicable*) to 5 (*highly* *applicable*). Examples are presented.

Reliability: Coefficient alpha was .92.

Validity: Correlations with other variables ranged from-.12 to -.47.

Authors: Matsui, T., and Onglatco, M.-L.

Article: Career orientedness of motivation to enter the university among Japanese high school girls: A path analysis.

Journal: *Journal of Vocational Behavior*, June 1992, *40*(3), 351–363.

Related Research: Slaney, R. B., et al. (1981). An investigation of two measures of career indecision. *Journal of Vocational Behavior*, *18*, 92–103.

■ ■ ■

5899

Test Name: CAREER-RELATED CONCERNS CHECKLIST

Purpose: To assess career-related concerns.

Number of Items: 9

Format: Responses are made on a 5-point scale ranging from 1 (*not at all*) to 5 (*very strong*). Includes two factors: Changing Work Role Identity and Lessened Career Opportunities. Examples are presented.

Reliability: Alpha coefficients were .78 and .80.

Validity: Correlations with other variables ranged from -.03 to .42.

Authors: Buunk, B. P., and Janssen, P. P. M.

Article: Relative deprivation, career issues, and mental health among men in midlife.

Journal: *Journal of Vocational Behavior*, June 1992, *40*(3), 338–350.

5900

Test Name: CAREER SALIENCE SCALE

Purpose: To measure career salience.

Number of Items: 8

Format: 5-point Likert format. Sample item presented.

Reliability: Alpha was .77.

Author: Vardi, Y.

Article: "Glory is not enough": Dual careers in Israeli air force families.

Journal: *Psychological Reports*, June 1992, *70*(3) Part I, 851–863.

Related Research: Pendleton, B. F., et al. (1980). Scales for the investigation of dual career families. *Journal of Marriage and the Family*, *42*, 269–275.

■ ■ ■

5901

Test Name: CAREER SALIENCE SCALE

Purpose: To measure the importance of work and career.

Number of Items: 27

Format: Items compare career with other sources of satisfaction, indicate job attitudes, career thought, and planning.

Reliability: Coefficient alpha was .81.

Authors: Kush, K., and Cochran, L.

Article: Enhancing a sense of agency through career planning.

Journal: *Journal of Counseling Psychology*, October 1993, *40*(4), 434–439.

Related Research: Greenhaus, J. H. (1973). A factorial investigation of career salience. *Journal of Vocational Behavior*, *3*, 95–98.

5902

Test Name: CAREER SATISFACTION SCALE

Purpose: To measure career satisfaction.

Number of Items: 5

Format: Responses are made on a 5-point scale ranging from 1 (*very dissatisfied*) to 5 (*very satisfied*). Sample items are presented.

Reliability: Alpha coefficients were .88 and .89.

Validity: Correlation with other variables ranged from -.33 to .39.

Authors: Aryee, S., et al.

Article: An investigation of the predictors and outcomes of career commitment in three career stages.

Journal: *Journal of Vocational Behavior*, February 1994, *44*(1), 1–16.

Related Research: Greenhaus, J., et al. (1990). Effects of race on organizational experience, job performance, evaluation and career outcomes. *Academy of Management Journal*, *33*, 64–86.

■ ■ ■

5903

Test Name: CAREER SATISFACTION SCALE

Purpose: To measure career satisfaction.

Number of Items: 8

Format: Responses are made on a 5-point scale.

Reliability: Coefficient alpha was .85.

Authors: Rhodes, S. R., and Doering, M. M.

Article: Intention to change careers: Determinants and process.

Journal: *The Career Development Quarterly*, September 1993, *42*(1), 76–92.

Related Research: Gould, S. (1979). Characteristics of career planners in upwardly mobile occupations. *Academy of Management Journal, 22,* 539–550.

• • •

5904

Test Name: CAREER TRANSITION INVENTORY

Purpose: To provide a multidimensional measure of career change adjustment.

Number of Items: 40

Format: Includes 5 factors: Readiness, Confidence, Control, Perceived Support, and Decision Independence. Responses are made on a 6-point scale ranging from 1 (*strongly agree*) to 6 (*strongly disagree*). All items are presented.

Reliability: Alpha coefficients ranged from .66 to .90.

Validity: Correlations with other variables ranged from -.47 to .56.

Authors: Heppner, M. J., et al.

Article: Assessing psychological resources during career change: Development of the Career Transition Inventory.

Journal: *Journal of Vocational Behavior,* February 1994, *44*(1), 55–74.

• • •

5905

Test Name: CAREER WITHDRAWAL INTENTIONS SCALE

Purpose: To measure career withdrawal intentions.

Number of Items: 3

Format: Responses are made on a 5-point scale ranging from 1 (*very unlikely*) to 5 (*very likely*). Sample items are presented.

Reliability: Internal consistency coefficients ranged from .85 to .91. Test–retest reliability was .57.

Validity: Correlations with other variables ranged from -.13 to .57.

Authors: Aryee, S., et al.

Article: An investigation of the predictors and outcomes of career commitment on three career stages

Journal: *Journal of Vocational Behavior,* February 1994, *44*(1), 1–16.

Related Research: Blau, G. (1988). Further exploring the meaning and measurement of career commitment. *Journal of Vocational Behavior, 32,* 284–297.

• • •

5906

Test Name: CHERNISS BURNOUT MEASURE

Purpose: To measure teacher burnout.

Number of Items: 14

Format: Responses are made on a 5-point scale ranging from 1 (*never*) to 5 (*always*). An example is presented.

Reliability: Coefficient alpha was .90.

Authors: Lamude, K. G., and Scudder, J.

Article: Burnout of teacher as related to influence tactics within the college classroom.

Journal: *Perceptual and Motor Skills,* October 1994, *79*(2), 915–919.

Related Research: Burke, R. J., & Greenglass, E. R. (1989). Psychological burnout among men and women in teaching: An examination of the Cherniss model. *Human Relations, 42,* 261–273.

5907

Test Name: COMPUTER-AIDED DESIGN ANXIETY QUESTIONNAIRE

Purpose: To assess college students' beliefs about computer-aided design.

Number of Items: 14

Format: Includes four types of items. Responses are made on a 7-point scale ranging from 1 (*strongly agree*) to 7 (*strongly disagree*). All items are presented.

Reliability: Alpha coefficients ranged from -.46 to .83.

Author: Frey, D. K.

Article: Assessing students' responses toward computer-aided design of apparel.

Journal: *Perceptual and Motor Skills,* April 1995, *80*(2), 435–443.

Related Research: Heinssen, R. K., et al. (1987). Assessing computer anxiety: Development and validation of the Computer Anxiety Rating Scale. *Computers in Human Behavior, 3,* 49–59.

• • •

5908

Test Name: COMPUTER ANXIETY FACTOR

Purpose: To measure computer anxiety.

Number of Items: 14

Format: Responses are made on a 5-point Likert-type scale.

Reliability: Coefficient alpha was .91.

Author: Szajna, B.

Article: An investigation of the predictive validity of computer anxiety and computer aptitude.

Journal: *Educational and Psychological Measurement,* Winter 1994, *54*(4), 926–934.

Related Research: Kerman, M. C.,

& Howard, G. S. (1990). Computer anxiety and computer attitudes: An investigation of construct and predictive validity issues. *Educational and Psychological Measurement, 50,* 681–690.

● ● ●

5909

Test Name: COMPUTER ANXIETY RATING SCALE

Purpose: To identify psychological anxiety about computers.

Number of Items: 10

Format: Responses are made on a 7-point scale ranging from *strongly disagree* to *strongly agree.* A sample item is presented.

Reliability: Internal consistency reliabilities were .89 (pretraining) and .81 (posttraining).

Validity: Correlations with other variables ranged from -.53 to .21.

Author: Martocchio, J. J.

Article: Effects of conceptions of ability on anxiety, self-efficacy and learning in training.

Journal: *Journal of Applied Psychology,* December 1994, *79*(6), 819–825

Related Research: Heinssen, R., et al. (19897). Assessing computer anxiety: Development and validation of the computer anxiety rating scale. *Computers in Human Behavior, 3,* 49–59.

● ● ●

5910

Test Name: COMPUTER ANXIETY RATING SCALE

Purpose: To evaluate computer anxiety.

Number of Items: 19

Format: Includes 2 factors: High Anxiety, and Confidence, Enthusiasm, and/or Anticipation. All items are presented.

Reliability: Internal-consistency reliability was .87.

Authors: Harrison, A. W., and Rainer, R. K., Jr.

Article: An examination of the factor structures and concurrent validities for the Computer Attitude Scale, The Computer Anxiety Rating Scale, and The Computer Self-Efficacy Scale.

Journal: *Educational and Psychological Measurement,* Autumn 1992, *52*(3), 735–745.

Related Research: Heinssen, R. K., Jr., et al. (1987). Assessing computer anxiety: Development and validity of the Computer Anxiety Rating Scale. *Computers in Human Behavior, 3,* 49–59.

● ● ●

5911

Test Name: COMPUTER ANXIETY SCALE

Purpose: To measure computer anxiety.

Number of Items: 23

Format: Includes 3 factors: Computer Liking, Computer Confidence, and Computer Achievement. Responses are made on a 7-point Likert-type scale.

Reliability: Alpha coefficients ranged from .81 to .96.

Author: Szajna, B.

Article: An investigation of the predictive validity of computer anxiety and computer aptitude.

Journal: *Educational and Psychological Measurement,* Winter 1994, *54*(4), 926–934.

Related Research: Bandalos, D., & Benson, J. (1990). Testing the factor structure invariance of a computer attitude scale over two grouping conditions. *Educational and Psychological Measurement, 50,* 49–60.

5912

Test Name: COMPUTER HASSLES SCALE

Purpose: To measure computer users' stress.

Number of Items: 37

Format: 4-point severity scales. All items presented.

Reliability: Alphas ranged from .89 to .95 across subscales.

Author: Hudiburg, R. A.

Article: Psychology of computer use: XXXIV. The Computer Hassles Scale: Subscales, norms, and reliability.

Journal: *Psychological Reports,* December 1995, *77*(3) Part I, 779–782.

Related Research: Hudiburg, R. A., et al. (1993). Psychology of computer use: XXIX. Measuring computer users' stress: The Computer Hassles Scale. *Psychological Reports, 73,* 923–929.

● ● ●

5913

Test Name: COMPUTER TECHNOLOGY HASSLES SCALE

Purpose: To assess stressors associated with computer use.

Number of Items: 69

Format: 4-point severity scales.

Validity: Correlations with other variables ranged from −.24 (computer course grade) to .27 (Hopkins Symptom Checklist).

Authors: Hudiburg, R. A., and Jones, M.

Article: Psychology of computer use: XXIII. Validating a measure of computer related stress.

Journal: *Psychological Reports,* August 1991, *69*(1), 179–182.

Related Research: Hudiburg, R. A.

(1989). Psychology of computer use: XVII. The Computer Technology Hassles Scale: Revision, reliability, and correlates. *Psychological Reports*, *65*, 1387–1394.

Ballance, C. T., & Rogers, S. U. (1991). Psychology of computer use XXIV: Computer-related stress among technical college students. *Psychological Reports*, 69, 539–542.

Hudiburg, R. A. (1991). Relation of computer hassles, somatic complaints and daily hassles. *Psychological Reports*, *69*, 1119–1122

■ ■ ■

5914

Test Name: CONCERNS ABOUT COMPUTERS SCALE

Purpose: To measure the concerns of people attempting to develop computer skills.

Number of Items: 35

Format: Factors extracted were Concern for Errors, Concern for Utility, Concern for Difficulties, Concern for Damage to Equipment, and Concern for Novelty.

Reliability: Alphas ranged from .63 to .90 across subscales. Total alpha was .95.

Authors: Crable, E. A., et al.

Article: Psychology of computer use: XXII. Preliminary development of a measure of concerns about computers.

Journal: *Psychological Reports*, August 1991, *69*(1), 235–236.

Related Research: Igabaria, M., & Parasuramon, S. (1989). A path analytic study of individual characteristics, computer anxiety and attitudes toward microcomputers. *Journal of Management*, *15*, 373–388.

5915

Test Name: CONTEXTUAL PERFORMANCE SCALE

Purpose: To assess contextual performance.

Number of Items: 16

Format: Responses are made on a 5-point scale ranging from 1 (*not at all likely*) to 5 (*extremely likely*). All items are presented.

Reliability: Coefficient alpha was .95.

Authors: Motowidlo, S. J., and Van Scotter, J. R.

Article: Evidence that task performance should be distinguished from conceptual performance.

Journal: *Journal of Applied Psychology*, August 1994, *79*(4), 475–480.

Related Research: Borman, W. C., & Motowidlo, S. J. (1993). Expanding the criterion domain to include elements of contextual performance. In N. Schmitt & W. C. Borman (Eds.), *Personal selection in organizations* (pp. 71–98). San Francisco: Jossey-Bass.

■ ■ ■

5916

Test Name: CONTINUANCE COMMITMENT SCALE

Purpose: To measure likelihood of quitting one's job.

Number of Items: 3

Format: 7-point Likert format. All items are presented.

Reliability: Alpha was .71.

Authors: Angle, H. L., and Lawson, M. B.

Article: Organizational commitment and employees' performance ratings: Both type of commitment and type of performance count.

Journal: *Psychological Reports*, December 1994, *75*(3) Part II, 1539–1551.

Related Research: Allen, N. J., & Meyer, J. P. (1990). The measurement and antecedents of affective continuance and normative commitment to the organization. *Journal of Occupational Psychology*, *63*, 1–18.

■ ■ ■

5917

Test Name: COOPERATION SCALES

Purpose: To measure cooperation and resistance between older subordinates and younger supervisors.

Number of Items: 10

Format: 5-point agreement scales. All items are presented.

Reliability: Alphas ranged from .73 to .84 across two subscales.

Validity: Cooperation and resistance subscales were correlated ($r = .66, p < .01$).

Authors: Smith, W. J., and Harrington, K. V.

Article: Younger supervisor-older subordinate dyads: A relationship of cooperation or resistance.

Journal: *Psychological Reports*, June 1994, *74*(3) Part I, 803–812.

■ ■ ■

5918

Test Name: DATA-ENTRY STRESS SCALE

Purpose: To measure data-entry stress.

Number of Items: 9

Format: Responses are made on 7-point scales. All items are presented.

Reliability: Coefficient alpha was .88.

Validity: Correlations with other variables ranged from -.40 to .12.

Authors: Aiello, J. R., and Kolb, K. J.

Article: Electronic performance monitoring and social context: Impact on productivity and stress.

Journal: *Journal of Applied Psychology*, June 1995, *80*(3), 339–353.

■ ■ ■

5919

Test Name: ENERGY DEPLETION INDEX

Purpose: To measure occupational burnout.

Number of Items: 4

Format: 5-point response scale. All items presented.

Reliability: Cronbach's alpha was .82.

Validity: Correlations with feelings about performance ranged from .20 to .65.

Author: Garden, A. M.

Article: Relationship between burnout and performance.

Journal: *Psychological Reports*, June 1991, *68*(3) Part I, 963–977.

Related Research: Garden, A. M. (1985). *Burnout: The effect of personality.* Unpublished doctoral dissertation, Cambridge, Massachusetts Institute of Technology.

■ ■ ■

5920

Test Name: FACULTY COLLEGIALITY SCALE

Purpose: To assess faculty collegiality.

Number of Items: 8

Format: Likert-type responses. Examples are presented.

Reliability: Coefficient alpha was .79.

Authors: Hoy, W. K., et al.

Article: Faculty trust in colleagues: Linking the principal with school effectiveness.

Journal: *Journal of Research and Development in Education*, Fall 1992, 26(1), 38–45.

Related Research: Halpin, A. W., & Croft, D. B. (1963). *The organizational climate of schools.* Chicago: Midwest Administration Center of the University of Chicago.

■ ■ ■

5921

Test Name: FACULTY STRESS INDEX

Purpose: To measure faculty stress.

Number of Items: 65

Format: 5-point Likert format.

Reliability: Alphas ranged from .53 to .72 across subscales.

Authors: Smith, E., et al.

Article: The multiple sources of workplace stress among land grant university faculty.

Journal: *Research in Higher Education*, June 1995, *36*(3), 261–282.

Related Research: Koch, J. L., et al. (1982). Job stress among school administrators: Factorial dimensions and differential effects. *Journal of Applied Psychology, 67,* 493–499.

■ ■ ■

5922

Test Name: FACULTY TRUST IN COLLEAGUES SCALE

Purpose: To measure faculty trust in colleagues.

Number of Items: 7

Format: Likert-type responses on a 6-point scale ranging from *strongly agree* to *strongly disagree.* Examples are presented.

Reliability: Coefficient alpha was .85.

Authors: Hoy, W. K., et al.

Article: Faculty trust in colleagues: Linking the principal with school effectiveness.

Journal: *Journal of Research and Development in Education*, Fall 1992, 26(1), 38–45.

Related Research: Hoy, W. K., & Kupersmith, W. J. (1985). The meaning and measure of faculty trust. *Educational and Psychological Research, 5,* 1–10.

■ ■ ■

5923

Test Name: FACULTY TRUST IN THE PRINCIPAL SCALE

Purpose: To measure faculty trust in the principal.

Number of Items: 7

Format: Likert-type responses on a 6-point scale ranging from *strongly agree* to *strongly disagree.* Examples are presented.

Reliability: Coefficient alpha was .86.

Authors: Hoy, W. K., et al.

Article: Faculty trust in colleagues: Linking the principal with school effectiveness.

Journal: *Journal of Research and Development in Education*, Fall 1992, *26*(1), 38–45.

Related Research: Hoy, W. K., & Kupersmith, W. J. (1985). The meaning and measure of faculty trust. *Educational and Psychological Research, 5,* 1–10.

5924

Test Name: FACULTY TRUST SCALE

Purpose: To assess teacher trust in the principal and in colleagues.

Number of Items: 14

Format: 6-point agreement scales. Sample items are described.

Reliability: Alphas ranged from .94 to .95.

Authors: Tarter, C. J., et al.

Article: Middle school climate, faculty trust, and effectiveness: A path analysis.

Journal: *Journal of Research and Development in Education*, Fall 1995, *29*(1), 41–49.

Related Research: Hoy, W. K., & Kupersmith, W. J. (1985). The meaning and measure of faculty trust. *Educational and Psychological Research*, *5*, 1–10.

■ ■ ■

5925

Test Name: FAITH IN MANAGEMENT SCALE

Purpose: To identify one's perception of the cooperation of management and supervisor fairness.

Number of Items: 3

Reliability: Coefficient alpha was .80.

Validity: Correlations with other variables ranged from -.43 to .63.

Authors: Lehman, W. E. K., and Simpson, D. D.

Article: Employee substance use and on-the-job behaviors.

Journal: *Journal of Applied Psychology*, June 1992, *77*(3), 309–321.

Related Research: Cook, J., & Wall, T. D. (1980). New York attitude measures of trust, organizational commitment and

personal need non-fulfillment. *Journal of Occupational Psychology*, *53*, 39–52.

■ ■ ■

5926

Test Name: FRIEDMAN SCHOOL PRINCIPAL BURNOUT SCALE

Purpose: To measure school principals' perceived burnout.

Number of Items: 22

Format: Includes 3 factors: Exhaustion, Aloofness, and Deprecation. Responses are made on a 6-point scale ranging from 1 (*never*) to 6 (*always*). All items are presented.

Reliability: Coefficient alpha was .92.

Author: Friedman, I. A.

Article: Measuring school principal-experienced burnout.

Journal: *Educational and Psychological Measurement*, August 1995, *55*(4), 641–651.

Related Research: Friedman, I. A. (1995). School principal burnout: The concept and its components. *Journal of Organizational Behavior*, *16*, 191–198.

■ ■ ■

5927

Test Name: FRUSTRATION INDEX

Purpose: To assess overall job frustration.

Number of Items: 3

Reliability: Coefficient alpha was .67.

Validity: Correlations with other variables ranged from -.24 to .72.

Authors: Jex, S. M., et al.

Article: The meaning of occupational stress items to survey respondents.

Journal: *Journal of Applied*

Psychology, October 1992, *77*(5), 623–628.

Related Research: Peters, L. H., & O'Connor, E. J. (1980). Situational constraints and employee affective reactions: The influences of a frequently overlooked construct. *Academy of Management Review*, *5*, 391–397.

■ ■ ■

5928

Test Name: GARAGE PRIDE SCALE

Purpose: To measure the extent to which drivers are proud of the garage in which they work.

Number of Items: 6

Reliability: Alpha was .74.

Validity: Correlations with other variables ranged from .12 to .44.

Authors: Mathieu, J. E., and Farr, J. L.

Article: Further evidence for the discriminant validity of measures of organizational commitment, job involvement, and job satisfaction.

Journal: *Journal of Applied Psychology*, February 1991, *76*(1), 127–133.

Related Research: Jones, A. P., & James, L. R. (1979). Psychological climate: Dimensions and relationships of individuals and aggregate work environment perceptions. *Organizational Behavior and Human Performance*, *23*, 201–250.

■ ■ ■

5929

Test Name: GENERAL JOB SATISFACTION SCALE

Purpose: To measure general job satisfaction.

Number of Items: 2

Format: An example is presented.

Reliability: Coefficient alpha was .82.

Validity: Correlations with other variables ranged from -.65 to .57.

Authors: Mossholder, K. W., et al.

Article: Confounding constructs and levels of constructs in affectivity measurement: An empirical investigation.

Journal: *Educational and Psychological Measurement*, Summer 1994, *54*(2), 336–349.

Related Research: Cammann, C., et al. (1983). Assessing the attitudes and perceptions of organizational members. In S. E. Seashore et al. (Eds.), *Assessing Organizational Change* (pp. 71–138). New York: Wiley.

■ ■ ■

5930

Test Name: GENERAL JOB SATISFACTION SCALE

Purpose: To determine how satisfied in general a worker is with the job.

Number of Items: 3

Reliability: Coefficient alpha was .57.

Validity: Correlations with other variables ranged from -.31 to .29.

Author: Macon, T. H.

Article: Time management: Test of process model.

Journal: *Journal of Applied Psychology*, June 1994, *79*(3), 381–391.

Related Research: Hackman, J. R., & Oldham, G. R. (1975). Development of the job diagnostic survey. *Journal of Applied Psychology*, *60*, 159–170.

■ ■ ■

5931

Test Name: GENERAL JOB SATISFACTION SCALE

Purpose: To measure general job satisfaction.

Number of Items: 4

Format: Responses are made on 7-point scales. All items are presented.

Reliability: Coefficient alpha was .60.

Validity: Correlations with other variables ranged from -.47 to .46.

Authors: Schaubroeck, J., et al.

Article: Procedural justice explanations and employee reactions to economic hardship: A field experiment.

Journal: *Journal of Applied Psychology*, June 1994, *79*(3), 455–460.

Related Research: Hackman, J. R., & Oldham, G. O. (1980). *Job redesign.* Reading, MA: Addison-Wesley.

■ ■ ■

5932

Test Name: GENERAL JOB SATISFACTION SCALE

Purpose: To measure general job satisfaction.

Number of Items: 18

Format: Items are adjectives to be deemed descriptive of a person's job.

Reliability: Coefficient alpha was .90.

Authors: Major, D. A. et al.

Article: A longitudinal investigation of newcomer expectations, early socialization outcomes, and the moderating effects of role development factors.

Journal: *Journal of Applied Psychology*, June 1995, *80*(3), 418–431.

Related Research: Ironson, G. H., et al. (1989). Construction of a job in general scale: A comparison of global, composite, and specific measures. *Journal of Applied Psychology*, *74*, 193–200.

■ ■ ■

5933

Test Name: HEALTH PROFESSIONS STRESS INVENTORY

Purpose: To measure the sources and frequency of stress among nurses, physicians, and pharmacists.

Number of Items: 30

Format: 5-point Likert format. All items are presented.

Reliability: Alphas ranged from .70 to .86 across subscales.

Validity: Correlations with other variables ranged from .29 to .53.

Authors: Eells, T. D., et al.

Article: Symptom correlates and factor structure of the Health Professions Stress Inventory.

Journal: *Psychological Reports*, December 1994, *75*(3) Part II, 1563–1568.

Related Research: Wolfgang, A. P. (1988). The Health Professions Stress Inventory. *Psychological Reports*, *62*, 220–222.

■ ■ ■

5934

Test Name: HOPPOCK JOB SATISFACTION SCALE

Purpose: To assess job satisfaction.

Number of Items: 4

Format: Responses are made on a 7-point scale ranging from 1 (*extreme dissatisfaction*) to 7 (*extreme satisfaction*).

Reliability: Internal consistency was .81. Test–retest (1 month) reliability was .74.

Validity: Correlations with other variables ranged from -.49 to .74.

Author: Long, B. C.

Article: Coping strategies of male managers: A prospective analysis of predictors of psychosomatic symptoms and job satisfaction.

Journal: *Journal of Vocational Behavior*, April 1993, *42*(2), 184–199.

Related Research: McNichols, C., et al. (1978). A validation of Hoppock's job satisfaction measure. *Academy of Management Journal, 21,* 737–742.

■ ■ ■

5935

Test Name: INTENT TO LEAVE SCALE

Purpose: To measure the likelihood of leaving one's job.

Number of Items: 3

Format: Formats vary by item. All items are presented.

Reliability: Alpha was .74.

Validity: Correlations with other variables ranged from -.70 to .12.

Authors: Martin, T. N., and Hafer, J. C.

Article: The multiplicative interaction effects of job involvement and organizational commitment in the turnover intentions of full-time and part-time employees.

Journal: *Journal of Vocational Behavior*, June 1995, *46*(3), 310–331.

■ ■ ■

5936

Test Name: INTENT TO QUIT SCALE

Purpose: To assess intent to quit.

Number of Items: 2

Format: Responses are made on a 7-point scale ranging from 1

(*strongly disagree*) to 7 (*strongly agree*). Both items are presented.

Reliability: Reliability coefficients were .79 and .76.

Validity: Correlations with other variables ranged from -.64 to .49.

Authors: Begley, T. M., and Czajka, J. M.

Article: Panel analysis of the moderating effects of commitment on job satisfaction, intent to quit, and health following organizational change.

Journal: *Journal of Applied Psychology*, August 1993, *78*(4), 552–556.

■ ■ ■

5937

Test Name: INTENTION TO QUIT THE ORGANIZATION SCALE

Purpose: To measure the intention to quit the organization.

Number of Items: 3

Format: Responses were made on a 7-point Likert-type scale ranging from 1 (*strongly disagree*) to 7 (*strongly agree*). Examples are presented.

Reliability: Coefficient alpha was .75.

Validity: Correlations with other variables ranged from -.71 to .66.

Author: Saks, A. M.

Article: Longitudinal field investigation of the moderating and mediating effects of self-efficacy on the relationship between training and newcomer adjustment.

Journal: *Journal of Applied Psychology*, April 1995, *80*(2), 211–225.

Related Research: Colarelli, S. M. (1984). Methods of communication and mediating processes in realistic job

interviews. *Journal of Applied Psychology, 69,* 633–642.

■ ■ ■

5938

Test Name: INTENT TO QUIT THE PROFESSION SCALE

Purpose: To measure the intention to quit the profession.

Number of Items: 5

Format: Responses were made on a 7-point Likert-type scale ranging from 1 (*strongly disagree*) to 7 (*strongly agree*).

Reliability: Coefficient alpha was .73.

Validity: Correlations with other variables ranged from -.58 to .66.

Author: Saks, A. M.

Article: Longitudinal field investigation of the moderating and mediating effects of self-efficacy on the relationship between training and newcomer adjustment.

Journal: *Journal of Applied Psychology*, April 1995, *80*(2), 211–225.

Related Research: Colarelli, S. M. (1984). Methods of communication and mediating processes in realistic job interviews. *Journal of Applied Psychology, 69,* 633–642.

■ ■ ■

5939

Test Name: INTENT TO STAY SCALE

Purpose: To measure likelihood of remaining in a job.

Number of Items: 3

Format: All items are presented.

Reliability: Alpha was .77.

Authors: Randall, C. R., and Mueller, C. W.

Article: Extensions of justice

theory: Justice evaluations and employees' reactions in a natural setting.

Journal: *Social Psychology Quarterly*, September 1995, *58*(3), 178–194.

Related Research: McCloskey, J., & McCain, B. (1987). Satisfaction, commitment and professionalism of newly employed nurses. *Image*, *19*, 20–24.

● ● ●

5940

Test Name: INTENT TO TURNOVER SCALE

Purpose: To measure intent to turnover.

Number of Items: 2

Format: Examples are presented.

Reliability: Coefficient alpha was .82.

Validity: Correlations with other variables ranged from -.65 to .44.

Authors: Mossholder, K. W., et al.

Article: Confounding constructs and levels of constructs in affectivity measurement: An empirical investigation.

Journal: *Educational and Psychological Measurement*, Summer 1994, *54*(2), 336–349.

Related Research: Cammann, C., et al. (1983). Assessing the attitudes and perceptions of organizational members. In S. E. Seashore et al. (Eds.), *Assessing organizational change* (pp. 71–138). New York: Wiley.

● ● ●

5941

Test Name: JOB ALIENATION— MODIFIED

Purpose: To measure respondent's attitudes toward their university course.

Number of Items: 4

Format: Responses are made on a 5-point Likert-type scale. An example is presented.

Reliability: Alpha coefficients ranged from .65 to .76.

Validity: Correlations with other variables ranged from -.57 to .44.

Authors: Newton, T., and Keenan, T.

Article: Further analyses of the dispositional argument in organizational behavior.

Journal: *Journal of Applied Psychology*, December 1991, *76*(6), 781–787.

Related Research: Kanungo, R. A. (1979). The concepts of alienation and involvement revisited. *Psychological Bulletin*, *86*, 119–138.

● ● ●

5942

Test Name: JOB AND WORK AVOIDANCE SCALE

Purpose: To measure job avoidance.

Number of Items: 6

Format: Responses are made on a 5-point scale ranging from 1 (*very unlikely*) to 5 (*very likely*). All items are presented.

Reliability: Reliability coefficient was .70.

Validity: Correlations with other variables ranged from -.33 to .29.

Authors: Judge, T. A., and Locke, E. A.

Article: Effect of dysfunctional thought processes on subjective well-being and job satisfaction.

Journal: *Journal of Applied Psychology*, June 1993, *78*(3), 475–490.

Related Research: Hanisch, K. A., & Hulin C. L. (1991). General attitudes and organizational withdrawal: An evaluation of a causal model. *Journal of Vocational Behavior, 39*, 110–128.

● ● ●

5943

Test Name: JOB AND WORK SATISFACTION SCALES

Purpose: To assess general job satisfaction and work satisfaction.

Number of Items: 36

Reliability: Alphas were .88 (work) and .90 (general job).

Validity: Correlations with other variables ranged from .66 to .80.

Authors: Upperman, P. J., and Church, T.

Article: Investigating Holland's typological theory with army occupational specialties.

Journal: *Journal of Vocational Behavior*, August 1995, *47*(1), 61–75.

Related Research: Baltzer, W. K., & Smith, P. C. (1990). *User's manual: Job Description Index (JDI)*. Bowling Green, OH: Department of Psychology, Bowling Green University.

● ● ●

5944

Test Name: JOB DESCRIPTIVE INDEX—SHORTENED VERSION

Purpose: To measure job satisfaction.

Number of Items: 20

Format: Includes 5 dimensions: satisfaction with work, with pay, with promotion, with supervision, and with coworkers.

Reliability: Alpha coefficients ranged from .69 to .90.

Author: Knoop, R.

Article: The relationship between importance and achievement to work values and job satisfaction.

Journal: *Perceptual and Motor Skills*, August 1994, *79*(1) Part 2, 595–605.

Related Research: Smith, P., et al. (1969). *The measurement of satisfaction in work and retirement.* Chicago: Rand McNally.

Hatfield, J., et al. (1985). An empirical evaluation of a test for assessing job satisfaction. *Psychological Reports*, *56*, 39–45.

■ ■ ■

5945

Test Name: JOB DIAGNOSTIC SURVEY

Purpose: To measure overall job satisfaction.

Number of Items: 17

Format: Includes satisfaction with coworker, pay, security, supervision, workload, and growth satisfaction.

Reliability: Coefficient alpha was .87.

Authors: Ganster, D. C., et al.

Article: The nomological validity of the Type A personality among employed adults.

Journal: *Journal of Applied Psychology*, February 1991, *76*(1), 143–168.

Related Research: Hackman, J. R., & Oldham, G. R. (1975). Development of the Job Diagnostic Survey. *Journal of Applied Psychology*, *60*, 159–170.

■ ■ ■

5946

Test Name: JOB DISTRESS SCALE

Purpose: To assess job distress.

Number of Items: 6

Format: Responses are made on a 4-point scale.

Reliability: Coefficient alpha was .84.

Validity: Correlations with other variables ranged from -.21 to .53.

Authors: Frone M. R., et al.

Article: Antecedents and outcomes of work-family conflict: Testing a model of the work-family interface.

Journal: *Journal of Applied Psychology*, February 1992, *77*(1), 65–78.

Related Research: Kandel, D. B., et al. (1985). The stressfulness of daily social roles for women: Marital, occupational and household roles. *Journal of Health and Social Behavior*, *26*, 64–78.

■ ■ ■

5947

Test Name: JOB FRUSTRATION QUESTIONNAIRE

Purpose: To assess level of frustration.

Number of Items: 29

Format: 6-point agree–disagree format.

Reliability: Alphas ranged from .83 to .88.

Authors: Furnham, A., and Walsh, J.

Article: Consequences of person-environment incongruence: Absenteeism, frustration, and stress.

Journal: *The Journal of Social Psychology*, April 1991, *131*(2), 187–204.

Related Research: Spector, P. (1973). Relationships of organizational frustration with reported behavioral reactions of employees. *Journal of Applied Psychology*, *60*, 635–637.

5948

Test Name: JOB INDUCED TENSION SCALE

Purpose: To measure a person's perception of work-related pressures and frustrations.

Number of Items: 6

Reliability: Coefficient alpha was .84.

Validity: Correlations with other variables ranged from -.43 to .61.

Author: Macan, T. H.

Article: Time management: Test of a process model.

Journal: *Journal of Applied Psychology*, June 1994, *79*(3), 381–391.

Related Research: House, R. J., & Rizzo, J. R. (1972). Role conflict and ambiguity as critical variables in a model of organizational behavior. *Organization Behavior and Human Performance*, *7*, 467–505.

■ ■ ■

5949

Test Name: JOB INTERFERENCE SCALE

Purpose: To reveal the extent to which time demands from job activities interfere with each other.

Number of Items: 7

Format: Responses are made to each item on 5-point frequency response scales. All items are presented.

Reliability: Coefficient alpha was .87.

Validity: Correlations with other variables ranged from -.25 to .47.

Authors: O'Driscoll, M. P., et al.

Article: Time devoted to job and off-job activities, interrole conflict, and affective experiences.

Journal: *Journal of Applied*

Psychology, June 1992, *77*(3), 272–279.

• • •

5950

Test Name: JOB INVOLVEMENT SCALE

Purpose: To measure importance of work to a person's self-worth.

Number of Items: 6

Format: 4-point Likert format.

Reliability: Alpha was .73.

Authors: Parker, B., and Chusmir, L. H.

Article: Development and validation of a life success measures scale.

Journal: *Psychological Reports*, April 1992, *70*(2), 627–637.

Related Research: Lodahl, T. M., & Kejner, M. (1965). The definition of measurement of job involvement. *Journal of Applied Psychology*, *49*, 24–33.

• • •

5951

Test Name: JOB REWARDS SCALE

Purpose: To assess the perceived enjoyment and the importance of one's job.

Number of Items: 13

Format: All items presented.

Reliability: Alphas were .82 (enjoyment) and .68 (importance).

Author: Phelan, J.

Article: The paradox of the contented female worker: An assessment of alternative explanations.

Journal: *Social Psychology Quarterly*, June 1994, *57*(2), 95–107.

Related Research: House, J. S., et al. (1979). Occupational stress and health among factory workers. *Journal of Health and Social Behavior*, *20*, 139–160.

• • •

5952

Test Name: JOB SATISFACTION QUESTIONNAIRE

Purpose: To measure satisfaction with work.

Number of Items: 23

Format: 5-point Likert format. All items are presented.

Reliability: Alphas ranged from .75 to .84 across subscales.

Authors: Saad, I. A., and Isralowitz, R. E.

Article: Teachers' job satisfaction in transitional society within the Bedouin Arab schools of the Negev.

Journal: *The Journal of Social Psychology*, December 1992, *132*(6), 771–781.

Related Research: Wanous, J. B., & Lawler, E. G., III. (1972). Measurement and meaning of job satisfaction. *Journal of Applied Psychology*, *56*, 95–105.

• • •

5953

Test Name: JOB SATISFACTION QUESTIONNAIRE

Purpose: To measure attitudes toward job and employer.

Number of Items: 26

Format: Agreement scales. Sample items are presented.

Reliability: Alpha was .61.

Authors: Gul, F. A., et al.

Article: Locus of control, task difficulty, and their interaction with employees' attitudes.

Journal: *Psychological Reports*, October 1994, *75*(2), 971–978.

Related Research: Milani, K. R. (1975). The relationship of participation in budget-setting to industrial supervisor performance and attitudes: A field study. *The Accounting Review*, *50*, 274–284.

• • •

5954

Test Name: JOB SATISFACTION SCALE

Purpose: To measure job satisfaction.

Number of Items: 2

Format: Responses are made on a 7-point scale. Both items are presented.

Reliability: Alpha coefficients were .87 (6 months) and .89 (12 months).

Authors: Irving, P. G., and Meyer, J. P.

Article: Reexamination of the net-expectations hypothesis: A longitudinal analysis.

Journal: *Journal of Applied Psychology*, December 1994, *79*(6), 937–949.

Related Research: Meyer, J. P., & Allen, N. J. (1988). Links between work experiences and organizational commitment during the first year of employment: A longitudinal analysis. *Journal of Occupational Psychology*, *61*, 195–209.

• • •

5955

Test Name: JOB SATISFACTION SCALE

Purpose: To measure job satisfaction.

Number of Items: 3

Format: Responses were made on a 7-point scale ranging from 1 (*extremely dissatisfied*) to 7 (*extremely satisfied*). All items are presented.

Reliability: Alpha coefficients were .83 and .84. Test–retest reliability (4 weeks) was .79.

Validity: Correlations with other variables ranged from -.47 to .47. Test–retest (4 weeks) reliability was .79.

Authors: Oldham, G. R., et al.

Article: Listen while you work? Quasi-experimental relations between personal-stereo headset use and employee work responses.

Journal: *Journal of Applied Psychology*, October 1995, *80*(5), 547–564.

Related Research: Hackman, J. R., & Oldham, G. R. (1980). *Work redesign.* Reading, MA: Addison-Wesley.

• • •

5956

Test Name: JOB SATISFACTION SCALE

Purpose: To measure job satisfaction.

Number of Items: 4

Reliability: Coefficient alpha was .79.

Validity: Correlations with other variables ranged from -.62 to .68.

Authors: Nye, L. G., and Witt, L. A.

Article: Dimensionality and construct validity of the Perceptions of Organizational Politics Scale (POPS).

Journal: *Educational and Psychological Measurement*, Autumn 1993, *53*(3), 821–829.

Related Research: Hoppock, R. (1935). *Job satisfaction.* New York: Harper and Row.

5957

Test Name: JOB SATISFACTION SCALE

Purpose: To assess personal growth and general job satisfaction.

Number of Items: 4

Format: 5-point Likert format.

Reliability: Alpha was .73.

Validity: Correlations with other variables ranged from -.45 to .37.

Authors: Rush, M. C., et al.

Article: Psychological resiliency in the public sector: "Hardiness" and pressure for change.

Journal: *Journal of Vocational Behavior*, February 1995, *46*(1), 17–39.

Related Research: Hackman, J. R., & Oldham, G. R. (1975). Development of the job diagnostic survey. *Journal of Applied Psychology*, *60*, 151–170.

• • •

5958

Test Name: JOB SATISFACTION SCALE

Purpose: To measure overall job satisfaction.

Number of Items: 5

Format: Responses are made on a 4-point scale ranging from 1 (*not at all satisfied*) to 4 (*very satisfied*). An example ispresented.

Reliability: Alpha coefficients were .75 and .74.

Validity: Correlations with other variables ranged from -.09 to .51.

Authors: Judge, T. A., and Watanabe, S.

Article: Another look at the job satisfaction-life satisfaction relationship.

Journal: *Journal of Applied*

Psychology, December 1993, *78*(6), 939–948.

• • •

5959

Test Name: JOB SATISFACTION SCALE

Purpose: To measure job satisfaction.

Number of Items: 5

Format: Responses are made on a 5-point scale ranging from 1 (*very dissatisfied*) to 5 (*very satisfied*). An example is given.

Reliability: Alpha coefficients were .90 and .88.

Validity: Correlations with other variables ranged from -.44 to .44.

Authors: Bacharach, S., and Bamberger, P.

Article: Causal models of role stressor antecedents and consequences: The importance of occupational differences.

Journal: *Journal of Vocational Behavior*, August 1992, *41*(1), 13–34.

Related Research: Conley, S., et al. (1989). The school work environment and teacher career dissatisfaction. *Educational Administration Quarterly*, *25*, 58–81.

• • •

5960

Test Name: JOB SATISFACTION SCALE

Purpose: To measure job satisfaction.

Number of Items: 6

Format: 5-point scales.

Reliability: Composite reliability was .75.

Authors: Day, D. V., and Bedeian, A. G.

Article: Personality similarity and

work-related outcomes among African-American nursing personnel: A test of the supplementary model of person-environment congruence.

Journal: *Journal of Vocational Behavior*, February 1995, *46*(1), 55–70.

Related Research: Taylor, J. C., & Bowers, D. G. (1972). *Survey of organizations*. Ann Arbor: Institute for Social Research, University of Michigan.

● ● ●

5961

Test Name: JOB SATISFACTION SCALE

Purpose: To measure job satisfaction.

Number of Items: 9

Format: Responses are made on 6-point scale ranging from 1 (*very dissatisfied*) to 6 (*very satisfied*).

Reliability: Internal consistency was .74 (N = 11,633).

Validity: Correlations with other variables ranged from -.55 to .48 (N = 11,633).

Authors: Vancouver, J. B., et al.

Article: Multilevel analysis of organizational goal congruence.

Journal: *Journal of Applied Psychology*, October 1994, *79*(5), 666–679.

Related Research: Schmitt, N., & Ostroff, C. (1987). *Pilot study of measurement and model linkage issues for the comprehensive assessment of schools environments*. Reston, VA: National Association for Secondary School Principals.

● ● ●

5962

Test Name: JOB SATISFACTION SCALE

Purpose: To measure job satisfaction.

Number of Items: 10

Format: Items deal with job satisfaction, intrinsic work motivation, job involvement, and other job-related items. Used 5-point scales.

Reliability: Internal consistency was .89 and .92 (N's were 377 and 80, respectively). Interrater reliability was .81 and .78.

Validity: Correlations with other variables ranged from -.97 to .73.

Authors: Campion, M. A., and McClelland, C. L.

Article: Interdisciplinary examination of the costs and benefits of enlarged jobs: A job design quasi-experiment.

Journal: *Journal of Applied Psychology*, April 1991, *76*(2), 186–198.

● ● ●

5963

Test Name: JOB SATISFACTION SCALE

Purpose: To measure job satisfaction.

Number of Items: 12

Format: Responses are made on a 6-point satisfaction–dissatisfaction scale.

Reliability: Internal consistency was .85.

Validity: Correlations with other variables ranged from -.37 to .76.

Authors: O'Driscoll, M. P., et al.

Article: Time devoted to job and off-job activities, interrole conflict, and affective experiences.

Journal: *Journal of Applied Psychology*, June 1992, *77*(3), 272–279.

Related Research: Schnake, M.

(1983). An empirical assessment of the effects of affective response in the measurement of organizational climate. *Personnel Psychology*, *36*, 791–807.

● ● ●

5964

Test Name: JOB SATISFACTION SCALE

Purpose: To assess job satisfaction.

Number of Items: 15

Reliability: Alpha was .88.

Validity: Correlations with other variables ranged from -.01 to .64.

Authors: Mathieu, J. E., and Farr, J. L.

Article: Further evidence for the discriminant validity of measures of organizational commitment, job involvement, and job satisfaction.

Journal: *Journal of Applied Psychology*, February 1991, *76*(1), 127–133.

Related Research: Hackman, J. R., & Oldham, G. R. (1974). The Job Diagnostic Survey: An instrument for the diagnosis of jobs and the evaluation of job redesign projects. *JSAS Catalog of Selected Documents in Psychology*, *4*, 148 (MS. No. 810).

● ● ●

5965

Test Name: JOB SATISFACTION SCALE

Purpose: To measure job satisfaction.

Number of Items: 15

Format: Includes subscales: Extrinsic and Intrinsic Job Satisfaction. Responses are made on a 7-point scale.

Reliability: Alpha coefficients were .76 and .88.

Validity: Correlations with other variables ranged from .15 to .51.

Authors: Cordery, J. L., and Sevastos, P. P.

Article: Responses to the original and revised job diagnostic survey: Is education a factor in responses to negatively worded items?

Journal: *Journal of Applied Psychology*, February 1993, *78*(1), 141–143.

Related Research: Warr, P., et al. (1979). Scales for the measurement of some work attitudes and aspects of psychological well-being. *Journal of Occupational Psychology, 52,* 129–148.

● ● ●

5966

Test Name: JOB SATISFACTION SCALE

Purpose: To measure job satisfaction.

Number of Items: 15

Format: 5-point Likert format.

Reliability: Alpha was .85.

Author: Riipinen, M.

Article: Occupational needs as moderators between locus of control and job involvement.

Journal: *Psychological Reports,* April 1994, *74*(2), 371–379.

Related Research: Kanungo, R. N., et al. (1975). Relationship of job involvement to perceived importance as satisfaction of employee needs. *International Review of Applied Psychology, 24,* 49–59.

● ● ●

5967

Test Name: JOB SATISFACTION SCALE

Purpose: To measure job satisfaction.

Number of Items: 18

Format: Sample items are presented.

Reliability: Alpha was .89.

Authors: Randall, C. R., and Mueller, C. W.

Article: Extensions of justice theory: Justice evaluations and employees' reactions in a natural setting.

Journal: *Social Psychology Quarterly,* September 1995, *58*(3), 178–194.

Related Research: Brayfield, A. H., & Rothe, H. F. (1951). An index of job satisfaction. *Journal of Applied Psychology, 35,* 307–311.

● ● ●

5968

Test Name: JOB SATISFACTION SCALE

Purpose: To measure job satisfaction.

Number of Items: 21

Format: Responses regarding satisfaction are made on a 7-point scale.

Reliability: Coefficient alpha was .82.

Validity: Correlations with other variables ranged from .14 to .61.

Authors: Hesketh, B., et al.

Article: Work adjustment theory: An empirical test using a fuzzy rating scale.

Journal: *Journal of Vocational Behavior,* June 1992, *40*(3), 318–337.

Related Research: Caplan, R. D. (1987). Person-environment fit theory and organizations:

Commensurate dimensions, time perspectives, and mechanisms. *Journal of Vocational Behavior, 31,* 248–267.

● ● ●

5969

Test Name: JOB SATISFACTION SCALE—MODIFIED

Purpose: To measure students' satisfaction with their course and with their university life.

Number of Items: 4

Format: Responses are made on a 5-point Likert-type scale. An example is presented.

Reliability: Coefficient alpha was .69.

Validity: Correlations with other variables ranged from -.29 to .03.

Authors: Newton, T., and Keenan, T.

Article: Further analyses of the dispositional argument in organizational behavior.

Journal: *Journal of Applied Psychology,* December 1991, *76*(6), 781–787.

Related Research: Newton, T. J., & Keenan, A. (1983). Is work involvement an attitude of the person or the environment? *Journal of Occupational Behavior, 4,* 169–178.

● ● ●

5970

Test Name: JOB STRESS SCALE

Purpose: To measure job stress.

Number of Items: 16

Format: Responses were made on a 5-point scale ranging from 1 (*produces no stress*) to 5 (*produces a great deal of stress*).

Reliability: Reliability was .84.

Validity: Correlations with other variables ranged from -.29 to .44 (*N* = 1062).

Authors: Judge, T. A., et al.

Article: Job and life attitudes of male executives.

Journal: *Journal of Applied Psychology*, October 1994, *79*(5), 767–782.

Related Research: French, J. R. P., & Kahn, R. L. (1962). A programmatic approach to studying the industrial environment and mental health. *Journal of Social Issues, 18*, 1–47.

Matteson, M. T., & Ivancevich, J. M. (1987). *Controlling work stress.* San Francisco: Jossey-Bass.

Sandman, B. A. (1992). The measurement of job stress: Development of the Job Stress Index. In C. J. Cranny et al. (Eds.), *Job satisfaction: How workers feel about their jobs and how it affects their performance* (pp. 241–254). Lexington, MA: Lexington Books.

■ ■ ■

5971

Test Name: JOB TENSION AND STRESS SCALES

Purpose: To assess job-related stress.

Number of Items: 21

Format: Two 5-point response scales were used. Sample items are presented.

Reliability: Alphas ranged from .63 to .75 across subscales.

Authors: Rush, M. C., et al.

Article: Psychological resiliency in the public sector: "Hardiness" and pressure for change.

Journal: *Journal of Vocational Behavior*, February 1995, *46*(1), 17–39.

Related Research: Ivancevich, J. M., & Matteson, M. T. (1980). *Stress and work: A managerial*

perspective. Glenview, IL: Scott, Foresman.

Kahn, R., et al. (1964). *Organizational stress: Studies in role conflict and ambiguity.* New York: Wiley.

■ ■ ■

5972

Test Name: JOB TENSION SCALE

Purpose: To identify the extent to which factors related to drivers' jobs affect their health and well-being.

Number of Items: 7

Reliability: Alpha was .84.

Validity: Correlations with other variables ranged from -.31 to -.60.

Authors: Mathieu, J. E., and Farr, J. L.

Article: Further evidence for the discriminant validity of measures of organizational commitment, job involvement, and job satisfaction.

Journal: *Journal of Applied Psychology*, February 1991, *76*(1), 127–133.

Related Research: House, R. J., & Rizzo, J. R. (1972). Role conflict and role ambiguity as critical variables in a model of organizational behavior. *Organizational Behavior and Human Performance, 1*, 467–505.

■ ■ ■

5973

Test Name: JOB TENSION SCALE

Purpose: To measure job tension.

Number of Items: 9

Format: 5-point scales range from *never* to *nearly all the time.*

Reliability: Alpha was .86.

Authors: Day, D. V., and Bedeian, A. G.

Article: Personality similarity and work-related outcomes among African-American nursing personnel: A test of the supplementary model of person-environment congruence.

Journal: *Journal of Vocational Behavior*, February 1995, *46*(1), 55–70.

Related Research: Lyons, T. F. (1971). Role clarity, need for clarity, satisfaction, tension and withdrawal. *Organizational Behavior and Human Performance, 6*, 99–110.

■ ■ ■

5974

Test Name: JOB TENSION SCALE

Purpose: To measure level of job-related tension.

Number of Items: 9

Reliability: Coefficient alpha was .70.

Validity: Correlations with other variables ranged from -.48 to .18.

Authors: Lehman, W. E. K., and Simpson, D. D.

Article: Employee substance use and on-the-job behaviors.

Journal: *Journal of Applied Psychology*, June 1992, *77*(3), 309–321.

Related Research: Kahn, R. L., et al. (1964). *Organizational stress: Studies in role conflict and ambiguity.* New York: Wiley.

■ ■ ■

5975

Test Name: JOB WITHDRAWAL INTENTIONS SCALE

Purpose: To measure job withdrawal intentions.

Number of Items: 3

Format: Responses are made on a 5-point scale ranging from 1 (*very* *unlikely*) to 5 (*very likely*).

Reliability: Internal reliability coefficients ranged from .70 to .95. Test–retest reliability was .60.

Validity: Correlations with other variables ranged from -.29 to .39.

Authors: Aryee, S., and Tan, K.

Article: Antecedents and outcomes of career commitment.

Journal: *Journal of Vocational Behavior*, June 1992, *40*(3), 288–305.

Related Research: Blau, G. (1988). Further exploring the meaning and measurement of career commitment. *Journal of Vocational Behavior*, *32*, 284–297.

■ ■ ■

5976

Test Name: LEISURE–INCOME TRADEOFF SCALE

Purpose: To measure leisure-income tradeoff.

Number of Items: 3

Format: Responses are made on a 6-point scale ranging from 1 (*strongly disagree*) to 6 (*strongly agree*). All items are presented.

Reliability: Alpha coefficients were .73 and .75.

Validity: Correlations with other variables ranged from -.24 to .35.

Author: Blau, G.

Article: Developing and testing a taxonomy of lateness behavior.

Journal: *Journal of Applied Psychology*, December 1994, *79*(6), 959–970.

Related Research: Leigh, J., & Lust, J. (1988). Determinants of employee tardiness. *Work and Occupations*, *15*, 78–95.

Youngblood, S. (1984). Work, nonwork and withdrawal. *Journal of Applied Psychology*, *69*, 106–117.

5977

Test Name: MEASURE OF INGRATIATORY BEHAVIORS IN ORGANIZATIONAL SETTINGS.

Purpose: To measure the frequency with which ingratiatory tactics are used by subordinates in superior–subordinate relationship.

Number of Items: 24

Format: Responses are made on a 5-point Likert-type scale ranging from 1 (*never do it*) to 5 (*almost always do it*). All items are presented.

Reliability: Cronbach's alpha was .92 (*N* = 148). Split-half reliability was .86 (*N* = 148). Test–retest (1 month) reliability was .69 and .73 (*N* = 148).

Validity: Correlations with other variables ranged from .29 to .63.

Authors: Kumar, K., and Beyerlein, M.

Article: Construction and validation of an instrument for measuring ingratiatory behaviors in organizational settings.

Journal: *Journal of Applied Psychology*, October 1991, *75*(5), 619–627.

■ ■ ■

5978

Test Name: MEASURE OF JOB SATISFACTION

Purpose: To assess job satisfaction.

Number of Items: 15

Format: Includes both intrinsic and extrinsic job satisfaction.

Reliability: Alpha coefficients were .69 and .78.

Validity: Correlations with other variable ranged from -.20 to .25.

Authors: Kelloway, E. K., and Barling, J.

Article: Members' participation in local union activities: Measurement, prediction, and replication.

Journal: *Journal of Applied Psychology*, April 1993, *78*(2), 262–279.

Related Research: Warr, P. E., et al. (1979). Scales for the measurement of some work attitudes and aspects of psychological well-being. *Journal of Occupational Psychology*, *52*, 129–148.

■ ■ ■

5979

Test Name: MET EXPECTATIONS OF JOB SCALE

Purpose: To measure the extent to which participants' expectations of job had been met, including stress, hours required, salary, advancement, skill development, influence, status, supervision, colleagues, type of work conditions, and benefits.

Number of Items: 12

Format: 3-point response format ranges from *has not met my expectations* to *has extended my expectations*.

Reliability: Alpha was .72.

Validity: Correlations with other variables ranged from -.30 to .56.

Authors: Rosin, H., and Korabik, K.

Article: Organizational experiences and propensity to leave: A multivariate study of men and women managers.

Journal: *Journal of Vocational Behavior*, February 1995, *46*(1), 1–16.

Related Research: Lee, T. W., & Mowday, R. T. (1987). Voluntarily leaving an organization: An empirical investigation of Steers and

Mowday's model of turnover. *Academy of Management Journal*, *30*, 721–743.

• • •

5980

Test Name: MICHIGAN ORGANIZATIONAL ASSESSMENTS QUESTIONNAIRE—ADAPTED

Purpose: To identify teachers' intention to leave the school.

Number of Items: 3

Format: Response are made on a scale ranging from 0 (*strongly agree*) to 4 (*strongly disagree*).

Reliability: Coefficient alpha was .85.

Validity: Correlations with other variables ranged from -.03 to -.47.

Authors: Vancouver, J. B., et al.

Article: Multilevel analysis of organizational goal congruence.

Journal: *Journal of Applied Psychology*, August 1994, *79*(4), 666–679.

Related Research: Cammann, C., et al. (1979). *The Michigan Organizational Assessment Questionnaire*. Unpublished manuscript, University of Michigan, Ann Arbor.

• • •

5981

Test Name: MUSIC CONTROL SCALE

Purpose: To identify a person's control over the music listened to at work.

Number of Items: 2

Format: Responses are made on a 7-point scale ranging from 1 (*strongly disagree*) to 7 (*strongly agree*). Both items are presented.

Reliability: Alpha coefficients were .60 and .61. Test–retest (4 weeks) reliability was .26.

Validity: Correlation with other variables ranged from -.16 to .18.

Authors: Oldham, G. R., et al.

Article: Listen while you work? Quasi-experimental relations between personal-stereo-headset use and employee work response.

Journal: *Journal of Applied Psychology*, October 1995, *80*(5), 547–564.

• • •

5982

Test Name: NURSING STRESS SCALE

Purpose: To assess nursing stress.

Number of Items: 34

Format: 4-point Likert format ranges from 1 (*never*) to 4 (*very frequently*).

Reliability: Test–retest reliability (2 weeks) was .81. Alpha was .89.

Authors: Bowman, G. D., and Stern, M.

Article: Adjustment to occupational stress: The relationship of perceived control to effectiveness of coping strategies.

Journal: *Journal of Counseling Psychology*, July 1995, *42*(3), 294–303.

Related Research: Gray-Toft, P. A., & Anderson, J. G. (1981). The Nursing Stress Scale: Development of an instrument. *Journal of Behavioral Assessment*, *3*, 11–23.

• • •

5983

Test Name: OCCUPATIONAL CHOICE SATISFACTION SCALE

Purpose: To measure occupational choice satisfaction.

Number of Items: 3

Format: Two items are answered on 5-point scales. The third item is scored *2* for any response and *0* for no response. All items are presented.

Reliability: Reliability coefficients were .76 and .78.

Validity: Correlation with other variables ranged from -.46 to .57 (*N* = 120).

Authors: Meir, E. I., et al.

Article: The benefits of congruence.

Journal: *The Career Development Quarterly*, March 1995, *43*(3), 257–266.

Related Research: Meir, E. I., & Mclamed, S. (1986). The accumulation of person-environment congruences and well-being. *Journal of Occupational Behavior*, *7*, 315-323.

• • •

5984

Test Name: OCCUPATIONAL PLANS QUESTIONNAIRE

Purpose: To assess occupational fit.

Number of Items: 22

Format: Items deal with commitment to stated occupational choice; knowledge and experience relevant to the occupation; consistency of occupation with self-perceived abilities, values, and interests; anticipated potential in the occupation; alternative choices; and the significance of the occupational role in the respondent's life. Items are multiple choice.

Reliability: Internal consistencies were .83 and .68.

Validity: Correlations with other variables ranged from -.45 to .50.

Authors: Savickas, M. L., et al.

Article: Dimensions of career decidedness.

Journal: *Measurement and Evaluation in Counseling and Development*, October 1992, *25*(3), 102–112.

Related Research: Herchenson, D. (1967). Sense of identity, occupational fit and enculturation in adolescence. *Journal of Counseling Psychology, 14*, 319–324.

■ ■ ■

5985

Test Name: OCCUPATION STRESS SCALE

Purpose: To measure perceived occupational stress.

Number of Items: 15

Format: Includes 3 scales: Role Overload, Responsibility, and Role Insufficiency. Responses are made on a 5-point scale ranging from 1 (*not at all applicable*) to 5 (*highly applicable*). Sample items are presented.

Reliability: Alpha coefficients were .88 and .87.

Validity: Correlations with other variables ranged from -.35 to .62 (*N* = 435).

Authors: Matsui, T., and Onglatco, M.-L.

Article: Career self-efficacy as a moderator of the relations between occupational stress and strain.

Journal: *Journal of Vocational Behavior*, August 1992, *41*(1), 79–88.

■ ■ ■

5986

Test Name: OFF-JOB INTERFERENCE SCALE

Purpose: To reveal the extent to which time demands from off-job activities interfere with each other.

Number of Items: 7

Format: Responses are made on a 5-point frequency response scale.

All items are presented.

Reliability: Coefficient alpha was .79.

Validity: Correlations with other variables ranged from -.21 to .37.

Authors: O'Driscoll, M. P., et al.

Article: Time devoted to job and off-job activities, interrole conflict, and affective experiences.

Journal: *Journal of Applied Psychology*, June 1992, *77*(3), 272–279.

■ ■ ■

5987

Test Name: ORGANIZATIONAL SOCIALIZATION QUESTIONNAIRE

Purpose: To measure organizational socialization.

Number of Items: 34

Format: Includes six factors: Performance Proficiency, Politics, Language, People, Organizational Goals and Values, and History. All items are presented.

Reliability: Alpha coefficients ranged from .78 to .86 (*N* = 182).

Validity: Correlations with other variables ranged from -.09 to .48 (*N* = 182).

Authors: Chao, G. T., et al.

Article: Organizational socialization: Its content and consequences.

Journal: *Journal of Applied Psychology*, October 1994, *79*(5), 730–743.

■ ■ ■

5988

Test Name: ORGANIZATION SATISFACTION SCALE

Purpose: To determine organizational satisfaction.

Number of Items: 3

Format: Responses are made on a

7-point scale ranging from 1 (*extremely dissatisfied*) to 7 (*extremely satisfied*). An example is presented.

Reliability: Alpha coefficients were .83 and .85. Test–retest (4 weeks) reliability was .73.

Validity: Correlations with other variables ranged from -.57 to .47.

Authors: Oldham, G. R., et al.

Article: Listen while you work? Quasi-experimental relations between personal-stereo-headset use and employee work response.

Journal: *Journal of Applied Psychology*, October 1995, *80*(5), 547–564.

■ ■ ■

5989

Test Name: PAY COGNITIONS SCALE

Purpose: To measure how salespersons compared their pay to different sources of comparison.

Number of Items: 7

Format: Responses are made on a 9-point scale ranging from -4 (40% less) to 4 (40% more). They could also check *I don't know* or *There is no comparison*. A sample item is presented.

Reliability: Internal consistency was .86.

Validity: Correlations with other variables ranged form -.11 to .51.

Author: George, J. M.

Article: State or trait: Effects of positive mood on prosocial behaviors at work.

Journal: *Journal of Applied Psychology*, April 1991, *76*(2), 299–307.

Related Research: Scholl, R. W., et al. (1987). Referent selection in determining equity perception: Differential effects on behavioral and attitudinal outcomes.

Personnel Psychology, 40, 113–124.

• • •

5990

Test Name: PAY FREEZE HARDSHIP SCALE

Purpose: To assess the degree to which a pay freeze caused economic hardship.

Number of Items: 3

Format: Responses are made on 7-point scale ranging from 1 (*disagree strongly*) to 7 (*agree strongly*).

Reliability: Coefficient alpha was .92. Examples are presented.

Validity: Correlations with other variables ranged from -.27 to .23.

Authors: Schaubroeck, J., et al.

Article: Procedural justice explanations and employee reactions to economic hardship: A field experiment.

Journal: *Journal of Applied Psychology*, June 1994, *79*(3), 455–460.

• • •

5991

Test Name: PAY SATISFACTION QUESTIONNAIRE

Purpose: To measure multidimensional compensation satisfaction.

Number of Items: 18

Time Required: Approximately 3 to 5 minutes.

Format: Responses are made on a 5-point scale ranging from 1 (*very dissatisfied*) to 5 (*very satisfied*).

Validity: Correlations of the Benefits Satisfaction Subscale with the Attitudes Toward Benefits Scale ranged from -.18 to .77.

Authors: Hart, D. E., and Carraher, S. M.

Article: The development of an instrument to measure attitudes toward benefits.

Journal: *Educational and Psychological Measurement*, June 1995, *55*(3), 480–484.

Related Research: Heneman, H. G., III, & Schwab, D. P. (1985). Pay satisfaction: Its multidimensional nature and measurement. *International Journal of Psychology, 20,* 129–141.

• • •

5992

Test Name: PERCEIVED JOB CONTROL

Purpose: To measure job characteristics, job control, and burnout.

Number of Items: 13

Format: Responses are made on a 5-point Likert scale (1—*under my control*; 5—*not under my control*).

Reliability: Coefficient alpha was .79.

Authors: Glass, D., et al.

Article: Depression, burnout, and perceptions of control in hospital nurses.

Journal: *Journal of Consulting and Clinical Psychology*, February 1993, *61*(1), 147–155.

Related Research: McDermott, D. (1984). Professional burnout and its relation to job characteristics, satisfaction, and control. *Journal of Human Stress, 10,* 79–85.

• • •

5993

Test Name: PERCEIVED SOCIAL SUPPORT SCALE

Purpose: To assess perceptions of work-related social support.

Number of Items: 3

Format: Responses are made on a 0–3 scale.

Reliability: Alpha coefficients were .84 and .55.

Validity: Correlations with other variables ranged from -.07 to .33.

Authors: Parkes, K. R., et al.

Article: Social support and the demand-discretion model of job stress: Tests of additive and interactive effects in two samples.

Journal: *Journal of Vocational Behavior*, February 1994, *44*(1), 91–113.

Related Research: House, J. S. (1981). *Work stress and social support*. Reading, MA: Addison-Wesley.

• • •

5994

Test Name: PERCEIVED WORKLOAD INDEX

Purpose: To measure perceived workload.

Number of Items: 7

Reliability: Coefficient alpha was .81.

Validity: Correlations with other variables ranged from -.12 to .56.

Authors: Jex, S. M., et al.

Article: The meaning of occupational stress items to survey respondents.

Journal: *Journal of Applied Psychology*, October 1992, *77*(5), 623–628.

Related Research: Spector, P. E., et al. (1988). Relations of job stressors to affective, health, and performance outcomes: A comparison of multiple data sources. *Journal of Applied Psychology, 73,* 11–19.

5995

Test Name: PERFORMANCE APPRAISAL DISCOMFORT SCALE

Purpose: To identify the degree of rater discomfort felt when in performance appraisal situations.

Number of Items: 20

Format: Responses are made on a 5-point scale ranging from 1 (*no discomfort*) to 5 (*high discomfort*). Includes 4 factors: Provision of Negative Feedback, Solicitation of Feedback, Encourage Performance Monitoring, and Justify/Defend ratings. All items are presented.

Reliability: Coefficient alphas ranged from .84 to .91.

Validity: Correlations with other variables ranged from .33 to .49.

Authors: Villanova, P., et al.

Article: Rater leniency and performance appraisal discomfort.

Journal: *Educational and Psychological Measurement*, Autumn 1993, *53*(3), 789–799.

Related Research: Bernardin, H. J. (1989). Innovative approaches to personnel selection and performance appraisal. *Journal of Management Systems*, *1*, 25–36.

■■■

5996

Test Name: PHYSICAL IMPAIRMENT SCALE

Purpose: To assess physical impairment in regard to employment.

Number of Items: 7

Format: 3-point difficulty scales. All items are presented.

Reliability: Alpha was .80.

Author: Mirowsky, J.

Article: Age and sense of control.

Journal: *Social Psychology*

Quarterly, March 1995, *58*(1), 31–43.

Related Research: Johnson, R. J., & Wolinsky, F. D. (1993). The structure of health status among older adults: Disease, disability, functional limitation, and perceived health. *Journal of Health and Social Behavior*, *34*, 105–121.

■■■

5997

Test Name: PHYSICIANS REACTIONS TO UNCERTAINTY SCALES

Purpose: To assess stress from uncertainty and reluctance to disclose uncertainty.

Number of Items: 24

Format: 6-point Likert format. All items are presented.

Reliability: Alphas ranged from .75 to .90 across subscales.

Authors: Gerrity, M. S., et al.

Article: Uncertainty and professional work: Perceptions of physicians in clinical practice.

Journal: *American Journal of Sociology*, January 1992, *97*(4), 1022–1051.

Related Research: Gerrity, M. S., et al. (1990). Physicians' reactions to uncertainty in patient care: A new measure and new insights. *Medical Care*, *28*, 724–736.

■■■

5998

Test Name: POLICY DECISION MAKING SCALE

Purpose: To measure the degree to which one participates in policy decision making.

Number of Items: 4

Format: Responses are made on a 4-point scale ranging from 1 (*seldom*) to 4 (*never*).

Reliability: Alpha coefficients were .72 and .61.

Validity: Correlations with other variables ranged from -.20 to .27.

Authors: Bacharach, S., and Bamberger, P.

Article: Causal models of role stressor antecedents and consequences: The importance of occupational differences.

Journal: *Journal of Vocational Behavior*, August 1992, *41*(1), 13–34.

Related Research: Bacharach, S., et al. (1990). Organizational and demographic models of teacher militancy. *Industrial and Labor Relations Review*, *43*, 570–586.

■■■

5999

Test Name: POWER MEASURE

Purpose: To measure the ability to control the job situation.

Number of Items: 6

Reliability: Coefficient alpha was .77.

Validity: Correlations with other variables ranged from -.31 to .42.

Authors: Lehman, W. E. K., and Simpson, D. D.

Article: Employee substance use and on-the-job behaviors.

Journal: *Journal of Applied Psychology*, June 1992, *77*(3), 309–321.

Related Research: Shepard, J. M. (1972). Alienation as a process: Work as a case in point. *The Sociological Quarterly*, *13*, 161–173.

■■■

6000

Test Name: PROFESSIONALISM SCALE

Purpose: To assess structural and

attitudinal aspects of the profession.

Number of Items: 17

Format: 5-point rating scale. All items presented.

Reliability: Subscale alphas ranged from .58 to .66.

Validity: Correlations with other variables ranged from -.02 to .30.

Authors: Kennedy, K. N., and Ramsey, R.

Article: Psychometric evaluation of the Hall Professionalism Scale.

Journal: *Psychological Reports*, August 1995, *77*(1), 331–338.

Related Research: Hall, R. H. (1968). Professionalization and bureaucratization. *American Sociological Review, 33,* 92–104.

■ ■ ■

6001

Test Name: PROFESSIONAL ORIENTATION SCALE

Purpose: To measure professional orientation

Number of Items: 9

Format: Likert-type items. Samples are presented.

Reliability: Reliability coefficients were .54 and .72.

Validity: Correlations with other variables ranged from .09 to .41.

Authors: DiPaola, M. F., and Hoy, W. K.

Article: Teacher militancy: A professional check on bureaucracy.

Journal: *Journal of Research and Development in Education*, Winter 1994, *27*(2), 83–88.

Related Research: Kuhlman, E., & Hoy, W. K. (1972). The socialization of professionals into bureaucracies. *Journal of Educational Administration, 8,* 18–27.

6002

Test Name: PROPENSITY TO LEAVE INDEX

Purpose: To measure and rate a job.

Number of Items: 3

Format: 5-point Likert format.

Reliability: Alphas ranged from .78 to .87.

Authors: Parker, B., and Chusmir, L. H.

Article: Development and validation of a Life Success Measures Scale.

Journal: *Psychological Reports*, April 1992, *70*(2), 627–637.

Related Research: Lyons, T. F. (1971). Role clarity, need for clarity, satisfaction, tensions and withdrawal. *Organizational Behavior and Human Performance, 6,* 99–110.

■ ■ ■

6003

Test Name: PROPENSITY TO STAY SCALE

Purpose: To assess likelihood of staying in a job.

Number of Items: 3

Format: 5-point Likert format.

Reliability: Alphas ranged from .78 to .87.

Authors: Chusmir, L. H., and Parker, B.

Article: Success strivings and their relationship to affective work behaviors: Gender differences.

Journal: *The Journal of Social Psychology*, February 1992, *132*(1), 87–99.

Related Research: Lyons, T. F. (1971). Role clarity, need for clarity, satisfaction, tension and withdrawal. *Organizational Behavior and Human Performance, 6,* 99–110.

6004

Test Name: PSYCHOLOGICAL STRAIN

Purpose: To measure work-related psychological strain.

Number of Items: 33

Format: Includes job dissatisfaction, work-load dissatisfaction, boredom, depression, anxiety, initiation, and somatic complaints. Responses are made on 3- to 5-point response scales. Sample items are presented.

Reliability: Alpha coefficients ranged from .75 to .86.

Validity: Correlations with other variables ranged from -.51 to .33.

Authors: Edwards, J. R., and Harrison, R. V.

Article: Job demands and worker health: Three-dimensional reexamination of the relationship between person-environment fit and strain.

Journal: *Journal of Applied Psychology*, August 1993, *78*(4), 628–648.

■ ■ ■

6005

Test Name: QUANTITATIVE ROLE OVERLOAD SCALE

Purpose: To measure conflict of organizational demands and allocated time.

Number of Items: 3

Format: Responses are made on a 4-point scale ranging from 1 (*false*) to 4 (*definitely true*). An example is presented.

Reliability: Alpha coefficients were .68 and .60.

Validity: Correlations with other variables ranged from -.33 to .46.

Authors: Bacharach, S., and Bamberger, P.

Article: Causal models of role stressor antecedents and consequences: The importance of occupational differences.

Journal: *Journal of Vocational Behavior*, August 1992, *41*(1), 13–34.

Related Research: Bacharach, S., et al. (1990). Organizational and demographic models of teacher militancy. *Industrial and Labor Relations Review*, *43*, 570–586.

■■■

6006

Test Name: REACTIONS TO INTERRACIAL SITUATIONS AT WORK QUESTIONNAIRE

Purpose: To measure aspects of interracial situations on the job.

Number of Items: 41

Format: 7-point Likert format. All items are presented.

Reliability: Alphas ranged from .57 to .87 across subscales.

Authors: Block, C. J., et al.

Article: White racial identity theory: A framework for understanding reactions toward interracial situations in organizations.

Journal: *Journal of Vocational Behavior*, February 1995, *46*(1), 71–88.

Related Research: McConahay, J. B. (1982). Self interest versus racial attitudes as correlates as anti-bussing attitudes in Louisville: Is it the busses or the Blacks? *Journal of Politics*, *44*, 692–720.

■■■

6007

Test Name: REALISTIC JOB PREVIEW SCALE

Purpose: To measure realistic job preview.

Number of Items: 4

Format: Responses are made on a 5-point scale ranging from 1 (*very inaccurate*) to 5 (*very accurate*). An example is presented.

Reliability: Alpha coefficients were .87 and .83.

Validity: Correlations with other variables ranged from -.38 to .44.

Authors: Bacharach, S., and Bamberger, P.

Article: Causal models of role stressor antecedents and consequences: The importance of occupational differences.

Journal: *Journal of Vocational Behavior*, August 1992, *41*(1), 13–34.

Related Research: Bacharach, S., et al. (1990). Organizational and demographic models of teacher militancy. *Industrial and Labor Relations Review*, *43*, 570–586.

■■■

6008

Test Name: REASONS FOR LEAVING SCALE

Purpose: To assess reasons for leaving a job.

Number of Items: 17

Format: 3-point scales range from *not at all a factor* to *definitely a factor*.

Reliability: Alphas ranged from .71 to .82 across subscales.

Validity: Correlations with other variables ranged from -.39 to .36.

Authors: Rosin, H., and Korabik, K.

Article: Organizational experiences and propensity to leave: A multivariate study of men and women managers.

Journal: *Journal of Vocational Behavior*, February 1995, *46*(1), 1–16.

6009

Test Name: REFORMIST DISSENT SCALE

Purpose: To identify reformist dissent among nurses.

Number of Items: 27 plus filler items.

Format: Responses are made on a scale ranging from 0 (*definitely would not do*) to 10 (*definitely would do*).

Reliability: Coefficient alpha was .92.

Validity: Correlation with other variables ranged from .02 to .37.

Author: Parker, L. E.

Article: When to fix it and when to leave: Relationship among perceived control, self-efficacy, dissent, and exit.

Journal: *Journal of Applied Psychology*, December 1993, *78*(6), 949–959.

■■■

6010

Test Name: RELATIVE DEPRIVATION SCALE

Purpose: To assess relative deprivation.

Number of Items: 8

Format: Responses are made on a 7-point Likert scale. All items are presented.

Reliability: Coefficient alpha was .89.

Validity: Correlations with other variables ranged from .11 to .70.

Authors: Buunk, B. P., and Janssen, P. P. M.

Article: Relative deprivation, career issues, and mental health among men in midlife.

Journal: *Journal of Vocational Behavior*, June 1992, *40*(3), 338–350.

Related Research: Crosby, F. (1984). Relative deprivation in organizational settings. *Research in Organizational Behavior, 6,* 51–93.

■ ■ ■

6011

Test Name: REWARD-SPECIFIC JOB SATISFACTION

Purpose: To assess rewards from self-actualization, security, friendship opportunities, altruism opportunities, and status.

Number of Items: 9

Format: 7-point Likert format. All items are presented.

Reliability: Alphas ranged from .64 to .84.

Authors: Randall, C. R., and Mueller, C. W.

Article: Extensions of justice theory: Justice evaluations and employees' reactions in a natural setting.

Journal: *Social Psychology Quarterly,* September 1995, *58*(3), 178–194.

Related Research: Mueller, C. W., & McCloskey, J. (1990). Nurses' job satisfaction: A proposed measure. *Nursing Research, 39,* 113–117.

■ ■ ■

6012

Test Name: ROLE STRAIN SCALE

Purpose: To assess role strain.

Number of Items: 12

Format: Includes both role conflict and role ambiguity.

Reliability: Coefficient alpha was .85.

Validity: Correlations with other variables ranged from -.39 to -.77.

Authors: Mathieu, J. E., and Farr, J. L.

Article: Further evidence for the discriminant validity of measures of organizational commitment, job involvement, and job satisfaction.

Journal: *Journal of Applied Psychology,* February 1991, *76*(1), 127–133.

Related Research: House, R. J., et al. (1983). Role conflict and role ambiguity scales: Reality or artifacts? *Journal of Applied Psychology, 68,* 334–337.

■ ■ ■

6013

Test Name: ROSEN JOB ENVIRONMENT QUESTIONNAIRE

Purpose: To measure self-perception of relationships with peers, superiors, and departments.

Number of Items: 5

Format: Responses are made on a 7-point scale ranging from 1 (*never can think of instances*) to 7 (*always, cannot think of any instance when this was not the case*).

Reliability: Reliability was .90.

Author: Fagenson, E. A.

Article: Perceptions of proteges' vs. nonproteges' relationships with their peers, superiors, and departments.

Journal: *Journal of Vocational Behavior,* August 1994, *45*(1), 55–78.

Related Research: Rosen, H. (1961). Desirable attributes of work: Four levels of management describe their job environments. *Journal of Applied Psychology, 45,* 156–160.

■ ■ ■

6014

Test Name: SALESPERSON TRUST OF SALE MANAGER SCALE

Purpose: To measure trust in sales manager.

Number of Items: 4

Format: Likert format. All items presented.

Reliability: Alpha was .83.

Authors: Strutton, D., et al.

Article: Relationship between psychological climate and trust between salespersons and their sales managers in sales organizations.

Journal: *Psychological Reports,* June 1993, *72*(3) Part I, 931–939.

Related Research: Lagace, R. R. (1991). An exploratory study of reciprocal trust between sale managers and salespersons. *Journal of Personal Selling and Sales Management, 11,* 49–58.

■ ■ ■

6015

Test Name: SATISFACTION WITH MY SUPERVISOR SCALE

Purpose: To measure one's satisfaction with one's supervisor.

Number of Items: 18

Format: Responses are made on a 5-point scale ranging from 1 (*very dissatisfied*) to 5 (*very satisfied*).

Reliability: Internal consistency coefficients were .95. Stability coefficient was .78.

Authors: Vandenberg, R. J., and Scarpello, V.

Article: Multitrait-multimethod validation of the Satisfaction with My Supervisor Scale.

Journal: *Educational and Psychological Measurement,* Spring 1992, *52*(1), 203–212.

Related Research: Scarpello, V., & Vandenberg, R. J. (1987). The satisfaction with my supervisor scale: Its utility for research and practical applications. *Journal of Management, 13,* 447–466.

6016

Test Name: SCHOOL PARTICIPANT EMPOWERMENT SCALE

Purpose: To measure school participant empowerment.

Number of Items: 38

Format: Includes 6 subscales: Decision Making, Professional Growth, Status Self-Efficacy, Autonomy, and Impact. Responses are made on a 5-point Likert-type scale. All items are presented.

Reliability: Alpha coefficients ranged from .81 to .94.

Authord: Short, P. M., and Rinehart, J. S.

Article: School Participant Empowerment Scale: Assessment of level of empowerment within the school environment.

Journal: *Educational and Psychological Measurement*, Winter 1992, *52*(4), 951–960.

Related Research: Dunst, R. (1991, February). *Issues in empowerment*. Presentation before the annual meeting of children's Mental Health and Service Policy Convention, Tampa, Florida.

■ ■ ■

6017

Test Name: SITUATIONAL CONSTRAINTS SCALE

Purpose: To measure the extent situational constraints are perceived in the work environment.

Number of Items: 11

Format: Responses are made on a 5-point scale ranging from *less than once per month or never* to *several times per day*.

Reliability: Internal consistency was .84.

Validity: Correlations with other variables ranged from .42 to .56.

Authors: Chen, P. Y., and Spector, P. E.

Article: Negative affectivity as the underlying cause of correlations between stressors and strains.

Journal: *Journal of Applied Psychology*, June 1991, *76*(3), 398–407.

Related Research: Spector, P. E., et al. (1988). Relation of job stressors to affective, health, and performance outcomes: A comparison of multiple data sources. *Journal of Applied Psychology, 71*, 11–19.

■ ■ ■

6018

Test Name: SKILLS AND ABILITIES CONFIDENCE SCALE

Purpose: To assess respondent's confidence in their abilities and skills.

Number of Items: 13

Format: Responses are made on a 5-point scale ranging from 1 (*strongly disagree*) to 5 (*strongly agree*). A sample item is presented.

Reliability: Internal consistency was .81.

Authors: Noe, R. A., and Wilk, S. L.

Article: Investigation of the factors that influence employees' participation in development activities.

Journal: *Journal of Applied Psychology*, April 1993, *78*(2), 291–302.

Related Research: Pond, S. B., & Hay, M. S. (1989). The impact of task preview information as a function of recipient self-efficacy. *Journal of Vocational Behavior, 35*, 17–19.

6019

Test Name: SKILL UTILIZATION INVENTORY

Purpose: To measure the use of occupational skills.

Number of Items: 4

Format: 5-point scales. A sample item is presented.

Reliability: Reliabilities ranged from .77 to .78.

Validity: Correlations with other variables ranged from -.45 to .50.

Authors: Meir, E. I., et al.

Article: The benefits of congruence.

Journal: *The Career Development Quarterly*, March 1995, *43*(3), 257-266.

Related Research: Caplan, R. D., et al. (1975). *Job demands and worker health: Main effects and occupational differences* (HEW Publication No. NIOSH 75-160). Washington, DC: National Institute for Occupational Safety and Health.

■ ■ ■

6020

Test Name: STAGES OF CONCERN QUESTIONNAIRES

Purpose: To assess concerns about an innovation (change) in work.

Number of Items: 35 (15)

Format: 7-point scales range from 1 (*not true of me now*) to 7 (*very true of me now*).

Reliability: Internal consistency reliabilities ranged from .50 to .83 across subscales and long and short versions.

Authors: Bailey, D. B., Jr., and Palsha, S. A.

Article: Qualities of the Stages of Concern Questionnaire and implications for educational innovations.

Journal: *Journal of Educational Research*, March/April 1992, *85*(4), 226–232.

Related Research: Hall, G. E., et al. (1986). *Measuring stages of concern about an innovation: A manual for the use of the SoC Questionnaire*. Austin, TX: Southwest Educational Development Laboratory.

● ● ●

6021

Test Name: SUBJECTIVE CAREER SUCCESS

Purpose: To measure how successful one feels in one's career.

Number of Items: 11

Format: Responses are made on a 5-point Likert scale ranging from 1 (*strongly disagree*) to 5 (*strongly agree*). A sample item is presented.

Reliability: Reliability estimates ranged from .65 to .79.

Validity: Correlations with other variables ranged from -.33 to .54.

Author: Peluchette, J. V. E.

Article: Subjective career success: The influence of individual difference, family, and organizational variables.

Journal: *Journal of Vocational Behavior*, October 1993, *43*(2), 198–208.

Related Research: Gattiker, U., & Larwood, L. (1986). Subjective career success: A study of managers and support personnel. *Journal of Business and Psychology*, *1*, 78–94.

● ● ●

6022

Test Name: SUBJECTIVE UNDEREMPLOYMENT SCALE

Purpose: To assess the extent to

which respondents believe they are overqualified for their jobs.

Number of Items: 4

Format: Yes–no format. All items are presented.

Reliability: Alpha was .75.

Authors: Jones-Johnson, G., and Johnson, W. R.

Article: Subjective underemployment and psychosocial stress: The role of perceived social and supervisor support.

Journal: *The Journal of Social Psychology*, February 1992, *132*(1), 11–21.

Related Research: Schockey, J. W. (1985). *The utilization of labor: Composition and consequences of underemployment in the United States*. Unpublished doctoral dissertation, Pennsylvania State University.

● ● ●

6023

Test Name: SUBORDINATE-SUPERVISOR TRUST

Purpose: To assess subordinate-supervisor trust.

Number of Items: 3

Format: Responses are made on a 7-point scale ranging from 1 (*disagree strongly*) to 7 (*agree strongly*). All items are presented.

Reliability: Coefficient alpha was .90.

Validity: Correlations with other variables ranged from -.08 to .61.

Authors: Fried, Y., et al.

Article: Personal and interpersonal predictors of supervisors' avoidance of evaluating subordinates.

Journal: *Journal of Applied Psychology*, August 1992, *77*(4), 462–468.

6024

Test Name: SUPERVISOR SUPPORT SCALE

Purpose: To assess supervisor support.

Number of Items: 9

Format: 5-point agreement format. All items are presented.

Reliability: Alphas ranged from .91 to .93.

Authors: Jones-Johnson, G., and Johnson, W. R.

Article: Subjective underemployment and psychosocial stress: The role of perceived social and supervisor support.

Journal: *The Journal of Social Psychology*, February 1992, *132*(1), 11–21.

Related Research: Papper, E. (1983). *Individual and organizational effects of perceived work load*. Unpublished doctoral dissertation, Bowling Green State University.

● ● ●

6025

Test Name: TASK DIFFICULTY QUESTIONNAIRE

Purpose: To measure task difficulty.

Number of Items: 7

Format: 5-point rating scales.

Reliability: Alpha was .64.

Authors: Gul, F. A., et al.

Article: Locus of control, task difficulty, and their interaction with employees' attitudes.

Journal: *Psychological Reports*, October 1994, *75*(2), 971–978.

Related Research: Van de Van, A., & Delbecg, A. L. (1974). A task contingent model of work-unit structure. *Administrative Science Quarterly*, *19*, 183–197.

6026

Test Name: TEACHER EFFICACY AND CONTROL SCALES

Purpose: To assess how much teachers look forward to work and how much control they have at work.

Number of Items: 9

Format: Formats vary. All items are presented.

Reliability: Alpha was .73 (efficacy) and .74 (control).

Authors: Lee, V. E., et al.

Article: The effect of the social organization of schools on teachers' efficacy and satisfaction.

Journal: *Sociology of Education*, July 1991, *64*(3), 190–208.

Related Research: Moles, O. (1988). *High School and Beyond Administrator and Teacher Survey (1984). Data file users manual.* Washington, DC: Office of Educational Research and Improvement, U.S. Department of Education.

■ ■ ■

6027

Test Name: TRAINEE PERSONAL REACTION SCALE—REVISED

Purpose: To provide a measure of the trainee's reactions to the supervision process, to the trainee's performance in supervision, and to the behavior of the supervisor.

Number of Items: 12

Format: Items are rated on a 5-point Likert scale ranging from 1 (*highly characteristic*) to 5 (*not characteristic at all*). Sample items are presented.

Reliability: Internal consistency reliability estimates ranged from .71 to .89.

Authors: Olk, M. E., and Friedlander, M. L.

Article: Trainees' Experiences of role conflict and role ambiguity in supervisory relationships.

Journal: *Journal of Counseling Psychology*, July 1992, *39*(3), 389–397.

Related Research: Holloway, E. L., & Wampold, B. E. (1984, August). *Dimensions of satisfaction.* Paper presented at the annual meeting of the American Psychological Association, Toronto, Canada.

■ ■ ■

6028

Test Name: TRANSPORTATION CONCERNS SCALE

Purpose: To measure transportation concerns.

Number of Items: 3

Format: Response scales vary. One scale is answered in miles; one is described in minutes; and a third is answered in ease/difficulty in getting to work. All items are presented.

Reliability: Alpha coefficients were .70 and .69.

Validity: Correlations with other variables ranged from -.07 to .25.

Author: Blau, G.

Article: Developing and testing a taxonomy of lateness behavior.

Journal: *Journal of Applied Psychology*, December 1994, *79*(6), 959–970.

Related Research: Farrell, D., & Robb, D. (1980, August). *Lateness to work: A study of withdrawal from work.* Paper presented at the meeting of the National Academy of Management, Detroit, Michigan.

Gupta, N., & Jenkins, G. (1983). Tardiness as a manifestation of employee withdrawal. *Journal of Business Research, 11*, 61–75.

■ ■ ■

6029

Test Name: TRUST IN MANAGEMENT SCALE.

Purpose: To assess employee trust in management.

Number of Items: 4

Format: Responses are made on a 7-point scale ranging from 1 (*strongly disagree*) to 7 (*strongly agree*). Sample items are presented.

Reliability: Internal consistency was .86.

Validity: Correlations with other variables ranged from .08 to .68.

Authors: Konovsky, M. A., and Cropanzano, R.

Article: Perceived Fairness of Employee Drug Testing as a Predictor of Employee Attitudes and Job Performance.

Journal: *Journal of Applied Psychology*, October 1991, *76*(5), 698–707.

Related Research: Tyler, T. R. (1989). The psychology of procedural justice: A test of the group-value model. *Journal of Personality and Social Psychology, 57*, 830–838.

■ ■ ■

6030

Test Name: TURNOVER INTENTION INDEX

Purpose: To assess turnover intention.

Number of Items: 2

Format: Responses are made on a 7-point scale ranging from 1 (*disagree strongly*) to 7 (*agree strongly*). Both items are presented.

Reliability: Coefficient alpha was .77.

Validity: Correlations with other variables ranged from -.56 to .23.

Authors: Schaubroeck, J., et al.

Article: Procedural justice explanations and employee reactions to economic hardship: A field experiment.

Journal: *Journal of Applied Psychology*, June 1994, *79*(3), 455–460.

Related Research: Colarelli, S. M. (1984). Methods of communication and mediating processes in realistic job previews. *Journal of Applied Psychology, 69*, 633–642.

∎ ∎ ∎

6031

Test Name: TURNOVER INTENTION SCALE

Purpose: To measure the likelihood of changing jobs.

Number of Items: 3

Format: 4-point Likert format. All items presented.

Reliability: Alpha was .84.

Authors: Pierce, L. G., and Gayer, P. D.

Article: Combining intention with investment to predict withdrawal behavior.

Journal: *The Journal of Social Psychology*, February 1991, *131*(1), 117–124.

Related Research: Lyons, T. F. (1971). Role clarity, need for clarity, satisfaction, tension, and withdrawal. *Organizational Behavior and Human Performance, 6*, 99–110.

∎ ∎ ∎

6032

Test Name: TURNOVER INTENTIONS MEASURE

Purpose: To measure turnover intentions.

Number of Items: 3

Format: Responses are made on a 5-point scale ranging from 1 (*strongly disagree*) to 5 (*strongly agree*). An example is presented.

Reliability: Reliability estimate was .90.

Authors: Major, D. A., et al.

Article: A longitudinal investigation of newcomer expectations, early socialization outcomes, and the moderating effects of role development factors.

Journal: *Journal of Applied Psychology*, June 1995, *80*(3), 418–431.

Related Research: Ostroff, C., & Kozlowski, S. W. J. (1992). Organizational socialization as a learning process: The role of information acquisition. *Personnel Psychology, 45*, 849–847.

∎ ∎ ∎

6033

Test Name: TURNOVER INTENTIONS SCALE

Purpose: To measure turnover intentions.

Number of Items: 3

Reliability: Coefficients alpha was .87.

Validity: Correlations with other variables ranged from -.55 to .44.

Authors: Jex, S. M., et al.

Article: The measuring of occupational stress items to survey respondents.

Journal: *Journal of Applied Psychology*, October 1992, *77*(5), 623–628.

Related Research: Beehr, T. A., & O'Driscoll, M. P. (1990, May). *Employee uncertainty as a factor in occupational stress.* Paper

presented at the 62nd Annual Meeting of the Midwestern Psychological Association, Chicago.

∎ ∎ ∎

6034

Test Name: TURNOVER INTENTIONS SCALE

Purpose: To identify turnover intentions.

Number of Items: 3

Format: Responses are made on a 7-point scale ranging from 1 (*strongly disagree*) to 7 (*strongly agree*). All items are presented.

Reliability: Alpha coefficients were .76 and .80. Test–retest (4 weeks) reliability was .77.

Validity: Correlations with other variables ranged from -.56 to .16.

Authors: Oldham, G. R., et al.

Article: Listen while you work? Quasi-experimental relations between personal-stereo headset use and employee work responses.

Journal: *Journal of Applied Psychology*, October 1995, *80*(5), 547–564.

Related Research: Colarelli, S. M. (1984). Methods of communication and mediating processes in realistic job previews. *Journal of Applied Psychology, 69*, 633–642.

∎ ∎ ∎

6035

Test Name: TURNOVER INTENTIONS SCALE

Purpose: To assess intentions to quit.

Number of Items: 3

Format: 7-point scales were used to respond. All items are presented.

Reliability: Internal consistency was .84.

Validity: Correlations with other

variables ranged from -.00 to .49.

Authors: Konovsky, M. A., and Cropanzano, R.

Article: Perceived fairness of employee drug testing as a predictor of employee attitudes and job performance.

Journal: *Journal of Applied Psychology*, October 1991, *76*(5), 698–707.

Related Research: Shore, L. M., et al. (1990). Job and organizational attitudes in relation to behavioral intentions. *Journal of Organizational Behavior, 11*, 57–67.

■■■

6036

Test Name: UNION SATISFACTION SCALES

Purpose: To measure satisfaction with national union, expectations and performance, union strength, quality of leadership, need for structural change, and labor relations climate.

Number of Items: 50

Format: Varied formats, but mostly 4- and 5-point rating scales.

Reliability: Alphas ranged from .51 to .71 across subscales.

Authors: Heshizer, B. P., and Martin, H. J.

Article: Correlates of local union officers' satisfaction.

Journal: *Psychological Reports*, April 1992, *70*(2), 459–465.

Related Research: Quinn, R. P., & Stains, G. (1978). *The 1977 quality of employment survey.* Ann Arbor: Institute for Social Research, University of Michigan.

■■■

6037

Test Name: WAYS OF COPING CHECKLIST—MODIFIED

Purpose: To assess occupational coping.

Number of Items: 42

Format: 4-point Likert scales range from 1 (*not at all*) to 4 (*used a great deal*).

Reliability: Alphas ranged from .77 to .85.

Authors: Bowman, G. D., and Stern, M.

Article: Adjustment to occupational stress: The relationship of perceived control to effectiveness of coping strategies.

Journal: *Journal of Counseling Psychology*, July 1995, *42*(3), 294–303.

Related Research: Long, B. C., et al. (1992). Causal model of stress and coping: Women in management. *Journal of Counseling Psychology, 39*, 227–239.

■■■

6038

Test Name: WITHDRAWAL INTENTIONS SCALE

Purpose: To measure intention to quit a job.

Number of Items: 4

Format: 5-point Likert format.

Reliability: Alpha was .66.

Validity: Correlations with other variables ranged from -.60 to .34.

Authors: Rush, M. C., et al.

Article: Psychological resiliency in the public sector: "Hardiness" and pressure for change.

Journal: *Journal of Vocational Behavior*, February 1995, *46*(1), 17–39.

Related Research: Mobley, W. H. (1977). Intermediate linkages in the relationship between job satisfaction and employee

turnover. *Journal of Applied Psychology, 62*, 237–240.

■■■

6039

Test Name: WORK ADDICTION RISK TEST

Purpose: To measure addictive working patterns.

Number of Items: 25

Format: Responses are made on a 5-point Likert scale ranging from *strongly agree* to *strongly disagree*.

Reliability: Test–retest reliability was .83. Coefficient alpha was .85.

Authors: Robinson, B. E., and Post, P.

Article: Validity of the work addiction risk test.

Journal: *Perceptual and Motor Skills*, February 1994, *78*(1), 337–338.

Related Research: Robinson, B. E., et al. Test–retest reliability of the Work Addiction Risk Test. *Perceptual and Motor Skills, 74*, 926.

■■■

6040

Test Name: WORKAHOLISM SCALE

Purpose: To measure the risk of addiction to work.

Number of Items: 25

Format: 4-point scales (*never true* to *always true*).

Reliability: Split-half was .85.

Authors: Robinson, B. E., and Post, P.

Article: Split-half reliability of the Work Addiction Risk Test: Development of a measure of workaholism.

Journal: *Psychological Reports*, June 1995, *76*(3) Part II, 1226.

Related Research: Robinson, B.E., & Post, P. (1994). Validity of the Work Addiction Risk Test. *Perceptual and Motor Skills, 78,* 337–338.

∙ ∙ ∙

6041

Test Name: WORKAHOLISM SCALES

Purpose: To identify the workaholic, work enthusiast, and other job-related profiles.

Number of Items: 61

Format: 5-point Likert format.

Reliability: Alphas ranged from .67 to .89.

Validity: Correlations between scales ranged from -.10 to .64. Correlations with health complaints ranged from -.22 to .38.

Authors: Spence, J. T., and Robbins, A. S.

Article: Workaholism: Definition, measurement, and preliminary results.

Journal: *Journal of Personality Assessment,* February 1992, *58*(1), 160–178.

∙ ∙ ∙

6042

Test Name: WORK AND CAREER EXPERIENCES SCALES

Purpose: To measure participation in training and development, fairness, satisfaction, job discretion, supervisor support, met expectations, advancement opportunities, performance-reward contingencies, and organizational commitment.

Number of Items: 96

Format: Multiple-choice and agree–disagree format. Sample items presented.

Reliability: Reliabilities ranged from .48 to .92 across subscales.

Author: Burke, R. J.

Article: Organizational treatment of minority managers and professionals: Costs to the majority?

Journal: *Psychological Reports,* April 1991, *68*(2), 439–449.

Related Research: Greenhaus, J. H., et al. (1990). Effects of race on organizational experiences, job performance evaluations, and career outcomes. *Academy of Management Journal, 33,* 64–86.

Alluto, J. A., et al. (1973). On operationalizing the concept of commitment. *Social Forces, 51,* 448–454.

Hackman, J. R., & Lawler, E. E. (1971). Employee reactions to job characteristics. *Journal of Applied Psychology, 55,* 259–286.

∙ ∙ ∙

6043

Test Name: WORK CHALLENGE SCALE

Purpose: To measure work challenge.

Number of Items: 4

Format: Responses are made on a 5-point scale ranging from 1 (*very inaccurate*) to 5 (*very accurate*). Sample items are presented.

Reliability: Alpha coefficients were .77 and .72.

Authors: Aryee, S., and Tan, K.

Article: Antecedents and outcomes of career commitment.

Journal: *Journal of Vocational Behavior,* June 1992, *40*(3), 288–305.

Related Research: Bacharach, S., et al. (1990). Work processes, role conflict, and role overload. *Work and Occupations, 17,* 199–228.

6044

Test Name: WORK ENVIRONMENT PERCEPTIONS AND JOB ATTITUDE SCALES

Purpose: To measure leadership, work strain, and job characteristics.

Number of Items: 41

Format: Likert format.

Reliability: Alphas ranged from .59 to .90.

Authors: Butler, M. C., and Ehrlich, S. B.

Article: Positional influences on job satisfaction and job performance: A multivariate, predictive approach.

Journal: *Psychological Reports,* December 1991, *69*(3) Part I, 855–865.

Related Research: Butler, M. C. (1981). Environmental factors and retention decisions of health care providers. In H. W. Sinaiko et al. (Eds.), *Military personnel attrition and retention: Research in progress* (pp. 69–78). Washington, DC: Smithsonian Institution Press.

∙ ∙ ∙

6045

Test Name: WORK-LOAD SCALE

Purpose: To measure work-related requirements.

Number of Items: 5

Format: Responses are made on a 5-point scale ranging from *never* to *extremely often*.

Reliability: Internal consistency was .85.

Validity: Correlations with other variables ranged from .08 to .42.

Authors: Chen, P. Y., and Spector, P. E.

Article: Negative affectivity as the

underlying cause of correlations between stressors and strains.

Journal: *Journal of Applied Psychology*, June 1991, *76*(3), 398–407.

Related Research: Spector, P. E., et al. (1988). Relation of job stressors to affective, health, and performance outcomes: A comparison of multiple data sources. *Journal of Applied Psychology, 71*, 111–119.

■ ■ ■

6046

Test Name: WORK–NONWORK CONFLICT SCALE

Purpose: To measure work–nonwork conflict.

Number of Items: 6

Format: A sample item is presented. 7-point scales.

Reliability: Alphas ranged from .78 to .82.

Validity: Correlations with other variables ranged from -.13 to .31.

Authord: Cohen, A., and Kirchmeyer, C.

Article: A multidimensional approach to the relation between organizational commitment and nonwork participation.

Journal: *Journal of Vocational Behavior*, April 1995, *46*(2), 189–202.

Related Research: Shamir, B. (1983). Some antecedents of work–nonwork conflict. *Journal of Vocational Behavior, 23*, 98–111.

■ ■ ■

6047

Test Name: WORK-RELATED DEPRESSION SCALE

Purpose: To assess work-related depression.

Number of Items: 6

Format: Response are made on a 4-point scale ranging from 1 (*never* or *little of the time*) to 4 (*most of the time*).

Reliability: Reliabilities were .81 and .86.

Validity: Correlations with other variables ranged from -.66 to .56.

Authors: Begley, T. M., and Czajka, J. M.

Article: Panel analysis of the moderating effects of commitment on job satisfaction, intent to quit, and health following organizational change.

Journal: *Journal of Applied Psychology*, August 1993, *78*(4), 552–556.

Related Research: Caplan, R. D., et al. (1975). *Job demands and worker health.* Washington, DC: U.S. Department of Health, Education, and Welfare.

■ ■ ■

6048

Test Name: WORK-RELATED IRRITATION SCALE

Purpose: To assess work-related irritation.

Number of Items: 3

Format: Responses are made on a 4-point scale ranging from 1 (*never* or *a little of the time*) to 4 (*most of the time*).

Reliability: Reliablitities were .80 and .85.

Validity: Correlations with other variables ranged from -.51 to .56.

Authors: Begley, T. M., and Czajka, J. M.

Article: Panel analysis of the moderating effects of commitment on job satisfaction, intent to quit, and health following organizational change.

Journal: *Journal of Applied*

Psychology, August 1993, *78*(4), 552–556.

Related Research: Caplan, R. D., et al. (1975). *Job demands and worker health.* Washington, DC: U.S. Department of Health, Education, and Welfare.

■ ■ ■

6049

Test Name: WORK-RELATED NEEDS SCALE

Purpose: To determine the work-related needs of prospective workers.

Number of Items: 12

Format: Responses are made on a 5-point Likert scale ranging from 1 (*not at all*) to 5 (*extremely important*).

Reliability: Coefficient alphas across the three subscales ranged from .68 to .77.

Authors: Saks, A. M., et al.

Article: Effects of job previews on self-selection and job choice.

Journal: *Journal of Vocational Behavior*, June 1994, *44*(3), 297–316.

Related Research: Adlerfer, C. P. (1967). Convergent and discriminant validation of satisfaction and desire measures by interviews and questionnaires. *Journal of Applied Psychology, 51*, 509–520.

■ ■ ■

6050

Test Name: WORK-ROLE SALIENCE SCALE

Purpose: To measure work-role salience.

Number of Items: 6

Format: Responses are made on a 5-point Likert scale ranging from 1 (*strongly disagree*) to 5 (*strongly agree*). Examples are presented.

Reliability: Coefficient alpha was .65.

Validity: Correlations with other variables ranged from -.26 to .39.

Authors: Aryee, S., and Tan, K.

Article: Antecedents and outcomes of career commitment.

Journal: *Journal of Vocational Behavior*, June 1992, *40*(3), 288–305.

Related Research: Greenhaus, J. (1971). An investigation of the role of career salience in vocational behavior. *Journal of Vocational Behavior*, *1*, 209–216.

6051

Test Name: WORK STRESS MEASURE

Purpose: To measure work stress.

Number of Items: 4

Format: Responses are made on a 5-point scale ranging from 1 (*strongly agree*) to 5 (*strongly disagree*). An example is presented.

Reliability: Coefficient alpha was .83.

Validity: Correlations with the occurrence of stressful events in

hospital nursing were .30 and .40.

Authors: Reilly, N. P., and Orsak, C. L.

Article: A career stage analysis of career and organizational commitment in nursing.

Journal: *Journal of Vocational Behavior*, December 1991, *39*(3), 311–330.

Related Research: Motowidlo, S. J., et al. (1986). Occupational stress: Its causes and consequences for job performance. *Journal of Applied Psychology*, *71*, 618–629.

CHAPTER 6
Aptitude

6052

Test Name: AT-RISK SURVEY

Purpose: To identify at-risk 4-year-old children.

Number of Items: 22

Reliability: Internal-consistency reliability was .81.

Validity: Correlations with other variables ranged from -.24 to -.58.

Authors: Payne, D. A., et al.

Article: Development and validation of a family environment checklist for use in selecting at-risk participants for innovative educational preschool programs.

Journal: *Educational and Psychological Measurement*, Winter 1993, *53*(4), 1079–1084.

Related Research: Payne, B. D., & Payne, D. A. (1991). The ability of teachers to identify academically at-risk elementary students. *Journal of Research in Childhood Education*, *5*(2), 116–126.

■ ■ ■

6053

Test Name: JUDGMENT OF LINE ORIENTATION TEST

Purpose: To measure visual spatial ability.

Number of Items: 30

Format: Participants identify two lines identical in orientation to two partial lines. Usually individually administered, but may be group administered through the use of an overhead projector.

Validity: Correlations with other variables ranged from -.33 to .29.

Authors: Glamser, F. D., and Turner, R. W.

Article: Youth sport participation and associated sex differences on a measure of spatial ability.

Journal: *Perceptual and Motor Skills*, December 1995, *81*(3) Part 2, 1099–1105.

Related Research: Benton, A. L., et al. (1994). *Contributions to neuropsychological assessment, a clinical manual.* New York: Oxford University Press.

■ ■ ■

6054

Test Name: KINDERGARTEN SCREENING BATTERY

Purpose: To assess learning ability of kindergarteners.

Number of Items: 95

Format: Students respond to open-ended questions, memorization tasks, and recognition activities.

Reliability: Internal consistency was .74.

Authors: Kelly, M. S., and Peverly, S. T.

Article: Identifying bright kindergartners at risk for learning difficulties: Predictive validity of a kindergarten screening tool.

Journal: *Journal of School Psychology*, Fall 1992, *30*(3), 245–258.

Related Research: Belkin, A. S., & Sugar, F. (1985). *Kindergarten Screening Battery.* Unpublished manuscript.

6055

Test Name: MENTAL DEXTERITY TEST

Purpose: To measure mental dexterity.

Time Required: 60 minutes.

Number of Items: 100

Format: Multiple-choice format.

Reliability: Reliability coefficients at or above .90.

Validity: Correlation with the WAIS was .84.

Author: Thumin, F. J.

Article: Correlations for a new personality test with age, education, intelligence, and the MMPI-2.

Journal: *Perceptual and Motor Skills*, December 1994, *79*(3) Part 1, 1383–1389.

Related Research: Thumin, F. J. (1970). The Mental Dexterity Test: A study of reliability and validity. *Perceptual and Motor Skills*, *30*, 163–166.

■ ■ ■

6056

Test Name: METACOGNITIVE QUESTIONNAIRE

Purpose: To assess the participant's metacognitive awareness about reading.

Number of Items: 20

Format: Includes four areas: evaluation, planning, regulation, and conditional knowledge. The respondent's three choices for responding are weighted 0, 1, or 2. Examples are presented.

Reliability: Test–retest (8 months) Pearson product-moment correlation was .55. Internal consistency reliability was .56.

Validity: Correlations with other variables ranged from -.09 to .48.

Authors: McBride-Chang, C., et al.

Article: Print exposure as a predictor of word reading and reading comprehension in disabled and nondisabled readers.

Journal: *Journal of Educational Psychology*, June 1993, *85*(2), 230–238.

Related Research: Jacobs, J. E., & Paris, S. G. (1987). Children's metacognition about reading: Issues in definition, measurement, and instruction. *Educational Psychologist, 22*, 255–278.

■ ■ ■

6057

Test Name: PHONOLOGICAL AWARENESS TEST

Purpose: To measure segmenting, blending, and matching tasks.

Number of Items: 66

Format: Includes the three tasks of segmenting, blending, and matching. The test is in Spanish.

Reliability: Alpha coefficients ranged from .77 to .94.

Validity: Correlations with other variables ranged from .23 to .68.

Authors: Durgunoglu, A. Y., et al.

Article: Cross-language transfer of phonological awareness.

Journal: *Journal of Educational Psychology*, September 1993, *85*(3), 453–465.

■ ■ ■

6058

Test Name: POTENTIAL MANAGERIAL EFFECTIVENESS SCALE

Purpose: To measure perceived potential managerial effectiveness.

Number of Items: 3

Format: Responses are made on a 5-point Likert-type scale ranging from 1 (*strongly disagree*) to 5 (*strongly agree*).

Reliability: Coefficient alpha was .85.

Validity: Correlations with other variables ranged from -.20 to .78.

Authors: Thomas, D. C., and Ravlin, E. C.

Article: Responses of employees to cultural adaptation by a foreign manager.

Journal: *Journal of Applied Psychology*, February 1995, *80*(1), 133–146.

■ ■ ■

6059

Test Name: STUDY MANAGEMENT AND ACADEMIC RESULTS TEST

Purpose: To predict academic performance.

Number of Items: 29

Format: All items are presented.

Reliability: Alphas ranged from .70 to .83. Test–retest ranged from .72 to .89.

Validity: Correlations between scales ranged from .34 to .53. Correlations with other variables ranged from −.51 to +.51.

Authors: Kleijn, W. C., et al.

Article: Cognition, study habits, test anxiety, and academic performance.

Journal: *Psychological Reports*, December 1994, *75*(3) Part I, 1219–1226.

CHAPTER 7
Attitudes

6060

Test Name: ACADEMIC ATTITUDES SCALE

Purpose: To assess academic self-esteem, cohesion, cooperation, and effort.

Number of Items: 13

Format: 5-point Likert format.

Reliability: Alphas ranged from .51 to .83 across subscales.

Authors: Johnson, D. W., et al.

Article: Impact of cooperative and individualistic learning on high-ability students' achievement, self-esteem and social acceptance.

Journal: *The Journal of Social Psychology*, December 1993, *133*(6), 839–844.

Related Research: Johnson, D. W., et al. (1983). Social independence and classroom climate. *Journal of Psychology*, *114*, 134–142.

■ ■ ■

6061

Test Name: ACCEPTANCE OF INTERPERSONAL VIOLENCE

Purpose: To measure postintervention rape-supportive attitudes.

Number of Items: 6

Format: 7-point Likert format. Sample items are presented.

Reliability: Alpha was .65.

Authors: Rosenthal, E. H., et al.

Article: Changing the rape-supportive attitudes of traditional

and non-traditional male and female college students.

Journal: *Journal of Counseling Psychology*, April 1995, *42*(2), 171–177.

Related Research: Burt, M. R. (1980). Cultural myths and support for rape. *Journal of Personality and Social Psychology*, *38*, 217–230.

■ ■ ■

6062

Test Name: ADULT-ATTITUDES TOWARD COMPUTERS SURVEY

Purpose: To assess nurses' attitudes toward computers.

Number of Items: 15

Format: Includes 2 factors: Interest/Usefulness and Comfort. Responses are made on a 5-point Likert-type scale ranging from 5 (*strongly agree*) to 1 (*strongly disagree*). All items are presented.

Reliability: Internal consistency reliability estimates ranged from .80 to .93.

Authors: Coover, D., and Delcourt, M. A. B.

Article: Construct and criterion-related validity of the Adult-Attitudes Toward Computers Survey for a Sample of Professional Nurses.

Journal: *Educational and Psychological Measurement*, Autumn 1992, *52*(3), 653–661.

Related Research: Delcourt, M. A. B., & Lewis, L. H. (1987, February). Measuring adults' attitudes towards computers: An

initial investigation. *Proceedings of the lifelong learning research conference.* College Park, MD.

■ ■ ■

6063

Test Name: ADVERSARIAL SEXUAL BELIEFS AND ACCEPTANCE OF RAPE MYTHS SCALE

Purpose: To assess violent attitudes regarding male–female relationships.

Number of Items: 17

Format: 7-point Likert format.

Reliability: Alphas ranged from .74 to .82.

Authors: Christopher, F. S., et al.

Article: Exploring the darkside of courtship: A test of a model of premarital sexual aggressiveness.

Journal: *Journal of Marriage and the Family*, May 1993, *55*(2), 469–479.

Related Research: Burt, M. R. (1980). Cultural myths and support for rape. *Journal of Personality and Social Psychology*, *38*, 217–230.

■ ■ ■

6064

Test Name: ADVERSARIAL SEXUAL BELIEFS SCALES

Purpose: To measure postintervention rape-supportive attitudes.

Number of Items: 9

Format: 7-point Likert format. Sample items are presented.

Reliability: Alpha was .72.

Authors: Rosenthal, E. H., et al.

Article: Changing the rape-supportive attitudes of traditional and non-traditional male and female college students.

Journal: *Journal of Counseling Psychology*, April 1995, *42*(2), 171–177.

Related Research: Burt, M. R. (1980). Cultural myths and support for rape. *Journal of Personality and Social Psychology, 38*, 217–230.

■ ■ ■

6065

Test Name: AIDS ATTITUDES AND CONSERVATIVE VIEWS SCALE

Purpose: To measure AIDS attitudes, conservative views, and willingness to care for AIDS patients.

Number of Items: 11

Format: 5-point scales. All items are presented.

Reliability: Alphas ranged from .69 to .92 across subscales.

Authors: Harrison, M., et al.

Article: Development of a measure of nurses' AIDS attitudes and conservative views.

Journal: *Psychological Reports*, June 1994, *74*(3) Part I, 1043–1048.

Related Research: Froman, R. D., et al. (1992). Development of a measure of attitudes toward persons with AIDS. *IMAGE: Journal of Nursing Scholarship, 24*, 149–152.

■ ■ ■

6066

Test Name: AIDS ATTITUDES AND KNOWLEDGE SCALE

Purpose: To measure attitudes toward gays, people with AIDS, and AIDS knowledge.

Number of Items: 30

Format: 3-point agreement scales. All items are presented.

Reliability: Subscale alphas ranged from .50 to .65.

Validity: Correlations between subscales ranged from .34 to .51.

Authors: Nicholas, L. J., et al.

Article: AIDS knowledge and attitudes towards homosexuals of Black first-year university students: 1990–1992.

Journal: *Psychological Reports*, October 1994, *75*(2), 819–823.

Related Research: Grieger, I., & Ponterotto, J. (1988). Students' knowledge of AIDS and their attitudes towards gay men and lesbian women. *Journal of College Student Development, 29*, 415–422.

■ ■ ■

6067

Test Name: ANIMAL EMPATHY SCALE

Purpose: To measure empathy toward animals.

Number of Items: 10

Format: Participants rate ten photographs of animals on 4-point scales.

Reliability: Spearman-Brown split-half reliability was .92.

Validity: Correlations with other variables ranged from -.45 to .72.

Author: Wagstaff, G. F.

Article: Attitudes toward animals and human beings.

Journal: *The Journal of Social Psychology*, August 1991, *131*(4), 573–575.

6068

Test Name: ANIMAL WELFARE SCALE

Purpose: To assess animal rights and welfare attitudes.

Number of Items: 6

Format: 5-point Likert format. Sample items presented.

Reliability: Spearman-Brown Split-half reliability was .78.

Validity: Correlations with other variables ranged from -.52 to .72.

Author: Wagstaff, G. F.

Article: Attitudes toward animals and human beings.

Journal: *The Journal of Social Psychology*, August 1991, *131*(4), 573–575.

■ ■ ■

6069

Test Name: ATTITUDE RESEARCH INSTRUMENT

Purpose: To identify attitudes toward women's capabilities in educational administration.

Number of Items: 26

Format: Responses are made on a 5-point Likert scale ranging from *strongly disagree* to *strongly agree*. All items are presented.

Reliability: Internal consistency coefficients ranged from .87 to .99.

Authors: Whitaker, K. S., and Hein, A.

Article: Principals' perceptions of female capabilities in school administration.

Journal: *Journal of Research and Development in Education*, Fall 1992, *25*(1), 40–50.

Related Research: Ringness, T. A. (1964). *Construction of an instrument for research studies toward women in school administrative costs.* Madison: University of Wisconsin.

6070

Test Name: ATTITUDES ABOUT GUILT SURVEY

Purpose: To assess attitudes about guilt.

Number of Items: 8

Format: Multiple-choice format. All items are presented.

Reliability: Alpha was .86.

Validity: Correlations with variables ranged from .05 to .65.

Authors: Kubany, E. S., et al.

Article: Initial examination of a multidimensional model of trauma-related guilt: Applications to combat veterans and battered women.

Journal: *Journal of Psychopathology and Behavioral Assessment,* December 1995, *17*(4), 353–376.

■ ■ ■

6071

Test Name: ATTITUDES ABOUT REALITY SCALE

Purpose: To measure attitudes about reality.

Number of Items: 40

Format: 7-point Likert format. All items are presented.

Reliability: Test–retest and internal consistency were in the low .70s.

Authors: Harrison, W. D., and Atherton, C. R.

Article: The Attitude About Reality Scale: A note on the use of logical positivism as a construct.

Journal: *The Journal of Social Psychology,* June 1992, *132*(3), 335–341.

Related Research: Unger, R. K. (1990, August). *Cross-cultural aspects of the Attitudes About Reality Scale.* Paper presented at the 98th Annual Convention of the American Psychological Association, Boston.

■ ■ ■

6072

Test Name: ATTITUDE SCALE—LG

Purpose: To assess homophobia.

Number of Items: 32

Format: 5-point Likert scales. Sample items are presented.

Reliability: Alpha was .95.

Authors: Gelso, C. J., et al.

Article: Countertransference reaction in lesbian clients: The role of homophobia, counselor gender and countertransference management.

Journal: *Journal of Counseling Psychology,* July 1995, *42*(3), 356–364.

Related Research: Daly, J. (1990). *Measuring attitudes towards lesbians and gay men: Development and initial psychometric evaluation on an instrument.* Unpublished doctoral dissertation, Southern Illinois University at Carbondale.

■ ■ ■

6073

Test Name: ATTITUDES TOWARD CHEATING SCALE

Purpose: To measure cheating attitudes.

Number of Items: 34

Format: Responses are made on a 5-point Likert-type scale.

Validity: Correlations with other variables ranged from -.35 to .23.

Authors: Roig, M., and Neaman, M. A. W.

Article: Alienation, learning or grade orientation, and achievement as correlates of attitudes toward cheating.

Journal: *Perceptual and Motor Skills,* June 1994, *78*(3) Part 2, 1096–1098.

Related Research: Gardner, W. M., & Melvin, K. B. (1988). A scale for measuring attitude toward cheating. *Bulletin of the Psychometric Society, 26,* 429–432.

■ ■ ■

6074

Test Name: ATTITUDES TOWARD EMPLOYEE DRUG TESTING SCALE

Purpose: To measure attitudes toward employee drug testing.

Number of Items: 19

Format: Responses are made on a 5-point scale. All items are presented.

Reliability: Coefficient alpha was .90.

Validity: Correlations with other variables ranged from -.45 to .40.

Authors: Murphy, K. R., and Thornton, G. C., III

Article: Development and validation of a measure of attitudes toward employee drug testing.

Journal: *Educational and Psychological Measurement,* Spring 1992, *52*(1), 189–201.

■ ■ ■

6075

Test Name: ATTITUDES TOWARD FEMINISM AND THE WOMEN'S MOVEMENT SCALE

Purpose: To assess feminist attitudes.

Number of Items: 10

Format: Responses are made on a 5-point Likert scale ranging from *strongly agree* to *strongly disagree.* An example is presented.

Reliability: Cronbach's alpha was .89 ($N = 117$).

Validity: Correlations with other variables ranged from -.23 to .77.

Authors: Fassinger, R. E., and Richie, B. S.

Article: Being the best: Preliminary results from a national study of the achievement of prominent Black and White women.

Journal: *Journal of Counseling Psychology,* April 1994, *41*(2), 191–204.

Related Research: O'Brien, K. M., & Fassinger, R. E. (1993). A causal model of the career orientation and career choice of adolescent women. *Journal of Counseling Psychology, 40,* 456–469.

● ● ●

6076

Test Name: ATTITUDES TOWARD FEMINISM SCALE— REVISED

Purpose: To measure college women's subjective reactions to feminist ideology and the women's movement.

Number of Items: 32

Format: Includes 10 items embedded in 22 masking items. Responses are made on a 5-point scale ranging from 1 (*strongly disagree*) to 5 (*strongly agree*).

Reliability: Test–retest (2 weeks) reliability was .81.

Authors: Hackett, G., et al.

Article: Reactions of women to nonsexist and feminist counseling: Effects of counselor orientation and mode of information delivery.

Journal: *Journal of Counseling Psychology,* July 1992, *39*(3), 321–330.

Related Research: Enns, C. Z., & Hackett, G. (1990). Comparison of feminist and nonfeminist

women's reactions to variants of nonsexist and feminist counseling. *Journal of Counseling Psychology, 37,* 33–40.

● ● ●

6077

Test Name: ATTITUDES TOWARD FORCIBLE DATE RAPE SCALE

Purpose: To measure attitudes toward date rape.

Number of Items: 6

Format: 5-point Likert format. All items are presented.

Reliability: Alpha was .92.

Validity: Correlations with criterion variables were in the expected direction and ranged from -.39 to .51.

Authors: Fischer, G. J., and Chen, J.

Article: The Attitudes Toward Forcible Date Rape (FDR) Scale: Development of a measurement model.

Journal: *Journal of Psychopathology and Behavioral Assessment,* March 1994, *16*(1), 33–51.

Related Research: Feild, H. S. (1978). Attitudes toward rape: A comparative analysis of police, rapists, crisis counselors and citizens. *Journal of Personality and Social Psychology, 36,* 156–179.

● ● ●

6078

Test Name: ATTITUDES TOWARD FOREIGN LANGUAGE SCALE

Purpose: To measure attitudes toward foreign language.

Number of Items: 32

Format: Responses are made on a 5-point Likert-type scale ranging from *strongly agree* to *strongly*

disagree. All items are presented.

Reliability: Alpha coefficients ranged from .81 to .95.

Validity: Correlation with foreign language achievement was .37.

Authors: Corbin, S. S., and Chiachiere, F. J.

Article: Validity and reliability of a scale measuring attitudes toward foreign language.

Journal: *Educational and Psychological Measurement,* April 1995, *55*(2), 258–267.

Related Research: Briem, H. (1974). *Development of an instrument to measure attitudes toward the study of foreign languages.* Unpublished doctoral dissertation, University of Michigan, Ann Arbor. (University Microfilms No. 75-652)

● ● ●

6079

Test Name: ATTITUDES TOWARD INDIVIDUALIZED EDUCATION PROGRAM MEASURE

Purpose: To measure special education teachers' attitudes toward the individualized education program of special education.

Number of Items: 25

Format: Includes five components: Value for Instructional Planning, Curriculum Planning, Value for Individualized Instruction, Team Planning, and Overall Attitude. Responses are made on a 5-point Likert-type scale ranging from 1 (*strongly disagree*) to 5 (*strongly agree*). All items are presented.

Reliability: Internal consistency reliabilities ranged from .64 to .88.

Authors: Ryan, L. B., and Rucker, C. N.

Article: The development and validation of a measure of special education teachers' attitudes toward the individualized educational program.

Journal: *Educational and Psychological Measurement*, Winter 1991, *51*(4), 877–882.

Related Research: Morgan, D. P., & Rhodes, G. (1983). Teachers' attitudes toward IEPs: A two year follow-up. *Exceptional Children*, *50*, 64–68.

■ ■ ■

6080

Test Name: ATTITUDES TOWARD LESBIANS AND GAY MEN

Purpose: To measure attitudes toward lesbians and gay men.

Number of Items: 70

Format: 5-point Likert format. All items are presented.

Reliability: Alphas ranged from .94 to .95.

Authors: Kyes, K. B., and Tumbelaka, L.

Article: Comparison of Indonesian and American college students' attitudes toward homosexuality.

Journal: *Psychological Reports*, February 1994, *74*(1), 227–237.

Related Research: Hudson, W. W., & Richettes, W. A. (1988). Index of homophobia. In C. M. Davis et al. (Eds.), *Sexuality-related measures: A compendium* (pp. 155–156). Lake Mills, IA: Graphic Publications.

■ ■ ■

6081

Test Name: ATTITUDES TOWARD PSYCHIATRISTS AND THE INSANITY DEFENSE SCALE

Purpose: To measure attitudes toward psychiatrists and the insanity defense.

Number of Items: 10

Format: 7-point agreement scales.

Reliability: Alpha was .35. Item-total correlations ranged from .22 to .69. Subscale alphas ranged from .54 to .81.

Validity: Correlation with verdict ranged from .07 to .33 across items and from .28 to .33 across subscales.

Authors: Cutler, B. L., et al.

Article: Jury selection in insanity defense cases.

Journal: *Journal of Research in Personality*, June 1992, *26*(2), 165–182.

■ ■ ■

6082

Test Name: ATTITUDES TOWARD SEEKING PROFESSIONAL PSYCHOLOGICAL HELP SCALE

Purpose: To assess attitudes toward traditional counseling services.

Number of Items: 29

Format: 4-point agreement scales range from 0 (*agree*) to 3 (*disagree*).

Reliability: Test–retest reliabilities ranged from .84 to .86 (5 days to 2 months). Internal consistency ranged from .83 to .86.

Authors: Kelly, A. E., and Achter, J. A.

Article: Self-concealment and attitudes toward counseling in university students.

Journal: *Journal of Counseling Psychology*, January 1995, *42*(1), 40–46.

Related Research: Fischer, E. H., & Turner, J. L. (1970). Orientations to seeking professional help: Development and research utility of an attitude scale. *Journal of Counseling and Clinical Psychology*, *35*, 79–96.

6083

Test Name: ATTITUDES TOWARD STATISTICS

Purpose: To measure attitudes toward statistics.

Number of Items: 29

Format: Includes 2 dimensions: course and field. Responses are made on a 5-point Likert scale ranging from *strongly disagree* to *strongly agree*.

Reliability: Alpha coefficients ranged from .82 to .94.

Validity: Correlations with the Survey of Attitudes Toward Statistics ranged from -.03 to .79.

Authors: Schau, C., et al.

Article: The development and validation of the survey of attitudes toward statistics.

Journal: *Educational and Psychological Measurement*, October 1995, *55*(5), 868–875.

Related Research: Wise, S. L. (1985). The development and validation of a scale measuring attitude toward statistics. *Educational and Psychological Measurement*, *45*, 401–405.

■ ■ ■

6084

Test Name: ATTITUDES TOWARD TRANSPORTING NUCLEAR WASTE

Purpose: To measure attitudes toward transporting nuclear waste.

Number of Items: 30

Format: Likert format. All items are presented.

Reliability: Split-half reliability ranged from .80 to .88 (Spearman-Brown).

Validity: Correlations with other variables ranged from .22 to .90.

Author: Larsen, K. S.

Article: Attitudes toward the transportation of nuclear waste: The development of a Likert-type scale.

Journal: *The Journal of Social Psychology*, February 1994, *134*(1), 27–34.

• • •

6085

Test Name: ATTITUDES TOWARD WOMEN SCALE

Purpose: To measure attitudes toward women.

Number of Items: 25

Format: Responses are made on a 4-point Likert scale. Examples are presented.

Validity: Correlates .97 with the original 55-item scale.

Authors: Sachs, R., et al.

Article: Biographic and personal characteristics of women in management.

Journal: *Journal of Vocational Behavior*, August 1992, *41*(1), 89–100.

Related Research: Spence, J. T., et al. (1973). A short version of the Attitudes Toward Women Scale. *Bulletin of the Psychonomic Society, 2*, 219–220.

• • •

6086

Test Name: ATTITUDES TOWARD WOMEN SCALE

Purpose: To measure male attitudes toward women.

Number of Items: 25

Format: Responses are made on a 7-point Likert scale (*strongly agree* to *strongly disagree*).

Reliability: Reliability was .95.

Authors: Schaeffer, A. M., and Nelson, E. S.

Article: Rape-supportive attitudes:

Effects of on-campus residence and education.

Journal: *Journal of College Student Development*, May 1993, *34*(3), 175–179.

Related Research: Spence, J. T., et al. (1973). A short version of the Attitudes Toward Women Scale (AWS). *Bulletin of the Psychonomic Society, 2*, 219–220.

• • •

6087

Test Name: ATTITUDES TOWARDS AIDS SCALE—HIGH SCHOOL VERSION

Purpose: To measure attitudes toward AIDS.

Number of Items: 20

Format: 3-point Likert format.

Reliability: Alpha was .79. Item-total correlations ranged from .06 to .60.

Author: Goh, D. S.

Article: Internal consistency and stability of the Attitudes Towards AIDS Scale—High School Version.

Journal: *Psychological Reports*, February 1994, *74*(1), 329–330.

Related Research: Goh, D. S. (1993). The development and reliability of the Attitudes Towards AIDS Scale. *College Student Journal, 27*, 208–214.

• • •

6088

Test Name: ATTITUDES TOWARDS CENSORSHIP SCALE

Purpose: To measure student attitudes toward censorship.

Number of Items: 34

Format: Likert format. All items are presented.

Reliability: Alpha was .74.

Validity: No interpretable factor structure was revealed by a factor analysis.

Authors: Naylor, A. P., et al.

Article: Attitudes of students in education classes toward censorship.

Journal: *Journal of Research and Development in Education*, Summer 1995, *28*(4), 189–195.

• • •

6089

Test Name: ATTITUDES TOWARDS DISABLED PERSONS SCALE

Purpose: To assess attitudes regarding the differences between disabled and nondisabled people and toward disabled people in general.

Number of Items: 30

Format: 6-point Likert format.

Reliability: Internal consistency ranged from .75 to .85.

Authors: Berry, J. O., and Jones, W. H.

Article: Situational and dispositional components of reactions toward persons with disabilities.

Journal: *The Journal of Social Psychology*, August 1991, *131*(4), 673–684.

Related Research: Yuker, H. E., et al. (1966). *The measurement of attitudes toward disabled persons.* Human Resources Study No. 7. Albertson, NY: Human Resource Center.

• • •

6090

Test Name: ATTITUDES TOWARD OBESITY

Purpose: To measure

professionals' attitudes towards obesity.

Number of Items: 28

Format: Varied formats. All items are presented.

Reliability: Alpha was .64. Test–retest (1 week) was .82.

Authors: Price, J. H., and Telljohann, S. K.

Article: School food-service directors' perceptions of childhood obesity.

Journal: *Psychological Reports*, June 1994, *74*(3) Part II, 1347–1359.

Related Research: Price, J. H., et al. (1987). Elementary school principals' perceptions of childhood obesity. *Journal of School Health*, *57*, 367–370.

■ ■ ■

6091

Test Name: ATTITUDES TOWARDS INCEST SCALE

Purpose: To measure attitudes toward incest.

Number of Items: 39

Format: 5-point Likert format.

Validity: Correlations with the Incest Blame Scale ranged from -.48 to .59.

Authors: McKenzie, B. J., and Calder, P.

Article: Factors related to attribution of blame in father-daughter incest.

Journal: *Psychological Reports*, December 1993, *73*(3) Part II, 1111–1121.

Related Research: Ciccone, B. (1981). *The development of an instrument to study attitudes towards incest.* Unpublished doctoral dissertation, Temple University, Philadelphia.

6092

Test Name: ATTITUDES TOWARD WOMEN SCALE

Purpose: To measure attitudes toward gender roles.

Number of Items: 15

Format: 5-point Likert format.

Reliability: Item-total correlations ranged from .31 to .73.

Authors: Kyes, K. B., and Tumbelaka, L.

Article: Comparison of Indonesian and American college students' attitudes toward homosexuality.

Journal: *Psychological Reports*, February 1994, *74*(1), 227–237.

Related Research: Spence, J. T., et al. (1973). A short version of the Attitudes Toward Women Scale (AWS). *Bulletin of the Psychonomic Society*, *2*, 219–220.

■ ■ ■

6093

Test Name: ATTITUDES TOWARD WOMEN SCALE

Purpose: To measure gender-role attitudes.

Number of Items: 55

Format: The statements deal with the rights and roles of women. Responses are made on a 4-point scale ranging from 1 (*agree strongly*) to 4 (*disagree strongly*).

Reliability: Corrected split-half reliability was .92 ($N = 294$); Test–retest (3–4 months) reliability was .93 ($N = 61$).

Validity: Correlations with other variables ranged from -.14 to .06.

Authors: Pyant, C. T., and Yanico, B. J.

Article: Relationship of racial identity and gender-role attitudes to Black women's psychological well-being.

Journal: *Journal of Counseling*

Psychology, July 1991, *38*(3), 315–322.

Related Research: Spence, J. T., & Helmreich, R. (1972). The Attitudes Toward Women Scale: An objective instrument to measure attitudes toward the rights and roles of women in contemporary society. *JSAS Catalog of Selected Documents in Psychology*, *2*, 66 (Ms. No. 153).

■ ■ ■

6094

Test Name: ATTITUDES TOWARD WOMEN SCALE—SHORT

Purpose: To assess views about the role of women in society.

Number of Items: 15

Format: 4-point Likert format.

Validity: Correlation with long version is .97.

Authors: Brems, C., and Wagner, P.

Article: Blame of victim and perpetrator in rape versus theft.

Journal: *The Journal of Social Psychology*, June 1994, *133*(3), 363–374.

Related Research: Spence, J., et al. (1973). A short version of the Attitudes Toward Women Scale (AWS). *Bulletin of the Psychonomic Society*, *2*, 219–220.

■ ■ ■

6095

Test Name: ATTITUDE TOWARD CHRISTIANITY SCALE

Purpose: To measure attitude toward Christianity among 11- to 16-year-olds.

Number of Items: 7

Format: All items presented.

Reliability: Alphas ranged from .46 to .93 across samples.

Validity: Correlations with church attendance ranged from .54 to .83 across samples.

Authors: Francis, L. J., et al.

Article: Reliability and validity of a short scale of attitude toward Christianity among students in the UK, USA, Australia, and Canada.

Journal: *Psychological Reports*, October 1995, *77*(2), 431–434.

Related Research: Francis, L. J., et al. (1991). Reliability and validity of a short measure of attitude toward Christianity among secondary school pupils in England, Scotland and Northern Ireland. *Collected Original Resources in Education*, *15*, 3, Fiche 2, G09.

• • •

6096

Test Name: ATTITUDE TOWARD COMPUTERS SCALE—HEBREW VERSION

Purpose: To measure attitude toward computers.

Number of Items: 24

Format: 5-point Likert format. All items presented.

Reliability: Alpha was .93. Item total correlations ranged from .36 to .81.

Validity: Correlations with other variables ranged from .37 to .50.

Authors: Evans, T. E., et al.

Article: Psychometric properties of the Hebrew version of the Francis Attitude Toward Computers Scale.

Journal: *Psychological Reports*, December 1995, *77*(3) Part I, 1003–1010.

Related Research: Francis, L. J. (1993). Measuring attitude toward computers among undergraduate college students: The affective domain. *Computers and Education*, *20*, 251–255.

6097

Test Name: ATTITUDE TOWARD MATERIALISM SCALE

Purpose: To measure attitude toward materialism.

Number of Items: 10

Format: 7-point agreement scales. All items presented.

Reliability: Alpha was .76.

Author: Yoon, K.

Article: Comparison of beliefs about advertising, attitudes toward advertising, and materialism held by African Americans and Caucasians.

Journal: *Psychological Reports*, October 1995, *77*(2), 455–466.

Related Research: Richins, M., & Dawson, S. (1992). A consumer values orientation for materialism and its measurement: Scale development and validation. *Journal of Consumer Research*, *19*, 303–316.

• • •

6098

Test Name: ATTITUDE TOWARD RECYCLING SCALE

Purpose: To measure attitudes toward recycling.

Number of Items: 20

Format: All items are presented.

Reliability: Split-half reliability was .93.

Validity: Correlations with other variables ranged from .30 to .74.

Author: Larsen, K. S.

Article: Environmental waste: Recycling attitudes and correlates.

Journal: *The Journal of Social Psychology*, February 1995, *135*(1), 83–88.

6099

Test Name: ATTITUDE TOWARDS TALENTED YOUTH MATHEMATICS PROGRAM

Purpose: To measure attitudes of participants in a program for mathematically talented youth.

Number of Items: 42

Format: 5-point Likert format. All items are presented.

Reliability: Internal reliabilities ranged from .74 to .90 across subscales. Test–retest (4–8 months) reliabilities ranged from .26 to .68.

Authors: Terwilliger, J. S., and Titus, J. C.

Article: Gender differences in attitudes and attitude changes among mathematically talented youth.

Journal: *Gifted Child Quarterly*, Winter 1995, *39*(1), 29–35.

Related Research: Fennema, E. (1974). Gender-related differences in mathematics learning. Why??? *The Elementary School*, *75*, 183–190.

• • •

6100

Test Name: ATTITUDE TOWARD THE QUESTIONNAIRE SCALE

Purpose: To assess how participants feel while completing questionnaire items.

Number of Items: 9

Format: 4-point scales.

Reliability: Alphas ranged from .76 to .79.

Authors: Nicholas, L. J., et al.

Article: Lying as a factor in research on sexuality.

Journal: *Psychological Reports*, October 1994, *75*(2), 839–842.

Related Research: Delamater, J. D.

(1974). Methodological issues in the study of premarital sexuality. *Sociological Methods and Research*, *3*, 30–61.

■ ■ ■

6101

Test Name: ATTITUDE TOWARD WAR SCALE

Purpose: To measure attitude toward war.

Number of Items: 10

Format: 9-point agreement scales.

Reliability: Alphas ranged from .80 to .81.

Author: Lee, Y. T.

Article: Reactions of American minority and nonminority students to the Persian Gulf War.

Journal: *The Journal of Social Psychology*, October 1993, *133*(5), 707–713.

Related Research: Kosterman, R., & Feshbach, S. (1969). Toward a measure of patriotic and nationalistic attitudes. *Political Psychology*, *10*, 257–274.

■ ■ ■

6102

Test Name: ATTITUDINAL MILITANCY SCALE

Purpose: To measure teacher militancy.

Number of Items: 11

Format: Responses are made on a 5-point Likert scale. Sample items are presented.

Reliability: Alpha coefficients were .73 and .90.

Validity: Correlations with other variables ranged from .08 to .41.

Authors: DiPaola, M. F., and Hoy, W. K.

Article: Teacher militancy: A professional check on bureaucracy.

Journal: *Journal of Research and Development in Education*, Winter 1994, *27*(2), 83–88.

Related Research: Wohnsiedler, B. (1975). An instrument to measure militant attitudes of public school teachers. *Dissertation Abstracts International*, *36-09*, 5735A.

■ ■ ■

6103

Test Name: BELIEF IN THE PARANORMAL SCALE

Purpose: To assess belief in the paranormal

Number of Items: 24

Format: 5-point Likert format.

Reliability: Alpha was .90.

Authors: Morier, D., and Keeports, D.

Article: Normal science and the paranormal: The effect of a scientific method course on student beliefs.

Journal: *Research in Higher Education*, August 1995, *35*(4), 443–453.

Related Research: Jones, W. H., et al. (1977). Belief in the Paranormal Scale: An objective instrument to measure belief in magical phenomena and causes. *JSAS Catalog of Selected Documents in Psychology*, *7*(100) (MS. No. 1577).

■ ■ ■

6104

Test Name: BELIEFS ABOUT ACADEMIC ACCELERATIONS SCALE

Purpose: To assess educators' beliefs about accelerated education for gifted students.

Number of Items: 22

Format: Likert format.

Reliability: Alpha was .94.

Authors: Jones, E. D., and Southern, W. T.

Article: Programming, grouping, and acceleration in rural school districts: A survey of attitudes and practices.

Journal: *Gifted Child Quarterly*, Spring 1992, *36*(2), 112–117.

Related Research: Southern, W. T., et al. (1989). Practitioner objections to the academic acceleration of young gifted children. *Gifted Child Quarterly*, *33*, 29–35.

■ ■ ■

6105

Test Name: BELIEFS ABOUT ADVERTISING SCALE

Purpose: To measure beliefs about advertising.

Number of Items: 21

Format: 7-point agreement scales. All items presented.

Reliability: Alphas ranged from .72 to .88 across subscales.

Author: Yoon, K.

Article: Comparison of beliefs about advertising, attitude toward advertising, and materialism held by African Americans and Caucasians.

Journal: *Psychological Reports*, October 1995, *77*(2), 455–466.

Related Research: Pollay, R. W., & Mittal, B. (1993). Here's the beef: Determinants, and segments in consumer criticism of advertising. *Journal of Marketing*, *57*, 99–114.

■ ■ ■

6106

Test Name: BELIEFS ABOUT CONSCIOUSNESS AND REALITY SCALES

Purpose: To measure extent to which persons endorse statements along the physical-transcendent dimension.

Number of Items: 94

Format: 4-point Likert format. Sample items presented.

Reliability: Alphas ranged from .82 to .95 across subscales.

Authors: Baruss, I., and Moore, R. J.

Article: Measurement of beliefs about consciousness and reality.

Journal: *Psychological Reports*, August 1992, *71*(1), 59–64.

Related Research: Baruss, I. (1990). *The personal nature of notions of consciousness.* Lanham, MD: University Press of America.

■ ■ ■

6107

Test Name: BELIEFS ABOUT THE CAUSES OF SUCCESS SCALE—CLASSROOM

Purpose: To determine what students believe are the causes of classroom success.

Number of Items: 20

Format: Includes four factors: Motivation/Effort, Deception, Ability, and External Factors. Responses are made on a 5-point Likert-type scale ranging from 1 (*strongly agree*) to 5 (*strongly disagree*). Most items are presented.

Reliability: Alpha coefficients ranged from .63 to .86.

Authors: Duda, J. L., and Nicholls, J. G.

Article: Dimensions of achievement motivation in schoolwork and sport.

Journal: *Journal of Educational Psychology*, September 1992, *84*(3), 290–299.

Related Research: Nicholls, J. G. (1989). *The competitive ethos and*

democratic education. Cambridge, MA: Harvard University Press.

■ ■ ■

6108

Test Name: BELIEFS ABOUT THE CAUSES OF SUCCESS SCALE—SPORT

Purpose: To determine what students believe are the causes of success in sport.

Number of Items: 20

Format: Includes four factors: Motivation/Effort, Deception, Ability, and External Factors. Responses are made on a 5-point Likert-type scale ranging from 1 (*strongly agree*) to 5 (*strongly disagree*). Most items are presented.

Reliability: Alpha coefficients ranged from .67 to .87.

Authors: Duda, J. L., and Nicholls, J. G.

Article: Dimensions of achievement motivation in schoolwork and sport.

Journal: *Journal of Educational Psychology*, September 1992, *84*(3), 290–299.

Related Research: Nicholls, J. G. (1989). *The competitive ethos and democratic education.* Cambridge, MA: Harvard University Press.

■ ■ ■

6109

Test Name: BELIEFS REGARDING HOW ONE READS AND HOW READING DEVELOPS SCALE

Purpose: To determine the beliefs and decisions of preservice and inservice secondary teachers regarding content area reading and instruction.

Number of Items: 30

Format: *Yes* or *no* response is required to each statement.

Reliability: Consistency was .86.

Validity: .91

Authors: Konopak, B., et al.

Article: Preservice and inservice secondary teacher's orientations toward content area reading.

Journal: *Journal of Educational Research*, March/April 1994, *87*(4), 220–227.

Related Research: Kinzer, C. K. (1988). Instructional frameworks and instructional choices: Comparisons between preservice and inservice teachers. *Journal of Reading Behavior, 20,* 357–377.

■ ■ ■

6110

Test Name: BELIEF THAT CHANGE CAN BE EFFECTED SCALE

Purpose: To identify nurses' beliefs that they can effect desired change in policy or behavior.

Number of Items: 8

Format: Responses are made on a scale from 0 (*not at all confident*) to 10 (*very confident*).

Reliability: Coefficient alpha was .85.

Validity: Correlation with other variables ranged from -.57 to .28.

Author: Parker, L. E.

Article: When to fix it and when to leave: Relationships among perceived control, self-efficacy, dissent, and exit.

Journal: *Journal of Applied Psychology*, December 1993, *78*(6), 949–959.

■ ■ ■

6111

Test Name: BLACKS IN BUSINESS SCALE

Purpose: To assess attitudes toward Black people as managers.

Number of Items: 33

Format: 7-point Likert format. Sample items presented.

Reliability: Alpha was .94.

Authors: Tomkiewicz, J., et al.

Article: Hispanic persons in business: Is there cause for optimism?

Journal: *Psychological Reports*, December 1991, *69*(3) Part I, 847–852.

Related Research: Stevens, G. E. (1984, June). Attitudes toward Blacks in management are changing. *Personnel Administrator*, 163–171.

● ● ●

6112

Test Name: BUREAUCRATIC ORIENTATION SCALE

Purpose: To measure bureaucratic orientation.

Number of Items: 15

Format: Likert-type items. Examples are presented.

Reliability: Reliability coefficients were .73 and .83.

Validity: Correlations with other variables ranged from -.06 to .09.

Authors: DiPaola, M. F., and Hoy, W. K.

Article: Teacher militancy: A professional check on bureaucracy.

Journal: *Journal of Research and Development in Education*, Winter 1994, *27*(2), 83–88.

Related Research: Kuhlman, E., & Hoy, W. K. (1972). The socialization of professionals into bureaucracies. *Journal of Educational Administration*, *8*, 18–27.

6113

Test Name: CHILD-REARING BELIEFS SCALES

Purpose: To identify parents' child-rearing beliefs.

Number of Items: 21

Format: Responses are made on a 6-point scale ranging from 1 (*not at all important*) to 6 (*extremely important*). Includes 3 subscales: Developing Problem-Solving Skills, Developing Creative Skills, and Developing Practical Skills. All items are presented.

Reliability: Alpha coefficients ranged from .37 to .81.

Authors: Okagaki, L., and Sternberg, R. J.

Article: Parental beliefs and children's school performance.

Journal: *Child Development*, February 1993, *64*(1), 36–56.

Related Research: Sternberg, R. J. (1985). *Beyond IQ: A triarchic theory of human intelligence.* New York: Cambridge University Press.

● ● ●

6114

Test Name: CHILDREN'S ATTITUDES TOWARD INSTITUTIONAL AUTHORITY SCALE

Purpose: To measure children's attitudes toward parents, police, and other authorities.

Number of Items: 30

Format: Balanced 5-point Likert format. Sample items are presented.

Reliability: Alphas ranged from .64 to .82 across authority types. Total alpha ranged from .78 to .90.

Authors: Rigby, K., and Black, D.

Article: Attitudes toward institutional authorities among Aboriginal school children in Australia.

Journal: *The Journal of Social Psychology*, December 1993, *133*(6), 845–852.

Related Research: Rigby, K. (1987). "Faking good" with self-reported pro-authority attitudes and behaviors among school children. *Personality and Individual Differences*, *8*, 445–447.

● ● ●

6115

Test Name: CHILDREN'S OCCUPATION, ACTIVITY, AND TRAIT-ATTITUDE MEASURE

Purpose: To assess children's gender attitudes.

Number of Items: 25

Format: Respondents are asked whether *only men, only women,* or *both men and women* should perform 10 feminine, 10 masculine, and 5 neutral activities.

Reliability: Cronbach's alpha coefficient for the activity subscale was .88.

Author: Bigler, R. S.

Article: The role of classification skill in moderating environmental influences on children's gender stereotyping: A study of the functional use of gender in the classroom.

Journal: *Child Development*, August 1995, *66*(4), 1072–1087.

Related Research: Bigler, R. S., et al. (1991). *Children's Occupation, Activity, and Trait-Attitude Measure (COAT-AM).* Unpublished scale. (Available from the Department of Psychology, 330 Mezes Hall, University of Texas at Austin, Austin, TX 78712)

6116

Test Name: COMPUTER ATTITUDE SCALE

Purpose: To measure positive and negative attitudes toward computers.

Number of Items: 20

Format: Includes 3 factors: Negative Feelings, Positive Feelings, and Lack of Understanding. All items are presented.

Reliability: Internal-consistency reliability was .81.

Authors: Harrison, A. W., and Rainer, R.K., Jr.

Article: An examination of the factor structures and concurrent validities for The Computer Attitude Scale, The Computer Anxiety Rating Scale, and The Computer Self-Efficacy Scale.

Journal: *Educational and Psychological Measurement*, Autumn 1992, *52*(3), 735–745.

Related Research: Nickell, G. S., & Pinto, J. N. (1986). The Computer Attitude Scale. *Computers in Human Behavior, 2*, 301–306.

* * *

6117

Test Name: CONSERVATISM SCALE—SHORT FORM

Purpose: To measure conservation.

Number of Items: 16

Format: Likert format. All items described.

Reliability: Alpha was .82.

Authors: Collins, D. M., and Hayes, P. F.

Article: Development of a short-form conservation scale suitable for mail surveys.

Journal: *Psychological Reports,*

April 1993, *72*(2), 419–422.

Related Research: Wilson, G. D., & Patterson, J. R. (1968). A new measure of conservation. *British Journal of Social and Cultural Psychology, 7*, 264–269.

* * *

6118

Test Name: CROSS-CULTURAL WORLD-MINDEDNESS SCALE

Purpose: To measure world-mindedness.

Number of Items: 26

Reliability: Alpha ranged from .80 to .84.

Validity: Democrats scored higher than Republicans in Southern California, but not in a Texas sample.

Author: Der-Karabetian, A., and Metzer, J.

Article: The Cross-Cultural World-Mindedness Scale and political party affiliation.

Journal: *Psychological Reports,* June 1993, *72*(3) Part II, 1069–1070.

Related Research: Der-Karabetian, A. (1992). World-mindedness and the nuclear threat: A multinational study. *Journal of Social Behavior and Personality, 7*, 293–308.

* * *

6119

Test Name: DISABILITY FACTOR SCALE

Purpose: To measure attitudes toward disabled persons.

Number of Items: 105

Format: 6-point bipolar rating scales.

Reliability: Test–retest was .80.

Authors: Little, G. L., et al.

Article: Cognitive behavioral

treatment of felony drug offenders: A five-year recidivism report.

Journal: *Psychological Reports,* December 1993, *73*(3) Part II, 1089–1090.

Related Research: Siller, J. (1986). The measurement of attitudes towards physically disabled person. In C. P. Herman et al. (Eds.), *Physical appearance: Stigma and social behavior* (pp. 21–24). The Ontario Symposium, Vol. 3. Hilldale, NJ: Erlbaum.

* * *

6120

Test Name: DYSFUNCTIONAL ATTITUDES SCALE

Purpose: To measure the degree of endorsement of extreme self-evaluative standards.

Number of Items: 40

Format: 7-point agreement scales. Sample items presented.

Reliability: Internal consistency ranged from .79 to .93. Test–retest (6 to 8 weeks) ranged from .73 to .84.

Authors: Kuiper, N. A., and Dance, K. A.

Article: Dysfunctional attitudes, role stress evaluations, and psychological well-being.

Journal: *Journal of Research in Personality*, June 1994, *28*(2), 245–262.

Related Research: Cone, D. B., et al. (1986). Factor structure of the Dysfunctional Attitude Scale in a student population. *Journal of Clinical Psychology, 42*, 307–309.

Power, M. J., et al. (1994). The Dysfunctional Attitude Scale: A comparison of Forms A and B and proposals for a new subscaled version. *Journal for Research in Personality, 28*, 263–276.

6121

Test Name: DYSFUNCTIONAL ATTITUDE SURVEY

Purpose: To measure dysfunctional thought processes.

Number of Items: 100

Format: Responses are made on a 7-point scale ranging from 1 (*totally disagree*) to 7 (*totally agree*). Examples are presented.

Reliability: Coefficient alpha was .93.

Validity: Correlations with other variables ranged from -.41 to .60.

Authors: Judge, T. A., and Locke, E. A.

Article: Effect of dysfunctional thought processes on subjective well-being and job satisfaction.

Journal: *Journal of Applied Psychology*, June 1993, *78*(3), 475–490.

Related Research: Weisman, A., & Beck, A. T. (1978). *Development and validation of the Dysfunctional Attitude Scale.* Paper presented at the annual convention of the Association for Advancement of Behavior Therapy, Chicago.

■ ■ ■

6122

Test Name: EMPLOYEE ATTITUDE SCALE

Purpose: To measure employee attitudes.

Number of Items: 102

Format: 85 responses are made on a 6-point scale ranging from *don't agree* to *strongly agree* and 17 responses are made on a 7-point scale ranging from *extremely dissatisfied* to *extremely satisfied*. Includes 3 factors: Perceived Supervisory Support, Participative Management, and Work Group Performance.

Validity: Correlations with other variables ranged from .01 to .38.

Authors: Geehr, J. L., et al.

Article: Quality circles: The effects of varying degrees of voluntary participation on employee attitudes and program efficacy.

Journal: *Educational and Psychological Measurement*, February 1995, *55*(1), 124–134.

Related Research: Tortorich, R., et al. (1981). Measuring organizational impact of quality circles. *Quality Circles Journal, 4*, 24–34.

■ ■ ■

6123

Test Name: FENNEMA-SHERMAN MATHEMATICS ATTITUDE SCALES

Purpose: To measure attitude toward mathematics.

Number of Items: 33

Format: Responses are made on a 5-point Likert-type scale. All items are presented.

Validity: Correlations with social desirability ranged from -.22 to .28.

Authors: Melancon, J. G., et al.

Article: Measurement integrity of scores from the Fennema-Sherman Mathematics Attitude Scales: The attitudes of public school teachers.

Journal: *Educational and Psychological Measurement*, Spring 1994, *54*(1), 187–192.

Related Research: Fennema, E., & Sherman, J. A. (1976). Fennema-Sherman Mathematics Attitude Scales: Instruments designed to measure attitudes toward the learning of mathematics by females and males. *Psychological Documents, 6*(1), 31.

6124

Test Name: FIGURAL INTERSECTIONS TEST

Purpose: To provide a nonverbal measure of mental capacity.

Number of Items: 36

Format: Items consist of geometric shapes.

Reliability: Reliability estimates ranged from the mid-.80s to the low .90s.

Validity: Correlations with other variables ranged from -.02 to .80.

Author: Johnson, J.

Article: Developmental versus language-based factors in metaphor interpretation.

Journal: *Journal of Educational Psychology*, December 1991, *83*(4), 470-483.

Related Research: Pascual-Leone, J., & Ijaz, H. (1989). Mental capacity testing as a form of intellectual-developmental assessment. In R. Samuda et al. (Eds.), *Assessment and placement of minority students* (pp. 143–171). Toronto, Ontario, Canada: C.J. Hogrefe.

■ ■ ■

6125

Test Name: FISHER-TURNER ATTITUDES TOWARD SEEKING PROFESSIONAL PSYCHOLOGICAL HELP SCALE

Purpose: To assess attitudes toward traditional counseling services.

Number of Items: 29

Format: Likert-type items employing a 4-point scale.

Reliability: Internal consistency estimates ranged from .83 to .86. Test–retest reliability was .86 at 5 days and .82 at 6 weeks.

Validity: Correlations with other variables ranged from -.28 to .32.

Authors: Robertson, J. M., and Fitzgerald, L. F.

Article: Overcoming the masculine mystique: Preferences for alternative forms of assistance among men who avoid counseling.

Journal: *Journal of Counseling Psychology*, April 1992, *39*(2), 240–246.

Related Research: Fisher, E. H., & Turner, J. L. (1970). Orientations to seeking professional help: Development and research utility of an attitude scale. *Journal of Consulting and Clinical Psychology, 35,* 79–90.

■ ■ ■

6126

Test Name: GENDER ROLE ATTITUDES SCALE

Purpose: To measure gender role attitudes.

Number of Items: 7

Format: Likert format. All items presented.

Reliability: Alpha was .73.

Authors: Booth, A., and Amato, P. R.

Article: Parental gender role nontraditionalism and offspring outcomes.

Journal: *Journal of Marriage and the Family*, November 1994, *56*(4), 865–877.

Related Research: Booth, A., et al. (1991). *Marital instability over the life course methodology report and code book for three wave panel study.* Lincoln: University of Nebraska, Bureau of Sociological Research.

■ ■ ■

6127

Test Name: GENDER ROLE SCALES

Purpose: To measure attitudes toward working wives.

Number of Items: 8

Format: 5-point agreement scales. All items presented.

Reliability: Alphas ranged from .68 to .76 across subscales.

Validity: Two factors have similar loadings for both White and African American respondents.

Authors: Blee, K. M., and Tickmyer, A. R.

Article: Racial differences in men's attitudes about women's gender roles.

Journal: *Journal of Marriage and the Family*, February 1995, *57*(1), 21–30.

Related Research: Grienstein, T. N. (1995). Gender ideology, marital disruption, and the employment of married women. *Journal of Marriage and the Family, 57,* 31–42.

■ ■ ■

6128

Test Name: GENERAL UNION ATTITUDES SCALE

Purpose: To measure attitudes toward labor unions.

Number of Items: 16

Format: Sample items are presented.

Reliability: Coefficient alpha was .93.

Validity: Correlations with other variables ranged from -.06 to .71.

Authors: Barling, J., et al.

Article: Preemployment predictors of union attitudes: The role of family socialization and work beliefs.

Journal: *Journal of Applied Psychology*, October 1991, *76*(5), 725–731.

Related Research: Getman, J. G., et al. (1976). *Union representation elections: Law and reality.* New York: Russell Sage.

McShane, S. (1986). General union attitudes: A construct validation. *Journal of Labor Research, 7,* 403–417.

■ ■ ■

6129

Test Name: GROUP THERAPY SURVEY

Purpose: To measure client attitudinal and behavioral expectations about group psychotherapy.

Number of Items: 25

Format: 4-point Likert format ranges from 1 (*strongly agree*) to 4 (*strongly disagree*).

Reliability: Alpha was .79 on the Positive Attitudes subscale.

Authors: Leong, F. T. L., et al.

Article: Group counseling expectations among Asian American students: The role of culture-specific factors.

Journal: *Journal of Counseling Psychology*, April 1995, *42*(2), 217–222.

Related Research: Slocum, Y. S. (1987). A survey of expectations about group therapy among clinical and nonclinical populations. *International Journal of Group Psychotherapy, 37,* 39–54.

■ ■ ■

6130

Test Name: GULF WAR ATTITUDE SCALES

Purpose: To assess attitudes toward the Gulf War.

Number of Items: 25

Format: 5-point response scales. Sample items are presented.

Reliability: Alphas ranged from .72 to .79 across subscales.

Validity: Correlations with other variables ranged from -.25 to .51.

Authors: Heskin, K., and Power, V.

Article: The determinants of Australians' attitudes toward the Gulf War.

Journal: *The Journal of Social Psychology*, June 1994, *133*(3), 317–330.

•••

6131

Test Name: HELPING ATTITUDES INSTRUMENT

Purpose: To measure helping attitudes.

Number of Items: 20

Format: 6-point bipolar scales. All items are presented.

Reliability: Alpha was .80. Split-half was .87.

Validity: Correlations with other variables ranged from -.54 to .50.

Author: Barber, N.

Article: Machiavellianism and altruism: Effect of relatedness of target person on Machiavellian and helping attitudes.

Journal: *Psychological Reports*, August 1994, *75*(1) Part II, 405–422.

•••

6132

Test Name: HISPANICS IN BUSINESS SCALE

Purpose: To assess attitudes toward Hispanic people as managers.

Number of Items: 33

Format: 7-point Likert format. Sample items presented.

Reliability: Alpha was .91.

Authors: Tomkiewicz, J., et al.

Article: Hispanic persons in business: Is there cause for optimism?

Journal: *Psychological Reports*, December 1991, *69*(3) Part I, 847–852.

Related Research: Stevens, G. E. (1984, June). Attitudes towards Blacks in management are changing. *Personnel Administrator*, 163–171.

•••

6133

Test Name: HOMOPHOBIA SCALE

Purpose: To assess counselor homophobia.

Number of Items: 16

Format: Responses are made on a 5-point scale ranging from 1 (*strongly agree*) to 5 (*strongly disagree*).

Reliability: Item-total correlation was .76. Internal consistency (alpha) was .93. Test–retest (4 weeks) reliability was .93.

Authors: Hayes, J. A., and Gelso, C. J.

Article: Male counselors' discomfort with gay and HIV-infected clients.

Journal: *Journal of Counseling Psychology*, January 1993, *40*(1), 86–93.

Related Research: Daly, J. (1990). *Measuring attitudes toward lesbians and gay men: Development and initial psychometric evaluation of an instrument.* Unpublished doctoral dissertation, Southern Illinois University at Carbondale.

•••

6134

Test Name: HOMOSEXUAL ATTITUDES INDICATOR

Purpose: To measure attitudes toward homosexual feelings and behavior, toward homosexuality in general, and toward disclosure of homosexuality.

Number of Items: 34

Format: 5-point Likert format.

Reliability: Alpha was .89.

Author: Dupras, A.

Article: Internalized homophobia and psychosexual adjustment among gay men.

Journal: *Psychological Reports*, August 1994, *75*(1) Part I, 23–28.

Related Research: Nungesser, L. (1983). *Homosexual acts, actors and identities.* New York: Praeger.

•••

6135

Test Name: HUMANITARIAN SCALE

Purpose: To assess positive and sympathetic attitudes toward human beings.

Number of Items: 6

Format: 5-point Likert format. Sample items presented.

Reliability: Spearman-Brown split-half validity was .73.

Validity: Correlations with other variables ranged from -.68 to .59.

Author: Wagstaff, G. F.

Article: Attitudes toward animals and human beings.

Journal: *The Journal of Social Psychology*, August 1991, *131*(4), 573–575.

•••

6136

Test Name: HUMAN RIGHTS QUESTIONNAIRE

Purpose: To measure attitudes toward human rights.

Number of Items: 38

Format: 7-point Likert format. All items are presented.

Reliability: Alphas ranged from .76 to .83 across subscales.

Validity: Correlations with other variables ranged from -.44 to .50.

Authors: Diaz-Veizades, J., et al.

Article: The measurement and structure of human rights attitudes.

Journal: *The Journal of Social Psychology*, April 1995, *135*(2), 313–328.

• • •

6137

Test Name: HYPERCOMPETITIVE ATTITUDE SCALE

Purpose: To assess individual differences in hypercompetitive attitudes.

Number of Items: 26

Format: 5-point scales range from 1 (*never true of me*) to 5 (*always true of me*). Sample items are presented.

Reliability: Alpha was .85.

Validity: Correlations with other variables ranged from -.23 to .34.

Authors: Ryckman, R. M., et al.

Article: Personality correlates of the Hypercompetitive Attitude Scale: Validity tests of Horney's theory of neurosis.

Journal: *Journal of Personality Assessment*, February 1994, *62*(1), 84–94.

Related Research: Ryckman, R. M., et al. (1990). Construction of a Hypercompetitive Attitude Scale. *Journal of Personality Assessment, 55,* 630–639.

6138

Test Name: INCEST ATTITUDES SURVEY

Purpose: To assess attitudes toward incest.

Number of Items: 23

Format: Includes 4 subscales: Definition, Fantasy, Dynamics, and Effects. Responses are made on a 4-point scale ranging from 0 (*strongly disagree*) to 3 (*strongly agree*). Examples are presented.

Reliability: Internal consistency reliability coefficients ranged from .48 to .89.

Validity: Correlations with other variables ranged from -.42 to .31.

Authors: Adams, E. M., and Betz, N. E.

Article: Gender differences in counselors' attitudes toward and attributions about incest.

Journal: *Journal of Counseling Psychology*, April 1993, *40*(2), 210–216.

Related Research: Ciccone, B. S. (1982). The development of an instrument to study incest attitudes. *Dissertation Abstracts International, 42,* 4743B.

• • •

6139

Test Name: INTERVENTION RATING PROFILE

Purpose: To assess the acceptability of behavioral interventions for presenting problems in case descriptions.

Number of Items: 20

Format: Responses are made on a 6-point Likert-type scale ranging from *strongly disagree* to *strongly agree*.

Reliability: Cronbach's alpha was .91.

Authors: Dunson, R. M., et al.

Article: Effect of behavioral consultation on student and teacher behavior.

Journal: *Journal of School Psychology*, Fall 1994, *32*(3), 247–266.

Related Research: Witt, J. C., et al. (1984). Factors affecting teachers' judgments of the acceptability of behavioral interventions: Time, involvement, behavior problems severity and type of intervention. *Behavior Therapy, 75,* 205–209.

• • •

6140

Test Name: ISSUE INVOLVEMENT SCALE

Purpose: To measure issue involvement.

Number of Items: 20

Format: Responses are made on a 7-point scale. Examples are presented.

Reliability: Alpha was .95.

Validity: Correlations with other variables were .31 and .59.

Authors: Gotlieb, J. B., and Dubinsky, A. J.

Article: Influence of price on aspects of consumers' cognitive process.

Journal: *Journal of Applied Psychology*, August 1991, *76*(4), 541–549.

Related Research: Zaichkowsky, J. L. (1985). Measuring the involvement construct. *Journal of Consumer Research, 12,* 341–352.

• • •

6141

Test Name: LANGUAGE ATTITUDE OF TEACHERS SCALE

Purpose: To measure teacher language attitudes.

Number of Items: 13

Format: Includes 3 factors: Language Politics, English Proficiency Intolerance, and Language Support. Responses are made on a 5-point Likert-type scale ranging from 1 (*strongly disagree*) to 5 (*strongly agree*). All items are presented.

Reliability: Alpha coefficients ranged from .60 to .81. Test–retest reliability was .72 ($N=28$).

Authors: Byrnes, D., and Kiger, G.

Article: Language Attitudes of Teachers Scale (LATS).

Journal: *Educational and Psychological Measurement*, Spring 1994, *54*(1), 227–231.

Related Research: Schuman, H., et al. (1988). *Racial attitudes in America*. Cambridge, MA: Harvard University Press.

■ ■ ■

6142

Test Name: LIFE ROLE SALIENCE SCALES

Purpose: To assess one's attitude toward four life roles.

Number of Items: 40

Format: Includes 4 scales: Occupational, Marital, Parental, and Home-Care. Responses are made on a 5-point agree–disagree scale. Examples are presented.

Reliability: Alpha coefficients ranged from .67 to .94.

Validity: Correlations with other variables ranged from -.20 to .23.

Authors: Campbell, K. M., and Campbell, D. J.

Article: Psychometric properties of the life role salience scales: Some construct validation evidence from

a sample of nonprofessional women.

Journal: *Educational and Psychological Measurement*, April 1995, *55*(2), 317–328.

Related Research: Amatea, E., et al. (1986). Assessing the work and family role expectations of career-oriented men and women: The Life Role Salience Scales. *Journal of Marriage and the Family*, *48*, 831–838.

■ ■ ■

6143

Test Name: MAINSTREAMING ATTITUDE INVENTORY FOR DAY CARE PROVIDERS

Purpose: To measure attitude of day care providers.

Number of Items: 15

Format: Responses are made on a 5-point scale ranging from *strongly agree* to *strongly disagree*.

Reliability: Coefficient alpha was .78.

Author: Folsom-Meek, S. L.

Article: Validity and reliability of a Mainstreaming Attitude Inventory for child-care providers.

Journal: *Perceptual and Motor Skills*, June 1995, *80*(3) Part 2, 1113–1114.

Related Research: Jansma, P., & Shultz, B. (1982). Validation and use of a mainstreaming attitude inventory with physical educators. *American Corrective Therapy Journal*, *36*, 150–158.

■ ■ ■

6144

Test Name: MATHEMATICS ATTITUDE SCALES

Purpose: To assess students' personal views of themselves as learners of mathematics, students' views of the usefulness of mathematics, students' views of

mathematics as a male domain, and parental support for mathematics study.

Number of Items: 40

Format: 5-point Likert format.

Reliability: Alphas ranged from .34 to .87 across subscales and samples.

Validity: Correlations with other variables ranged from -.52 to .35.

Authors: Tocci, C. M., and Englehard, G., Jr.

Article: Achievement, parental support, and gender differences in attitudes toward mathematics.

Journal: *Journal of Educational Research*, May/June 1991, *85*(5), 280–286.

Related Research: Garden, R. A. (1987). The second IEA mathematics study. *Cooperative Education Review*, *31*, 47–68.

■ ■ ■

6145

Test Name: MATHEMATICS ATTITUDE SURVEY

Purpose: To assess students' self-concept, locus of control, attitude toward mathematics, sex role orientation, and family orientation.

Number of Items: 23

Format: Responses are made on a 4-point scale ranging from *strongly agree* to *strongly disagree*.

Reliability: Coefficient alpha was .75.

Authors: Randhawa, B. S., et al.

Article: Role of mathematics self-efficacy in the structural model of mathematics achievement.

Journal: *Journal of Educational Psychology*, March 1993, *85*(1), 41–48.

Related Research: Ethington, C. A., & Wolfe, L. M. (1988).

Women's selection of quantitative undergraduate fields of study: Direct and indirect influences. *American Educational Research Journal*, *25*, 157–175.

■ ■ ■

6146

Test Name: MATHEMATICS ATTITUDE SURVEY

Purpose: To assess various attitudes about mathematics.

Number of Items: 42

Format: 5-point Likert format ranges from *strongly disagree* to *strongly agree.*

Reliability: Alphas ranged from .34 to .89 across subscales. Total alphas ranged from .81 to .84.

Authors: Gierl, M. J., and Bisanz, J.

Article: Anxieties and attitudes related to mathematics in Grades 3 and 6.

Journal: *Journal of Experimental Education*, Winter 1995, *63*(2), 139–158.

Related Research: Fennema, E., & Sherman, J. (1976). Fennema-Sherman Mathematics Attitude Scales: Instruments designed to measure attitudes towards the learning of mathematics by females and males. *JSAS Catalogue of Selected Documents in Psychology*, *6*, 31–32.

■ ■ ■

6147

Test Name: MODERN RACISM SCALE

Purpose: To measure the extent to which a White person holds racial attitudes or beliefs toward Blacks.

Number of Items: Two versions: 6-item version and 7-item version.

Format: Has both a 5-point and a 4-point Likert scale format.

Reliability: Alpha coefficients were

.75 (*N* = 879) and .79 (*N* = 709) for 6-item format. Alpha coefficients ranged from .81 to .86 for the 7-item format and test–retest reliabilities ranged from .72 to .93.

Validity: Correlations with other variables ranged from -.30 to .70.

Authors: Sabnani, H. B., and Ponterotto, J. G.

Article: Racial/ethnic minority-specific instrumentation in counseling research: A review, critique, and recommendations.

Journal: *Measurement and Evaluation in Counseling and Development*, January 1992, *24*(4), 161–187.

Related Research: McConahay, J. B. (1986). Modern racism, ambivalence, and the modern racism scale. In J. F. Dovidio & S. L. Gaertner (Eds.), *Prejudice, discrimination, and racism* (pp. 91–125). New York: Academic Press.

■ ■ ■

6148

Test Name: OPINIONS ABOUT DEAF PEOPLE SCALE

Purpose: To measure beliefs about deaf adults' capabilities.

Number of Items: 20

Format: Responses are made on a 4-point Likert scale. All items are presented.

Reliability: Coefficient alpha was .83. Split-half reliability was .82.

Validity: Correlation with Attitude Toward Deafness Scale was .75.

Authors: Berkay, P. J., et al.

Article: The development of the Opinions About Deaf People Scale: A scale to measure hearing adults' beliefs about the capabilities of deaf adults.

Journal: *Educational and Psychological Measurement*, February 1995, *55*(1), 105–114.

6149

Test Name: OPINIONS ABOUT MENTAL ILLNESS SCALE

Purpose: To identify opinion about the cause, treatment, description, and prognosis of mental illness.

Number of Items: 51

Format: Includes a 6-point scale ranging from 1 (*strongly agree*) to 6 (*strongly disagree*). Includes 5 factors: Authoritarianism, Benevolence, Mental Hygiene Ideology, Social Restrictiveness, and Interpersonal Etiology.

Reliability: KR-20 reliability coefficients ranged from .21 to .89.

Authors: Nickerson, K. J., et al.

Article: Cultural mistrust, opinions about mental illness, and Black students' attitudes toward seeking psychological help from White counselors.

Journal: *Journal of Counseling Psychology*, July 1994, *41*(3), 378–385.

Related Research: Cohen, J., & Struening, E. L. (1962). Opinions about mental illness in the personnel of two large mental hospitals. *Journal of Abnormal and Social Psychology*, *64*, 349–360.

■ ■ ■

6150

Test Name: OPINIONS ABOUT TESTING QUESTIONNAIRE

Purpose: To assess teachers' opinions about testing.

Number of Items: 18

Format: 6-point Likert format. All items are described.

Reliability: Internal consistency reliabilities ranged from .63 to .75.

Author: Green, K. E.

Article: Differing opinions on

testing between preservice and inservice teachers.

Journal: *Journal of Educational Research*, September/October 1992, *86*(1), 37–42.

Related Research: Green, K. E., & Stager, S. F. (1986). Measuring attitudes of teachers toward testing. *Measurement and Evaluation in Counseling and Development*, *19*, 141–150.

■ ■ ■

6151

Test Name: PARENT READING BELIEF INVENTORY

Purpose: To measure parents' beliefs about the goals and process of reading aloud to young children.

Number of Items: 55

Format: Includes 7 subscales: Affect, Participation, Resources, Efficacy, Knowledge, Environment, and Reading Instruction. Responses are made on a 4-point Likert-type scale ranging from 1 (*strongly agree*) to 4 (*strongly disagree*). Examples are presented.

Reliability: Alpha coefficients ranged from .50 to .85. Test–retest reliability was .79.

Validity: Correlations with other variables ranged from .07 to .39.

Authors: De Baryshe, B. D., and Binder, J. C.

Article: Development of an instrument for measuring parental beliefs about reading aloud to young children.

Journal: *Perceptual and Motor Skills*, June 1994, *78*(3) Part 2, 1303–1311.

■ ■ ■

6152

Test Name: PARENTS' ATTITUDES TOWARD UNIONS

Purpose: To assess children's perceptions of their parents' attitudes toward unions.

Number of Items: 6

Format: Responses are made on a 5-point scale.

Reliability: Alpha was .82 (mothers) and .84 (fathers).

Validity: Correlations ranged from .03 to .72.

Author: Barling, J.

Article: Pre-employment predictors of union attitudes: The role of family socialization and work beliefs.

Journal: *Journal of Applied Psychology*, October 1991, *76*(5), 725–731.

Related Research: Brett, J. M. (1980). Why employees want unions. *Organizational Dynamics*, *8*, 47–59.

■ ■ ■

6153

Test Name: PREGNANCY BELIEF SCALE

Purpose: To assess attitudes and beliefs about sexual intercourse and conception.

Number of Items: 5

Format: 4-point agreement scales. All items presented.

Reliability: Alpha was .55.

Authors: Pleck, J. H., et al.

Article: Adolescent males' condom use: Relationships between perceived costs-benefits and consistency.

Journal: *Journal of Marriage and the Family*, August 1991, *53*(3), 733–745.

Related Research: Scheehan, M. K., et al. (1986). Perceptions of sexual responsibility: Do young men and women agree? *Pediatric Nursing*, *12*, 17–21.

■ ■ ■

6154

Test Name: PRIMARY TEACHER QUESTIONNAIRE

Purpose: To assess teacher beliefs about appropriate practice in primary-grade settings.

Number of Items: 42

Format: 4-point Likert format. All items are presented.

Reliability: Alphas ranged from .80 to .87 across two subscales.

Validity: Group difference data presented.

Author: Smith, K.

Article: Development of the Primary Teacher Questionnaire.

Journal: *Journal of Educational Research*, September/October 1993, *87*(1), 23–29.

■ ■ ■

6155

Test Name: PSYCHOTHERAPISTS' QUESTIONNAIRE

Purpose: To measure psychotherapists' attitudes and observations of nonverbal behavior in the introductory greeting situation.

Number of Items: 28

Format: Yes–no and multiple-choice formats. All items presented.

Reliability: Interrater kappas ranged from .00 to 1.00. Intrarater kappas ranged from .00 to 1.00.

Authors: Astrom, J., et al.

Article: Psychotherapists' attitudes toward observations of nonverbal communication in a greeting situation: I. Psychometrics of a questionnaire.

Journal: *Psychological Reports*, December 1991, *69*(3) Part I, 963–975.

Related Research: Åström J., et al. (1992). Psychotherapists' attitudes towards observations of nonverbal communication in a greeting situation: II. Relationships to background variables. *Psychological Reports*, *70*, 103–194.

• • •

6156

Test Name: PUBLIC VIEWS OF INTELLIGENCE QUESTIONNAIRE

Purpose: To measure lay views and opinions of intelligence.

Number of Items: 23

Format: Likert format. All items are presented.

Validity: Three scales were identified by factor analysis: (a) Intelligence Is Real, Inherited, and Fixed, (b) Intelligence Is Relative and Cannot Be Defined Scientifically, and (c) Males and Females Have Different Abilities.

Authors: Räty, H., et al.

Article: Public views on intelligence: A Finnish study.

Journal: *Psychological Reports*, February 1993, *72*(1), 59–65.

Related Research: Shipstone, K., & Burt, S. L. (1973). Twenty-five years on: A replication of Flugel's (1947) work on lay "popular views of intelligence and related topics." *British Journal of Educational Psychology*, *43*, 183–187.

• • •

6157

Test Name: PUNITIVE-INTERNAL ATTITUDES TO OFFENDERS SCALE

Purpose: To measure attitudes toward offenders.

Number of Items: 8

Format: All items presented.

Reliability: Alpha was .74.

Validity: Correlations with other variables ranged from -.27 to .78.

Authors: Mohr, P. B., and Luscri, G.

Article: Blame and punishment: Attitudes to juvenile and criminal offending.

Journal: *Psychological Reports*, December 1995, *77*(3) Part II, 1091–1096.

• • •

6158

Test Name: QUICK DISCRIMINATION INDEX

Purpose: To measure one's attitudes toward racial diversity and women's equality.

Number of Items: 30

Format: Includes 3 factors: general racial diversity and multiculturalism attitudes, affective racial diversity attitudes, and general women's equity issues attitudes. Responses are made on a 5-point Likert-type scale ranging from 1 (*strongly disagree*) to 5 (*strongly agree*). All items are presented.

Reliability: Alpha coefficients ranged from .65 to .88. Test–retest (15 weeks) reliability coefficients ranged from .65 to .96.

Validity: Correlations with other variables ranged from -.19 to .50.

Authors: Ponterotto, J. G., et al.

Article: Development and initial validation of the Quick Discrimination Index (QDI).

Journal: *Educational and Psychological Measurement*, December 1995, *55*(6), 1016–1031.

• • •

6159

Test Name: RAPE MYTH ACCEPTANCE SCALE

Purpose: To measure adherence to typical myths about rape.

Number of Items: 19

Format: Formats vary. Sample items are presented.

Reliability: Alpha was .56.

Authors: Rosenthal, E. H., et al.

Article: Changing the rape-supportive attitudes of traditional and non-traditional male and female college students.

Journal: *Journal of Counseling Psychology*, April 1995, *42*(2), 171–177.

Related Research: Burt, M. R. (1980). Cultural myths and support for rape. *Journal of Personality and Social Psychology*, *38*, 217–230.

Heppner, M. J., et al. (1995). The differential effects of rape prevention programming on attitudes, behavior and knowledge. *Journal of Counseling Psychology*, *42*, 508–518.

• • •

6160

Test Name: READING BELIEF SCALES

Purpose: To measure beliefs regarding how one reads, and beliefs regarding how reading develops.

Number of Items: 30

Format: All items are presented.

Reliability: Scoring methods are described. Consistency across instruments and teacher groups ranged from .84 to .89.

Authors: Konopak, B. C., et al.

Article: Preservice and inservice secondary teachers' orientations toward content area reading.

Journal: *Journal of Educational Research*, March/April 1994, *87*(4), 220-227.

Related Research: Kinzer, C. K., & Carrick, D. A. (1986). Teacher beliefs and instructional influences. In J. Niles & R. Lalik (Eds.), *Solving problems in literacy: Learners, teachers and researchers* (pp. 127–134). New York: National Reading Conference.

■ ■ ■

6161

Test Name: REVISED SITUATIONAL ATTITUDE SCALE

Purpose: To determine participants' racial attitudes.

Number of Items: 10

Format: Personal and social situations are presented that have some relevance to a racial response. Reactions to each situation are measured on 10 bipolar semantic differential scales.

Reliability: Median communality (internal consistency) was .60.

Authors: Balenger, V. J., et al.

Article: Racism attitudes among incoming White students: A study of 10-year trends.

Journal: *Journal of College Student Development*, May 1992, *33*(3), 245–252.

Related Research: Minatoya, L. Y., & Sedlacek, W. E. (1979). *Attitudes of Whites toward Blacks: A revision of the Situational Attitude Scale (SAS*; Counseling Center Research Report No. 7-79). College Park: University of Maryland.

■ ■ ■

6162

Test Name: SERIOUS THEFT SCALE

Purpose: To assess the seriousness of theft.

Number of Items: 7

Format: 6-point frequency scales. All items are presented.

Reliability: Alphas ranged from .53 to .74.

Validity: Correlations with other variables ranged from -.24 to .46.

Authors: McCarthy, B., and Hagan, J.

Article: Mean streets: The theoretical significance of situational delinquency among homeless youth.

Journal: *American Journal of Sociology*, November 1992, *98*(3), 597–627.

■ ■ ■

6163

Test Name: SEXIST ATTITUDES TOWARD WOMEN SCALE

Purpose: To examine attitudes of women in regard to feminist ideology.

Number of Items: 40

Format: Responses are made on a 6-point Likert-type scale.

Validity: Correlation with Rape-Myth Acceptance Scale was .41.

Authors: Anderson, W. P., and Cummings, K.

Article: Women's acceptance of rape myths and their sexual experiences.

Journal: *Journal of College Student Development*, January 1993, *34*(1), 53–57.

Related Research: Benson, P., & Vincent, S. (1980). Development and validation of the Sexist Attitudes Toward Women Scale (SATWS). *Psychology of Women Quarterly*, *5*(2), 276–291.

■ ■ ■

6164

Test Name: SEX-ROLE ATTITUDE SCALE

Purpose: To assess sex-role attitudes where sex-role stereotyping is less pronounced than in the United States.

Number of Items: 17

Format: Likert format. All items presented.

Reliability: Alpha was .84.

Authors: Van Yperen, N. W., and Buunk, B. P.

Article: Sex-role attitudes, social comparison, and satisfaction with relationships.

Journal: *Social Psychology Quarterly*, June 1991, *54*(2), 169–180.

Related Research: Van Yperen, N. W., & Buunck, B. P. (1991). Equity theory, communal and exchange orientation in cross-cultural perspective. *Journal of Social Psychology*, *131*, 5–20.

■ ■ ■

6165

Test Name: SEXUAL PERMISSIVENESS SCALE

Purpose: To measure attitudes toward sexuality.

Number of Items: 20

Format: 7-point agreement scales.

Reliability: Alpha was .91.

Authors: Oliver, M. B., and Sedikides, C.

Article: Effects of sexual permissiveness on desirability of partner as a function of low and high commitment to relationship.

Journal: *Social Psychology Quarterly*, September 1992, *55*(3), 321–333.

Related Research: Hendrick, S., & Hendrick, C. (1987). Multidimensionality of sexual attitudes. *Journal of Sex Research*, *23*, 502–526.

6166

Test Name: SITUATIONAL ATTITUDE SCALE

Purpose: To measure attitudes toward groups that are targets of oppression and prejudice.

Number of Items: 10

Format: Respondents share reactions to personal and social situations by checking a point on each semantic differential that describes their feelings.

Reliability: Cronbach's alpha reliability coefficients ranged from .76 to .91.

Authors: Engstrom, C. M., et al.

Article: Faculty attitudes toward male revenue and nonrevenue student-athletes.

Journal: *Journal of College Student Development*, May/June 1995, *36*(3), 217–227.

Related Research: Engstrom, C. M., & Sedlacek, W. E. (1991). A study of prejudice toward college student-athletes. *Journal of Counseling and Development, 70*, 189–193.

■ ■ ■

6167

Test Name: SOCIAL SCALE

Purpose: To measure attitudes toward Blacks.

Number of Items: 55

Format: Responses are made on a 7-point Likert scale.

Reliability: Coefficient alphas on the subscales ranged from .95 to .91.

Authors: Neville, H., and Furlong, M.

Article: The impact of participation in a cultural awareness program on the racial attitudes and social behaviors of first-year college students.

Journal: *Journal of College Student Development*, September 1994, *35*(5), 371–377.

Related Research: Byrnes, D. A., & Kiger, G. (1988). Contemporary measures of attitudes toward Blacks. *Educational and Psychological Measurement, 48*, 107–118.

■ ■ ■

6168

Test Name: SOCIO-POLITICAL ATTITUDES SCALES

Purpose: To measure attitudes toward the Persian Gulf War, support for the Los Angeles Police Department, and dimensions of racism.

Number of Items: 18

Format: 5-point Likert format. All items presented.

Reliability: Alphas ranged from .61 to .97.

Validity: Correlations with other variables ranged from -.004 to .60.

Authors: Sidanius, J., and Liu, J. H.

Article: The Gulf War and the Rodney King beating: Implications of the general conservatism and social dominance perspectives.

Journal: *The Journal of Social Psychology*, December 1992, *132*(6), 685–700.

■ ■ ■

6169

Test Name: STATISTICS ATTITUDE SCALE

Purpose: To measure attitudes toward statistics.

Number of Items: 20

Format: 5-point Likert format. Sample items presented.

Reliability: Alpha was .95.

Authors: Glencross, M. J., and Cherian, V. I.

Article: Attitudes toward applied statistics of postgraduate students in education in the Lebowa region of South Africa.

Journal: *Psychological Reports*, August 1995, *77*(1), 315–322.

Related Research: Glencross, M. J., & Cherian, V. I. (1992). Attitudes toward applied statistics of postgraduate education students in Transkei. *Psychological Reports, 70*, 67–75.

■ ■ ■

6170

Test Name: STUDENT ATTITUDE INVENTORY

Purpose: To assess students' opinions about the honor system at a university and their perceptions of themselves within the system.

Number of Items: 30

Format: Responses are made on a 4-point Likert scale.

Reliability: Internal consistency reliability estimate, coefficient alpha, was .82.

Authors: May, K. M., and Loyd, B. H.

Article: Academic dishonesty: The honor system and students' attitudes.

Journal: *Journal of College Student Development*, March 1993, *34*(2), 125–129.

Related Research: Haines, V. J., et al. (1986). College cheating: Immaturity, lack of commitment, and the neutralizing attitude. *Research in Higher Education, 25*, 342–354.

■ ■ ■

6171

Test Name: STUDENT ATTITUDES TOWARDS WAR SCALE

Purpose: To assess student attitudes toward war.

Number of Items: 23

Format: Likert format.

Reliability: Total alpha was .90. Subscale alphas ranged from .42 to .70.

Validity: One in 27 correlations with personality traits was significant at the .05 level.

Author: Lester, D.

Article: Factors affecting students attitudes toward war.

Journal: *The Journal of Social Psychology*, August 1994, *133*(4), 541–543.

▪▪▪

6172

Test Name: SUPERVISOR ATTITUDES AND BEHAVIOR SCALE

Purpose: To measure subordinates' perceptions of supervisors' attitudes and behaviors.

Number of Items: 32

Format: 5-point Likert format. All items are presented.

Reliability: Alphas ranged from .74 to .96 across subscales.

Authors: Tjosvold, D., et al.

Article: Leadership influence: Goal interdependence and power.

Journal: *The Journal of Social Psychology*, February 1992, *132*(1), 39–50.

Related Research: Tjosvold, D., et al. (1983). Cooperative and competitive relationships between leaders and their subordinates. *Human Relations, 36*, 1111–1124.

▪▪▪

6173

Test Name: SURVEY FOR WRITING ATTITUDES

Purpose: To measure attitudes toward writing in Grades 4 to 8.

Number of Items: 19

Format: 5-point responses ranging from 1 (*almost always*) to 5 (*almost never*). All items are presented.

Reliability: Cronbach's alphas ranged from .50 to .75 across subscales. Total alpha was .78

Author: Knudson, R. E.

Article: Development and use of a writing attitudes survey in Grades 4 to 8.

Journal: *Psychological Reports*, June 1991, *68*(3) Part I, 807–816.

Related Research: Daly, J. A., & Miller, M. D. (1975). The empirical development of an instrument to measure writing apprehension. *Research in the Teaching of English, 9*, 242–249.

▪▪▪

6174

Test Name: SURVEY OF THE ATTITUDES TOWARD STATISTICS

Purpose: To measure students' attitudes toward statistics.

Number of Items: 28

Format: Includes 4 factors: Affect, Cognitive Competence, Value, and Difficulty. Responses are made on a 7-point Likert scale ranging from 1 (*strongly disagree*) to 7 (*strongly agree*).

Reliability: Alpha coefficients ranged from .64 to .85.

Validity: Correlations with the Attitudes Toward Statistics ranged from -.03 to .79.

Authors: Schau, C., et al.

Article: The development and validation of the Survey of Attitudes Toward Statistics.

Journal: *Educational and Psychological Measurement*, October 1995, *55*(5), 868–875.

6175

Test Name: "TALL POPPY" SCALE

Purpose: To assess attitudes toward high achievers.

Number of Items: 20

Format: 7-point agreement scales. All items presented.

Reliability: Alphas ranged from .59 to .80 across subscales, and across Australian and Japanese samples.

Authors: Feather, N. T., and McKee, I. R.

Article: Global self-esteem and attitudes toward the high achiever for Australian and Japanese students.

Journal: *Social Psychology Quarterly*, March 1993, *56*(1), 65–76.

Related Research: Feather, N. T. (1989). Attitudes towards the high achiever: The fall of the tall poppy. *Australian Journal of Psychology, 41*, 239–267.

▪▪▪

6176

Test Name: TEACHER ATTITUDES ABOUT RESEARCH QUESTIONNAIRE

Purpose: To identify teachers' attitudes toward educational research.

Number of Items: 20

Format: Includes 6 areas: importance of educational research to teaching, difficulties in interpreting educational research, preferred ways of learning educational research, interest in conducting action research, general attitudes toward educational research, and ability to find systematic answers to classroom problems. Responses are made on a 5-point scale ranging from 1 (*strongly agree*) to

5 (*strongly disagree*). All items are presented.

Reliability: Alpha coefficient was .78 (*N*= 39). Test–retest (1 semester) reliability was .67 (*N*= 23).

Author: Sardo-Brown, D.

Article: Classroom teachers' attitudes about research reported in psychological journals before, during, and after completing a graduate research course in which they plan an action research study.

Journal: *Journal of Research and Development in Education*, Summer 1992, *25*(4), 248–254.

Related Research: Pettus, A. M., & Allain, V. A. (1991). *Teachers and research: Thresholds of change.* Paper presented at the annual meeting of the Association of Teacher Educators, New Orleans, Louisiana.

■ ■ ■

6177

Test Name: TEACHER BELIEFS ABOUT INSTRUCTIONAL MEDIA

Purpose: To measure teachers' beliefs about instructional media.

Number of Items: 72

Time Required: Approximately 20 minutes.

Format: Includes 2 factors: Technological Beliefs and Traditional Beliefs.

Reliability: Reliability coefficients ranged from .80 to .92.

Author: Lawless, K. A.

Article: Development of a measure to assess teacher beliefs about instructional media.

Journal: *Educational and Psychological Measurement*, October 1995, *55*(5), 876–880.

6178

Test Name: TEACHER SURVEY

Purpose: To query teachers on the effects of standardized tests.

Number of Items: 81

Format: Likert-type items are used. Includes 13 subscales.

Reliability: Alpha coefficients ranged from .32 to .88.

Authors: Herman, J. L., et al.

Article: Assessing the effects of standardized testing on schools.

Journal: *Educational and Psychological Measurement*, Summer 1994, *54*(2), 471–482.

Related Research: Herman, J. L., et al. (1990). *The effects of testing on teaching and learning* (CSE Tech. Rep. No. 327, Grant No. OERI-G-86-0003). Los Angeles: University of California Center for Research on Evaluating Standards, and Student Testing.

■ ■ ■

6179

Test Name: TEST ATTITUDE SURVEY

Purpose: To assess test-taking motivation and attitudinal dispositions.

Number of Items: 45

Format: Likert-type measure with responses ranging from 1 (*strongly disagree*) to 7 (*strongly agree*). Includes 9 factors: Motivation, Lack of Concentration, Belief in Test, Test Ease, External Attributions, General Need Achievement, Future Effects, Preparation, and Comparative Anxiety.

Reliability: Alpha coefficients ranged from .50 to .94. Test–retest reliablities ranged from .20 to .74.

Validity: Correlations with other variables ranged from -.50 to .55.

Authors: Schmit, M. J., and Ryan, A. M.

Article: Test-taking dispositions: A missing link?

Journal: *Journal of Applied Psychology*, October 1992, *77*(5), 629–637.

Related Research: Arvey, R. D., et al. (1990). Motivational components of test taking. *Personal Psychology, 43*, 695–716.

■ ■ ■

6180

Test Name: USEFULNESS OF MATHEMATICS SCALE

Purpose: To measure the relevance of mathematics to life and work.

Number of Items: 10

Format: 5-point Likert format.

Reliability: Alpha was .92.

Validity: Correlations with other variables ranged from -.39 to .51.

Authors: Lopez, F. G., and Lent, R. W.

Article: Sources of mathematics self-efficacy in high school students.

Journal: *The Career Development Quarterly*, September 1992, *41*(1), 3–12.

Related Research: Fennema, E., & Sherman, J. A. (1976). Fennema-Sherman Mathematics Attitudes Scales: Instruments designed to measure attitudes towards the learning of mathematics of males and females. *JSAS Catalog of Selected Documents in Psychology, 6*, 31 (Ms. No. 1225).

■ ■ ■

6181

Test Name: WOMEN IN THE MILITARY SCALE

Purpose: To assess attitudes about women in the military.

Number of Items: 12

Format: 7-point agreement scales. All items are presented.

Reliability: Alpha was .80.

Authors: Hurrell, R. M., and Lukens, J. H.

Article: Dimensions of attitudes toward women in the military: Factor analysis of the Women in the Military Scale.

Journal: *Psychological Reports*, June 1995, *76*(3) Part II, 1263–1266.

Related Research: Hurrell, R. M., & Lukens, J. H. (1994). Attitudes towards women in the military during the Persian Gulf War. *Perceptual and Motor Skills*, *78*, 99–104.

■ ■ ■

6182

Test Name: WORK ATTITUDES INVENTORY

Purpose: To measure work attitudes.

Number of Items: 15

Format: Responses are made on a 7-point Likert-type scale ranging from *strongly agree* to *strongly disagree*. Includes two factors: Job Satisfaction and Inner Work Standards.

Reliability: Item-total correlations ranged from .37 to .70.

Authors: Tosti-Vasey, J. L., and Willis, S. L.

Article: Professional currency among midcareer college faculty: Family and work factors.

Journal: *Research in Higher Education*, April 1991, *32*(2), 123–139.

Related Research: Willis, S. L., & Tosti-Vasey, J. L. (1985, April). *Professional obsolescence among mid-career faculty.* Paper presented at the annual meeting of the Eastern Psychological Association, New York.

6183

Test Name: WORLD-VIEW QUESTIONNAIRE

Purpose: To measure world-view.

Number of Items: 40

Format: Bipolar format.

Reliability: Alpha was .86. Guttman split-half was .86.

Validity: 14 of 40 items differed by gender significantly.

Authors: Jensen, L. C., et al.

Article: Do men's and women's world-views differ?

Journal: *Psychological Reports*, February 1991, *68*(1), 312–314.

Related Research: Bernard, J. (1981). *The female world.* New York: Free Press.

■ ■ ■

6184

Test Name: WRITING ATTITUDE SCALE

Purpose: To assess writing attitudes of children.

Number of Items: 19

Format: 5-point scales ranged from 1 (*almost always*), to 5 (*almost never*). All items are presented.

Reliability: Alpha was .78 (children's version) and .84 (primary grade students).

Author: Knudson, R. E.

Article: Writing expectancies, attitudes, and achievement of first to sixth graders.

Journal: *Journal of Educational Research*, November/December 1995, *89*(2), 90–97.

Related Research: Knudson, R. E. (1993). Development of a writing attitude survey for Grades 9 to 12: Effects of gender, grade and ethnicity. *Psychological Reports*, *73*, 587–794.

6185

Test Name: WRITING ATTITUDE SURVEY FOR STUDENTS

Purpose: To measure attitude toward writing.

Number of Items: 19

Format: 5-point frequency scales (*almost always* to *almost never*). All items presented.

Reliability: Alphas ranged from .83 to .84 across two factors.

Validity: No ethnic differences, limited grade-level differences, or significant sex differences were found.

Author: Knudson, R. E.

Article: Development of a writing attitude survey for Grades 9 to 12: Effects of gender, grade, and ethnicity.

Journal: *Psychological Reports*, October 1993, *73*(2), 587–594.

■ ■ ■

6186

Test Name: UNION ATTITUDES SCALE

Purpose: To measure students' perception of parental union attitudes.

Number of Items: 6

Reliability: Coefficient alpha was .86.

Validity: Correlations with other variables ranged from .12 to .72 (*N* = 69).

Authors: Kelloway, E. K., and Watts, L.

Article: Preemployment predictors of union attitudes: Replication and extension.

Journal: *Journal of Applied Psychology*, August 1994, *79*(4), 631–634.

Related Research: Brett, J. M. (1980). Why employees want unions. *Organizational Dynamics*, *8*, 47–59.

CHAPTER 8
Behavior

6187

Test Name: ABUSE AND USE OF DRUGS SURVEY

Purpose: To measure drug abuse and drug use.

Number of Items: 48

Format: Forty items had a given response set. Eight items were open-ended.

Reliability: Cronbach's alpha was .92.

Authors: Hillman, S. B., and Sawilowsky, S. S.

Article: Multidimensional differences between adolescent substance abusers and users.

Journal: *Psychological Reports,* February 1991, *68*(1), 115–122.

Related Research: Labouvie, E. W., & McGee, C. R. (1986). Relation of personality to alcohol and drug use in adolescence. *Journal of Consulting and Clinical Psychology, 54,* 289–293.

· · ·

6188

Test Name: ACADEMIC MISCONDUCT SURVEY

Purpose: To measure incidence of various types of academic misconduct.

Number of Items: 37

Format: Includes 3 sections: Instances of Various Behaviors, Who Cheats?, and Rationales for Academic Misconduct. All items are presented.

Reliability: Alpha coefficients for academic misconduct and

neutralization were .93 and .83 respectively.

Authors: Daniel, L. G., et al.

Article: Academic misconduct among teacher education students: A descriptive-correlational study.

Journal: *Research in Higher Education,* December 1991, *32*(6), 703–724.

Related Research: Haines, V. J., et al. (1986). College cheating: Immaturity, lack, of commitment, and the neutralizing attitude. *Research in Higher Education, 25,* 342–354.

· · ·

6189

Test Name: ACADEMIC MISCONDUCT SURVEY

Purpose: To measure academic misconduct such as copying answers, writing papers for another student, and other more serious actions.

Number of Items: 41

Format: Graphic scale format. All items are presented.

Reliability: Alphas ranged from .51 to .89 across subscales.

Authors: Ferrell, C. M., and Daniel, L. G.

Article: A frame of reference for understanding behaviors related to the academic misconduct of undergraduate teacher education students.

Journal: *Research in Higher Education,* June 1995, *36*(3), 345–375.

Related Research: Daniel, L. G., et al. Academic misconduct among teacher education students: A descriptive correlational study. *Research in Higher Education, 32,* 703–724.

· · ·

6190

Test Name: ACADEMIC PRACTICES SURVEY

Purpose: To assess extent of cheating and plagiarism.

Number of Items: 24

Format: 5-point frequency scales. All items presented.

Reliability: Alpha was .81. Split-half reliability was .87.

Authors: Roig, M., and Detommaso, L.

Article: Are college cheating and plagiarism related to academic procrastination?

Journal: *Psychological Reports,* October 1995, *77*(2), 691–698.

Related Research: Evans, E. D., & Craig, D. (1990). Adolescent cognitions for academic cheating as a function of grade level and achievement status. *Journal of Adolescent Research, 5,* 325–345.

· · ·

6191

Test Name: ACTIVITY AND DRUG USE CHECKLISTS

Purpose: To assess activities high school students engage in with parent/guardians, with peers, with themselves, and at school, as well as how they spend their money and what drugs they use.

Time Required: 35–40 minutes.

Format: Checklist format.

Reliability: Test–retest (1 week) reliabilities ranged from .70 to .94 and higher.

Authors: Lewandowski, L. M., and Westman, A. S.

Article: Drug use and its relation to high school students' activities.

Journal: *Psychological Reports,* April 1991, *68*(2), 363–367.

Related Research: Checklists and summary statistics available from Microfiche Publications, P.O. Box 3513, Grand Central Station, New York, NY 10163 (Document NAPS-04855).

■ ■ ■

6192

Test Name: ACTIVITY SCALE

Purpose: To measure activity level.

Number of Items: 10

Reliability: Coefficient alpha was .69.

Validity: Correlations with other variables ranged from -.02 to .40.

Authors: Conte, J. M., et al.

Article: Time urgency: Conceptual and construct development.

Journal: *Journal of Applied Psychology,* February 1995, *80*(1), 178–185.

Related Research: Buss, A. H., & Plomin, R. (1975). *A temperament theory of personality development.* New York: Wiley.

■ ■ ■

6193

Test Name: ADAPTIVE SOCIAL BEHAVIOR INVENTORY

Purpose: To determine degree of prosocial behavior in young children.

Number of Items: 23

Format: Responses are made on a 3-point scale from 1 (*rarely*) to 3 (*almost always*).

Reliability: Cronbach alpha was .84.

Author: Smith, M. C.

Article: The association between the quality of sibling relationships and developmental outcomes in preschool-age foster children.

Journal: *Child Study Journal,* December 1995, *25*(4), 237–263.

Related Research: Hogan, A. (1992). The Adaptive Social Behavior Inventory (ASBI): A new assessment of social competence in high risk three-year-olds. *Journal of Psychoeducational Assessment, 10,* 230–239.

■ ■ ■

6194

Test Name: ADOLESCENT BEHAVIORAL PROBLEMS SCALE

Purpose: To measure deviance among adolescents.

Number of Items: 12

Format: 6-point frequency scales.

Reliability: Alpha was .71.

Authors: Farrell, M. P., and Barnes, G. M.

Article: Family systems and social support: A test of the effects of cohesion and adaptability on the functioning of parents and adolescents.

Journal: *Journal of Marriage and the Family,* February 1993, *55*(1), 119–132.

Related Research: Barnes, G. M., et al. (1987). Parent-adolescent interactions in the development of alcohol abuse and other deviant behaviors. *Family Perspectives, 21,* 321–335.

6195

Test Name: ADOLESCENT RISK BEHAVIOR AND ATTITUDES QUESTIONNAIRE

Purpose: To assess degree of engagement in risky behavior.

Number of Items: 78

Format: 5-point frequency scales (*never done* to *does very often*)

Reliability: Alpha was .96.

Authors: Moore, S. M., and Gullone, E.

Article: Fear of weight gain: Its correlates among school aged adolescents.

Journal: *Psychological Reports,* June 1995, *76*(3) Part II, 1305–1306.

Related Research: Gullone, E., & Moore, S. (1995). *The Adolescent Risk Behavior and Attitude Questionnaire.* (Unpublished manuscript available from the authors, Victoria University of Technology, Australia.)

■ ■ ■

6196

Test Name: ADULT INVENTORY OF PROCRASTINATION

Purpose: To measure procrastination.

Number of Items: 15

Format: 5-point scales. Sample items are presented.

Reliability: Internal reliability was .74. Test–retest reliability (1 month) was .71.

Validity: Correlations with behavioral measures ranged from -.26 to .12.

Author: Ferrari, J. R.

Article: Psychometric validation of two procrastination inventories for adults: Arousal and avoidance measures.

Journal: *Journal of Psychopathology and Behavioral Assessment*, June 1992, *14*(2), 97–110.

Related Research: McCown, W., & Johnson, J. (1989). *Validation of an adult inventory of procrastination.* Unpublished manuscript, Department of Mental Health/Psychology, Hahneman University, Philadelphia.

■ ■ ■

6197

Test Name: ADULT PLAYFULNESS SCALE

Purpose: To assess playfulness (spontaneity, fun, expressiveness, creativity, silliness).

Number of Items: 32

Format: Semantic differential format. All items presented.

Reliability: Alphas ranged from .73 to .83 across subscales.

Validity: Correlations with other related constructs exceeded .29 (creativity) and .45 (spontaneity). Other correlations reported.

Authors: Glynn, M. A., and Webster, J.

Article: The Adult Playfulness Scale: An initial assessment.

Journal: *Psychological Reports*, August 1992, *71*(1), 83–103.

■ ■ ■

6198

Test Name: AMSTERDAM CHILD BEHAVIOR CHECKLIST

Purpose: To measure attention, restlessness, aggressive, and fear behaviors.

Number of Items: 21

Format: 4-point scales: *fits a little* to *fits (nearly) completely*.

Reliability: Alphas ranged from .77 to .91 across subscales.

Validity: Correlations with

Teacher Report Form ranged from .06 to .79.

Author: DeJong, P. F.

Article: Validity of the Amsterdam Child Behavior Checklist: A short rating scale for children.

Journal: *Psychological Reports*, December 1995, *77*(3) Part II, 1139–1144.

Related Research: DeJong, P. F., & Das-Smaal, E. A. (1991). The Amsterdam Child Behavior Checklist: Short behavior checklist for children. *Nederlands Tijdschrift voor de Psychologie, 46*, 76–83.

■ ■ ■

6199

Test Name: APPLICANT SELF-REPORT INTERVIEW BEHAVIOR

Purpose: To measure applicants' perception of their interview behavior.

Number of Items: 14

Format: Includes 5 scales: self-promotion, fit with organization, opinion conformity, other-enhancement, and nonverbal behavior. Responses are made on a 7-point scales ranging from 1 (*strongly disagree*) to 7 (*strongly agree*). Examples are given.

Reliability: Alpha coefficients ranged from .46 to .80.

Authors: Stevens, C. K., and Kristof, A. L.

Article: Making the right impression: A field study of applicant impression management during job interviews.

Journal: *Journal of Applied Psychology*, October 1995, *80*(5), 587–606.

Related Research: Schlenker, B. R. (1980). Impression management: The self-concept, social identity, and interpersonal

relations. Monterey, CA: Brooks/Cole.

Tedeschi, J., & Melburg, U. (1984). Impressions management and influence in the organization. In S. Bacharack & E. J. Lawller (Eds.), *Research in the sociology of organizations* (Vol. 3, pp. 31–58). Greenwich, CT: JAI Press.

■ ■ ■

6200

Test Name: AROUSAL PREDISPOSITION SCALE

Purpose: To measure individual differences in arousability.

Number of Items: 12

Format: Responses are made on a 5-point scale ranging from *never* to *always*. An example is presented.

Validity: Correlation with stress related symptoms was .48.

Authors: Hicks, R. A., et al.

Article: Arousability and stress-related physical symptoms: A validation study of Coren's Arousal Predisposition Scale.

Journal: *Perceptual and Motor Skills*, April 1992, *74*(2), 659–662.

Related Research: Coren, S. (1990). The Arousal Predisposition Scale: Normative data. *Bulletin of the Psychometric Society, 28*, 551–552.

■ ■ ■

6201

Test Name: ARTISTIC AND SCIENTIFIC ACTIVITY SURVEY

Purpose: To assess how often participants engage in artistic and scientific activity.

Number of Items: 59

Format: 4-point scales are described.

Validity: Correlations with other variables ranged from .00 to .27.

Authors: Guastello, S. J., et al.

Article: Cognitive abilities and creative behaviors: CAB-S and consequences.

Journal: *The Journal of Creative Behavior,* Fourth Quarter, 1991, *26*(4), 260–267.

Related Research: Hocevar, D. (1981). Measurement of creativity: Review and critique. *Journal of Personality Assessment, 45,* 450–464.

• • •

6202

Test Name: AVOIDABILITY MEASURE

Purpose: To measure avoidability.

Number of Items: 7

Format: Responses are made on a 5-point scale ranging from 5 (*strongly agree*) to 1 (*strongly disagree*). All items are presented.

Reliability:. Internal consistency reliabilities were .90 and .94.

Validity: Correlations with other variables ranged from -.54 to .40.

Author: Campion, M. A.

Article: Meaning and measurement of turnover: Comparison of alternative measures and recommendations for research.

Journal: *Journal of Applied Psychology,* April 1991, *76*(2), 199–212.

• • •

6203

Test Name: BEHAVIORAL CHARACTERISTICS RATING SCALE FOR SUPERIOR STUDENTS.

Purpose: To rate learning, motivation, creativity, and leadership among superior students.

Format: Four response categories

per item (*seldom or never observed* to *observed all the time*).

Reliability: Alphas ranged from .54 to .84. Test–retest ranged from .00 to .76.

Validity: Correlations of teachers and student ratings ranged from -.07 to .26.

Author: O'Brien, G.

Article: Reliability and validity of four subscales of a scale for rating behavioral characteristics of superior students as self-reporting tools.

Journal: *Psychological Reports,* February 1991, *68*(1), 285–286.

Related Research: Renzulli, J. S., & Hartman, R. K. (1971). Scale for Rating Behavioral Characteristics of Superior Children. *Exceptional Children, 38,* 243–248.

• • •

6204

Test Name: BEHAVIORAL INTENTIONS SCALE

Purpose: To measure behavioral intentions.

Number of Items: 3

Format: Responses are made on a semantic differential scale. An example is presented.

Reliability: Coefficient alpha was .98.

Authors: Gotlieb, J. B., et al.

Article: Consumer satisfaction and perceived quality: Complementary or divergent constructs?

Journal: *Journal of Applied Psychology,* December 1994, *79*(6), 875–885.

Related Research: Fishbein, M., & Ajzen, I. (1975). *Belief, attitude, intention and behavior: An introduction to theory and research.* New York: Addison-Wesley.

6205

Test Name: BEHAVIORAL INTENTIONS SCALE

Purpose: To identify the likelihood that a participant would engage in certain behavior.

Number of Items: 9

Format: Includes two subsections: trust and association. Responses are made on a 5-point Likert-type response format ranging from 1 (*strongly disagree*) to 5 (*strongly agree*). Examples are presented.

Reliability: Alpha coefficients were .85 (trust) and .40 (association).

Validity: Correlations with other variables ranged from -.21 to .78.

Authors: Thomas, D. C., and Ravlin, E. C.

Article: Responses of employees to cultural adaptation by a foreign manager.

Journal: *Journal of Applied Psychology,* February 1995, *80*(1), 133–146.

Related Research: Bond, M. H. (1983). Linking person perception to behavioral intention dimensions. *Journal of Cross-Cultural Psychology, 14,* 41–63.

• • •

6206

Test Name: BEHAVIORAL OBSERVATION SCALE

Purpose: To rate instructor performance.

Number of Items: 10

Format: Responses are made on a 7-point scale ranging from 1 (*never*) to 7 (*all the time*).

Reliability: Correlation coefficients were .75 and .88.

Authors: Steiner, D. D., et al.

Article: Distributional ratings of performance: Further examination of a new rating format.

Journal: *Journal of Applied Psychology*, June 1993, *78*(3), 438–442.

Related Research: Lathom, G. P., & Wexley, K. N. (1977). Behavioral observational scales for performance appraisal purposes. *Personnel Psychology, 30*, 255–268.

Murphy, K. R., et al. (1982). Do observational scales measure observation? *Journal of Applied Psychology, 67*, 562–567.

■ ■ ■

6207

Test Name: BEHAVIORAL PROBLEMS INDEX

Purpose: To measure the number of behavioral problems experienced in the last 3 months.

Number of Items: 28

Format: Yes–no format. All items presented.

Reliability: Alphas ranged from .85 to .89.

Authors: Le Clere, F. B., and Kowalewski, B. M.

Article: Disability in the family: The effects on children's well-being.

Journal: *Journal of Marriage and the Family*, May 1994, *56*(2), 457–468.

Related Research: Peterson, J. L., & Zill, N. (1986). Marital disruption, parent-child relationships, and behavior problems in children. *Journal of Marriage and the Family, 48*, 295–307.

■ ■ ■

6208

Test Name: BEHAVIORAL SELF-REPORT OF FEMININITY

Purpose: To measure the frequency that women engage in feminine behaviors.

Number of Items: 59

Format: Frequency scales.

Reliability: Alpha was .92. Test–retest (2 weeks) was .90.

Authors: Greene, K. S., and Gynther, M. D.

Article: Predictor-criterion relationships as a function of item comparability.

Journal: *Psychological Reports*, October 1995, *77*(2), 363–366.

Related Research: Greene, K. S., & Gynther, M. D. (1994). Another femininity scale? *Psychological Reports, 75*, 164–170.

■ ■ ■

6209

Test Name: BEHAVIOR EVALUATION RATING SCALE

Purpose: To determine participants' conceptions of ideal, typical or average, and worst-possible performers.

Number of Items: 39

Format: Includes positive and negative behaviors and characteristics relevant to teaching. Responses are made on a 7-point scale ranging from 7 (*an extremely great extent*) to 1 (*an extremely little extent*).

Reliability: Alpha coefficients ranged from .95 to .96.

Authors: Maurer, T. J., and Alexander, R. A.

Article: Contrast effects in behavioral measurement: An investigation of alternative process explanations.

Journal: *Journal of Applied Psychology*, February 1991, *76*(1), 3–10.

Related Research: Buckley, R. M., & Armenakis, A. A. (1987). Detecting scale recalibration in survey research. *Group and Organization Studies, 12*, 464–481.

■ ■ ■

6210

Test Name: BEHAVIOR QUESTIONNAIRE

Purpose: To assess the behavior of preschool children.

Number of Items: 29

Format: 3-point true–false format.

Reliability: Test–retest correlations (1 month) exceeded .64.

Authors: Vitaro, F., et al.

Article: Teachers' and mothers' assessment of children's behaviors from kindergarten to Grade two: Stability and change within and across informants.

Journal: *Journal of Psychopathology and Behavioral Assessment*, December 1991, *13*(4), 325–342.

Related Research: Behar, L. B., & Stringfield, S. (1974). A behavior rating scale for the preschool child. *Developmental Psychology, 10*, 601–610.

Weir, K., & Duveen, G. (1981). Further development and validation of the Prosocial Behavior Questionnaire for Teachers. *Journal of Child Psychology and Psychiatry, 22*, 357–374.

■ ■ ■

6211

Test Name: BEHAVIOR RATING SCALE

Purpose: To rate the frequency of teacher behaviors.

Number of Items: 11

Format: Ratings are made on 7-point scale ranging from 1 (*never*) to 7 (*all the time*).

Reliability: Test–retest correlations ranged from .15 to .44

Validity: Correlations with the Performance Judgment Scale ranged from .06 to .70.

Authors: Murphy, K. R., and Anhalt, R. L.

Article: Is halo error a property of the rater, ratees, or the specific behaviors observed?

Journal: *Journal of Applied Psychology,* August 1992, 77(4), 494–500.

Related Research: Murphy, K. R., & Reynolds, D. H. (1988). Does true halo affect observed halo? *Journal of Applied Psychology, 73,* 1–4.

■ ■ ■

6212

Test Name: BRISTOL SOCIAL ADJUSTMENT GUIDE

Purpose: To enable teachers to identify behaviors of 7-year-old children.

Number of Items: 146

Format: For each item, a teacher underlines as many syndromes (there are 12) as apply to the child.

Reliability: Alpha was .68.

Authors: Chase-Lansdale, P. L., et al.

Article: The long-term effects of parental divorce on the mental health of young adults: A developmental perspective.

Journal: *Child Development,* December 1995, 66(6), 1614–1634.

Related Research: Stott, D. H. (1969). *The social adjustment of children.* London: University of London Press.

■ ■ ■

6213

Test Name: BULIMIA TEST

Purpose: To assess bulimic symptomatology.

Number of Items: 36

Format: 5-point Likert format ranges from 1 (*normal*) to 5 (*bulimic*).

Reliability: Test–retest and internal consistency reliabilities were .95.

Authors: Lester, R., and Petrie, T. A.

Article: Personality and physical correlates of bulimic symptomatology among Mexican American female college students.

Journal: *Journal of Counseling Psychology,* April 1995, 42(2), 199–203.

Related Research: Thelen, M. H., et al. (1991). A revision of the bulimia test: The BULIT-R. *Psychological Assessment, 3,* 119–124.

■ ■ ■

6214

Test Name: CHEATING QUESTIONNAIRE

Purpose: To assess degree of cheating in the classroom.

Number of Items: 21

Time Required: 10 minutes.

Format: 7-point scales. All items are presented.

Validity: Correlations with other variables ranged from -.28 to .76.

Authors: Genereux, R. L., and McLeod, B. A.

Article: Circumstances surrounding cheating: A questionnaire study of college students.

Journal: *Research in Higher Education,* December 1995, 36(6), 687–704.

Related Research: May, K. M., & Loyd, B. (1994). Honesty tests in academia and business: A comparative study. *Research in Higher Education, 35,* 499–511.

6215

Test Name: CHILD BEHAVIOR CHECKLIST AGES 2–3

Purpose: To assess child psychopathology in broad and narrow-band syndromes.

Number of Items: 99

Format: Check list format.

Reliability: Test–retest (1 year) ranged from .56 to .76 across subscales. Test–retest (7 days) ranged from .79 to .92.

Authors: Crawford, L., and Lee, S. W.

Article: Test–Retest reliability of the Child Behavior Checklist Ages 2–3.

Journal: *Psychological Reports,* October 1991, 69(2), 496–498.

Related Research: Achenbach, T. M., & Edelbrock, C. S. (1983). *Manual for the Child Behavior Checklist and Revised Behavior Profile.* Burlington: University of Vermont, Department of Psychiatry.

■ ■ ■

6216

Test Name: CHILD RATING QUESTIONNAIRE

Purpose: To assess behavior of children via teacher ratings.

Number of Items: 6

Format: 5-point scales. Items are described.

Reliability: Test–retest (1 month) ranged from .83 to 1.00.

Authors: Boyum, L. A., and Parke, R. E.

Article: The role of family emotional expressiveness in the development of children's social competence.

Journal: *Journal of Marriage and the Family,* August 1995, 57(3), 595–608.

Related Research: Cassidy, J., & Asher, S. (1992). Loneliness and peer relations in young children. *Child Development, 63,* 350–365.

• • •

6217

Test Name: CHRONIC SELF-DESTRUCTIVENESS SCALE

Purpose: To measure tendency to behave in a self-destructive manner.

Number of Items: 52

Format: 5-point scales. Sample items presented.

Reliability: Alphas ranged from .73 to .95. Test–retest (1 month) ranged from .90 to .98.

Author: Boudewyn, A. C., and Liem, J. H.

Article: Psychological, interpersonal, and behavioral correlates of chronic self-destructiveness: An exploratory study.

Journal: *Psychological Reports,* December 1995, *77*(3), 1283–1297.

Related Research: Kelly, K., et al. (1985). Chronic self-destructiveness: Conceptualization, measurement, and initial validation of a construct. *Motivation and Emotion, 9,* 135–151.

• • •

6218

Test Name: CLASSROOM BEHAVIOR INVENTORY

Purpose: To measure dimensions of children's classroom behavior.

Number of Items: 42

Format: Responses are made on a 5-point Likert scale ranging from *not at all* to *very much like.*

Reliability: Internal consistency was .90.

Authors: Arcia, E., et al.

Article: Neurobehavioral Evaluation System (NES) and school performance.

Journal: *Journal of School Psychology,* Fall 1991, *29*(4), 337–352.

Related Research: Schaefer, E. S., et al. (1977). *Classroom Behavior Inventory.* Unpublished Manuscript, Frank Porter Graham Child Development Center, The University of North Carolina at Chapel Hill.

• • •

6219

Test Name: CLASSROOM LIFE INSTRUMENT

Purpose: To assess competitiveness and cooperativeness.

Number of Items: 15

Format: Includes two factors: Cooperativeness and Competitiveness. Responses are made on a 5-point scale ranging from 1 (*completely false*) to 5 (*completely true*).

Reliability: Alpha coefficients were .83 and .89.

Author: Kline, T. J. B.

Article: Cooperativeness and competitiveness: Dimensionality and gender specificity of the Classroom Life Instrument.

Journal: *Educational and Psychological Measurement,* April 1995, *55*(2), 335–339.

Related Research: Johnson, D. W., & Johnson, R. (1983). Social interdependence and perceived academic and personal support in the classroom. *Journal of Social Psychology, 120,* 77–82.

Johnson, D. W., et al. (1983). Social interdependence and classroom climate. *Journal of Psychology, 114,* 135–142.

6220

Test Name: COGNITIVE SLIPPAGE SCALE

Purpose: To measure speech deficits and confused thinking in individuals with schizophrenia and schizotypal personality disorder.

Number of Items: 35

Reliability: Cronbach's alpha ranged from .86 to .89. Test–retest (4 weeks) ranged from .75 to .80.

Validity: Schizophrenic sample scored higher than college student sample ($t = -34.36$, $p < .001$).

Authors: Osmon, A., et al.

Article: Reliability and validity of the Cognitive Slippage Scale in two populations.

Journal: *Psychological Reports,* February 1992, *70*(1), 131–136.

Related Research: Meirs, T. C., & Raulin, M. L. (1985, March). *The development of a scale to measure cognitive slippage.* Paper presented at the Eastern Psychological Association Convention, Boston, MA.

• • •

6221

Test Name: COMBAT EXPERIENCE SCALE

Purpose: To measure extent of the respondent's combat experience.

Number of Items: 48

Format: 5-point frequency scale. All items presented.

Reliability: Alpha was .92.

Validity: Correlations with other variables ranged from -.17 to .53.

Authors: Gimbel, C., and Booth, A.

Title: Why does military combat experience adversely affect marital relations?

Journal: *Journal of Marriage and the Family*, August 1994, *56*(3), 691–703.

■ ■ ■

6222

Test Name: COMPLIANCE WITH SUPERVISOR'S WISHES SCALE

Purpose: To measure attitudinal and behavioral compliance.

Number of Items: 10

Format: 5-point Likert format. Sample items are presented.

Reliability: Alpha was .80.

Authors: Rahim, M. A., and Afza, M.

Article: Leader power, commitment, satisfaction, compliance, and propensity to leave a job among U.S. accountants.

Journal: *The Journal of Social Psychology*, October 1993, *133*(5), 611–625.

Related Research: Rahm, M. A., & Buntzman, G. F. (1988). Supervisory power bases, styles of handling conflict with subordinates, and subordinate compliance and satisfaction. *Journal of Psychology, 123*, 195–210.

■ ■ ■

6223

Test Name: COMPUTER PLAYFULNESS SCALE

Purpose: To measure cognitive playfulness on the computer.

Number of Items: 7

Format: Respondents indicate degree of agreement or disagreement on 7-point scales based on adjectives.

Reliability: Coefficient alpha was .97.

Authors: Martocchio, J. J., and Webster, J.

Article: Effects of feedback and cognitive playfulness on performance in microcomputer software training.

Journal: *Personnel Psychology*, Fall 1992, *45*(3), 553–578.

Related Research: Webster, J., & Martocchio, J. J. (1992). Microcomputer playfulness: Development of a measure with workplace implications. *MIS Quarterly, 16*, 201–226.

■ ■ ■

6224

Test Name: DAYTIME SLEEPINESS SCALE

Purpose: To measure general burdens of sleepiness, behavioral effects of sleepiness, and interference sleepiness causes in specific life domains.

Number of Items: 11

Format: Yes–no and one frequency scale. All items are presented.

Validity: Correlations with other variables ranged from -.27 to .40.

Authors: Van Knippenberg, et al.

Article: The Rotterdam Daytime Sleepiness Scale: A new daytime sleepiness scale.

Journal: *Psychological Reports*, February 1995, *76*(1), 83–87.

Related Research: Johns, M. W. (1991). A new method for measuring daytime sleepiness: The Epworth Sleepiness Scale. *Sleep, 14*, 540–545.

■ ■ ■

6225

Test Name: DECISIONAL PROCRASTINATION SCALE

Purpose: To measure indecision.

Number of Items: 5

Format: Sample items presented.

Reliability: Alpha was .80. Test–retest was .69.

Authors: Farrari, J. R., and Olivette, M. J.

Article: Parental authority and the development of female dysfunctional procrastination.

Journal: *Journal of Research in Personality*, March 1994, *28*(1), 87–100.

Related Research: Mann, L. (1982). *Decision-Making Questionnaire*. Unpublished scale, Flinders University of South Australia.

■ ■ ■

6226

Test Name: DELINQUENCY SCALE

Purpose: To assess delinquent or antisocial behaviors.

Number of Items: 23

Format: Responses were made on a 6-point scale ranging from *never* to *10 or more times*.

Reliability: Internal consistency coefficients were .82 and .84.

Author: Windle, M.

Article: A study of friendship characteristics and problem behaviors among middle adolescents.

Journal: *Child Development*, December 1994, *65*(6), 1764–1777.

Related Research: Elliott, D. S., et al. (1985). *Explaining delinquency and drug use.* Beverly Hills, CA: Sage.

■ ■ ■

6227

Test Name: DELINQUENCY SCALE

Purpose: To assess degree and types of delinquency.

Number of Items: 27

Format: Responses are made on a 4-point scale from 1 (*never*) to 4 (*often*).

Reliability: Alpha reliabilities by age (10-, 11-, 12-, 13-, 14-year-old boys) ranged from .86 to .92.

Authors: Haapasalo, J., and Tremblay, R. E.

Article: Physically aggressive boys from ages 6 to 12: Family background, parenting behavior, and prediction of delinquency.

Journal: *Journal of Consulting and Clinical Psychology,* October 1994, *62*(5), 1044–1052.

Related Research: LeBlanc, M., & Tremblay, R. E. (1988). A study of factors associated with the stability of hidden delinquency. *International Journal of Adolescence and Youth, 1,* 269–291.

■ ■ ■

6228

Test Name: DESIRABLE BEHAVIOR RECOGNITION MEASURE

Purpose: To measure the extent of the recognition and reward of different behaviors.

Number of Items: 6

Format: Includes 3 subscales: Recognition for Prosocial Individual Behavior, Recognition for Prosocial Organizational Behavior, and Recognition for Role-Prescribed Behavior. Examples are presented.

Reliability: Coefficient alpha was .83.

Validity: Correlations with other variables ranged from -.07 to .37.

Authors: McNeely, B. L., and Meglino, B. M.

Article: The role of dispositional and situational antecedents in prosocial organizational behavior: An examination of the intended beneficiaries of prosocial behaviors.

Journal: *Journal of Applied*

Psychology, December 1994, *79*(6), 836–844.

■ ■ ■

6229

Test Name: DRINKING INVENTORY

Purpose: To measure frequency and severity of one's and one's family's drinking patterns.

Number of Items: 31

Format: Includes 3 factors. Sample items are presented.

Reliability: Internal consistency coefficients ranged from .86 to .97.

Authors: McNamara, P., et al.

Article: Markers of cerebral lateralization and alcoholism.

Journal: *Perceptual and Motor Skills,* December 1994, *79*(3) Part 2, 1435–1440.

Related Research: Williams, J. G., & Morrice, A. (1992). Measuring drinking patterns among college students. *Psychological Reports, 70,* 231–238.

■ ■ ■

6230

Test Name: DRINKING PRACTICES QUESTIONNAIRE

Purpose: To measure positive and negative antecedents and consequences of alcohol use.

Number of Items: 73

Format: 7-point Likert format (1 *never* to 7 *very often*).

Reliability: Alphas ranged from .87 to .97 across subscales.

Validity: Correlations with other variables ranged from -.27 to .63.

Authors: Williams, J. G., and Morrice, A.

Article: Measuring drinking among college students.

Journal: *Psychological Reports,* February 1992, *70*(1), 231–238.

6231

Test Name: DRINKING SELF-EFFICACY SCALE

Purpose: To predict alcohol consumption.

Number of Items: 31

Format: Six-point scales range from 1 (*I am very sure I would drink*)to 6 (*I am very sure I would not drink*). All items are presented.

Reliability: Test–retest reliabilities (2 weeks to 2 months) ranged from .84 to .93. Alphas ranged from .87 to .94.

Validity: Three factors were identified with eigenvalues greater than 1.00. These were self-efficacy (a) in situations of social pressure, (b) in situations of opportunistic drinking, and (c) in situations where there is need for emotional relief.

Authors: Young, R. M., et al.

Article: Development of a drinking self-efficacy questionnaire.

Journal: *Journal of Psychopathology and Behavioral Assessment,* March 1991, *13*(1), 1–15.

■ ■ ■

6232

Test Name: DRIVING ANGER SCALE

Purpose: To measure anger of drivers.

Number of Items: 33 (short form 14 items).

Format: 5-point Likert format. All items are presented.

Reliability: Alphas were .90 and .80 (short form). Subscale reliabilities ranged from .78 to .87 (long form).

Authors: Deffenbacher, J. L., et al.

Article: Development of a Driving Anger Scale.

Journal: *Psychological Reports*, February 1994, *74*(1), 83–91.

Related Research: Novaco, R. W., et al. (1979). Transportation, stress, and community psychology. *American Journal of Community Psychology*, *7*, 361–380.

• • •

6233

Test Name: DRUG USE SURVEY

Purpose: To measure substance-use knowledge, attitudes, peer and personal-use behaviors, and demographic variables in participants.

Number of Items: 44

Format: Survey is divided into subscales; each subscale uses a yes–no response format or Likert scale.

Reliability: Cronbach alphas for the subscales ranged from .68 to .86.

Authors: Robinson, S., et al.

Article: Patterns of drug use among female and male undergraduates.

Journal: *Journal of College Student Development*, March 1993, *34*(2), 130–137.

Related Research: Robinson, S. E., et al. (1993). Influence of substance abuse education on undergraduates' knowledge, attitudes and behaviors. *Journal of Alcohol and Drug Education*, *39*, 123–130.

• • •

6234

Test Name: EATING ATTITUDES TEST

Purpose: To identify eating-disorder symptoms.

Number of Items: 40

Format: A checklist format.

Validity: Correlations with other variables ranged from -.28 to .54.

Authors: Pumariega, A. J., et al.

Article: Clinical correlates of body-size distortion.

Journal: *Perceptual and Motor Skills*, June 1993, *76*(3) Part 2, 1311–1319.

Related Research: Garner, D. M., & Garfinkel, P. E. (1979). The Eating Attitudes Test: An index of the symptoms of anorexia nervosa. *Psychological Medicine*, *9*, 273–279.

• • •

6235

Test Name: EATING ATTITUDES TEST—26

Purpose: To assess the symptoms of anorexia nervosa.

Number of Items: 26

Format: Frequency scales range from 0 (*never*) to 3 (*always*). All items are presented.

Reliability: Alpha was .83.

Validity: Correlations with other variables ranged from -.32 to .90. Correlations between subscales ranged from -.05 to .90.

Authors: Koslowsky, M., et al.

Article: The factor structure and criterion validity of the short form of the eating attitudes test.

Journal: *Journal of Personality Assessment*, February 1992, *58*(1), 27–35.

Related Research: Garner, D. M., et al. (1983). Development and validation of a multidimensional eating disorder inventory for anorexia nervosa and bulimia. *International Journal of Eating Disorders*, *2*, 15–34.

6236

Test Name: ENVIRONMENTALLY RESPONSIVE BEHAVIOR QUESTIONNAIRE

Purpose: To assess environmentally responsible behavior.

Number of Items: 34

Format: Yes–no format. Sample items are presented.

Reliability: Alpha was .78.

Authors: Caltabiano, N. J., and Caltabiano, M. L.

Article: Assessing environmentally responsible behavior.

Journal: *Psychological Reports*, June 1995, *76*(3) Part II, 1080–1082.

Related Research: Stern, P. C. (1992). Psychological dimensions of global environmental change. *Annual Review of Psychology*, *43*, 269–302.

• • •

6237

Test Name: EYSENCK IMPULSIVENESS QUESTIONNAIRE

Purpose: To measure impulsive behavior in children.

Number of Items: 23

Format: Uses a 4-point scale.

Reliability: Coefficient alpha was .80.

Validity: Correlations with other variables ranged from -.13 to .72.

Authors: M. T. Carrillo-de-la-Peña, et al.

Article: Comparison among various methods of assessment of impulsiveness.

Journal: *Perceptual and Motor Skills*, October 1993, *77*(2), 567–575.

Related Research: Eysenck, S. B.

G., et al. (1984). Age norms for impulsiveness, venturesomeness and empathy in children. *Personality and Individual Differences, 5,* 315–321.

...

6238

Test Name: FAGERSTRÖM TOLERANCE QUESTIONNAIRE

Purpose: To measure six aspects of smoking.

Number of Items: 8

Format: Open-ended. All items presented.

Reliability: Alpha was .70.

Validity: Men score higher than women ($p <$ .001), age groups differ significantly ($p <$ .001 and $p <$ .05).

Authors: Becona, E., et al.

Article: Scores of Spanish smokers on Fagerström's Tolerance Questionnaire.

Journal: *Psychological Reports,* December 1992, *71*(3) Part II, 1227-1233.

Related Research: Fagerström, K. O., & Schneider, N. G. (1989). Measuring nicotine dependence in tobacco smoking: A review of Fagerström's Tolerance Questionnaire. *Journal of Behavioral Medicine, 12,* 159–182.

...

6239

Test Name: FOCUSING INVENTORY—STATE

Purpose: To measure focusing.

Number of Items: 11

Format: Responses are made on a 5-point scale ranging from 1 (*fits me not at all*) to 5 (*fits me extremely well*). All items are presented.

Reliability: Coefficient alpha was .92.

Authors: Weinstein, M., and Smith, J. C.

Article: Isometric squeeze relaxation (progressive relaxation) vs. meditation: Absorption and focusing as predictors of state effects.

Journal: *Perceptual and Motor Skills,* December 1992, *75*(3) Part 2, 1263–1271.

Related Research: Smith, J. C., & Weinstein, M. (1987). *Development of the Focusing Inventory.* Unpublished manuscript, Roosevelt University, Chicago.

...

6240

Test Name: FUNDAMENTAL INTERPERSONAL RELATIONS ORIENTATION—BEHAVIOR SCALE

Purpose: To determine individual behavioral dimensions in three areas—inclusion, control, and affection.

Number of Items: 54

Format: Responses are made on a Likert scale.

Reliability: Reproducibility score was .94 for six scales. Test–retest (mean coefficient of stability) for the six scales was .86.

Authors: Steward, R. J., et al.

Article: Alienation and interactional style: A study of successful Anglo, Asian, and Hispanic university students.

Journal: *Journal of College Student Development,* March 1992, *33*(2), 149–156.

Related Research: Schutz, W. (1966). *The interpersonal underworld.* Palo Alto, CA: Science and Behavior Books.

6241

Test Name: GENERAL BEHAVIORAL PROCRASTINATION SCALE

Purpose: To assess the frequency of postponing activity.

Number of Items: 20

Format: 5-point scales. Sample items are presented.

Reliability: Alpha was .82. Test–retest reliability was .80.

Validity: Correlations with behavioral measures ranged from -.26 to .23.

Author: Ferrari, J. R.

Article: Psychometric validation of two procrastination inventories for adults: Arousal and avoidance measures.

Journal: *Journal of Psychopathology and Behavioral Assessment,* June 1992, *14*(2), 97–110.

Related Research: Lay, C. H. (1986). At last, my research in procrastination. *Journal of Research in Personality, 20,* 479–495.

...

6242

Test Name: GENERAL LEADERSHIP IMPRESSION SCALE

Purpose: To measure leadership perceptions.

Number of Items: 5

Format: Responses are made on a 5-point rating scale ranging from *extreme amount* to *nothing.* A sample item is presented.

Reliability: Cronbach's alpha was .88.

Authors: Zaccaro, S. V., et al.

Article: Self-monitoring and trait-bases variance in leadership: An investigation of leader flexibility across multiple group situations.

Journal: *Journal of Applied Psychology*, April 1991, *76*(2), 308–315.

Related Research: Lord, R. G., et al. (1984). A test of leadership categorization theory: Internal structure, information processing and leadership perceptions. *Organizational Behavior and Human Performance, 34,* 343–378.

■ ■ ■

6243

Test Name: HEALTH BEHAVIOR CHECKLIST

Purpose: To provide a description of usual health practice behaviors.

Number of Items: 27

Format: Responses are made on a 5-point scale ranging from 1 (*not at all like me*) to 5 (*very much like me*). Includes 4 scales: Wellness Maintenance and Enhancement, Traffic Risk, Accident Control, and Substance Risk. All items are presented.

Reliability: Alpha coefficients ranged from .30 to .79.

Validity: Correlations with other variables ranged from -.23 to .34.

Authors: Woodruff, S. I., and Conway, T. L.

Article: A longitudinal assessment of the impact of health/fitness status and health behavior on perceived quality of life.

Journal: *Perceptual and Motor Skills*, August 1992, *75*(1), 3–14.

Related Research: Vickers, R. R., et al. (1990). Demonstration of replicable dimensions among men aboard Navy ships. *Military Psychology, 2,* 79–94.

6244

Test Name: HIV PREVENTION SCALE—SHORT VERSION

Purpose: To assess self-reported safer sex practices in heterosexual samples.

Number of Items: 13

Format: 5-point responses (*always* to *never*). All items presented.

Reliability: Alphas ranged from .78 to .83 across subscales.

Author: Bassman, L.

Article: Object relations and self-reported AIDS self-care behavior.

Journal: *Psychological Reports,* June 1991, *68*(3) Part I, 915–923.

Related Research: Bassman, L. (1991). *HIV prevention Scale. Test in Microfiche, Set P.* Princeton, NJ: Educational Testing Service.

Bassman, L. (1992). Realty testing and self-reported AIDS Self-care behavior. *Psychological Reports, 70,* 59–65.

■ ■ ■

6245

Test Name: HOMEWORK STYLE AND BEHAVIOR SCALE

Purpose: To measure how children perform homework.

Number of Items: 12

Format: 5-point agreement scales. Sample items are presented.

Reliability: Alphas ranged from .73 to .83.

Authors: Hong, E., et al.

Article: Homework style and homework behavior of Korean and American children.

Journal: J*ournal of Research and Development in Education,* Summer 1995, *28*(4), 197–207.

Related Research: Milgram, R. M., & Perkins, P. G. (1991).

Homework Style Scale. Unpublished document, Tel-Aviv University, School of Education and University of Nevada, Las Vegas, College of Education.

■ ■ ■

6246

Test Name: IMPRESSION MANAGEMENT SCALE REVISED

Purpose: To provide for supervisors' reports of subordinates' impression of management behavior.

Number of Items: 12

Format: Responses are made on a 5-point scale ranging from 1 (*never*) to 5 (*always*). Includes 3 factors: Manipulation, Supervisory Awareness, and Supervisory Favors. All items are presented.

Reliability: Alpha coefficients ranged from .68 to .89.

Validity: Correlations with other variables ranged from -.37 to .29.

Authors: Shore, L. M., and Wayne, S. J.

Article: Commitment and employee behavior: Comparison of affective commitment and continuous commitment with perceived organizational support.

Journal: *Journal of Applied Psychology,* October 1993, *78*(5), 774–780.

Related Research: Wayne, S. J., & Ferris, G. R. (1990). Influence tactics, affect, and exchange quality in supervisor-subordinate interactions: A laboratory experiment and field study. *Journal of Applied Psychology, 75,* 487–499.

■ ■ ■

6247

Test Name: INFANTS CHARACTERISTICS QUESTIONNAIRE

Purpose: To measure infant difficultness.

Number of Items: 32

Format: Responses are made on 7-point scales.

Reliability: Alpha coefficients ranged from .22 to .79.

Authors: Sagi, A., et al.

Article: Sleeping out of home in a kibbutz communal arrangement: It makes a difference for infant-mother attachment.

Journal: *Child Development,* August 1994, *65*(4), 992–1004.

Related Research: Bates, J. E., et al. (1979). Measurement of infant difficultness. *Child Development, 50,* 794–803.

• • •

6248

Test Name: INFLUENCE BEHAVIOR QUESTIONNAIRE

Purpose: To measure influence tactics.

Format: Includes 9 influence tactics: Rational Persuasion, Inspirational Appeal, Consultation, Integration, Exchange, Personal Appeal, Coalition, Legitimating, and Pressure.

Reliability: Alpha coefficients ranged from .55 to .89.

Validity: Correlations with other variables ranged from -.25 to .52.

Authors: Yuki, G., and Tracey, J. B.

Article: Consequences of influence tactics used with subordinates, peers, and the boss.

Journal: *Journal of Applied Psychology,* August 1992, *77*(4), 525–535.

Related Research: Yuki, G., & Falbe, C. M. (1990). Influence tactics in upward, downward, and lateral influence attempts. *Journal*

of Applied Psychology, 75, 132–140.

• • •

6249

Test Name: INGRATIATORY BEHAVIOR SCALE

Purpose: To assess behavior designed to increase one's personal attractiveness to others.

Number of Items: 35

Format: 7-point rating scales range from 1 (*never*) to 7 (*always*).

Reliability: Alphas ranged from .72 to .93 across five subscales.

Validity: Correlations between subscales averaged .40.

Authors: Shankar, A., et al.

Article: Organizational context and ingratiatory behavior in organizations.

Journal: *The Journal of Social Psychology,* October 1994, *133*(5), 641–647.

• • •

6250

Test Name: INNER SPEECH ABOUT SELF SCALE

Purpose: To assess an individual's use of inner speech.

Number of Items: 18

Format: 6-point Likert format. All items are presented.

Reliability: Alpha was .93. Item-total correlations ranged from .30 to .78.

Validity: Correlations with other variables ranged from -.26 to .48.

Author: Siegrist, M.

Article: Inner speech as a cognitive process mediating self-consciousness and inhibiting self-deception.

Journal: *Psychological Reports,* February 1995, *76*(1), 259–265.

6251

Test Name: JOB EXPERIENCE SURVEY

Purpose: To measure perceptual definitions of behavior as sexual harassment.

Number of Items: 20

Format: 5-point scales. A sample item is presented.

Reliability: Alpha was .90.

Authors: Gehlauf, D. N., and Popovich, P. M.

Article: The effects of personal and situational factors on university administrators' responses to sexual harassment.

Journal: *Research in Higher Education,* June 1994, *35*(3), 373–386.

Related Research: Popovich, P. M., et al. (1986). Assessing the incidence and perceptions of sexual harassment behaviors among American undergraduates. *Journal of Psychology, 120,* 387–396.

• • •

6252

Test Name: LEADER POWER AND INFLUENCE SCALES

Purpose: To measure the power and influence of supervisors.

Number of Items: 35

Format: 5-point Likert format. All items are presented.

Reliability: Alphas ranged from .68 to .93 across subscales.

Authors: Tjosvold, D., et al.

Article: Leadership influence: Goal interdependence and power.

Journal: *The Journal of Social Psychology,* February 1992, *132*(1), 39–50.

Related Research: Tjosvold, D., et al. (1983). Cooperative and competitive relationships between leaders and their subordinates. *Human Relations, 36,* 1111–1124.

■ ■ ■

6253

Test Name: LEADER POWER INVENTORY

Purpose: To measure the bases of supervisory power.

Number of Items: 25

Format: 5-point Likert format.

Reliability: Internal consistency of subscales ranged from .77 to .93.

Authors: Rahim, M. A., and Afza, M.

Article: Leader power, commitment, satisfaction, compliance, and propensity to leave a job among US accountants.

Journal: *The Journal of Social Psychology,* October 1993, *133*(5), 611–625.

Related Research: Rahim, M. A. (1988). The development of the Leader Power Inventory. *Multivariate Behavioral Research, 23,* 1–13.

■ ■ ■

6254

Test Name: LEADERSHIP MEASURE

Purpose: To measure leadership.

Number of Items: 17

Format: Includes 3 factors: Support, Goal Emphasis, and Work Facilitation.

Reliability: Alpha coefficients ranged from .78 to .96.

Validity: Correlations with other variables ranged from .31 to .48.

Authors: Oz, S., and Eden, D.

Article: Restraining the Golem: Boosting performance by changing the interpretation of low scores.

Journal: *Journal of Applied Psychology,* October 1994, *79*(5), 744–754.

Related Research: Bowers, D. G., & Seashore, S. E. (1966). Predicting organizational effectiveness with a four-factor theory of leadership. *Administrative Science Quarterly, 11,* 238–263.

■ ■ ■

6255

Test Name: LEARNED HELPLESSNESS QUESTIONNAIRE

Purpose: To indicate the difference between learned helplessness and mastery orientation.

Number of Items: 10

Format: Items are responded to by choosing one of two alternative attributions.

Validity: Correlations with other variables ranged from -.18 to .22.

Authors: Qian, G., and Alvermann, D.

Article: Role of epistemological beliefs and learned helplessness in secondary school students' learning science concepts from text.

Journal: *Journal of Educational Psychology,* June 1995, *87*(2), 282–292.

Related Research: Crandall, V. C., et al. (1965). Children's beliefs in their own control of reinforcement in intellectual academic achievement situations. *Child Development, 36,* 91–109.

■ ■ ■

6256

Test Name: LIFESTYLE EXERCISE INVENTORY

Purpose: To identify percentage of time one engages in specific behaviors.

Number of Items: 10

Format: Participant indicates percentage of time one engages in each activity. Examples are presented.

Reliability: Alpha coefficients were .64 and .69. Test–retest reliability (1 month) was .77.

Validity: Correlations with other variables ranged from -.27 to .32.

Authors: Cardinal, B. J., and Cardinal, M. K.

Article: Lifestyle Exercise Inventory: Preliminary development.

Journal: *Perceptual and Motor Skills,* December 1993, *77*(3) Part 2, 1066.

Related Research: Blair, S. N., et al. (1992). Physical activity and health: A lifestyle approach. *Medicine, Exercise, Nutrition and Health, 1,* 54–57.

■ ■ ■

6257

Test Name: LIFETIME SEXUAL INVOLVEMENT SCALE

Purpose: To measure sexual involvement.

Number of Items: 21

Format: Gutman format.

Reliability: Reproducibility was .94.

Authors: Christopher, F. S., et al.

Article: Exploring the darkside of courtship: A test of a model of premarital sexual aggressiveness.

Journal: *Journal of Marriage and the Family,* May 1993, *55*(2), 469–479.

Related Research: Bentler, P. M. (1968). Heterosexual behavior assessment. *Behavior Research and Therapy, 6,* 21–25.

■ ■ ■

6258

Test Name: MALE FUNCTION PROFILE\IMPOTENCE QUESTIONNAIRE

Purpose: To collect information normally not evident in the early stages of the diagnosis of impotence.

Number of Items: 259

Format: Responses made on a 3-point scale: *true–false–does not apply*.

Reliability: Reliabilities ranged from .07 to .87. "Profile Type" matches with subsequent clinical diagnosis. All reported in detail.

Validity: Detailed validity checks are presented.

Authors: Fineman, K. R., and Rettinger, H. I.

Article: Development of the Male Function Profile/Impotence Questionnaire.

Journal: *Psychological Reports*, June 1991, *68*(3) Part II, 1151–1175.

■ ■ ■

6259

Test Name: MEMBER'S PERFORMANCE SCALE

Purpose: To provide leader appraisal of member's performance.

Number of Items: 7

Format: 7-point scales were used for responses. All items are presented.

Reliability: Alpha coefficients were .93.

Authors: Liden, R. C., et al.

Article: A longitudinal study on the early development of leader-member exchanges.

Journal: *Journal of Applied Psychology*, August 1993, *78*(4), 662–674.

Related Research: Isui, A. S. (1984). A role set analysis of managerial reputation. *Organizational Behavior and Human Performance, 34,* 64–96.

6260

Test Name: DIMENSIONS OF SOCIAL SUPPORT SCALE

Purpose: To measure the extent to which respondents were receiving informational and emotional support from a variety of sources.

Number of Items: 20

Format: Responses are made on a 5-point Likert scale (*not at all* to *extremely*) using the same 9-item set of questions for the four support sources—mother, father, friend, significant adult.

Reliability: Cronbach's alphas ranged from .95 to .85.

Author: Rodney, H. E.

Article: A profile of collegiate Black children of alcoholics.

Journal: *Journal of College Student Development*, May/June 1995, *36*(3), 228–235.

Related Research: Cohen, F. (1977). *Dimensions of Social Support Scale.* Unpublished document, Stanford University, School of Medicine, San Francisco.

■ ■ ■

6261

Test Name: MULTIFACTOR LEADERSHIP QUESTIONNAIRE

Purpose: To measure leadership behaviors.

Number of Items: 70

Format: Responses are made on a 5-point Likert scale.

Reliability: Alphas ranged from .67 (*management by exception*) to .94 (*charisma*).

Author: Komives, S.

Article: Gender differences in the relationship of hall directors' transformational and transactional leadership and achieving styles.

Journal: *Journal of College Student Development*, March 1991, *32*, 155–165.

Related Research: Bass, B. M. (1985). *Multifactor Leadership Questionnaire.* Binghamton, NY: State University of New York, School of Management.

■ ■ ■

6262

Test Name: MYSTICISM SCALE

Purpose: To assess mystical experience.

Number of Items: 32

Format: 5-point rating scales.

Reliability: Alphas ranged from .69 to .76 across subscales.

Authors: Hood, R. W., Jr., et al.

Article: Further factor analysis of Hood's Mysticism Scale.

Journal: *Psychological Reports*, December 1993, *73*(3) Part II, 1176–1178.

Related Research: Hood, R. W., Jr. (1975). The construction and preliminary validation of a measure of reported mystical experience. *Journal for the Scientific Study of Religion, 14,* 29–41.

■ ■ ■

6263

Test Name: NAVY EQUAL OPPORTUNITY/SEXUAL HARASSMENT SURVEY

Purpose: To assess equal opportunity and sexual harassment in the Navy.

Number of Items: 65 (*equal opportunity*); sexual harassment not specified.

Format: 5-point Likert format.

Reliability: Alphas ranged from .52 to .88 across subsamples of respondents.

Author: Rosenfeld, P.

Article: Effects of gender and ethnicity on Hispanic women in the US Navy.

Journal: *The Journal of Social Psychology*, June 1994, *133*(3), 349–354.

Related Research: Rosenfeld, P., et al. (1992). *Assessment of equal opportunity climate: Results of a 1989 Navy-wide survey* (N PRDC TR 92-14). San Diego, CA: Navy Personnel Research Center.

■ ■ ■

6264

Test Name: NEEDS OF ADOLESCENT RUNAWAYS

Purpose: To determine the needs of runaway adolescents.

Number of Items: 45

Time Required: 30 to 45 minutes.

Format: Uses a 4-point Likert-type scale ranging from not at all to a great deal.

Reliability: Factor 1 alpha coefficient was .90 (14 items). Factor 2 alpha coefficient was .90 (7 items). Factor 3 alpha coefficient was .79 (7 items).

Authors: Post, P., and McCoard, D.

Article: Needs and self-concept of runaway adolescents.

Journal: *The School Counselor*, January 1994, *41*(3), 213–219.

Related Research: Brennan, T., et al. (1978). *The social psychology of runaways*. Lexington, MA: Lexington Books.

■ ■ ■

6265

Test Name: OPINION LEADERSHIP SCALE— REVISED

Purpose: To measure opinion leadership.

Number of Items: 3

Reliability: Coefficient alpha was .64.

Validity: Correlations with other variables ranged from .38 to .60.

Authors: Flynn, L. R., and Goldsmith, R. E.

Article: A validation of the Goldsmith and Hofacker Innovativeness Scale.

Journal: *Educational and Psychological Measurement*, Winter 1993, *53*(4), 1105–1116.

Related Research: Childers, T. (1986). Assessment of the psychometric properties of an opinion leadership scale. *Journal of Marketing Research, 23*, 184–188.

■ ■ ■

6266

Test Name: ORGANIZATIONAL CITIZENSHIP BEHAVIOR SCALE

Purpose: To assess organizational citizenship behavior.

Number of Items: 16

Format: Responses are made on a 5-point scale ranging from 1 (*disagree completely*) to 5 (*agree completely*).

Reliability: Alpha coefficients were .88 (*altruism*) and .87 (*compliance*).

Validity: Correlations with other variables ranged from -.37 to .30.

Authors: Shore, L. M., and Wayne, S. J.

Article: Commitment and employee behavior: Comparison of effective commitment and continuance commitment with perceived organizational support.

Journal: *Journal of Applied Psychology*, October 1993, *78*(5), 774–780.

Related Research: Smith, C. A., et al. (1983). Organizational

citizenship behavior: Its nature and antecedents. *Journal of Applied Psychology, 68*, 653–663.

■ ■ ■

6267

Test Name: ORGANIZATIONAL CITIZENSHIP BEHAVIOR— REVISED

Purpose: To measure organizational citizenship behavior.

Number of Items: 10

Format: Responses are made on a 5-point scale ranging from 1 (*never*) to 5 (*always*). Includes two factors: Conscientiousness and Altruism. All items are presented.

Reliability: Alpha coefficients were .82 and .89.

Authors: Becker, T. E., and Randall, D. M.

Article: Validation of a measure of organizational citizenship behavior against an objective behavioral criterion.

Journal: *Educational and Psychological Measurement*, Spring 1994, *54*(1), 160–167.

Related Research: Smith, C. A., et al. (1983). Organizational citizenship behavior: Its nature and antecedents. *Journal of Applied Psychology, 68*, 653–663.

■ ■ ■

6268

Test Name: PARENT DAILY REPORT

Purpose: To determine child problem behaviors.

Number of Items: 31

Format: Responses are made on a checklist.

Reliability: Test–retest reliabilities ranged from .85 to .98.

Author: Moore, K. J.

Article: Use of pooled time series in

the study of naturally occurring clinical events and problem behavior in a foster care setting.

Journal: *Journal of Consulting and Clinical Psychology*, August 1994, *62*(4), 718–728.

Related Research: Chamberlain, P. (1980). *Standardization of a parent report measure.* Unpublished doctoral dissertation, University of Oregon.

■ ■ ■

6269

Test Name: PASSIVE–AGGRESSIVE BEHAVIOR SCALE

Purpose: To measure passive–aggressive behavior.

Number of Items: 19

Format: 2-point agree–disagree scales.

Reliability: Alpha was .71.

Authors: Milgram, N. A., et al.

Article: Situational and personal determinants of academic procrastination.

Journal: The Journal of General Psychology, April 1994, *119*(2), 123–133.

Related Research: Dangour, W. (1990). Procrastination. Unpublished master's thesis, Tel-Aviv University, Ramat-Aviv.

■ ■ ■

6270

Test Name: PERCEIVED BEHAVIORAL CONTROL SCALE

Purpose: To measure behavioral control using a multiplicative scale in which the belief in a control factor is multiplied by the power of a factor to control.

Number of Items: 11

Format: 7-point bipolar scale

(*belief*) and 7-point importance (*power*) scale.

Reliability: Alpha was .87.

Validity: Correlations with other variables ranged from .04 to .36.

Authors: Valois, P., et al.

Article: Psychometric properties of a perceived behavioral control multiplicative scale developed according to Ajzen's theory of planned behavior.

Journal: *Psychological Reports,* June 1993, *72*(3) Part II, 1079–1083.

■ ■ ■

6271

Test Name: PERCEIVED TEACHER BEHAVIOR INVENTORY

Purpose: To measure teacher behavior via student report.

Number of Items: 22

Format: 5-point agreement scales. Sample items presented.

Reliability: Alphas ranged from .75 to .89 across subscales.

Validity: Correlations between subscales ranged from .27 to .41.

Author: Mboya, M. M.

Article: Gender differences in teachers' behaviors in relation to adolescents' self-concepts.

Journal: *Psychological Reports,* December 1995, *77*(3) Part I, 831–839.

Related Research: Mboya, M. M. (1994). A new multidimensional measure of African adolescents' perceptions of teacher behaviors. *Perceptual and Motor Skills, 78,* 419–426.

■ ■ ■

6272

Test Name: PERFORMANCE-MAINTENANCE SCALES

Purpose: To measure leadership styles across cultures: task performance and orientation toward team maintenance.

Number of Items: 20

Format: 5-point scale (*never* to *always*).

Reliability: Alphas ranged from .59 to .91.

Authors: Powell, G. N., and Kido, Y.

Article: Managerial stereotypes in a global economy: A comparative study of Japanese and American business students' perspectives.

Journal: *Psychological Reports,* February 1994, *74*(1), 219–226.

Related Research: Peterson, M. F., et al. (1987). *A validity study of English versions of Japanese PM leadership style measures in electronics plants.* Paper presented at the Annual Meeting of the Southern Management Association, New Orleans.

■ ■ ■

6273

Test Name: PERSONAL ILLNESS-ACCIDENTS SCALE

Purpose: To provide a retroactive indication of personal illness and/or accidents.

Number of Items: 3

Format: Responses are made on a 5-point scale ranging from 1 (*never*) to 5 (*very frequently*). All items are presented.

Reliability: Alpha coefficients were .61 and .65.

Validity: Correlations with other variables ranged from -.04 to .18.

Author: Blau, G.

Article: Developing and testing a taxonomy of lateness behavior.

Journal: *Journal of Applied Psychology,* December 1994, *79*(6), 959–970.

6274

Test Name: PHYSICAL ACTIVITY INVENTORY

Purpose: To measure participation in physical activity.

Number of Items: 18

Format: Includes six parts each containing two closed-ended and one open-ended question. Examples are presented.

Reliability: Test–retest reliability was .76.

Validity: Correlations with other variables ranged from .15 to .41.

Author: Merriman, W. J.

Article: Relationship among socialization, attitude, and placement with participation in physical activity of students with emotional disorders.

Journal: *Perceptual and Motor Skills,* February 1993, *76*(1), 287–292.

Related Research: Kenyon, G. (1968). *Values held for physical activity by selected urban secondary students in Canada, Australia, England and the United States.* (ERIC Document Reproduction Service No. ED 019-709).

■ ■ ■

6275

Test Name: POSITIVE IMPRESSION SURVEY

Purpose: To measure use and effectiveness of ways of impressing others.

Number of Items: 28

Format: 5-point frequency scales (*very infrequently* to *very frequently*). Sample items are presented.

Reliability: Test–retest (22 days) was .84.

Validity: Correlations between use

and effectiveness scores ranged from .29 to .72.

Author: DuBrin, A. J.

Article: Sex differences in the use and effectiveness of tactics of impression management.

Journal: *Psychological Reports,* April 1994, *74*(2), 531–544.

■ ■ ■

6276

Test Name: PREOCCUPATIVE SCALE

Purpose: To identify action-oriented and state-oriented individuals.

Number of Items: 7

Format: Forced-choice format.

Reliability: Internal reliability was .43.

Authors: Menec, Y. H., et al.

Article: The effects of adverse learning conditions on action-oriented and state-oriented college students.

Journal: *Journal of Experimental Education,* Summer 1995, *63*(4), 281–299.

Related Research: Kuhl, J. (1985). Volitional mediators of cognition-behavior consistency: Self-regulatory processes and action versus state orientation. In J. Kuhl & J. Beckman (Eds.), *Action control: From cognition to behavior* (pp. 101–128). Berlin: Springer Verlag.

■ ■ ■

6277

Test Name: PRESSURE AND MANIPULATION AND ANTISOCIAL ACTS SCALES

Purpose: To measure premarital sexual aggression.

Number of Items: 20

Format: 9-point Likert format.

Reliability: Alpha was .91 (antisocial acts) and .89 (pressure and manipulation).

Authors: Christopher, F. S., et al.

Article: Exploring the darkside of courtship: A test of a model of premarital sexual aggression.

Journal: *Journal of Marriage and the Family,* May 1993, *55*(2), 469–479.

Related Research: Christopher, F. S., & Frandsen, M. M. (1991). Strategies of influence in sex and dating. *Journal of Social and Personal Relationships, 7,* 89–105.

■ ■ ■

6278

Test Name: PROBLEM HISTORY SCALE

Purpose: To provide a self-report of addictions and emotional problems.

Number of Items: 25

Format: Items deal with addictions, partner violence, and emotional stress.

Reliability: Test–retest (4 to 9 weeks) reliability ranged from .69 to .86. Coefficient alpha ranged from .69 to .91.

Validity: Correlations with other variables ranged from -.68 to .70.

Authors: Hadley, J. A., et al.

Article: Common aspects of object relations and self-representations in offspring from disparate dysfunctional families.

Journal: *Journal of Counseling Psychology,* July 1993, *40*(3), 348–356.

Related Research: Cook, D. R. (1989). The Problem History Scale. *Psychology of Addictive Behaviors, 3,* 69–79.

6279

Test Name: PROCRASTINATION SCALE

Purpose: To measure tendency to procrastinate.

Number of Items: 20

Format: 5-point scales. Sample items presented.

Reliability: Alphas ranged from .79 to .82. Test–retest reliability was .80.

Author: Ferrari, J. R.

Article: Procrastinators and perfect behavior: An exploratory factor analysis of self-presentation, self-awareness and self-handicapping components.

Journal: *Journal of Research in Personality,* March 1992, *26*(1), 75–84.

Related Research: Lay, C. H. (1986). At last, my research article on procrastination. *Journal of Research on Personality, 20,* 474–495.

Lay, C. (1988). The relation of procrastination and optimism to judgments of time to complete an essay and anticipation of setbacks. *Journal of Social Behavior and Personality, 3,* 201–214.

■ ■ ■

6280

Test Name: PROCRASTINATION SCALE

Purpose: To provide a self-report measure of procrastination tendencies.

Number of Items: 35

Format: Responses are made on a 5-point Likert scale. All items are presented.

Reliability: Coefficient alpha was .90.

Validity: Correlations with other variables were -.47 to -.54.

Author: Tuckman, B. W.

Article: The development and concurrent validity of the Procrastination Scale.

Journal: *Educational and Psychological Measurement,* Summer 1991, *51*(2), 473–480.

■ ■ ■

6281

Test Name: PROSOCIAL BEHAVIOR SCALE

Purpose: To measure prosocial behavior.

Number of Items: 20

Format: Includes 3 factors: Prosocial Organizational Behaviors, Role-Prescribed Prosocial Behavior, and Prosocial Individual Behavior. Responses are made on a 5-point scale ranging from 1 (*never*) to 5 (*always*). All items are presented.

Validity: Correlations with other variables ranged from -.19 to .30.

Authors: McNeely, B. L., and Meglino, B. M.

Article: The role of dispositional and situational antecedents in prosocial organizational behavior: An examination of the intended beneficiaries of prosocial behavior.

Journal: *Journal of Applied Psychology,* December 1994, *79*(6), 836–844.

Related Research: Gorsuch, R. L. (1974). *Factor analysis.* Philadelphia: W.B. Saunders.

■ ■ ■

6282

Test Name: PSYCHOLOGICAL REACTANCE SCALE

Purpose: To measure psychological reactance.

Number of Items: 14

Format: 5-point Likert format. Sample items are presented.

Reliability: Test–retest was .89 (2 weeks). Alpha was .77.

Authors: Hong, S.-M., et al.

Article: Psychological reactance: Effects of age and gender.

Journal: *The Journal of Social Psychology,* April 1994, *133*(2), 223–228.

Related Research: Hong, S.-M. (1990). Hong's Psychological Reactance Scale: A further factor analytic validation. *Psychological Reports, 70,* 512–514.

■ ■ ■

6283

Test Name: PUPIL BEHAVIOR PATTERNS SCALE

Purpose: To measure pupil behavior including disrespect, sociability, and attentiveness.

Number of Items: 27

Format: Response scales range from 1 (*never*) to 6 (*always*). All items are presented.

Reliability: Total alpha was .89. Subscale alphas ranged from .81 to .87.

Author: Friedman, I. A.

Article: Student behavior patterns contributing to teacher burnout.

Journal: *Journal of Educational Research,* May/June 1995, *88*(5), 281–289.

Related Research: Friedman, I. A. (1991). High- and low-burnout schools: School culture aspects of teacher burnout. *Journal of Educational Research, 84,* 325–333.

■ ■ ■

6284

Test Name: QUALITY CIRCLE PROCESS SCALE

Purpose: To measure the degree to

which quality-circle group problem-solving guides are followed.

Number of Items: 13

Format: Includes 3 factors: Following Guidelines, Group Cohesiveness, and Use of Effective Problem Solving Techniques. Responses are made on a 6-point scale ranging from *not at all* to *strongly agree.*

Reliability: Correlations with other variables ranged from .02 to .38.

Authors: Geehr, J. L., et al.

Article: Quality circles: The effects of varying degrees of voluntary participation on employee attitudes and program efficacy.

Journal: *Educational and Psychological Measurement,* February 1995, *55*(1), 124–134.

Related Research: Adams, E. (1991). Quality circle performance. *Journal of Management, 17,* 25–39.

■ ■ ■

6285

Test Name: QUANTITATIVE INVENTORY OF ALCOHOL DISORDERS

Purpose: To assess drinking behavior.

Number of Items: 22

Format: 5-point scales.

Reliability: Test–retest reliability was .86.

Authors: Mintz, L. B., et al.

Article: Relations among parental alcoholism, eating disorders, and substance abuse in nonclinical college women: With additional evidence against the uniformity myth.

Journal: *Journal of Counseling Psychology,* January 1995, *42*(1), 65–70.

Related Research: Stinnett, J. L., & Schechter, J. O. (1982/1983). A Quantitative Inventory of Alcohol Disorders (QIAD): A severity scale for alcohol abuse. *American Journal of Drug and Alcohol Abuse, 9,* 413–430.

■ ■ ■

6286

Test Name: RECREATIONAL THERAPY RATING FORM

Purpose: To assess behavior of recreational therapy patients.

Number of Items: 119

Format: True–false format. Sample items are presented.

Reliability: Median item total correlation was .79.

Authors: Berard, M., and Dreger, R. M.

Article: Prediction of recreational therapy behavior of hospitalized adolescents from a behavior classification instrument.

Journal: *Psychological Reports,* December 1994, *75*(3) Part II, 1603–1618.

Related Research: Dinning, R. E. (1972). *Reliability of the therapy rating forms.* Unpublished manuscript, Louisiana Central State Hospital, Psychology Department, Pineville.

■ ■ ■

6287

Test Name: REFLECTIVE TEACHING INSTRUMENT

Purpose: To measure reflective teaching practices.

Format: Likert format.

Reliability: Total alphas ranged from .70 to .82. Subscale alphas ranged from .47 to .83.

Validity: Correlations with other variables ranged from .07 to .35.

Authors: Candler-Lotven, A. C., et al.

Article: Reliability and validity of the Reflective Teaching Instrument.

Journal: *Psychological Reports,* August 1995, *77*(1), 63–66.

Related Research: Kirby, P. C., & Teddlie, C. (1989). Development of the Reflective Teaching Instrument. *Journal of Research and Development in Education, 22,* 45–51.

■ ■ ■

6288

Test Name: RESPONSIBILITY QUESTIONNAIRE

Purpose: To assess responsibility in OCD patients.

Number of Items: 126

Format: 9-point rating scales.

Reliability: Alpha was .81. Test–retest reliability was .59.

Validity: Correlations with other variables ranged from .16 to .56.

Authors: Rheaume, J., et al.

Article: Inflated responsibility in obsessive-compulsive disorder: Psychometric studies of a semiidiographic measure.

Journal: *Journal of Psychopathology and Behavioral Assessment,* December 1994, *16*(4), 265–276.

Related Research: Rheaume, J., et al. (1995). Inflated responsibility and its role in OCD: Validation of a theoretical definition of responsibility. *Behavior Research and Therapy, 33,* 159–169.

■ ■ ■

6289

Test Name: REVISED BEHAVIOR PROBLEM CHECKLIST

Purpose: To allow teachers to report student behavior problems.

Number of Items: 89

Format: Responses are made on a 3-point scale indicating the severity of problem behavior (*no problem, mild problem, severe problem*).

Reliability: Median coefficient alpha was .83.

Authors: Frentz, C., et al.

Article: Popular, controversial, neglected, and rejected adolescents: Contrasts of social competence and achievement differences.

Journal: *Journal of School Psychology,* Summer 1991, *29*(2), 109–120.

Related Research: Quay, H. C., & Peterson, D. (1983). *The Revised Behavior Problem Checklist.* Coral Gables, FL: University of Miami, Department of Psychology.

• • •

6290

Test Name: REVISED LOVE/ HATE CHECKLIST

Purpose: To survey hateful and loving behaviors.

Number of Items: 40

Format: A checklist format.

Validity: Correlations with other variables ranged from -.21 to .30.

Authors: Necessary, J. R., and Parish, T. S.

Article: Are we as we act or as we see ourselves to be?

Journal: *Perceptual and Motor Skills,* December 1994, *79*(3) Part 1, 1232–1234.

Related Research: Parish, T. S., & Necessary, J. R. (1993). Perceived actions of parents and attitudes of youth. *Adolescence, 28,* 185–188.

6291

Test Name: SCALE FOR RATING BEHAVIORAL CHARACTERISTICS OF SUPERIOR STUDENTS

Purpose: To assess the extent to which students possess attributes associated with superior academic performance.

Number of Items: 37

Format: Responses are made on a 4-point scale indicating the extent to which the characteristic is true of a pupil.

Reliability: Test–retest coefficients ranged from .77 to .79. Interrater agreement coefficients ranged from .67 to .91.

Authors: McSheffrey, R., and Hoge, R.

Article: Performance within an enriched program for the gifted.

Journal: *Child Study Journal,* June 1992, *22*(2), 93–102.

Related Research: Renzulli, J. S., et al. (1971). Teacher identification of superior students. *Exceptional Children, 38,* 211–214.

• • •

6292

Test Name: SELF-CONCEALMENT SCALE

Purpose: To measure the predisposition to conceal from others distressing or negative information.

Number of Items: 10

Format: 5-point Likert format.

Reliability: Test–retest reliability (4 weeks) was .81. Interitem reliability was .83.

Authors: Kelly, A. E., and Achter, J. A.

Article: Self-concealment and attitudes toward counseling in university students.

Journal: *Journal of Counseling Psychology,* January 1995, *42*(1), 40–46.

Related Research: Larson, D. G., & Chastain, R. L. (1990). Self-concealment: Conceptualization, measurement, and health implications. *Journal of Social and Clinical Psychology, 9,* 439–455.

• • •

6293

Test Name: SELF-CONTROL RATING SCALE

Purpose: To allow teachers to rate children's level of impulsivity vs. self-control.

Number of Items: 33

Format: Responses are made on a 7-point Likert scale with one word descriptive anchors at each end of the continuum.

Reliability: Internal consistency was .98.

Authors: Frentz, C., et al.

Article: Popular, controversial, neglected, and rejected adolescents: Contrasts of social competence and achievement differences.

Journal: *Journal of School Psychology,* Summer 1991, *29*(2), 109–120.

Related Research: Kendall, P. C., & Wilcox, L. E. (1979). Self-control in children: Development of a rating scale. *Journal of Consulting and Clinical Psychology, 47,* 1020–1029.

• • •

6294

Test Name: SELF-CONTROL SCHEDULE

Purpose: To measure the repertoire of self-control skills suitable for coping with stressful events.

Number of Items: 36

Format: 6-point Likert scales. Sample item presented.

Reliability: Internal consistencies ranged between .78 and .81. Test–retest reliability was .86 over 4 weeks.

Author: Stevens, M. J.

Article: Predictors of existential openness.

Journal: *Journal of Research in Personality*, March 1992, *26*(1), 32–43.

Related Research: Rosenbaum, M. (1980). A schedule for assessing self-control behaviors: Preliminary findings. *Behavior Therapy, 11*, 109–121.

■ ■ ■

6295

Test Name: SELF-HANDICAPPING SCALE

Purpose: To measure self-handicapping.

Number of Items: 10

Format: Responses are made on a 6-point scale ranging from 1 (*certainly, always true*) to 6 (*certainly, always false*).

Reliability: Alpha coefficients were .70 to .72.

Validity: Correlations with other variables ranged from -.36 to .61.

Author: Wesley, J. C.

Article: Effects of ability, high school achievement, and procrastinatory behavior on college performance.

Journal: *Educational and Psychological Measurement,* Summer 1994, *54*(2), 404–408.

Related Research: Strube, M. J. (1986). An analysis of the Self-Handicapping Scale. *Basic and Applied Social Psychology, 7,* 211–224.

6296

Test Name: SELF-HANDICAPPING SCALE

Purpose: To measure self-handicapping as a trait.

Number of Items: 14

Format: True–false format.

Reliability: Alphas ranged from .59 to .79. Sample items presented.

Authors: Lay, C. L., et al.

Article: Self-handicappers and procrastinators: A comparison of their practice behavior prior to an evaluation.

Journal: *Journal of Research in Personality*, September 1992, *26*(3), 242–257.

Related Research: Rhodewalt, F. (1990). Self-handicappers: Individual differences in the preference for anticipatory, self-protective acts. In R. Higgins et al. (Eds.), *Self-handicapping: The paradox that isn't* (pp. 69–106). New York: Plenum Press.

■ ■ ■

6297

Test Name: SELF-HANDICAPPING SCALE

Purpose: To assess the tendency to use self-handicapping behavior such as lack of effort, illness, and procrastination.

Number of Items: 25

Format: Sample items presented.

Reliability: Alpha was .78. Test–retest reliability (1 month) was .74.

Authors: Rhodewalt, F., and Fairfield, M.

Article: Claimed self-handicaps and the self-handicapper: The relation of reduction in intended effort to performance.

Journal: *Journal of Research in*

Personality, December 1991, *25*(4), 402–417.

Related Research: Rhodewalt, F., et al. (1984). Self-handicapping among competitive athletes: The role of practice in self-esteem protection. *Basic and Applied Social Psychology, 7,* 307–323.

■ ■ ■

6298

Test Name: SELF-MANAGEMENT PRACTICES SCALE

Purpose: To assess how individuals attempt to change their lifestyles.

Number of Items: 10

Format: 4-point rating scales. All items presented.

Validity: Correlations with other variables ranged from -.26 to .60 across items and subscales.

Authors: Williams, R. L., et al.

Article: Naturalistic application of self-change practices.

Journal: *Journal of Research in Personality*, June 1991, *25*(2), 167–176.

Related Research: Williams, R. L., et al. (1990). *Construction and validation of a self-report scale of self-management practices.* Unpublished manuscript, The University of Tennessee, Knoxville.

■ ■ ■

6299

Test Name: SELF-MANAGEMENT PRACTICES SCALE

Purpose: To assess self-management practices in daily life.

Number of Items: 16

Format: 5-point rating scales. All items presented.

Reliability: Alpha was .81. Test–retest reliabilities (1 week) ranged from .65 to .90 across subscales.

Validity: Correlations with other variables ranged from -.30 to .71. Correlations with other self-control scales ranged from .30 to .68 across subscales.

Author: Williams, R. L.

Article: Construction and validation of a brief self-report scale of self-management practices.

Journal: *Journal of Research in Personality,* September 1992, *26*(3), 216–234.

● ● ●

6300

Test Name: SELF-REGULATION SCALE

Purpose: To assess children's styles of self-regulation in the academic domain.

Number of Items: 26

Format: Responses are made on a 4-point Likert-type scale. Includes 4 subscales: External, Introjected, Identified, and Intrinsic. Examples are presented.

Reliability: Internal consistency estimates ranged from .62 to .82.

Authors: Grolnick, W. S., et al.

Article: Inner resources for school achievement: Motivational mediators of children's perceptions of their parents.

Journal: *Journal of Educational Psychology,* December 1991, *83*(4), 508–517.

Related Research: Ryan, R. M., & Connell, J. P. (1989). Perceived locus of causality and internalization: Examining reasons for acting in two domains. *Journal of Personality and Social Psychology, 57,* 749–761.

● ● ●

6301

Test Name: SELF-REGULATION SCALE

Purpose: To enable teachers to rate student academic behavior in class.

Format: 5-point frequency scales.

Reliability: KR was .82.

Validity: Correlation with academic achievement was .62. Correlations with other variables ranged from -.14 to .69.

Authors: Feldman, S. C., et al.

Article: The relationship of self-efficacy, self-regulation, and collaborative verbal behavior with grades: Preliminary findings.

Journal: *Psychological Reports,* December 1995, *77*(3) Part I, 971–978.

Related Research: Zimmerman, B. J., & Martinez-Pons, M. (1990). Construct validation of a strategy model of student self-regulated learning. *Journal of Educational Psychology, 80,* 284–290.

● ● ●

6302

Test Name: SELF-REPORT ABSENCE MEASURE

Purpose: To measure an absence self-report.

Number of Items: 3

Format: Responses are made on a 7-point scale ranging from *never* to *more than once a week.* An example is presented

Reliability: Coefficient alpha was .61.

Author: Johns, G.

Article: How often were you absent? A review of the use of self-reported absence data.

Journal: *Journal of Applied Psychology,* August 1994, *79*(4), 574–591.

Related Research: Harrisch, K. A., & Hulin, C. L. (1990). Job attitudes and organizational withdrawal: An examination of

retirement and other voluntary withdrawal behaviors. *Journal of Vocational Behavior, 37,* 60–78.

● ● ●

6303

Test Name: SELF-REPORT ABSENCE MEASURE

Purpose: To provide an absence self-report.

Number of Items: 6

Format: Responses are made on 5- or 7-point response scales. Examples are presented.

Reliability: Coefficient alpha was .53.

Author: Johns, G.

Article: How often were you absent? A review of the use of self-reported absence data.

Journal: *Journal of Applied Psychology,* August 1994, *79*(4), 574–591.

Related Research: Hanisch, K. A., & Hulin, C. L. (1991). General attitudes and organizational withdrawal: An evaluation of a causal model. *Journal of Vocational Behavior, 39,* 110–128.

● ● ●

6304

Test Name: SELF TALK SCALE

Purpose: To measure the disposition to talk to oneself about oneself.

Number of Items: 27

Format: 5-point frequency scales. Sample items are presented.

Reliability: Alpha was .89.

Validity: Correlations with other variables ranged from .30 to .46.

Author: Morin, A.

Article: Preliminary data on a relation between self-talk and complexity of the self-concept.

Journal: *Psychological Reports,*

February 1995, *76*(1), 267–272.

Related Research: Morin, A., et al. (1993). Self-talk as a mediator of private self-consciousness: A measure of self-talk and a correlational study. *Revue Quebecoise de Psychologie, 14,* 3–19.

● ● ●

6305

Test Name: SEXUAL EXPERIENCES QUESTIONNAIRE

Purpose: To assess the degree of sexual harassment in behavioral terms.

Number of Items: 18

Format: 3 point scales range from 1 (*never*) to 3 (*more than once*).

Reliability: Internal consistency ranged from .88 to .92. Test–retest reliability was .86 over 2 weeks.

Authors: Gelfand, M. J., et al.

Article: The structure of sexual harassment: A confirmatory analysis across cultures and settings.

Journal: *Journal of Vocational Behavior,* October 1995, *47*(2), 164–177.

Related Research: Fitzgerald, L. F., & Hesson-McInnis, M. (1989). The dimensions of sexual harassment: A structural analysis. *Journal of Vocational Behavior, 35,* 309–326.

● ● ●

6306

Test Name: SEXUAL EXPERIENCES QUESTIONNAIRE

Purpose: To measure sexual harassment.

Number of Items: 28

Format: Includes five forms of sexual harassment: gender,

seductive behavior, sexual bribery, sexual coercion, and sexual imposition. Examples are presented.

Reliability: Alpha coefficients ranged from .24 to .89. Test–retest (2 weeks) reliability was .86. Split-half corrected reliabilities ranged form .62 to .86.

Authors: Stockdale, M. S., and Veux, A.

Article: What sexual harassment experiences lead respondents to acknowledge being sexually harassed? A secondary analysis of a university survey.

Journal: *Journal of Vocational Behavior,* October 1993, *43*(2), 221–234.

Related Research: Fitzgerald, L. F., & Shullman, S. L. (1985, August). *The development and validation of an objectively scored measure of sexual harassment.* Paper presented to the annual meeting of the American Psychological Association, Los Angeles.

● ● ●

6307

Test Name: SEXUAL EXPERIENCE SURVEY

Purpose: To determine occurrences of male-against-female sexual assault for male and female college students.

Time Required: 25 minutes.

Format: Participants respond using a yes–no format.

Reliability: Test–retest was over 80%.

Authors: Finley, C., and Corty, E.

Article: Rape on campus: The prevalence of sexual assault while enrolled in college.

Journal: *Journal of College Student Development,* March 1993, *34*(2), 113–117.

Related Research: Koss, M. P., & Oros, C. J. (1982). Sexual experiences survey: A research instrument investigating sexual aggression and victimization. *Journal of Consulting and Clinical Psychology, 50,* 455–457.

● ● ●

6308

Test Name: SEXUAL PERMISSIVENESS SCALE

Purpose: To measure sexual permissiveness.

Number of Items: 5

Format: 5-point agreement scales. Sample items described.

Reliability: Alpha was .88.

Authors: Whitbeck, L. B., et al.

Article: The effects of divorced mothers' dating behaviors and sexual attitudes on the sexual attitudes and behavior of their adolescent children.

Journal: *Journal of Marriage and the Family,* August 1994, *56*(3), 615–621.

Related Research: Reiss, I. (1967). *The social context of premarital sexual permissiveness.* New York: Holt, Rinehart and Winston.

● ● ●

6309

Test Name: SEXUALLY HARASSING BEHAVIORS SCALE

Purpose: To identify sexually harassing behaviors experienced from supervisors and coworkers.

Number of Items: 8

Format: Responses are made on a 5-point scale ranging from 1 (*never*) to 5 (*ten or more times*).

Reliability: Alpha coefficients were .74 and .72.

Validity: Correlations with other variables ranged from -.30 to .37.

Authors: Morrow, P. C., et al.

Article: Sexual harassment behaviors and work related perceptions and attitudes.

Journal: *Journal of Vocational Behavior,* December 1994, *45*(3), 295–309.

■ ■ ■

6310

Test Name: SILENCING THE SELF SCALE

Purpose: To assess intrapersonal and interpersonal behaviors of women that are predictive of depression.

Number of Items: 31

Format: Likert format. Sample items are presented.

Validity: Factor structure of items was generally similar to that found in Jack's study.

Authors: Stevens, H. B., and Galvin, S. L.

Article: Structural findings regarding the Silencing the Self Scale.

Journal: *Psychological Reports,* August 1995, *77*(1), 11–17.

Related Research: Jack, D. C., & Dill, D. (1992). The Silencing the Self Scale: Schemas of intimacy associated with depression in women. *Psychology of Women Quarterly, 16,* 97–106.

■ ■ ■

6311

Test Name: SOCIALLY RESPONSIBLE CONSUMER BEHAVIOR SCALE

Purpose: To measure extent to which consumers purchase products and services perceived to benefit the environment.

Number of Items: 40

Format: 5-point scales (*always true* to *never true*). All items are presented.

Reliability: Alphas ranged from .90 to .95.

Author: Roberts, J. A.

Article: Sex differences in socially responsible behavior.

Journal: *Psychological Reports,* August 1993, *73*(1), 139–148.

Related Research: Roberts, J. A. (1991). D*evelopment of a profile of the socially responsible consumer for the 1990's and its marketing, management and public policy implications.* Unpublished doctoral dissertation, Marketing Department, University of Nebraska, Lincoln.

■ ■ ■

6312

Test Name: SPORT SOCIALIZATION INVENTORY—SPANISH VERSION

Purpose: To measure active sport involvement.

Number of Items: 49

Format: Employs a 5-point Likert format. Examples are presented.

Reliability: Test–retest reliabilities ranged from .79 to .95. Alpha coefficients ranged from .80 to .96.

Validity: Concurrent validity was .51.

Authors: Pizarro, A. L., et al.

Article: Development of a Spanish version of a Sport Socialization Inventory.

Journal: *Perceptual and Motor Skills,* December 1991, *73*(3) Part 1, 799–803.

Related Research: Greendorfer, S. L., et al. (1986). Gender differences in Brazilian children's socialization into sport. *International Review for Sociology of Sport, 21,* 53–63.

■ ■ ■

6313

Test Name: SPORTS ORIENTATION QUESTIONNAIRE

Purpose: To measure the nature of competitive behavior in sports.

Number of Items: 25

Format: Includes 3 dimensions: Competitiveness, Win Orientation, and Goal Orientation.

Validity: Correlations with other variables ranged from .13 to .65.

Authors: Smither, R. D., and Houston, J. M.

Article: The nature of competitiveness: The development and validation of the Competitiveness Index.

Journal: *Educational and Psychological Measurement,* Summer 1992, *52*(2), 407–418.

Related Research: Gill, D. L., & Deeter, T. E. (1988). Development of the Sports Orientation Questionnaire. *Research Quarterly for Exercise and Sport, 59,* 191–202.

■ ■ ■

6314

Test Name: STANDARDIZED ASSAULT INTERVIEW

Purpose: To determine assault severity and to provide demographic information.

Number of Items: 126

Format: Open-ended responses are made to questions.

Reliability: Interrater reliability was .81.

Authors: Foa, E., et al.

Article: Evaluation of a brief cognitive–behavioral program for the prevention of chronic PTSD in recent assault victims.

Journal: *Journal of Consulting and Clinical Psychology,* December 1995, *63*(6), 948–955.

Related Research: Foa, E. B., & Rothbaum, B. O. (1985). *The Standardized Assault Interview.* Unpublished interview, Department of Psychiatry, Medical College of Pennsylvania at East Pennsylvania Psychiatric Institute, Philadelphia.

■ ■ ■

6315

Test Name: STIGMA SCALE

Purpose: To measure extent of stigmatization of selected targets.

Number of Items: 6

Format: Formats vary across items and vignettes.

Reliability: Alpha was .94.

Validity: Factor analysis revealed one stigma factor with an eigenvalue of 2.80.

Authors: Crandall, C. S., and Cohen, C.

Article: The personality of the stigmatizer: Cultural world view, conventionalism and self-esteem.

Journal: *Journal of Research in Personality,* December 1994, *28*(4), 461–480.

■ ■ ■

6316

Test Name: STUDENT ALCOHOL QUESTIONNAIRE

Purpose: To measure drinking patterns, problems related to alcohol, and alcohol knowledge.

Number of Items: 71

Format: True–false format. Sample items are presented.

Reliability: Alphas ranged from .27 to .92 across subscales.

Authors: Engs, R. C., and Hanson, D. J.

Article: The Student Alcohol

Questionnaire: An updated reliability of the Drinking Patterns, Problems, Knowledge and Attitude subscales.

Journal: *Psychological Reports,* February 1994, *74*(1), 12–14.

Related Research: Engs, R. C. (1975). *The Student Alcohol Questionnaire.* Bloomington: Department of Health and Safety Education, Indiana University.

■ ■ ■

6317

Test Name: STUDENT PARTICIPATION QUESTIONNAIRE

Purpose: To assess the form and extent of participation among elementary grade pupils.

Number of Items: 29

Format: Includes three subscales: Effort, Initiative, and Nonparticipatory Behavior. Examples are presented.

Reliability: Alpha coefficients ranged from .89 to .94.

Authors: Finn, J. D., et al.

Article: Measuring participation among elementary grade students.

Journal: *Educational and Psychological Measurement,* Summer 1991, *51*(2), 393–402.

Related Research: Swift, M. S., & Spivack, G. (1969). Achievement-related classroom behavior of secondary-school normal and disturbed students. *Exceptional Children, 35,* 677–684.

Fincham, F. D, et al. (1989). Learned helplessness, test anxiety, and academic achievement: A longitudinal analysis. *Child Development, 60,* 138–145.

■ ■ ■

6318

Test Name: SUBSTITUTES FOR LEADERSHIP SCALE— REVISED

Purpose: To measure main and interactive effects of substitutes variables and leader behaviors on employee attitude, perception, and performance.

Number of Items: 41

Format: Responses are made on 7-point scales. Includes 13 factors. All items are presented.

Reliability: Alpha coefficients ranged from .70 to .91.

Authors: Podsakoff, P. M., and Mackenzie, S. B.

Article: An examination of the psychometric properties and nomological validity of some revised and reduced substitutes for leadership scales.

Journal: *Journal of Applied Psychology,* October 1994, *79*(5), 702–713.

Related Research: Podsakoff, P. M., et al. (1993). Substitutes for leadership and the management of professionals. *The Leadership Quarterly, 4,* 1–44.

■ ■ ■

6319

Test Name: SUBSTITUTES FOR LEADERSHIP SCALE— REVISED

Purpose: To measure main and interactive effects of substitutes variables and leader behaviors on employee attitudes, perception, and performance.

Number of Items: 74

Format: Responses are made on 7-point scales. Includes 13 factors. All items presented.

Reliability: Alpha coefficients ranged from .64 to .92 ($N = 411$).

Authors: Podsakoff, P. M., and Mackenzie, S. B.

Article: An examination of the psychometric properties and nomological validity of some revised and reduced substitutes for leadership scales.

Journal: *Journal of Applied Psychology,* October 1994, *79*(5), 702–713.

Related Research: Podsakoff, P. M., et al. (1993). Do substitutes for leadership really substitute for leadership? An empirical examination of Kerr and Jernier's situational leadership model. *Organizational Behavior and Human Decision Processes, 54,* 1–44.

• • •

6320

Test Name: SUPPORTIVE LEADERSHIP SCALE

Purpose: To measure supportive leadership.

Number of Items: 9

Format: Responses are made on a 4-point scale ranging from *rarely* to *very frequently.* Sample items are presented.

Reliability: Coefficient alpha was .94.

Authors: Hoy, W. K., et al.

Article: Faculty trust in colleagues: Linking the principal with school effectiveness.

Journal: *Journal of Research and Development in Education,* Fall 1992, *26*(1), 38–45.

Related Research: Halpin, A. W., & Croft, D. B. (1963). *The organizational climate of schools.* Chicago: Midwest Administration Center of the University of Chicago.

• • •

6321

Test Name: TASK LEADERSHIP PERFORMANCE SCALE

Purpose: To assess self-perceived leadership performance.

Number of Items: 4

Format: 5-point Likert format. All items are presented.

Reliability: Alpha was .95.

Authors: Riley, A., and Burke, P. J.

Article: Identities and self-verification in the small group.

Journal: *Social Psychology Quarterly,* June 1995, *58*(2), 61–73.

Related Research: Burke, P. J. (1971). Task and socio-emotional leadership role performance. *Sociometry, 34,* 22–40.

• • •

6322

Test Name: TEACHER CHECKLIST

Purpose: To enable teachers to note a range of classroom behaviors.

Number of Items: 17

Format: Includes 3 subscales: Aggression, Prosocial Behavior, and School Performance. Responses are made on a 5-point scale ranging from 1 (*not at all like this child*) to 5 (*very much like this child*).

Reliability: Alpha coefficients ranged from .82 to .95. Test–retest (6 weeks) reliabilities ranged from .93 to .97.

Authors: Hudley, C., and Graham, S.

Article: An attributional intervention to reduce peer-directed aggression among African American boys.

Journal: *Child Development,* February 1993, *64*(1), 124–138.

Related Research: Coie, J. (1990). *Teacher checklist.* Unpublished manuscript.

6323

Test Name: TEACHER–CHILD RATING SCALE

Purpose: To allow teachers to rate individual students' social, behavioral, and academic competence and problems.

Number of Items: 38

Format: A teacher-report rating scale.

Reliability: Internal consistency reliabilities exceeded .90 and test–retest exceeded .80 across three samples.

Author: Pianta, R. C.

Article: Patterns of relationships between children and kindergarten teachers.

Journal: *Journal of School Psychology,* Spring 1994, *32*(1), 15–31.

Related Research: Hightower, A. D., et al. (1986). The Teacher-Child Rating Scale: A brief objective measure of elementary children's school problem behaviors and competencies. *School Psychology Review, 15,* 393–409.

• • •

6324

Test Name: TEACHER OBSERVATION OF CLASSROOM ADAPTION

Purpose: To assess student behaviors.

Number of Items: 14

Format: Responses are made on a 6-point Likert scale ranging from 0 (*almost never*) to 5 (*almost always*).

Reliability: Alpha was .87.

Author: Lochman, J. E.

Article: Screening of child behavior problems for prevention programs at school entry.

Journal: *Journal of Consulting and Clinical Psychology*, August 1995, *63*(4), 549–559.

Related Research: Werthamer, et al. (1991). Effects of first-grade classroom environment on shy behavior, aggressive behavior, and concentration problems. *American Journal of Community Psychology, 19*, 585–602.

■ ■ ■

6325

Test Name: TEACHER REPORT FORM

Purpose: To measure teacher behavior.

Number of Items: 120

Format: 3-point scales (*not true* to *very true* or *often true*).

Reliability: Alphas ranged from .78 to .95 across subscales.

Validity: Correlations with the Amsterdam Child Behavior Checklist ranged from .06 to .79.

Author: DeJong, P. F.

Article: Validity of the Amsterdam Child Behavior Checklist: A short rating scale for children

Journal: *Psychological Reports*, December 1995, *77*(3) Part II, 1139–1144.

■ ■ ■

6326

Test Name: TEACHING YOUNGER SIBLINGS QUESTIONNAIRE

Purpose: To assess self-reported teaching of younger siblings.

Number of Items: 23

Format: 7-point frequency scales. All items presented.

Reliability: Alpha was .75.

Author: Smith, T. E.

Article: Growth in academic achievement and teaching younger siblings.

Journal: *Social Psychology Quarterly*, March 1993, *56*(1), 77–85.

Related Research: Smith, T. E. (1984). School grades and responsibility for younger siblings: An empirical study of the teaching function. *American Sociological Review, 49*, 248–260.

■ ■ ■

6327

Test Name: TEL-AVIV ACTIVITIES INVENTORY

Purpose: To examine leisure activities.

Number of Items: 62

Format: Responses are made using a yes–no format. (There are 10 subscales or factors.)

Reliability: The correlation between computer (subscale) and science (subscale) was .37. The correlation between Literature I and Literature II subscales was .39.

Author: Kelly, K.

Article: The relation of gender and academic achievement to career self-efficacy and interests.

Journal: *Gifted Child Quarterly*, Spring 1993, *37*(2), 59–68.

Related Research: Milgram, R. M. (1990). *Tel-Aviv Activities Inventory.* Tel-Aviv University, School of Education, Ramat-Aviv, Israel.

■ ■ ■

6328

Test Name: TERMINATION BEHAVIOR CHECKLIST— THERAPIST

Purpose: To enable counselors to identify termination activities.

Number of Items: 38

Format: Counselors respond by checking each item representing behaviors that occurred. An abbreviated form of all items is presented.

Reliability: Test–retest (3 weeks) reliability was .89.

Authors: Quintana, S. M., and Holahan, W.

Article: Termination in short-term counseling: Comparison of successful and unsuccessful cases.

Journal: *Journal of Counseling Psychology*, July 1992, *39*(3), 299–305.

Related Research: Marx, J. A., & Gelso, C. J. (1987). Termination of individual counseling in a university counseling center. *Journal of Counseling Psychology, 34*, 309.

■ ■ ■

6329

Test Name: THERAPEUTIC REACTANCE SCALE

Purpose: To measure psychological reactance.

Number of Items: 28

Format: Responses are made on a 4-point Likert scale ranging from 1 (*strongly disagree*) to 4 (*strongly agree*).

Reliability: Internal consistency estimates ranged from .75 to .84. Test–retest (3 weeks) reliability ranged from .57 to .60.

Author: Hunsley, J.

Article: Treatment acceptability of symptom prescription techniques.

Journal: *Journal of Counseling Psychology*, April 1993, *40*(2), 139–143.

Related Research: Dowd, E. T., et al. (1991). The Therapeutic Reactance Scale: A measure of psychological reactance. *Journal*

of Counseling and Development, 69, 541–545.

■ ■ ■

6330

Test Name: THERAPIST TERMINATION QUESTIONNAIRE—ADAPTED

Purpose: To measure affective reactions.

Number of Items: 22

Format: Responses are made on a 9-point Likert format. Includes three factors: Anxiety, Depression, and Task Satisfaction.

Validity: Correlations with other variables ranged from -.16 to .35.

Authors: Boyer, S. P., and Hoffman, M. A.

Article: Counselor affective reactions to termination: Impact of counselor loss history and perceived client sensitivity to loss.

Journal: *Journal of Counseling Psychology,* July 1993, *40*(3), 271–277.

Related Research: Greene, L. R. (1980). On terminating psychotherapy: More evidence of sex-role related countertransference. *Psychology of Women Quarterly, 4,* 548–557.

■ ■ ■

6331

Test Name: TRAINER BEHAVIOR SCALE

Purpose: To measure group leader behavior.

Number of Items: 28

Format: Responses are made on a 5-point Likert scale ranging from 5 (*strongly agree*) to 1 (*strongly disagree*). Includes 7 dimensions: congruence–empathy, conceptual input, conditionality, perceptiveness, openness,

affection, and dominance. Examples are presented.

Validity: Correlations with other variables ranged from -.40 to .37.

Authors: Kivlighan, D. M., Jr., et al.

Article: Projection in group counseling: The relationship between members' interpersonal problems and their perception of the group leader.

Journal: *Journal of Counseling Psychology,* January 1994, *41*(1), 99–104.

Related Research: Bolman, L. (1971). Some effects of trainers on their T groups. *Journal of Applied Behavioral Science, 7,* 309–325.

■ ■ ■

6332

Test Name: VERRAN/SNYDER-HALPERN SLEEP SCALE

Purpose: To measure three dimensions of sleep.

Number of Items: 15

Reliability: Alpha coefficients ranged from .65 to .84.

Validity: Correlations with sleep disturbance were .19 and .20.

Author: Mahon, N. E.

Article: Loneliness and sleep during adolescence.

Journal: *Perceptual and Motor Skills,* February 1994, *78*(1), 227–231.

Related Research: Verran, J. A. (1988). *Verran/Snyder-Halpern (VSH) Sleep Scale information sheet.* Unpublished data, University of Arizona, Tucson.

■ ■ ■

6333

Test Name: VOLUNTARINESS MEASURE

Purpose: To determine voluntariness.

Number of Items: 7

Format: Responses are made on a 5-point scale ranging from 5 (*strongly agree*) to 1 (*strongly disagree*). All items are presented.

Reliability: Internal consistency reliabilities were .92 and .90.

Validity: Correlations with other variables ranged from -.55 to .66.

Author: Campion, M. A.

Article: Meaning and measurement of turnover: Comparison of alternative measures and recommendations for research.

Journal: *Journal of Applied Psychology,* April 1991, *76*(2), 199–212.

■ ■ ■

6334

Test Name: WENDER UTAH RATING SCALE

Purpose: To assess adults' descriptions of their childhood behaviors.

Number of Items: 61

Reliability: Alpha was .87.

Validity: Correlations with other variables ranged from .49 to .54.

Authors: Weyandt, L. L., et al.

Article: Reported prevalence of attentional difficulties in a general sample of college students.

Journal: *Journal of Psychopathology and Behavioral Assessment,* September 1995, *17*(3), 293–304.

Related Research: Ward, M., et al. (1993). The Wender Utah Rating Scale: An aid in retrospective diagnosis of children with ADHD. *American Journal of Psychiatry, 160,* 245–256.

CHAPTER 9
Communication

6335

Test Name: AFFECTIVE SELF-DISCLOSURE SCALE FOR COUPLES

Purpose: To measure the frequency of emotional self-disclosure to partners.

Number of Items: 16

Format: Responses are made on a 4-point Likert scale (*never* to *very often*).

Reliability: Internal consistency reliability was .92.

Authors: Vera, E. M., and Betz, N. E.

Article: Relationships of self-regard and affective self-disclosure to relationship satisfaction in college students.

Journal: *Journal of College Student Development*, September 1992, *33*(5), 422–430.

Related Research: Davidson, B., et al. (1983). Affective self-disclosure and marital adjustment: A test of equity theory. *Journal of Marriage and the Family, 45,* 93–102.

• • •

6336

Test Name: ATTRACTION TO FEEDBACK SCALE

Purpose: To measure attitudes toward communicating interpersonal feedback messages.

Number of Items: 15

Format: Responses are made on a 7-point scale ranging from 1 (*strongly disagree*) to 7 (*strongly agree*).

Reliability: Internal consistency reliability was .94 (*N* = 75).

Authors: Robinson, F. F., and Hardt, D. A.

Article: Effects of cognitive and behavioral structure and discussion of corrective feedback outcomes on counseling and group development.

Journal: *Journal of Counseling Psychology*, October 1992, *39*(4), 473–481.

Related Research: Hulse, D. (1981). *The effects of cognitive-behavioral pretraining on attraction to feedback and attraction to the group.* Unpublished doctoral dissertation, Indiana University, Bloomington.

• • •

6337

Test Name: AUDITORY ANALYSIS OF SPEECH

Purpose: To evaluate the phonological analysis of speech.

Format: Involves sound-blending tasks and word identifying tasks in which only some part of the word is spoken. The child picks out the correct picture from three alternatives.

Reliability: K-R internal consistency coefficient was .74.

Validity: Correlations with other variables ranged from .31 to .37.

Authors: Korkman, M., and Hakkinen-Rihu, P.

Article: A new classification of developmental language disorders.

Journal: *Brain and Language*, July 1994, *47*(1), 96–116.

• • •

6338

Test Name: COMMUNICATIVE ADAPTABILITY SCALE

Purpose: To measure social communicative competence.

Format: Includes 6 dimensions: social confirmation, social composure, social experience, appropriate disclosure, wit, and articulation.

Reliability: Alpha coefficients ranged from .65 to .84.

Validity: Correlations with rated satisfaction with communication ranged from .19 to .46.

Author: Prisbell, M.

Article: Perceptions of satisfaction with communication and self-rated competence in dating relationships.

Journal: *Perceptual and Motor Skills*, August 1994, *79*(1) Part 2, 529–530.

Related Research: Duran, R. L. (1983). Communicative adaptability: A measure of social communicative competence. *Communication Quarterly, 31,* 320–326.

• • •

6339

Test Name: CONTACT WITH MEDICAL HEALTH CARE PROFESSIONALS INVENTORY

Purpose: To measure contact with medical professionals.

Number of Items: 28

Format: Respondents provided number of times they phoned or visited any of 28 specialists in the past year. All items are presented.

Reliability: Cronbach's alpha was .43 (office) .52 (phone) and .59 (total).

Validity: Women reported more total contact than men ($p < .01$).

Author: Korman, J. J.

Article: An inventory to measure contact with medical health care professionals.

Journal: *Psychological Reports*, June 1991, *69*(1), 43–49.

■ ■ ■

6340

Test Name: DISCLOSURE SCALE

Purpose: To measure "here-and-now" and "there-and-then" disclosures.

Number of Items: 60

Format: Likert format.

Reliability: Alpha was .97.

Validity: Correlations with other variables ranged from -.30 to .55.

Author: Slavin, R.

Article: "Here-and-now" and "there-and-then" disclosures on cohesion and on students' attitudes toward specific courses.

Journal: *Psychological Reports*, February 1995, *76*(1), 111–121.

Related Research: Slavin, R. (1993). The significance of "here-and-now" disclosure in promoting cohesion in group therapy. *Group, 17*, 143–150.

■ ■ ■

6341

Test Name: EMOTIONAL SELF-DISCLOSURE SCALE

Purpose: To assess emotional self-disclosure.

Number of Items: 40

Format: Responses are made on a 5-point Likert scale ranging from *not at all willing to discuss this topic* to *totally willing to discuss this topic.*

Reliability: Test–retest reliability (for partner targets) ranged from .58 to .75. Internal consistency reliability (for partner targets) ranged from .86 to .95.

Authors: Vera, E. M., and Betz, N. E.

Article: Relationships of self-regard and affective self-disclosure to relationship satisfaction in college students.

Journal: *Journal of College Student Development*, September 1992, *33*(5), 422–430.

Related Research: Snell, W. E. et al. (1988). Development of the Emotional Self-Disclosure Scale. *Sex Roles, 18*, 59–73.

■ ■ ■

6342

Test Name: GROUP TASK STRATEGY SCALE

Purpose: To assess group task strategy.

Number of Items: 8

Format: Responses were made on 5-point Likert scale ranging from 1 (*strongly disagree*) to 5 (*strongly agree*). All items are presented.

Reliability: Cronbach's alpha was .87.

Validity: Correlations with other variables ranged from -.46 to .59.

Authors: Saavedra, R., et al.

Article: Complex interdependence in task-performing groups.

Journal: *Journal of Applied Psychology*, February 1993, *78*(1), 61–72.

Related Research: Hackman, J. R. (1982). *A set of methods for research on work teams* (Tech. Rep. No.1). New Haven, CT: Yale University Group Effectiveness Research Project, School of Organization and Management.

■ ■ ■

6343

Test Name: INTERACTION INVOLVEMENT SCALE

Purpose: To measure communicator's interaction.

Number of Items: 18

Format: Includes 3 subscales: Attentive, Perceptive, and Responsive.

Reliability: Retest reliability was .81.

Authors: Ralston, S. M., et al.

Article: An exploratory study of recruiters' self-ratings of interpersonal communication and applicants' decisions about employment.

Journal: *Perceptual and Motor Skills*, August 1993, *77*(1), 135–142.

Related Research: Cegala, D. J. (1981). Interaction involvement: A cognitive dimension of communicative competence. *Communication Education, 30*, 109–121.

■ ■ ■

6344

Test Name: INTERPERSONAL COMMUNICATION SATISFACTION INVENTORY

Purpose: To measure satisfaction with communication.

Number of Items: 19

Format: 7-point agree–disagree format. All items are presented.

Reliability: Alpha was .73.

Authors: Blood, D. J., and Ferriss, S. J.

Article: Effects of background

music on anxiety, satisfaction with communication, and productivity.

Journal: *Psychological Reports*, February 1993, *72*(1), 171–177.

Related Research: Hecht, M. L. (1978). The conceptualization and measurement of interpersonal communication satisfaction. *Human Communication Research*, *4*, 253–264.

• • •

6345

Test Name: LEADER–LEADER–MEMBER EXCHANGE MEASURE

Purpose: To assess supervisors' perceptions of leader–member exchanges.

Number of Items: 7

Format: Responses are made on a 7-point scale ranging from 1 (*strongly disagree*) to 7 (*strongly agree*). An example is presented.

Reliability: Alpha coefficients ranged from .75 to .84.

Authors: Liden, R. C., et al.

Article: A longitudinal study on the early development of leader-member exchanges.

Journal: *Journal of Applied Psychology*, August 1993, *78*(4), 662–674.

Related Research: Waynes, S. J., & Ferris, G. R. (1990). Influence tactics, affect, and exchange quality in supervisor-subordinate interactions: A laboratory experiment and field study. *Journal of Applied Psychology*, *75*, 487–499.

• • •

6346

Test Name: LEADER–MEMBER EXCHANGE SCALE

Purpose: To measure leader–member exchange.

Number of Items: 7

Format: Four response options are give for each item.

Reliability: Internal consistency reliability was .83.

Authors: Major, D. A., et al.

Article: A longitudinal investigation of newcomers expectation, early socialization outcomes, and the moderating effects of role development factors.

Journal: *Journal of Applied Psychology*, June 1995, *80*(3), 418–431.

Related Research: Scandura, T. A., & Graen, G. B. (1984). Moderating effects of initial leader-member exchange status on the effects of a leadership intervention. *Journal of Applied Psychology*, *69*, 428–436.

• • •

6347

Test Name: LEATHERS CREDIBILITY SCALE

Purpose: To measure source credibility.

Number of Items: 12

Format: Includes 3 dimensions: competence, trustworthiness, and dynamism.

Reliability: Alpha coefficients ranged from .81 to .94.

Authors: Powell, F. C., and Wanzenreid, J. W.

Article: Do Current Measures of Dimensions of Source Credibility Produce Stable Outcomes in Replicated Tests?

Journal: *Perceptual and Motor Skills*, October 1995, *81*(2), 675–687.

Related Research: Leathers, D. G. (1992). *Successful nonverbal communications, principles and applications.* New York: Macmillan.

6348

Test Name: MCCROSKEY AND JENSON SOURCE CREDIBILITY SCALE

Purpose: To measure source credibility.

Number of Items: 25

Format: Includes five dimensions: competency, character, sociability, composure, and extroversion.

Reliability: Alpha coefficients ranged from .81 to .95.

Authors: Powell, F. C., and Wanzenreid, J. W.

Article: Do current measures of dimensions of source credibility produce stable outcomes in replicated tests?

Journal: *Perceptual and Motor Skills*, October 1995, *81*(2), 675–687.

Related Research: McCroskey, J. C., & Jenson, T. J. (1975). Image of mass media news sources. *Journal of Broadcasting*, *19*, 169–180.

• • •

6349

Test Name: MEMBER VIEW OF LEADER–MEMBER EXCHANGE SCALE

Purpose: To measure the subordinate's perception of leader–member exchanges.

Number of Items: 7

Format: Responses are made on a 7-point scale ranging from 1 (*strongly disagree*) to 7 (*strongly agree*). Examples are presented.

Reliability: Alpha coefficients ranged from .80 to .90.

Authors: Liden, R. C., et al.

Article: A longitudinal study on the early development of leader-member exchanges.

Journal: *Journal of Applied*

Psychology, August 1993, *78*(4), 662–674.

Related Research: Scandura, T. A., & Graen, G. B. (1984). Moderating effects of initial leader-member exchange status on the effects of a leadership intervention. *Journal of Applied Psychology*, *69*, 428–436.

■ ■ ■

6350

Test Name: NONVERBAL COMMUNICATION QUESTIONNAIRE

Purpose: To measure nonverbal communication in psychotherapy patients.

Number of Items: 21

Format: Various formats. All items are presented.

Reliability: Test–retest (3 to 27 months) ranged from .48 to 1.00.

Authors: Åström, J., et al.

Article: Attitude towards and observation of nonverbal communication in a psychotherapeutic greeting situation: III. An interview study of outpatients.

Journal: *Psychological Reports*, August 1993, *73*(1), 151–168.

Related Research: Åström, J., et al. (1991). Attitudes to and observation of nonverbal communication in a psychotherapeutic greeting situation: I. Psychometrics of a questionnaire. *Psychological Reports*, *69*, 963–975.

■ ■ ■

6351

Test Name: PERSONAL REPORT OF COMMUNICATION APPREHENSION

Purpose: To measure a participant's level of apprehension in interpersonal, small group,

public, and organizational communication context.

Number of Items: 24

Format: Includes four categories, each of which is represented by six questions. Uses a Likert scale ranging from *strongly agree* to *strongly disagree*.

Reliability: Internal reliability was .90.

Authors: Monroe, C., et al.

Article: Communication apprehension among high school dropouts.

Journal: *School Counselor*, March 1992, *39*(4), 273–280.

Related Research: McCrosby, J. (1982). *Introduction to rhetorical communication*. Englewood Cliffs, NJ: Prentice-Hall.

■ ■ ■

6352

Test Name: PLANNING PROCESS QUALITY QUESTIONNAIRE

Purpose: To identify the quality of the planning process.

Number of Items: 9

Format: Includes three components: Individual roles, supplies, and group coordinators. Responses were made on 5-point scales.

Reliability: Alpha coefficients ranged from .55 to .79. Interrater Pearson correlations ranged from .39 to .77.

Author: Weingart, L. R.

Article: Impact of group goals, task component complexity, effort, and planning on group performance.

Journal: *Journal of Applied Psychology*, October 1992, *77*(5), 682–693.

Related Research: Smith, K. G., et al. (1990). Goal setting, planning and organizational performance:

An experimental simulation. *Organizational Behavior and Human Decision Processes*, *46*, 118–134.

■ ■ ■

6353

Test Name: PSYCHOLOGICAL MEDICAL INVENTORY

Purpose: To measure communication and relationship skills.

Number of Items: 11

Format: 7-point scales. Sample items are presented.

Reliability: Alpha was .85.

Authors: Rabinowitz, S., et al.

Article: Teaching interpersonal skills to occupational and environmental health professionals.

Journal: *Psychological Reports*, June 1994, *74*(3) Part II, 1299–1306.

Related Research: Ireton, H., & Sherman, M. (1988). Self-ratings of graduating family practice residents' psychological medicine abilities. *Family Practice Research Journal*, *7*, 236–244.

■ ■ ■

6354

Test Name: SATISFACTION WITH COMMUNICATION SCALE

Purpose: To measure satisfaction with communication.

Number of Items: 19

Format: Likert format is employed.

Reliability: Coefficient alpha was .95.

Validity: Correlations with affinity-seeking ranged from .35 to .47.

Author: Prisbell, M.

Article: Affinity-seeking strategies

associated with students' perceptions of satisfaction with communication in the classroom.

Journal: *Perceptual and Motor Skills*, August 1994, *79*(1) Part 1, 33–34.

Related Research: Prisbell, M. (1991). *The relationships among classroom communication satisfaction, immediacy, and student learning.* Paper presented at the annual meeting of the Western States Communication Association, Phoenix, Arizona.

■ ■ ■

6355

Test Name: SELF-DISCLOSURE SCALES

Purpose: To measure extent, consciousness, positiveness, honesty, and depth of disclosure.

Number of Items: 31

Format: 7-interval Likert format.

Reliability: Alpha reliabilities ranged from .72 to .93.

Authors: Prisbell, M., and Dallinger, J. M.

Article: The developmental nature of self-disclosure.

Journal: *Psychological Reports*, February 1991, *68*(1), 211–214.

Related Research: Wheeless, L. R. (1978). A follow-up study of the relationships among trust, disclosure, and interpersonal solidarity. *Human Communication Research, 4,* 143–157.

■ ■ ■

6356

Test Name: SELF-EVALUATION OF COMMUNICATION EXPERIENCES AFTER LARYNGECTOMY SCALE

Purpose: To enable participants to evaluate their communication experiences.

Number of Items: 35

Format: Includes 3 subscales: Attitudinal, Environmental, and General Experiences.

Validity: Correlations with other variables ranged from -.84 and .83.

Authors: Blood, G. W., et al.

Article: Perceived control, adjustment, and communication problems in laryngeal cancer survivors.

Journal: *Perceptual and Motor Skills*, December, 1993, *77*(3) Part 1, 764–766.

Related Research: Blood, G. W. (1993). Development and assessment of a scale addressing communication needs of patients with laryngectomies. *American Journal of Speech Language Pathology, 2,* 65–76.

■ ■ ■

6357

Test Name: SOURCE CREDIBILITY MANIPULATION SCALE

Purpose: To assess the effectiveness of the source credibility manipulation.

Number of Items: 6

Format: Responses are made on a 7-point scale. All items are presented.

Reliability: Reliability was .84.

Authors: Gotlieb, J. B., and Dubinsky, A. J.

Article: Influence of price on aspects of consumers' cognitive process.

Journal: *Journal of Applied Psychology*, August 1991, *76*(4), 541–549.

Related Research: Harmon, R. R., & Coney, K. A. (1982). The persuasive effects of source credibility in buy and lease

situations. *Journal of Marketing Research, 19,* 255–260.

■ ■ ■

6358

Test Name: TEAM-MEMBER EXCHANGE SCALE

Purpose: To measure team-member exchange.

Number of Items: 11

Format: Responses are made on a 5-point scale ranging from 1 (*very little extent*) to 5 (*very great extent*).

Reliability: Coefficient alpha was .85.

Authors: Major, D. A., et al.

Article: A longitudinal investigation of newcomers expectation, early socialization outcomes, and the moderating effects of role development factors.

Journal: *Journal of Applied Psychology*, June 1995, *80*(3), 418–431.

Related Research: Seers, A. (1989). Team-member exchange quality: A new construct for role-making research. *Organizational Behavior and Human Decision Processes, 43,* 118–135.

■ ■ ■

6359

Test Name: TRANSITIVE PANTOMIME EXPRESSION TEST

Purpose: To evaluate the ability to express meaningful information by pantomime.

Number of Items: 15

Format: Following presentation of each picture, the respondent shows what the object was by pretending to use it. Scoring of each item is on a 0-to-3 scale.

Reliability: Coefficient of concordance for interjudge scoring was .91.

Validity: Correlations with other variables ranged from .27 to .76.

Authors: Wang, L., and Goodglass, H.

Article: Pantomime, praxis, and aphasia.

Journal: *Brain and Language*, May 1992, *42*(4), 402–418.

■ ■ ■

6360

Test Name: WORKING ALLIANCE INVENTORY

Purpose: To assess bond, task, and goal dimensions of an alliance.

Number of Items: 36

Format: Scales range from 1 (*never*) to 7 (*always*).

Reliability: Alphas ranged from .88 to .91.

Authors: Mallinkrodt, B., et al.

Article: Working alliance, attachment memories and social competencies of women in brief therapy.

Journal: *Journal of Counseling Psychology*, January 1995, *42*(1), 79–84.

Related Research: Horvath, A. O., & Greenberg, L. (1989). Development and validation of the Working Alliance Inventory. *Journal of Counseling Psychology*, *36*, 223–232.

Kivlighan, D. M., & Shaughnessy, P. (1995). Analysis of the development of the Working Alliance using hierarchical linear modeling. *Journal of Counseling Psychology*, *42*, 338–349.

CHAPTER 10
Concept Meaning

6361

Test Name: EPISTEMOLOGICAL BELIEF QUESTIONNAIRE

Purpose: To identify epistemological beliefs.

Number of Items: 53

Format: Includes 4 factors: Simple Knowledge, Certain Knowledge, Quick Learning, and Innate Ability.

Validity: Correlations with other variables ranged from -.42 to .22.

Authors: Qian, G., and Alvermann, D.

Article: Role of epistemological beliefs and learned helplessness in secondary school students' learning science concepts from text.

Journal: *Journal of Educational Psychology*, June 1995, *87*(2), 282–292.

Related Research: Schommer, M., & Dunnell, P. A. (1992, April). *Epistemological beliefs among gifted and non-gifted students.* Paper presented at the annual meeting of the American Educational Research Association, San Francisco.

■ ■ ■

6362

Test Name: LEARNING CONTEXT QUESTIONNAIRE

Purpose: To measure epistemological styles.

Number of Items: 50

Format: Each item is rated on a 6-point Likert-type scale ranging from A (*strongly agree*) to F (*strongly disagree*).

Reliability: Test–retest reliability was .84.

Authors: Wilkinson, W. D., and Maxwell, S.

Article: The influence of college students' epistemological style on selected problem-solving processes.

Journal: *Research in Higher Education*, June 1991, *32*(3), 333–350.

Related Research: Chapman, D. W., & Griffith, J. V. (1982). *Summary data analysis activities related to development of the learning context questionnaire. Final Report: Project MATCH.* Unpublished manuscript, Davidson College, Davidson, North Carolina.

■ ■ ■

6363

Test Name: SPELLING MEASURE

Purpose: To capture children's emerging knowledge of words.

Number of Items: 5

Format: A 7-point scale ranging from 0 (*random strings of letters*) to 6 (*conventional spellings*). All items are presented.

Reliability: Interrater agreement was .93.

Authors: Stahl, S. A., and Murrey, B. A.

Article: Defining phonological awareness and its relationship to early reading.

Journal: *Journal of Educational Psychology*, June 1994, *86*(2), 221–234.

Related Research: Tangel, D. M., & Blackman, B. (1992, April). *Effect of phoneme awareness training on the invented spelling of kindergarten and first grade children on the standard spelling of first and second grade children.* Paper presented at the annual meeting of the National Reading Conference, San Antonio, Texas.

■ ■ ■

6364

Test Name: WAYS-OF-KNOWING INSTRUMENT

Purpose: To assess the various ways-of-knowing stages (silence, received knowledge, subjective knowledge, procedural knowledge, and constructed knowledge).

Number of Items: 48

Format: Responses are made on a 4-point Likert-type scale (*strongly disagree* to *strongly agree*).

Reliability: Cronbach's alpha internal reliability coefficients for the five subscales ranged from .69 to .80.

Author: Buczynski, P. L.

Article: The development of a paper-and-pencil measure of Belenki, Curchy, Goldberger and Raril's (1986) conceptual model of Women's Ways-of-Knowing Instrument.

Journal: *Journal of College Student Development*, May 1993, *34*(3), 197–200.

Related Research: Buczynski, P. L. (1991). *The Ways-of-knowing Instrument.* Unpublished Instrument, Utah State University, Logan.

CHAPTER 11
Creativity

6365

Test Name: CREATIVITY STYLES QUESTIONNAIRE

Purpose: To assess seven dimensions of creativity.

Number of Items: 72

Format: 3-point true–false–unsure scales.

Reliability: Internal consistency ranged from .35 to .70.

Authors: Kumar, V. K., et al.

Article: Creativity styles of freshmen students.

Journal: *The Journal of Creative Behavior*, Fourth Quarter 1991, *25*(4), 320–323.

Related Research: Kumar, V. K., & Holman, E. R. (1989). *Creativity Styles Questionnaire.* Unpublished questionnaire, Department of Psychology, West Chester University, West Chester, Pennsylvania.

...

6366

Test Name: CREATIVITY TEST BATTERY

Purpose: To measure four aspects of creativity in India: fluency, flexibility, originality, and elaboration.

Number of Items: 18

Time Required: Each item is timed. Times range from 2 to 4 minutes.

Format: Format varies by item. All items are described.

Reliability: Test–retest reliabilities ranged from .55 to .84.

Validity: Correlation between total creativity score and subscale scores ranged from .60 to .84.

Authors: Sudhir, M. A., and Khiangte, V.

Article: Testing creativity in India.

Journal: *The Journal of Creativity Behavior*, First Quarter, 1991, *25*(1), 27–33.

...

6367

Test Name: HOW DO YOU THINK? FORM E.

Purpose: To measure creativity.

Number of Items: 100

Format: 5-point Likert format.

Reliability: Alpha was .89.

Authors: Smith, D. E., and Tegano, D. W.

Article: Relationship of scores on two personality measures: Creativity and self-image.

Journal: *Psychological Reports*, August 1992, *71*(1), 43–49.

Related Research: Davis, G. A. (1977). *How Do You Think, Form E.* Madison: University of Wisconsin.

...

6368

Test Name: MULTIDIMENSIONAL SENSE OF HUMOR SCALE

Purpose: To measure humor as creativity, as a coping mechanism, humor appreciation, and attitudes towards humor.

Number of Items: 24

Format: 5-point Likert format.

Reliability: Alpha was .92.

Author: Hampes, W. P.

Article: Relation between intimacy and the Multidimensional Sense of Humor Scale.

Journal: *Psychological Reports*, June 1994, *74*(3) Part II, 1360–1362.

Related Research: Thorson, J. A., & Powell, F. C. (1993). Development and validation of a multidimensional sense of humor scale. *Journal of Clinical Psychology*, *49*, 13–23.

...

6369

Test Name: PARENTAL EVALUATION OF CHILDREN'S CREATIVITY

Purpose: To assess attitudinal, intellectual, and motivational creativity.

Number of Items: 25

Format: Parents rate their children on 7-point scales.

Reliability: Alphas ranged from .59 to .77 across subscales.

Validity: Correlations with other variables ranged from -.03 to .29.

Authors: Gaynor, J. L. R., and Runco, M. A.

Article: Family size, birth-order, age-interval, and creativity of children.

Journal: *The Journal of Creative Behavior*, Second Quarter, 1992, *26*(2), 108–118.

Related Research: Runco, M. A.

(1989). Parents' and teachers' ratings of the creativity of children. *Journal of Social Behavior and Personality, 4,* 73–83.

■ ■ ■

6370

Test Name: STUDENT PRODUCT ASSESSMENT FORM

Purpose: To evaluate student products completed in programs for gifted and talented students.

Number of Items: 15

Format: All items and formats are presented.

Reliability: Interrater reliabilities ranged from .39 to 1.00 across items.

Authors: Reis, S. M., and Renzulli, J. S.

Article: The assessment of creative products in programs for gifted and talented students.

Journal: *Gifted Child Quarterly,* Summer 1991, *35*(3), 128–134.

Related Research: Reis, S. M. (1981). *An analysis of the productivity of gifted students participating in programs using the revolving door identification model.* Unpublished doctoral dissertation, University of Connecticut, Storrs.

CHAPTER 12
Development

6371

Test Name: CONCEPTS DEVELOPMENT QUESTIONNAIRE

Purpose: To measure parents' underlying theories concerning childhood development.

Number of Items: 20

Format: 4-point agreement scales. Sample items presented.

Reliability: Alpha was .82.

Authors: Crinc, K. A., and Booth, C. L.

Article: Mothers' and fathers' perceptions of daily hassles of parenting across early childhood.

Journal: *Journal of Marriage and the Family*, November 1991, *53*(4), 1042–1050.

Related Research: Sameroff, A. J., & Feil, L. A. (1985). Parental concepts of development. In I. E. Sigel (Ed.), *Parental belief systems*. Hillsdale, NJ: Erlbaum.

■ ■ ■

6372

Test Name: EGO DEVELOPMENT SCALE

Purpose: To assess ego development.

Number of Items: 36

Reliability: Interrater reliabilities ranged from .70 to .92.

Validity: Correlations with other variables ranged from -.35 to .56.

Authors: Allen, J. P., et al.

Article: Longitudinal assessment of autonomy and relatedness in adolescent family interactions as predictors of adolescent ego development and self-esteem.

Journal: *Child Development*, February 1994, *65*(1), 179–194.

Related Research: Loevinger, J., et al. (1970). *Measuring ego development* (Vol. 2). San Francisco: Jossey-Bass.

■ ■ ■

6373

Test Name: EGO DEVELOPMENT SCALE

Purpose: To measure stage resolution for the first seven stages of Erikson's theory of ego development.

Number of Items: 93

Format: 4-point Likert format.

Reliability: Alphas ranged from .65 to .83 across subscales. Total alphas ranged from .92 to .93.

Validity: Correlations between subscales ranged from .08 to .68.

Authors: Cohen, C. R., et al.

Article: Relationships between career indecision subtypes and ego identity development.

Journal: *Journal of Counseling Psychology*, October 1995, *42*(4), 440–447.

Related Research: Ocshe, R., & Plug, C. (1986). Cross-cultural investigation of the validity of Erikson's theory of personality development. *Journal of Personality and Social Psychology*, *50*, 1240–1252.

6374

Test Name: ERWIN IDENTITY SCALE

Purpose: To assess students' level of identity.

Number of Items: 59

Format: Responses are made on a 5-point scale.

Reliability: Cronbach's alpha for the three dimensions were .90, .74, and .81.

Author: Buczynski, P. L.

Article: The relationship between identity and cognitive development in college freshmen: A structural equation modeling analysis.

Journal: *Journal of College Student Development*, May 1991, *32*(3), 212–222.

Related Research: Erwin, T. D., & Delworth, U. (1980). An instrument to measure Chickering's vector of identity. *National Association of Personnel Administrators Journal*, *17*, 19–24.

■ ■ ■

6375

Test Name: EXTENDED OBJECTIVE MEASURE OF EGO IDENTITY STATUS

Purpose: To measure identity status.

Number of Items: 64

Format: 6-point agreement scales.

Reliability: Internal consistency ranged from .64 to .90. Test–retest ranged from .82 to .90.

Authors: Hamer, R. J., and Bruch, M. A.

Article: The role of shyness and private self-consciousness in identity development.

Journal: *Journal of Research in Personality*, December 1994, *28*(4), 436–452.

Related Research: Bennion, L. D., & Adams, G. R. (1986). A revision of the extended version of the objective measure of ego-identity status: An identity instrument for use with late adolescents. *Journal of Adolescent Research*, *1*, 267–281.

■ ■ ■

6376

Test Name: GENERATIVITY SCALE

Purpose: To measure interest in establishing and guiding the next generation.

Number of Items: 16

Format: 4-point Likert format.

Reliability: Test–retest was .82.

Author: Bailey, W. T.

Article: Psychological development in men: Generativity and involvement with young children.

Journal: *Psychological Reports*, December 1992, *71*(3) Part I, 929–930.

Related Research: Ryff, C. D., & Heincke, S. G. (1983). Subjective organization of personality in adulthood in aging. *Journal of Personality and Social Psychology*, *44*, 807–816.

■ ■ ■

6377

Test Name: ICELANDIC PARENT DEVELOPMENT INVENTORY

Purpose: To enable mothers to be informants of their children's

development for children between 36 and 72 months.

Number of Items: 190

Format: Includes 8 subtests: Gross Motor, Fine Motor, Language Expression, Language Comprehension, Personal–Social, Achievement, Information, and Self-Help.

Reliability: Alpha coefficients ranged from .76 to .90.

Validity: Correlations with the Griffith Mental Development Scale ranged from -.12 to .69.

Authors: Gudmundsson, E., and Gretarsson, S. J.

Article: The reliability and validity of the Icelandic Parent Development Inventory for children from 36 Months to 72 Months.

Journal: *Educational and Psychological Measurement*, Summer 1993, *53*(2), 571–584.

■ ■ ■

6378

Test Name: SCALE OF INTELLECTUAL DEVELOPMENT

Purpose: To assess students' cognitive development.

Number of Items: 115

Format: Responses are made on a 4-point scale (*agree* to *disagree*).

Reliability: Cronbach's alpha coefficients for the four dimensions were .81, .90, .76, and .73.

Author: Buczynski, P. L.

Article: The relationship between identity and cognitive development in college freshmen: A structural equation modeling analysis.

Journal: *Journal of College Student Development*, May 1991, *32*(3), 212–222.

Related Research: Erwin, T. D. (1983). The scale of intellectual

development using Perry's scheme. *Journal of College Student Personnel*, *24*, 6–12.

■ ■ ■

6379

Test Name: SELF-DESCRIPTION BLANK

Purpose: To measure respondents' progress through Erickson's first six developmental stages.

Number of Items: 70

Format: Includes six developmental scales.

Reliability: Test–retest (1 week) reliabilities ranged from .77 to .93.

Authors: Lopez, F. G., et al.

Article: Conflictual independence, mood regulation, and generalized self-efficacy: Test of a model of late-adolescent identity

Journal: *Journal of Counseling Psychology*, July 1992, *39*(3) 375–381.

Related Research: McClain, E. W. (1975). An Ericksonian cross-cultural study of adolescent development. *Adolescence*, *10*, 527–541.

■ ■ ■

6380

Test Name: SEPARATION–INDIVIDUATION INVENTORY

Purpose: To measure socioemotional development over the first 3 years of life in five stages: normal autism, symbiosis, differentiation, practicing, rapprochement.

Number of Items: 50

Format: 11-point rating scales (*not the least like* to *exactly alike*). Sample items are presented.

Reliability: Spearman-Brown split-half reliability ranged from .74 to .96 across subscales. Interrater reliability ranged from .85 to 1.00.

Validity: Intersubscale correlations ranged from -.28 to .81. Highest correlations were obtained between adjacent stages of development.

Authors: Bartolomucci, E., and Taylor, J.

Article: Preliminary reliability and validity of an instrument measuring separation-individuation outcomes.

Journal: *Psychological Reports*, October 1991, *69*(2), 391–398.

Related Research: Taylor, J., & Denton, S. (1978). *Separation-individuation inventory*. Pittsburgh, PA: Institute for the Black Family, University of Pittsburgh.

■ ■ ■

6381

Test Name: SKILL DEVELOPMENT SCALE

Purpose: To measure skill development.

Number of Items: 4

Format: Responses are made on a 5-point scale ranging from 1 (*never*) to 5 (*nearly all the time*). Sample items are presented.

Reliability: Coefficient alpha was .81.

Validity: Correlations with other variables ranged from -.24 to .34.

Authors: Aryee, S., and Tan, K.

Article: Antecedents and outcomes of career commitment.

Journal: *Journal of Vocational Behavior*, June 1992, *40*(3), 288–305.

6382

Test Name: SKILL DEVELOPMENT SCALE

Purpose: To measure skill development.

Number of Items: 6

Format: Responses are made on a 5-point scale ranging from 1 (*never*) to 5 (*nearly all the time*). Sample items are presented.

Reliability: Alpha coefficients were .81 and .76.

Validity: Correlations with other variables ranged from -.15 to .35.

Authors: Aryee, S., et al.

Article: An investigation of the predictors and outcomes of career commitment in three career stages.

Journal: *Journal of Vocational Behavior*, February 1994, *44*(1), 1–16.

■ ■ ■

6383

Test Name: WASHINGTON SENTENCE COMPLETION TEST—SHORT FORM

Purpose: To measure ego development by a projective assessment method.

Number of Items: 12

Format: Sentence-completion format.

Reliability: Internal consistency ranged from .73 to .77.

Validity: Correlations with long form was .92.

Author: Mabry, C. H.

Article: Gender differences in ego level.

Journal: *Psychological Reports*, June 1993, *72*(3) Part I, 752–754.

Related Research: Holt, R. R. (1980). Loevinger's measured ego development: Reliability and national norms for male and female short forms. *Journal of Personality and Social Psychology*, *39*, 909–920.

■ ■ ■

6384

Test Name: WASHINGTON UNIVERSITY SENTENCE COMPLETION TEST—FORM 81

Purpose: To measure ego development.

Number of Items: 36

Format: Items are sentence stems completed by respondents.

Reliability: Alpha coefficients ranged from .81 to .90.

Authors: Novy, D. M., and Francis, D. J.

Article: Psychometric properties of the Washington University Sentence Completion Test.

Journal: *Educational and Psychological Measurement*, Winter 1992, *52*(4), 1029–1039.

Related Research: Novy, D. M. (1990). *An investigation of the validity of Loevinger's model and measure of ego development*. Unpublished doctoral dissertation, University of Houston.

CHAPTER 13
Family

6385

Test Name: ACCEPTANCE/ INVOLVEMENT SCALE

Purpose: To measure the extent adolescents perceive their parents as loving, responsive, and involved in helping them out of a problem.

Number of Items: 10

Format: Several responses are true–false and others are made on a 3-point scale. Examples are presented.

Reliability: Coefficient alpha was .72.

Authors: Steinberg, L., et al.

Article: Over-time changes in adjustment and competence among adolescents from authoritative, authoritarian, indulgent, and neglectful families.

Journal: *Child Development*, June 1994, *65*(3), 754–770.

Related Research: Lamborn, S., et al. (1991). Patterns of competence and adjustment among adolescents from authoritative, authoritarian, indulgent and neglectful homes. *Child Development, 62*, 1049–1065.

■■■

6386

Test Name: ADOLESCENT-COPING ORIENTATION FOR PROBLEM EXPERIENCES SCALE

Purpose: To provide information on how a person relates with family members and peers to cope with stress.

Number of Items: 95

Format: Includes 7 scales: Developing and Maintaining a Sense of Competence and Self-Esteem, Investing in Family Relationships, Investing in Extra-Familial Relationships and Seeking Social Support, Developing Positive Perceptions About Life Situations, Relieving Tensions Through Diversions, Relieving Tension Through Substance Use and/or the Expression of Anger, and Avoiding Confrontations and Withdrawing. Responses are made on a 4-point Likert scale ranging from 1 (*very false*) to 4 (*very true*).

Validity: Correlations with other variables ranged from -.43 to .55.

Authors: Perosa, S. L., and Perosa, L. M.

Article: Relationships among Minuchin's structural family model: Identity, achievement, and coping style.

Journal: *Journal of Counseling Psychology*, October 1993, *40*(4), 479–489.

Related Research: McCubbin, H., & Patterson, J. (1981*). Systematic assessment of family stress, resources and coping.* Minneapolis: Family Stress and Coping Project, University of Minnesota.

■■■

6387

Test Name: ADOLESCENT FAMILY LIFE SATISFACTION INDEX

Purpose: To assess extent to which adolescents perceive family life in a positive manner.

Number of Items: 13

Format: All items are presented.

Reliability: Alphas ranged from .88 to .90 across subscales.

Validity: Correlation between subscales was .36.

Authors: Henry, C. S., and Plunkett, S. W.

Article: Validation of the Adolescent Family Life Satisfaction Index: An update.

Journal: *Psychological Reports*, April 1995, *76*(2), 672–674.

■■■

6388

Test Name: ADOLESCENT PARENT RELATIONS SCALE

Purpose: To measure level of attachment of adolescents to their parents.

Number of Items: 14

Format: 5-point Likert format.

Reliability: Test–retest was .73.

Authors: Nava, G. R., and Bailey, K. G.

Article: Measuring psychological kinship: Scale refinement and validation.

Journal: *Psychological Reports*, February 1991, *68*(1), 215–227.

Related Research: Atkinson, B. R., & Bell, N. J. (1986*). Attachment and autonomy in adolescence.* Paper presented at the meeting of the Society for Research on Adolescence. Madison, Wisconsin.

6389

Test Name: ASPECTS OF MARRIED LIFE QUESTIONNAIRE

Purpose: To assess spouses' satisfaction with aspects of married life.

Number of Items: 10

Format: 9-point satisfaction scales.

Reliability: Alphas were .69 (husband) and .72 (wife).

Authors: McHale, S. M., and Crouter, A. C.

Article: You can't always get what you want: Incongruence between sex-role attitudes on family work roles and its implications for marriage.

Journal: *Journal of Marriage and the Family*, August 1992, *54*(3), 537–547.

Related Research: Huston, T. L., et al. (1986). Changes in the marital relationship during the first year of marriage. In R. Gilmore & S. Duck (Eds.), *The emerging field of personal relationships* (pp. 109–132). Hillsdale, NJ: Erlbaum.

■ ■ ■

6390

Test Name: ATTACHMENT Q-SET

Purpose: To assess security of attachment to mother in a nonstressful environment.

Number of Items: 90

Time Required: 45 minutes to an hour.

Format: Respondents place index cards with descriptions of behaviors on them into nine piles, based on whether the behaviors were like or unlike their child's behavior in the last 2 weeks.

Reliability: Interrater reliability was .93.

Authors: Das Eiden, R., et al.

Article: Maternal working models of attachment, marital adjustment, and the parent–child relationship.

Journal: *Child Development*, October 1995, *66*(5), 1504–1518.

Related Research: Waters, E., & Deanne, K. E. (1985). Defining and assessing individual differences in attachment relationships: Q-methodology and the organization of behavior in infancy and early childhood. In I. Bretherton & E. Waters (Eds.), *Growing points of attachment theory and research* (pp. 41–65). *Monographs of the society for research in Child Development*, *50* (1-2, Serial No. 209).

■ ■ ■

6391

Test Name: ATTACHMENT TO PARENTS SCALE

Purpose: To measure attachment to parents.

Number of Items: 28

Format: 5-point rating scales. Sample item presented.

Reliability: Internal consistency ranged from .86 to .91. Test–retest (3 weeks) was .93.

Authors: Hamer, R. J., and Bruch, M. A.

Article: The role of shyness and private self-consciousness in identity development.

Journal: *Journal of Research in Personality*, December 1994, *28*(4), 436–452.

Related Research: Armsden, G. C., & Greenberg, M. T. (1987). The inventory of parent and peer attachment: Individual differences and their relationship to psychological well-being in adolescence. *Journal of Youth and Adolescence*, *16*, 427–454.

6392

Test Name: ATTITUDE TO RELATIONSHIPS SCALE

Purpose: To assess effects of divorce on wariness about long-term relationships, marriage, and family life.

Number of Items: 12

Format: 4-point self-rating scales. Sample items presented.

Reliability: Alpha was .86.

Validity: Correlations with other variables ranged from .23 to .51.

Author: Dunlop, R., and Burns, A.

Article: The sleeper effect—myth or reality?

Journal: *Journal of Marriage and the Family*, May 1995, *57*(2), 375–386.

■ ■ ■

6393

Test Name: CAREGIVER SUPPORT APPRAISAL SCALE—P

Purpose: To measure support perceived from family and friends.

Number of Items: 15

Format: Responses are "yes," "no," or "don't know." Examples are presented.

Reliability: Coefficient alphas were .59 and .79. Test–retest (3 weeks) reliability was .81.

Validity: Correlations with other variables ranged from .06 to .64.

Author: Caruso, G.-A. L.

Article: The development of three scales to measure the supportiveness of relationships between parents and child care providers.

Journal: *Educational and Psychological Measurement*, Spring 1992, *52*(1), 149–160.

Related Research: Procidano, M. E., & Heller, K. (1983). Measures of perceived social support from family and friends: Three validation studies. *American Journal of Community Psychology, 11*, 1–24.

■ ■ ■

6394

Test Name: CAREGIVER SUPPORT APPRAISAL SCALE—V

Purpose: To measure support perceived from the caregiver.

Number of Items: 9

Format: Responses are made on a 4-point Likert-type scale. Several items are presented.

Reliability: Coefficient alphas were .74 and .80. Test–retest (3 weeks) reliability was .86.

Validity: Correlations with other variables ranged from .10 to .64.

Author: Caruso, G.-A. L.

Article: The development of three scales to measure the supportiveness of relationships between parents and child care providers.

Journal: *Educational and Psychological Measurement,* Spring 1992, *52*(1), 149–160.

Related Research: Vaux, A., et al. (1986). The social support appraisals (SS-A) scale: Studies of reliability and validity. *American Journal of Community Psychology, 14*, 195–219.

■ ■ ■

6395

Test Name: CHILDREN OF ALCOHOLICS LIFE EVENTS SCHEDULE

Purpose: To assess stress specific to being in an alcoholic home.

Number of Items: 34

Format: Sample items are described.

Reliability: Alphas ranged from .71 to .81. Test–retest (2 weeks) was .88.

Authors: Havey, J. M., and Dodd, D. K.

Article: Children of alcoholics, negative life events, and early experimentation with drugs.

Journal: *Journal of School Psychology,* Winter 1995, *33*(4), 305–317.

Related Research: Roosa, M. W., et al. (1988). The Children of Alcoholics Life Events Schedule: A stress scale for children of alcohol abusing parents. *Journal of Studies on Alcohol, 49*, 422–429.

■ ■ ■

6396

Test Name: CHILDREN OF ALCOHOLICS SCREENING TEST

Purpose: To measure perceptions, feelings, attitudes and experiences related to parent drinking.

Number of Items: 30

Format: Inventory developed from case studies and experiences reported by clinically diagnosed children of alcoholics.

Reliability: Spearman-Brown split-half reliability was .98.

Author: Rodney, H. E.

Article: A profile of collegiate Black children of alcoholics.

Journal: *Journal of College Student Development,* May/June 1995, *36*(3), 228–235.

Related Research: Pilat, J., and Jones, J. W. (1984-85). Identification of children of alcoholics: Two empirical studies. *Alcohol, Health and Research World, 9*, 27–33, 36.

6397

Test Name: CHILDREN'S PERCEPTIONS OF PARENTS SCALE

Purpose: To measure children's perceptions of their parents.

Number of Items: 21

Format: A 4-point Likert-type ordinal scale is used. Sample items are presented.

Reliability: Alpha coefficients ranged from .55 to .70.

Validity: Correlations with other variables ranged from -.08 to .27.

Authors: Grolnick, W. S., et al.

Article: Inner resources for school achievement: Motivational mediators of children's perceptions of their parents.

Journal: *Journal of Educational Psychology,* December 1991, *83*(4), 508–517.

■ ■ ■

6398

Test Name: CHILDREN'S REPORT OF PARENTAL BEHAVIOR INVENTORY

Purpose: To enable children to report parental behavior.

Number of Items: 42

Format: Includes 5 dimensions: Acceptance, Rejection, Inconsistent Discipline, Control, and Hostile Control. Responses are made on a 3-point scale.

Reliability: Alpha coefficients ranged from .50 to .84.

Validity: Correlations with other variables ranged from -.58 to .50.

Authors: Knight, G. P., et al.

Article: Socialization and family correlates of mental health outcomes among Hispanic and Anglo American children: Consideration of cross-ethnic scalar equivalence.

Journal: *Child Development*, February 1994, *65*(1), 212–224.

Related Research: Schaefer, E. S. (1965). Children's report of parental behavior: An inventory. *Child Development*, *36*, 413–424.

• • •

6399

Test Name: CHILDREN'S ROLE INVENTORY

Purpose: To measure (by retrospective report) children's roles in alcoholic families: hero, mascot, lost child, and scapegoat.

Number of Items: 60

Format: Likert format.

Reliability: Alphas ranged from .86 to .91.

Authors: Fischer, J. L., and Wampler, R. S.

Article: Abusive drinking in young adults: Personality type and family role as moderators of family-of-origin influences.

Journal: *Journal of Marriage and the Family*, May 1994, *56*(2), 469–479.

Related Research: Potter, A. E., & Williams, D. E. (1991). Development of a measure examining children's roles in alcoholic families. *Journal of Studies on Alcohol*, *52*, 50–77.

• • •

6400

Test Name: COGNITIONS OF HOME SCALE

Purpose: To assess the importance of home and family.

Number of Items: 7

Format: 5-point scales.

Reliability: Alphas ranged from .81 to .89.

Authors: Farmer, H. S., et al.

Article: Women's career choices:

Focus on science, math and technology careers.

Journal: *Journal of Counseling Psychology*, April 1995, *42*(2), 155–170.

Related Research: Super, D., & Culha, M. (1976). *Work Salience Inventory*. (Available from Helen S. Farmer, 210 Department of Educational Psychology, University of Illinois, 1310 S. 6th Street, Champaign, IL 61820).

• • •

6401

Test Name: COMMITMENT INVENTORY

Purpose: To measure commitment to a marriage.

Number of Items: 60

Format: 7-point Likert scales, 6-point difficulty scales, and 6-point happiness scales are used. All items presented.

Reliability: Alphas ranged from .70 to .94 across subscales.

Validity: Correlations with other commitment measures ranged from -.61 to .92.

Authors: Stanley, S. M., and Marleman, H. J.

Article: Assessing commitment in personal relationships.

Journal: *Journal of Marriage and the Family*, August 1992, *54*(3), 595–608.

• • •

6402

Test Name: CONFLICT BEHAVIOR QUESTIONNAIRE

Purpose: To measure student perceptions of parents and parent–child conflict.

Number of Items: 44

Format: True–false format.

Reliability: Alphas ranged from .94 to .95. Test–retest reliabilities ranged from .37 to .85 (8 weeks).

Authors: Finke, H. L., and Hurley, J. R.

Article: Everyday thinking of college students and their parents and students' simulations of each parent's thinking.

Journal: *Psychological Reports*, February 1995, *76*(1), 247–257.

Related Research: Robin, A. L., & Weiss, J. G. (1980). Criterion-related validity of behavioral and self-report measures of problem-solving communication skills in distressed and non-distressed parent-adolescent dyads. *Journal of Counseling Psychology*, *35*, 203–208.

• • •

6403

Test Name: CONFLICT RESOLUTION STYLES INVENTORY

Purpose: To assess conflict resolution styles in couples.

Number of Items: 16

Format: 5-point rating scales. All items presented.

Reliability: Alphas ranged from .65 to .91. Test–retest (1 year) ranged from .46 to .83.

Validity: Correlations with other variables ranged from -.71 to .41.

Author: Kurdek, L. A.

Article: Conflict resolution styles in gay, lesbian, heterosexual nonparent and heterosexual parent couples.

Journal: *Journal of Marriage and the Family*, August 1994, *56*(3), 705–722.

• • •

6404

Test Name: CONFLICTUAL INDEPENDENCE SCALE

Purpose: To indicate to what extent late adolescents' emotional, attitudinal, and functional independence from each parent are free from feelings of guilt, mistrust, anger, and resentment.

Number of Items: 50

Format: Half of the items refer to mother–student relationships and the other half to father–student relationships.

Reliability: Alpha coefficients ranged from .88 to .92. Test–retest (2 to 3 weeks) reliabilities ranged from .85 to .96.

Validity: Correlations with other variables ranged from -.40 to .31.

Authors: Lopez, F. G., et al.

Article: Conflictual independence, mood regulation, and generalized self-efficacy: Test of a model of late-adolescent identity.

Journal: *Journal of Counseling Psychology*, July 1992, *39*(3), 375–381.

Related Research: Hoffman, J. A. (1984). Psychological separation of late adolescents from their parents. *Journal of Counseling Psychology, 31*, 170–178.

• • •

6405

Test Name: CONTINUED ATTACHMENT SCALE

Purpose: To measure children's attachment to parents.

Number of Items: 6

Format: All items are presented. Formats vary.

Reliability: Alphas ranged from .74 to .80. Test–retest ranged from .82 to .85.

Validity: Correlation between mother and father version was .67. Correlations with other variables ranged from -.30 to .51.

Authors: Berman, W. H., et al.

Article: Measuring continued attachment to parents: The

Continued Attachment Scale-Parent Version.

Journal: *Psychological Reports*, August 1994, *75*(1) Part I, 171–182.

• • •

6406

Test Name: CONTROL SCALE

Purpose: To measure perception of control in work–family conflict areas.

Number of Items: 14

Format: Responses are made on a 5-point scale ranging from 1 (*very little*) to 5 (*very much*). All items are presented.

Reliability: Coefficient alpha was .75.

Validity: Correlations with other variables ranged from -.45 to .35 (*N* = 398).

Authors: Thomas, L. T., and Ganster, D. L.

Article: Impact of family-supportive work variables on work-family conflict and strain: A control perspective.

Journal: *Journal of Applied Psychology*, February 1995, *80*(1), 6–15.

Related Research: Thomas, L. T. (1991). *The relationship between work-family role conflict, family supportive policies, and stress: A control perspective.* Unpublished doctoral dissertation, University of Nebraska-Lincoln.

• • •

6407

Test Name: DIAGNOSTIC SCALE FOR INCEST SURVIVORS

Purpose: To assess reactions to incest.

Number of Items: 20

Format: 4-point frequency scales range from *never* to *often*. All

items are presented.

Reliability: Alpha was .92.

Validity: Scale discriminates between known groups [*F*(3, 81) = 29.75, *p* < .0001].

Authors: Pearce, E., and Lovejoy, F.

Article: The development and testing of a Diagnostic Scale for Incest Survivors.

Journal: *The Journal of Social Psychology*, October 1994, *133*(5), 677–675.

• • •

6408

Test Name: DIVORCE PROPENSITY SCALE

Purpose: To measure likelihood of divorce.

Number of Items: 5

Format: 5-point scales. Sample items presented.

Reliability: Reliability was .75.

Authors: MacEwen, K., and Barling, J.

Article: Type A behavior and marital satisfaction: Differential effects of achievement striving and impatience/irritability.

Journal: *Journal of Marriage and the Family*, November 1993, *55*(4), 1001–1010.

Related Research: Booth, A., et al. (1983). Measuring marital instability. *Journal of Marriage and the Family, 45*, 387–393.

Booth, A., et al. (1985). Predicting divorce and permanent separation. *Journal of Family Issues, 6*, 331–346.

• • •

6409

Test Name: DUAL-CAREER FAMILY SCALE

Purpose: To investigate the dual-career family.

Number of Items: 31

Format: Includes 6-subscales: Marriage Type, Domestic Responsibility, Satisfaction, Self-Image, Career Salience, and Career Line.

Reliability: Alpha coefficients ranged from .57 to .76.

Validity: Criterion-related validity ranged from .01 to .49.

Authors: Okocha, A., and Perrone, P.

Article: Career salience among Nigerian dual-career women.

Journal: *The Career Development Quarterly*, September 1992, *41*(1), 84–93.

Related Research: Pendleton, B. F., et al. (1980). Scales for investigation of the dual-career family. *Journal of Marriage and the Family*, *40*(1), 269–276.

• • •

6410

Test Name: DUAL EMPLOYED COPING SCALES

Purpose: To assess coping mechanisms of male and female responses to work–family conflict in dual-earner families.

Number of Items: 49

Format: 5-point Likert format.

Reliability: Alphas ranged from .54 to .91 across subscales.

Validity: Correlations with other variables ranged from -.15 to -.38.

Author: Burley, K. A.

Article: Gender differences and similarities in coping responses to anticipated work-family conflict.

Journal: *Psychological Reports*, February 1994, *74*(1), 115–123.

Related Research: Skinner, D. A., & McCubbin, H. I. (1987). Dual

Employed Coping Scales (DECS). In H. McCubbin & A. Thompson (Eds.), *Family assessment inventories for research and practice* (pp. 259–270). Madison: University of Wisconsin-Madison, Family Stress, Coping and Health Project.

• • •

6411

Test Name: EASTERBROOK AND GOLDBERG PARENT ATTITUDE SCALE

Purpose: To determine child-rearing practices and behavioral intentions in mothers.

Number of Items: 36

Format: Responses are made on a 4-point scale ranging from *never* to *very often*.

Reliability: Cronbach alpha on the authoritative scale was .80 and Cronbach alpha on the authoritarian scale was .78.

Author: Smith, M. C.

Article: Child-rearing practices associated with better developmental outcomes in preschool-age foster children.

Journal: *Child Study Journal*, December 1994, *24*(4), 299–326.

Related Research: Easterbrook, A., & Goldberg, S. (1984). Toddler development in families: Impact of father involvement and parenting characteristics. *Child Development*, *55*, 740–752.

• • •

6412

Test Name: EMOTIONAL AUTONOMY SCALE

Purpose: To assess emotional autonomy from mothers and fathers.

Number of Items: 40

Format: 4-point Likert format.

Reliability: Alphas ranged from .79 to .82 across subscales.

Authors: McClanahan, G., and Holmbeck, G. N.

Article: Separation-individuation, family functioning and psychological adjustment in college students: A construct validity study of the Separation-Individuation Test of Adolescence.

Journal: *Journal of Personality Assessment*, December 1992, *59*(3), 468–485.

Related Research: Steinberg, L., & Silverberg, S. (1986). The vicissitudes of autonomy in early adolescence. *Child Development*, *57*, 841–851.

• • •

6413

Test Name: ENRICHING AND NURTURING RELATIONSHIPS, ISSUES, COMMUNICATION AND HAPPINESS QUESTIONS: ALTERNATE VERSION

Purpose: To assess a marriage or a defacto relationship between partners who have children from previous marriages.

Number of Items: 125

Format: 5-point Likert format. Sample items presented.

Reliability: Alphas ranged from .52 to .83 across subscales.

Authors: Schultz, N. C., et al.

Article: Couple strengths and stressors in complex and simple stepfamilies in Australia.

Journal: *Journal of Marriage and the Family*, August 1996, *53*(3), 555-564.

Related Research: Olsen, D. H., et al. (1986). *PREPARE/ENRICH (rev. ed.). Counselor's manual.* Minneapolis: PREPARE/ENRICH, Inc.

Fowers, B. J., & Olsen, D. H. (1993). ENRICH marital

satisfaction scale: A reliability and validity study. *Journal of Family Psychology*, *7*, 1–10.

■ ■ ■

6414

Test Name: FAMILY ADAPTABILITY AND COHESION EVALUATION SCALES

Purpose: To assess family cohesion and adaptability.

Number of Items: 30

Format: Responses are made on 5-point scales.

Reliability: Alpha coefficients ranged from .72 to .84.

Validity: Correlations with other variables ranged from -.36 to .19.

Authors: Knight, G. P., et al.

Article: Socialization and family correlates of mental health outcomes among Hispanic and Anglo American children: Considerations of cross-ethnic scalar equivalence.

Journal: *Child Development*, February 1994, *65*(1), 212–224.

Related Research: Olson, D. H., et al. (1982). FACES II: Family adaptability and cohesion evaluation scales. In D. H. Olson et al. (Eds.), *Family inventories* (pp. 5–23). St. Paul: Family Social Science, University of Minnesota.

■ ■ ■

6415

Test Name: FAMILY ADAPTABILITY AND COHESION EVALUATION SCALE III

Purpose: To measure family interactional styles.

Number of Items: 20

Format: Responses are made on a 5-point Likert-type scale.

Reliability: .83 for cohesion and .80 for adaptability.

Author: Vickers, H.

Article: Young children at risk: Differences in family functioning.

Journal: *Journal of Educational Research*, May/June 1994, *87*(5), 262–270.

Related Research: Olson, D. H., et al. (1985). *FACES III. Family Social Science*. St. Paul: University of Minnesota.

■ ■ ■

6416

Test Name: FAMILY CRISIS-ORIENTED PERSONAL SCALES

Purpose: To measure coping styles used by families when coping with difficulties.

Number of Items: 27

Format: 5-point Likert format.

Reliability: Alphas ranged from .76 (active coping) to .78 (passive coping).

Authors: Florian, V., and Dangoor, N.

Article: Personal familial adaptation of women with severe physical disabilities: A further validation of the ABCX model.

Journal: *Journal of Marriage and the Family*, August 1994, *56*(3), 735–746.

Related Research: McCubbin, H. I., & Thompson, A. I. (1987). *Family assessment inventories for research and practice*. Madison: University of Wisconsin Press.

■ ■ ■

6417

Test Name: FAMILY EXPERIENCES QUESTIONNAIRE

Purpose: To assess positive and negative aspects of parents'

perceptions of their parenting partnership.

Number of Items: 133

Format: Responses are made on a 4-point scale ranging from *strongly disagree* to *strongly agree*.

Reliability: Alpha coefficients ranged from .83 to .91.

Authors: Floyd, F. J., and Zmich, D. E.

Article: Marriage and the parenting partnership: Perceptions and interactions of parents with mentally retarded and typically developing children.

Journal: *Child Development*, December 1991, *62*(4), 1434–1448.

Related Research: Frank, S .J., et al. (1986). *The parenting alliance: Bridging the relationship between marriage and parenting*. Unpublished manuscript, Michigan State University.

■ ■ ■

6418

Test Name: FAMILY EXPRESSIVENESS QUESTIONNAIRE

Purpose: To measure the frequency of and variety of emotional experiences in the family of origin.

Number of Items: 40

Format: 9-point rating scales.

Reliability: Alphas ranged from .85 to .94. Test–retest reliabilities ranged from .89 to .92.

Author: Cooley, E. L.

Article: Family expressiveness and proneness to depression among college students.

Journal: *Journal of Research in Personality*, September 1992, *26*(3), 281–287.

Related Research: Halberstadt, A. G. (1986). Family socialization of emotional expression and nonverbal communication styles and skills. *Journal of Personality and Social Psychology*, 51, 827–836.

• • •

6419

Test Name: FAMILY EXPRESSIVENESS QUESTIONNAIRE—SELF-REPORT VERSION

Purpose: To assess the frequency that respondents express emotion.

Number of Items: 40

Format: 9-point scales.

Reliability: Alphas ranged from .87 to .91.

Authors: Boyum L. A., and Parke, R. D.

Article: The role of family emotional expressiveness in the development of children's social competence.

Journal: *Journal of Marriage and the Family*, August 1995, 57(3), 593–608.

Related Research: Cassidy, J., et al. (1992). Family connections: The roles of emotional expressiveness within the family and children's understanding of emotions. *Child Development*, 63, 603–618.

• • •

6420

Test Name: FAMILY FUNCTIONING SCALES

Purpose: To assess relationship and system maintenance factors of family functioning.

Number of Items: 60

Format: Includes 13 factors: Cohesion, Expression, Conflict, Organization, Sociability, External Locus of Control, Idealization, Disengagement, Democratic, Laissez-Faire,

Authoritarian, Enmeshment, and Organization.

Reliability: Alpha coefficients ranged from .60 to .90 (minus Organization).

Validity: Correlations with other variables ranged from -.31 to .25.

Authors: Penick, N. I., and Jepsen, D. A.

Article: Family functioning and adolescent career development.

Journal: *The Career Development Quarterly*, March 1992, 40(3), 208–222.

Related Research: Bloom, B. L. (1985). A factor analysis of self-report measures of family functioning. *Family Process*, 24, 225–239.

• • •

6421

Test Name: FAMILY FUNCTIONING STYLE SCALE

Purpose: To evaluate family functioning.

Number of Items: 26

Format: 4-point scales range from 0 (*not at all like*) to 4 (*almost always like*).

Reliability: Alpha was .92.

Validity:: Correlation with Family Hardiness Scale was .74.

Authors: Davis, S., and Gettinger, M.

Article: Family-focused assessment for identifying family resources and concerns: Parent preferences, assessment information, and evaluation across three methods.

Journal: *Journal of School Psychology*, Summer 1995, 33(2), 99–121.

Related Research: Dunst, C. J., et al. (1988). *Enabling and empowering families: Principles and guidelines for practice.* Cambridge, MA: Brookline.

6422

Test Name: FAMILY INTERACTION QUESTIONNAIRE

Purpose: To measure adolescents' descriptions of parents.

Number of Items: 68

Format: Semantic differential format. Judges then rate the participants' responses.

Reliability: Interrater reliabilities ranged from .41 to .92. Alphas ranged from -.40 to .72.

Validity: Correlations with other variables ranged from -.40 to .72.

Authors: Quinlan, D. M., et al.

Article: The analysis of descriptions of parents: Identification of a more differentiated factor structure.

Journal: *Journal of Personality Assessment*, October 1992, 59(2), 340–351.

Related Research: Blatt, S. J., et al. (1979). Parental representations and depression in normal young adults. *Journal of Abnormal Psychology*, 85, 383–389.

• • •

6423

Test Name: FAMILY INVOLVEMENT SCALE

Purpose: To assess family involvement.

Number of Items: 10

Format: Half of the items assessed spouse involvement and half of the items assessed parental involvement. Responses are made on a 6-point agree/disagree response scale.

Reliability: Coefficient alpha was .88.

Validity: Correlations with other variables ranged from -.31 to .14.

Authors: Frone, M. R., et al.

Article: Antecedents and outcomes of work-family conflict: Testing a model of the work-family interface.

Journal: *Journal of Applied Psychology*, February 1992, *77*(1), 65–78.

Related Research: Frone, M. R., & Rice, R. W. (1987). Work-family conflict: The effect of job and family involvement. *Journal of Occupational Behavior, 8,* 45–53.

■ ■ ■

6424

Test Name: FAMILY LIFE QUESTIONNAIRE

Purpose: To assess harmony in family life.

Number of Items: 24

Format: Likert format.

Reliability: Alphas ranged from .84 to .91. Test–retest reliabilities ranged from .61 to .84.

Validity: Correlation with the Mother-Daughter Relationship Scale was .40.

Authors: Smith, L. M., et al.

Article: Identity strivings within the mother-daughter relationship.

Journal: *Psychological Reports*, April 1995, *76*(2), 495–503.

Related Research: Guerny, B. G., Jr. (1977). *Relationship enhancement: Skill-training for therapy, problem prevention and enrichment.* San Francisco: Jossey-Bass.

■ ■ ■

6425

Test Name: FAMILY NEEDS SURVEY

Purpose: To assess family needs.

Number of Items: 35

Format: Checklist format.

Reliability: Test–retest (6 months) ranged from .67 to .81.

Authors: Davis, S., and Gettinger, M.

Article: Family-focused assessment for identifying family resources and concerns: Parent preferences, assessment information, and evaluation across three methods.

Journal: *Journal of School Psychology*, Summer 1995, *33*(2), 99–121.

Related Research: Bailey, D. B., & Blasco, P. (1990). Parents' perceptions on a written survey of family needs. *Journal of Early Intervention, 14,* 196–203.

■ ■ ■

6426

Test Name: FAMILY-OF-ORIGIN SCALE

Purpose: To assess the amounts of autonomy and intimacy of family environments.

Number of Items: 40

Format: Uses a 5-point Likert scale. Scores range from 40 to 200.

Reliability: Test–retest reliability coefficient was .97. Internal consistency reliability was .75.

Author: Hovestadt, A. J.

Article: Autonomy and intimacy of self and externally disciplined students: Families of origin and the implementation of an adult mentor program.

Journal: *School Counselor*, September 1991, *39*(1), 20–29.

Related Research: Hovestadt, A. J. (1985). A Family-of-Origin Scale. *Journal of Marital and Family Therapy, 11,* 287–297.

■ ■ ■

6427

Test Name: FAMILY-OF-ORIGIN SCALE SHORT FORMS 1 AND 2

Purpose: To assess the characteristics of family of origin.

Number of Items: 15

Format: 5-point scales range from 1 (*strongly disagree*) to 5 (*strongly agree*). All items are presented.

Reliability: Alphas were .95.

Validity: Correlations with other variables ranged from -.72 to .78.

Author: Ryan, B. A., et al.

Article: Parallel short forms of the family of origin scale: Evidence of their reliability and validity.

Journal: *Journal of Psychopathology and Behavioral Assessment*, September 1995, *17*(3), 283–291.

Related Research: Hovestadt, A. J., et al. (1985). A family of origin scale. *Journal of Marriage and Family Therapy, 11,* 287–297.

■ ■ ■

6428

Test Name: FAMILY RITUAL QUESTIONNAIRE

Purpose: To assess the routines and the meanings associated with family rituals such as dinner together and celebrations of holidays.

Number of Items: 56

Format: Interviewing and scoring methods are described.

Reliability: Alphas ranged from .81 to .93 across the major subscales.

Authors: Fiese, B. H., et al.

Article: Family rituals in the Early Stages of Parenthood.

Journal: *Journal of Marriage and the Family*, August 1993, *55*(3), 633–642.

Related Research: Fiese, B. H., & Kline, C. A. (1993). Development of the Family Ritual Questionnaire (FRQ): Initial reliability and validity studies. *Journal of Family Psychology, 6,* 290–299.

■ ■ ■

6429

Test Name: FAMILY SATISFACTION SCALE

Purpose: To measure family satisfaction.

Number of Items: 3

Format: Responses are made on a 5-point Likert scale ranging from strongly agree to strongly disagree.

Reliability: Alpha coefficients were .86 and .90.

Authors: Thompson, C. A., et al.

Article: Putting all one's eggs in the same basket: A comparison of commitment and satisfaction among self- and organizationally employed men.

Journal: *Journal of Applied Psychology,* October 1992, *77*(5), 738–743.

Related Research: Hackman, J. R., & Oldham, G. R. (1975). Development of the Job Diagnostic Survey. *Journal of Applied Psychology, 60,* 159–170.

■ ■ ■

6430

Test Name: FAMILY STRESSOR SCALE

Purpose: To provide an overall family stressor score.

Number of Items: 8

Format: Included parental stressor items (parental workload and extent of child/children's misbehavior) and marital stressor items (lack of spouse support and degree of tension or conflict in the relationship). Items used either 4-point or 5-point frequency-based response scales.

Reliability: Coefficient alpha was .66.

Validity: Correlations with other variables ranged from -.22 to .60.

Authors: Frone, M. R., et al.

Article: Antecedents and outcomes of work-family conflict: Testing a model of the work-family interface.

Journal: *Journal of Applied Psychology,* February 1992, *77*(1), 65–78.

Related Research: Kessler, R. C. (1985). [1985 Detroit area survey]. Unpublished questionnaire. Ann Arbor: University of Michigan, Institute for Social Research.

■ ■ ■

6431

Test Name: FAMILY STRUCTURE SURVEY

Purpose: To assess the presence of inappropriate family interactions.

Number of Items: 50

Format: Includes 4 subscales: Child Involvement, Family Fear of Separation, Parent-Child Role Reversal, and Parental Marital Conflict. Responses are made on a 5-point scale ranging from 1 (*completely false*) to 5 (*completely true*).

Reliability: Alpha coefficients ranged from .51 to .90.

Validity: Correlations with other variables ranged from -.52 to .37.

Authors: Kenny, M. E., and Donaldson, G. A.

Article: Contributions of parental attachment and family structure to the social and psychological functioning of first-year college students.

Journal: *Journal of Counseling Psychology,* October 1991, *38*(4), 479–486.

Related Research: Lopez, F. G., et al. (1989). Effects of marital conflict and family coalition

patterns on college student adjustment. *Journal of College Student Development, 30,* 46–52.

■ ■ ■

6432

Test Name: FAMILY→WORK CONFLICT SCALE

Purpose: To measure family → work conflict.

Number of Items: 4

Reliability: Reliability was .76.

Validity: Correlations with other variables ranged from -.16 to .27 (*N*= 1062).

Authors: Judge, T. A., et al.

Article: Job and life attitudes of male executives.

Journal: *Journal of Applied Psychology,* October 1994, *79*(5), 767–782.

Related Research: Guteck, B. A., et al. (1991). Rational versus gender role explanations for work-family conflict. *Journal of Applied Psychology, 76,* 560–568.

■ ■ ■

6433

Test Name: FAMILY-WORK SPILLOVER SCALE

Purpose: To measure how much family obligations interfere with work.

Number of Items: 4

Reliability: Alpha was .79 (women) and .81 (men).

Validity: No difference found between men and women. (t_{275} = .68).

Author: Burley, K. A.

Article: Family-work spillover in dual-career couples: A comparison of two time perspectives.

Journal: *Psychological Reports,* April 1991, *68*(1), 471–480.

Related Research: Kopelman,

R E., et al. (1983). A model of work, family and interrole conflict: A construct validity study. *Organizational Behavior and Human Performance*, *32*, 198–215.

•••

6434

Test Name: FILIAL RESPONSIBILITY SCALE

Purpose: To assess filial responsibility expectations.

Number of Items: 6

Format: 4-point agreement scales. Sample items presented.

Reliability: Alpha was .67.

Authors: Lee, G. R., et al.

Article: Depression among older parents: The role of intergenerational exchange.

Journal: *Journal of Marriage and the Family*, August 1995, *57*(3), 823–833.

Related Research: Seelbach, W. C. (1977). Gender differences in expectations for filial responsibility. *The Gerontologist*, *17*, 421–425.

•••

6435

Test Name: GLOBAL PARENTING AUTHORITY SCALE

Purpose: To measure authoritative, authoritarian, and permissive parenting among preschool and school-age children.

Number of Items: 62

Format: 5-point frequency scales (*never* to *always*). All items presented.

Reliability: Alphas ranged from .75 to .91 across subscales.

Authors: Robinson, C. C., et al.

Article: Authoritative, authoritarian, and permissive

parenting practices: Development of a new measure.

Journal: *Psychological Reports*, December 1995, *77*(3) Part I, 819–830.

Related Research: Buri, J. R. (1991). Parental Authority Questionnaire. *Journal of Personality Assessment*, *57*, 110–119.

•••

6436

Test Name: HEREFORD PARENT ATTITUDE SURVEY

Purpose: To assess changes in parent's attitudes towards their children after parent training through group discussion.

Number of Items: 75

Format: 5-point agree–disagree response scale.

Reliability: Mean split-half reliability was .80.

Validity: Interscale correlations ranged from .33 to .62.

Authors: Brand, H. J., and Ellis, E. G.

Article: Use of the Hereford Parent Attitude Survey as an outcome measure in parent education research.

Journal: *Psychological Reports*, February 1991, *68*(2), 435–438.

Related Research: Hereford, C. F. (1963). *Changing parental attitudes through group discussion*. Austin: University of Texas Press.

•••

6437

Test Name: HOME–CAREER CONFLICT MEASURE

Purpose: To assess home–career conflict.

Number of Items: 4 ambiguous story cues.

Time Required: Approximately 20 minutes.

Format: Respondents project their feelings, needs, and conflicts into each of the 4 ambiguous story cues. Responses are scored according to three subscales of affect, events, and activity. All items are presented.

Reliability: Interater reliabilities were .92 or better. Inter–item reliabilities ranged from .23 to .39.

Validity: Correlations with other variables ranged from -.09 to .23.

Authors: Tipping, L. M., and Farmer, H. S.

Article: A Home-Career Conflict Measure: Career counseling implications.

Journal: *Measurement and Evaluation in Counseling and Development*, October 1991, *24*(3), 111–118.

Related Research: Farmer, H. S., et al. (1982). Manual for scoring the Home-Career Conflict Measure. *JSAS Catalog of Selected Documents in Psychology*, *12*, 48 (Ms. No. 2511).

•••

6438

Test Name: HOME LEAVING COGNITION SCALE

Purpose: To assess students' beliefs about leaving home.

Number of Items: 31

Format: Responses are made on a Likert-type scale. Includes 8 subscales: Self-Governance, Emotional Detachment, Financial Independence, Separate Residence, Disengagement, School Affiliation, Starting a Family, and Graduation.

Reliability: Alpha coefficients ranged from .54. to .85.

Authors: Holmbeck, G. N., and Wandrei, M. L.

Article: Individual and relational predictors of adjustment in first-year college students.

Journal: *Journal of Counseling Psychology*, January 1993, *40*(1), 73–78.

Related Research: Moore, D. (1987). Parent-adolescent separation: The construction of adulthood by late adolescents. *Developmental Psychology, 23,* 298–307.

• • •

6439

Test Name: HOUSEHOLD COPING MECHANISM SCALE

Purpose: To measure household coping mechanism.

Number of Items: 8

Format: Responses are made on a 5-point scale ranging from 1 (*very inaccurate*) to 5 (*very accurate*). Sample items are presented.

Reliability: Coefficient alpha was .94.

Authors: Aryee, S., and Tan, K.

Article: Antecedents and outcomes of career commitment.

Journal: *Journal of Vocational Behavior*, June 1992, *40*(3), 288–305.

Related Research: Steffy, B., & Jones, J. (1988). The impact of family and career planning variables on the organizational, career, and community commitment of professional women. *Journal of Vocational Behavior, 32,* 196–212.

• • •

6440

Test Name: HUSBAND'S EMOTION WORK SCALE

Purpose: To assess emotion work of husbands.

Number of Items: 15

Format: 7-point frequency scales. All items presented.

Reliability: Alpha was .94.

Validity: Correlations with other variables ranged from -.12 to .71.

Author: Erickson, R. J.

Article: Reconceptualizing family work: The effect of emotion work on perceptions of marital quality.

Journal: *Journal of Marriage and the Family*, November 1993, *55*(4), 888–900.

• • •

6441

Test Name: HUSBAND SUPPORT SCALE

Purpose: To measure wife's perceptions of husband support.

Number of Items: 4

Format: 5-point scales ranging from 1 (*not at all applicable*) to 5 (*highly applicable*). All items are described.

Reliability: Alpha was .75.

Validity: Correlations with other variables ranged from -.26 to .09.

Authors: Matusi, T., et al.

Article: Work-family conflict and the stress-buffering effects of husband support and coping behavior among Japanese married working women.

Journal: *Journal of Vocational Behavior*, October 1995, *47*(2), 178–192.

Related Research: Cohen, S., & Wills, T. A. (1985). Stress, social support, and buffering hypothesis. *Psychological Bulletin, 98,* 310–357.

• • •

6442

Test Name: INCEST BLAME SCALE

Purpose: To measure attitudes toward father–daughter incest.

Number of Items: 20

Format: 5-point Likert format. All items presented.

Reliability: Reliabilities ranged from .13 to .77.

Validity: Correlations with Attitudes Towards Incest Scale ranged from -.48 to .59.

Authors: McKenzie, B. J., and Calder, P.

Article: Factors related to attribution of blame in father-daughter incest.

Journal: *Psychological Reports*, December 1993, *73*(3) Part II, 1111–1121.

Related Research: Jackson, T., and Ferguson, W. (1983). Attribution of blame in incest. *American Journal of Community Psychology, 11,* 393–422.

• • •

6443

Test Name: INEFFECTIVE ARGUING INVENTORY

Purpose: To assess how couples handle conflict.

Number of Items: 8

Format: 5-point agreement scales. All items presented.

Reliability: Alphas ranged from .86 to .89. Test–retest (1 year) ranged from .63 to .84.

Validity: Correlations with other variables ranged from -.35 to .63.

Author: Kurdek, L. A.

Article: Conflict resolution styles in gay, lesbian, heterosexual nonparent and heterosexual parent couples.

Journal: *Journal of Marriage and the Family*, August 1994, *56*(3), 705–722.

6444

Test Name: INTERACTIONAL PROBLEM-SOLVING INVENTORY

Purpose: To measure marital adjustment.

Number of Items: 17

Format: 5-point scales (*applies directly to us* to *does not apply at all to us*).

Reliability: Alpha was .86 to .88 for husbands and wives respectively. Combined score reliability was .90.

Validity: Correlations with related constructs ranged from .56 to .77.

Authors: Lange, A., et al.

Article: Status inconsistency, traditionality and marital distress in the Netherlands.

Journal: *Psychological Reports*, June 1991, *68*(3) Part II, 1243–1253.

Related Research: Lange, A. (1983). *Interactionele Probleem Oplossing Vragenlijst.* Deuventer, Netherlands: Van Loghum Slaterus.

■ ■ ■

6445

Test Name: INTERGENERATIONAL INDIVIDUATION SCALE

Purpose: To assess how independent children are from parents.

Number of Items: 8

Format: 5-point Likert format. Sample items presented.

Reliability: Alpha was .77.

Authors: Farrell, M. P., and Barnes, G. M.

Article: Family systems and social support: A test of the effects of cohesion and adaptability on the functioning of parents and adolescents.

Journal: *Journal of Marriage and the Family*, February 1993, *55*(1), 119–132.

Related Research: Bray, J. H., et al. (1984). *Parental authority in the family manual.* Houston: Texas Women's University, Houston Center.

■ ■ ■

6446

Test Name: INTERPARENTAL CONFLICT SCALE (O'LEARY-PORTER SCALE)

Purpose: To measure conflict between parents.

Number of Items: 10

Format: 5-point Likert format. Sample items presented.

Reliability: Internal consistency ranged from .77 to .87.

Authors: Brody, G. H., et al.

Article: Religion's role in organizing family relationships: Family process in rural, two-parent African American families.

Journal: *Journal of Marriage and the Family*, November 1994, *56*(4), 878–888.

Related Research: Porter, B., & O'Leary, K. D. (1980). Marital discord and childhood behavior problems. *Journal of Abnormal Child Psychology*, *8*, 287–295.

■ ■ ■

6447

Test Name: INTERPERSONAL CONFLICT SCALE

Purpose: To measure interpersonal conflict between spouses.

Number of Items: 4

Format: 5-point Likert format.

Reliability: Alpha was .75.

Author: Abbey, A., et al.

Article: Infertility and subjective well-being: The mediating roles of self-esteem, internal control and interpersonal conflict.

Journal: *Journal of Marriage and the Family*, May 1992, *54*(2), 408–417.

Related Research: Abbey, A., et al. (1985). Effects of different sources of social support and social conflict on emotional well-being. *Basic and Applied Social Psychology*, *6*, 111–129.

■ ■ ■

6448

Test Name: INTERROLE CONFLICT SCALE

Purpose: To assess work–family conflict.

Number of Items: 4

Format: 5-point Likert format.

Reliability: Alpha was .86.

Validity: Correlations with other variables ranged from -.04 to -.38.

Author: Burley, K. A.

Article: Gender difference and similarities in coping responses to anticipated work-family conflict.

Journal: *Psychological Reports*, February 1994, *74*(1), 115–123.

Related Research: Kopelman, R. E., et al. (1983). A model of work, family and interrole conflict: A construct validation study. *Organizational Behavior and Human Performance*, *32*, 198–215.

■ ■ ■

6449

Test Name: INTIMACY SCALE

Purpose: To measure intimacy between mothers and daughters.

Number of Items: 17

Format: 7-point agreement response options.

Reliability: Alphas ranged from .91 to .97.

Validity: Correlations with other variables ranged from -.05 to .74.

Authors: Smith, L. M., et al.

Article: Identity strivings within the mother-daughter relationship.

Journal: *Psychological Reports*, April 1995, *76*(2), 495–503.

Related Research: Walker, A. J., & Thompson, L. (1983). Intimacy and intergenerational aid and contact among mothers and daughters. *Journal of Marriage and the Family, 45,* 841–847.

■ ■ ■

6450

Test Name: INTIMATE RELATIONS SCALE

Purpose: To assess the interpersonal nature of the marital relationship in three dimensions: (a) maintenance, (b) conflict, and (c) ambivalence and love.

Number of Items: 25

Format: 9-point frequency scales.

Reliability: Alphas ranged from .61 to .90.

Authors: Volling, B. L., and Belsky, J.

Article: Multiple determinants of father involvement during infancy in dual-earner and single-earner families.

Journal: *Journal of Marriage and the Family*, May 1991, *53*(2), 461–474.

Related Research: Braiker, H., & Kelly, H. (1979). Conflict in the development of close relationships. In R. Burgess & T. Huston (Eds.), *Social exchange and developing relationships* (pp. 135–168). New York: Academic Press.

6451

Test Name: INVENTORY OF PARENT AND PEER ATTACHMENT

Purpose: To measure attachment toward mother, father, and close friends.

Number of Items: 75

Format: Responses are made on Likert-type scales.

Reliability: Test–retest reliabilities ranged from .86 to .93.

Author: Brack, G., et al.

Article: Relationships between attachment and coping resources among late adolescents.

Journal: *Journal of College Student Development*, May 1993, *34*(3), 212–220.

Related Research: Armsden, G., & Greenberg, M. T. (1988*). Manual for Inventory of Parent and Peer Attachment.* Unpublished manuscript available from authors.

■ ■ ■

6452

Test Name: INVENTORY OF PEER AND PARENTAL ATTACHMENT—REVISED SCALE

Purpose: To assess current maternal and paternal attachment.

Number of Items: 50

Format: Includes both maternal and paternal scales. Responses are made on a 5-point set of options ranging from *always true* to *never true.*

Reliability: Test–retest (3 weeks) reliability coefficient was .93.

Authors: Calloni, J. C., and Handal, P. J.

Article: Differential parental attachment: Empirical support for the self-in-relation model.

Journal: *Perceptual and Motor Skills*, December 1992, *75*(3) Part 1, 904–906.

Related Research: Armsden, G. C., & Greenberg, M. T. (1987). The inventory of parent and peer attachment: Individual differences and their relationship to psychological well being in adolescence. *Journal of Youth and Adolescence, 16,* 427–454.

■ ■ ■

6453

Test Name: ISSUES CHECKLIST

Purpose: To measure conflict between parents and adolescents.

Number of Items: 44

Format: 5-point anger scales.

Reliability: Alphas ranged from .61 to .71 across subscales.

Authors: Galambos, N. L., and Almeida, O. M.

Article: Does parent-adolescent conflict increase in early adolescence?

Journal: *Journal of Marriage and the Family*, November 1992, *54*(4), 737–747.

Related Research: Prinz, R., et al. (1979). Multivariate assessment of conflict in distressed and nondistressed mother-adolescent dyads. *Journal of Applied Behavioral Analysis, 12,* 691–700.

■ ■ ■

6454

Test Name: KANSAS MARITAL AND PARENTAL SATISFACTION SCALES

Purpose: To measure satisfaction with self as spouse and parent.

Number of Items: 6

Format: All items are presented.

Reliability: Alphas were .96 (marital) and .85 (parental).

Validity: Husband–wife score correlations were .57 (marital) and .49 (parental).

Authors: Chang, L.-W., et al.

Article: Dimensionality of brief family interaction and satisfaction sales among couples from eight western and midwestern states.

Journal: *Psychological Reports*, February 1994, *74*(1), 131–144.

...

6455

Test Name: KANSAS MARITAL SATISFACTION SCALE

Purpose: To assess marital happiness.

Number of Items: 3

Format: Responses are made on a 7-point Likert scale ranging from *extremely dissatisfied* to *extremely satisfied.*

Reliability: Alphas ranged from .89 to .93.

Authors: Dominico, D., and Windle, M.

Article: Intrapersonal and interpersonal functioning among middle-aged female adult children of alcoholics.

Journal: *Journal of Consulting and Clinical Psychology*, August 1993, *61*(4), 659–666.

Related Research: Schumm, W. R., et al. (1986). Concurrent and discriminant validity of the Kansas Marital Satisfaction Scale. *Journal of Marriage and the Family*, *48*, 381–387.

...

6456

Test Name: LIFE ROLE IMPORTANCE AND INVOLVEMENT SCALES

Purpose: To measure importance

of an involvement in career, children, home, and marriage.

Number of Items: 40

Format: Sample items are presented.

Reliability: Alphas ranged from .70 to .86 across subscales.

Author: Burke, R. J.

Article: Career and life values and expectations of university business students.

Journal: *Psychological Reports*, August 1994, *75*(1) Part I, 147–160.

Related Research: Amatea, E. S., et al. (1986). Assessing the work and family role expectations of career-oriented men and women: The Life Role Salience Scale. *Journal of Marriage and the Family*, *48*, 831–838.

...

6457

Test Name: LIFE STRAIN SCALE

Purpose: To measure marital, parental, work, and health strains.

Number of Items: 17

Format: Varies by item. Sample items presented.

Reliability: Alphas ranged from .72 to .84 across subscales.

Author: Jackson, P. B.

Article: Specifying the buffering hypothesis: Support, strain and depression.

Journal: *Social Psychology Quarterly*, December 1992, *55*(4), 363–378.

Related Research: Kandel, D. B., et al. (1985). The stressfulness of daily social roles for women: Marital, occupational and household roles. *Journal of Health and Social Behavior*, *26*, 64–78.

6458

Test Name: MARITAL BURNOUT SCALE

Purpose: To measure emotional strain (burnout) in marriages.

Number of Items: 12

Format: 7-point frequency scales. All items presented.

Reliability: Alpha was .93.

Validity: Correlations with other variables ranged from -.76 to .12.

Author: Erickson, R. J.

Article: Reconceptualizing family work: The effect of emotion work on perceptions of marital quality.

Journal: *Journal of Marriage and the Family*, November 1993, *55*(4), 888–900.

...

6459

Test Name: MARITAL COMMUNICATION INVENTORY

Purpose: To measure communication between spouses.

Number of Items: 14

Format: All items are presented.

Reliability: Alphas ranged from .77 to .85 across subscales.

Validity: Husband–wife score correlations ranged from .29 to .56.

Authors: Chang, L.-W., et al.

Article: Dimensionality of brief family interaction and satisfaction sales among couples from eight western and midwestern states.

Journal: *Psychological Reports*, February 1994, *74*(1), 131–144.

Related Research: Schumm, W. R., et al. (1983). The Marital Communication Inventory. In E. E. Filsinger (Ed.), *Marriage and family assessment: A sourcebook for family therapy* (pp. 191–208). Beverly Hills, CA: Sage.

6460

Test Name: MARITAL CONSENSUS SCALE

Purpose: To assess marital agreement and disagreement.

Number of Items: 15

Format: 6-point Likert scales.

Reliability: Alphas ranged from .94 to .95.

Authors: Farrell, M. P., and Barnes, G. M.

Article: Family systems and social support: A test of the effects of cohesion and adaptability on the functioning of parents and adolescents.

Journal: *Journal of Marriage and the Family*, February 1993, *55*(1), 119–132.

Related Research: Spanier, G. (1976). Measuring dyadic adjustment: New scales for assessing the quality of marriage and similar dyads. *Journal of Marriage and the Family*, *38*, 15–28.

■ ■ ■

6461

Test Name: MARITAL INSTABILITY SCALE

Purpose: To assess degree to which couples discuss possibility of divorce.

Number of Items: 4

Format: Yes–no format.

Reliability: Alpha was .76.

Authors: Hoffman, K. L., et al.

Article: Physical wife abuse in a non-western society: An integrated theoretical approach.

Journal: *Journal of Marriage and the Family*, February 1994, *56*(1), 131–146.

Related Research: Edwards, J. N., et al. (1987). Coming apart: A prognostic instrument of marital

breakup. *Family Relations*, *36*, 168–170.

■ ■ ■

6462

Test Name: MARITAL QUALITY INVENTORY

Purpose: To assess marital quality including: social support, strain, harmony, negative behavior, conflict, and feelings of being bothered.

Number of Items: 13

Format: Varies by item. All items presented.

Reliability: Alphas ranged from .44 to .70.

Author: Umberson, D.

Article: Marriage as support or strain? Marital quality following the death of a parent.

Journal: *Journal of Marriage and the Family*, August 1995, *57*(3), 709–723.

Related Research: House, J. S., et al. (1988). Structures and processes of social support. In W. R. Scott & J. Blake (Eds.), *Annual review of sociology* (pp. 293–318). Palo Alto, CA: Annual Reviews.

■ ■ ■

6463

Test Name: MARITAL RELATIONSHIPS EQUITY SCALE

Purpose: To measure a couple's tendency to take the other into account.

Number of Items: 13

Format: 7-point rating scales. Sample items presented.

Reliability: Alphas were .68 (women) and .76 (men).

Authors: Guelzow, M. G., et al.

Article: An exploratory path analysis of the stress process for

dual-career men and women.

Journal: *Journal of Marriage and the Family*, February 1991, *53*(1), 131–164.

Related Research: Blumstein, P., & Schwartz, P. (1983). *American couples*. New York: William Morrow.

■ ■ ■

6464

Test Name: MARITAL RELATIONSHIP SCALE

Purpose: To measure the quality of parents' marital relationship.

Number of Items: 6

Format: 4-point frequency scales. All items are presented.

Reliability: Alpha was .87.

Author: Amato, P. R.

Article: Psychological distress and the recall of childhood family characteristics.

Journal: *Journal of Marriage and the Family*, November 1991, *53*(4), 1011–1019.

Related Research: Johnson, D. R., et al. (1986). Dimensions of marital quality: Toward methodological and conceptual refinement. *Journal of Family Issues*, *7*, 31–49.

■ ■ ■

6465

Test Name: MATERNAL SEPARATION ANXIETY SCALE

Purpose: To measure maternal separation anxiety.

Number of Items: 35

Format: Includes 3 subscales: Maternal Separation Anxiety, Perception of Separation Effects of the Child, and Employment-Related Separation Concerns. Likert scale is used.

Reliability: Alpha coefficients ranged from .25 to .78.

Authors: Sagi, A., et al.

Article: Sleeping out of home in a kibbutz communal arrangement: It makes a difference for infant-mother attachment.

Journal: *Child Development*, August 1994, *65*(4), 992–1004.

Related Research: Hock, E., & Clinger, J. B. (1981). Infant coping behaviors: Their assessment and their relation to maternal attributes. *Journal of Genetic Psychology*, *138*, 231–243.

• • •

6466

Test Name: MODIFIED IMPACT ON FAMILY SCALE

Purpose: To assess the effects of behaviorally difficult children on their families.

Number of Items: 23

Format: 5-point Likert format. Sample items presented.

Reliability: Cronbach's alpha was .93 ($p < .0001$). Split-half was .96 ($p < .0001$). Test–retest (4 days) was .96 ($p < .0001$).

Validity: Correlations with other variables ranged from .66 to .71.

Authors: Sheeber, L. B., and Johnson, J. H.

Article: Applicability of the Impact on Family Scale for assessing families with behaviorally difficult children.

Journal: *Psychological Reports*, August 1992, *71*(1), 155–159.

Related Research: Stein, R., & Riessman, C. (1980). Development of an Impact on Family Scale. *Medical Care*, *18*, 465–472.

• • •

6467

Test Name: MOTHER–DAUGHTER CONFLICT SCALE

Purpose: To measure mother–daughter conflict.

Number of Items: 8

Format: 7-point Likert format.

Reliability: Alphas ranged from .67 to .82.

Validity: Correlations with other variables ranged from -.61 to .78.

Authors: Smith, L. M., et al.

Article: Identity strivings within the mother-daughter relationship.

Journal: *Psychological Reports*, April 1995, *76*(2), 495-503.

Related Research: Boyd, C. (1987). Relationships among the correlates within the construct of mother-daughter identification: Mutual identification, attachment, conflict and identity in adult Polish-American women. *Dissertation Abstracts International*, *48*. (University Microfilms No. 8714530).

• • •

6468

Test Name: MOTHER–DAUGHTER RELATIONSHIP SCALE

Purpose: To measure the quality of the mother–daughter relationship.

Number of Items: 9

Format: Likert format.

Reliability: Alpha was .84. Test–retest reliabilities ranged from .61 to .84.

Validity: Correlation with Family Life Questionnaire was .40.

Authors: Smith, L. M., et al.

Article: Identity strivings within the mother-daughter relationship.

Journal: *Psychological Reports*, April 1995, *76*(2), 495–503.

Related Research: Inazu, J. K., & Fox, G. L. (1980). Maternal influences on the sexual behavior of teenage daughters: Direct and indirect sources. *Journal of Family Issues*, *1*, 81–102.

• • •

6469

Test Name: "NEW FATHER" ROLE SCALE

Purpose: To measure dimensions of the "new father" role.

Number of Items: 6

Format: Varies by item. All items presented (from the National Survey of Children).

Reliability: Alphas ranged from .57 to .67 across two subscales.

Validity: Correlations with other variables ranged from -.25 to .86.

Authors: Harris, K. M., and Morgan, S. P.

Article: Fathers, sons, and daughters: Differential paternal involvement in parenting.

Journal: *Journal of Marriage and the Family*, August 1991, *53*(3), 531–544.

• • •

6470

Test Name: NONRESIDENTIAL FATHER'S PARENTING SCALE

Purpose: To measure perceptions of the parenting of nonresidential fathers.

Number of Items: 22

Format: Mothers and adolescent children each respond to set of questions. 5-point agreement scales. All items presented.

Reliability: Alpha was .90 (adolescent reports) and .86 (mother reports).

Validity: Correlation between adolescent girls' and mothers' scores was .29. Correlation between scores of adolescent boys' and mothers' scores was .01.

Authors: Simons, R. L., et al.

Article: The impact of mothers' parenting, involvement by nonresidential fathers, and parental conflict on the adjustment of adolescent children.

Journal: *Journal of Marriage and the Family*, May 1994, *56*(2), 356–374.

• • •

6471

Test Name: O'LEARY-PORTER SCALE

Purpose: To assess frequency of interparental conflict in the presence of children.

Number of Items: 10

Format: Responses are made on a 5-point scale ranging from *never/very little* to *a lot*. Sample items are presented.

Reliability: Internal consistency ranged from .77 to .87.

Authors: Brody, G. H., et al.

Article: Financial resources, parent psychological functioning, parent co-caregiving, and early adolescent competence in rural two-parent African-American families.

Journal: *Child Development*, April 1994, *65*(2), 590–605.

Related Research: Porter, B., & O'Leary, K. D. (1980). Marital discord and childhood behavior problems. *Journal of Abnormal Child Psychology, 8*, 287–295.

• • •

6472

Test Name: PARENT–ADOLESCENT ATTACHMENT INVENTORY

Purpose: To assess adolescents' perception of the quality of relationships to parents.

Number of Items: 6

Format: 5-point closeness scales. Sample items presented.

Reliability: Alphas ranged from .81 to .86.

Authors: Small, S. A., and Luster, T.

Article: Adolescent sexual activity: An ecological risk-factor approach.

Journal: *Journal of Marriage and the Family*, February 1994, *56*(1), 181–192.

Related Research: Armsden, G., & Greenberg, M. T. (1987). Inventory of parent and peer attachment: Individual differences in their relationship to psychological well-being in adolescent. *Journal of Youth and Adolescence, 16*, 427–453.

• • •

6473

Test Name: PARENT–ADOLESCENT COMMUNICATION SCALE

Purpose: To assess the qualities of open and problem parent-child communication.

Number of Items: 20

Format: Responses are made on 5-point response scales. Examples are presented.

Reliability: Alpha coefficients ranged from .60 to .88.

Validity: Correlations with other variables ranged from -.47 to .48.

Authors: Knight, G. P., et al.

Article: Socialization and family correlates of mental health outcomes among Hispanic and Anglo American children: Consideration of cross-ethnic scalar equivalence.

Journal: *Child Development*, February 1994, *65*(1), 212–224.

Related Research: Barnes, H., & Olson, D. H. (1982). Parent-adolescent communication. In D. H. Olson et al. (Eds.), *Family inventories* (pp. 33–48). St. Paul: Family Social Science, University of Minnesota.

• • •

6474

Test Name: PARENTAL ACCEPTANCE–REJECTION QUESTIONNAIRE

Purpose: To measure a child's perception of parental acceptance–rejection.

Number of Items: 60

Format: 4-point Likert format. Sample items presented.

Reliability: Alpha was .81.

Authors: Rohner, R. P., et al.

Article: Effects of corporal punishment, perceived caretaker warmth and cultural beliefs on the psychological adjustment of children in St. Kitts, West Indies.

Journal: *Journal of Marriage and the Family*, August 1991, *53*(3), 681–693.

Related Research: Rohner, R. P. (1989). *Handbook for the Study of Parental Acceptance and Rejection.* Center for the Study of Parental Acceptance and Rejection, University of Connecticut, Storrs.

• • •

6475

Test Name: PARENTAL ATTACHMENT QUESTIONNAIRE

Purpose: To measure attachment.

Number of Items: 55

Format: Includes 3 factors: Affective Quality of Attachment, Parental Fostering of Autonomy, and Parental Role in Providing Emotional Support. Responses are made on a 5-point Likert scale ranging from 1 (*not at all*) to 5 (*very much*).

Reliability: Alpha coefficients were .96 and .88. Test–retest (2 weeks) reliability ranged from .82 to .92.

Validity: Correlations with other variables ranged from -.40 to .51.

Authors: Kenny, M. E., and Hart, K.

Article: Relationship between parental attachment and eating disorders in an inpatient and college sample.

Journal: *Journal of Counseling Psychology*, October 1992, *39*(4), 521–526.

Related Research: Kenny, M. (1990). College seniors' perceptions of parental attachments: The value and stability of family ties. *Journal of College Student Development*, *31*, 39–46.

■ ■ ■

6476

Test Name: PARENTAL ATTITUDES TOWARD CHILDREARING

Purpose: To measure childrearing attitudes.

Number of Items: 51

Format: 6-point Likert format.

Reliability: Alphas ranged from .67 to .69 across subscales.

Authors: McGuire, J., and Earls, F.

Article: Exploring the reliability of measures of family relations, parental attitudes, and parent-child relations in a disadvantaged minority population.

Journal: *Journal of Marriage and the Family*, November 1993, *55*(4), 1042–1046.

Related Research: Easterbrooks, M., & Goldberg, W. (1984). Toddler development in the

family: Impact of father involvement and parenting characteristics. *Child Development*, *55*, 740–752.

■ ■ ■

6477

Test Name: PARENTAL AUTHORITY QUESTIONNAIRE

Purpose: To measure parenting styles.

Number of Items: 30

Format: Sample items presented.

Reliability: Alphas ranged from .74 to .87. Test–retest reliabilities ranged from .77 to .92.

Author: Farrari, J. R., and Olivette, M. J.

Article: Parental authority and the development of female dysfunctional procrastination.

Journal: *Journal of Research in Personality*, March 1994, *28*(1), 87–100.

Related Research: Buri, J. R. (1991). Parental Authority Questionnaire. *Journal of Personality Assessment*, *57*, 110–119.

■ ■ ■

6478

Test Name: PARENTAL AUTHORITY QUESTIONNAIRE

Purpose: To measure permissive, authoritarian, and authoritative parental authority.

Number of Items: 60

Format: 5-point Likert format. All items are presented.

Reliability: Test–retest reliability (2 weeks) ranged from .77 to .92. Alphas ranged from .74 to .87.

Validity: Correlations with other variables ranged from -.53 to .95. Correlations between subscales ranged from -.52 to .12.

Author: Buri, J. R.

Article: Parental Authority Questionnaire.

Journal: *Journal of Personality Assessment*, August 1991, *57*(1), 110–119.

■ ■ ■

6479

Test Name: PARENTAL BONDING INSTRUMENT

Purpose: To describe parental behaviors of parental bonding.

Number of Items: 50

Format: Includes two 25-item parallel forms; one for mother and one for father. Each form includes a Care scale and an Overprotection scale. Responses are made on a 4-point scale ranging from 1 (*very like*) to 4 (*very unlike*). Sample items are presented.

Reliability: Test–retest (3 weeks) reliabilities were .76 (Care scale) and .63 (Overprotection scale). Split-half reliabilities were .88 (Care scale) and .79 (Overprotection scale).

Validity: Correlations with ratings of independent judges were .77 (Care) and .50 (Overprotection). Correlations of self-ratings by participants and those by their mothers ranged from .44 to .55. Correlations with other variables ranged from -.37 to .62.

Author: Mallinckrodt, B.

Article: Childhood emotional bonds with parents, development of adult social competencies, and availability of social support.

Journal: *Journal of Counseling Psychology*, October 1992, *39*(4), 453–461.

Related Research: Parker, G., et al. (1979). A parental bonding instrument. *British Journal of Medical Psychology*, *52*, 1–10.

6480

Test Name: PARENTAL INVOLVEMENT AND CHILD CARE INDEX

Purpose: To assess parents' involvement with young children.

Number of Items: 23

Format: Likert format.

Reliability: Test–retest reliabilities ranged from .60 to .90. Internal consistency was .67.

Authors: Ahmedzzaman, M., and Roopnarne, J. L.

Article: Sociodemographic factors, functioning style, social support, and fathers' involvement with preschoolers in African-American families.

Journal: *Journal of Marriage and the Family*, August 1992, *54*(3), 699–707.

Related Research: Radin, N. (1982). *Paternal involvement in child care index.* Ann Arbor: University of Michigan School of Social Work.

■ ■ ■

6481

Test Name: PARENTAL NURTURANCE SCALE

Purpose: To measure parental nurturance from the child's point of view.

Number of Items: 24

Format: Likert format.

Reliability: Alphas ranged from .92 to .94. Test–retest ranged from .93 to .95.

Validity: Correlations with self-esteem ranged from .44 to .67.

Authors: Buri, J. R., and Murphy, P.

Article: Stability of parental nurturance as a salient predictor of self-esteem.

Journal: *Psychological Reports*, October 1992, *71*(2), 535–543.

Related Research: Buri, J. R. (1989). Self-esteem and appraisals of parental behavior. *Journal of Adolescent Research*, *4*, 33–49.

■ ■ ■

6482

Test Name: PARENTAL RELATIONSHIP QUESTIONNAIRE

Purpose: To measure parental attachment and adjustment to college.

Number of Items: 110

Format: Likert format.

Reliability: Alphas ranged from .79 to .83.

Authors: McClanahan, G., and Holmbeck, G. N.

Article: Separation-individuation, family functioning and psychological adjustment in college students: A construct validity study of the Separation-Individuation Test of Adolescence.

Journal: *Journal of Personality Assessment*, December 1992, *59*(3), 468–485.

Related Research: Kenny, M. E. (1987). The extent and function of parental attachment among first-year college students. *Journal of Youth and Adolescence*, *16*, 17–29.

■ ■ ■

6483

Test Name: PARENT BEHAVIOR CHECKLIST

Purpose: To measure parental disciplinary and nurturing behavior and developmental expectations.

Number of Items: 100

Format: 4-point scales ranging from 1 (*almost always/always*) to 4

(*almost never/never*). Sample items are presented.

Reliability: Internal consistencies ranged from .81 to .97. Test–retest ranged from .81 to .98 over 1 week.

Authors: Tucker, M. A., and Fox, R. A.

Article: Assessment of families with mildly handicapped and nonhandicapped preschoolers.

Journal: *Journal of School Psychology*, Spring 1995, *33*(1), 29–37.

Related Research: Fox, R. A. (1992). Development of an instrument to measure the behavior and expectations of parents of young children. *Journal of Pediatric Psychology*, *17*, 231–239.

■ ■ ■

6484

Test Name: PARENT–CHILD AFFECT SCALE

Purpose: To assess feelings that exist between adult children and their parents.

Number of Items: 15

Format: 4-point frequency scales. Sample items described.

Reliability: Alphas ranged from .92 to .96.

Authors: Cooney, T. M.

Article: Young adults' relations with parents: The influence of recent parental divorce.

Journal: *Journal of Marriage and the Family*, February 1994, *56*(1), 45–56.

Related Research: Walker, A. J., & Thompson, L. (1983). Intimacy and intergenerational aid and contact among mothers and daughters. *Journal of Marriage and the Family*, *45*, 841–849.

6485

Test Name: PARENT–CHILD SCALE

Purpose: To measure parent–child relationships.

Number of Items: 24

Format: Responses are made on a 5-point scale ranging from 1 (*always*) to 5 (*never*).

Reliability: Internal consistency of the subscales ranged from .62 to .82. Test–retest reliabilities ranged from .63 to .87.

Authors: Miller-Johnson, S., et al.

Article: Parent-child relationships and the management of insulin-dependent diabetes mellitus.

Journal: *Journal of Consulting and Clinical Psychology*, June 1994, *62*(3), 603–610.

Related Research: Hetherington, M., & Clingempeel, W. G. (1992). Coping with marital transitions. *Monographs of the Society for Research in Child Development*, *57*, 1–238.

• • •

6486

Test Name: PARENTING DAILY HASSLES SCALE

Purpose: To measure parental perceptions of the problems of parenting.

Number of Items: 20

Format: 4-point frequency scales. 5-point intensity scales.

Reliability: Alpha was .81 (frequency) and .89 (intensity).

Author: Crinc, K. A., and Booth, C. L.

Article: Mothers' and fathers' perceptions of daily hassles of parenting across early childhood.

Journal: *Journal of Marriage and the Family*, November 1991, *53*(4), 1024–1050.

Related Research: Crinc, K. A., & Greenberg, M. T. (1990). Minor parenting stresses with young children. *Child Development*, *61*, 1628–1637.

• • •

6487

Test Name: PARENTING INVENTORY

Purpose: To measure expectations, discipline, and nurturing.

Number of Items: 100

Format: 4-point frequency scale (*almost always/always* to *almost never/never*.

Reliability: Test–retest ranged from .81 to .98. Internal consistency ranged from .82 to .97.

Validity: Correlations with other variables ranged from -.35 to .86.

Authors: Peters, C. L., and Fox, R. A.

Article: Parenting Inventory: Validity and social desirability.

Journal: *Psychological Reports*, April 1993, *72*(2), 683–689.

• • •

6488

Test Name: PARENTING SCALES

Purpose: To assess parental disciplining, satisfaction with parenting, beliefs about parenting, and parental discipline.

Number of Items: 13

Format: 5-point frequency scales, 4-point satisfaction scales, and 5-point agreement scales. All items presented.

Reliability: Alpha ranged from .57 to .85 across subscales.

Validity: Correlations between subscales and between subscales and other variables ranged from -.42 to .69.

Authors: Simons, R. L., et al.

Article: Childhood experience, conceptions of parenting, and attitudes of spouse as determinants of parental behavior.

Journal: *Journal of Marriage and the Family*, February 1993, *55*(1), 91–106.

Related Research: Simons, R. L., et al. (1991). Intergenerational transmission of harsh parenting. *Developmental Psychology*, *27*, 159–171.

• • •

6489

Test Name: PARENTING STYLES QUESTIONNAIRE

Purpose: To measure authoritative, authoritarian, permissive, and adjunctive parenting styles.

Number of Items: 18

Format: Sample items presented.

Reliability: Alphas ranged from .58 to .79.

Authors: Fine, M. A., and Kurdek, L. A.

Article: The adjustment of adolescents in stepfather and stepmother families.

Journal: *Journal of Marriage and the Family*, November 1992, *54*(4), 725–736.

Related Research: Buri, J. R., et al. (1988). Effects of parental authoritarianism and authoritativeness on self-esteem. *Personality and Social Psychological Bulletin*, *14*, 271–282.

• • •

6490

Test Name: PARENT PARTICIPATION INTERVIEW

Purpose: To assess the type and amount of parent involvement in their children's education.

Number of Items: 51

Format: Parents indicate the number of hours they participate in 51 activities. All items are presented.

Reliability: Alphas ranged from .76 to .92 across subscales. Total alpha was .90.

Validity: Correlations between subscales ranged from .01 to .83.

Authors: Hickman, C. W., et al.

Article: High school parent involvement: Relationships with achievement, grade level, SES, and gender.

Journal: *Journal of Research and Development in Education*, Spring 1995, *28*(3), 125–134.

■ ■ ■

6491

Test Name: PARENT PERCEPTION INVENTORY

Purpose: To assess warmth and support between family members.

Number of Items: 18

Format: Responses are made on a 5-point Likert scale on dimensions of warmth and criticism.

Reliability: Alpha coefficients ranged from .78 to .88.

Authors: McCloskey, L. A., et al.

Article: The effects of systemic family violence on children's mental health.

Journal: *Child Development*, October 1995, *66*(5), 1239–1261.

Related Research: Hazzard, A., et al. Children's perceptions of parental behaviors. *Journal of Abnormal Child Psychology*, *11*, 49–60.

■ ■ ■

6492

Test Name: PARENTS' BELIEFS ABOUT CHOLESTEROL

Purpose: To measure the effect parents think cholesterol has on their children.

Number of Items: 28

Format: 5-point Likert format. All items are presented.

Reliability: Alpha was .84. Test–retest (2 weeks) was .83.

Authors: Price, J. H., et al.

Article: Parents' beliefs about cholesterol and its effects on their children.

Journal: *Psychological Reports*, April 1994, *74*(2), 611–621.

Related Research: Garcia, R. E., and Moodie, D. S. (1989). Routine cholesterol surveillance in childhood. *Pediatrics*, *84*, 751–755.

■ ■ ■

6493

Test Name: PARENT SUPPORT AND AFFECTION SCALES

Purpose: To assess parents' support of children and children's support of parents.

Number of Items: 16

Format: 4-point frequency scales. All items presented.

Reliability: Alphas were .90 (parent support) and .92 (child support).

Authors: Donnelly, D., and Finkelhor, D.

Article: Does equality in custody arrangement improve the parent-child relationship?

Journal: *Journal of Marriage and the Family*, November 1992, *54*(4), 837–845.

Related Research: Devereaux, E. C., et al. (1962). Patterns of parent behavior in the United States of America and the Federal Republic of Germany: A cross-national comparison.

International Social Science Journal, *14*, 488–506.

■ ■ ■

6494

Test Name: PEER AND FAMILY SCALES

Purpose: To measure peer pressure and intimacy, family intimacy, and parental control and supervision.

Number of Items: 22

Format: 5-point Likert format. All items presented.

Reliability: Alphas ranged from .69 to .80 across subscales.

Validity: Correlations between subscales ranged from -.10 to .40.

Authors: Giordano, P. L., et al.

Article: The family and peer relations of Black adolescents.

Journal: *Journal of Marriage and the Family*, May 1993, *55*(2), 277–287.

■ ■ ■

6495

Test Name: PERCEIVED ADEQUACY OF RESOURCES SCALE

Purpose: To measure adults' perceptions of the family dynamics affecting them.

Number of Items: 28

Format: Includes 7 subscales: Physical Environment, Health and Energy, Time, Finances, Interpersonal, Knowledge and Skills, and Community.

Reliability: Alpha coefficients ranged from .52 to .89.

Validity: Correlations with other variables ranged from -.47 to .08.

Authors: Burrell, B., et al.

Article: Measurement

characteristics of the Perceived Adequacy of Resources Scale.

Journal: *Educational and Psychological Measurement*, April 1995, *55*(2), 249–257.

Related Research: Rowland, V. T., et al. (1985). Perceived adequacy of resources: Development of a scale. *Home Economics Research Journal, 14,* 221–225.

● ● ●

6496

Test Name: PERCEIVED FAMILY PROBLEMS SCALE

Purpose: To measure extent of family problems.

Number of Items: 6

Format: 5-point frequency scales. All items are described.

Reliability: Alphas ranged from .85 to .86.

Authors: Bringle, R. G., and Bagby, G. J.

Article: Self-esteem and perceived quality of romantic and family relationships in young adults.

Journal: *Journal of Research in Personality*, December 1992, *26*(4), 340–356.

Related Research: Emery, R. E. (1982). Interparental conflict and the children of discord and divorce. *Psychology Bulletin, 92,* 310–330.

● ● ●

6497

Test Name: PERCEIVED SOCIAL SUPPORT FROM FAMILY AND FRIENDS SCALES

Purpose: To measure social support from family and friends.

Number of Items: 40

Format: Yes–no format.

Reliability: Alphas ranged from .85 to .90.

Validity: Correlations with other variables ranged from -.07 to .75.

Author: Gavazzi, S. M.

Article: Perceived social support from family and friends in a clinical sample of adolescents.

Journal: *Journal of Personality Assessment*, June 1994, *62*(3), 465–471.

Related Research: Procidano, M. E., & Heller, K. (1983). Measures of perceived social support from friends and from family: Three validation studies. *American Journal of Community Psychology, 11,* 1–24.

● ● ●

6498

Test Name: PERCEPTUAL INDICATORS OF FAMILY QUALITY OF LIFE SCALE

Purpose: To measure respondents' perceptions of the degree to which their needs are met in their families.

Number of Items: 35

Format: Likert format.

Reliability: Theta was .97.

Author: Loyer-Carlson, V.

Article: Pets and perceived family life quality.

Journal: *Psychological Reports*, June 1991, *70*(3) Part I, 947–952.

Related Research: Rettig, K. D., et al. (1989). *Family life quality: Theory, assessment, and replication.* Paper presented at the Preconference Workshop on Theory Construction and Research Methodology, National Council on Family Relations, New Orleans, LA.

● ● ●

6499

Test Name: PLEASURE IN CHILDREARING SCHEDULE

Purpose: To identify parental pleasure in childrearing.

Number of Items: 10

Format: Responses are made on a 7-point scale ranging from *pleasurable* to *very unpleasant.*

Reliability: Test–retest (6 months) reliability was .70.

Authors: Fagot, B. I., and Kavanagh, K.

Article: Parenting during the second year: Effects of children's age, sex, and attachment classification.

Journal: *Child Development,* February 1993, *64*(1), 258–271.

Related Research: Fagot, B. I. (1983). *Pleasure in childrearing schedule.* Unpublished rating scale. (Available from Oregon Social Learning Center, 207 East 5th, Suite 202, Eugene, OR 97401).

● ● ●

6500

Test Name: POSTSEPARATION PARENTAL CONFLICT SCALE

Purpose: To measure postseparation parental conflict.

Number of Items: 4

Format: 8-point scales. Sample item presented.

Reliability: Alpha was .60.

Authors: Kline, M., et al.

Article: The long shadow of marital conflict: A model of children's postdivorce adjustment.

Journal: *Journal of Marriage and the Family,* May 1991, *53*(2), 297–309.

Related Research: Jacobson, D. S. (1978). The impact of marital separation/divorce on children: II. Interparental hostility and child adjustment. *Journal of Divorce, 2,* 3–19.

6501

Test Name: PSYCHOLOGICAL SEPARATION INVENTORY

Purpose: To measure adolescent psychological separation from parents.

Number of Items: 138

Format: Includes four scales: Functional Independence, Attitudinal Independence, Emotional Independence, and Conflictual Independence.

Reliability: Alpha coefficients ranged from .84 to .92. Test–retest reliability coefficients ranged from .74 to .96.

Authors: Hoyt, W. T., et al.

Article: Interpersonal influence in a single case of brief counseling: An analytic strategy and a comparison of two indexes of influence.

Journal: *Journal of Counseling Psychology*, April 1993, *40*(2), 166–181.

Related Research: Hoffman, J. A. (1984). Psychological separation of late adolescents from their parents. *Journal of Counseling Psychology, 31*, 170–178.

• • •

6502

Test Name: QUALITY MARRIAGE INDEX

Purpose: To assess and evaluate marriages.

Number of Items: 6

Format: Agreement scales. Sample items are presented.

Reliability: Alpha was .96.

Authors: Karney, B. R., et al.

Article: An empirical investigation of sampling strategies in marital research.

Journal: *Journal of Marriage and the Family*, November 1995, *57*(4), 909–920.

Related Research: Norton, R. (1983). Measuring marital quality: A critical look at the dependent variable. *Journal of Marriage and the Family, 45,* 141–151.

• • •

6503

Test Name: QUALITY OF PARENT–CHILD RELATIONSHIPS SCALE

Purpose: To measure the quality of mother–child and father–child relationships.

Number of Items: 7

Format: 4-point frequency scales. All items presented.

Reliability: Alpha was .86 for mothers and .87 for fathers.

Author: Amato, P. R.

Article: Psychological distress and the recall of childhood family characteristics.

Journal: *Journal of Marriage and the Family*, November 1991, *53*(4), 1011–1019.

Related Research: Furstenburg, F. F., et al. (1985). Parenting apart: Patterns of childrearing after marital disruption. *Journal of Marriage and the Family, 47,* 893–904.

• • •

6504

Test Name: RAISING CHILDREN SCALE

Purpose: To assess childraising behavior in three dimensions: harsh, firm, and lax.

Number of Items: 39

Format: 7-point Likert format.

Reliability: Alphas ranged from .60 to .72 across subscales.

Authors: McGuire, J., and Earls, F.

Article: Exploring the reliability of measures of family relations, parental attitudes and parent-child relations in a disadvantaged minority population.

Journal: *Journal of Marriage and the Family*, November 1993, *55*(4), 1042–1046.

Related Research: Greenberger, E., & Goldberg, W. (1989). Work, parenting and the socialization of children. *Developmental Psychology, 25,* 22–35.

• • •

6505

Test Name: READINESS FOR PARENTING CHANGE SCALE

Purpose: To measure readiness to learn more about parenting.

Number of Items: 6

Format: Likert format. Sample items presented.

Reliability: Alpha was .71.

Author: South, R., et al.

Article: A controlled parenting skills outcome study examining individual difference and attendance effects.

Journal: *Journal of Marriage and the Family*, May 1995, *57*(2), 449–464.

Related Research: McConnaughy, E. A., et al. (1989). Stage of change in psychotherapy: A follow-up report. *Psychotherapy: Theory Research and Practice, 26,* 494–506.

• • •

6506

Test Name: ROLE BEHAVIOR SCALE

Purpose: To measure willingness to

perform the parent role and willingness to provide the time, energy, and resources for a child.

Number of Items: 8

Format: 5-point agreement scales. All items presented.

Reliability: Alphas ranged from .61 to .72 across subscales.

Authors: Nuttbrock, L., and Freudiger, P.

Article: Identity salience and motherhood: A test of Stryker's theory.

Journal: *Social Psychology Quarterly*, June 1991, *54*(2), 146–157.

Related Research: Miller, W. B. (1981). *The psychology of reproduction*. Springfield, VA: National Technical Information Services.

■ ■ ■

6507

Test Name: ROLE QUALITY SCALE

Purpose: To measure rewarding and distressing aspects of adult daughter relationships with their mothers.

Number of Items: 19

Format: 4-point rating scale. All items presented.

Reliability: Alphas ranged from .75 to .94. Test–retest (2 months or less) ranged from .79 to .94.

Authors: Barnett, R. C., et al.

Article: Adult daughter-parent relationships and their associations with daughters' subjective well-being and psychological distress.

Journal: *Journal of Marriage and the Family*, February 1991, *53*(1), 29–42.

Related Research: Barnett, R. C. (1988). On the relationships of

adult daughters to their mothers. *Journal of Geriatric Psychiatry*, *21*, 37–50.

Barnett, R. C., & Marshall, N. L. (1991). The relationships between women's work and family roles and their subjective well-being and psychological distress. In M. Frankenheuser et al. (Eds.), *Women, work and health* (pp. 111–138). New York: Plenum Press.

■ ■ ■

6508

Test Name: SELF-REPORT FAMILY INVENTORY

Purpose: To provide an index of family members' perceptions of their family's functioning.

Number of Items: 36

Format: Includes 5 subscales: Health/Competence, Conflict, Cohesion, Ladership, and Expressiveness. Responses are made on a 5-point Likert-type scale.

Reliability: Alpha coefficients ranged from .84 to .88. Test–retest (30 to 90 days) correlations ranged from .44 to .85.

Validity: Correlations with other variables ranged from -.30 to .45.

Authors: Hadley, J. A., et al.

Article: Common aspects of object relations and self-representations in offspring from disparate dysfunctional families.

Journal: *Journal of Counseling Psychology*, July 1993, *40*(3), 348-356.

Related Research: Beavers, W. R., et al. (1990). *Beavers System Model manual, 1990 edition*. Unpublished manuscript, Southwest Family Institute, Dallas, Texas.

6509

Test Name: SEPARATION–INDIVIDUATION TEST OF ADOLESCENCE

Purpose: To assess adolescent separation–individuation issues.

Number of Items: 103

Format: Includes 7 subscales: Separation Anxiety, Engulfment Anxiety, Dependency Denial, Nurturance Seeking, Enmeshment Seeking, Health Separation, and Self-centeredness.

Reliability: Alpha coefficients for six of the seven subscales were presented and ranged from .60 to .77.

Authors: Holmbeck, G. N., and Wandrei, M. L.

Article: Individual and relational predictors of adjustment in first-year college students.

Journal: *Journal of Counseling Psychology*, January 1993, *40*(1), 73-78.

Related Research: Levine, J. B., et al. (1986). The Separation-Individuation Test of Adolescence. *Journal of Personality Assessment*, *50*, 123-137.

■ ■ ■

6510

Test Name: SEVEN SECRETS SURVEY RETROSPECTIVE

Purpose: To assess, by retrospective reports, fathers' perceptions of their effectiveness with children.

Number of Items: 35

Format: 5-point rating scales are used.

Reliability: Test–retest reliability (3 weeks) was .96.

Validity: Correlations with the Personality Assessment Questionnaire ranged from -.42 to .23.

Authors: Brost, L., and Johnson, W.

Article: Retrospective appraisals of fathers' effectiveness and psychological health of adults.

Journal: *Psychological Reports*, December 1995, *77*(3) Part I, 803–807.

Related Research: Roid, G. H., & Canfield, K. R. (1994). Measuring the dimensions of effective fathering. *Educational and Psychological Measurement*, *54*, 212–218.

• • •

6511

Test Name: SHARED ACTIVITIES QUESTIONNAIRE

Purpose: To assess child–grandparent interactions and activities.

Number of Items: 29

Format: 5-point Likert format (*not characteristic* to *very characteristic*). All items presented.

Reliability: Cronbach's alpha was .93.

Validity: Significant differences occur on selected items by sex of grandparent, age of grandparent, sex of grandchild, size of community, race of grandchild, birth order of grandchild, and family structure.

Author: Kennedy, G. E.

Article: Shared activities of grandparents and grandchildren.

Journal: *Psychological Reports*, February 1992, *70*(1), 211–227.

• • •

6512

Test Name: SIBLING RELATIONSHIP INVENTORY

Purpose: To measure sibling relationships.

Number of Items: 38

Format: Responses are made on a 5-point scale.

Reliability: Coefficient alpha was .90.

Authors: McHale, S. M., and Pawletko, T. M.

Article: Differential treatment of siblings in two female contexts.

Journal: *Child Development*, February 1992, *63*(1), 68–81.

Related Research: Schaeffer, E., & Edgerton, M. (1981). *The Sibling Inventory of Behavior*. Unpublished manuscript, University of North Carolina, Chapel Hill.

• • •

6513

Test Name: SPOUSE SUPPORT SCALE

Purpose: To measure spouse support.

Number of Items: 4

Format: Responses are made on a 5-point scale ranging from 1 (*very inaccurate*) to 5 (*very accurate*).

Reliability: Alpha coefficients were .78 and .86.

Authors: Aryee, S., and Tan, K.

Article: Antecedents and outcomes of career commitment.

Journal: *Journal of Vocational Behavior*, June 1992, *40*(3), 288–305.

Related Research: Suchet, M., & Barling, J. (1986). Employed mothers: Interrole conflict, spouse support and marital functioning. *Journal of Occupational Behavior*, *7*, 167–178.

• • •

6514

Test Name: STEPFAMILY AND STEPFATHER COGNITION SCALES

Purpose: To measure ambiguity of stepfather role, optimism regarding stepfamilies, and myths about stepfamilies.

Number of Items: 23

Format: 7-point agreement scales. Sample items presented.

Reliability: Alphas ranged from .72 to .85 across subscales.

Validity: Correlations with family role satisfactions scales ranged from -.62 to .61.

Authors: Kurder, L. A., and Fine, M. A.

Article: Cognitive correlates of satisfaction for mothers and stepfathers in stepfather families.

Journal: *Journal of Marriage and the Family*, August 1991, *53*(3), 565–572.

• • •

6515

Test Name: STORM AND STRESS SCALE

Purpose: To measure parents' perceptions of adolescence.

Number of Items: 9

Format: 7-point Likert format. All items are presented.

Reliability: Alpha was .87.

Authors: Scheer, S. D., and Unger, D. G.

Article: Parents' perceptions of their adolescence: Implication for parent-youth conflict and family satisfaction.

Journal: *Psychological Reports*, February 1995, *76*(1), 131–136.

Related Research: Holmbeck, G. H., & Hill, J. P. (1988). Storm and stress beliefs about adolescence: Prevalence, self-reported antecedents, and effect of an undergraduate course. *Journal of Youth and Adolescence*, *17*, 285–306.

6516

Test Name: STRESSORS OF CLERGY CHILDREN AND COUPLES SCALE

Purpose: To measure stressors relevant to multiple family members in clergy family.

Number of Items: 19

Format: 6-point severity-of-upset scales. All items are presented.

Reliability: Alpha was .80.

Authors: Ostrander, D. L., et al.

Article: The stressors of clergy children and couples: Reliability and validity.

Journal: *Psychological Reports*, February 1993, *72*(1), 271–275.

Related Research: Ostrander, D. L., et al. (1990). The Stressors of Clergy Children Inventory: Reliability and validity. *Psychological Reports, 67,* 787–794.

■ ■ ■

6517

Test Name: STRICTNESS/ SUPERVISION SCALE

Purpose: To assess parental monitoring and supervision of the adolescent.

Number of Items: 9

Format: Several responses are true–false and others are made on a 3-point scale. Examples are presented.

Reliability: Coefficient alpha was .76.

Authors: Steinberg, L., et al.

Article: Over-time changes in adjustment and competence among adolescents from authoritative, authoritarian, indulgent, and neglectful families.

Journal: *Child Development*, June 1994, *65*(3), 754–770.

Related Research: Lamborn, S., et al. (1991). Patterns of competence and adjustment among adolescents from authoritative, authoritarian, indulgent and neglectful homes. *Child Development, 62,* 1049–1065.

■ ■ ■

6518

Test Name: STRUCTURAL FAMILY INTERACTION SCALE—REVISED

Purpose: To identify family interactions.

Number of Items: 68

Format: Includes 7 scales: Enmeshment/Disengagement, Flexibility/Rigidity, Family Conflict Avoidance/Expression, Mother-Child Cohesion/ Estrangement, Father-Child Cohesion/Estrangement, Spouse Conflict Resolved/Unresolved, and Cross-Generational Triads/Parent Coalition. Responses are made on a 4-point Likert scale ranging from 1 (*very false*) to 4 (*very true*). An example is presented.

Reliability: Alpha coefficients ranged from .71 to .93. Test–retest estimates (4 weeks) ranged from .81 to .92.

Validity: Correlations with other variables ranged from -.43 to .55.

Authors: Perosa, S. L., and Perosa, L. M.

Article: Relationships among Minuchin's structural family model, identity achievement, and coping style.

Journal: *Journal of Counseling Psychology*, October 1993, *40*(4), 479–489.

Related Research: Perosa, L., & Perosa, S. (1990, August). *The revision and validation of the Structural Family Interaction Scale.* Paper presented at the 98th Annual Convention of the American Psychological Association, Boston.

6519

Test Name: SUPPORTIVE PARENTING SCALE

Purpose: To measure parental support via child self-report.

Number of Items: 9

Format: 5-point frequency scales. Sample items presented.

Reliability: Alphas ranged from .78 to .89.

Authors: Simons, R. L., et al.

Article: Gender differences in the international transmission of parenting beliefs.

Journal: *Journal of Marriage and the Family*, November 1992, *54*(4), 823–836.

Related Research: Simons, R. L. (1992). *Childhood experience, conceptions of parenting, and attitudes of spouse as determinants of parental behavior.* Paper presented at the National Council of Family Relations, Orlando, Florida.

■ ■ ■

6520

Test Name: UNION-FAMILY CONFLICT SCALE

Purpose: To assess union-family conflict.

Number of Items: 6

Format: Responses are made on a 7-point scale ranging from 1 (*strongly disagree*) to 7 (*strongly agree*). Examples are presented.

Reliability: Coefficient alpha was .76.

Validity: Correlations with other variables ranged from -.42 to .09.

Authors: Mellor, S., et al.

Article: Cross-level analysis of the influence of local union structure on women's and men's union commitment.

Journal: *Journal of Applied*

Psychology, April 1994, *79*(2), 203–210.

•••

6521

Test Name: WHO DOES WHAT

Purpose: To assess husbands' and wives' perceptions of their relative responsibility for household tasks, family decision making, and caring for children.

Number of Items: 12

Format: Responses are made on a 9-point scale (1—*she does it all*; 9—*he does it all*).

Reliability: Cronbach's alphas on the subscales ranged from .62 to .86.

Authors: Babcock, J. C., et al.

Article: Power and violence: The relation between communication patterns, power discrepancies and domestic violence.

Journal: *Journal of Consulting and Clinical Psychology*, February 1993, *61*(1), 40–50.

Related Research: Cowan, C. P., et al. (1978). Becoming a family: The impact of a first child's birth on the couple's relationship. In W. B. Miller & L. F. Newman (Eds.), *The first child and family formation*. Chapel Hill, NC: Carolina Population Center.

•••

6522

Test Name: WORK AND FAMILY ORIENTATION QUESTIONNAIRE

Purpose: To measure achievement motivation in four dimensions: competition, personal unconcern, mastery, and work.

Number of Items: 23

Format: 5-point Likert format.

Reliability: Alphas ranged from .50 to .76 across subscales.

Authors: Platow, M. J., and Shane, R.

Article: Social value orientations and the expression of achievement motivation.

Journal: *The Journal of Social Psychology*, February 1995, *135*(1), 71–81.

Related Research: Helmreich, R., & Spence, J. (1978). The Work and Family Orientation Questionnaire: An objective instrument to assess components of achievement motivation and attitudes toward family and career. *JSAS Catalog of Selected Documents in Psychology*, *8*, 35 (MS. No. 1677).

•••

6523

Test Name: WORK AND FAMILY ROLE CONFLICT SCALE

Purpose: To assess interrole conflict.

Number of Items: 8

Format: Responses are made on a 5-point scale ranging from 1 (*strongly disagree*) to 5 (*strongly agree*). All items are presented.

Reliability: Coefficient alpha was .87.

Authors: Thomas, L. T., and Ganster, D. L.

Article: Impact of family-supportive work variables on work-family conflict and strain: A control perspective.

Journal: *Journal of Applied Psychology*, February 1995, *80*(1), 6–15.

Related Research: Kopelman, R. E., et al. (1983). A model of work, family, and interrole conflict: A construct validity study. *Organizational Behavior and Human Performance*, *32*, 198–215.

•••

6524

Test Name: WORK AND FAMILY ROLE CONFLICT SCALE

Purpose: To measure work and family role conflict.

Number of Items: 16

Format: Responses are made on a 5-point scale ranging from 1 (*always*) to 5 (*never*). All items are presented.

Reliability: Coefficient alpha was .88.

Authors: Thomas, L. T., and Ganster, D. L.

Article: Impact of family-supportive work variables on work-family conflict and strain: A control perspective.

Journal: *Journal of Applied Psychology*, February 1995, *80*(1), 6–15.

Related Research: Bohen, H. H., & Viverso-Long, A. (1981). *Balancing jobs and family life*. Philadelphia: Temple University Press.

•••

6525

Test Name: WORK–FAMILY CONFLICT SCALE

Purpose: To measure work-family conflict.

Number of Items: 4

Format: 5-point Likert format. A sample item is presented.

Reliability: Alpha was .82.

Author: Burley, K. A.

Article: Family variables as mediators of the relationship between work-family conflict and marital adjustment among dual-career men and women.

Journal: *The Journal of Social Psychology*, August 1995, *135*(4), 483-497.

Related Research: Kapelman, R. E., et al. (1983). A model of work, family, and interrole conflict: A construct validation study. *Organizational Behavior* *and Human Performance, 32,* 198–215.

●●●

6526

Test Name: WORK–FAMILY CONFLICT SCALE

Purpose: To measure work–family conflict.

Number of Items: 8

Format: Responses are made on a 6-point scale ranging from 1 (*strongly disagree*) to 6 (*strongly agree*). A sample item is presented.

Reliability: Alpha coefficients were .81 and .80.

Validity: Correlations with other variables ranged from -.25 to .28.

Author: Blau, G.

Article: Developing and testing a taxonomy of lateness behavior.

Journal: *Journal of Applied Psychology,* December 1994, *79*(6), 959–970.

Related Research: Kopelman, R., et al. (1983). A model of work, family and interrole conflict: A construct validation study. *Organizational Behavior and Human Performance, 32,* 198–215.

●●●

6527

Test Name: WORK–FAMILY CONFLICT SCALES

Purpose: To measure family-to-work and work-to-family conflict.

Number of Items: 10

Format: 5-point scales ranged from 1 (*not at all applicable*) to 5 (*highly applicable*).

Reliability: Alphas ranged form .83 to .85.

Validity: Correlations with other variable ranged from -.20 to .55.

Authors: Matusi, T., et al.

Article: Work-family conflict and the stress-buffering effects of husband support and coping behavior among Japanese married working women.

Journal: *Journal of Vocational Behavior,* October 1995, *47*(2), 178–192.

Related Research: Greenhaus, J. H., & Beutell, N. J. (1985). Sources of conflict between work and family roles. *Academy of Management Review, 10,* 76–88.

●●●

6528

Test Name: WORK–HOME CONFLICT SCALE

Purpose: To measure work–home conflict.

Number of Items: 4

Format: Responses are made on a 4-point scale ranging from 1 (*definitely true*) to 4 (*definitely false*). An example is presented.

Reliability: Alpha coefficients were .87 and .77.

Validity: Correlations with other variables ranged from -.44 to .60.

Authors: Bacharach, S., and Bamberger, P.

Article: Causal models of role stressor antecedents and consequences: The importance of occupational differences.

Journal: *Journal of Vocational Behavior,* August 1992, *41*(1), 13–34.

Related Research: Bacharach, S., et al. (1990). Work-home conflict among nurses and engineers: Mediating the impact of role stress on burnout and satisfaction at work. *Journal of Organizational Behavior, 12,* 39–53.

●●●

6529

Test Name: YOUN SCALE

Purpose: To measure how elderly persons perceive the conflicts and problems in their relationships to married sons and daughters.

Number of Items: 13

Format: All items are presented.

Reliability: Internal consistency ranged from .84 to .89.

Validity: Correlations with other variables ranged from -.48 to -.53.

Authors: Youn, G., and Song, D.

Article: Aging Koreans' perceived conflicts in relationships with their offspring as a function of age, gender, cohabitation status and marriage.

Journal: *The Journal of Social Psychology,* June 1992, *132*(3), 299–305.

Related Research: Youn, G., & Song, D. (1990). The Youn Scale for the aging Korean: Some validity findings. *Journal of Modern Social Science, 1,* 59-71.

●●●

6530

Test Name: YOUTH–PARENT CONFLICT SCALE

Purpose: To measure youth–parent conflict.

Number of Items: 20

Format: True–false format.

Reliability: Alpha was .86.

Authors: Scheer, S. D., and Unger, D. G.

Article: Parents' perceptions of their adolescence: Implications for parent-youth conflict and family satisfaction.

Journal: *Psychological Reports,* February 1995, *76*(1), 131–136.

Related Research: Prinz, R. J. (1979). The Conflict Behavior Questionnaire. In A. L. Robin & S. L. Foster (Eds.), *Negotiating parent-adolescent conflict* (pp. 299–308). New York: Guilford.

CHAPTER 14
Institutional Information

6531

Test Name: ACADEMIC ADVISING INVENTORY

Purpose: To evaluate advising programs from a theoretical perspective that allows comparison across institutions.

Number of Items: 44

Format: (2 parts). Part 1—one part of a pair is selected for each item. Part 2—respondents report how frequently they engage in various types of advising activities.

Reliability: Cronbach alphas ranged from .78 to .42.

Author: Frost, S. H.

Article: Fostering the critical thinking of college women through academic advising and faculty contact.

Journal: *Journal of College Student Development*, July 1991, *32*(4), 395–366.

Related Research: Winston, R. B., & Sandor, J. A. (1984). *Academic Advising Inventory*. Athens, GA: Student Development Associates.

· · ·

6532

Test Name: ACADEMIC MOTIVATION PROFILE

Purpose: To provide course evaluation.

Number of Items: 36

Format: Includes 4 dimensions: Attention, Relevance, Confidence, and Satisfaction. Responses are made on a 4-point scale.

Reliability: Alpha coefficients ranged from .63 to .93.

Authors: Carey, L. M., et al.

Article: Procedures for designing course evaluation instruments: Masked personality format versus transparent achievement format.

Journal: *Educational and Psychological Measurement*, Spring 1994, *54*(1), 134–145.

Related Research: Keller, J. M. (1979). Motivation and instructional design: A theoretical perspective. *Journal of Instructional Development, 2,* 26–34.

· · ·

6533

Test Name: ACADEMIC SETTING EVALUATION QUESTIONNAIRE

Purpose: To measure faculty satisfaction with working conditions, social climate, and relationships with students.

Number of Items: 33

Format: Includes 3 factors: Satisfaction With Working Conditions, Social Climate, and Relationship With Students. All items are presented.

Reliability: Alpha coefficients ranged from .87 to .90.

Validity: Correlations with other variables ranged from .40 to .70.

Authors: Fernandez, J., and Mateo, M. A.

Article: The development and factorial validation of the Academic Setting Evaluation Questionnaire.

Journal: *Educational and Psychological Measurement*, Summer 1993, *53*(2), 425–435.

· · ·

6534

Test Name: ACADEMIC SITUATIONAL CONSTRAINTS SCALE

Purpose: To assess academic situational constraints.

Number of Items: 60

Format: Includes 15 categories. Responses are made on a 7-point scale ranging from 1 (*strongly disagree*) to 7 (*strongly agree*). Examples are presented.

Reliability: Alpha coefficients ranged from .82 to .97 ($N = 405$).

Validity: Correlations with other variables ranged from -.30 to .47.

Authors: Hatcher, L., et al.

Article: A measure of academic situational constraints: Out-of-class circumstances that inhibit college student development.

Journal: *Educational and Psychological Measurement*, Winter 1991, *51*(4), 953–962.

· · ·

6535

Test Name: APPLICANT ATTRACTION TO THE ORGANIZATIONAL SCALE

Purpose: To measure applicant attraction to the organization.

Number of Items: 5

Format: Responses are made on a 7-point scale.

Reliability: Coefficient alpha was .95.

Validity: Correlations with other variables ranged from -.17 to .36.

Authors: Turban, D. B., and Keon, T. L.

Article: Organizational attractiveness: An interactionist perspective.

Journal: *Journal of Applied Psychology*, April 1993, *78*(2), 184–193.

■ ■ ■

6536

Test Name: ASSESSMENT RATING PROFILE

Purpose: To measure an individual's perceptions of the acceptability of assessment scales and methods.

Number of Items: 18

Format: Responses are made on a 6-point Likert scale that ranges from 1 (*strongly agree*) to 6 (*strongly disagree*).

Reliability: Cronbach's coefficient alpha was .94.

Authors: Shapiro, E. S., and Eckert, T. L.

Article: Acceptability of curriculum-based assessment by school psychologists.

Journal: *Journal of School Psychology*, Summer 1994, *32*(2), 167-183.

Related Research: Kratochwill, T. R., & Van Someran, K. (1984). *Assessment Rating Profile*. Unpublished test, University of Wisconsin-Madison.

■ ■ ■

6537

Test Name: AVAILABILITY OF RESOURCES SCALE

Purpose: To assess availability of resources.

Number of Items: 6

Format: Responses are made on a 5-point Likert scale ranging from 1 (*strongly disagree*) to 5 (*strongly agree*).

Reliability: Reliability estimates were .68 and .80.

Validity: Correlations with other variables ranged from -.17 to .33.

Author: Peluchette, J. V. E.

Article: Subjective career success: The influence of individual difference, family, and organizational variables.

Journal: *Journal of Vocational Behavior*, October 1993, *43*(2), 198–208.

Related Research: McGee, G., & Ford, R. (1987). Faculty research productivity and intention to change positions. *The Review of Higher Education*, *11*, 1–16.

■ ■ ■

6538

Test Name: CAMPUS CLIMATE SURVEY

Purpose: To measure campus climate for Latino students.

Number of Items: 36

Format: Formats vary. All items are presented.

Reliability: Alphas ranged from .58 to .76 across subscales.

Author: Hurtado, S.

Article: The institutional climate for talented Latino students.

Journal: *Research in Higher Education*, February 1994, *35*(1), 21–41.

Related Research: Hurtado, S. (1992). The campus racial climate: Contexts for conflict.

Journal of Higher Education, *63*, 539–569.

■ ■ ■

6539

Test Name: CAMPUS ENVIRONMENT SURVEY

Purpose: To assess students' perception of their campus environment.

Number of Items: 41

Format: Responses are made on a 5-point Likert scale ranging from 1 (*strongly disagree*) to 5 (*strongly agree*). Includes 4 factors: Indifference and Lack of Recognition, Detection of Sex Bias and Discrimination, Invisibility of Women in the Curriculum, and Sexual Harassment and Differential Treatment. All items are presented.

Reliability: Coefficient alpha was .81.

Validity: Correlations with other variables ranged from -.37 to .47.

Authors: Fischer, A. R., and Good, G. E.

Article: Gender, self, and others: Perceptions of the campus environment.

Journal: *Journal of Counseling Psychology*, July 1994, *41*(3), 343–355.

Related Research: Leonard, M. M., & Ossana, S. (1987). *Technical manual for the Campus Environment Survey*. Unpublished manual, University of Maryland Counseling Center.

■ ■ ■

6540

Test Name: CHILDREN'S PRACTICES INVENTORY

Purpose: To measure curricular practices for 4- and 5-year-old children.

Number of Items: 18

Format: Observers rate classrooms on a 5-point Likert-type scale ranging from *not at all like this classroom* to *very much like this classroom*.

Reliability: Cronbach's alpha was .96.

Author: Zepeda, M.

Article: An exploratory study of demographic characteristics, retention, and developmentally appropriate practice in kindergarten.

Journal: *Child Study Journal*, March 1993, *23*(1), 57–78.

Related Research: Hyson, M. C., et al. (1990). The Classroom Practices Inventory: An observation instrument based on NAEYC's guidelines for developmentally appropriate practices for 4- and 5-year old children. *Early Childhood Research Quarterly*, *5*, 475–494.

• • •

6541

Test Name: CLIENT SATISFACTION QUESTIONNAIRE

Purpose: To measure consumer satisfaction with mental health services.

Number of Items: 8

Format: Responses are made on scale ranging from 0 to 4. Dimensions include physical surroundings, type of treatment, treatment staff, quality of service, amount of service, outcome of service, general satisfaction, and procedures.

Reliability: Internal consistency ranged from .84 to .93.

Authors: Rhodes, R. H., et al.

Article: Client retrospective recall of resolved and unresolved misunderstanding events.

Journal: *Journal of Counseling*

Psychology, July 1994, *41*(4), 473–483.

Related Research: Larsen, D. L., et al. (1979). Assessment of client/patient satisfaction: Development of general scale. *Evaluation and Program Planning*, *2*, 197–207.

• • •

6542

Test Name: COLLECTIVE BARGAINING GOALS

Purpose: To determine collective bargaining goals.

Number of Items: 13

Format: Includes 3 factors: Traditional Bargaining Goals, Academic Bargaining Goals, and Policy Bargaining Goals.

Reliability: Internal consistency coefficients ranged from .71 to .88.

Validity: Correlations with other variables ranged from -.28 to .46.

Authors: Ponak, A., et al.

Article: Collective Bargaining Goals of University Faculty.

Journal: *Research in Higher Education*, August 1992, *33*(4), 415–431.

• • •

6543

Test Name: COLLEGE CLASSROOM ENVIRONMENT SCALES

Purpose: To measure college students' perceptions of classroom environments.

Number of Items: 62

Format: Responses are made on a 5-point scale (*never/almost never true* to *always/almost always true*).

Reliability: Test–retest reliability across the 5 scales ranged from .38 to .81. Coefficient alphas across the scales ranged from .80 to .92.

Authors: Winston, R. B., et al.

Article: A measure of college classroom climate: The College Classroom Environment Scales.

Journal: *Journal of College Student Development*, January 1994, *35*(1), 11–18.

Related Research: Winston, R. B., Jr., et al. (1988). *College Classroom Environment Scales* (version 1). Unpublished instrument.

• • •

6544

Test Name: COMPANY PRACTICES SCALE

Purpose: To determine the extent to which the employer provided each practice.

Number of Items: 43

Format: Responses are made on a 5-point scale ranging from 1 (*no extent /not provided*) to 5 (*a great extent*). Includes 3 subscales: Financial Inducements, General Support, and Family-Oriented Support. All items are presented.

Reliability: Alpha coefficients ranged from .60 to .84.

Validity: Correlations with other variables ranged from -.36 to .34.

Authors: Guzzo, R. A., et al.

Article: Expatriate managers and the psychological contract.

Journal: *Journal of Applied Psychology*, August 1994, *79*(4), 617–626.

• • •

6545

Test Name: DEVELOPMENT ACTIVITIES BENEFITS SCALE

Purpose: To assess potential employee benefits gleaned from development activities participation.

Number of Items: 14

Format: Includes three benefits

scales: Personal, Career, and Job-Related.

Reliability: Internal consistency ranged from .70 to .88.

Authors: Noe, R. A., and Wilk, S. L.

Article: Investigation of the factors that influence employees' participation in development activities.

Journal: *Journal of Applied Psychology*, April 1993, *78*(2), 291–302.

Related Research: Nordhaug, O. (1989). Reward functions of personnel training. *Human Relations, 42,* 373–388.

■ ■ ■

6546

Test Name: DISTRIBUTIVE JUSTICE INDEX

Purpose: To measure the extent salespersons think rewards are related to performance inputs.

Number of Items: 6

Format: Responses are made on a 5-point scale ranging from 1 (*rewards are very fairly distributed*) to 5 (*rewards are not distributed at all fairly*). A sample item is presented.

Reliability: Internal consistency was .94.

Validity: Correlations with other variables ranged from -.06 to .58.

Author: George, J. M.

Article: State or trait: Effects of positive mood on prosocial behaviors at work.

Journal: *Journal of Applied Psychology*, April 1991, *76*(2), 299–307.

Related Research: Price, J. L. & Mueller, C. W. (1986). *Handbook of organizational measurement.* Marshfield, MA: Pittman.

6547

Test Name: EMPLOYEE REACTIONS MEASURE

Purpose: To measure employee reactions to the organization's selection procedure.

Number of Items: 11

Format: Includes two subscales: Privacy and Appropriateness. Responses are made on a 5-point Likert-type scale. All items are presented.

Reliability: Alpha coefficients were .84 (Privacy) and .94 (Appropriateness).

Author: Rosse, J. G., et al.

Article: A field study of job applicants' reactions to personality and cognitive ability testing.

Journal: *Journal of Applied Psychology*, December 1994, *79*(6), 987–992.

Related Research: Miller, J. L., & Rosse, J. (1992, August). *Behavioral responses to privacy invasion resulting from employment procedures.* Paper presented at the annual meeting of the Academy of Management, Las Vegas, Nevada.

■ ■ ■

6548

Test Name: ENVIRONMENTAL INTERFERENCES INDEX

Purpose: To provide an environmental interference index.

Number of Items: 3

Format: Responses are made on a 7-point Likert-type scale ranging from 1 (*strongly disagree*) to 7 (*strongly agree*). All items are presented.

Reliability: Alpha coefficients were .64 and .66. Test–retest (4 weeks) correlation was .61.

Validity: Correlations with other

variables ranged from -.24 to .22.

Authors: Oldham, G. R., et al.

Article: Listen while you work? Quasi-experimental relations between personal-stereo-headset use and employee work responses.

Journal: *Journal of Applied Psychology*, October 1995, *80*(5), 547–564.

Related Research: Oldham, G. R. (1988). Effect of changes in workspace partitions and spatial density on employee reactions: A quasi-experiment. *Journal of Applied Psychology, 73,* 253–258.

■ ■ ■

6549

Test Name: ENVIRONMENTAL SUPPLIES—RESPONDENT PREFERENCES FIT QUESTIONNAIRE

Purpose: To measure environmental-supplies-respondent-preferences fit.

Number of Items: 21

Format: Responses are made on 5-point and 7-point scales. Includes 4 dimensions: job complexity, role ambiguity, responsibility for persons, and quantitative work load. Sample items are presented.

Reliability: Alpha coefficients ranged from .71 to .89.

Validity: Correlations with other variables ranged from -.51 to .39.

Authors: Edwards, J. R., and Harrison, R. V.

Article: Job demands and worker health: Three-dimensional reexamination of the relationship between person-environment fit and strain.

Journal: *Journal of Applied Psychology*, August 1993, *78*(4), 628–648.

Related Research: French, Jr., et al. (1982). *The mechanisms of*

job stress and strain. New York: Wiley.

■ ■ ■

6550

Test Name: ENVIRONMENTAL SUPPORT SCALES

Purpose: To measure support for achievement in math and science from parents, school, and society.

Number of Items: 18

Format: 5-point Likert format.

Reliability: Alphas ranged from .79 to .91 across subscales.

Authors: Farmer, H. S., et al.

Article: Women's career choices: Focus on science, math and technology careers.

Journal: *Journal of Counseling Psychology*, April 1995, *42*(2), 155–170.

Related Research: US Department of Labor. (1972). *The myth and the reality.* Washington, DC: U.S. Department of Labor, Women's Bureau.

■ ■ ■

6551

Test Name: EQUAL OPPORTUNITY MEASURE

Purpose: To measure aspects of the equal opportunity environment.

Number of Items: 4

Format: Responses are made on a 5-point Likert-type scale.

Reliability: Coefficient alpha was .78.

Validity: Correlations with other variables ranged from -.55 to .55.

Authors: Nye, L. G., and Witt, L. A.

Article: Dimensionality and construct validity of the Perceptions of Organizational Politics Scale (POPS).

Journal: *Educational and Psychological Measurement*, Autumn 1993, *53*(3), 821–829.

Related Research: Witt, L. A. (1991). Equal opportunity perceptions and job attitudes. *Journal of Social Psychology*, *131*, 431–433.

■ ■ ■

6552

Test Name: ETHICAL CLIMATE QUESTIONNAIRE

Purpose: To measure perceptions of decisions made by organization members that require ethical criteria.

Number of Items: 36

Format: 6-point true–false scales. All items are presented.

Reliability: Alphas ranged from .69 to .80 across subscales.

Authors: Cullen, J. B., et al.

Article: The Ethical Climate Questionnaire: An assessment of its development and validity.

Journal: *Psychological Reports*, October 1993, *73*(2), 667–674.

Related Research: Victor, B., & Cullen, J. B. (1987). A theory and measure of ethical climates in organizations. *Research in Corporate Social Performance and Policy*, *9*, 51–71.

■ ■ ■

6553

Test Name: EVENT DIMENSION SCALES

Purpose: To assess characteristics of anger-evoking events.

Number of Items: 80

Format: 7-point and 3-point rating scales. Sample items presented.

Reliability: Alphas ranged from .79 to .92.

Validity: Correlations with anger

ranged from .04 to .80 across subscales.

Authors: Ben-Zur, H., and Breznitz, S.

Article: What makes people angry: Dimensions of anger-evoking events.

Journal: *Journal of Research in Personality*, March 1991, *25*(1), 1–22.

■ ■ ■

6554

Test Name: EXAMINEE FEEDBACK QUESTIONNAIRE

Purpose: To evaluate aspects of the test situation.

Number of Items: 10–15

Format: Responses are made on a 5-point scale ranging from 5 (*excellent*) to 1 (*poor*).

Reliability: Test–retest reliability coefficients ranged from .46 to .88.

Validity: Correlations with the Israeli Psychometric Entrance Test ranged from .59 to .84.

Author: Nevo, B.

Article: Examinee Feedback Questionnaire: Reliability and validity measures.

Journal: *Educational and Psychological Measurement*, June 1995, *55*(3), 499–504.

■ ■ ■

6555

Test Name: FAIRNESS PERCEPTIONS MEASURES

Purpose: To measure perception of fairness of hiring practices.

Number of Items: 8

Format: Includes 2 measures: overall procedural fairness and overall distributive fairness perceptions. Responses are made on a 5-point scale. Examples are presented.

Reliability: Alpha coefficients were .85 (procedural fairness) and .86 (distributive fairness).

Validity: Correlations with other variables ranged from -.08 to .31.

Author: Gilliland, S. W.

Article: Effects of procedural and distributive justice on reactions to a selection system.

Journal: *Journal of Applied Psychology*, October 1994, *79*(5), 691–701.

Related Research: Folger, R. (1987). Distributive and procedural justice in the workplace. *Social Justice Research, 1,* 143–159.

● ● ●

6556

Test Name: FAIRNESS PERCEPTIONS SCALE

Purpose: To assess participants' perceptions of training assignment fairness.

Number of Items: 20

Format: Includes 2 dimensions: distributive and procedural. Responses are made on a 5-point Likert scale ranging from 1 (*strongly disagree*) to 5 (*strongly agree*).

Reliability: Coefficient alpha was .91.

Validity: Correlations with other variables ranged from -.19 to .42.

Author: Quiñones, M. A.

Article: Pretraining context effects: Training assignment as feedback.

Journal: *Journal of Applied Psychology*, April 1995, *80*(2), 226–238.

Related Research: Hattrup, K. E. (1992). *Affirmative Action in organizational hiring: Self-regulatory processes underlying beneficiary reactions.* Unpublished doctoral dissertation,

Michigan State University, East Lansing.

● ● ●

6557

Test Name: GRADUATE SATISFACTION SCALE

Purpose: To assess satisfaction with various aspects of the graduate school experience.

Number of Items: 8

Format: Responses are made on a 6-point Likert scale (*very dissatisfied* to *very satisfied*).

Reliability: Cronbach's alpha was .83.

Authors: Hodgson, C. S., and Simon, J. M.

Article: Graduate student academic and psychological functioning.

Journal: *Journal of College Student Development*, May/June 1995, *36*(3), 244–259.

Related Research: Jacobi, M. (1984). *Contextual analysis of stress and health among re-entry women to college.* Unpublished doctoral dissertation, University of California, Irvine.

● ● ●

6558

Test Name: HIRING EXPECTATIONS MEASURE

Purpose: To assess a priori hiring expectations.

Number of Items: 5

Format: Responses are made on a 5-point scale. An example is given.

Reliability: Coefficient alpha was .88.

Validity: Correlations with other variables ranged from .07 to .37.

Author: Gilliland, S. W.

Article: Effects of procedural and

distributive justice on reactions to a selection system.

Journal: *Journal of Applied Psychology*, October 1994, *79*(5), 691–701.

● ● ●

6559

Test Name: HOSPITAL SATISFACTION SCALE

Purpose: To measure satisfaction with a hospital.

Number of Items: 3

Format: Responses are made on a 7-point scale ranging from *strongly agree* to *strongly disagree*. All items are presented.

Reliability: Coefficient alpha was .97.

Authors: Gotlieb, J. B., et al.

Article: Consumer satisfaction and perceived quality: Complimentary or divergent constructs?

Journal: *Journal of Applied Psychology*, December 1994, *79*(6), 875–885.

Related Research: Oliver, R. L. (1980). A cognitive model of the antecedents and consequences of satisfaction decisions. *Journal of Marketing Research, 17,* 460–469.

● ● ●

6560

Test Name: IDENTIFICATION WITH ORDERLINESS SCALE

Purpose: To measure the orderliness of office environments.

Number of Items: 15

Format: One item requires respondent to choose one of three photographs that best depict respondent's own office. Fourteen items use rating scales.

Reliability: Alpha was .84.

Authors: Schell, B. H., and Deluca, V. M.

Article: Task-achievement, obsessive-compulsive, Type A traits and job satisfaction of professionals in public practice accounting.

Journal: *Psychological Reports*, October 1991, *69*(2), 611-630.

Related Research: McElroy, J. C., et al. (1983). Generalizing impact object language to other audiences: Peer response to office design. *Psychological Reports, 53,* 315–322.

■ ■ ■

6561

Test Name: INTERVENTION RATING PROFILE

Purpose: To measure psychological treatment acceptability.

Number of Items: 15

Format: Responses are made on a 6-point Likert scale, ranging from *strongly disagree* to *strongly agree.*

Reliability: Cronbach's alpha was .98.

Authors: Elliott, S., and Treating, M. V. B.

Article: The Behavior Intervention Rating Scale: Development and validation of a pretreatment acceptability and effectiveness measure.

Journal: *Journal of School Psychology*, Spring 1991, *29*(1), 43–51.

Related Research: Marten, B. K., et al. Teacher judgments concerning the acceptability of school-based interventions. *Professional Psychology: Research and Practice, 16,* 191–198.

■ ■ ■

6562

Test Name: INTRINSIC JOB CHARACTERISTICS SCALE

Purpose: To determine the extent of the presence of intrinsic job characteristics in one's job.

Number of Items: 12

Reliability: Coefficient alpha was .74.

Authors: Judge, T. A., and Watanabe, S.

Article: Another look at the job satisfaction-life satisfaction relationship.

Journal: *Journal of Applied Psychology*, December 1993, *78*(6), 939-948.

Related Research: Hackman, J. R., & Oldham, G. R. (1975). Development of the Job Diagnostic Survey. *Journal of Applied Psychology, 60,* 159–170.

■ ■ ■

6563

Test Name: JOB AND ORGANIZATIONAL ATTRIBUTES SCALE

Purpose: To assess attributes of a job, company, and its location.

Number of Items: 51

Format: Sample items are described.

Reliability: Alphas ranged from .79 to .91 across subscales.

Validity: Correlates with other variables ranged from .11 to .63.

Authors: Turban, D. B., et al.

Article: factors related to job acceptance decisions of college recruits.

Journal: *Journal of Vocational Behavior*, October 1995, *47*(2), 193-213.

Related Research: Jurgensen, C. E. (1978). Job preferences (What makes a job good or bad?). *Journal of Applied Psychology, 63,* 267–276.

6564

Test Name: JOB AUTONOMY QUESTIONNAIRE

Purpose: To assess the extent of job autonomy.

Number of Items: 6

Format: The accuracy of each statement is indicated on a 7-point scale. All items are presented.

Reliability: Interrater reliability was .55. Coefficient alpha was .70 and .54. Split-half reliability coefficient was .82.

Validity: Correlations with other variables ranged from .02 to .16.

Authors: Barrick, M. R., and Mount, M. K.

Article: Autonomy as a moderator of the relationships between the big five personality dimensions and job performance.

Journal: *Journal of Applied Psychology*, February 1993, *78*(1), 111–118.

Related Research: Hackman, J. R., & Oldham, G. R. (1976). Motivations throughout the design of work: Test of a theory. *Organizational Behavior and Human Performance, 16,* 250–279.

■ ■ ■

6565

Test Name: JOB CHARACTERISTICS INVENTORY

Purpose: To assess work experience in six dimensions: variety, autonomy, task identity, feedback, dealing with others, and friendship opportunities.

Number of Items: 30

Format: 5-point scales.

Reliability: Alphas ranged from .72 to .86.

Validity: Correlations with other variables ranged from -.32 to .45.

Authors: Brooks, L., et al.

Article: The relation of career-related work or internship experiences to the career development of college seniors.

Journal: *Journal of Vocational Behavior*, June 1995, *46*(3), 332–349.

Related Research: Sims, H. P., et al. (1976). The measurement of job characteristics. *Academy of Management Journal, 19*, 195–212.

•••

6566

Test Name: JOB CHARACTERISTICS SCALE

Purpose: To measure one's perceptions of the motivational characteristics of one's job.

Number of Items: 7

Format: Responses are made on a 5-point scale ranging from 1 (*to a very small extent*) to 5 (*to a very large extent*). Examples are presented.

Reliability: Alpha coefficients were .73 and .78.

Validity: Correlations with other variables ranged from -.20 to .43.

Authors: Aryee, S., et al.

Article: An investigation of the predictors and outcomes of career commitment in three career stages.

Journal: *Journal of Vocational Behavior*, February 1994, *44*(1), 1–16.

Related Research: Hackman, J. R., & Oldham, G. R . (1980). *Work redesign*. Reading, MA: Addison-Wesley.

•••

6567

Test Name: JOB COMPLEXITY SCALE

Purpose: To measure job complexity.

Number of Items: 2

Format: Responses are made on a 7-point scale ranging from 1 (*not at all complex*) to 7 (*very complex*) for Item 1 and from 1 (*very little training*) to 7 (*a great deal of training*) for Item 2.

Reliability: Correlations with other variables ranged from -.19 to .15.

Authors: Oldham, G. R., et al.

Article: Listen while you work? Quasi-experimental relations between personal-stereo headset use and employee work responses.

Journal: *Journal of Applied Psychology*, October 1995, *80*(5), 547–564.

•••

6568

Test Name: JOB CONTENT INNOVATION SCALE

Purpose: To assess the frequency of trying out new methods at work and the frequency of making decisions about the timing of work procedures.

Number of Items: 6

Format: 5-point scales. All items are described.

Reliability: Alphas ranged from .64 (new methods) to .76 (timing).

Validity: Correlations with other variables ranged from -.09 to .23.

Authors: Feij, J. A., et al.

Article: The development of career-enhancing strategies and content innovation: A longitudinal study of new workers.

Journal: *Journal of Vocational Behavior*, June 1995, *46*(3), 231–256.

•••

6569

Test Name: JOB CONTROL SCALE

Purpose: To measure job control.

Number of Items: 4

Format: Employs a 4-point scale ranging from *a lot* to *not at all*. Examples are presented.

Reliability: Alpha was .86.

Authors: Evans, G. W., and Carrere, S.

Article: Traffic congestion, perceived control and psycho-physiological stress among urban bus drivers.

Journal: *Journal of Applied Psychology*, October 1991, *76*(5), 658–663.

Related Research: Karasek, R. & Theorell, T. (1990). *Healthy work*. New York: Basic Books.

•••

6570

Test Name: JOB DEMAND AND DISCRETION SCALES

Purpose: To assess job demand and discretion.

Number of Items: 14

Format: Responses are made on a 4-point scale.

Reliability: Alpha coefficients were .85 and .86 (demand) and .80 and .79 (discretion).

Validity: Correlations with other variables ranged from -.22 to .36.

Authors: Parkes, K. R., et al.

Article: Social support and the demand-discretion model of job stress: Tests of additive and interactive effects in two samples.

Journal: *Journal of Vocational Behavior*, February 1994, *44*(1), 91–113.

Related Research: Karasek, R. A. (1979). Job demand, job decision latitude and mental strain: Implications for job redesign. *Administrative Science Quarterly, 24*, 285–308.

6571

Test Name: JOB DESCRIPTION SCALES

Purpose: To assess ease of work, flexibility of work, and supervisor and coworker support at work.

Number of Items: 17

Format: All items are presented.

Reliability: Reliabilities ranged from .70 to .74 across subscales.

Authors: Glass, J., and Camarigg, V.

Article: Gender, parenthood, and job-family compatibility.

Journal: *American Journal of Sociology*, July 1992, *98*(1), 131–151.

Related Research: Quinn, R., & Seashore, S. (1979). *1977 quality of employment cross section codebook*. Ann Arbor, MI: Institute for Social Research, Survey Research Center.

• • •

6572

Test Name: JOB DIAGNOSTIC SURVEY—REVISED

Purpose: To measure five core job dimensions.

Number of Items: 15

Format: Uses a 3-anchor 7-point response format. The five dimensions are skill variety, task identity, task significance, autonomy, and feedback.

Reliability: Coefficient alphas ranged from .63 to .79.

Validity: Correlations with other variables ranged from -.01 to .63.

Authors: Renn, R. W., et al.

Article: Measurement properties of the Revised Job Diagnostic Survey: More promising news from the public sector.

Journal: *Educational and*

Psychological Measurement, Winter 1993, *53*(4), 1011–1021.

Related Research: Hackman, J. R., & Oldham, G. R. (1975). Development of the Job Diagnostic Survey. *Journal of Applied Psychology*, *60*, 159–170.

Hackman, J. R., & Oldham, G. R. (1980). *Work redesign*. Reading, MA: Addison-Wesley.

• • •

6573

Test Name: JOB SCOPE SCALE

Purpose: To measure job scope.

Number of Items: 15

Reliability: Coefficient alpha was .79.

Validity: Correlations with other variables ranged from .34 to .66.

Authors: Mathieu, J. E., and Farr, J. L.

Article: Further evidence for the discriminant validity of measures of organizational commitment, job involvement, and job satisfaction.

Journal: *Journal of Applied Psychology*, April 1991, *76*(1), 127–133.

Related Research: Sims, H. P., et al. (1976). Antecedents of work-related expectancies. *Academy of Management Journal*, *19*, 195–212.

• • •

6574

Test Name: JOB SCOPE SCALE

Purpose: To measure job scope.

Number of Items: 35

Format: Assesses autonomy, feedback, task identity, task interdependence, outcome certainty, variety, and dealing with others.

Reliability: Coefficient alpha was .83.

Validity: Correlations with other variables ranged from .24 to .64.

Authors: Mathieu, J. E., and Farr, J. L.

Article: Further evidence for the discriminant validity of measures of organizational commitment, job involvement, and job satisfaction.

Journal: *Journal of Applied Psychology*, February 1991, *76*(1), 127–133.

Related Research: Sims, H. P., et al. (1976). Antecedents of work-related expectancies. *Academy of Management Journal*, *19*, 195–212.

Withey, M., et al. (1983). Measures of Perrow's work unit technology: An empirical assessment of a new scale. *Academy of Management Journal*, *26*, 45–63.

• • •

6575

Test Name: LEVEL OF CARE AND UTILIZATION SURVEY

Purpose: To assess level of care for individuals with severe mental illness.

Number of Items: 88

Format: All items are presented.

Reliability: Test–retest ranged from .70 to the .90s. Overall alpha was .78. Subscale alphas ranged from .40 to .97.

Validity: Correlations with the GAF Scale ranged from -.59 to .58.

Authors: Holcomb, W. R., et al.

Article: Reliability and concurrent validity of the Level of Care and Utilization Survey.

Journal: *Psychological Reports*, October 1994, *75*(2), 779–786.

6576

Test Name: LOCAL UNION STRUCTURE SCALE

Purpose: To assess local union structure.

Number of Items: 15

Format: Includes 3 dimensions: innovation, formalization, and centralization. Responses are made on a 7-point scale ranging from 1 (*strongly disagree*) to 7 (*strongly agree*). Examples are presented.

Reliability: Interrater reliabilities ranged from .76 to .84 (*N* = 29). Alpha coefficients ranged from .83 to .93.

Validity: Correlations with other variables ranged from -.43 to .43.

Authors: Mellor, S., et al.

Article: Cross-level analysis of the influence of local union structure on women's and men's union commitment.

Journal: *Journal of Applied Psychology*, April 1994, *79*(2), 203–210.

■ ■ ■

6577

Test Name: LOGO: F

Purpose: To evaluate whether faculty engage in behavior or hold attitudes that promote learning or grade-orientation in students.

Number of Items: 20

Format: Ten 5-point Likert items and ten 5-point frequency items. All items presented.

Reliability: Alphas ranged from .54 to .68.

Authors: Eison, J., et al.

Article: Assessing faculty orientations toward grades and learning: Some initial results.

Journal: *Psychological Reports*, October 1993, *73*(2), 643–656.

Related Research: Eisan, J., et al. (1982). *LOGO II: A user's manual*. Knoxville: Learning Research Center, University of Tennessee.

■ ■ ■

6578

Test Name: MERITOCRACY SCALE

Purpose: To measure the degree to which evaluation is based on individual merit.

Number of Items: 2

Format: Responses are made on a 5-point scale ranging from 1 (*not at all*) to 5 (*a great deal*). An example is given.

Reliability: Alpha coefficients were .90 and .92.

Validity: Correlations with other variables ranged from -.41 to .37.

Authors: Bacharach, S., and Bamberger, P.

Article: Causal models of role stressor antecedents and consequences: The importance of occupational differences.

Journal: *Journal of Vocational Behavior*, August 1992, *41*(1), 13–34.

Related Research: Bacharach, S., et al. (1990). Organizational and demographic models of teacher militancy. *Industrial and Labor Relations Review*, *43*, 570–586.

■ ■ ■

6579

Test Name: MULTIMETHOD JOB DESIGN QUESTIONNAIRE

Purpose: To measure job characteristics.

Number of Items: 55

Format: Includes motivational, mechanistic, biological, and perceptual–motor areas.

Reliability: Alpha coefficients

ranged from .56 to .86. Pretest– posttest correlations ranged from .28 to .55 (*N* = 178).

Validity: Correlations with other variables ranged from -.41 to .63 (*N* = 515).

Authors: Campion, M. A., and McClelland, C. L.

Article: Follow-up and extension of the interdisciplinary costs and benefits of enlarged jobs.

Journal: *Journal of Applied Psychology*, June 1993, *78*(3), 339–351.

Related Research: Campion, M. A. (1988). Interdisciplinary approaches to job design: A constructive replication with extensions. *Journal of Applied Psychology*, *73*, 467–481.

■ ■ ■

6580

Test Name: MY CLASS INVENTORY—MODIFIED

Purpose: To measure classroom climate.

Number of Items: 20

Format: 3-point Likert format ranges from *most of the time* to *seldom*. All items are presented.

Reliability: Alphas ranged from .56 to .67.

Validity: Mean correlations with other scales ranged from .31 to .67.

Authors: Goh, S. C., et al.

Article: Psychosocial climate and student outcomes in elementary mathematics classrooms: A multilevel analysis.

Journal: *Journal of Experimental Education*, Fall 1995, *64*(1), 29–40.

Related Research: Fraser, B. J., et al. (1989). Assessing and improving the psychosocial environment of mathematics classrooms. *Journal for Research in Mathematics Education, 20,* 191–201.

■ ■ ■

6581

Test Name: ORGANIZATIONAL CLIMATE DESCRIPTIVE QUESTIONNAIRE FOR MIDDLE SCHOOLS

Purpose: To measure six dimensions of organizational climate: supportive principal behavior, restrictive principal behavior, directive teacher behavior, collegial teacher behavior, committed teacher behavior, and disengaged teacher behavior.

Number of Items: 50

Format: 4-point frequency scale ranging from *rarely* to *frequently occurs.*

Reliability: Alphas ranged from .87 to .96 across subscales.

Author: Sabo, D. J.

Article: Organizational climate of middle schools and the quality of student life.

Journal: *Journal of Research and Development in Education,* Spring 1995, *28*(3), 125–134.

Related Research: Hoy, W. K., et al. (1994). *The organizational climate of middle schools: The development and test of the OCDQ-RM.* Unpublished Paper.

Hoy, W. K., & Clover, S. I. R. (1968). Elementary school climate: A revision of the OCDQ. *Educational Administration Quarterly, 22,* 93–110.

■ ■ ■

6582

Test Name: ORGANIZATIONAL CLIMATE QUESTIONNAIRE

Purpose: To assess organizational climate in three dimensions:

participative, nurturant task, and authoritarian.

Number of Items: 24

Format: 7-point frequency scales range from 1 (*never*) to 7 (*always*).

Reliability: Reliabilities ranged from .54 to .89.

Authors: Shankar, A., et al.

Article: Organizational context and ingratiatory behavior in organizations.

Journal: *The Journal of Social Psychology,* October 1994, *133*(5), 641–647.

Related Research: Sinha, J. B. P. (1987). *Leader Behavior Scale.* Patna, India: Assert.

■ ■ ■

6583

Test Name: ORGANIZATIONAL CULTURE SURVEY

Purpose: To measure organizational culture in terms of Teamwork, Trust, and Credibility, Performance and Goals and Organizational Functioning.

Number of Items: 55

Format: 6-point Likert format.

Reliability: Alphas ranged from .70 to .94 across subscales.

Validity: Correlations between subscales ranged from -.17 to .80. Correlations with objective performance ranged from .20 to .77.

Authors: Petty, M. M., et al.

Article: Relationships between organizational culture and organizational performance.

Journal: *Psychological Reports,* April 1995, *76*(2), 483–492.

■ ■ ■

6584

Test Name: ORGANIZATIONAL DIVERSITY INVENTORY

Purpose: To measure the elements of organizational diversity.

Number of Items: 20

Format: Responses are made on a 5-point Likert-type scale. Includes 5 factors: Existence of Discrimination, Discrimination Against Specific Groups, Managing Diversity, Actions Regarding Minorities, and Attitudes Toward Religion. All items are presented.

Reliability: Alpha coefficients ranged from .64 to .80.

Authors: Hegarty, W. H., and Dalton, D. R.

Article: Development and psychometric properties of the Organizational Diversity Inventory (ODI).

Journal: *Educational and Psychological Measurement,* December 1995, *55*(6), 1047–1052.

Related Research: Galagan, P. A. (1993). Heading diversity. *Training and Development Journal, 47*(4), 38–45.

■ ■ ■

6585

Test Name: ORGANIZATIONAL STRUCTURE SCALE

Purpose: To measure formalization, centralization, hierarchy, and technology in bureaucratic organizations.

Number of Items: 26

Format: All items presented. Response alternatives vary.

Validity: First- and second-order factor analyses suggest revisions.

Authors: Miller, L., and Weiss, R.

Article: Factor analysis study of the Aiken and Hage measures of perceived organizational structure and technology.

Journal: *Psychological Reports,* June 1991, *68*(3) Part II, 1379–1386.

Related Research: Dewar, R. D., et al. (1980). An examination of the reliability and validity of the Aiken and Hage scales of centralization, formalization, and task routineness. *Administrative Science Quarterly*, *25*, 120–126.

• • •

6586

Test Name: ORGANIZATIONAL SUPPORT SCALE

Purpose: To measure organizational support.

Number of Items: 7

Format: Responses are made on a 5-point scale ranging from 1 (*very inaccurate*) to 5 (*very accurate*). Sample items are presented.

Reliability: Coefficient alpha was .82.

Authors: Aryee, S., and Tan, K.

Article: Antecedents and outcomes of career commitment.

Journal: *Journal of Vocational Behavior*, June 1992, *40*(3), 288–305.

Related Research: Farr, J. L., et al. (1983). Relationships among individual motivation, work environment, and updating in engineers. *Psychological Documents*, *13*, 16.

• • •

6587

Test Name: ORGANIZATIONAL VALUE ORIENTATION QUESTIONNAIRE ·

Purpose: To study the degree of normative orientation present in a given organization.

Number of Items: 10

Format: Uses a 5-point Likert-type scale.

Reliability: Coefficient was .89.

Authors: Reyes, P., and Shaw, J.

Article: School cultures:

Organizational value, orientation, and commitment.

Journal: *Journal of Educational Research*, May/June 1992, *85*(5), 295–302.

Related Research: Reyes, P. (1990a). Individual work orientation and teacher outcomes. *Journal of Educational Research*, *83*(6), 327–335.

• • •

6588

Test Name: ORGANIZATION WORK—FAMILY POLICIES SCALE

Purpose: To determine the extent of organizational policies to deal with work and family issues.

Number of Items: 5

Format: Responses are made on a 5-point scale ranging from 1 (*none*) to 5 (*a very large amount*). All items are presented.

Reliability: Coefficient alpha was .75.

Validity: Correlations with other variables ranged from -.17 to .28 (*N* = 1062).

Authors: Judge, T. A., et al.

Article: Job and life attitudes of male executives.

Journal: *Journal of Applied Psychology*, October 1994, *79*(5), 767–782.

• • •

6589

Test Name: PATIENT SATISFACTION INTERVIEW

Purpose: To assess satisfaction with partial hospitalization programs including satisfaction with: physical environment, therapists, treatment strategies, and preparation for community autonomy.

Number of Items: 40

Format: Better–worse response categories.

Reliability: Item-total correlations averaged .87. Alphas ranged from .71 to .76. Test–retest ranged from .68 to .87 (1 day) and .04 to .90 (6 months).

Authors: Corrigan, P. W., and Jakus, M. R.

Article: The patient satisfaction interview for partial hospitalization programs.

Journal: *Psychological Reports*, April 1993, *72*(2), 387–390.

Related Research: Lehman, A. F. (1988). A quality of life interview for the chronically mentally ill. *Evaluation in Program Planning*, *11*, 51-62.

• • •

6590

Test Name: PERCEIVED ORGANIZATIONAL SUPPORT SCALE

Purpose: To measure perceived organizational support.

Number of Items: 17

Format: Responses are made on a 5-point scale ranging from 1 (*strongly disagree*) to 5 (*strongly agree*).

Reliability: Coefficient alpha was .95.

Validity: Correlations with other variables ranged from -.08 to .64.

Authors: Shore, L. M., and Wayne, S. J.

Article: Commitment and employee behavior: Comparison of affective commitment and continuance commitment with perceived organizational support.

Journal: *Journal of Applied Psychology*, October 1993, *78*(5), 774–780.

Related Research: Eisenberger, R., et al. (1986). Perceived organizational support. *Journal of Applied Psychology, 71,* 500–507.

• • •

6591

Test Name: PERCEIVED ORGANIZATIONAL SUPPORT SCALE

Purpose: To assess perceived organizational support.

Number of Items: 21

Format: Includes 3 domains: current job assignment, off-the job life, and plans for repatriation.

Reliability: Alpha coefficients ranged from .91 to .95.

Authors: Guzzo, R. A., et al.

Article: Expatriate managers and the psychological contract.

Journal: *Journal of Applied Psychology,* August 1994, *79*(4), 617–626.

Related Research: Eisenberger, R., et al. (1986). Perceived organizational support. *Journal of Applied Psychology, 71,* 500–507.

• • •

6592

Test Name: PERCEIVED QUALITY OF CLASSROOM'S PHYSICAL ENVIRONMENT INSTRUMENT

Purpose: To assess the quality of the classroom physical environment.

Number of Items: 11

Format: Responses are made on a 5-point scale. Examples are presented.

Reliability: Coefficient alpha was .77.

Validity: Correlations with other variables ranged from -.32 to .66.

Authors: Cheng, Y. C.

Article: Classroom environment and student affective performance: An effective profile.

Journal: *Journal of Experimental Education,* Spring 1994, *62*(3), 221–239.

• • •

6593

Test Name: PERCEIVED QUALITY SCALE

Purpose: To measure perceived hospital quality.

Number of Items: 10

Format: Includes 5 elements: tangibles, reliability, responsiveness, assurance, and empathy. All items are presented.

Reliability: Coefficient alpha was .95.

Authors: Gotlieb, J. B., et al.

Article: Consumer satisfaction and perceived quality: Complementary or divergent constructs?

Journal: *Journal of Applied Psychology,* December 1994, *79*(6), 875–885.

Related Research: Parasuraman, A., et al. (1988). SERVQUAL: A multiple-item scale for measuring consumer perception of service quality. *Journal of Retailing, 64,* 35–48.

• • •

6594

Test Name: PERCEIVED UNION SUPPORT SCALE

Purpose: To measure perceived union support.

Number of Items: 15

Format: Responses are made on a 5-point scale ranging from 1 (*strongly disagree*) to 5 (*strongly agree*). All items are presented.

Reliability: Coefficient alpha was .96.

Validity: Correlations with other variables ranged from .51 to .87.

Authors: Shore, L. M., et al.

Article: Validation of a measure of perceived union support.

Journal: *Journal of Applied Psychology,* December 1994, *79*(6), 971–977.

Related Research: Shore, L. M., & Tetrick, L. E. (1991). A construct validity study of the survey of perceived organizational support. *Journal of Applied Psychology, 76,* 637–643.

• • •

6595

Test Name: PERCEPTIONS OF THE NEW JOB'S ATTRIBUTES SCALE

Purpose: To measure perceptions of the new job's attributes.

Number of Items: 13

Format: Includes Type of Work, Location, and Financial Rewards. Responses are made on a 5-point scale ranging from 1 (*much poorer*) to 5 (*much better*).

Reliability: Alpha coefficients ranged from .82 to .93.

Validity: Correlations with other variables ranged from -.11 to .66.

Authors: Turban, D. B., et al.

Article: Factors relating to relocation decisions of research and development employees.

Journal: *Journal of Vocational Behavior,* October 1992, *41*(2), 183–199.

• • •

6596

Test Name: PERCEPTIONS OF ORGANIZATIONAL POLITICS SCALES—REVISED

Purpose: To measure organizational political behavior.

Number of Items: 12

Format: Includes three factors: General Political Behavior, Going Along to Get Ahead, and Pay and Promotion. Responses are made on a 5-point Likert-type scale ranging from 1 (*strongly disagree*) to 5 (*strongly agree*). All items are presented.

Reliability: Internal reliabilities were .87 and .93.

Validity: Correlations with other variables ranged from -.55 to -.85

Authors: Nye, L. G., and Witt, L. A.

Article: Dimensionality and construct validity of the Perceptions of Organizational Politics Scale (POPS).

Journal: *Educational and Psychological Measurement*, Autumn 1993, *53*(3), 821–829.

Related Research: Kacmar, K. M., & Ferris, G. R. (1991). Perceptions of Organizational Politics Scales (POPS): Development and construct validation. *Educational and Psychological Measurement*, *51*, 193–205.

■ ■ ■

6597

Test Name: PERSONAL AUTHORITY IN THE FAMILY SYSTEM QUESTIONNAIRE VERSION C

Purpose: To assess triangulation, individuation, intimacy, and personal authority.

Number of Items: 84

Format: Likert format.

Reliability: Alphas ranged from .73 to .92 (mean was .82). Test–retest (2 months) ranged from .56 to .80 (mean was .67).

Validity: Mean correlations with other variables ranged from .80 to .85.

Authors: Lease, S. H., and Yanico, B. J.

Article: Evidence of validity for the Children of Alcoholics Screening Test.

Journal: *Measurement and Evaluation in Counseling and Development*, January 1995, *27*(1), 200–209.

Related Research: Bray, J. H., et al. (1984). *Manual for the Personal Authority in the Family System Questionnaire*. Houston, TX: Houston Family Institute.

■ ■ ■

6598

Test Name: PSYCHOLOGICAL CLIMATE SCALE

Purpose: To measure the psychological climate in organizations, including autonomy, cohesion, fairness, innovation, pressure, recognition, and trust.

Number of Items: 26

Format: Likert format. All items presented.

Reliability: Alphas ranged from .70 to .84 across subscales.

Validity: Factor loadings presented for each subscale.

Authors: Strutton, D., et al.

Article: Relationship between psychological climate and trust between salespersons and their managers in sales organizations.

Journal: *Psychological Reports*, June 1993, *72*(3) Part I, 931–939.

■ ■ ■

6599

Test Name: QUALITY OF SCHOOL LIFE QUESTIONNAIRE

Purpose: To assess students' views of school life.

Number of Items: 40

Format: Uses a self-report Likert scale. Items form clusters or subscales.

Reliability: The reliability coefficient (Cronbach's alpha) was .89.

Author: Ainley, J., et al.

Article: High school factors that influence students to remain in school.

Journal: *Journal of Educational Research*, November/December 1991, *85*(2), 69–80.

Related Research: Batten, M., & Girling-Butcher, S. (1981). *Perceptions of the quality of school life: A case study of schools and students*. Hawthorn, Victoria: ACER.

■ ■ ■

6600

Test Name: REACTION MEASURE

Purpose: To assess trainees' perceptions of their training.

Number of Items: 10

Format: Includes such perceptions as the value of the training module; the predicted use of skill taught; and the effectiveness and contribution of the trainer, method, and videos. Responses were made on a 5-point Likert scale.

Reliability: Alpha coefficients were .92 and .80.

Validity: Correlations with other variables ranged from -.13 to .29.

Author: Baldwin, T. T.

Article: Effects of alternative modeling strategies on outcomes of interpersonal-skills training.

Journal: *Journal of Applied Psychology*, April 1992, *77*(2), 147–154.

6601

Test Name: RECEPTIVITY TO CHANGE SCALE

Purpose: To measure receptivity/resistance to nonspecific changes in an organizational environment.

Number of Items: 18

Reliability: Alpha coefficient was .87.

Validity: Correlations with other variables ranged from -.23 to .58 (*N* = 148).

Author: McLain, D. L.

Article: The MSTAT-1: A new measure of an individual's tolerance for ambiguity.

Journal: *Educational and Psychological Measurement*, Spring 1993, *53*(1), 183–189.

Related Research: Dunham, R. B., et al. (1989). *The development of an attitude toward change instrument.* Unpublished Manuscript, University of Wisconsin-Madison.

■ ■ ■

6602

Test Name: REID-GUNDLACH SOCIAL SERVICES SATISFACTION SCALE

Purpose: To assess client's overall satisfaction with social services.

Number of Items: 34

Format: Responses are made on a 5-point Likert-type scale ranging from 1 (*strongly agree*) to 5 (*strongly disagree*). Includes 3 subscales: Relevance of Service, Impact of Service, and Gratification with Service.

Reliability: Guttman's lambda reliability estimates ranged from .82 to .86. Pearson product-moment correlations ranged from .75 to .87.

Authors: Nickerson, K. J., et al.

Article: Cultural mistrust, opinions about mental illness, and Black students' attitudes toward seeking psychological help from White counselors.

Journal: *Journal of Counseling Psychology*, July 1994, *41*(3), 378–385.

Related Research: Reid, P. N., & Gunlach J. H. (1983). A scale for the measurement of consumer satisfaction with social services. *Journal of Social Service Research*, 7, 37–54.

■ ■ ■

6603

Test Name: ROBUSTNESS SEMANTIC DIFFERENTIAL SCALE

Purpose: To assess if an organization is perceived to be interesting, challenging and meaningful for its participants.

Number of Items: 10

Format: Seven scale anchors range from *very* to *slight*.

Reliability: Test–retest reliabilities ranged from .77 to .78.

Authors: Hart, D. R., and Willower, D. J.

Article: Principals' organizational commitment and school environmental robustness.

Journal: *Journal of Educational Research*, January/February 1994, *87*(3), 174–179.

Related Research: Licata, J. W., & Willower, D. J. (1978). Toward an operational definition of environmental robustness. *Journal of Educational Research*, *71*, 218–222.

■ ■ ■

6604

Test Name: ROUTINIZATION SCALE

Purpose: To measure routinization.

Number of Items: 3

Format: Responses are made on a 4-point scale ranging from 1 (*definitely true*) to 4 (*definitely false*).

Reliability: Alpha coefficients were .84 and .82.

Validity: Correlations with other variables ranged from -.28 to .20.

Authors: Bacharach, S., and Bamberger, P.

Article: Causal models of role stressor antecedents and consequences: The importance of occupational differences.

Journal: *Journal of Vocational Behavior*, August 1992, *41*(1), 13–34.

Related Research: Bacharach, S., & Aiken, M. (1976). Structural and process constraints on influence in organizations: A level-specific analysis. *Administrative Science Quarterly*, *21*, 623–642.

■ ■ ■

6605

Test Name: SCHOOL ORGANIZATION SCALES

Purpose: To assess sense of community, disorderly student conduct, principal leadership, staff influence, encouragement of innovation, and administrator responsiveness in schools.

Number of Items: 25

Format: Formats vary. All items are presented.

Reliability: Alphas ranged from .63 to .85 across subscales.

Authors: Lee, V. E., et al.

Article: The effect of the social organization of schools on teachers' efficacy and satisfaction.

Journal: *Sociology of Education*, July 1991, *64*(3), 190–208.

Related Research: Moles, O. (1988). *High School and Beyond*

Administrator and Teacher Survey (1984). Data file users manual. Washington, DC: Office of Educational Research and Improvement, U.S. Department of Education.

■■■

6606

Test Name: SCIENCE LABORATORY ENVIRONMENT INVENTORY

Purpose: To assess student perceptions of cohesiveness, open-endedness, integration, role clarity, and material environment in science laboratories.

Number of Items: 35

Format: 5-point frequency scales range from *almost never* to *very often.*

Reliability: Alphas ranged from .60 to .90 across subscales.

Validity: Mean correlations with other variables ranged from .11 to .45.

Authors: McRobbie, C. J., and Fraser, B. J.

Article: Associations between student outcomes and psychosocial science environment.

Journal: *Journal of Educational Research,* November/December 1993, *87*(2), 78–85.

■■■

6607

Test Name: SERVQUAL

Purpose: To measure service quality.

Number of Items: 26

Format: Contains 3 factors: Dependability/Trust, Personal Attention/Helpfulness, and Equipment/Facilities. Sample items are presented.

Reliability: Alpha coefficients for the 3 factors ranged from .66 to .88.

Validity: Correlations with other variables ranged from -.15 to .51.

Authors: Schneider, B., et al.

Article: A passion for service: Using content analysis to explicate service climate themes.

Journal: *Journal of Applied Psychology,* October 1992, *77*(5), 705–716.

Related Research: Parasurman, A., et al. (1989). SERVQUAL: A multiple item scale for measuring consumer perceptions of service quality. *Journal of Retailing, 64,* 12–40.

■■■

6608

Test Name: STORE MANAGEMENT FAIRNESS

Purpose: To measure the extent salespersons feel that they are fairly treated by store management.

Number of Items: 3

Format: Responses are made on a 7-point scale ranging from 1 (*strongly disagree*) to 7 (*strongly agree*). A sample item is presented.

Reliability: Internal consistency was .89.

Validity: Correlations with other variables ranged from .01 to .58.

Author: George, J. M.

Article: State or trait: Effects of positive mood or prosocial behaviors at work.

Journal: *Journal of Applied Psychology,* April 1991, *76*(2), 299–307.

■■■

6609

Test Name: SUBORDINATE'S CONFIDENCE IN APPRAISAL

Purpose: To assess the subordinate's confidence in the operation of the performance appraisal system.

Number of Items: 4

Format: Responses are made on a 7-point scale ranging from 1 (*disagree strongly*) to 7 (*agree strongly*). All items are presented.

Reliability: Coefficient alpha was .76.

Validity: Correlation with other variables ranged from -.01 to .61.

Authors: Fried, Y., et al.

Article: Personal and interpersonal predictors of supervisors' avoidance of evaluating subordinates.

Related Research: Pearce, J. L., & Porter, L. W. (1986). Employee responses to formal performance appraisal feedback. *Journal of Applied Psychology, 71,* 211–218.

■■■

6610

Test Name: SURVEY OF ORGANIZATIONS

Purpose: To assess the psychological climate of an organization.

Number of Items: 15

Format: 5-point scales.

Reliability: Alphas ranged from .50 to .78 across subscales. Total alpha was .84.

Validity: Correlations with other variables ranged from -.61 to .78.

Authors: Day, D. V., and Bedeian, A. G.

Article: Personality similarity and work-related outcomes among African-American nursing personnel: A test of the supplementary model of person-environment congruence.

Journal: *Journal of Vocational Behavior,* February 1995, *46*(1), 55–70.

Related Research: Taylor, J. C., & Bowers, D. G. (1972). *Survey of organizations.* Ann Arbor: Institute for Social Research, University of Michigan.

...

6611

Test Name: SURVEY OF PERCEIVED ORGANIZATIONAL SUPPORT

Purpose: To measure employee perception of the extent to which the organization values his/her contributions and well-being.

Number of Items: 16

Format: Responses are made on a 5-point Likert-type scale.

Reliability: Coefficient alpha was .95.

Validity: Correlations with other variables ranged from -.85 to .68.

Authors: Nye, L. G., and Witt, L. A.

Article: Dimensionality and construct validity of the Perceptions of Organizational Politics Scale (POPS).

Journal: *Educational and Psychological Measurement,* Autumn 1993, *53*(3), 821–829.

Related Research: Eisenberger, R., et al. (1986). Perceived organizational support. *Journal of Applied Psychology, 71,* 500–507.

...

6612

Test Name: TASK AUTONOMY SCALE

Purpose: To measure task autonomy.

Number of Items: 2

Format: Examples are presented.

Reliability: Coefficient alpha was .81.

Validity: Correlations with other variables ranged from -.56 to .40.

Authors: Mossholder, K. W., et al.

Article: Confounding constructs and levels of constructs in affectivity measurement: An empirical investigation.

Journal: *Educational and Psychological Measurement,* Summer 1994, *54*(2), 336–349.

Related Research: Cammann, C., et al. (1983). Assessing the attitudes and perceptions of organizational members. In S. E. Seashore et al. (Eds.), *Assessing organizational change* (pp. 71–138). New York: Wiley.

...

6613

Test Name: TEACHERS' PERCEIVED SCHOOL EFFECTIVENESS SCALE

Purpose: To measure teachers' perceptions of how well, how much, how flexible, and how efficiently the school functions.

Number of Items: 8

Format: Responses are made on a 5-point Likert-type scale. Examples are presented.

Reliability: Coefficient alpha was .88.

Authors: Hoy, W. K., et al.

Article: Faculty trust in colleagues: Linking the principal with school effectiveness.

Journal: *Journal of Research and Development in Education,* Fall 1992, *26*(1), 38–45.

Related Research: Hoy, W. K., & Ferguson, J. (1985). A theoretical framework and exploration of organizational effectiveness in schools. *Educational Administration Quarterly, 21,* 117–134.

6614

Test Name: TEACHING ENVIRONMENT SCALE

Purpose: To measure teaching autonomy.

Number of Items: 35

Format: Includes a 4-point Likert scale (*definitely true* to *definitely false*).

Reliability: Internal consistency coefficient was .93.

Authors: Pearson, C., and Hall, B.

Article: Initial construct validation of the Teaching Autonomy Scale.

Journal: *Journal of Educational Research,* Jan/Feb. 1993, *86*(3), 172–178.

Related Research: Hall, B., et al. (1989, February). *Perceptions of autonomy within the beginning teacher's work environment.* Paper presented at the annual meeting of the Association of Teacher Educators, St. Louis, Missouri.

...

6615

Test Name: TEAM EFFICACY SCALE

Purpose: To measure the degree to which teams are effectively used to provide for maximal efficiency.

Number of Items: 3

Format: Responses are made on a 4-point scale ranging from 1 (*definitely false*) to 4 (*definitely true*).

Reliability: Alpha coefficients were .67 and .62.

Validity: Correlations with other variables ranged from -.44 to .42.

Authors: Bacharach, S., and Bamberger, P.

Article: Causal models of role stressor antecedents and

consequences: The importance of occupational differences.

Journal: *Journal of Vocational Behavior*, August 1992, *41*(1), 13–34.

Related Research: Bacharach, S., et al. (1990). Organizational and demographic models of teacher militancy. *Industrial and Labor Relations Review, 43*, 570–586.

• • •

6616

Test Name: TRAINEE EQUITY INDEX

Purpose: To enable trainees to rate how equitably they were tested.

Number of Items: 23

Format: A 3-point scale was used to rate each outcome.

Reliability: Coefficient alpha was .82.

Author: Dvir, T., et al.

Article: Self-fulfilling prophecy and gender: Can women be Pygmalion and Galatea?

Journal: *Journal of Applied Psychology*, April 1995, *80*(2), 253–270.

Related Research: Eden, D., & Ravid, G. (1982). Pygmalion vs. self-expectancy: Effects of instructor-and self-expectancy on trainee performance. *Organizational Behavior and Human Performance, 30*, 351–364.

• • •

6617

Test Name: TRAINING CHARACTERISTICS SCALE

Purpose: To measure five dimensions of training characteristics.

Number of Items: 23

Format: Includes 5 dimensions: variety, autonomy, feedback,

dealing with others, and training challenge.

Reliability: Alpha coefficients ranged from .58 to .81.

Validity: Correlations with other variables ranged from -.61 to .64.

Author: Mathieu, J. E.

Article: A cross-level nonrecursive model of the antecedents of organizational commitment and satisfaction.

Journal: *Journal of Applied Psychology*, October 1991, *76*(5), 607–618.

Related Research: Sims, H. P., et al. (1976). The measurement of job characteristics. *Academy of Management Journal, 19*, 195–212.

Jones, A. P., & James, L. R. (1979). Psychological climate: Dimensions and relationships of individual and aggregated work environment perception. *Organizational Behavior and Human Performance, 16*, 74–113.

• • •

6618

Test Name: TREATMENT ACCEPTABILITY QUESTIONNAIRE

Purpose: To assess the acceptability of psychological treatments for adult and child populations.

Number of Items: 6

Format: Participant responds to vignettes on 7-point scales. All items and vignettes are presented.

Reliability: Alpha was .81.

Validity: Correlations with other variables ranged from -.06 to .87.

Author: Hunsley, J.

Article: Development of the Treatment Acceptability Questionnaire.

Journal: *Journal of*

Psychopathology and Behavioral Assessment, March 1992, *14*(1), 55–64.

• • •

6619

Test Name: TREATMENT EVALUATION INVENTORY

Purpose: To rate treatment as acceptable, likable, suitable, cruel, unfair, and effective.

Number of Items: 15- and 9-item versions.

Format: 7-point Likert format.

Validity: The short and long versions yield unequal evaluation scores for some types of treatment.

Authors: Spirrison, C. L., and Noland, K.

Article: The original vs. an abbreviated version of the Treatment Evaluation Inventory: Systematic measurement error.

Journal: *Psychological Reports*, December 1991, *69*(3) Part I, 763–766.

Related Research: Kazdin, A. G. (1980). Acceptability of alternative treatments for deviant child behavior. *Journal of Applied Behavior Analysis, 13*, 259–273.

Kelly, M. L., et al. (1989). Development of a modified Treatment Evaluation Inventory. *Journal of Psychopathology and Behavioral Assessment, 11*, 235–247.

• • •

6620

Test Name: UNDERSTANDING THE PAY SYSTEM SCALE

Purpose: To measure employees' perceptions of their understanding of the pay system.

Number of Items: 5

Format: Responses are made on a

7-point Likert scale ranging from *great extent* to *not at all*.

Reliability: Coefficient alpha was .91 (time 1). Coefficient alpha was .87 (time 2).

Authors: Brown, K. A., and Huber, V. L.

Article: Lowering floors and raising ceilings: A longitudinal assessment of the effects of earnings-at-risk plan on pay satisfaction.

Journal: *Personnel Psychology,* Summer 1992, *45*(2), 279–311.

Related Research: Brown, K. A., & Mitchell, T. R. (1991). Just-in-time versus batch manufacturing: The role of performance obstacles. *Academy of Management Journal, 34*, 906–917.

■ ■ ■

6621

Test Name: UNION INSTRUMENTALITY SCALE

Purpose: To measure union instrumentality.

Number of Items: 12

Format: Respondents indicate the impact that the local union has on 12 conditions of the employment relationship. Responses range from 1 (*very negative*) to 5 (*very positive*).

Reliability: Coefficient alpha was .92.

Authors: Shore, L. M., et al.

Article: Validation of a measure of perceived union support.

Journal: *Journal of Applied Psychology,* December 1994, *79*(6), 971–977.

Related Research: DeCotiis, T. A., & LeLovarn, J. (1981). A predictive study of rating behavior in a representation election using union instrumentality and work perceptions. *Organizational Behavior and Human Performance, 27*, 103–118.

Fullagar, C., & Barling, J. (1989). A longitudinal test of a model of the antecedents and consequences of union loyalty. *Journal of Applied Psychology, 74*, 213–227.

■ ■ ■

6622

Test Name: WORK CLIMATE STRUCTURE SCALE

Purpose: To assess work climate.

Number of Items: 25

Format: 5-point Likert format. Sample items are presented.

Reliability: Alphas ranged from .69 to .86 across subscales.

Authors: Lam, P., et al.

Article: Work life, career commitment, and job satisfaction as antecedents of career withdrawal cognition among teacher interns.

Journal: *Journal of Research and Development in Education,* Summer 1995, *28*(4), 230–235.

Related Research: Kyriacou, C., and Sutcliffe, J. (1978). A model of teacher stress. *Educational Studies, 4*, 1–6.

■ ■ ■

6623

Test Name: WORK SITE SMOKING BAN FAIRNESS SCALE

Purpose: To assess perceptions of fairness of a work site smoking ban policy.

Number of Items: 4

Format: Topics of the questions are presented.

Reliability: Coefficient alpha was .87.

Validity: Correlations with other variables ranged from .07 to .84 (*N* = 732).

Author: Greenberg, J.

Article: using socially fair treatment to promote acceptance of a work site smoking ban.

Journal: *Journal of Applied Psychology,* April 1994, *79*(2), 288–297.

Related Research: Greenberg, J. (1987). A taxonomy of organizational justice theories. *Academy of Management Review, 12*, 9–22.

CHAPTER 15
Motivation

6624

Test Name: ACADEMIC MOTIVATION SCALE

Purpose: To measure motivation toward education.

Number of Items: 28

Format: Responses are made on a 7-point scale ranging from 1 (*not at all*) to 7 (*exactly*). Includes 7 factors: Amotivation, External Regulation, Introjected Regulation, Identified Regulation, Intrinsic Motivation—Knowledge, Intrinsic Motivation—Accomplishment, and Intrinsic Motivation—Stimulation.

Reliability: Test–retest (1 month) reliability ranged from .71 to .83 ($N = 57$). Alpha coefficients ranged from .72 to .91.

Authors: Vallerand, R. J., et al.

Article: The Academic Motivation Scale: a measure of intrinsic, extrinsic, and amotivation in education.

Journal: *Educational and Psychological Measurement,* Winter 1992, *52*(4), 1003–1017.

Related Research: Vallerand, R. J., et al. (1989). Construction and validation of the Echelle de Motivation en Education (EME). *Canadian Journal of Behavioral Sciences, 21,* 323–349.

■ ■ ■

6625

Test Name: ACHIEVABILITY OF FUTURE GOALS SCALE

Purpose: To measure optimism regarding present behavior being organized to achieve future goals.

Number of Items: 8

Format: Items are rated on a 7-point Likert scale.

Reliability: Coefficient alphas were .69 and .71.

Authors: Savickas, M. L., and Jarjoura, D.

Article: The Career Decision Scale as a type indicator.

Journal: *Journal of Counseling Psychology,* January 1991, *38*(1), 85–90.

Related Research: Heimberg, L. (1961). *Development and construct validation of an inventory for the measurement of future time perspective.* Unpublished master's thesis, Vanderbilt University, Nashville, TN.

■ ■ ■

6626

Test Name: ACHIEVEMENT GOAL TENDENCIES QUESTIONNAIRE

Purpose: To measure achievement goal tendencies.

Number of Items: 20

Format: Responses are made on a 5-point scale ranging from 1 (*never*) to 5 (*always*). Includes 3 factors. All items are presented.

Reliability: Alpha coefficients ranged from .71 to .89.

Authors: Hayamizu, T., and Weiner, B.

Article: A test of Dweck's model of achievement goals as related to perceptions of ability.

Journal: *Journal of Experimental Education,* Spring 1991, *59*(3), 226–234.

Related Research: Hayamizu, T., et al. (1989). Cognitive motivational processes mediated by achievement goal tendencies. *Japanese Psychological Research, 31,* 179–189.

■ ■ ■

6627

Test Name: ACHIEVEMENT MOTIVATION SCALE

Purpose: To assess achievement motivation.

Number of Items: 7

Reliability: Alpha was .62.

Validity: Correlation with other variables ranged from -.56 to .62.

Author: Mathieu, J. E.

Article: A cross-level nonrecursive model of the antecedents of organizational commitment and satisfaction.

Journal: *Journal of Applied Psychology,* October 1991, *76*(5), 607–618.

Related Research: Murray, H. J. (1938). *Exploration in personality.* New York: Oxford University Press.

Steers, R M., & Braunstein, D. N. (1976). A behaviorally-based measure of manifest needs in work settings. *Journal of Vocational Behavior, 9,* 251–266.

6628

Test Name: ACHIEVEMENT MOTIVES SCALE

Purpose: To measure strength of success and failure motives.

Number of Items: 15

Format: Responses are made on a 4-point scale ranging from 4 (*is very true of me*) to 1 (*is not at all true of me*). Examples are presented.

Reliability: Alpha coefficients ranged from .60 to .88. Test–retest (6 months) reliabilities were .71 and .65.

Validity: Correlations with grades in English and mathematics ranged from -.63 to .54.

Author: Halvari, H.

Article: Maximal aerobic power as a function of achievement motives, future time orientation, and perceived intrinsic instrumentality of physical tasks for future goals among males.

Journal: *Perceptual and Motor Skills*, April 1991, *72*(2), 367–381.

Related Research: Gjesme, T. (1977). General satisfaction and boredom at school as a function of the pupil's personality characteristics. *Scandinavian Journal of Educational Research*, *21*, 113–146.

■ ■ ■

6629

Test Name: ACHIEVING TENDENCY SCALES FOR MALES AND FEMALES

Purpose: To measure achievement motivation.

Number of Items: 26

Format: 9-point agreement scales.

Validity: Correlations with other scales ranged from .24 to .94.

Author: Menchaca, V. D.

Article: Achievement motivation in Mexican-American eighth grade students.

Journal: *Psychological Reports*, June 1993, *72*(3) Part I, 971–978.

Related Research: Mehrabian, A. (1968). Male and female scales of the tendency to achieve. *Educational and Psychological Measurement, 28*, 493–502.

■ ■ ■

6630

Test Name: ACTIVITY-FEELING STATE SCALE

Purpose: To measure selected psychological needs.

Number of Items: 13

Format: Responses are made on a 7-point scale ranging from strongly disagree to strongly agree. Includes four subscales: Self-Determination, Competence, Relatedness, and Tension. An example is presented.

Reliability: Alpha coefficients ranged from .53 to .94.

Validity: Correlations with measures of intrinsic motivation ranged from -.43 to .69.

Authors: Reeve, J., and Sickenius, B.

Article: Development and validation of a brief measure of the three psychological needs underlying intrinsic motivation: The AFS Scales.

Journal: *Educational and Psychological Measurement*, Summer 1994, *54*(2), 506–515.

■ ■ ■

6631

Test Name: AFFINITY-SEEKING SCALE

Purpose: To assess affinity seeking.

Number of Items: 25

Reliability: Coefficient alpha was .89.

Validity: Correlations with communication satisfaction ranged from .35 to .47.

Author: Prisbell, M.

Article: Affinity-seeking strategies associated with students' perceptions of satisfaction with communication in the classroom.

Journal: *Perceptual and Motor Skills*, August 1994, *79*(1) Part 1, 33–34.

Related Research: McCroskey, J. C., & McCroskey, L. L. (1986). The affinity-seeking of classroom teachers. *Communication Research Reports, 3*, 158–167.

■ ■ ■

6632

Test Name: AROUSAL SEEKING TENDENCY SCALE—II

Purpose: To measure one's optimal stimulation level.

Number of Items: 32

Format: Responses are made on a 5-point rating scale ranging from -2 (*strongly disagree*) to +2 (*strongly agree*).

Reliability: Alpha coefficients were .88 and .89.

Validity: Correlations with other variables ranged from -.03 to .78.

Authors: Baumgartner, H., and Steenkamp, J.-B. E. M.

Article: An investigation into the construct validity of the Arousal Seeking Tendency Scale, Version II.

Journal: *Educational and Psychological Measurement*, Winter 1994, *54*(4), 993–1001.

Related Research: Mehrabian, A. (1978). Characteristic individual reactions to preferred and unpreferred environments.

Journal of Personality, 46,
717–731.

■ ■ ■

6633

Test Name: CHILDREN'S SPORT
GOAL ORIENTATION
INVENTORY

Purpose: To measure seven goal
orientations related to sports: skill
development, mastery
demonstration, competitive
achievement, social development,
social judgment, affiliation, and
experiential goal orientation.

Number of Items: 21

Format: 7-point importance rating
scales. All items presented.

Validity: Four oblique factors were
extracted. Correlations between
factors ranged from .25 to .57.

Authors: Lewthwaite, R., and
Piparo, A. J.

Article: Goal orientations in young
competitive athletes: Physical
achievement, social-relational, and
experiential concerns.

Journal: *Journal of Research in
Personality,* June 1993, *27*(2),
103–117.

Related Research: Dweck, C. S., &
Leggett, E. L. (1988). A social
cognitive approach to motivation
and personality. *Psychological
Review, 95,* 256–273.

■ ■ ■

6634

Test Name: DILIGENCE
INVENTORY—HIGHER
EDUCATION FORM

Purpose: To measure students'
diligence in studying.

Number of Items: 48

Format: All items are presented.

Reliability: Total reliability was
.90. Subscale reliabilities ranged
from .59 to .86.

Validity: Several known-group
difference analyses are presented.

Authors: Bernard, H., and
Schuttenberg, E. M.

Article: Development of the
Diligence Inventory—Higher
Education Form.

Journal: *Journal of Research and
Development in Education,* Winter
1995, *28*(2), 91–100.

Related Research: Bernard, H.
(1991). *Development and
application of a diligence-ability
regression model for explaining
and predicting competence among
juniors and seniors in selected
Michigan high schools.* (PhD
dissertation, Andrews University),
Ann Arbor: University Microfilms
International.

■ ■ ■

6635

Test Name: EXPECTANCY-
THEORY SCALE

Purpose: To measure training
motivation.

Number of Items: 6

Format: Responses are made on a
7-point Likert-type scale ranging
from 1 (*strongly disagree*) to 7
(*strongly agree*). An example is
presented.

Reliability: Alpha coefficients
ranged from .92 to .97.

Validity: Correlations with other
variables ranged from -.22 to .58.

Authors: Tannenbaum, S. I., et al.

Article: Meeting trainees'
expectations: The influence of
training fulfillment on the
development of commitment, self-
efficacy, and motivation.

Journal: *Journal of Applied
Psychology,* December 1991,
76(6), 759–769.

Related Research: Lawler, E. E.
(1981). *Pay and organizational*

development. Reading, MA:
Addison-Wesley.

■ ■ ■

6636

Test Name: GAMBLING
MOTIVATION SCALE

Purpose: To assess the motivation
to gamble.

Number of Items: 28

Format: 7-point Likert format.
Sample items are presented.

Reliability: Alphas ranged from .64
to .81 across subscales.

Authors: Chantal, Y., et al.

Article: Motivation and gambling
involvement.

Journal: *The Journal of Social
Psychology,* December 1995,
135(6), 755–763.

Related Research: Chantal, Y., et
al. (1994). Construction et
validatron de l'Echelle de
Motivatron Relative aux Jeux de
Hasard et d'Argent [On the
development and validation of the
Gambling Motivation Scale
(GMS)]. *Society and Leisure, 17,*
189–212.

■ ■ ■

6637

Test Name: GOAL
COMMITMENT SCALE

Purpose: To assess goal
commitment.

Number of Items: 4

Format: Responses are made on a
5-point Likert scale ranging from 5
(*strongly agree*) to 1 (*strongly
disagree*).

Reliability: Coefficient alpha
was .80.

Validity: Correlations with other
variables ranged from .05 to .35.

Authors: Barrick, M. R., et al.

Article: Conscientiousness and

performance of sales representatives: Test of the mediating effects of goal setting.

Journal: *Journal of Applied Psychology*, October 1993, *78*(5), 715–722.

Related Research: Hollenbeck, J. R., et al. (1989). Investigation of the construct validity of self-report measure of goal commitment. *Journal of Applied Psychology, 74*, 951–956.

Hollenbeck, J. R., et al. (1989). An empirical examination of the antecedents of commitment to difficult goals. *Journal of Applied Psychology, 74*, 18–23.

■ ■ ■

6638

Test Name: GOAL COMMITMENT SCALE

Purpose: To provide a self-report measure of goal commitment.

Number of Items: 9

Reliability: Internal consistency was .69

Validity: Correlations with other variables ranged from -.12 to .34.

Authors: Wright, P. M., et al.

Article: Productivity and extra-role behavior: The effects of goals and incentives on spontaneous helping.

Journal: *Journal of Applied Psychology*, June 1993, *78*(3), 374–381.

Related Research: Hollenbeck, J., et al. (1989). An empirical examination of antecedents if commitment to difficult goals. *Journal of Applied Psychology, 74*, 18–23.

■ ■ ■

6639

Test Name: GOAL INSTABILITY SCALE

Purpose: To measure lack of goal directedness and inhibition in work.

Number of Items: 10

Format: 6-point Likert format.

Reliability: Internal consistency was .76. Test–retest reliability (2 weeks) was .80.

Validity: Correlations with other variables ranged from -.42 to .40.

Authors: Multon, K. D., et al.

Article: An empirical derivation of career decision subtypes in a high school sample.

Journal: *Journal of Vocational Behavior*, August 1995, *47*(1), 76–92.

Related Research: Robbins, S. B., & Patton, M. J. (1985). Self-psychology and career development: Construction of the Superiority and Goal Instability Scales. *Journal of Counseling Psychology, 32*, 221–231.

■ ■ ■

6640

Test Name: GOAL ORIENTATION SCALE—SPORT

Purpose: To determine the students' general motivational orientation in sport.

Number of Items: 21

Format: Responses are made on a 5-point Likert-type scale ranging from 1 (*strongly agree*) to 5 (*strongly disagree*). Includes 4 factors: Ego Orientation, Task Orientation, Work Avoidance, and Cooperation. All items are presented.

Reliability: Alpha coefficients ranged from .66 to .89.

Authors: Duda, J. L., and Nicholls, J. G.

Article: Dimensions of achievement motivation in school work and sport.

Journal: *Journal of Educational Psychology*, September 1992, *84*(3), 290–299.

Related Research: Nicholls, J. G. (1989). *The competitive ethos and democratic education.* Cambridge, MA: Harvard University Press.

■ ■ ■

6641

Test Name: GOALS INVENTORY

Purpose: To measure learning and performance goal orientations.

Format: Responses are made on a 5-point Likert-type scale. Includes two factors: Learning and Performance. All items are presented.

Validation: Correlations with other variables ranged from -.36 to .52.

Authors: Roedel, T. D., et al.

Article: Validation of a measure of learning and performance goal orientations.

Journal: *Educational and Psychological Measurement*, Winter 1994, *54*(4), 1013-1021.

Related Research: Schraw, G., & Roedel, T. D. (1993, April). *Beliefs about intelligence and academic goals.* Paper presented at the annual meeting of the American Educational Research Association. Atlanta, Georgia.

■ ■ ■

6642

Test Name: HURLBERT INDEX OF SEXUAL DESIRE

Purpose: To measure sexual desire.

Number of Items: 25

Format: Responses are made on a 5-point Likert-type scale.

Reliability: Test–retest was .86.

Internal consistency alpha was .89.

Author: Beck, J. G.

Article: Hypoactive sexual desire disorder: An overview.

Journal: *Journal of Consulting and Clinical Psychology,* December 1995, *63*(6), 919–927.

Related Research: Apt, C., & Hurlbert, D. (1992). Motherhood and female sexuality beyond one year postpartum. *Journal of Sex Education and Therapy, 18,* 104–114.

* * *

6643

Test Name: IMPULSIVITY AND SENSATION SEEKING SCALES

Purpose: To measure impulsivity and sensation seeking.

Number of Items: 20

Format: 4-point response scale.

Reliability: Test–retest (6 months) was .71 (Impulsivity) and .70 (Sensation Seeking).

Validity: Correlations with Zuckerman's Sensation Seeking Scale were .60 and .42.

Authors: Lennings, C. J.

Article: The Shalling Sensation Seeking and Impulsivity Scales: Their relationship to time perspective and time awareness, a preliminary report.

Journal: *Psychological Reports,* August 1991, *69*(1), 131–136.

Related Research: Schalling, D., et al. (1983). Impulsive cognitive style and inability to tolerate boredom: Psychophysiological studies of temperamental vulnerability. In M. Zuckerman (Ed.), *Biological basis of sensation seeking, impulsivity and anxiety* (pp. 123–145). Hillsdale, NJ: Erlbaum.

6644

Test Name: INSTRUCTIONAL MATERIALS MOTIVATION SCALE

Purpose: To measure the motivational impact of instructional materials.

Number of Items: 36

Format: Uses a 4-element Likert-type scale. Items are divided into four primary dimensions of motivation: attention, relevance, confidence, and satisfaction.

Reliability: Coefficient alpha was .90.

Authors: Hirumi, A., and Bowers, D.

Article: Enhancing motivation and acquisition of coordinate concepts by using concept trees.

Journal: *Journal of Educational Research,* May/June 1991, *84*(5), 273–279.

Related Research: Keller, J. M. (1988). *Development of Instructional Materials Motivation Checklist (IMMC) and Survey (IMMS).* Tallahassee: The Florida State University, Department of Educational Research.

* * *

6645

Test Name: INTENTIONS TO SEEK COUNSELING INVENTORY

Purpose: To assess intentions to seek counseling.

Number of Items: 17

Format: 6-point scales range from 1 (*very unlikely*) to 6 (*very likely*).

Reliability: Alpha was .84.

Author: Kelly, A. E., and Achter, J. A.

Article: Self-concealment and attitudes toward counseling in university students.

Journal: *Journal of Counseling Psychology,* January 1995, *42*(1), 40–46.

Related Research: Cash, T. F., et al. (1975). When counselors are heard but not seen: Initial impact of physical attractiveness. *Journal of Counseling Psychology, 22,* 273–279.

* * *

6646

Test Name: INTERNAL WORK MOTIVATION SCALE

Purpose: To measure internal work motivation.

Number of Items: 3

Format: Examples are presented.

Reliability: Coefficient alpha was .68.

Validity: Correlations with other variables ranged from -.14 to .22.

Authors: Mossholder, K. W., et al.

Article: Confounding constructs and levels of constructs in affectivity measurement: An empirical investigation.

Journal: *Educational and Psychological Measurement,* Summer 1994, *54*(2), 336–349.

Related Research: Cammann, C., et al. (1983). Assessing the attitudes and perceptions of organizational members. In S. E. Seashore et al. (Eds.), *Assessing organizational change* (pp. 71–138). New York: Wiley.

* * *

6647

Test Name: JOB DESIRABILITY EXERCISE

Purpose: To measure the need for socialized power.

Number of Items: 27

Format: Each item is a different hypothetical job whose desirability is rated on an 11-point Likert-type scale ranging from -5 (*very undesirable*) to +5 (*very desirable*).

Reliability: Test–retest correlation was .75 (*N* = 246).

Validity: Correlations with other variables ranged from -.18 to .19.

Authors: Butler, J. K., Jr., and Stahl, M. J.

Article: Validation of the Job Desirability Exercise: A decision modeling experiment for measuring the need for socialized power.

Journal: *Educational and Psychological Measurement,* Winter 1993, *53*(4), 983–992.

■ ■ ■

6648

Test Name: LEARNING ATTITUDES SCALE

Purpose: To assess motivation to learn and to transfer, and to evaluate development experiences.

Number of Items: 37

Format: Responses are made on a 5-point scale ranging from 1 (*strongly disagree*) to 5 (*strongly agree*). Examples are presented.

Reliability: Internal consistency ranged from .68 to .82.

Authors: Noe, R. A., and Wilk, S. L.

Article: Investigation of the factors that influence employees' participation in development activities.

Journal: *Journal of Applied Psychology,* April 1993, *78*(2), 291–302.

Related Research: Noe, R. A., & Schmitt, N. (1986). The influence of trainee attitudes on training effectiveness: Test of a model. *Personnel Psychology, 39,* 497–523.

6649

Test Name: LIFESTYLES APPROACHES INDEX

Purpose: To measure performance focus, efficiency, goal directedness, and timeliness of task completion.

Number of Items: 16

Reliability: Total alpha was .81. Alphas ranged from .64 to .71 across subscales. Test–retest reliabilities ranged from .65 to .89.

Validity: Correlations with MBTI indexes ranged from -.42 to .08.

Authors: Williams, R. L., et al.

Article: Relationship of self-management to personality types and indices.

Journal: *Journal of Personality Assessment,* June 1995, *64*(3), 494–506.

Related Research: Williams, R. L., et al. (1992). Construction and validation of a brief self-report scale of self-management practices. *Journal of Research in Personality, 26,* 216–234.

■ ■ ■

6650

Test Name: LOGO II

Purpose: To assess students' motivation for grades and learning.

Number of Items: 32

Format: Includes two scales assessing high learning-oriented attitudes or behavior and two scales assessing high grade-oriented attitudes or behavior.

Reliability: Alpha coefficients ranged from .52 to .77.

Validity: Correlations with other variables ranged from -.20 to .37.

Authors: Stark, J. S., et al.

Article: The student goals

exploration: Reliability and concurrent validity.

Journal: *Educational and Psychological Measurement,* Summer 1991, *51*(2), 413–422.

Related Research: Eison, J. (1981). A new instrument for assessing students' orientations toward grades and learning. *Psychological Reports, 48,* 919–924.

■ ■ ■

6651

Test Name: LONG-TERM PERSONAL DIRECTION SCALE

Purpose: To assess time perspective.

Number of Items: 20

Format: Items are rated on a 7-point Likert scale.

Reliability: Coefficient alphas were .87 and .84.

Authors: Savickas, M. L., and Jarjoura, D.

Article: The Career Decision Scale as a type indicator.

Journal: *Journal of Counseling Psychology,* January 1991, *38*(1), 85–90.

Related Research: Wessman, A. E. (1973). Personality and the subjective experience of time. *Personality Assessment, 7,* 89–97.

■ ■ ■

6652

Test Name: mAch nAff SCALE

Purpose: To measure the strength of women's achievement and affiliation needs.

Number of Items: 30

Format: Items consist of bipolar adjectives.

Reliability: Split-half reliability

was .80. Test–retest reliability was .88.

Author: Harris, S. M., et al.

Article: Relationships between achievement and affiliation needs and sex-role orientation of college women whose fathers were absent from home.

Journal: *Perceptual and Motor Skills*, June 1991, *72*(3) Part 2, 1307–1315.

Related Research: Lindgren, H. C. (1976). Measuring need to achieve by mAch-nAff Scale—A forced-choice questionnaire. *Psychological Reports, 39,* 907–910.

■ ■ ■

6653

Test Name: MANIFEST NEEDS QUESTIONNAIRE

Purpose: To measure protégés' and nonprotégés' needs.

Number of Items: 20

Format: Includes 4 needs: Power, Achievement, Autonomy, and Affiliation. Responses are made on a 7-point scale ranging from 1 (*never*) to 7 (*always*). Examples are presented.

Reliability: Reliability ranged from .20 to .84.

Author: Fagenson, E. A.

Article: Mentoring—Who needs it? A comparison of proteges' and nonproteges' needs for power, achievement, affiliation, and autonomy.

Journal: *Journal of Vocational Behavior*, August 1992, *41*(1), 48–60.

Related Research: Steers, R., & Braunstein, D. N. (1976). A behaviorally-based measure of manifest needs in work settings. *Journal of Vocational Behavior, 9,* 251–266.

6654

Test Name: MOTIVATION ASSESSMENT SCALE

Purpose: To assess the motivators of maladaptive behavior in persons with mental retardation.

Number of Items: 16

Format: Observer rates a client on 7-point frequency scales. All items presented.

Reliability: Alphas ranged from .69 to .81 across subscales.

Authors: Bihm, E. M., et al.

Article: Factor structure of the Motivation Assessment Scale for Persons with Mental Retardation.

Journal: *Psychological Reports,* June 1991, *68*(3) Part II, 1235–1238.

Related Research: Durand, V. M., & Crimmons, D. B. (1988) Identifying variables maintaining self-injurious behavior. *Journal of Autism and Developmental Disorders, 18,* 99–117.

■ ■ ■

6655

Test Name: MOTIVATION TO LEARN SCALE

Purpose: To assess participants' motivation to learn training program material.

Number of Items: 10

Format: Responses are made on a 5-point Likert scale ranging from 1 (*strongly disagree*) to 5 (*strongly agree*).

Reliability: Coefficient alpha was .93.

Validity: Correlations with other variables ranged from -.29 to .56.

Author: Quiñones, M. A.

Article: Pretraining context effects: Training assignment as feedback.

Journal: *Journal of Applied*

Psychology, April 1995, *80*(2), 226–238.

Related Research: Noe, R. A., & Schmitt, N. (1986). The influence of trainee attitudes on training effectiveness: Test of a model. *Personnel Psychology, 44,* 51–65.

■ ■ ■

6656

Test Name: NEED FOR ACHIEVEMENT SCALE

Purpose: To measure need for achievement.

Number of Items: 4

Format: Includes 2 factors: Self-Esteem and Personal Efficacy. All items are presented.

Reliability: Coefficient alpha was .46 ($N = 411$).

Validity: Correlations with other variables ranged from .31 to .43 ($N = 411$).

Author: Ward, E. A.

Article: Construct validity of need for achievement and locus of control scales.

Journal: *Educational and Psychological Measurement,* Winter 1994, *54*(4), 983–992.

Related Research: Faver, C. A. (1982). Achievement orientation, attainment values, and women's employment. *Journal of Vocational Behavior, 20,* 67–80.

■ ■ ■

6657

Test Name: NEED FOR ACHIEVEMENT SCALE

Purpose: To measure need for achievement.

Number of Items: 5

Format: Responses are made on a 5-point scale.

Reliability: Coefficient alpha was .56.

Validity: Correlations with other variables ranged from -.14 to .38.

Authors: Turban, D. B., and Keon, T. L.

Article: Organizational attractiveness: An interactionist perspective.

Journal: *Journal of Applied Psychology*, April 1993, *78*(2), 184–193.

Related Research: Steers, R. M., & Braunstein, D. N. (1976). A behaviorally based measure of manifest needs in work settings. *Journal of Vocational Behavior, 9,* 251–266.

■ ■ ■

6658

Test Name: NEED FOR ACHIEVEMENT SCALE

Purpose: To measure need for achievement.

Number of Items: 14

Format: Includes 3 factors: Planning, Interpersonal Standards, and Effort. All items are presented.

Reliability: Coefficient alpha was .55 (*N* = 411).

Validity: Correlations with other variables ranged from .17 to .39 (*N* = 411).

Author: Ward, E. A.

Article: Construct validity of need for achievement and locus of control scales.

Journal: *Educational and Psychological Measurement,* Winter 1994, *54*(4), 983–992.

Related Research: Ray, J. J. (1979). A quick measure of achievement motivation. Validated in Australia and reliable in Britain and South Africa.

Australian Psychologist, 14, 337–344.

■ ■ ■

6659

Test Name: NONSEXUAL EXPERIENCE SENSATION SEEKING SCALE REVISED

Purpose: To measure sensation seeking.

Number of Items: 11

Format: 4-point rating scales. All items are presented.

Reliability: Item-total correlations ranged from .28 to .70. Alpha was .81.

Validity: Correlations with other variables ranged from -.25 to .57.

Authors: Kalichman, S. C., and Rompa, D.

Article: Sexual Sensation Seeking and Sexual Compulsivity Scales: Reliability, validity, and predicting HIV risk behavior.

Journal: *Journal of Personality Assessment,* December 1995, *65*(3), 586–601.

■ ■ ■

6660

Test Name: NOVELTY EXPERIENCING SCALE

Purpose: To measuring one's optimal stimulation level.

Number of Items: 80

Format: Includes 4 subscales: External Sensation, External Cognition, Internal Cognition, and Internal Sensation.

Reliability: Ranged from .85 to .89.

Validity: Correlations with other variables ranged from .06 to .51.

Authors: Baumgartner, H., and Steenkamp, J.-B. E. M.

Article: An investigation into the conduct validity of the Arousal

Seeking Tendency Scale, Version II.

Journal: *Educational and Psychological Measurement,* Winter 1994, *54*(4), 993–1001.

■ ■ ■

6661

Test Name: PARTICIPATION MOTIVATION QUESTIONNAIRE

Purpose: To assess a student's motivation to participate in the single physical activity they do most often.

Number of Items: 30

Format: 5-point Likert format (1–*not at all important* to 5–*very important*). All items are presented.

Reliability: Alphas ranged from .67 to .94 across scales and subsamples.

Validity: Correlations between subscales ranged from .02 to .49.

Author: Dwyer, J. J. M.

Article: Internal structure of Participation Motivation Questionnaire completed by undergraduates.

Journal: *Psychological Reports,* February 1992, *70*(1), 283–290.

Related Research: Gill, D. L., et al. (1983). Motives for participating in competitive youth swimming. *International Journal of Sport Psychology, 16,* 126–140.

■ ■ ■

6662

Test Name: PAY VALANCE SCALE

Purpose: To assess to what extent pay satisfies Maslow's needs.

Number of Items: 15

Format: Likert format.

Reliability: Total alpha was .80.

Alphas ranged from .69 to .75 across subscales.

Validity: Correlations with age ranged from -.21 to .13.

Authors: Fox, J. B., et al.

Article: Age and pay valance in a production field setting.

Journal: *The Journal of Social Psychology*, February 1994, *133*(1), 79–88.

⋯

6663

Test Name: PERSISTENCE SCALE FOR CHILDREN

Purpose: To measure how firm and steadfast children are in a purpose or task.

Number of Items: 40

Format: True–false format. A sample item is presented.

Reliability: Internal reliability was .66. Test–retest (6 months) was .77.

Validity: Correlations with other constructs ranged from -.42 to .58 (*p* < .01).

Authors: McGiboney, G. W., and Carter, C.

Article: Measuring persistence and personality characteristics of adolescents.

Journal: *Psychological Reports*, February 1993, *72*(1), 128–130.

Related Research: Lufti, D., & Cohen, A. (1987). A scale for measuring persistence in children. *Journal of Personality Assessment, 51*(2), 178–185.

⋯

6664

Test Name: PERSONAL INCENTIVES FOR EXERCISE QUESTIONNAIRE

Purpose: To measure incentives for exercise.

Number of Items: 48

Format: Responses are made on a Likert-type scale ranging from 1 (*strongly disagree*) to 5 (*strongly agree*). Examples are given.

Reliability: Alpha coefficients ranged form .74 to .94 (*N* = 135).

Authors: Finkenberg, M. E., et al.

Article: Analysis of course type, gender, and personal incentives to exercise.

Journal: *Perceptual and Motor Skills*, February 1994, *78*(1), 155-159.

Related Research: Duda, J. L., & Tappe, M. K. (1989). The Personal Incentives for Exercise Questionnaire: Preliminary development. *Perceptual and Motor Skills, 68*, 1122.

⋯

6665

Test Name: POWER SOURCE SCALES

Purpose: To measure power sources including reward, coercive, referent, legitimate, and expert.

Number of Items: 25

Format: 5-point Likert format.

Reliability: Alphas ranged from .62 to .83 across subscales.

Author: Zemanek, J. E., Jr.

Article: How salespersons' use of a power base can affect customers' satisfaction in a social system: An empirical examination.

Journal: *Psychological Reports*, February 1995, *76*(1), 211–217.

Related Research: Gaski, J. F. (1986). Interrelations among a channel entity's power sources: Impact of the exercise of reward and coercion on expert, referent, and legitimate power sources. *Journal of Marketing Research, 23*, 62–77.

6666

Test Name: PROBLEM-SOLVING SELF-EFFICACY SCALE

Purpose: To measure confidence and perseverance when solving problems.

Number of Items: 40

Format: 4-point scales. All items are presented.

Reliability: Alpha was .93.

Validity: Correlations with Career Decision-Making Self-Efficacy Scale was .51.

Author: Erford, B. T.

Article: Parent autonomy-enhancement and development of self-efficacy.

Journal: *Psychological Reports*, December 1995, *77*(3) Part II, 1347–1353.

Related Research: Scherer, M., et al. (1982). The Self-Efficacy Scale: Construction and validation. *Psychological Reports, 51*, 663–671.

⋯

6667

Test Name: REASONS FOR EXERCISE INVENTORY

Purpose: To determine reasons for exercise.

Number of Items: 25

Format: Includes 4 factors: Fitness/Health Management, Appearance/Weight Management, Stress/Mood Management, and Socializing. All items are presented.

Reliability: Alpha coefficients ranged form .67 to .81.

Authors: Cash, T. F., et al.

Article: Why do women exercise? Factor analysis and further validation of the Reasons for Exercise Inventory.

Journal: *Perceptual and Motor Skills,* April 1994, *78*(2), 539–544.

Related Research: Silberstein, L. R., et al. (1988). Behavioral and psychological implications of body dissatisfaction: Do men and women differ? *Sex Roles, 19,* 219–232.

■ ■ ■

6668

Test Name: SALESPEOPLE MOTIVATION SCALE

Purpose: To measure to what extent salespeople work harder or smarter.

Number of Items: 8

Format: 9-point scales.

Reliability: Alphas ranged from .57 to .89 across subscales and among salespersons and sales supervisors.

Authors: Harmon, H. A., et al.

Article: Replication of Sujan's attributional analysis of salespeople's motivation to work smarter versus harder.

Journal: *Psychological Reports,* October 1995, *75*(2), 987–992.

Related Research: Sujan, H. (1986). Smarter versus harder: An exploratory attributional analysis of salespeople's motivation. *Journal of Marketing Research, 23,* 41–49.

■ ■ ■

6669

Test Name: SCHOOL MOTIVATION SCALE

Purpose: To measure a global set of beliefs and feelings that being in school is satisfying, worthwhile, and important.

Number of Items: 4

Format: Responses are made on a 5-point Likert-type scale ranging

from 1 (*not at all true*) to 5 (*completely true*).

Reliability: Internal consistency was .61.

Validity: Correlations with other variables ranged from .21 to .46.

Authors: Goodenow, C., and Grady, K. E.

Article: The relationship of school belonging and friends' values to academic motivation among urban adolescent students.

Journal: *Journal of Experimental Education,* Fall 1993, *62*(1), 60–71.

Related Research: Ford, M., & Tisak, M. (1982, April). *Evaluation of an educational intervention to enhance social-cognitive skills.* Paper presented at the annual meeting of the American Educational Research Association, New York.

■ ■ ■

6670

Test Name: SELF-MOTIVATION INVENTORY

Purpose: To measure general goal-striving persistence and willpower.

Number of Items: 40

Format: 5-point response alternatives.

Reliability: Repeated measure correlations ranged from .86 to .92 over 1 to 5 months.

Authors: Welsh, M. C., et al.

Article: Cognitive strategies and personality variables in adherence to exercise.

Journal: *Psychological Reports,* June 1991, *68*(3) Part II, 1327–1335.

Related Research: Dishman, R. K., & Ickes, W. (1981). Self-motivation and adherence to therapeutic exercise. *Journal of Behavioral Medicine, 4,* 421–438.

6671

Test Name: SENSATION-SEEKING SCALE

Purpose: To assess the desire to engage in risky behavior, to pursue new sensations, to nonconform.

Number of Items: 40

Format: Forced-choice format.

Reliability: Test–retest was .94 (total) and no coefficients were lower than .83 across subscales.

Validity: Correlations between subscales ranged from .21 to .47. Correlations with Strong's Adventure Scale ranged from .32 to .65.

Author: Cronin, C.

Article: Construct validation of the Strong Interest Inventory Adventure Scale using the Sensation Seeking Scale among female college students.

Journal: *Measurement and Evaluation in Counseling and Development,* April 1995, *28*(1), 3–8.

Related Research: Zuckerman, M. (1979). *Sensation seeking: Beyond the optimal level of arousal.* Hillsdale, NJ: Erlbaum.

■ ■ ■

6672

Test Name: SENSATION SEEKING SCALE FOR CHILDREN

Purpose: To assess sensation seeking in children.

Number of Items: 26

Format: All items are presented.

Reliability: Test–retest reliabilities ranged from .14 to .59 across samples. Spearman-Brown reliabilities ranged from .63 to .85. Alphas ranged from .67 to .83.

Validity: Correlations with demographic variables ranged from -.02 to .33. Group difference data are presented.

Authors: Russo, M. F., et al.

Article: A Sensation Seeking Scale for Children: Further refinement and psychometric development.

Journal: *Journal of Psychopathology and Behavioral Assessment,* June 1993, *15*(2), 69–86.

Related Research: Russo, M. F., et al. (1991). Preliminary development of a sensation seeking scale for children. *Personality and Individual Differences, 12,* 399–405.

• • •

6673

Test Name: SENSATION SEEKING SCALE—FORM V

Purpose: To measure one's optimal stimulation level.

Number of Items: 40

Format: Includes 4 subscales: Thrill and Adventure Seeking, Experience Seeking, Disinhibition, and Boredom Susceptibility.

Reliability: Ranged from .51 to .80.

Authors: Baumgartner, H., and Steenkamp, J.-B. E. M.

Article: An investigation into the construct validity of the Arousal Seeking Tendency Scale, Version II.

Journal: *Educational and Psychological Measurement,* Winter 1994, *54*(4), 993–1001.

Related Research: Zuckerman, M. (1979). *Sensation seeking: Beyond the optimal level of arousal.* Hillsdale, NJ: Erlbaum.

• • •

6674

Test Name: SEXUAL INTENTIONS SCALE

Purpose: To assess intention to become sexually involved.

Number of Items: 4

Format: 5-point rating scales. All items presented.

Reliability: Alpha was .74.

Authors: East, P. L., et al.

Article: Sisters' and girlfriends' sexual and childbearing behavior: Effects on early adolescent girls' sexual outcomes.

Journal: *Journal of Marriage and the Family,* November 1993, *55*(4), 953–963.

Related Research: Olsen, J., et al. (1992). The effects of abstinence sex education programs on virgin versus nonvirgin students. *Journal of Research and Development in Education, 25,* 69–75.

• • •

6675

Test Name: SEXUAL SENSATION-SEEKING SCALE

Purpose: To measure (a) sensation seeking related to sexual and nonsexual experiences and (b) sexual compulsivity.

Number of Items: 10

Format: 4-point scales. All items are presented.

Reliability: Alphas ranged from .75 to .89. Item-total correlations ranged from .29 to .77.

Validity: Correlations with other variables ranged from -.42 to .68.

Authors: Kalichman, S. C., et al.

Article: Sexual sensation seeking: Scale development and predicting AIDS-risk behavior among homosexually active men.

Journal: *Journal of Personality Assessment,* June 1994, *62*(3), 385–397.

Related Research: Kalichman, S.

C., & Rompa, D. (1995). Sexual Sensation Seeking and Sexual Compulsivity Scales: Reliability, validity, and predicting HIV-risk behavior. *Journal of Personality Assessment, 65,* 586–601.

• • •

6676

Test Name: SEXUAL SENSATION SEEKING SCALE REVISED

Purpose: To measure sexual sensation seeking.

Number of Items: 11

Format: 4-point rating scales. All items are presented.

Reliability: Item-total correlations ranged from .22 to .67. Alpha was .79.

Validity: Correlations with other variables ranged from -.34 to .70.

Authors: Kalichman, S. C., and Rompa, D.

Article: Sexual Sensation Seeking and Sexual Compulsivity Scales: Reliability, validity and predicting HIV risk behavior.

Journal: *Journal of Personality Assessment,* December 1995, *65*(3), 586–601.

• • •

6677

Test Name: STRENGTH OF WILL SCALE

Purpose: To assess a person's determination to reach a goal.

Number of Items: 6

Format: 6-point scales. A sample item is presented.

Reliability: Test–retest reliability was .75.

Authors: Gold, B. T., and Ziegler, M.

Article: Measuring environmental/ biological attribution: A fundamental dimension.

Journal: *The Journal of Social Psychology,* December 1994, *133*(6), 837–845.

Related Research: Wrightsman, L. S. (1974). *Assumptions about human nature: A social psychological analysis.* Monterey, CA: Brooks/Cole.

■ ■ ■

6678

Test Name: STUDENT LEARNING AND MOTIVATION SCALES

Purpose: To assess student involvement, affiliation, satisfaction, parent involvement, academic self-esteem, and achievement motivation.

Number of Items: 24

Format: 4-point rating scales range from *not at all true* to *very true.*

Reliability: Alphas ranged from .55 to .83 across subscales.

Validity: Correlations between scales ranged from .14 to .63.

Authors: Huang, S.-Y. L., and Waxman, H. C.

Article: Motivation and learning-environment differences between Asian-American and White middle school students in mathematics.

Journal: *Journal of Research and Development in Education,* Summer 1995, *28*(4), 208–219.

Related Research: Uguroglu, M. E., & Walberg, H. J. (1986). Predicting achievement and motivation. *Journal of Research and Development in Education, 19,* 1–12.

Fraser, B. J. (1986). *Classroom environments.* London: Croom Helm.

Waxman, H. C., et al. (1992). Investigating the effects of the classroom learning environment on the academic achievement of at-risk students. In H. C. Waxman & C. D. Ellett (Eds.), *The study of learning environment,* Vol. 5, (pp. 92–100). Houston, TX: University of Houston.

CHAPTER 16
Perception

6679

Test Name: ACADEMIC SELF-CONCEPT SCALE

Purpose: To assess self-concept for academic events.

Number of Items: 10

Format: Each school task is rated on a 10-point scale ranging from 1 (*completely incompetent*) to 10 (*completely competent*). Examples are given.

Reliability: Guttman lower bound reliability was .86.

Authors: Howard-Rose, D., and Winne, P. H.

Article: Measuring component and sets of cognitive processes in self-regulated learning.

Journal: *Journal of Educational Psychology*, December 1993, *85*(4), 591–604.

Related Research: Howard, D. C. (1989). *Variations in cognitive engagement as indicators of self-regulated learning.* Unpublished doctoral dissertation, Simon Fraser University, Burnaby, British Columbia, Canada.

■ ■ ■

6680

Test Name: ACADEMIC SELF CONCEPT SCALE

Purpose: To assess academic self-concept.

Number of Items: 40

Format: Responses are made on a Likert scale.

Reliability: Alpha coefficients were .91 and .92. Test–retest reliability was .88.

Validity: Correlations with other variables ranged from -.21 to .45.

Author: Lyon, M. A.

Article: Academic self-concept and its relationship to achievement in a sample of junior high school students.

Journal: *Educational and Psychological Measurement*, Spring 1993, *53*(1), 201–210.

Related Research: Reynolds, W. M. (1982, March). *Noncognitive correlates of achievement: An examination of academic self-concept.* Paper presented at the annual meeting of the American Educational Research Association, New York.

■ ■ ■

6681

Test Name: ACADEMIC SELF-EFFICACY SCALE

Purpose: To assess academic self-efficacy.

Number of Items: 8

Format: An example is presented.

Reliability: Coefficient alpha was .87.

Validity: Correlations with other variables ranged from -.04 to .25.

Authors: Tannenbaum, S. I., et al.

Article: Meeting trainees' expectations: The influence of training fulfillment on the development of commitment, self-efficacy, and motivation.

Journal: *Journal of Applied Psychology*, December 1991, *76*(6), 759–769.

Related Research: McIntire, S. M., & Levine, E. L. (1984). Task specific self-esteem: An empirical investigation. *Journal of Vocational Behavior*, *25*, 290–303.

■ ■ ■

6682

Test Name: ACADEMIC SELF-EFFICACY SCALE

Purpose: To measure specific academic self-efficacy components.

Number of Items: 29

Format: Includes the following components: Memorization, Class Concentration, Understanding, Explaining Concepts, Discriminating Concepts, and Notetaking.

Reliability: Alpha coefficients ranged from .73 to .87.

Author: Mone, M. A.

Article: Comparative validity of two measures of self-efficacy in predicting academic goals and performance.

Journal: *Educational and Psychological Measurement*, Summer 1994, *54*(2), 516–529.

Related Research: Wood, R. E., & Locke, E. A. (1987). The relation of self-efficacy and grade goals to academic performance. *Educational and Psychological Measurement*, *47*, 1013–1024.

■ ■ ■

6683

Test Name: ACCEPTING THE PAST AND REMINISCING ABOUT THE PAST SCALES

Purpose: To measure how

individuals evaluate and reflect on the past.

Number of Items: 27

Format: All items are presented.

Reliability: Alphas were greater than .70 for accepting and reminiscing. Item-total correlations ranged from -.67 to .63 (none were less than .29 in absolute value).

Validity: Correlations with other variables ranged from -.53 to .71.

Authors: Santor, D. M., and Zuroff, D. C.

Article: Depressive symptoms: Effects of negative affectivity and failing to accept the past.

Journal: *Journal of Personality Assessment*, October 1994, *63*(2), 294–312.

■ ■ ■

6684

Test Name: ACCIDENT LOCUS OF CONTROL SCALE

Purpose: To measure both internal and external locus of control.

Number of Items: 12

Format: Half of the items measure internal locus of control. The other half measure external locus of control.

Reliability: Alpha coefficients were .80 (external locus of control) and .61 (internal locus of control), and .66 (for total).

Authors: Salminen, S., and Klen, T.

Article: Accident locus of control and risk taking among forestry and construction workers.

Journal: *Perceptual and Motor Skills*, June 1994, *78*(3) Part 1, 852–834.

Related Research: Klen, T. (1992). *Tapaturmariskin arviointi, riskinottotaipumus, persoonallisius ja tyotapaturmat*

metsureilla [The assessment of accident risk, the risk taking tendency, personality, and occupational accidents of forestry workers]. Unpublished licenciate thesis, University of Helsinki, Department of Psychology.

■ ■ ■

6685

Test Name: ADULT NOWICKI-STRICKLAND INTERNAL–EXTERNAL SCALE

Purpose: To measure locus of control.

Number of Items: 40

Format: A yes–no format is used.

Reliability: Split-half reliabilities ranged from .74 to .86. Test–retest reliabilities ranged from .63 to .76.

Author: Wehmeyer, M. L.

Article: Gender differences in locus of control scores for students with learning disabilities.

Journal: *Perceptual and Motor Skills*, October 1993, *77*(2), 359–366.

Related Research: Nowicki, S., & Duke, M. P. (1974). A locus of control scale for non–college as well as college adults. *Journal of Personality Assessment*, *38*, 136–137.

■ ■ ■

6686

Test Name: ADULT SELF-PERCEPTION PROFILE

Purpose: To measure perceived self-esteem.

Number of Items: 50

Reliability: Alpha exceeds .80 on all subscales.

Validity: Correlations with other variables ranged from -.61 to -.06.

Authors: Brems, C., and Lloyd, P.

Article: Validation of the MMPI-2 Low Self-Esteem Content Scale.

Journal: *Journal of Personality Assessment*, December 1995, *65*(3), 550–556.

Related Research: Harter, S. (1986). *Manual for the Adult Self-Perception Profile*. Denver, CO: University of Denver.

■ ■ ■

6687

Test Name: ADULT SOURCES OF SELF-ESTEEM INVENTORY

Purpose: To measure self-esteem.

Number of Items: 20

Format: 10-point rating scales. All items are presented.

Validity: Correlations between male and female rankings of importance and satisfaction ratings were .93 and .97, respectively.

Authors: Watkins, D., and Yu, J.

Article: Gender differences in the source and level of self-esteem of Chinese college students.

Journal: *The Journal of Social Psychology*, June 1993, *133*(3), 347–352.

Related Research: Elovson, A., & Flemming, J. (1989). *Rationale for multidimensional self-esteem scale scoring and weighting*. Unpublished manuscript, California State University.

■ ■ ■

6688

Test Name: AFRICAN SELF-CONSCIOUSNESS SCALE

Purpose: To assess level of African self-consciousness.

Number of Items: 42

Format: Responses are made on an 8-point scale from *strongly disagree* to *strongly agree*.

Reliability: Test–retest (6 weeks) reliability coefficient was .90 (*N*= 109).

Validity: Correlations were .68 and .70 with other variables.

Authors: Sabnani, H. B., and Ponterotto, J. G.

Article: Racial/ethnic minority-specific instrumentation in counseling research: A review, critique, and recommendations.

Journal: *Measurement and Evaluation in Counseling and Development*, January 1992, *24*(4), 161–187.

Related Research: Baldwin, J. A., & Bell, Y. R. (1985). The African Self-Consciousness Scale: An Africentric personality questionnaire. *The Western Journal of Black Studies*, *9*, 61–68.

• • •

6689

Test Name: AIDS ATTRIBUTION SCALE

Purpose: To measure blame imputed to AIDS patients for their disease.

Number of Items: 7

Format: Likert format (respondents react to vignettes).

Reliability: Cronbach's alpha was .70

Authors: Dowell, K. A., et al.

Article: When are AIDS patients to blame for their disease? Effects of patients sexual orientation and mode of transmission.

Journal: *Psychological Reports*, August 1991, *69*(1), 211–219.

Related Research: Kelly, J., et al. (1987). Medical students' attitudes toward AIDS and homosexual patients. *Journal of School Health*, *62*, 549–556.

6690

Test Name: ALCOHOL EXPECTANCIES FOR SOCIAL EVALUATIVE SITUATIONS

Purpose: To assess positive outcomes of alcohol in social contexts.

Number of Items: 10

Format: 5-point rating scales. Sample items presented.

Reliability: Alphas ranged from .84 to .89.

Validity: Correlations with the Alcohol Expectancy Questionnaire ranged from .79 to .86.

Authors: Bruch, M. A., et al.

Article: Shyness, alcohol expectancies, and alcohol use: Discovery of a suppressor effect.

Journal: *Journal of Research in Personality*, June 1992, *26*(2), 137–149.

Related Research: Brown, S. A., et al. (1980). Expectancies of reinforcement from alcohol: Their domain and relationship to drinking patterns. *Journal of Consulting and Clinical Psychology*, *48*, 419–426.

• • •

6691

Test Name: ALCOHOL EXPECTANCY QUESTIONNAIRE

Purpose: To measure positive expectancies associated with alcohol use.

Number of Items: 90

Format: Responses are made on a 5-point Likert scale (*strongly disagree* to *strongly agree*).

Reliability: Test–retest reliability was .64 for the entire instrument. Coefficient alphas ranged from .72 to .92.

Authors: Martin, C. M., and Hoffman, M. A.

Article: Alcohol expectancies, living environment, peer influence, and gender: A model of college-student drinking.

Journal: *Journal of College Student Development*, May 1993, *34*(3), 206–211.

Related Research: Brown, S. A., et al. (1980). Expectations of reinforcement from alcohol: Their domain and relation to drinking patterns. *Journal of Consulting and Clinical Psychology*, *48*, 419–426.

• • •

6692

Test Name: ALCOHOL EXPECTANCY QUESTIONNAIRE—REVISED

Purpose: To measure perceptions about the effects of drinking alcohol.

Number of Items: 120

Format: Responses are made using a forced item choice format (agree–disagree).

Reliability: Internal consistency coefficients ranged from .72 to .92. Test–retest reliability was .64.

Authors: Reese, F. L., and Friend, R.

Article: Alcohol expectancies and drinking practices among Black and White undergraduate males.

Journal: *Journal of College Student Development*, September 1994, *35*(5), 319–323.

Related Research: Brown, S. A., et al. (1987). The Alcohol Expectancy Questionnaire: An instrument for the assessment of adolescent and adult expectancies. *Journal of Studies on Alcohol*, *48*, 419–426.

• • •

6693

Test Name: ANS-IE

Purpose: To measure locus of control.

Number of Items: 40

Format: This instrument is the adult version of the Nowicki-Strickland Internal-External Scale. There are 6 factors for females and 8 factors for males.

Validity: Correlations with other variables ranged from -.17 to -.23.

Author: Wehmeyer, M. L.

Article: Factor structure and construct validity of a locus of control scale with individuals with mental retardation.

Journal: *Educational and Psychological Measurement*, Winter 1993, *53*(4), 1055–1066.

Related Research: Nowicki, S., & Duke, M. P. (1974). A locus of control scale for noncollege as well as college adults. *Journal of Personality Assessment, 38,* 136–137.

■ ■ ■

6694

Test Name: ANTICIPATED SHIFT IN SELF-EVALUATION SCALE

Purpose: To measure anticipated shifts in self-evaluation following a scenario.

Format: 7-point scales range from -3 (*definitely lessen*) to +3 (*definitely enhance*). Sample items are described.

Reliability: Alphas ranged from .75 to .82.

Authors: Stake, J. E., et al.

Article: Trait self-esteem, positive and negative events, and event-specific shifts in self-evaluation and affect.

Journal: *Journal of Research in Personality*, June 1995, *29*(2), 223–241.

Related Research: Stake, J. E.

(1994). Development and validation of the six-factor self-concept scale. *Education and Psychological Measurement, 54,* 56–72.

■ ■ ■

6695

Test Name: ART SELF-PERCEPTION INVENTORY

Purpose: To assess self-concept in four major arts-related areas of junior high school and high school students.

Number of Items: 40

Format: Includes 4 areas: music, visual arts, dance, and dramatic arts.

Reliability: Coefficient alphas were all .92 ($N = 205$).

Validity: Correlations with other variables ranged from -.39 to .51.

Authors: Vispoel, W. P.

Article: The development and validation of the Arts Self-Perception Inventory for adolescents.

Journal: *Educational and Psychological Measurement*, Winter 1993, *53*(4), 1023–1033.

■ ■ ■

6696

Test Name: ATTENTION TO BODY SHAPE SCALE

Purpose: To measure consciousness of one's body.

Number of Items: 7

Format: 5-point agreement scales. All items are presented.

Reliability: Alphas ranged from .70 to .83.

Validity: Correlations with other variables ranged from -.02 to .60.

Author: Beebe, D. W.

Article: The Attention to Body

Shape Scale: A new measure of body focus.

Journal: *Journal of Personality Assessment*, December 1995, *65*(3), 486–501.

■ ■ ■

6697

Test Name: ATTITUDES TOWARD PARENTAL LEAVE TAKERS SCALE

Purpose: To assess perception of the research, teaching, and parenting effectiveness of colleagues who take parental leave.

Number of Items: 10

Format: The items are asked about male and female colleagues separately. All items are presented.

Reliability: Alpha coefficients were .85 and .90.

Validity: Correlations with other variables ranged from -.11 to .65.

Author: Grover, S. L.

Article: Predicting the perceived fairness of parental leave policies.

Journal: *Journal of Applied Psychology*, April 1991, *76*(2), 247–255.

■ ■ ■

6698

Test Name: ATTRIBUTES OF INTELLIGENCE SCALES

Purpose: To identify parents' conceptions of the intelligence of their first-grade child.

Number of Items: 35

Format: Includes 3 cognitive functions: problem-solving skills, verbal skills, and creativity; and 3 noncognitive attributes: motivation for school, self-management skills, and social skills. All items are presented.

Reliability: Interitem reliabilities ranged from .76 to .94.

Authors: Okagaki, L., and Sternberg, R.J.

Article: Parental beliefs and children's school performance.

Journal: *Child Development*, February 1993, *64*(1), 36–56.

Related Research: Sternberg, R. J. (1985). *Beyond IQ: A triarchic theory of human intelligence.* New York: Cambridge University Press.

• • •

6699

Test Name: ATTRIBUTIONAL STYLE QUESTIONNAIRE

Purpose: To measure the attributional dimensions of locus, stability and globality.

Number of Items: 36

Format: All items are presented.

Reliability: Alpha was .65.

Validity: Corelations with other variables ranged from .14 to .26.

Author: Whitley, B. E., Jr.

Article: A short form of the expanded Attributional Style Questionnaire.

Journal: *Journal of Personality Assessment*, April 1991, *56*(2), 365–369.

Related Research: Peterson, C. (1991). On shortening the Attributional Style Questionnaire. *Journal of Personality Assessment*, *56*, 179–183.

• • •

6700

Test Name: ATTRIBUTIONAL STYLE QUESTIONNAIRE

Purpose: To assess one's explanation for causes of events.

Number of Items: 48

Format: Scores range from -18 to +18.

Reliability: Internal consistency was .75 and .72.

Author: Palmer, L. K.

Article: Effects of a walking program on attributional style, depression, and self-esteem in women.

Journal: *Perceptual and Motor Skills*, December 1995, *81*(3) Part 1, 891–898.

Related Research: Seligman, M. E. P. (1987). *The Attributional Style Questionnaire* (ASQ). (Available from Martin Seligman, Department of Psychology, University of Pennsylvania, Philadelphia, PA 19104-6196.)

Tennen, H., et al. (1987). Depressive attributional style: The role of self-esteem. *Journal of Personality*, *55*, 631–660.

• • •

6701

Test Name: ATTRIBUTION INVENTORY

Purpose: To identify one's attributions for success.

Number of Items: 12

Format: Responses are made on a 5-point Likert-type scale.

Validity: Correlations with other variables ranged from -.23 to .31.

Authors: Roedel, T. D., et al.

Article: Validation of a measure of learning and performance goal orientations.

Journal: *Educational and Psychological Measurement*, Winter 1994, *54*(4), 1013–1021.

Related Research: Weiner, B. (1985). An attributional theory of achievement motivation and emotion. *Psychological Review*, *92*(4), 548–573.

6702

Test Name: ATTRIBUTIONS FOR ABUSE SCALE

Purpose: To describe an abused woman's causal attribution for abuse.

Number of Items: 21

Format: 5-point scales. Sample items presented.

Reliability: Alphas ranged from .71 to .75 across subscales.

Author: Herbert, T. B., et al.

Article: Coping with an abusive relationship: I. How and why do women stay?

Journal: *Journal of Marriage and the Family*, May 1991, *53*(2), 311–323.

Related Research: Frieze, I. H. (1979). Perceptions of battered wives. In I. H. Frieze (Ed.), *New approaches to social problems: Applications of attribution theory* (pp. 79–108). San Francisco: Jossey-Bass.

• • •

6703

Test Name: AUTONOMIC PERCEPTION QUESTIONNAIRE—REVISION

Purpose: To assess frequency that certain bodily symptoms are experienced in anxiety.

Number of Items: 30

Format: 9-point Likert format ranges from *not at all true about me* to *very true about me.* All items are presented.

Reliability: Alphas ranged from .83 to .89 across subscales.

Validity: Correlations with other variables ranged from .17 to .50.

Authors: Shields, S. A., and Simon, A.

Article: Is awareness of bodily change in emotion related to awareness of other bodily processes?

Journal: *Journal of Personality Assessment*, August 1991, *57*(1), 96–109.

Related Research: Shields, S. A. (1984). Reports of bodily change in anxiety, sadness and anger. *Motivation and Emotion, 8*, 1–21.

• • •

6704

Test Name: BETTS QUESTIONNAIRE UPON MENTAL IMAGERY—REVISED

Purpose: To measure vividness of mental imagery.

Number of Items: 35

Format: Includes 7 sensory modalities: visual, auditory, tactile, kinesthetic, gustatory, olfactory, and organic. Responses are made on a 7-point scale ranging from 1 (*perfectly clear and vivid*) to 7 (*no image at all*).

Validity: Correlations with other variables ranged from -.18 to .00.

Authors: Campos, A., and González, M. A.

Article: Vividness of imagery and creativity.

Journal: *Perceptual and Motor Skills*, December 1993, *77*(3) Part 1, 923–928.

Related Research: Sheehan, P. W. (1967). A shortened form of Betts' Questionnaire Upon Mental Imagery. *Journal of Clinical Psychology, 23*, 386–389.

• • •

6705

Test Name: BIALER-CROMWELL LOCUS OF CONTROL SCALE

Purpose: To assess locus of control.

Number of Items: 19

Format: Responses are made using a yes–no format.

Reliability: Test–retest reliability coefficient was .84.

Authors: Belle, D., and Burr, R.

Article: Why children do not confide: An exploratory analysis.

Journal: *Child Study Journal*, December 1991, *21*(4), 217–234.

Related Research: Bialer, I. (1961). Conceptualization of success and failure in mental retarded and normal children. *Journal of Personality, 29*, 303–320.

• • •

6706

Test Name: BODY AWARENESS QUESTIONNAIRE

Purpose: To assess self-reported attentiveness to normal nonemotive bodily processes.

Number of Items: 18

Reliability: Alpha was .80. Test–retest reliability was .80.

Validity: Correlations with the Autonomic Response Questionnaire Revision ranged from .17 to .29. Correlation with the Body subscale of the Love Symptom Checklist was .06.

Authors: Shields, S. A., and Simon, A.

Article: Is awareness of bodily change in emotion related to awareness of other bodily processes.

Journal: *Journal of Personality Assessment*, August 1991, *57*(1), 96–109.

Related Research: Shields, S. A., et al. (1989). The Body Awareness Questionnaire: Reliability and validity. *Journal of Personality Assessment, 53*, 802–815.

6707

Test Name: BODY-CATHEXIS SCALE

Purpose: To measure person's feelings toward parts and functions of their body.

Number of Items: 46

Format: Responses are made on a 5-point scale.

Reliability: Split-half reliability was .81.

Authors: Melnick, M. J., and Mookerjee, S.

Article: Effects of advanced weight training on body-cathexis and self-esteem.

Journal: *Perceptual and Motor Skills*, June 1991, *72*(3) Part 2, 1335–1345.

Related Research: Secord, P. F., & Jourard, S. M. (1953). The appraisal of body-cathexis: Body-cathexis and the self. *Journal of Consulting Psychology, 17*, 343–347.

• • •

6708

Test Name: BODY CATHEXIS SCALE—GREEK VERSION

Purpose: To measure satisfaction with parts or processes of the body.

Number of Items: 40

Format: 5-point Likert format.

Reliability: Split-half reliability was .89. Test–retest (2 weeks) was .90. Cronbach's alpha was .92.

Validity: Six factors were extracted. Alphas for the items in the factors ranged from .59 to .85. No differences by age were found.

Authors: Theodorakis, Y., et al.

Article: Age differences and structural validity for the Greek Version of the Body Cathexis Scale.

Journal: *Psychological Reports*, February 1991, *68*(1), 43–49.

Related Research: Secord, F. P., et al. (1953). The appraisal of body-cathexis: Body cathexis and the self. *Journal of Consulting Psychology*, *17*, 343–347.

■ ■ ■

6709

Test Name: BODY ESTEEM SCALE

Purpose: To enable people to evaluate their bodies.

Number of Items: 35

Format: Responses are made on a 5-point scale ranging from 1 (*have strong negative feelings*) to 5 (*have strong positive feelings*).

Reliability: Alpha coefficients ranged from .78 to .87.

Validity: Correlations with Rosenberg's Self-Esteem Scale ranged from .32 to .51.

Authors: Finkenberg, M. E., et al.

Article: Body esteem and enrollment in classes with different levels of physical activity.

Journal: *Perceptual and Motor Skills*, June 1993, *76*(3) Part 1, 783–792.

Related Research: Franzoi, S. L., & Shields, S. E. (1984). The Body Esteem Scale: Multidimensional structure and sex differences in a college population. *Journal of Personality Assessment*, *48*, 173–178.

■ ■ ■

6710

Test Name: BODY-IMAGE ASSESSMENT SCALE

Purpose: To assess body dissatisfaction.

Number of Items: Nine male and nine female front-view-contour drawings.

Format: Participants rank-order each of the nine drawings from thinnest to heaviest.

Reliability: Correlation of rankings 1 week apart was .78.

Validity: Correlation with body mass index was .59.

Authors: Thompson, M. A., and Gray, J. J.

Article: Development and validation of a new body-image assessment scale.

Journal: *Journal of Personality Assessment*, April 1995, *64*(2), 258–269.

Related Research: Thompson, J. K., & Tantleff, S. (1992). Female and male ratings of upper torso: Actual ideal and stereotypical conceptions. *Journal of Social Behavior and Personality*, *7*, 345–354.

■ ■ ■

6711

Test Name: BODY IMAGE AVOIDANCE QUESTIONNAIRE

Purpose: To assess behavior performed to control and conceal one's appearance.

Number of Items: 19

Format: 5-point frequency scales range from 5 (*always*) to 1 (*never*).

Reliability: Alpha was .89. Stability (2 weeks) was .88.

Validity: Correlations with other variables ranged from .31 to .52.

Authors Cash, T. F., and Szymanski, M. L.

Article: The development and validation of the Body-Image Ideals Questionnaire.

Journal: *Journal of Personality Assessment*, June 1995, *64*(3), 466–477.

Related Research: Rosen, J. C., et al. (1991). Development of a body image avoidance questionnaire. *Psychological Assessment*, *3*, 32–37.

■ ■ ■

6712

Test Name: BODY-IMAGE IDEALS QUESTIONNAIRE

Purpose: To measure self-perceived discrepancies from and importance of internalized ideals for physical characteristics including height, skin complexion, hair texture/thickness, facial features, muscle tone/definition, body proportions, weight, chest size, strength, and coordination.

Number of Items: 10

Format: 4-point discrepancy scales range from -1 (*exactly like I am*), to 3 (*very unlike me*). 4-point importance scales range from 0 (*not important*) to 3 (*very important*).

Reliability: Alphas ranged from .75 to .82.

Validity: Correlations with other variables ranged from -.72 to .71.

Authors: Cash, T. F., and Szymanski, M. L.

Article: The development and validation of the Body-Image Ideals Questionnaire.

Journal: *Journal of Personality Assessment*, June 1995, *64*(3), 466–477.

■ ■ ■

6713

Test Name: BODY IMAGE QUESTIONNAIRE

Purpose: To measure body image.

Number of Items: 20

Format: Responses are either *agree*, *undecided*, or *disagree*. All items are presented.

Reliability: Coefficient alpha was .72.

Validity: Correlations with percent body fat were -.76 and -.51.

Authors: Huddy, D. C., et al.

Article: Relationship between body image and percent body fat among college male varsity athletes and nonathletes.

Journal: *Perceptual and Motor Skills*, December 1993, *77*(3) Part 1, 851–857.

• • •

6714

Test Name: BODY IMAGE SCALE

Purpose: To calculate body image.

Number of Items: 5

Format: Responses are made on a 5-point Likert-type scale ranging from *very thin* to *very fat*.

Reliability: Coefficient alpha was .90.

Authors: Koslowsky, M., et al.

Article: Predicting actual weight from self-report data.

Journal: *Educational and Psychological Measurement*, Spring 1994, *54*(1), 168–173.

Related Research: Rapter, A., & Yanko, Y. (1989). *Anorexia nervosa in subpopulations in Israel.* Unpublished manuscript, Tel-Aviv University, Tel-Aviv, Israel.

Stunkard, A., & Mendelson, M. (1967). Obesity and body image: Characteristics of disturbances in the body image of some obese persons. *American Journal of Psychiatry*, *123*, 1296–1300.

• • •

6715

Test Name: BODY PARTS SATISFACTION SCALE

Purpose: To measure an individual's satisfaction with his/her body.

Number of Items: 24

Format: 6-point satisfaction scale ranges from 1 (*extremely dissatisfied*) to 6 (*extremely satisfied*).

Reliability: Alpha was .93.

Authors: Lester, R., and Petrie, T. A.

Article: Personality and physical correlates of bulimic symptomatology among Mexican American female college students.

Journal: *Journal of Counseling Psychology*, April 1995, *42*(2), 199–203.

Related Research: Mintz, L. B., & Betz, N. E. (1988). Prevalence and correlates of eating disordered behaviors among undergraduate women. *Journal of Counseling Psychology*, *35*, 463–471.

• • •

6716

Test Name: BODY SATISFACTION QUESTIONNAIRE

Purpose: To rate one's satisfaction with one's body.

Number of Items: 15

Format: Responses are made on a 5-point scale.

Validity: Correlations with self-concept ranged from .11 to .82.

Authors: Folk, L., et al.

Article: Body satisfaction and self-concept of third- and sixth-grade students.

Journal: *Perceptual and Motor Skills*, April 1993, *76*(2), 547-553.

Related Research: Rauste von Wright, M. (199). Body image satisfaction in adolescent girls and boys: A longitudinal study. *Journal of Youth and Adolescence*, *18*, 71–83.

6717

Test Name: BODY SELF-RELATIONS QUESTIONNAIRE—SHORT FORM

Purpose: To measure perceptions of body image.

Number of Items: 54

Format: Includes 3 domains: physical appearance, physical fitness, and physical health.

Reliability: Alpha coefficients ranged from .85 to .90.

Validity: Correlations with other variables ranged from -.40 to .52.

Authors: Adame, D. D., et al.

Article: Physical fitness, body image, and locus of control in college women dancers and nondancers.

Journal: *Perceptual and Motor Skills*, February 1991, *72*(1), 91–95.

Related Research: Winstead, B. A., & Cash, T. F. (1984). *Reliability and validity of the Body Self-Relations Questionnaire: A new measure of body image.* Paper presented at the meeting of the Southeastern Psychological Association, New Orleans, Louisiana.

• • •

6718

Test Name: BRAZILIAN HEALTH LOCUS OF CONTROL

Purpose: To measure health locus of control.

Number of Items: 18

Format: 5-point agreement scales.

Reliability: Alphas were .54 or greater across subscales.

Authors: Paine, P., et al.

Article: Psychometric properties of the Brazilian Health Locus of Control Scale.

Journal: *Psychological Reports*, August 1994, *75*(1) Part I, 91–94.

Related Research: Wallston, K. A., et al. (1978). Development of the Multidimensional Health Locus of Control (MHLC) Scales. *Health Education Monographs*, *6*, 160–170.

• • •

6719

Test Name: CANADIAN SELF-ESTEEM INVENTORY

Purpose: To measure self-concept.

Number of Items: 30

Format: Responses are "yes" or "no."

Validity: Validity estimates ranged from .81 to .89.

Author: MWamwenda, T. S.

Article: Sex differences in self-concept among African adolescents.

Journal: *Perceptual and Motor Skills*, August 1991, *73*(1), 191–194.

Related Research: Battle, J. (1976). Test-retest reliability of the Canadian Self-Esteem Inventory for Children. *Psychological Reports*, *38*, 1343–1345.

• • •

6720

Test Name: CAREER AND EDUCATIONAL SELF-EFFICACY SCALE

Purpose: To assess the confidence level of students in completing educational requirements for a job and how likely they are to enter this occupation.

Number of Items: 20

Format: Responses are made on 10-point confidence scales. All items are presented.

Reliability: Alphas ranged from .70 to .77 across subscales.

Author: Kelly, K. R.

Article: The relation of gender and academic achievement to career self-efficacy and interests.

Journal: *Gifted Child Quarterly*, Spring 1993, *37*(2), 59–64.

Related Research: Betz, N. E., & Hackett, G. (1981). The relationship of career-related self-efficacy expectations to perceived career options in college women and men. *Journal of Counseling Psychology*, *28*, 399–410.

• • •

6721

Test Name: CAREER ATTITUDE SCALE

Purpose: To measure career self-efficacy.

Number of Items: 18

Format: Responses are made on a 5-point scale ranging from 1 (*not at all confident*) to 5 (*very confident*). Includes male and female subscales. All items are presented.

Reliability: Alpha coefficients ranged from .75 to .90. Test–retest (21 days) reliability was .74 (female subscale) and .83 (male subscale). $N = 37$.

Validity: Correlations with other variables ranged from .02 to .50.

Authors: Bonett, R. M., and Stickel, S. A.

Article: A psychometric analysis of the career attitude scale.

Journal: *Measurement and Evaluation in Counseling and Development*, April 1992, *25*(1), 14–18.

• • •

6722

Test Name: CAREER DECISION-MAKING SELF-EFFICACY SCALE

Purpose: To measure career decision-making self-efficacy.

Number of Items: 25

Format: Includes 5 domains. Responses are made on a 5-point scale ranging from 1 (*entirely unsure*) to 5 (*completely sure*).

Reliability: Coefficient alpha was .89.

Validity: Correlations with other variables ranged from .16 to .53.

Authors: Matsui, T., and Omglato, M.-L.

Article: Career orientedness of motivation to enter the university among Japanese high school girls: A path analysis.

Journal: *Journal of Vocational Behavior*, June 1992, *40*(3), 351–363.

Related Research: Taylor, K. M., & Betz, N. E. (1983). Applications of self-efficacy theory to the understanding and treatment of career indecision. *Journal of Vocational Behavior*, *22*, 63–81.

• • •

6723

Test Name: CAREER DECISION-MAKING SELF-EFFICACY SCALE

Purpose: To measure a respondent's career decision-making attitudes and skills.

Number of Items: 50

Format: Responses are made on a scale of 0 to 9 in order to rate their confidence in their ability to complete career decision-making tasks.

Reliability: Test–retest reliability coefficient was .83.

Author: Luzzo, D. A.

Article: The relative contributions of self-efficacy and locus of control to the prediction of career maturity.

Journal: *Journal of College Student Development*, January/February 1995, *36*(1), 61–66.

Related Research: Taylor, K. M., & Betz, N. E. (1983). Applications of self-efficacy theory to the understanding and treatment of career indecision. *Journal of Vocational Behavior*, *22*, 63–81.

■ ■ ■

6724

Test Name: CAREER DECISION-MAKING SELF-EFFICACY SCALE

Purpose: To measure self-efficacy expectations related to tasks or behaviors considered to be associated with career decision making.

Number of Items: 52

Format: Responses are made on a 10-point scale ranging from complete confidence to no confidence at all.

Reliability: Internal consistency reliability was .97.

Authors: Bergeron, L. M., and Romano, J. L.

Article: The relationships among career decision-making self-efficacy, educational indecision, vocational indecision, and gender.

Journal: *Journal of College Student Development*, January 1994, *35*(1), 19–24.

Related Research: Taylor, K. M., & Betz, N. E. (1983). Applications of self-efficacy theory to the understanding and treatment of career indecision. *Journal of Vocational Behavior*, *22*, 63–81.

■ ■ ■

6725

Test Name: CAREER INSIGHT SCALE

Purpose: To measure one's career insight.

Number of Items: 3

Format: Responses are made on a 5-point scale ranging from 5 (*strongly agree*) to 1 (*strongly disagree*). An example is presented.

Reliability: Coefficient alpha was .65.

Validity: Correlation with other variables ranged from .00 to .32.

Authors: Maurer, T. J., and Tarulli, B. A.

Article: Investigation of perceived environment, perceived outcome, and person variables in relationship to voluntary development activity by employees.

Journal: *Journal of Applied Psychology*, February 1994, *79*(1), 3–14.

Related Research: Noe, R., et al. (1990). An investigation of the correlates of career motivation. *Journal of Vocational Behavior*, *37*, 340–356.

■ ■ ■

6726

Test Name: CAREER LOCUS OF CONTROL SCALE

Purpose: To measure a participant's locus of control for career development.

Number of Items: 18

Format: Responses are made using a true–false format.

Reliability: Test–retest reliability coefficient was .93.

Author: Luzzo, D. A.

Article: The relative contributions of self-efficacy and locus of control to the prediction of career maturity.

Journal: *Journal of College Student Development*, January/February 1995, *36*(1), 61–66.

Related Research: Trice, A. D., et al. (1989). A career locus of control scale for undergraduate students. *Perceptual and Motor Skills*, *69*, 555–561.

■ ■ ■

6727

Test Name: CAREER MYTHS SCALE

Purpose: To measure irrational beliefs regarding the career choice process.

Number of Items: 27

Format: Responses are made on a 5-point Likert-type scale ranging from 5 (*strongly agree*) to 1 (*strongly disagree*). All items are presented. Includes 4 components: test myths, misconceptions of exactitude, self-esteem myths, and strong career attraction myths.

Reliability: Coefficient alpha was .75.

Validity: Correlations with other variables ranged from -.43 to .12.

Authors: Stead, G. B., et al.

Article: The relation between career indecision and irrational beliefs among university students.

Journal: *Journal of Vocational Behavior*, April 1993, *42*(2), 155–169.

Related Research: Stead, G. B. (1991). *The Career Myths Scale*. Vista University, Port Elizabeth.

■ ■ ■

6728

Test Name: CAREER SEARCH SELF-EFFICACY SCALE

Purpose: To measure confidence in career search tasks.

Number of Items: 35

Format: 10-point scales ranged from 1 (*very little*) to 10 (*very* *much*). Sample items are presented.

Reliability: Alpha was .97.

Validity: Correlations with other variables ranged from -.50 to .75.

Authors: Solberg, V. S., et al.

Article: Career decision-making and career search activity: Relative effects of career search self-efficacy and human agency.

Journal: *Journal of Counseling Psychology*, October 1995, *42*(4), 448–455.

Related Research: Solberg, V. S., et al. (1994). Career search efficacy: Ripe for applications and intervention programming, *Journal of Career Development*, *21*, 63–72.

■ ■ ■

6729

Test Name: CAREER SELF-EFFICACY EXPECTATIONS SCALE

Purpose: To measure degree of confidence in one's capability and success to accomplish each task.

Number of Items: 30

Format: Responses are made on a 5-point scale ranging from 1 (*entirely unsure*) to 5 (*completely sure*). Examples are presented.

Reliability: Coefficient alpha was .82.

Validity: Correlations with other variables ranged from -.35 to .16 (*N* = 435).

Authors: Matsui, T., and Onglatco, M.-L.

Article: Career self-efficacy as a moderator of the relations between occupational stress and strain.

Journal: *Journal of Vocational Behavior*, August 1992, *41*(1), 79–88.

Related Research: Matsui, T., & Onglatco, M. (1991).

Instrumentality, expressiveness, and self-efficacy in career activities among Japanese working women. *Journal of Vocational Behavior*, *39*, 241–250.

■ ■ ■

6730

Test Name: CAREER SELF-EFFICACY SCALE

Purpose: To measure the degree of certainty respondents have concerning their ability to complete job-related tasks.

Number of Items: 3

Format: 10-point scales ranges from 1 (*not at all sure*) to 10 (*completely sure*).

Reliability: Alpha was .75.

Validity: Correlations with other variables ranged from -.37 to .45.

Authors: Brooks, L., et al.

Article: The relation of career-related work or internship experiences to the career development of college seniors.

Journal: *Journal of Vocational Behavior*, June 1995, *46*(3), 332–349.

Related Research: Betz, N. E., & Hackett, G. (1981). The relationship of career-related self-efficacy expectations to perceived career options in college women and men. *Journal of Counseling Psychology*, *28*, 399–410.

■ ■ ■

6731

Test Name: CAREER SELF-EFFICACY SCALE

Purpose: To assess confidence in ability to complete educational requirements and job duties of 10 technical science careers.

Number of Items: 10

Format: Response to each item was rated on a 10-point scale ranging

from 0 (*no confidence*) to 9 (*complete confidence*).

Reliability: Cronbach alpha was .94.

Validity: Correlations with other variables ranged from .36 to .48.

Authors: Cooper, S. E., and Robinson, D. A. G.

Article: The relationship of mathematics self-efficacy beliefs to mathematics anxiety and performance.

Journal: *Measurement and Evaluation in Counseling and Development*, April 1991, *24*(1), 4–11.

■ ■ ■

6732

Test Name: CAREER SELF-EFFICACY SCALE

Purpose: To measure self-efficacy.

Number of Items: 15

Format: A person's certainty to perform job duties of the 15 occupations presented is indicated by a high score.

Reliability: Test–retest (17 days) reliability was .85.

Authors: Kush, K., and Cochran, L.

Article: Enhancing a sense of agency through career planning.

Journal: *Journal of Counseling Psychology*, October 1993, *40*(4), 434–439.

Related Research: Rotberg, H., et al. (1987). Career self-efficacy expectations and perceived range of career options in community college students. *Journal of Counseling Psychology*, *34*, 164–170.

■ ■ ■

6733

Test Name: CHANCE SELF-REPORT SCALE

Purpose: To determine whether one believes chance could be an important factor in career selection.

Number of Items: 2

Format: Responses are made on a 7-point scale.

Reliability: Reliability was .81.

Validity: Correlation with the Coopersmith Self-Esteem Inventory was -.02.

Authors: Miller, M. J., et al.

Article: Chance receptivity as a function of self-concept: An exploratory study.

Journal: *Perceptual and Motor Skills*, February 1991, *72*(1), 291–295.

■ ■ ■

6734

Test Name: CHILDHOOD OBESITY SCALE

Purpose: To assess perceptions of childhood obesity.

Number of Items: 39

Time Required: 20 minutes

Format: 7-point agreement scales. All items are presented.

Reliability: Internal reliability was .65.

Author: Savage, M. P.

Article: Perceptions of childhood obesity of undergraduate students in physical education.

Journal: *Psychological Reports*, June 1995, *76*(3) Part II, 1251–1259.

Related Research: Price, J. H. et al (1990). Elementary physical education teachers' perceptions of childhood obesity. *Health Education*, *21*(6), 26–32.

■ ■ ■

6735

Test Name: COGNITIVE ERRORS QUESTIONNAIRE

Purpose: To assess general and pain-related cognitive distortion.

Number of Items: 48

Format: Responses are made on a 5-point scale according to the extent to which the thought listed resembles the thought participants would have had in the same situation.

Reliability: Cronbach's alpha was .96 for one scale and .94 for the other.

Authors: Smith, T. W., et al.

Article: Cognitive distortion and depression in chronic pain: Association with diagnosed disorders.

Journal: *Journal of Consulting and Clinical Psychology*, February 1994, *62*(1), 195–198.

Related Research: Lefebvre, M. F. (1981). Cognitive distortion and cognitive errors in depressed psychiatric and low back pain patients. *Journal of Consulting and Clinical Psychology*, *49*, 517–525.

■ ■ ■

6736

Test Name: COLOR-A-PERSON BODY DISSATISFACTION TEST

Purpose: To assess dissatisfaction with one's body.

Number of Items: 2

Format: Two outlines of either a male or female body are presented to subjects who then color each part according to a code of dissatisfaction.

Reliability: All reliabilities are in the .70s and .80s.

Validity: Correlations with self-esteem ranged from -.69 to -.05.

Authors: Wooley, O. W., and Rall, S.

Article: The Color-A-Person Body Dissatisfaction Test: Stability,

internal consistency, validity and factor structure.

Journal: *Journal of Personality Assessment*, June 1991, *56*(3), 395–413.

■ ■ ■

6737

Test Name: COMPETENCY RATING SCALE

Purpose: To measure academic, social, and psychological competence.

Number of Items: 27

Format: 5-point rating scales.

Reliability: Alphas ranged from .58 to .86 across subscales.

Validity: Correlations with other variables ranged from -.39 (Eating Disorder Inventory) to .53 (Body Areas Satisfaction).

Authors: Gibson, S. G., and Thomas, C. D.

Article: Self-rated competence, current weight, and body-image among college women.

Journal: *Psychological Reports*, August 1991, *69*(1), 336–338.

Related Research: Hesse-Biber, S., et al. (1987). The differential importance of weight and body-image among college men and women. *Genetic Social and General Psychology Monographs*, *113*, 511–528.

■ ■ ■

6738

Test Name: COMPLACENCY POTENTIAL RATING SCALE

Purpose: To assess self-satisfaction that may result in unjustified nonvigilance.

Number of Items: 20

Format: 5-point Likert format.

Reliability: Total alpha was .98.

Alphas ranged from .82 to .97 across subscales.

Authors: Singh, I. L., et al.

Article: Individual differences in monitoring failures of automation.

Journal: *The Journal of General Psychology*, July 1993, *120*(3), 357–373.

Related Research: Singh, I. L., et al. (1993). Automation-induced "complacency": Development of a complacency potential scale. *International Journal of Aviation Psychology*, *3*, 111–112.

■ ■ ■

6739

Test Name: COMPUTER SELF-EFFICACY SCALE

Purpose: To determine the influence of computer training on computer self-efficacy.

Number of Items: 30

Format: Responses are made on a 5-point Likert-type scale ranging from 1 (*strongly disagree*) to 5 (*strongly agree*). Includes 4 factors: Beginning Skills, Maintenance Skills, Advanced Skills, and File and Software Skills. All items are presented.

Reliability: Alpha coefficients ranged from .91 to .96.

Authors: Torkzadeh, G., and Koufteros, X.

Article: Factorial validity of a computer self-efficacy scale and the impact of computer training.

Journal: *Educational and Psychological Measurement*, Fall 1994, *54*(3), 813–821.

Related Research: Murphy, C., et al. (1989). Development and validation of the Computer Self-Efficacy Scale. *Educational and Psychological Measurement*, *49*, 893–899.

6740

Test Name: COMPUTER SELF-EFFICACY SCALE

Purpose: To measure one's perceptions of one's specific computer-related knowledge and skills.

Number of Items: 32

Format: Includes 3 dimensions: beginning computer skills, moderate computer skill, and advanced skills. All items are presented.

Reliability: Internal-consistency reliability coefficients ranged from .92 to .55.

Validity: Correlations with other variables ranged from -.61 to .55.

Authors: Harrison, A. W., and Rainer, R. K., Jr.

Article: An examination of the factor structures and concurrent validities for The Computer Attitude Scale, The Computer Anxiety Rating Scale, and The Computer Self-Efficacy Scale.

Journal: *Educational and Psychological Measurement*, Autumn 1992, *52*(3), 735–745.

Related Research: Murphy, C. A., et al. (1989). Development and validation of the Computer Self-Efficacy Scale. *Educational and Psychological Measurement*, *49*, 893–899.

■ ■ ■

6741

Test Name: COUNSELING SELF-ESTIMATE INVENTORY

Purpose: To measure counselors' self-estimates of their counseling activities that occur during a counseling session.

Number of Items: 67

Format: Includes 5 factors: Microskills, Process, Difficult Client Behavior, Cultural

Competence, and Awareness of Values. Responses are made on a 6-point scale ranging from 1 (*strongly disagree*) to 6 (*strongly agree*). 53 items are presented.

Reliability: Alpha coefficients ranged from .62 to .93.

Validity: Correlations with other variables ranged from -.73 to .51.

Authors: Larson, L. M., et al.

Article: Development and validation of the Counseling Self-Estimate Inventory.

Journal: *Journal of Counseling Psychology*, January 1992, *39*(1), 105–120.

■ ■ ■

6742

Test Name: CRIME VICTIMIZATION LOCUS OF CONTROL SCALE

Purpose: To measure locus of control specific to victimization.

Number of Items: 3

Format: All items are presented. Coding rules described.

Validity: Correlation ratios and odds ratios suggested that age, race, educational level, gender, and other variables predict internal and external scores.

Authors: Houts, S. S., and Kassab, C. D.

Article: Three-item locus of control scale for crime victimization.

Journal: *Psychological Reports*, October 1994, *75*(2), 1011–1018.

■ ■ ■

6743

Test Name: ENVIRONMENTAL/BIOLOGICAL ATTRIBUTION SCALE

Purpose: To assess environmental/biological attributions.

Number of Items: 20

Format: 7-point Likert format. Sample items are presented.

Reliability: Alpha was .83.

Validity: Correlations with other variables ranged from -.05 to .75.

Authors: Gold, B. T., and Ziegler, M.

Article: Measuring environmental/biological attribution: A fundamental dimension.

Journal: *The Journal of Social Psychology*, December 1994, *133*(6), 837–845.

■ ■ ■

6744

Test Name: E SCALE

Purpose: To measure individual differences in experiencing role overload and role conflict.

Number of Items: 58

Format: 5-point Likert format.

Reliability: Alpha was .87.

Authors: Ryckman, R. M., et al.

Article: Personality correlates of the Hypercompetitive Attitude Scale: Validity tests of Horney's theory of neurosis.

Journal: *Journal of Personality Assessment*, February 1994, *62*(1), 84–94.

Related Research: Thornton, B. (1992). *The Type-E (everything to everybody) personality: Psychometric properties of a brief assessment of individual differences mediating the experience of multiple roles.* Unpublished manuscript, University of Southern Maine.

Braiker, H. B. (1986). *The Type-E woman: How to overcome the stress of being everything to everybody.* New York: Dodd Mead.

6745

Test Name: EXERCISE IDENTITY SCALE

Purpose: To measure the salience of one's identification with exercise.

Number of Items: 9

Format: Employs a Likert format ranging from *strongly disagree* to *strongly agree*. All items are presented.

Reliability: Test–retest (1 week) reliability was .93. Coefficient alpha was .94.

Validity: Correlations with other variables ranged from .29 to .68.

Authors: Anderson, D. F., and Cychosz, C. M.

Article: Development of an Exercise Identity Scale.

Journal: *Perceptual and Motor Skills*, June 1994, *78*(3) Part 1, 747–751.

■ ■ ■

6746

Test Name: EXPECTANCY/ CONTEXT QUESTIONNAIRE

Purpose: To measure phasic fluctuations in expectancies that occur over short periods caused by changes in context or changes after intervention.

Number of Items: 20

Format: Responses are made on a 5-point Likert scale.

Reliability: Coefficient alphas among the scales ranged from the .80s to the low .90s.

Authors: Darkes, J., and Goldman, M. S.

Article: Expectancy challenge and drinking reduction: Experimental evidence for a mediational process.

Journal: *Journal of Consulting and*

Clinical Psychology, April 1993, *61*(2), 344–353.

Related Research: Levine, B., & Goldman, M. S. (1989, August). *Situational variations in expectancies.* Paper presented at the 97th Annual Convention of the American Psychological Association, New Orleans, Louisiana.

■ ■ ■

6747

Test Name: EXPECTANCY SCALE

Purpose: To measure students' expectancy of success in schoolwork.

Number of Items: 5

Format: Responses are made on a 5-point Likert-type scale ranging from 1 (*not at all true*) to 5 (*completely true*).

Reliability: Alpha was .72.

Validity: Correlations with other variables ranged from .24 to .54.

Authors: Goodenow, C., and Grady, K. E.

Article: The relationship of school belonging and friends' values to academic motivation among urban adolescent students.

Journal: *Journal of Experimental Education*, Fall 1993, 62(1), 60–71.

Related Research: Pintrich, P., & DeGroot, E. (1990). Motivational and self-regulated learning components of classroom academic performance. *Journal of Educational Psychology*, *82*, 33–40.

■ ■ ■

6748

Test Name: EXPECTATIONS ABOUT COUNSELING—BRIEF FORM

Purpose: To measure students' expectations about counseling.

Number of Items: 53

Format: Includes 17 scales. Responses are made on a 7-point Likert-type scale ranging from *not true* to *definitely true*.

Reliability: Internal consistency reliabilities ranged from .69 to .82 ($N = 446$). Test–retest (2 months) reliability coefficients ranged from .47 to .71.

Author: Tinsley, H. E. A., et al.

Article: Client expectations about counseling and involvement during career counseling.

Journal: *The Career Development Quarterly*, June 1995, *42*(4), 326–336.

Related Research: Tinsley, H. E. A., et al. (1980). Factor analysis of the domain of client expectancies about counseling. *Journal of Counseling Psychology, 27*, 561–570.

▪ ▪ ▪

6749

Test Name: EXPECTATIONS ABOUT COUNSELING—BRIEF FORM

Purpose: To measure expectations about counseling.

Number of Items: 66

Format: 7-point Likert format ranges from 1 (*not true*) to 7 (*very true*).

Reliability: Internal consistency ranged from .69 to .82. Test–retest reliability (2 months) ranged from .47 to .87.

Authors: Satterfield, W. A., et al.

Article: Client stages of change and expectations about counseling.

Journal: *Journal of Counseling Psychology*, October 1995, *42*(4), 476–478.

Related Research: Tinsley, H. E. A.

(1982). *Expectations about counseling.* Unpublished test manual, Southern Illinois University at Carbondale, Department of Psychology.

▪ ▪ ▪

6750

Test Name: EXPECTATIONS FOR COLLEGE SCALES

Purpose: To assess expectations for academic and intellectual development, collegiate atmosphere, and career development.

Number of Items: 14

Format: 4-point scales. All items are presented.

Reliability: Alphas ranged from .66 to .82 across subscales.

Validity: Correlations with other variables ranged from -.03 to .44.

Authors: Braxton, J. M., et al.

Article: Expectations for college and student persistence.

Journal: *Research in Higher Education*, October 1995, *36*(5), 595–612.

▪ ▪ ▪

6751

Test Name: EXPECTATIONS FOR REEMPLOYMENT SCALE

Purpose: To assess expectations for reemployment.

Number of Items: 3

Format: Responses are made on a 5-point scale ranging from 1 (*no chance*) to 5 (*100% chance*). All items are presented.

Validity: Correlations with other variables ranged from -.26 to .51.

Authors: Prussia, G. E., et al.

Article: Psychological and behavioral consequences of job loss: A covariance structure analysis using Weiner's (1985) attribution model.

Journal: *Journal of Applied Psychology*, June 1993, *78*(3), 382–394.

Related Research: Kinicki, A. J. (1989). Predicting occupational role choices after involuntary job loss. *Journal of Vocational Behavior, 35*, 204–218.

▪ ▪ ▪

6752

Test Name: FACULTY SUPPORT SCALE

Purpose: To measure perceptions of faculty support.

Number of Items: 10

Format: Includes two parts: faculty encouragement and faculty discouragement. Items consist of possible faculty reactions or responses. Students indicate whether they ever encountered each and how many times each was encountered. Examples are presented.

Validity: Internal consistencies were .77 (encouragement) and .80 (discouragement).

Reliability: Correlations with other variables ranged from -.34. to .32.

Author: Hackett, G., et al.

Article: Gender, ethnicity, and social cognitive factors predicting the academic achievement of students in engineering.

Journal: *Journal of Counseling Psychology*, October 1992, *39*(4), 527–538.

▪ ▪ ▪

6753

Test Name: FEMINIST IDENTITY SCALE

Purpose: To assess feminist identity.

Number of Items: 39

Format: 5-point Likert format. Sample items are presented.

Reliability: Alphas ranged from .54 to .81 across subscales.

Authors: Sik, H. N., et al.

Article: Feminist identities and preferred strategies for advancing women's positive self-concept.

Journal: *The Journal of Social Psychology*, October 1995, *135*(5), 561–572.

Related Research: Bargad, A., & Hyde, J. S. (1991). A study of feminist identity development in women. *Psychology of Women Quarterly, 15*, 181–201.

■ ■ ■

6754

Test Name: GAY STEREOTYPE SCALE

Purpose: To assess degree of gay stereotyping.

Number of Items: 20

Format: 7-point rating scales. Items are described.

Reliability: Alpha was .55.

Authors: Seligman, C. K., et al.

Article: Courtesy stigma: The social implications of associating with a gay person.

Journal: *The Journal of Social Psychology*, February 1991, *131*(1), 45–56.

Related Research: Gurwitz, S. B., & Marcus, M. (1978). Effects of anticipated interaction, sex, and homosexual stereotypes on first impressions. *Journal of Applied Social Psychology, 8*, 47–56.

■ ■ ■

6755

Test Name: GENERALIZED SELF-EFFICACY SCALE— SHORT FORM

Purpose: To measure one's expectations of performing competently across a broad range of situations that are challenging,

and that require effort and perseverance.

Number of Items: 10

Format: Responses are made on a 7-point scale ranging from 1 (*completely agree*) to 7 (*completely disagree*). Examples are presented.

Reliability: Coefficient alpha was .75.

Validity: Correlations with other variables ranged from -.15 to .44.

Authors: Lopez, F. G., et al.

Article: Conflictual independence, mood regulation, and generalized self-efficacy: Test of a model of late-adolescent identity.

Journal: *Journal of Counseling Psychology*, July 1992, *39*(3), 375–381.

Related Research: Tipton, R. M., & Worthington, E. L. (1984). The measurement of generalized self-efficacy: A study of constant validity. *Journal of Personality Assessment, 48*, 545–548.

■ ■ ■

6756

Test Name: GENERAL SELF-EFFICACY SCALE

Purpose: To assess self-efficacy expectations that are dependent on past experiences and on tendencies to attribute success to skill as opposed to chance.

Number of Items: 23

Format: Responses are made on a 7-point Likert scale.

Reliability: Cronbach alpha coefficients of the 3 subscales ranged from .86 to .71.

Authors: May, K. M., and Sowa, C. J.

Article: Personality characteristics and family environments of short-term counseling clients.

Journal: *Journal of College*

Student Development, January 1994, *35*(1), 59–62.

Related Research: Sherer, M., et al. (1982). The Self-Efficacy Scale: Construction and validation. *Psychological Reports, 51*, 663–671.

■ ■ ■

6757

Test Name: GENERAL SELF-EFFICACY SCALE

Purpose: To measure beliefs people have about their ability to overcome obstacles and succeed.

Number of Items: 30

Format: Includes filler items and items measuring social self-efficacy. Responses are made on a 5-point Likert-type scale. There are 17 General Self-Efficacy items. Sample items are presented.

Reliability: Coefficient alpha was .77.

Validity: Correlations with other variables ranged from -.47 to .29.

Author: Tuckman, B. W.

Article: The development and concurrent validity of the Procrastination Scale.

Journal: *Educational and Psychological Measurement*, Summer 1991, *51*(2), 473–480.

Related Research: Scherer, M., et al. (1982). The Self-Efficacy Scale: Construction and validation. *Psychological Reports, 51*, 663–671.

■ ■ ■

6758

Test Name: GENERAL SELF-EFFICACY SCALE-REVISED

Purpose: To assess general self-efficacy.

Number of Items: 17

Format: Responses are made on a

4-point *agree–disagree* scale. Examples are presented.

Reliability: Alpha coefficients were .89 and .86.

Authors: Eden, E., and Aviram, A.

Article: Self-efficacy training to speed reemployment: Helping people to help themselves.

Journal: *Journal of Applied Psychology*, June 1993, *78*(3), 352–360.

Related Research: Sherer, M., et al. (1982). The Self-Efficacy Scale: Construction and validation. *Psychological Reports, 51,* 663–671.

■ ■ ■

6759

Test Name: GLOBAL SELF-WORTH SCALE

Purpose: To assess children's sense of self-worth.

Number of Items: 6

Format: Responses are made on a 4-point scale.

Reliability: Alpha coefficients ranged from .71 to .82.

Authors: Knight, G. P., et al.

Article: Socialization and family correlates of mental health outcomes among Hispanic and Anglo American children: Considerations of cross-ethnic scalar equivalence.

Journal: *Child Development,* February 1994, *65*(1), 212–224.

Related Research: Harter, S. (1985). *Manual for the self-perception profile for children.* Unpublished manuscript, University of Denver.

■ ■ ■

6760

Test Name: GLOBAL SELF-WORTH SUBSCALE

Purpose: To assess self-esteem.

Number of Items: 5

Format: Items are scored on a 4-point scale.

Reliability: Alpha coefficients were .71 and .73.

Validity: Correlations with other variables ranged from -.27 to .23.

Authors: Seidman, E., et al.

Article: The impact of school transitions in early adolescence on the self-system and perceived social context of poor urban youth.

Journal: *Child Development*, April 1994, *65*(2), 507–522.

Related Research: Harter, S. (1987). *The perceived competence scale for adolescents.* Unpublished manuscript, University of Denver.

■ ■ ■

6761

Test Name: GOAL ORIENTATION SCALE—CLASSROOM

Purpose: To enable respondents to reflect on when they personally felt most successful in their schoolwork.

Number of Items: 21

Format: Responses are made on a 5-point Likert-type scale ranging from 1 (*strongly agree*) to 5 (*strongly disagree*). Includes 4 factors: Ego Orientation, Task Orientation, Work Avoidance, and Cooperation. All items are presented.

Reliability: Alpha coefficients ranged from .71 to .89.

Authors: Duda, J. L., and Nicholls, J. G.

Article: Dimensions of achievement motivation in school work and sport.

Journal: *Journal of Educational Psychology*, September 1992, *84*(3), 290–299.

Related Research: Nicholls, J. G. (1989). *The competitive ethos and democratic education.* Cambridge, MA: Harvard University Press.

■ ■ ■

6762

Test Name: HARTER PERCEIVED COMPETENCE SCALE

Purpose: To measure perceived competence in students.

Number of Items: 7

Format: Responses are made on a 4-point scale.

Reliability: Alpha was .75.

Authors: Vallerand, R. J., et al.

Article: A comparison of the school intrinsic motivation and perceived competence of gifted and regular students.

Journal: *Gifted Child Quarterly*, Fall 1994, *38*(4), 172–175.

Related Research: Harter, S. (1982). The Perceived Competence Scale for Children. *Child Development, 53,* 87–97.

■ ■ ■

6763

Test Name: HEALTH LOCUS OF CONTROL SCALE

Purpose: To measure health locus of control.

Number of Items: 11

Format: Responses are made on a 6-point Likert-type format ranging from *strongly disagree* to *strongly agree.*

Validity: Correlations with other variables ranged from -.15 to .23.

Authors: Weisberg, E., et al.

Article: Personal determinants of leisure-time exercise activities.

Journal: *Perceptual and Motor Skills*, December 1992, *75*(3) Part 1, 779–784.

Related Research: Wallston, B. S., et al. (1976). On the Health Locus of Control (HLC) Scale. *Journal of Consulting and Clinical Psychology, 4,* 580–585.

■ ■ ■

6764

Test Name: HEALTH PERCEPTION QUESTIONNAIRE

Purpose: To identify one's health perceptions.

Number of Items: 34

Format: Responses are made on a Likert-type scale ranging from 1 (*strongly agree*) to 5 (*strongly disagree*). Examples are presented.

Reliability: Alpha coefficients ranged from .68 to .93 on 9 of 12 categories presented.

Author: Kenney, J. W.

Article: Perceptions of health among lay consumers.

Journal: *Perceptual and Motor Skills*, October 1991, *73*(2), 427–432.

Related Research: Woods, N. F., et al. (1988). Being healthy: Women's images. *Advances in Nursing Science, 11*(1), 36–46.

■ ■ ■

6765

Test Name: HOCKEY COMPETENCE SCALE

Purpose: To assess perceived competence in hockey.

Number of Items: 3

Format: 5-point Likert format. All items presented.

Reliability: Alphas ranged from .48 to .52 over two administrations. Test–retest reliability was .46.

Authors: Losier, G., and Vallerand, R. J.

Article: The temporal relationship between perceived competence and self-determined motivation.

Journal: *The Journal of Social Psychology*, December 1994, *133*(6), 793–801.

Related Research: Harter, S. (1982). The perceived competence scale for children. *Child Development, 53,* 87–97.

■ ■ ■

6766

Test Name: HOW CAREER GROUPS WORK SCALE

Purpose: To measure participants' perceptions of group experience contributing to learning and change.

Number of Items: 14

Format: Responses are made on a 4-point scale ranging from *did not apply to my learning in group* to *one of the two most important experiences.*

Reliability: Hoyt estimate of reliability was .86.

Authors: Mawson, D. L., and Kahn, S. E.

Article: Group process in a women's career intervention.

Journal: *The Career Development Quarterly*, March 1993, *41*(3), 238–245.

Related Research: Kivlighan, D., et al. (1987). Participants' perceptions of change mechanisms in career counseling groups: The role of emotional components in career problem solving. *Journal of Career Development, 14,* 35–44.

■ ■ ■

6767

Test Name: IDEA INVENTORY

Purpose: To measure general irrational beliefs.

Number of Items: 33

Format: Responses are made on a 3-point Likert-type scale ranging from 1 (*agree*) to 3 (*disagree*). All items are presented.

Reliability: Test–retest (4–6 weeks) reliability coefficients ranged from .81 to .86.

Authors: Watson, M. B., and Foxcroft, C. D.

Article: The relation between career indecision and irrational beliefs among university students.

Journal: *Journal of Vocational Behavior*, April 1993, *42*(2), 155–169.

Related Research: Kassinove, H., et al. (1977). Developmental trends in rational thinking: Implications for rational emotive school mental health programs. *Journal of Community Psychology, 5,* 266–274.

■ ■ ■

6768

Test Name: IDENTITY DIFFUSION SCALE

Purpose: To assess identity cohesion.

Number of Items: 10

Format: 6-point Likert format. Sample items presented.

Reliability: Alphas ranged from .77 to .78.

Authors: Farrell, M. P., and Barnes, G. M.

Article: Family systems and social support: A test of the effects of cohesion and adaptability on the functioning of parents and adolescents.

Journal: *Journal of Marriage and the Family*, February 1993, *55*(1), 119–132.

Related Research: Farrell, M. P., & Rosenberg, S. D. (1981). *Men* *at mid-life.* Boston: Auburn House.

• • •

6769

Test Name: IDENTITY STYLE INVENTORY

Purpose: To assess processing orientation.

Number of Items: 39

Format: 5-point scales. Sample items presented.

Reliability: Test–retest reliabilities (2 months) ranged from .68 to .78.

Author: Berzonsky, M. D.

Article: Self-identity: The relationship between process and content.

Journal: *Journal of Research in Personality*, December 1994, *28*(4), 453–460.

Related Research: Berzonsky, M. D. (1992). Identity and coping strategies. *Journal of Personality*, *60*, 771-778.

• • •

6770

Test Name: IMPOSTER PHENOMENON SCALE

Purpose: To measure the feeling of intellectual phoniness despite great achievement.

Number of Items: 14

Format: 7-point Likert format. All items are presented.

Reliability: Internal consistency ranged from .72 to .85.

Validity: Correlations with other variables ranged from .17 to .63.

Author: Fried-Buchalter, S.

Article: Fear of success, fear of failure, and the impostor phenomenon: A factor analytic approach to convergent and discriminant validity.

Journal: *Journal of Personality*

Assessment, April 1992, *58*(2), 368–379.

Related Research: Harvey, J. C. (1982). *The imposter phenomenon and achievement: A failure to internalize success.* (Doctoral dissertation, Temple University, 1981). *Dissertation Abstracts International*, *49*, 4969B-4970B.

Chance, P. R., & O'Toole, M. A. (1988). The imposter phenomenon: An internal barrier to empowerment and achievement. *Women and Therapy*, *6*, 51–64.

• • •

6771

Test Name: INITIAL SELF-EFFICACY SCALE

Purpose: To measure task-specific self-efficacy for the job of entry-level accountant.

Number of Items: 47

Format: Responses are made on an 11-point scale ranging from 0 (*no confidence*) to 10 (*complete confidence*). Sample items are presented.

Reliability: Coefficient alpha was .98. Test–retest reliability was .43

Validity: Correlations with other variables ranged from -.14 to .43.

Author: Saks, A. M.

Article: Longitudinal field investigation of the moderating and mediating effects of self-efficacy on the relationship between training and newcomer adjustment.

Journal: *Journal of Applied Psychology*, April 1995, *80*(2), 211–225.

• • •

6772

Test Name: INTELLECTUAL ACHIEVEMENT RESPONSIBILITY QUESTIONNAIRE

Purpose: To measure locus of control.

Number of Items: 34

Format: Responses to each experience are made by indicating the event was caused by the student or by other people or events.

Reliability: Test–retest reliabilities ranged from .66 to .74. Split-half reliabilities ranged from .54 to .60.

Author: Wehmeyer, M. L.

Article: Gender differences in locus of control scores for students with learning disabilities.

Journal: *Perceptual and Motor Skills*, October 1993, *77*(2), 359–366.

Related Research: Crandall, V. C., et al. (1965). Children's beliefs in their own control of reinforcements in intellectual-academic achievement situations. *Child Development*, *43*, 91–109.

• • •

6773

Test Name: INTERNAL CONTROL INDEX

Purpose: To measure locus of control.

Number of Items: 28

Format: 5-point rating scales (*never* to *always*).

Reliability: Alpha was .82. Item-total correlations ranged from .06 to .58.

Author: Jacobs, K. W.

Article: Psychometric properties of the Internal Control Index

Journal: *Psychological Reports*, August 1993, *73*(1), 251–255.

Related Research: Duttweiler, P. C. (1984). The Internal Control Index: A newly developed measure of locus of control. *Educational*

and Psychological Measurement,
44, 209–221.

• • •

6774

Test Name: INTERNAL–
EXTERNAL LOCUS OF
CONTROL SCALE

Purpose: To determine internal
external locus of control among
college students.

Number of Items: 29

Format: There are 23 forced-
choice items (with one point given
for each external response) and 6
filler items.

Reliability: Internal reliability
estimates ranged from .65 to .79.

Authors: Martin, N. K., and
Dixon, P. N.

Article: Factors influencing
students' college choice.

Journal: *Journal of College
Student Development,* May 1991,
32(3), 253–257.

Related Research: Rotter, G. S.
(1966). Generalized expectancies
for internal versus external
control of reinforcement.
Psychological Monographs, 80,
1–28.

• • •

6775

Test Name: INTERNAL,
POWERFUL OTHERS AND
CHANCE SCALES

Purpose: To measure locus of
control.

Number of Items: 24

Format: Includes 3 measures of
locus of control: internal, powerful
others, and chance. Responses
are made on a Likert scale ranging
from 1 (*strongly disagree*) to 5
(*strongly agree*).

Reliability: KR-20 reliabilities
ranged from .64 to .78.

Validity: Correlations with other
variables were -.35 to .42

Authors: Wanberg, C. R., and
Muchinsky, P. M.

Article: A typology of career
decision status: Validity extension
of the vocational decision status
model.

Journal: *Journal of Counseling
Psychology,* January 1992, *39*(1),
71–80.

Related Research: Levenson, H.
(1974). Activism and powerful
others: Distinctions within the
concept of internal-external
control. *Journal of Personality
Assessment, 38,* 377–383.

• • •

6776

Test Name: JACKSON INCEST
BLAME SCALE

Purpose: To measure four
dimensions of attribution of blame
in cases of incest.

Number of Items: 20

Format: Responses to each item
are made on a 6-point scale
ranging from 0 (*strongly disagree*)
to 5 (*strongly agree*). Examples
are presented.

Reliability: Alpha coefficients
ranged from .44 to .71.

Validity: Correlations with other
variables ranged from -.46 to .18.

Authors: Adams, E. M., and
Betz, N. E.

Article: Gender difference in
counselors' attitudes toward and
attributions about incest.

Journal: *Journal of Counseling
Psychology,* April 1993, *40*(2),
210–216.

Related Research: Jackson, T. H.,
& Ferguson, W. P. (1983).
Attribution of blame in incest.
*American Journal of Community
Psychology, 11,* 313–322.

6777

Test Name: JANICE FIELD
FEELINGS OF INADEQUACY
SCALE—REVISED

Purpose: To measure self-esteem.

Number of Items: 20

Format: Responses are made to
each item on a scale that includes
*very often, fairly often, sometimes,
once in a great while,* and
practically never.

Reliability: Split-half reliabilities
were .72 and .88

Validity: Correlations with other
variables ranged from -.75 to .47.

Authors: Wanberg, C. R., and
Muchinsky, P. M.

Article: A typology of career
decision status: Validity extension
of the vocational decision status
model.

Journal: *Journal of Counseling
Psychology,* January 1992, *39*(1),
71–80.

Related Research: Eagly, A. H.
(1967). Involvement as a
determinant of response to
favorable and unfavorable
information. *Journal of
Personality and Social Psychology
Monographs, 7*(3, Whole No.
643).

• • •

6778

Test Name: JOB LOSS
PERCEPTIONS SCALE

Purpose: To measure perceptions
of job loss.

Number of Items: 6

Format: Includes three dimensions:
External Attribution,
Reversibility, and Intensity.
Responses are made on a 5-point
scale ranging from 1 (*strongly
disagree*) to 5 (*strongly agree*).

Reliability: Alpha coefficients
ranged from .65 to .77.

Authors: Leana, C. R., and Feldman, D. C.

Article: Gender differences in responses to unemployment.

Journal: *Journal of Vocational Behavior*, February 1991, *38*(1), 65–77.

Related Research: Kelly, H. H. (1973). The process of causal attribution. *American Psychologist, 28,* 107–128.

• • •

6779

Test Name: JOB STRESSORS INTERVIEW

Purpose: To measure role ambiguity, person-role conflict, gender-role conflict, job dissatisfaction, anxiety, depression, anger, technical performance, and social performance.

Number of Items: 34

Format: Varied formats. All items are presented.

Reliability: Alphas ranged from .67 to .84 across subscales.

Author: Abranis, D. J.

Article: Relationship of job stressors to job performance: Linear or an inverted-U?

Journal: *Psychological Reports*, August 1994, *75*(1) Part II, 547–558.

Related Research: Cohen, S. (1980). After effect of stress on human performance and social behavior: A review of research and theory. *Psychological Bulletin, 88,* 82–108.

• • •

6780

Test Name: LEISURE SATISFACTION SCALE

Purpose: To measure satisfaction

with various dimensions of participant's use of time.

Number of Items: 24

Format: Responses are made on a 5-point Likert-type scale ranging from 1 (*almost never true*) to 5 (*almost always true*). A sample item is presented.

Reliability: Coefficient alpha was .93.

Authors: Robbins, S. B., et al.

Article: Goal continuity as a mediator of early retirement adjustment: Testing a multidimensional model.

Journal: *Journal of Counseling Psychology*, January 1994, *41*(1), 18–26.

Related Research: Beard, J., & Ragheb, M. (1980). Measuring leisure satisfaction. *Journal of Leisure Research, 12,* 20–33.

• • •

6781

Test Name: LEISURE VALUES AND PREFERENCES SCALE

Purpose: To measure awareness of leisure preferences and knowledge of leisure resources.

Number of Items: 6

Format: Responses are made on 3-point Likert-type rating scales. Sample items are presented.

Reliability: Alpha was .85.

Authors: Robbins, S. B., et al.

Article: Goal continuity as a mediator of early retirement adjustment: Testing a multidimensional model.

Journal: *Journal of Counseling Psychology*, January 1994, *41*(1), 18–26.

Related Research: Kelly, J. (1983). *Leisure identities and interactions*. Winchester, MA: Allen & Unwin.

6782

Test Name: LITWIN AND STRINGER ORGANIZATIONAL QUESTIONNAIRE—FORM B

Purpose: To measure climate perceptions.

Number of Items: 50

Format: Includes 7 factors: Structure, Responsibility, Warm-Support, Reward, Pressure Standards, Risk, and Accommodation. Responses are made on a 7-point scale.

Reliability: Alpha coefficients ranged from .68 to .89 (*N* = 1104).

Authors: Day, D. V., and Bedeian, A. G.

Article: Work climate and Type A status as predictors of job satisfaction: A test of the interactional perspective.

Journal: *Journal of Vocational Behavior*, February 1991, *38*(1), 39–52.

Related Research: Litwin, G. H., & Stringer, R. A., Jr. (1968). *Motivation and organizational change*. Boston, MA: Division of Research, Graduate School of Business Administration, Harvard University.

• • •

6783

Test Name: LOCUS OF CONTROL INVENTORY

Purpose: To measure locus of control.

Number of Items: 24

Format: Includes 3 scales: Internal, Powerful Others, and Chance. Responses are made on a 6-point scale ranging from -3 (*strongly disagree*) to +3 (*strongly agree*).

Reliability: Kuder-Richardson reliabilities ranged from .64 to .78. Test–retest (1 week) reliabilities ranged from .60 to .79.

Author: Gadzella, B. M.

Article: Locus of control differences among stress groups.

Journal: *Perceptual and Motor Skills*, December 1994, *79*(3) Part 2, 1619–1624.

Related Research: Levenson, H. (1981). Differentiating among internality, powerful others, and chance. In H. Lefcourt (Ed.), *Research with locus of control, Vol. 1. Assessment method* (pp. 15–63). New York: Academic Press.

■ ■ ■

6784

Test Name: LOCUS OF CONTROL SCALE

Purpose: To measure personal and social control.

Number of Items: 10

Format: All items presented.

Reliability: KR-20 ranged from .67 to .68.

Validity: Correlations with other variables ranged from .36 to -.27.

Author: Ferguson, E.

Article: Rotter's Locus of Control Scale: A ten-item two factor model.

Journal: *Psychological Reports*, December 1993, *73*(3) Part II, 1267–1278.

Related Research: Rotter, J. B. (1966). Generalized expectancies for internal versus external control of reinforcement. *Psychological Monographs: General and Applied, 80*, (1, Whole No. 609).

■ ■ ■

6785

Test Name: LOCUS OF CONTROL SCALE

Purpose: To measure locus of control.

Number of Items: 28

Format: Includes two factors: Autonomous Behavior and Self-Confidence. All items are presented.

Reliability: Coefficient alpha was .85 (*N* = 411).

Validity: Correlations with other variables ranged from .39 to .44 (*N* = 411).

Author: Ward, E. A.

Article: Construct validity of need for achievement and locus of control scales.

Journal: *Educational and Psychological Measurement*, Winter 1994, *54*(4), 983–992.

Related Research: Duttweiler, P. C. (1984). The Internal Control Index: A newly developed measure of locus of control. *Educational and Psychological Measurement, 44*, 209–221.

■ ■ ■

6786

Test Name: LOCUS OF CONTROL SCALE

Purpose: To measure how much participants feel they can influence the decisions of superiors, coworkers, and subordinates; the relationships they have with them; and their responsibilities in the organizations.

Number of Items: 28

Format: 5-point Likert format.

Reliability: Alpha was .86.

Author: Riipinen, M.

Article: Occupational needs as moderators between locus of control and job involvement.

Journal: *Psychological Reports*, April 1994, *74*(2), 371–379.

Related Research: Petersen, N. (1985). Specific versus generalized locus of control scales related to satisfaction. *Psychological Reports, 56*, 60–62.

■ ■ ■

6787

Test Name: LOCUS OF CONTROL SCALE

Purpose: To measure locus of control.

Number of Items: 29

Format: Forced-choice format.

Reliability: Alphas ranged from .65 to .73. Test–retest reliabilities ranged from .55 to .78.

Authors: Heppner, P. P., et al.

Article: Progress in resolving problems: A problem-focused style of coping.

Journal: *Journal of Counseling Psychology*, July 1995, *42*(3), 279–293.

Related Research: Ratter, J. B. (1966). Generalized expectancies for internal versus external control of reinforcement. *Psychological Monographs*, *80*(1, Whole No. 609).

■ ■ ■

6788

Test Name: LOCUS OF CONTROL SCALE

Purpose: To measure locus of control.

Number of Items: 40

Format: Yes–no format.

Reliability: Split-half ranged from .74 to .86. Test–retest ranged from .63 to .76. Alphas ranged from .74 to .86.

Author: Wehmeyer, M. L.

Article: Reliability and acquiescence in the measurement of locus of control with adolescents and adults with mental retardation.

Journal: *Psychological Reports*, August 1994, *75*(1) Part II, 527–537.

Related Research: Nowicki, S., & Duke, M. P. (1974). A locus of control scale for non-college as well as college adults. *Journal of Personality Assessment, 38,* 136–137.

■ ■ ■

6789

Test Name: LOCUS OF CONTROL SCALE—BRIEF VERSION

Purpose: To measure locus of control.

Number of Items: 9

Format: Likert format. All items presented.

Reliability: Alphas ranged from .59 to .72 across subscales.

Validity: Model fit the data (Chi-square = 70.88, $p + .18$).

Authors: Sapp, S. G., and Harrod, W. J.

Article: Reliability and validity of a brief version of Levenson's Locus of Control Scale.

Journal: *Psychological Reports,* April 1993, *72*(2), 539–550.

Related Research: Levenson, H. (1974). Activism and powerful others: Distinctions within the concept of internal-external control. *Journal of Personality Assessment, 38,* 377–383.

■ ■ ■

6790

Test Name: LOW BACK SELF-EFFICACY SCALE

Purpose: To determine level of confidence low-back-pain patients have in their ability to successfully complete certain daily activities.

Number of Items: 20

Format: Respondents indicate on a 10-point scale their confidence in successfully completing each task. All tasks are presented.

Reliability: Alpha coefficients ranged from .97 to .98.

Author: Altmaier, E. M., et al.

Article: Role of self-efficacy in rehabilitation outcome among chronic low back pain patients.

Journal: *Journal of Counseling Psychology,* July 1993, *40*(3), 335–339.

Related Research: Bandura, A. (1986). *Social foundations of thought and action: A social cognitive theory.* Englewood Cliffs, NJ: Prentice Hall.

■ ■ ■

6791

Test Name: MAMMOGRAPHY QUESTIONNAIRE

Purpose: To measure the components of the Health Belief Model as applied to mammography.

Number of Items: 22

Format: 6-point Likert format. All items presented.

Reliability: Alphas ranged from .60 to .83 across subscales and test groups. Test–retest ranged from .49 to .75.

Validity: Correlations with recency of use of mammography ranged from -.08 to .47 across subscales.

Authors: Hyman, R. B., and Baker, S.

Article: Construction of the Hyman-Baker Mammography Questionnaire, a measure of health belief model variables.

Journal: *Psychological Reports,* December 1992, *71*(3) Part II, 1203–1215.

■ ■ ■

6792

Test Name: MANAGING STUDENTS SCALE

Purpose: To measure teachers' perceptions of how students can be managed.

Number of Items: 21

Format: Likert format. All items are presented.

Reliability: Internal consistency was .70. Subscale alphas ranged from .60 to .90.

Author: Johnson, V. G.

Article: Student teachers' conceptions of classroom control.

Journal: *Journal of Educational Research,* November/December 1994, *88*(2), 109–137.

Related Research: Lampert, M. (1985). How teachers manage to teach: Perspectives on problems in practice. *Harvard Educational Review, 55,* 178–194.

■ ■ ■

6793

Test Name: MASTERY SCALE

Purpose: To assess sense of control over events in one's environment.

Number of Items: 7

Format: 5-point agreement scales.

Reliability: Alpha was .80.

Authors: Simons, R. L., et al.

Article: Explaining women's double jeopardy: Factors that mediate the association between harsh treatment as a child and violence by a husband.

Journal: *Journal of Marriage and the Family,* August 1993, *55*(3), 713–712.

Related Research: Pearlin, L. I., et al. (1981). The stress process. *Journal of Health and Social Behavior, 22,* 337–356.

■ ■ ■

6794

Test Name: MATHEMATICS COURSE OUTCOME EXPECTATIONS SCALE

Purpose: To determine positive outcomes that might result from taking mathematics-related courses.

Number of Items: 15

Format: Responses are made on a 10-point scale ranging from 0 (*strongly disagree*) to 9 (*strongly agree*).

Reliability: Coefficient alpha was .90. Test–retest (2 weeks) reliability was .91.

Validity: Correlations with other variables ranged from -.19 to .67.

Authors: Lent, R. W., et al.

Article: Predicting mathematics-related choice and success behavior: Test of an expanded social cognitive model.

Journal: *Journal of Vocational Behavior*, April 1993, *42*(2), 223–236.

Related Research: Lent, R. W., et al. (1991). Mathematics self-efficacy: Sources and relation to science-based career choice. *Journal of Counseling Psychology*, *38*, 424–430.

■ ■ ■

6795

Test Name: MATHEMATICS SELF-EFFICACY SCALE

Purpose: To measure math self-efficacy.

Number of Items: 5

Format: 5-point Likert format.

Reliability: Alpha was .89.

Author: Farmer, H. S., et al.

Article: Women's career choices: Focus on science, math and technology careers.

Journal: *Journal of Counseling Psychology*, April 1995, *42*(2), 155–170.

Related Research: Betz, N., & Hackett, G. (1983). The relationship of mathematics self-

efficacy expectations to the selection of science-based college majors. *Journal of Vocational Behavior*, *23*, 329–345.

■ ■ ■

6796

Test Name: MATHEMATICS SELF-EFFICACY SCALE— REVISED

Purpose: To measure mathematics self-efficacy.

Number of Items: 52

Format: 5-point Likert format.

Reliability: Alphas ranged from .90 to .92.

Authors: Pajares, F., and Miller, M. D.

Article: Mathematics self-efficacy and mathematics performances: The need for specificity of assessment.

Journal: *Journal of Counseling Psychology*, April 1995, *42*(2), 190–198.

Related Research: Betz, N. E., & Hackett, G. (1983). The relationship of mathematics self-efficacy expectations to the selection of science-based college majors. *Journal of Vocational Behavior*, *23*, 329–345.

■ ■ ■

6797

Test Name: MATHEMATICS SELF-EFFICACY—COLLEGE COURSES SCALE—REVISED

Purpose: To measure one's confidence in his or her ability to complete mathematics-related college courses with grades of B or better.

Number of Items: 15

Format: Responses are made on a 10-point scale.

Reliability: Coefficient alpha was .92. Test–retest (2 weeks) reliability was .94.

Validity: Correlations with other variables ranged from -.37 to .61.

Authors: Lent, R. W., et al.

Article: Predicting mathematics-related choice and success behavior: Test of an expanded social cognitive model.

Journal: *Journal of Vocational Behavior*, April 1993, *42*(2), 223–236.

Related Research: Betz, N. E., & Hackett, G. (1983). The relationship of mathematics self-efficacy expectations to the selection of science-based college majors. *Journal of Vocational Behavior*, *23*, 329–345.

■ ■ ■

6698

Test Name: MATH SELF-CONCEPT SCALE

Purpose: To measure one's math self-concept.

Number of Items: 7

Format: Responses are made on a 5-point Likert scale ranging from 1 (*strongly disagree*) to 5 (*strongly agree*). Examples are presented.

Reliability: Alpha coefficients were .88 (men) and .91 (women).

Authors: Bandalos, D. L., et al.

Article: Effects of math self-concept, perceived self-efficacy, and attributions for failure and success on test anxiety.

Journal: *Journal of Educational Psychology*, December 1995, *87*(4), 611–623.

Related Research: Benson, J. (1989). Structural components of statistical test anxiety in adults: An exploratory model. *Journal of Experimental Education*, *57*, 247–261.

6799

Test Name: MATH SELF-EFFICACY SCALE

Purpose: To identify students' confidence in their ability to solve course-related math problems.

Number of Items: 20

Format: Responses are made on a 10-point scale ranging from 0 (*no confidence at all*) to 9 (*complete confidence*).

Reliability: Internal consistency ranged from .82 to .92. Test–retest reliability ranged from .47 to .74.

Validity: Correlations with other variables ranged from -.23 to .57.

Authors: Lopez, F. G., and Lent, R. W.

Article: Sources of mathematics self-efficacy in high school students.

Journal: *The Career Development Quarterly*, September 1992, *41*(1), 3–12.

■ ■ ■

6800

Test Name: MEANING OF WORK SCALE

Purpose: To identify one's perception of work.

Number of Items: 19

Format: Includes three latent variables: Self-Actualization, Independence, and Society. All items are presented.

Reliability: Coefficients of determination ranged from .85 to .96.

Authors: Kraska, M. F., and Wilmoth, J. N.

Article: LISREL model of three latent variables from 19 Meaning of Work Items for vocational students.

Journal: *Educational and*

Psychological Measurement, Autumn 1991, *51*(3), 767–774.

Related Research: Kazanas, H. C., et al. (1975). An instrument to measure the meaning and value of work. *Journal of Industrial Teacher Education, 12*(4), 68–73.

■ ■ ■

6801

Test Name: MEDICAL CAREER SELF-EFFICACY SCALES

Purpose: To measure how confident high school students are in their ability to be successful in performing medical activities.

Number of Items: 23

Format: Rating scales range from 0 (*no confidence at all*) to 9 (*complete confidence*). All items are presented.

Reliability: Alphas ranged from .78 to .93.

Validity: Interscale Correlations ranged from .31 to .89.

Authors: Speight, J. D., et al.

Article: Medcamps' effect on junior high school students' medical career self-efficacy.

Journal: *The Career Development Quarterly*, March 1995, *43*(3), 285–295.

■ ■ ■

6802

Test Name: MEMBER-PERCEIVED SIMILARITY WITH LEADER SCALE

Purpose: To measure member perceived similarity with leader.

Number of Items: 6

Format: Responses are made on a 7-point scale ranging from 1 (*strongly disagree*) to 7 (*strongly agree*). All items are presented.

Reliability: Coefficient alpha was .91. Test–retest reliabilities

ranged from .55 to .74 for time spans from 2 weeks to 6 months.

Authors: Liden, R. C., et al.

Article: A longitudinal study on the early development of leader-member exchanges.

Journal: *Journal of Applied Psychology*, August 1993, *78*(4), 662–674.

Related Research: Turban, D. B., & Jones, A. P. (1988). Supervisor-subordinates similarity: Types, effects, and mechanism. *Journal of Applied Psychology, 73*, 228–234.

■ ■ ■

6803

Test Name: ME SCALE

Purpose: To measure the self-concept of gifted and talented youth.

Number of Items: 40

Format: Responses are either *agree* or *disagree*. All items are presented.

Reliability: KR-20 reliability was .79.

Authors: Feldhusen, J. F., and Willard-Holt, C.

Article: Me: A self-concept scale, revised norms.

Journal: *Perceptual and Motor Skills*, February 1992, *74*(1), 299-303.

Related Research: Feldhusen, J. F., & Kolloff, M. B. (1982). Me: A self-concept scale for gifted students. *Perceptual and Motor Skills, 53*, 319–323.

■ ■ ■

6804

Test Name: MISSOURI COMPREHENSIVE GUIDANCE EVALUATION SURVEY

Purpose: To obtain self-efficacy

ratings of competencies expected of high school students.

Number of Items: 98

Format: 7-point Likert format ranges from 1 (*very low level of confidence*) to 7 (*very high level of confidence*).

Reliability: Internal consistency ranged from .96 to .98.

Validity: Correlations with other variables ranged from -.51 to .55.

Authors: Multon, K. D., et al.

Article: An empirical derivation of career decision subtypes in a high school sample.

Journal: *Journal of Vocational Behavior*, August 1995, *47*(1), 76–92.

Related Research: Gysbers, N., et al. (1992). *Missouri Comprehensive Guidance Competency Survey: Grades 9-12.* Jefferson City, MO: Missouri Department of Elementary and Secondary Education. (Available from Norman Gysbers, University of Missouri—Columbia, Department of Educational and Counseling Psychology, 305 Noyes Hall, Columbia, MO 65211.)

■ ■ ■

6805

Test Name: MOTOR PERCEIVED COMPETENCE SCALE

Purpose: To measure children's perceived motor competence.

Number of Items: 18

Format: Responses are made on a 5-point scale. All items are presented.

Reliability: Internal consistency and stability reliabilities were .88.

Validity: Correlations with other variables were -.33 and .35.

Authors: Rudisill, M. E., et al.

Article: The relationship between children's perceived and actual motor competence.

Journal: *Perceptual and Motor Skills*, June 1993, *76*(3) Part 1, 895–906.

■ ■ ■

6806

Test Name: MULTIDIMENSIONAL BODY–SELF RELATIONS QUESTIONNAIRE

Purpose: To assess body-image parameters.

Number of Items: 69

Format: Includes items from the three somatic domains of physical appearance, health, and physical fitness; items from the Body Areas Satisfaction Scale; and six weight-related items.

Validity: Correlations with the Bulimia Test—Revised ranged from -.73 to .38.

Authors: Geissler, T., et al.

Article: Bulimic symptoms and body-image characteristics among university women.

Journal: *Perceptual and Motor Skills*, October 1994, *79*(2), 771–775.

Related Research: Cash, T. F., et al. (1986). The great American shape-up. *Psychology Today*, *20*(4), 30–37.

■ ■ ■

6807

Test Name: MULTICULTURAL COUNSELING AWARENESS SCALE

Purpose: To measure multicultural counseling awareness.

Number of Items: 45

Format: Includes two subscales: Knowledge/Skills and Awareness.

Responses are made on a 7-point Likert-type scale.

Reliability: Alpha coefficients ranged from .78 to .92.

Validity: Correlations with the Quick Discrimination Index ranged from .21 to .50 (*N*= 57).

Authors: Ponterrotto, J. G., et al.

Article: Development and initial validation of the Quick Discrimination Index (QDI).

Journal: *Educational and Psychological Measurement*, December 1995, *55*(6), 1016–1031.

Related Research: Ponterrotto, J. G., & Pedersen, P. B. (1993). *Preventing prejudice: A guide for counselors and educators.* Newbury Park, CA: Sage.

■ ■ ■

6808

Test Name: MULTIDIMENSIONAL HEALTH LOCUS OF CONTROL SCALES

Purpose: To measure health locus of control.

Number of Items: 18

Format: Includes 3 dimensions: chance, internal, and powerful others.

Reliability: Test–retest reliability coefficients ranged from .62 to .80.

Authors: Casey, T. A., et al.

Article: An investigation of the factor structure of the Multidimensional Health Locus of Control Scales in a health promotion program.

Journal: *Educational and Psychological Measurement*, Summer 1993, *53*(2), 491–498.

Related Research: Wallston, K. A., et al. (1978). Development of the Multidimensional Health Locus of Control (MHLC) Scales. *Health Education Monographs*, *6*(2), 160–170.

6809

Test Name:
MULTIDIMENSIONAL LOCUS
OF CONTROL SCALE

Purpose: To measure locus of control.

Number of Items: 24

Format: Includes 3 factors: Internality, Powerful Others, and Chance. All items are presented.

Reliability: Coefficient alpha was .82 (N = 411).

Validity: Correlations with other variables ranged from .17 to .44.

Author: Ward, E. A.

Article: Construct validity of Need for Achievement and Locus of Control Scales.

Journal: *Educational and Psychological Measurement*, Winter 1994, *54*(4), 983–992.

Related Research: Levenson, H. (1974). Activism and powerful others: Distinctions within the concept of internal-external control. *Journal of Personality Assessment*, *38*, 377–383.

● ● ●

6810

Test Name:
MULTIDIMENSIONAL LOCUS
OF PAIN CONTROL
QUESTIONNAIRE

Purpose: To assess locus of control regarding pain.

Number of Items: 27

Format: 10-point VAS from *very true* to *very untrue*. All items are presented.

Reliability: Alphas ranged from .72 to .82 across subscales.

Validity: Correlations between scales ranged from -.29 to .15. Correlations with other variables ranged from -.15 to .35.

Authors: ter Kuile, M. M., et al.

Article: The development of the Multidimensional Locus of Pain Control Questionnaire: Factor structure, reliability and validity.

Journal: *Journal of Psychopathology and Behavioral Assessment*, December 1993, *15*(4), 387–404.

● ● ●

6811

Test Name:
MULTIDIMENSIONAL
MEASURE OF CHILDREN'S
PERCEPTION OF CONTROL.

Purpose: To measure locus of control.

Number of Items: 48

Format: 4-point scales. Sample items presented.

Reliability: Alphas ranged from .60 to .78. Split-half ranged between .62 and .68.

Author: Magzawa, A. S.

Article: Influence of involuntary migration on children's perception of control.

Journal: *Psychological Reports*, June 1992, *70*(3) Part I, 707–710.

Related Research: Connel, J. P. (1985). A new multidimensional measure of children's perception of control. *Child Development*, *56*, 1018–1041.

● ● ●

6812

Test Name:
MULTIDIMENSIONAL–
MULTIATTRIBUTIONAL
CAUSALITY SCALE

Purpose: To measure locus of control.

Number of Items: 48

Format: Includes 2 scales: Achievement and Affiliation. Each scale is divided into Ability, Effort, Task Difficulty, and Luck.

Responses are made on a 4-point Likert-type scale.

Reliability: Alpha coefficients ranged from .54 to .78.

Validity: Correlations with other variables ranged from .24 to .62.

Authors: Hyman, G. J., et al.

Article: The relationship between three multidimensional locus of control scales.

Journal: *Educational and Psychological Measurement*, Summer 1991, *51*(2), 403–412.

Related Research: Lefcourt, H. M. (1981). The construction and development of the Multidimensional-Multiattributional Causality Scales. In H. M. Lefcourt (Ed.), *Research with the locus of control construct, Vol. 1.* New York: Academic Press.

● ● ●

6813

Test Name: NON-COGNITIVE
QUESTIONNAIRE

Purpose: To assess positive self-concept, realistic self-appraisal regarding academic abilities, understanding and ability to deal with racism, preference for long-term goals, ability of support people for one's academic goals, demonstrated leadership in organized or informal groups, demonstrated community service prior to college, and knowledge acquired in nontraditional ways and fields.

Number of Items: 16

Format: Responses are made on Likert-type questions (13) and open-ended questions (3).

Reliability: Test–retest reliability for all items ranged from .70 to .94.

Authors: Young, B. D., and Sowa, C. J.

Article: Predictors of academic success for Black student athletes.

Journal: *Journal of College Student Development*, July 1992, *33*(4), 318–323.

Related Research: Tracey, T. J., & Sedlacek, W. E. (1985). The relationship of noncognitive variables to academic success: A longitudinal comparison by race. *Journal of College Student Personnel, 26*, 405–410.

■ ■ ■

6814

Test Name: NOWICKI-STRICKLAND LOCUS OF CONTROL SCALE

Purpose: To assess internal–external locus of control.

Number of Items: 40

Format: Responses are made on a 4-point scale ranging from *yes, totally agree,* to *no, totally disagree.*

Reliability: Test–retest correlation was .59 at a 7-month interval.

Author: Adalbjarnardottir, S.

Article: How schoolchildren propose to negotiate: The role of social withdrawal, social anxiety, and locus of control.

Journal: *Child Development,* December 1995, *66*(6), 1614–1634.

Related Research: Nowicki, S., & Strickland, B. R. (1973). A locus of control scale for children. *Journal of Consulting and Clinical Psychology, 40*, 148–154.

■ ■ ■

6815

Test Name: OCCUPATIONAL QUESTIONNAIRE

Purpose: To assess students' self-efficacy for 31 occupations.

Number of Items: 31

Format: Students rate on a 6-point scale ranging from 1 (*very unsure*) to 6 (*very sure*) how sure they are that they have the ability to successfully learn each of 31 occupations. All occupations are indicated.

Reliability: Coefficient alpha was .95. Average test–retest (7 days) reliability was .71 (*N* = 87). Test–retest reliability of generality of self-efficacy score was .84.

Validity: Correlations of generality of self-efficacy and other variables ranged from .11 to .53.

Authors: Church, A. T., et al.

Article: Self-efficacy for careers and occupational consideration in minority high school equivalency students.

Journal: *Journal of Counseling Psychology,* October 1992, *39*(4), 498–508.

Related Research: Teresa, J. S. (1991). *Increasing self-efficacy for careers in young adults from migrant farm workers' backgrounds.* Unpublished doctoral dissertation, Washington State University, Pullman.

■ ■ ■

6816

Test Name: OCCUPATIONAL SELF-EFFICACY SCALE

Purpose: To measure general self-efficacy.

Number of Items: 20

Format: Includes traditionally male and traditionally female occupations. Responses are either *yes* or *no* concerning whether respondents can or cannot complete the job duties or educational requirements for each item. "Yes" responses are qualified on a scale from 1 (*completely unsure*) to 10 (*completely sure*).

Reliability: Alpha coefficients ranged from .89 to .95.

Authors: Rooney, R. A., and Osipow, S. H.

Article: Task-specific Occupational Self-Efficacy Scale: The development and validation of a prototype.

Journal: *Journal of Vocational Behavior,* February 1992, *40*(1), 14–32.

Related Research: Betz, N. E., & Hackett, G. (1981). The relationship of career-related self-efficacy expectations to perceived career options in college women and men. *Journal of Counseling Psychology, 28*, 399–410.

■ ■ ■

6817

Test Name: OMNIBUS TEST

Purpose: To measure 12 aspects of the self.

Number of Items: 84

Format: 4-point scales range from *very true* to *very false.*

Reliability: Reliabilities ranged from .53 to .82 across subscales.

Validity: Correlations between subscales ranged from -.48 to .68.

Authors: Jensen, L., et al.

Article: Development of a self-theory and measurement scale.

Journal: *Journal of Personality Assessment,* December 1991, *57*(3), 521–530.

■ ■ ■

6818

Test Name: OUTCOME EXPECTATIONS SCALE

Purpose: To assess students' perceptions of outcomes accruing from an engineering undergraduate degree if successfully completed.

Number of Items: 12

Format: Includes nine positive and three negative outcomes. Responses are made on a 10-point scale ranging from 0 (*strongly disagree*) to 9 (*strongly agree*). Examples are presented.

Reliability: Internal consistency reliability coefficients were .81 (positive outcomes) and .77 (negative outcomes).

Validity: Correlations with other variables ranged from -.35 to .41.

Authors: Hackett, G., et al.

Article: Gender, ethnicity, and social cognitive factors predicting the academic achievement of students in engineering.

Journal: *Journal of Counseling Psychology*, October 1992, *39*(4), 527–538.

• • •

6819

Test Name: OVERT SELF-CRITICISM SCALE

Purpose: To measure self-reproach.

Number of Items: 7

Format: Sample item presented. Response categories not specified.

Reliability: Cronbach's Alpha was .90.

Authors: Powers, T. A., and Zuroff, D. C.

Article: A measure of overt self-criticism: Validation and correlates.

Journal: *Psychological Reports*, April 1992, *70*(2), 562.

Related Research: Powers, T. A., & Zuroff, D. C. (1988). Interpersonal consequences of overt self-criticism: A comparison with neutral and self-enhancing presentations of self. *Journal of Personality and Social Psychology*, *54*, 1054–1062.

6820

Test Name: PARENTAL-LEAVE-POLICY FAIRNESS SCALE

Purpose: To assess perceived parental-leave-policy fairness.

Number of Items: 9

Format: Includes these types of items: fairness, parental deservingness, and institutional responsibility. Responses are made on a 7-point scale ranging from 1 (*strongly disagree*) to 7 (*agree strongly*). All items are presented.

Reliability: Coefficient alpha was .95.

Validity: Correlations with other variables ranged from -.07 to .65.

Author: Grover, S. L.

Article: Predicting the perceived fairness of parental leave policies.

Journal: *Journal of Applied Psychology*, April 1991, *76*(2), 247–255.

• • •

6821

Test Name: PARENT SCHOOL EFFICACY SCALE

Purpose: To measure parents' perceptions of how much they help their children do well in school.

Number of Items: 12

Format: 5-point Likert format. A sample item is presented.

Reliability: Alpha was .81.

Validity: Correlations with other variables ranged from -.14 to .11.

Authors: Hoover-Dempsey, K. V., et al.

Article: Explorations in parent-school relations.

Journal: *Journal of Educational Research*, May/June 1992, *85*(5), 287–294.

6822

Test Name: PARENTS' PARTICIPATION IN UNIONS

Purpose: To assess children's perception of their parents' participation in unions.

Number of Items: 5.

Format: Responses to three items are made on a 3-point scale and responses to two items are made on a 5-point scale.

Reliability: Alphas were .70 (mothers) and .77 (fathers).

Validity: Correlation with other variables ranged from -.18 to .47.

Authors: Barling, J., et al.

Article: Pre-employment predictor of union attitudes: The role of family socialization and work beliefs.

Journal: *Journal of Applied Psychology*, October 1991, *76*(5), 725–731.

• • •

6823

Test Name: PEER COUNSELING HELPING STYLE QUESTIONNAIRE

Purpose: To determine the helping style most preferred by students who have met with peer counselors.

Number of Items: 25

Reliability: Internal consistency for each cluster ranged from .86 to .90.

Authors: Morey, R., and Miller, C.

Article: High school peer counseling: The relationship between student satisfaction and peer counselors' style of helping.

Journal: *School Counselor*, March 1993, *40*(4), 293–300.

Related Research: Morey, R., & Miller, C. (1988). *Peer Counseling Helping Style*

Questionnaire. Atascedero, CA: Author.

Morey, R., et al. (1989). Peer counseling: Students served, problems discussed and reported level of satisfaction. *The School Counselor, 37*, 137–143.

■ ■ ■

6824

Test Name: PERCEIVED ACADEMIC ABILITY SCALE

Purpose: To assess perceived academic ability.

Number of Items: 4

Format: Responses are made on a 5-point Likert-type scale ranging from 1 (*strongly agree*) to 5 (*strongly disagree*). Sample items are presented.

Reliability: Coefficient alpha was .86.

Authors: Duda, J. L., and Nicholls, J. G.

Article: Dimensions of achievement motivation in school work and sport.

Journal: *Journal of Educational Psychology*, September 1992, *84*(3), 290–299.

Related Research: Nicholls, J. G. (1989). *The competitive ethos and democratic education.* Cambridge, MA: Harvard University Press.

■ ■ ■

6825

Test Name: PERCEIVED COGNITIVE COMPETENCE QUESTIONNAIRE

Purpose: To assess perceived cognitive competence.

Number of Items: 50

Reliability: Coefficient alpha was .79.

Validity: Correlations with other variables ranged from .06 to .30.

Authors: Pierson, L. H., and Connell, J. P.

Article: Effect of grade retention on self-system processes, school engagement, and academic performance.

Journal: *Journal of Educational Psychology*, September 1992, *84*(3), 300–307.

Related Research: Skinner, E. A., et al. (1990). What it takes to do well in school and whether I've got it: A process model of perceived control and children's engagement and achievement in school. *Journal of Educational Psychology, 82*, 22–32.

■ ■ ■

6826

Test Name: PERCEIVED COMPETENCE SCALE

Purpose: To assess self-perceptions of competence.

Number of Items: 28

Format: Includes four domains: cognitive competence, social competence, physical competence, and general self-worth. An example is presented.

Reliability: Reliability estimates ranged from .73 to .84.

Author: Chan, L. K. S

Article: Relationship of motivation, strategic learning, and reading achievement in Grades 5, 7, and 9.

Journal: *Journal of Experimental Education*, Summer 1994, *62*(4), 319–339.

Related Research: Harter, S. (1982). The Perceived Competence Scale for Children. *Child Development, 53*, 87–97.

■ ■ ■

6827

Test Name: PERCEIVED CONTROL OVER TIME SCALE

Purpose: To assess the extent people believe they can affect how their time is spent.

Number of Items: 5

Format: Responses are made on a 5-point scale ranging from 1 (*seldom true*) to 5 (*very often true*).

Reliability: Coefficient alpha was .68.

Validity: Correlations with other variables ranged from -.43 to .29.

Author: Macan, T. H.

Article: Time management: Test of a process model.

Journal: *Journal of Applied Psychology*, June 1994, *79*(3), 381–391.

Related Research: Macan, T. M., et al. (1990). College students' time management: Correlations with academic performance and stress. *Journal of Educational Psychology, 82*, 760–768.

■ ■ ■

6828

Test Name: PERCEIVED CONTROL QUESTIONNAIRE

Purpose: To identify workers' perceived control over decision making.

Number of Items: 20

Format: 11-point scales are used ranging from 0 (*rarely*) to 10 (*always*) and another from 0 (*very little*) to 10 (*a great deal*).

Reliability: Internal consistency was .91.

Author: Parker, L. E.

Article: When to fix it and when to leave it: Relationships among perceived control, self-efficacy, dissent, and exit.

Journal: *Journal of Applied Psychology*, December 1993, *78*(6), 949–959.

Related Research: Tannenbaum, A. S., et al. (1974). *Hierarchy in organizations.* San Francisco: Jossey-Bass.

■ ■ ■

6829

Test Name: PERCEIVED CONTROL SCALE

Purpose: To assess perceived control.

Number of Items: 3

Format: Responses are made on a 7-point scale ranging from 1 (*strongly disagree*) to 7 (*strongly agree*). Examples are presented.

Reliability: Alpha coefficients were .68 and .71.

Validity: Correlations with other variables ranged from -.33 to .60.

Authors: Stevens, C. K, et al.

Article: Gender differences in the acquisition of salary negotiation skills: The role of goals, self-efficacy, and perceived control.

Journal: *Journal of Applied Psychology*, October 1993, *78*(5), 723–735.

■ ■ ■

6830

Test Name: PERCEIVED CONTROL SCALE

Purpose: To measure perceived control.

Number of Items: 5

Format: Responses are made on a 9-point scale ranging from 1 (*no control at all*) to 9 (*complete control*). All items are presented.

Reliability: Reliability coefficients were .80 and .95.

Authors: Goff, B. G., and Goddard, H. W.

Article: Relationship between selected values and perceived control.

Journal: *Perceptual and Motor Skills*, February 1992, *74*(1), 147–150.

Related Research: Schulz, R., & Decker, D. (1985). Long-term adjustment to physical disability: The role of social support, perceived control, and self-blame. *Journal of Personality and Social Psychology, 48*, 1162–1172.

■ ■ ■

6831

Test Name: PERCEIVED CONTROL SCALE

Purpose: To measure control and lack of control over good and bad outcomes.

Number of Items: 8

Format: 5-point agreement scales. All items presented.

Reliability: Alpha was .68.

Author: Ross, C. E.

Article: Marriage and the sense of control.

Journal: *Journal of Marriage and the Family*, November 1991, *53*(4), 831–838.

Related Research: Mirowsky, J., & Ross, C. E. (1991). Eliminating defense and agreement bias from measures of self-control: A 2x2 index. *Social Psychology Quarterly, 54*, 127–145.

■ ■ ■

6832

Test Name: PERCEIVED CONTROL SCALE

Purpose: To measure one's beliefs about the expectancy of attaining desired outcomes.

Number of Items: 40

Format: 6-point Likert format. All items are presented.

Reliability: Alphas ranged from .71 to .81 across subscales.

Validity: Correlations between subscales ranged from .32 to .39.

Author: Nelson, E. A.

Article: Control beliefs of adults in three domains: A new assessment of perceived control.

Journal: *Psychological Reports*, February 1993, *72*(1), 155–165,

■ ■ ■

6833

Test Name: PERCEIVED FRAUDULENCE SCALE

Purpose: To assess self-perceptions of fraudulence.

Number of Items: 51

Format: Sample items are presented.

Reliability: Alpha was .94.

Validity: Correlations with other variables ranged from -.55 to .83.

Authors: Kolligian, J., Jr., and Sternberg, R. J.

Article: Perceived fraudulence in young adults: Is there an "impostor syndrome"?

Journal: *Journal of Personality Assessment*, April 1991, *56*(2), 308–326.

■ ■ ■

6834

Test Name: PERCEIVED INTERNAL CONTROL

Purpose: To measure perceived internal control.

Number of Items: 5

Format: 5-point Likert format. Sample item presented.

Reliability: Alpha was .79.

Authors: Abbey, A., et al.

Article: Infertility and subjective well-being: The mediating roles of self-esteem, internal control and interpersonal conflict.

Journal: *Journal of Marriage and*

the Family, May 1992, *52*(2), 408–417.

Related Research: Abbey, A., & Andrews, F. M. (1985). Modeling the psychological determinants of life quality. *Social Indicators Research*, *16*, 1–34.

■ ■ ■

6835

Test Name: PERCEIVED PERFORMANCE SCALE

Purpose: To measure one's perceived level of performance on a training assignment test.

Number of Items: 5

Format: Responses are made on a 5-point Likert scale.

Reliability: Coefficient alpha was .90.

Validity: Correlations with other variables ranged from -.60 to .51.

Author: Quiñones, M. A.

Article: Pretraining context effects: Training assignment as feedback.

Journal: *Journal of Applied Psychology*, April 1995, *80*(2), 226–238.

■ ■ ■

6836

Test Name: PERCEIVED PERSONAL COMPETENCY RATING SCALE

Purpose: To assess the extent to which individuals perceive themselves to possess competencies in four general areas: social, personal, problem-solving, and functional.

Number of Items: 30

Format: Responses are made on a 5-point Likert scale.

Reliability: Test–retest reliability was .85.

Author: Steward, R. J.

Article: Two faces of academic

success: Case studies of American Indians on a predominantly Anglo university campus.

Journal: *Journal of College Student Development*, May 1993, *34*(3), 191–196.

Related Research: Paul, S. C., et al. (1981). *Personal Competency Rating Scale*. Unpublished instrument. University of Utah, Salt Lake City.

■ ■ ■

6837

Test Name: PERCEIVED PHYSICAL ACTIVITY SCALE

Purpose: To measure perceived physical activity.

Number of Items: 10

Format: Responses are made on a 5-point Likert scale. An example is presented.

Reliability: Coefficient alpha was .93.

Authors: Bosscher, R. J., et al.

Article: Measuring physical self-efficacy in old age.

Journal: *Perceptual and Motor Skills*, October 1993, *77*(2), 470.

Related Research: Ryckman, R. M., et al. (1982). Development and validation of a physical self-efficacy scale. *Journal of Personality and Social Psychology*, *42*, 891–900.

■ ■ ■

6838

Test Name: PERCEIVED PHYSICAL COMPETENCE SCALE

Purpose: To measure physical competence.

Number of Items: 9

Format: Includes two subscales: Perceived Fitness and Perceived Body Build. Responses are made

on a 5-point Osgood semantic differential scale.

Reliability: Alpha coefficients ranged from .29 to .76.

Validity: Correlations with the Rosenberg Self-Esteem Scale were .55 (boys) and .29 (girls).

Authors: Lintunen, T., et al.

Article: Use of the Perceived Physical Competence Scale with adolescents with disabilities.

Journal: *Perceptual and Motor Skills*, April 1995, *80*(2), 571–577.

Related Research: Lintunen, T. (1987). Perceived Physical Competence Scale for children. *Scandinavian Journal of Sports Sciences*, *9*, 57–64.

■ ■ ■

6839

Test Name: PERCEIVED PRODUCT KNOWLEDGE SCALE

Purpose: To measure perceived product knowledge.

Number of Items: 3

Format: A sample item is presented.

Reliability: Coefficient alpha was .82.

Validity: Correlation with a measure of knowledge was .49. Correlations with other variables ranged from .37 to .69.

Authors: Flynn, L. R., and Goldsmith, R. E.

Article: A validation of the Goldsmith and Hofacker Innovativeness Scale.

Journal: *Educational and Psychological Measurement*, Winter 1993, *53*(4), 1105–1116.

Related Research: Venkatraman, M. P. (1990). Opinion leadership, enduring involvement and characteristics of opinion leaders: A moderating or mediating relationship? In M. E. Goldberg, G. Gorn, & R. W. Pollay (Eds.), *Advances in consumer research*. Provo, UT: Association for Consumer Research, *17*, 60–67.

•••

6840

Test Name: PERCEIVED RELATEDNESS TO PEERS QUESTIONNAIRE

Purpose: To assess perceived relatedness to peers.

Number of Items: 7

Format: Responses are made on a 4-point scale ranging from *very true* to *not at all true*. An example is presented.

Reliability: Coefficient alpha was .79.

Validity: Correlations with other variables ranged from .06 to .25.

Authors: Pierson, L. H., and Connell, J. P.

Article: Effect of grade retention on self-system processes, school engagement, and academic performance.

Journal: *Journal of Educational Psychology*, September 1992, *84*(3), 300–307.

Related Research: Connell, J. P., & Wellborn, J. G. (1990). Competence, autonomy, and relatedness: A motivational analysis of self-system process. In M. R. Gunnar & L. A. Stroufe (Eds.), *Minnesota symposium on child psychology* (pp. 43–77). Hillsdale, NJ: Erlbaum.

•••

6841

Test Name: PERCEIVED SELF-EFFICACY SCALE

Purpose: To measure perceived self-efficacy.

Number of Items: 7

Format: Responses are made on a 10-point scale ranging from 1 (*never*) to 10 (*always*).

Reliability: Alpha coefficients were .90 (men) and .90 (women).

Validity: Correlation with Math Self-Concept was .49.

Authors: Bandalos, D. L., et al.

Article: Effects of math self-concept, perceived self-efficacy, and attributions for failure and success on test anxiety.

Journal: *Journal of Educational Psychology*, December 1995, *87*(4), 611–623.

Related Research: Bandura, A. (1986). *Social foundations of thought and action* (pp. 396–397). Englewood Cliffs, NJ: Prentice Hall.

•••

6842

Test Name: PERCEIVED SELF-EFFICACY SCALE

Purpose: To determine how confident nurses feel that they can do a job well.

Number of Items: 8

Format: Responses are made on a scale ranging from 0 (*cannot do at all*) to 10 (*certain can do*). The 8 items are presented.

Reliability: Coefficient alpha was .89.

Validity: Correlation with other variables ranged from -.15 to .34.

Author: Parker, L. E.

Article: When to fix it and when to leave: Relationships among perceived control, self-efficacy, dissent, and exit.

Journal: *Journal of Applied Psychology*, December 1993, *78*(6), 949–959.

6843

Test Name: PERCEIVED SELF-NEED FOR IMPROVEMENT

Purpose: To identify one's perceived self-need for improvement.

Number of Items: 3

Format: Responses are made on a 5-point scale ranging from 5 (*strongly agree*) to 1 (*strongly disagree*). An example is presented.

Reliability: Coefficient alpha was .63.

Validity: Correlations with other variables ranged from .09 to .26.

Authors: Maurer, T. J., and Tarulli, B. A.

Article: Investigation of perceived environment, perceived outcome, and person variables in relationship to voluntary development activity by employees.

Journal: *Journal of Applied Psychology*, February 1994, *79*(1), 3–14.

•••

6844

Test Name: PERCEIVED SELF-WORTH QUESTIONNAIRE

Purpose: To assess perceived self-worth.

Number of Items: 7

Format: Responses are made on a 4-point scale ranging from *very true* to *not at all true*. An example is presented.

Reliability: Coefficient alpha was .70.

Validity: Correlations with other variables ranged from -03 to .25.

Authors: Pierson, L. H., and Connell, J. P.

Article: Effect of grade retention on self-system processes, school engagement, and academic performance.

Journal: *Journal of Educational Psychology*, September 1992, *84*(3), 300–307.

• • •

6845

Test Name: PERCEIVED SPORT ABILITY SCALE

Purpose: To assess perceived ability in sport.

Number of Items: 4

Format: Responses are made on a 5-point Likert-type scale ranging from 1 (*strongly agree*) to 5 (*strongly disagree*). Sample items are presented.

Reliability: Coefficient alpha was .89.

Authors: Duda, J. L., and Nicholls, J. G.

Article: Dimensions of achievement motivation in school work and sport.

Journal: *Journal of Educational Psychology*, September 1992, *84*(3), 290-299.

Related Research: Nicholls, J. G. (1989). *The competitive ethos and democratic education.* Cambridge, MA: Harvard University Press.

• • •

6846

Test Name: PERCEIVED WORK ALTERNATIVES SCALE

Purpose: To assess employee beliefs about the availability of better work alternatives.

Number of Items: 10

Format: Responses are made on a 4-point scale ranging from 1 (*very unlikely*) to 4 (*very likely*). Eight items are presented.

Reliability: Alpha coefficients were .84 and .88.

Validity: Correlations with other variables ranged from -.57 to .23.

Authors: Pond, S. B., III, and Geyer, P. D.

Article: Differences in the relation between job satisfaction and perceived work alternatives among older and younger blue-collar workers.

Journal: *Journal of Vocational Behavior*, October 1991, *39*(2), 251–262.

Related Research: Pond, S. B. III, & Geyer, P. D. (1987). Employee age as a moderator of the relationship between perceived work alternatives and job satisfaction. *Journal of Applied Psychology*, *72*, 552–557.

• • •

6847

Test Name: PERCEPTION OF POWER SCALE

Purpose: To measure perception of power.

Number of Items: 30

Format: Includes 6 subscales: Expert, Reward, Coercive, Referent, Legitimate, and Information. Responses are made on a Likert format ranging from -3 (*strongly disagree*) to +3 (*strongly agree*).

Reliability: Alpha coefficients ranged from .76 to .92.

Authors: Temple, L. E., and Loewen, K. R.

Article: Perceptions of power: First impressions of a woman wearing a jacket.

Journal: *Perceptual and Motor Skills*, February 1993, *76*(1), 339–348.

Related Research: Holzbach, R. L., Jr. (1974). *An investigation of a model for managerial effectiveness: The effects of*

leadership style and leader attributed social power on subordinate job performance. Unpublished doctoral dissertation, Carnegie-Mellon University, Ann Arbor, MI. (University Microfilms).

• • •

6848

Test Name: PERCEPTIONS OF CHEATING SCALE

Purpose: To assess perceptions of academic cheating in examination-related situations.

Number of Items: 30

Format: Responses are made on a 7-point scale ranging from 1 (*do not punish the student*) to 7 (*expel the student from school*).

Reliability: Coefficient alphas were .93 ($N = 252$) and .94 ($N = 180$).

Authors: Roberts, D. M., and Toombs, R.

Article: A scale to assess perceptions of cheating in examination-related situations.

Journal: *Educational and Psychological Measurement*, Autumn 1993, *53*(3), 755-762.

Related Research: Roberts, D., & Rabiniowitz, W. (1992). An investigation of student perceptions of cheating in academic situations. *The Review of Higher Education*, *15*, 179–190.

• • •

6849

Test Name: PERCEPTIONS OF SEXUALLY INAPPROPRIATE BEHAVIOR AND INTIMIDATION SCALES

Purpose: To assess the degree to which behavior of men to women is inappropriate or intimidating.

Number of Items: 10

Format: 5-point scales. All items are presented.

Reliability: Alphas were .80 (Inappropriateness) and .78 (Intimidating).

Validity: Correlations with other variables ranged from -.11 to .66.

Authors: Matsui, T., et al.

Article: Women's perceptions of social-sexual behavior: A cross national replication.

Journal: *Journal of Vocational Behavior*, April 1995, *46*(2), 203–215.

Related Research: Gutek, B. A., et al. (1983). Interpreting social-sexual behavior in a work setting. *Journal of Vocational Behavior*, *22*, 30–48.

■ ■ ■

6850

Test Name: PERFORMANCE ATTRIBUTIONS SCALE

Purpose: To identify attributions responsible for participant training assignment test performance.

Number of Items: 20

Format: Includes 4 attributions: luck, effort, task difficulty, and ability.

Reliability: Alpha coefficients ranged from .71 to .86 ($N = 163$).

Validity: Correlations with other variables ranged from -.37 to .42 ($N = 163$).

Author: Quiñones, M. A.

Article: Pretraining context effects: Training assignment as feedback.

Journal: *Journal of Applied Psychology*, April 1995, *80*(2), 226–238.

Related Research: Weiner, B. (1985). An attributional theory of achievement motivation and emotion. *Psychological Review*, *92*, 548–573.

6851

Test Name: PERFORMANCE SELF-ESTEEM SCALE

Purpose: To measure achievement specific self-esteem.

Number of Items: 40

Format: 7-point rating scales.

Reliability: Alpha was .91.

Author: Bringle, R. G., and Bagby, G. J.

Article: Self-esteem and perceived quality of romantic and family relationships in young adults.

Journal: *Journal of Research in Personality*, December 1992, *26*(4), 340–356.

Related Research: Stake, J. E. (1985). Predicting reactions to everyday events from measures of self-esteem. *Journal of Personality*, *53*, 539–542.

■ ■ ■

6852

Test Name: PERSONAL ATTITUDE SURVEY

Purpose: To assess academic self-concept.

Number of Items: 15

Reliability: Alpha coefficient was .88.

Validity: Correlations with other variables ranged from .33 to .71.

Author: Lyon, M. A.

Article: Academic self-concept and its relationship to achievement in a sample of junior high school students.

Journal: *Educational and Psychological Measurement*, Spring 1993, *53*(1), 201–210.

Related Research: Reynolds, W. M. (1982, March). *Noncognitive correlates of achievement: An examination of academic self-concept.* Paper presented at the annual meeting of the American

Educational Research Association, New York.

■ ■ ■

6853

Test Name: PERSONAL ATTRIBUTES QUESTIONNAIRE

Purpose: To assess gender self-concept.

Number of Items: 24

Format: Bipolar adjectives are separated by 5-point scales.

Reliability: Test–retest reliability was .60. Alpha coefficients were .71 and .55.

Authors: Davey, F. H., and Stoppard, J. M.

Article: Some factors affecting the occupational expectations of female adolescents.

Journal: *Journal of Vocational Behavior*, December 1993, *43*(3), 235–250.

Related Research: Spence, J. T., & Helmreich, R. L. (1978). *Masculinity and femininity: Their psychological dimensions, correlates and antecedents.* Austin: University of Texas Press.

■ ■ ■

6854

Test Name: PERSONAL ATTRIBUTES QUESTIONNAIRE

Purpose: To assess personal attributes by self-description.

Number of Items: 55

Format: Bipolar adjectives rated on 5-point scales.

Reliability: Alphas ranged from .79 to .94.

Authors: Adams, C. B., et al.

Article: Young adults' expectation about sex-roles in mid-life.

Journal: *Psychological Reports*,

December 1991, *69*(3) Part I, 823-829.

Related Research: Spence, J. T., & Helinieich, R. L. (1974). The Personal Attributes Questionnaire: A measure of sex-role stereotypes and masculinity and femininity. *JSAS Catalog of Selected Documents in Psychology*, *4*(43) (Ms. No. 617).

Spence, J. T., et al. (1980). The Male-Female Relations Questionnaire: A self-report inventory of sex-role behaviors and preferences of its relationships to masculine and feminine personality traits, sex-role attitudes, and other measures. *JSAS Selected Documents in Psychology*, *10*(87) (MS. No. 2113).

Sherer, R. F., et al. (1992). Dimensionality of sex-role behavior: Factor stability of the Male-Female Relations—Female Form. *Psychological Reports*, *70*, 371–374.

■ ■ ■

6855

Test Name: PERSONAL POWERS SCALE

Purpose: To measure a person's belief in his or her personal paranormal powers.

Number of Items: 7

Format: All items are presented.

Reliability: Alpha was .83.

Validity: Correlation with the Belief in the Paranormal Scale was .58.

Authors: Morier, D., and Keeports, D.

Article: Normal science and the paranormal: The effect of a scientific method course on student beliefs.

Journal: *Research in Higher Education*, August 1995, *35*(4), 443–453.

6856

Test Name: PERSON PERCEPTION QUESTIONNAIRE

Purpose: To assess characteristics of persons such as stereotypes.

Number of Items: 90

Format: Bipolar 7-point scales and percentage rating scales.

Reliability: Alphas ranged from .69 to .92.

Authors: Jackson, L. A., and Ervin, K. S.

Article: Height stereotypes of women and men: The liabilities of shortness for both sexes.

Journal: *The Journal of Social Psychology*, August 1992, *132*(4), 433-445.

Related Research: Jackson, L. A., et al. (1987). Stereotypes and nonstereotype judgments: The effects of gender role attitudes on ratings of likability, adjustment and occupational potential. *Personality and Social Psychology Bulletin*, *13*, 45–52.

■ ■ ■

6857

Test Name: PHYSICAL ACTIVITY STEREOTYPING INDEX

Purpose: To assess gender labeling of physical activities.

Number of Items: 24

Format: 5 response choices are provided.

Reliability: Reliability coefficients were .77 (children) and .95 (adults).

Authors: Pellet, T. L., and Ignico, A. A.

Article: Relationship between children's and parents' stereotyping of physical activities.

Journal: *Perceptual and Motor*

Skills, December 1993, *77*(3) Part 2, 1283–1289.

Related Research: Ignico, A. A. (1989). Development and verification of a gender-role stereotyping index for physical activities. *Perceptual and Motor Skills*, *68*, 1067–1075.

■ ■ ■

6858

Test Name: PHYSICAL ATTRACTIVENESS QUESTIONNAIRE

Purpose: To measure the importance of physical attractiveness and appearance in respondents.

Number of Items: 5

Format: Responses for 3 items are made on a 6-point scale. For 2 items 7 factors are presented for each question and respondents are asked to rank them in order of importance.

Reliability: Cronbach's alpha was .66.

Author: Siever, M.

Article: Sexual orientation and gender as factors in socioculturally acquired vulnerability to body dissatisfaction and eating disorders.

Journal: *Journal of Consulting and Clinical Psychology*, April 1994, *62*(2), 252–260.

Related Research: Berscheid, E., et al. (1972, July). A Psychology Today questionnaire: Body Image. *Psychology Today*, *6*, 57–66.

■ ■ ■

6859

Test Name: PHYSICAL SELF-EFFICACY SCALE

Purpose: To measure physical self-efficacy.

Number of Items: 10

Format: An example is presented.

Reliability: Alpha coefficients were .85 and .87.

Validity: Correlations with other variables ranged from -.15 to .36.

Authors: Tannenbaum, S. I., et al.

Article: Meeting trainees' expectations: The influence of training fulfillment on the development of commitment, self-efficacy, and motivation.

Journal: *Journal of Applied Psychology*, December 1991, *76*(6), 759–769.

Related Research: McIntire, S. M., & Levine, E. L. (1984). Task specific self-esteem: An empirical investigation. *Journal of Vocational Behavior, 25,* 290–303.

■ ■ ■

6860

Test Name: PHYSICAL SELF-EFFICACY SCALE

Purpose: To assess one's perception of personal physical mastery.

Number of Items: 22

Format: Includes 2 subscales: Perceived Physical Ability and Perceived Self-Presentation Confidence.

Reliability: Internal consistency was .81.

Validity: Correlations with other variables ranged from -.16 to .53.

Authors: Sumerlin, J. R., et al.

Article: Subjective biological self and self-actualization.

Journal: *Perceptual and Motor Skills,* December 1994, *79*(3) Part 1, 1327–1337.

Related Research: Ryckman, R. M., et al. (1982). Development and validation of a physical self-efficacy scale. *Journal of Personality and Social Psychology, 42,* 891–900.

6861

Test Name: PHYSICAL SELF-ESTEEM SCALE

Purpose: To measure physical self-esteem.

Number of Items: 11

Format: 5-point Likert format. Sample items are presented.

Reliability: Alpha was .90.

Authors: Adams, T., et al.

Article: Principle centeredness: A values clarification approach to wellness.

Journal: *Measurement and Evaluation in Counseling and Development,* July 1995, *28*(3), 139–147.

Related Research: Field, L. K., & Steinhardt, M. A. (1992). The relationship of internally directed behavior to self-reinforcement, self-esteem, and expectancy for exercise. *American Journal of Health Promotion, 7,* 21–27.

■ ■ ■

6862

Test Name: POSSIBLE SELVES QUESTIONNAIRE

Purpose: To assess future perceptions of the self that one believes to be likely, the self that one hopes for, and the self that one fears.

Format: Sample items presented. 6-points scales follow each item.

Reliability: Interrater correlations ranged from .86 to .92 across subscales when responses were rated by negativeness to positiveness.

Validity: Correlations with other variables ranged from -.26 to .26.

Authors: Carver, C. S., et al.

Article: The possible selves of optimists and pessimists.

Journal: *Journal of Research in Personality,* June 1994, *28*(2), 133–141.

Related Research: Osyerman, D., & Markus, H. (1990). Possible selves and delinquency. *Journal of Personality and Social Psychology, 59,* 112–125.

■ ■ ■

6863

Test Name: POSSIBLE SELVES QUESTIONNAIRE

Purpose: To measure past, present, and future expectations of self-expectations.

Number of Items: 150

Format: Varied formats. Item formats are described.

Reliability: Test–retest reliabilities (1 week) ranged from .72 to .89.

Validity: Correlations with other variables ranged from -.33 to .74.

Authors: Hill, A. L., and Spokane, A. R.

Article: Career counseling and possible selves: A case study.

Journal: *The Career Development Quarterly,* March 1995, *43*(3), 221–232.

Related Research: Markus, H. R. (1987). *Possible Selves Questionnaire.* (Available from H. R. Markus, Research Center for Group Dynamics, Institute for Social Research, University of Michigan, Ann Arbor, MI 48106–1248).

■ ■ ■

6864

Test Name: PRETRAINING SELF-EFFICACY SCALE

Purpose: To measure one's expectations for their future level of performance.

Number of Items: 10

Format: Responses are made on a 5-point Likert scale. An example is presented.

Reliability: Coefficient alpha was .89 (*N* = 163).

Validity: Correlations with other variables ranged from -.47 to .51.

Author: Quiñones, M. A.

Article: Pretraining context effects: Training assignment as feedback.

Journal: *Journal of Applied Psychology*, April 1995, *80*(2), 226–238.

Related Research: Hattrup, K. E. (1992). *Affirmative action in organizational hiring: Self-regulatory processes underlying beneficiary reactions.* Unpublished doctoral dissertation, Michigan State University, East Lansing.

■ ■ ■

6865

Test Name: PRISON LOCUS OF CONTROL SCALE

Purpose: To measure locus of control in a prison environment.

Number of Items: 20

Format: 2-point agree–disagree format. All items presented.

Reliability: KR-20 reliability was .73. Test–retest (5 days) was .91.

Validity: Correlation with Nowicki-Strickland Scale was .63 (*p* < .001). Correlation with Prison Adjustment Scale was .27 (*p* < .001). Correlations with other variables ranged from .28 to .77.

Author: Pugh, D. N.

Article: Prisoners and locus of control: Initial assessments of a specific scale.

Journal: *Psychological Reports*, April 1992, *70*(2), 523–530.

6866

Test Name: PRISON LOCUS OF CONTROL SCALE

Purpose: To measure locus of control in prisoners.

Number of Items: 20

Format: 10-point agree–disagree scales. All items are presented.

Reliability: Alpha was .88.

Validity: Correlations with other variables ranged from -.68 to .74.

Author: Pugh, D. N.

Article: Revision and further assessments of the Prison Locus of Control Scale.

Journal: *Psychological Reports*, June 1994, *74*(3) Part I, 979–986.

■ ■ ■

6867

Test Name: PRIVATE–PUBLIC SELF-CONSCIOUSNESS SCALE

Purpose: To measure private–public self-consciousness.

Number of Items: 23

Format: Includes 3 subscales: Private Self-Consciousness, Public Self-Consciousness, and Social Anxiety.

Reliability: Alpha coefficients ranged from .62 to .79.

Validity: Correlations with other variables ranged from -.41 to .35.

Authors: Rentsch, J. R., and Heffner, T. S.

Article: Measuring self-esteem: Validation of a new scoring technique for "who am i?" responses.

Journal: *Educational and Psychological Measurement*, Autumn 1992, *52*(3), 641–651.

Related Research: Feneingstein, A., et al. (1975). Public and private self-consciousness: Assessment and theory. *Journal*

of Consulting and Clinical Psychology, *43*, 522–527.

■ ■ ■

6868

Test Name: PUPIL CONTROL IDEOLOGY FORM

Purpose: To measure teacher beliefs regarding pupil control.

Number of Items: 20

Format: Responses are made on a Likert scale ranging from 5 (*strongly agree*) to 1 (*strongly disagree*).

Reliability: Split-half reliabilities ranged from .83 to .95. Internal consistency correlations ranged from .61 to .95. A stability coefficient over 7 days was .86.

Authors: Agne, K. J., et al.

Article: Relationships between teacher belief systems and teacher effectiveness.

Journal: *Journal of Research and Development in Education*, Spring 1994, *27*(3), 141–152.

Related Research: Graham, S., et al. (1985). An analysis of the dimensionality of the Pupil Control Ideology Scale. *Educational and Psychological Measurement*, *45*, 889–896.

■ ■ ■

6869

Test Name: READING SELF-CONCEPT SCALE

Purpose: To measure a range of reading-related self-perceptions.

Number of Items: 50

Format: Responses are made on a 5-point scale ranging from 1 (*no, never*) to 5 (*yes, always*). Examples are presented.

Reliability: Reliability coefficients ranged from .82 to .88.

Authors: Chapman, J. W., and Tummer, W. E.

Article: Development of young children's reading self-concepts: An examination of emerging subcomponents and their relationship with reading achievement.

Journal: *Journal of Educational Psychology*, March 1995, *87*(1), 154–167.

Related Research: Chapman, J. W., & Tummer, W. E. (1992). *Reading Self-Concept Scale* (unpublished scale). Palmerston North, New Zealand: Educational Research and Development Centre, Massey University.

■ ■ ■

6870

Test Name: RELATIONSHIP BELIEFS QUESTIONNAIRE

Purpose: To measure adherence to relationship-specific irrational beliefs.

Number of Items: 71

Format: 6-point agreement scales.

Reliability: Alpha was .95. Subscale alphas ranged from .68 to .91.

Validity: Correlation with Relationship Beliefs Inventory was .44.

Authors: Romans, J. S., and DeBord, J.

Article: Development of the Relationship Beliefs Questionnaire.

Journal: *Psychological Reports*, June 1995, *76*(3) Part II, 1248–1250.

■ ■ ■

6871

Test Name: REVISED PERSONAL ATTRIBUTE INVENTORY

Purpose: To assess self-concepts.

Number of Items: 80

Format: An adjective checklist.

Validity: Correlations with other variables ranged from -.31 to .30.

Author: Necessary, J. R., and Parish, T. S.

Article: Are we as we act or as we see ourselves to be?

Journal: *Perceptual and Motor Skills*, December 1994, *79*(3) Part 1, 1232-1234.

Related Research: Parish, T. S., & Necessary, J. R. (1994). *Professors and students: Are they worlds apart?* Paper presented at the annual meeting of the Mid-Western Educational Research Association in Chicago.

■ ■ ■

6872

Test Name: REVISED PSYCHOTHERAPY EXPECTANCY INVENTORY

Purpose: To measure client and counselor expectation of clients' behavior in counseling.

Number of Items: 30

Format: Two forms: client form and counselor form. Includes 4 factors: Approval, Advice, Audience, and Relationship. Responses are made on a 7-point scale.

Reliability: Coefficient alpha was .87. Test–retest (1 week) reliability coefficient was .68. Test–retest (4 weeks) reliability coefficient was .78.

Validity: Correlation of client expectations with counselor ratings of client in session behavior was .41.

Authors: Al-Darmaki, F., and Kivlighan, Jr., D. M.

Article: Congruence in client-counselor expectations for relationship and the working alliance.

Journal: *Journal of Counseling*

Psychology, October 1993, *40*(4), 379–384.

Related Research: Berzins, J. I. (1971). *Revision of Psychotherapy Expectancy Inventory.* Unpublished manuscript, University of Kentucky, Lexington.

■ ■ ■

6873

Test Name: REVISED SCALE FOR AMBIGUITY TOLERANCE

Purpose: To measure tolerance for ambiguity.

Number of Items: 20

Format: 4-point agreement scales.

Reliability: Alpha was .87.

Authors: Friedland, N., and Keinan, G.

Article: The effects of stress, ambiguity tolerance, and trait anxiety on the formation of causal relationships.

Journal: *Journal of Research in Personality*, March 1991, *25*(1), 88–107.

Related Research: MacDonald, A. P., Jr. (1970). Revised scale for ambiguity tolerance: Reliability and validity. *Psychological Reports*, *26*, 791–798.

■ ■ ■

6874

Test Name: REVISED SELF-MONITORING SCALE

Purpose: To measure self-monitoring.

Number of Items: 13

Format: Includes 2 subscales: Self-Presentation and Expressive Sensitivity.

Reliability: Coefficient alpha was .75.

Validity: Correlations with other variables ranged from -.15 to .41.

Authors: Carson, A. D., and Mowsesion, R.

Article: Self-monitoring and private self-consciousness: Relations to Holland's vocational personality types.

Journal: *Journal of Vocational Behavior*, April 1993, *42*(2), 212–222.

Related Research: Lennox, R. D., & Wolfe, R. N. (1984). Revision of the Self-Monitoring Scale. *Journal of Personality and Social Psychology*, *46*, 1349–1364.

■ ■ ■

6875

Test Name: ROLE AMBIGUITY INDEX

Purpose: To measure role ambiguity.

Number of Items: 4

Reliability: Coefficient alpha was .77.

Validity: Correlations with other variables ranged from -.25 to .46.

Authors: Jex, S. M., et al.

Article: The meaning of occupational stress items to survey respondents.

Journal: *Journal of Applied Psychology*, October 1992, *77*(5), 623–628.

Related Research: Beehr, T. A., et al. (1976). Relationship of stress to individually and organizationally valued states: Higher order needs as a moderator. *Journal of Applied Psychology*, *61*, 41–47.

■ ■ ■

6876

Test Name: ROLE AMBIGUITY SCALE

Purpose: To measure role ambiguity.

Number of Items: 4

Format: Responses are made on a 7-point scale ranging from 1 (*very true*) to 7 (*very false*). An example is presented.

Reliability: Alpha coefficients were .73 and .80.

Validity: Correlations with other variables ranged from -.32 to .39.

Authors: Bacharach, S., and Bamberger, P.

Article: Causal models of role stressor antecedents and consequences: The importance of occupational differences.

Journal: *Journal of Vocational Behavior*, August 1992, *41*(1), 13–34.

Related Research: Rizzo, J., et al. (1970). Role conflict and ambiguity in complex organizations. *Administrative Science Quarterly*, *15*, 150–163.

■ ■ ■

6877

Test Name: ROLE AMBIGUITY SCALE

Purpose: To measure role ambiguity.

Number of Items: 6

Format: Responses are made on a 5-point scale ranging from 1 (*very false*) to 5 (*very true*).

Reliability: Coefficient alpha was .83 (*N* = 193).

Validity: Correlations with other variables ranged from -.45 to .67 (*N* = 193).

Author: Bauer, T. N., and Green, S. G.

Article: Effect of newcomer involvement in work-related activities: A longitudinal study of socialization.

Journal: *Journal of Applied Psychology*, April 1994, *79*(2), 211–223.

Related Research: Rizzo, J., et al.

(1970). Role conflict and ambiguity in complex organizations. *Administrative Science Quarterly*, *15*, 150–163.

■ ■ ■

6878

Test Name: ROLE AMBIGUITY SCALE

Purpose: To provide an index of role ambiguity.

Number of Items: 6

Format: Responses are made on a 7-point scale ranging from 1 (*disagree strongly*) to 7 (*agree strongly*). All items are presented.

Reliability: Alpha coefficients were .78 and .88.

Validity: Correlations with other variables ranged from -.33 to .52.

Authors: Fried, Y., and Tiegs, R. B.

Article: Supervisors' role conflict and role ambiguity differential relations with performance ratings of subordinates and the moderating effect of screening ability.

Journal: *Journal of Applied Psychology*, April 1995, *80*(2), 282–291.

Related Research: Rizzo, J., et al. (1970). Role conflict and ambiguity in complex organizations. *Administrative Science Quarterly*, *15*, 150–163.

■ ■ ■

6879

Test Name: ROLE AMBIGUITY SCALE

Purpose: To measure role ambiguity.

Number of Items: 8

Reliability: Coefficient alpha was .77.

Validity: Correlations with other variables ranged from -.17 to .42.

Authors: Schaubroeck, J., et al.

Article: Dispositional affect and work-related stress.

Journal: *Journal of Applied Psychology*, June 1992, *77*(3), 322–335.

Related Research: Rizzo, J., et al. (1970). Role conflict and ambiguity in complex organizations. *Administrative Science Quarterly*, *15*, 150–163.

■ ■ ■

6880

Test Name: ROLE AMBIGUITY SCALE

Purpose: To measure role ambiguity.

Number of Items: 10

Format: Includes two constructs: goal clarity and process clarity. Responses are made on a 6-point scale ranging from 1 (*very uncertain*) to 6 (*very certain*). All items are presented.

Reliability: Reliability ranged from .49 to .92.

Author: Sawyer, J. E.

Article: Goal and process clarity: Specifications of multiple constructs of role ambiguity and a structural equation model of their antecedents and consequences.

Journal: *Journal of Applied Psychology*, April 1992, *77*(2), 143–146.

Related Research: Rizzo, J. R., et al. (1970). Role conflict and ambiguity in complex organizations. *Administrative Science Quarterly*, *15*, 150–163.

■ ■ ■

6881

Test Name: ROLE CLARITY SCALE

Purpose: To measure clarity.

Number of Items: 4

Format: Responses are made on a 5-point scale ranging from 1 (*very little extent*) to 5 (*very great extent*). An example is presented.

Reliability: Alpha coefficients were .68 and .80.

Authors: Major, D. A., et al.

Article: A longitudinal investigation of newcomers expectation, early socialization outcomes, and the moderating effects of role development factors.

Journal: *Journal of Applied Psychology*, June 1995, *80*(3), 418–431.

Related Research: Baehr, T. A. (1976). Perceived situational moderation of the relationship between subjective role ambiguity and role strain. *Journal of Applied Psychology*, *61*, 35–40.

■ ■ ■

6882

Test Name: ROLE CLARITY SCALE

Purpose: To measure role clarity.

Number of Items: 10

Format: Responses were made on a 5-point scale ranging from 1 (*strongly disagree*) to 5 (*strongly agree*).

Validity: Correlations with other variables ranged from -.20 to .40.

Author: Morrison, E. W.

Article: Longitudinal study of the effects of information seeking on newcomer socialization.

Journal: *Journal of Applied Psychology*, April 1993, *78*(2), 173–183.

Related Research: Ashford, S. J. (1986). The role of feedback seeking in individual adaptation: A resource perspective. *Academy of Management Journal*, *29*, 465–487.

Rizzo, J. R., et al. (1970). Role

conflict and ambiguity in complex organizations. *Administrative Science Quarterly*, *15*, 150–163.

■ ■ ■

6883

Test Name: ROLE CONFLICT AND AMBIGUITY SCALES

Purpose: To measure role conflict and ambiguity.

Number of Items: 14

Format: 5-point scales range from *very true* to *very false*. Sample items are presented.

Reliability: Alphas ranged from .79 to .88.

Authors: Day, D. V., and Bedeian, A. G.

Article: Personality similarity and work-related outcomes among African-American nursing personnel: A test of the supplementary model of person-environment congruence.

Journal: *Journal of Vocational Behavior*, February 1995, *46*(1), 55–70.

Related Research: Rizzo, J. R., et al. (1970). Role conflict and ambiguity in complex organizations. *Administrative Science Quarterly*, *15*, 150–163.

■ ■ ■

6884

Test Name: ROLE CONFLICT SCALE

Purpose: To measure role conflict.

Number of Items: 5

Format: Responses are made on a 5-point scale ranging from 1 (*very little extent*) to 5 (*very great extent*).

Reliability: Alpha coefficients were .72 to .78.

Authors: Major, D. A., et al.

Article: A longitudinal investigation of newcomers

expectation, early socialization outcomes, and the moderating effects of role development factors.

Journal: *Journal of Applied Psychology*, June 1995, *80*(3), 418–431.

Related Research: Rizzo, J. R., et al. (1970). Role conflict and ambiguity in complex organizations. *Administrative Science Quarterly*, *15*, 150–163.

■ ■ ■

6885

Test Name: ROLE CONFLICT SCALE

Purpose: To measure role conflict.

Number of Items: 6

Reliability: Coefficient alpha was .82.

Validity: Correlations with other variables ranged from -.21 to .31.

Authors: Schaubroeck, J., et al.

Article: Dispositional affect and work-related stress.

Journal: *Journal of Applied Psychology*, June 1992, *77*(3), 322–335.

Related Research: Rizzo, J., et al. (1970). Role conflict and ambiguity in complex organizations. *Administrative Science Quarterly*, *15*, 150–163.

■ ■ ■

6886

Test Name: ROLE CONFLICT SCALE

Purpose: To measure role conflict.

Number of Items: 7

Format: Responses are made on a 5-point scale ranging from 1 (*very false*) to 5 (*very true*).

Reliability: Coefficient alpha was .81 (*N* = 193).

Validity: Correlations with other

variables ranged from -.32 to .49 (*N* = 193).

Authors: Bauer, T. N., and Green, S. G.

Article: Effect of newcomer involvement in work-related activities: A longitudinal study of socialization.

Journal: *Journal of Applied Psychology*, April 1994, *79*(2), 211–223.

Related Research: Rizzo, J., et al. (1970). Role conflict and ambiguity in complex organizations. *Administrative Science Quarterly*, *15*, 150–163.

■ ■ ■

6887

Test Name: ROLE CONFLICT SCALE

Purpose: To measure role conflict.

Number of Items: 8

Format: Responses are made on a 5-point scale ranging from *very false* to *very true*.

Reliability: Internal consistency was .79.

Validity: Correlations with other variables ranged from .32 to .56.

Authors: Chen, P. Y., and Spector, P. E.

Article: Negative affectivity as the underlying cause of correlations between stressors and strains.

Journal: *Journal of Applied Psychology*, June 1991, *76*(3), 398–407.

Related Research: Rizzo, J. R., et al. (1970). Role conflict and ambiguity in complex organizations. *Administrative Science Quarterly*, *15*, 150–163

■ ■ ■

6888

Test Name: ROLE CONFLICT SCALE

Purpose: To measure role conflict in the workplace.

Number of Items: 8

Format: Responses are made on a 7-point scale ranging from 1 (*very false*) to 7 (*very true*). An example is presented.

Reliability: Alpha coefficients were .87 and .85.

Validity: Correlations with other variables ranged from -.44 to .46.

Authors: Bacharach, S., and Bamberger, P.

Article: Causal models of role stressor antecedents and consequences: The importance of occupational differences.

Journal: *Journal of Vocational Behavior*, August 1992, *41*(1), 13–34.

Related Research: Kahn, R., et al. (1964). *Organizational stress: Studies in role conflict and ambiguity.* New York: Wiley.

■ ■ ■

6889

Test Name: ROLE CONFLICT SCALE

Purpose: To provide an index of role conflict.

Number of Items: 8

Format: Responses are made on a 7-point scale ranging from 1 (*disagree strongly*) to 7 (*agree strongly*). All items are presented.

Reliability: Alpha coefficients were .62 and .71.

Validity: Correlations with other variables ranged from -.43 to .52.

Authors: Fried, Y., and Tiegs, R. B.

Article: Supervisors' role conflict and role ambiguity differential relations with performance ratings of subordinates and the moderating effect of screening ability.

Journal: *Journal of Applied Psychology*, April 1995, *80*(2), 282–291.

Related Research: Rizzo, J., et al. (1970). Role conflict and ambiguity in complex organizations. *Administrative Science Quarterly*, *15*, 150–163.

■■■

6890

Test Name: ROLE SCALE

Purpose: To measure role conflict and role ambiguity.

Number of Items: 14

Format: Includes role conflict and role ambiguity items.

Reliability: Alpha coefficients were .79 and .76.

Authors: Lamude, K. G., and Scudder, J.

Article: Resistance in the college classroom: Variations in students' perceived strategies for resistance and teachers' stressors as a function of students' ethnicity.

Journal: *Perceptual and Motor Skills*, October 1992, *75*(2), 615–626.

Related Research: Rizzo, J. R., et al. (1970). Role conflict and ambiguity in complex organizations. *Administrative Science Quarterly*, *15*, 150–163.

■■■

6891

Test Name: ROLE SPILLOVER SCALE

Purpose: To measure role overload and role conflict.

Number of Items: 20

Format: 5-point Likert format.

Reliability: Alpha was .90 (wives) and .92 (husbands).

Authors: Paden, S. L., and Buehler, C.

Article: Coping with the dual-income lifestyle.

Journal: *Journal of Marriage and the Family*, February 1995, *57*(1), 101–110.

Related Research: Small, S. A., & Riley, D. (1990). Toward a multidimensional assessment of work spillover into family life. *Journal of Marriage and the Family*, *52*, 51–61.

■■■

6892

Test Name: ROLE STRAIN SCALES

Purpose: To assess role strain.

Number of Items: 13

Format: Includes 3 indexes: role conflict, role ambiguity, and role overload.

Reliability: Alpha coefficients ranged from .65 to .72.

Validity: Correlation with other variables ranged from -.62 to .02.

Author: Mathieu, J. E.

Article: A cross-level nonrecursive model of the antecedents of organizational commitment and satisfaction.

Journal: *Journal of Applied Psychology*, October 1991, *76*(5), 607–618.

Related Research: House, R. J., et al. (1983). Role conflict and role ambiguity scales: Reality or artifact? *Journal of Applied Psychology*, *68*, 334–337.

Agdell-Halim, A. A. (1978). Employee affective responses to organizational stress: Moderating effects of job characteristics. *Personnel Psychology*, *31*, 561–579.

6893

Test Name: ROTTER I-E- SCALE

Purpose: To measure perceived locus of control.

Number of Items: 23

Format: Forced-choice items.

Validity: Correlation with the Alcohol Responsibility Scale was .36.

Author: Johnson, E. E.

Article: Comparison of two locus of control scales in predicting relapse in an alcoholic population.

Journal: *Perceptual and Motor Skills*, February 1991, *72*(1), 43–50.

Related Research: Rotter, J. B. (1966). Generalized expectancies for internal versus external control of reinforcement. *Psychological Monographs*, *80*, 1–28.

■■■

6894

Test Name: ROTTER INTERNAL–EXTERNAL LOCUS OF CONTROL

Purpose: To identify internal or external control orientation.

Number of Items: 29

Format: The scale is composed of forced-choice question pairs.

Reliability: Coefficient alpha was .70. Test–retest (1 month) reliabilities were .60 (men) and .83 (women).

Validity: Correlations with other variables ranged from -.41 to .26.

Authors: Mallinckrodt, B., and Bennett, J.

Article: Social support and the impact of job loss in dislocated blue-collar workers.

Journal: *Journal of Counseling Psychology*, October 1992, *39*(4), 482–489.

Related Research: Rotter, J. B. (1966). Generalized expectancies for internal vs. external control of reinforcement. *Psychological Monographs*, *80*(1, Whole No. 609).

• • •

6895

Test Name: SALES PERFORMANCE PERCEPTIONS SCALES

Purpose: To measure perceptions of salespersons.

Number of Items: 13

Format: Likert format. All items presented.

Reliability: Alpha was .83.

Authors: Hawes, J. M., et al.

Article: Building exchange relationships: Perceptions of sales representatives' performance.

Journal: *Psychological Reports*, April 1993, *72*(2), 607–614.

Related Research: Simpson, E. K., & Kahler, R. C. (1980-81). A scale for source credibility validated in the selling context. *Journal of Selling and Sales Management*, *1*, 17–25.

• • •

6896

Test Name: SCHOLASTIC SELF CONCEPT SCALE

Purpose: To measure feelings of self-esteem with regard to school work.

Number of Items: 9

Format: 10-point rating scales. Sample items presented.

Reliability: Alpha was .67.

Authors: DuBois, D. L., et al.

Article: Effects of family environment and parent-child relationships on school adjustment during the transition to early adolescence.

Journal: *Journal of Marriage and the Family*, May 1994, *56*(2), 405–414.

Related Research: Narikawa, O., & Frith, S. (1972). *Measures of self-concept.* Los Angeles: Instructional Objectives Exchange.

• • •

6897

Test Name: SELF-CONCEPT OF ACADEMIC ABILITY SCALE

Purpose: To measure self-evaluations of general academic ability.

Number of Items: 8

Format: Responses are made on a 5-point scale.

Reliability: Reliability coefficients were .82 and .77.

Validity: Correlations with other variables ranged from .22 to .32.

Author: Mboya, M. M.

Article: Self-concept of academic ability: Relations with gender and academic achievement.

Journal: *Perceptual and Motor Skills*, December 1993, *77*(3) Part 2, 1131–1137.

Related Research: Brookover, W. B., et al. (1962). *Self-confidence of ability and school achievement.* U.S. Office of Education, Cooperative Research Project No. 845, Educational Publication Services, Michigan State University, East Lansing.

• • •

6898

Test Name: SELF-CONSCIOUSNESS SCALE

Purpose: To assess an individual's tendency to direct self-attention inward or outward.

Number of Items: 23

Format: Includes 3 subscales: Private Self-Consciousness, Public Self-Consciousness, and Social Anxiety. Responses are made on a 5-point scale ranging from 1 (*extremely uncharacteristic*) to 5 (*extremely characteristic*). Examples are presented.

Reliability: Test–retest (2 weeks) reliability ranged from .73 to .84.

Validity: Correlations with other variables ranged from -.63 to .42.

Authors: Wanberg, C. R., and Muchinsky, P. M.

Article: A typology of career decision status: Validity extension of the vocational decision status model.

Journal: *Journal of Counseling Psychology*, January 1992, *39*(1), 71–80.

Related Research: Fenigstein, A., et al. (1975). Public and private self-consciousness: Assessment and theory. *Journal of Consulting and Clinical Psychology*, *43*, 522–527.

• • •

6899

Test Name: SELF-CONSCIOUSNESS SCALE— ITALIAN VERSION

Purpose: To measure the tendency to pay attention to oneself or to feel aware of oneself.

Number of Items: 23

Format: All items presented in English.

Reliability: Alphas ranged from .78 to .85. Test–retest ranged from .75 to .85.

Validity: Correlations with other variables ranged from -.38 to .46.

Author: Comunian, A. L.

Article: Self-Consciousness Scale Dimensions: An Italian adaptation.

Journal: *Psychological Reports*, April 1994, *74*(2), 483–489.

Related Research: Scheier, M. F., & Carver, C. S. (1985). The Self-Consciousness Scale: Revised version for use with general populations. *Journal of Applied Psychology*, *15*, 687–699.

■ ■ ■

6900

Test Name: SELF-CONTROL SUBSCALE

Purpose: To assess self-regulation.

Number of Items: 5

Format: Items are rated on a 5-point scale. All items are presented.

Reliability: Alpha coefficients ranged from .71 to .92.

Authors: Brody, G. H., et al.

Article: Financial resources, parent psychological functioning, parent co-caregiving, and early adolescent competence in rural two-parent African-American families.

Journal: *Child Development*, April 1994, *65*(2), 590–605.

Related Research: Humphrey, L. L. (1982). Children's and teachers' perceptive on children's self-control: The development of two rating scales. *Journal of Consulting and Clinical Psychology*, *50*, 624–633.

■ ■ ■

6901

Test Name: SELF-CRITICAL COGNITION SCALE

Purpose: To assess self-critical and self-defeating tendencies in processing self-relevant information.

Number of Items: 13

Format: 6-point agree–disagree

scales. All items are presented.

Reliability: Alpha was .89. Test–retest (6.5 weeks) was .83.

Validity: Subscale correlations with other related variables ranged from .62 to -.71.

Authors: Ishiyama, F. I., and Munson, P. A.

Article: Development and validation of a self-critical cognition scale.

Journal: *Psychological Reports*, February 1993, *72*(1), 147–154.

■ ■ ■

6902

Test Name: SELF-DECEPTION AND OTHER-DECEPTION QUESTIONNAIRES

Purpose: To measure self-deception in terms of things universally true but psychologically threatening.

Number of Items: 20 (self), 20 (other).

Format: 7-point rating scales.

Reliability: Alpha was .63.

Validity: Correlations with other variables ranged from -.39 to .42.

Authors: King, L. A., et al.

Article: The structure of inhibition.

Journal: *Journal of Research in Personality*, March 1992, *26*(1), 85–102.

Related Research: Sackeim, H. A., & Gur, R. C. (1979). Self-deception, other-deception, and self-reported psychopathology. *Journal of Consulting and Clinical Psychology*, *47*, 213–215.

■ ■ ■

6903

Test Name: SELF-DESCRIPTION INVENTORY

Purpose: To measure occupational

needs including achievement, self-actualization, job security, and financial reward.

Number of Items: 39

Format: Adjective-pair format.

Reliability: Alphas were .89 (intrinsic needs) and .90 (extrinsic needs).

Validity: Correlations with other variables ranged from -.11 to .64.

Author: Riipinen, M.

Article: Occupational needs as moderators between locus of control and job involvement.

Journal: *Psychological Reports*, April 1994, *74*(2), 371–379.

Related Research: Ghiselli, E. (1971). *Explorations in managerial talent*. Pacific Palisades, CA: Goodyear.

■ ■ ■

6904

Test Name: SELF-DESCRIPTION INVENTORY

Purpose: To measure self-concept.

Number of Items: 50

Format: 5-point agreement scales. Sample items presented.

Reliability: Alphas ranged from .74 to .90 across subscales.

Validity: Correlations between subscales ranged from .02 to .32.

Authors: Mboya, M. M.

Article: Gender differences in teachers' behaviors in relation to adolescents' self-concepts.

Journal: *Psychological Reports*, December 1995, *77*(3) Part I, 831–839.

Related Research: Mboya, M. M. (1993). Development and construct validity of a self-description inventory for African adolescents. *Psychological Reports*, *72*, 183–191.

6905

Test Name: SELF-DESCRIPTIVE INVENTORY FOR AFRICAN ADOLESCENTS

Purpose: To measure self-concept for African adolescents.

Number of Items: 50

Time Required: 40 minutes

Format: 5-point Likert format. All items are presented.

Validity: Eight factors had eigen values of greater than 1.00. The squared multiple correlations of the eight factors are in the .70s.

Author: Mboya, M. M.

Article: Development and construct validity of a self-descriptive inventory for African adolescents.

Journal: *Psychological Reports*, February 1993, *72*(1), 183–191.

■ ■ ■

6906

Test Name: SELF-DESCRIPTIVE Q-SET

Purpose: To measure self-esteem.

Number of Items: 43

Format: Items are sorted into 7 categories ranging from 1 (*most undescriptive*) to 7 (*most descriptive*).

Reliability: Split-half reliability coefficients ranged from .56 to .88.

Authors: Block, J., and Robins, R. W.

Article: A longitudinal study of consistency and change in self-esteem from early adolescence to early childhood.

Journal: *Child Development*, June 1993, *64*(3), 909–923.

Related Research: Block, J. H., & Block, J. (1980). The role of ego-control and ego-resiliency in the organization of behavior. In W. A. Collins (Ed.), *Minnesota symposium on child psychology (Vol. 13)* (pp. 39–101). Hillsdale, NJ: Erlbaum.

■ ■ ■

6907

Test Name: SELF-EFFICACY EXPECTATIONS SCALE

Purpose: To measure self-efficacy expectations.

Number of Items: 27

Format: Responses are made on a 10-point scale ranging from 9 (*complete confidence*) to 10 (*no confidence at all*).

Reliability: Coefficient alpha was .96.

Author: Vasil, L.

Article: Self-efficacy expectations and causal attributions for achievement among male and female university faculty.

Journal: *Journal of Vocational Behavior*, December 1992, *41*(3), 259–269.

Related Research: Schoen, L. G., & Winocur, S. (1988). An investigation of the self-efficacy of male and female academics. *Journal of Vocational Behavior*, *32*, 307–320.

■ ■ ■

6908

Test Name: SELF-EFFICACY FOR COMPUTER TECHNOLOGIES

Purpose: To measure self-efficacy with different types of computer technologies.

Number of Items: 25

Format: 4-point Likert format.

Reliability: Alphas ranged from .97 to .98 across subscales.

Authors: Kinzie, M. B., et al.

Article: Computer technologies: Attitudes and self-efficacy across undergraduate disciplines.

Journal: *Research in Higher Education*, December 1994, *35*(6), 745–768.

Related Research: Delcourt, M. A. B., & Kinzie, M. B. (1993). Computer technologies in teacher education: The measurement of attitudes and self efficacy. *Journal of Research and Development in Education*, *27*, 31–37.

■ ■ ■

6909

Test Name: SELF-EFFICACY FOR WORK ACTIVITIES SCALE

Purpose: To assess self-efficacy for work activities.

Number of Items: 60

Format: Includes six domains: realistic, investigative, artistic, social, enterprising, and conventional. Responses are made on a 10-point scale ranging from 0 (*entirely unsure*) to 9 (*completely sure*). All items are presented.

Reliability: Alpha coefficients ranged from .88 to .95.

Authord: Matsui, T., and Tsukamoto, S.-I.

Article: Relation between career self-efficacy measures based on occupational titles and Holland codes and model environments: A methodological contribution.

Journal: *Journal of Vocational Behavior*, February 1991, *38*(1), 78–91.

Related Research: Matsui, T., et al. (1989). Relations of sex-typed socializations to career self-efficacy expectations of college students. *Journal of Vocational Behavior*, *35*, 1–16.

Holland, J. L. (1985). *Making vocational choices: A theory of vocational personalities and work environments* (2nd ed.). Englewood Cliffs, NJ: Prentice-Hall.

6910

Test Name: SELF-EFFICACY QUESTIONNAIRE

Purpose: To identify one's confidence in ability to complete various activities.

Number of Items: 30

Format: Responses are made on a scale ranging from 1 (*completely unsure*) to 10 (*completely sure*).

Reliability: Internal consistency reliabilities ranged from .25 to .88.

Authors: Lenox, R. A., and Subich, L. M.

Article: The relationship between self-efficacy beliefs and inventoried vocational interests.

Journal: *The Career Development Quarterly*, June 1994, *42*, 302–313.

Related Research: Lent, R. W., et al. (1989). Relation of self-efficacy to inventoried vocational interests. *Journal of Vocational Behavior, 34*, 279–288.

• • •

6911

Test Name: SELF-EFFICACY SCALE

Purpose: To measure self-efficacy.

Number of Items: 4

Format: Responses are made on a 5-point scale ranging from 5 (*strongly agree*) to 1 (*strongly disagree*). A sample item is presented.

Reliability: Coefficient alpha was .77.

Validity: Correlation with other variables ranged from .06 to .32.

Authors: Maurer, T. J., and Tarullin, B. A.

Article: Investigation of perceived environment, perceived outcomes, and person variables in relationship to voluntary development activity by employees.

Journal: *Journal of Applied Psychology*, February 1994, *79*(1), 3–14

Related Research: Bandura, A. (1977). Self-efficacy: Toward a unifying theory of behavioral change. *Psychological Review, 84*, 191–215.

Gist, M. (1987). Self-efficacy: Implications for organizational behavior and human resource management. *Academy of Management Review, 12*, 472–485.

• • •

6912

Test Name: SELF-EFFICACY SCALE

Purpose: To measure self-efficacy.

Number of Items: 6 (23).

Format: 5-point Likert format.

Reliability: Alpha was .71 (and .86 for 23-item version).

Authors: Mallinkrodt, B., et al.

Article: Co-occurrence of eating disorders and incest: The role of attachment, family environment, and social competencies.

Journal: *Journal of Counseling Psychology*, April 1995, *42*(2), 178–186.

Related Research: Shere, M., et al. (1982). The Self-Efficacy Scale: Construction and validation. *Psychological Reports, 51*, 663–671.

Mallinckrodt, B., et al. (1995). Attachment patterns in the psychotherapy relationship: Development of the Client Attachment Therapist Scale. *Journal of Counseling Psychology, 42*, 307–317.

6913

Test Name: SELF-EFFICACY SCALE

Purpose: To measure self-efficacy.

Number of Items: 8

Format: Responses are made on a 7-point scale ranging from 1 (*strongly disagree*) to 7 (*strongly agree*). An example is presented.

Reliability: Alpha coefficients ranged from .82 to .86.

Authors: Ford, J. K., et al.

Article: Impact of task experience and individual factors on training-emphasis ratings.

Journal: *Journal of Applied Psychology*, August 1993, *78*(4), 583–590.

Related Research: Jones, G. (1986). Socialization tactics, self-efficacy, and newcomers' adjustments to organizations. *Academy of Management Journal, 29*, 262–279.

• • •

6914

Test Name: SELF-EFFICACY SCALE

Purpose: To measure self-efficacy.

Number of Items: 10

Format: Responses are made on a 5-point scale ranging from 1 (*strongly agree*) to 5 (*strongly disagree*).

Reliability: Coefficient alpha was .85.

Authors: Saks, A. M., et al.

Article: Effects of job reviews on self-selection and job choice.

Journal: *Journal of Vocational Behavior*, June 1994, *44*(3), 297–316.

Related Research: Ellis, R. A., & Taylor, M. S. (1983). Role of self-esteem within the job search process. *Journal of Applied Psychology*, *68*, 632–640.

■ ■ ■

6915

Test Name: SELF-EFFICACY SCALE

Purpose: To provide a measure of initiation to the task.

Number of Items: 10

Format: Responses are made on a 10-point scale ranging from 1 (*not at all confident*) to 10 (*very confident*). Examples are given.

Reliability: Coefficient alpha was .95 (*N* = 193).

Validity: Correlations with other variables ranged from -.38 to .68 (*N* = 193).

Authors: Bauer, T. N., and Green, S. G.

Article: Effect of newcomer involvement in work-related activities: A longitudinal study of socialization.

Journal: *Journal of Applied Psychology*, April 1994, *79*(2), 211–223.

Related Research: Bandura, A. (1977). Self-efficacy: Toward a unifying theory of behavioral change. *Psychological Review*, *84*, 191–215.

■ ■ ■

6916

Test Name: SELF-EFFICACY SCALE

Purpose: To measure general and social self-efficacy.

Number of Items: 23

Format: Likert format.

Reliability: Alpha ranged from .57 to .74 across subscales.

Validity: Correlations with other variables ranged from -.54 to .19.

Authors : Woodruf, S. L., and Cushman, J. F.

Article: Task, domain, and general efficacy: A reexamination of the Self-Efficacy Scale.

Journal: *Psychological Reports*, April 1993, *72*(2), 423–432

Related Research: Shere, M., et al. (1982). The Self-Efficacy Scale: Construction and validation. *Psychological Reports*, *51*, 663–671.

■ ■ ■

6917

Test Name: SELF-EFFICACY TOWARD TEACHING INVENTORY

Purpose: To assess confidence in teaching.

Number of Items: 32

Format: 3-point rating scales.

Reliability: Alpha was .94.

Authors: Prieto, L. R., and Altmaier, E. M.

Article: The relationship of prior training and previous teaching experience to self-efficacy among graduate teaching assistants.

Journal: *Research in Higher Education*, August 1994, *35*(4), 481–497.

Related Research: Tollerud, T. (1990). The perceived self-efficacy of teaching skills of advanced doctoral students and graduates from counselor education programs. (Doctoral dissertation, University of Iowa). *Dissertation Abstracts International*, *51*, 12A.

■ ■ ■

6918

Test Name: SELF-EMPOWERMENT INDEX

Purpose: To measure teacher self-empowerment.

Number of Items: 25

Format: Includes 3 factors: Courage to Take Risks, Self-Reflection, and Autonomy. All items are presented.

Reliability: Alpha coefficients ranged from .64 to .91.

Author: Wilson, S. M.

Article: The Self-Empowerment Index: A measure of internally and externally expressed teacher autonomy.

Journal: *Educational and Psychological Measurement*, Autumn 1993, *53*(3), 727–737.

Related Research: Block, P. (1987). *The empowered manager.* San Francisco: Jossey-Bass.

■ ■ ■

6919

Test Name: SELF-ESTEEM INVENTORY

Purpose: To measure evaluative attitudes toward self in social, academic, family, and personal areas of experiences.

Number of Items: 25

Format: Responses are either *like me* or *unlike me*. An example is given.

Reliability: Split-half reliability was .90.

Author: Munson, W. W.

Article: Self-esteem, vocational identity, and career salience in high school students.

Journal: *The Career Development Quarterly*, June 1992, *40*(4), 361–368.

Related Research: Coopersmith, S. (1967). *The antecedents of self-esteem.* San Francisco: W. H. Freeman.

■ ■ ■

6920

Test Name: SELF-ESTEEM SCALE

Purpose: To measure self-esteem.

Number of Items: 6

Format: All items are presented. 5-point Likert format.

Reliability: Alpha was .80.

Authors: Hong, S. M., et al.

Article: Self-esteem: The effects of life satisfaction, sex and age.

Journal: *Psychological Reports*, February 1993, *72*(1), 95–101.

Related Research: Richardson, T. M., & Benbow, C. P. (1990). Long-term effects of acceleration on the social-emotional adjustment of mathematically precocious youths. *Journal of Educational Psychology*, *82*, 464–470.

■ ■ ■

6921

Test Name: SELF-ESTEEM SCALE

Purpose: To measure self-esteem.

Number of Items: 7

Format: Sample self-descriptive adjectives are described. 7-point response scales are used.

Reliability: Alpha was .78.

Authors: Shafer, R. B., and Keith, P. M.

Article: Self-esteem agreement in the marital relationship.

Journal: *The Journal of Social Psychology*, February 1992, *132*(1), 5–9.

Related Research: Sherwood, J. J. (1962). *Self-identity and actualization: A theory and research.* Unpublished doctoral dissertation, University of Michigan, Ann Arbor.

■ ■ ■

6922

Test Name: SELF-ESTEEM SCALE

Purpose: To measure global self-esteem.

Number of Items: 8

Format: Responses are made on a 7-point scale.

Reliability: Coefficient alpha was .80.

Validity: Correlations with other variables ranged from .05 to .38.

Authors: Turban, D. B., and Keon, T. L.

Article: Organizational attractiveness: An interactionist perspective.

Journal: *Journal of Applied Psychology*, April 1993, *78*(2), 184–193.

Related Research: Rosenberg, M. (1965). *Society and the adolescent self image.* Princeton, NJ: Princeton University Press.

■ ■ ■

6923

Test Name: SELF-ESTEEM SCALE

Purpose: To measure one's self-regard and self-worth.

Number of Items: 9

Format: Responses are made on a 7-point Likert scale ranging from 1 (*strongly disagree*) to 7 (*strongly agree*). An example is given.

Reliability: Reliability estimates were .78 and .85.

Validity: Correlations with other variables ranged from -.24 to .54.

Author: Peluchette, J. V. E.

Article: Subjective career success: The influence of individual difference, family, and organizational variables.

Journal: *Journal of Vocational Behavior*, October 1993, *43*(2), 198–208.

Related Research: Rosenberg, M. (1965). *Society and the adolescent*

self-image. Middletown, CN: Wesleyan University Press.

■ ■ ■

6924

Test Name: SELF-ESTEEM SCALE

Purpose: To measure self-esteem as reflected appraisals, self-perceived competence, and social comparisons.

Number of Items: 9

Reliability: Alphas ranged from .41 to .67 across subscales.

Authors: Schwalbe, M. L., and Staples, C. L.

Article: Gender differences in sources of self-esteem.

Journal: *Social Psychology Quarterly*, June 1991, *54*(2), 158–168.

Related Research: Schwalbe, M. L., et al. (1986). The effects of occupational conditions and individual characteristics on the importance of self-esteem sources in the workplace. *Basic and Applied Social Psychology*, *7*, 63–84.

■ ■ ■

6925

Test Name: SELF-ESTEEM SCALE

Purpose: To measure self-esteem.

Number of Items: 10

Format: Responses are made on a 4-point Likert-type scale ranging from 1 (*strongly agree*) to 4 (*strongly disagree*).

Reliability: Coefficient alpha was .85.

Validity: Correlations with other variables ranged from -.14 to .52.

Authors: King, W. C., Jr., and Miles, E. W.

Article: A quasi-experimental assessment of the effect of computerizing noncognitive paper-and-pencil measurements: A test of measurement equivalence.

Journal: *Journal of Applied Psychology*, December 1995, *80*(6), 643–651.

Related Research: Rosenberg, M. (1965). *Society and the adolescent self-image.* Princeton, NJ: Princeton University Press.

■ ■ ■

6926

Test Name: SELF-ESTEEM SCALE

Purpose: To assess self-esteem.

Number of Items: 10

Format: Guttman format.

Reliability: Reproducibility was 90%. Scalability was 65%.

Authors: McClanahan, G., and Holmbeck, G. N.

Article: Separation-individuation, family functioning and psychological adjustment in college students: A construct validity study of the Separation-Individuation Test of Adolescence.

Journal: *Journal of Personality Assessment*, December 1992, *59*(3), 468–485.

Related Research: Simmons, R. G., et al. (1973). Disturbance in the self-image at adolescence. *American Sociological Review, 38*, 553–568.

■ ■ ■

6927

Test Name: SELF-ESTEEM SCALE

Purpose: To assess self-esteem.

Number of Items: 10

Format: 5-point frequency rating scales.

Reliability: Test–retest reliability was .88.

Author: Medora, N. P., et al.

Article: Romanticism and self-esteem among pregnant adolescents, adolescent mothers and nonpregnant, nonparenting teens.

Journal: *The Journal of Social Psychology*, October 1994, *133*(5), 581–591.

Related Research: Bachman, J. G., et al. (1978). *Adolescence to adulthood: Change and stability in the lives of young men.* Ann Arbor: Institute for Social Research, University of Michigan.

■ ■ ■

6928

Test Name: SELF-EXPRESSION INVENTORY

Purpose: To measure defects of self.

Number of Items: 20

Format: Includes 2 subscales: Goal Instability and Superiority. Responses are made on a 6-point Likert-type scale ranging from 1 (*strongly agree*) to 6 (*strongly disagree*).

Reliability: Test–retest reliability coefficients were .80 (superiority) and .76 (goal instability). Alpha coefficients were .76 (superiority) and .81 (goal instability).

Validity: Correlations with other variables ranged from -.68 to .02.

Authors: Hadley, J. A., et al.

Article: Common aspects of object relations and self-representations in offspring from disparate dysfunctional families.

Journal: *Journal of Counseling Psychology*, July 1993, *40*(3), 348–356.

Related Research: Robbins, S. B., & Patton, M. J. (1985). Self-psychology and career development: Construction of the Superiority and Goal Instability

scales. *Journal of Counseling Psychology, 32*, 221–231.

■ ■ ■

6929

Test Name: SELF-IMAGE SCALE

Purpose: To measure self-esteem.

Number of Items: 32

Format: 4-point scales range from 0 (*never*), to 3 (*often*). Sample items are presented.

Reliability: Split-half reliability was .85.

Authors: Conte, H. P., et al.

Article: Development of a self-report conflict scale.

Journal: *Journal of Personality Assessment*, February 1995, *64*(1), 168–184.

Related Research: Plutchik, R., et al. (1979). A structural theory of ego defenses. In C. E. Izard (Ed.), *Emotions in personality and psychotherapy* (pp. 229–257). New York: Plenum.

■ ■ ■

6930

Test Name: SELF-LIKING/SELF-COMPETENCE SCALE

Purpose: To measure global self-esteem.

Number of Items: 20

Format: 5-point Likert format. All items are presented.

Reliability: Alphas ranged from .80 to .92.

Validity: Partial correlations with other variables ranged from -.30 to .48.

Authors: Tafarodi, R. W., and Swann, W. B., Jr.

Article: Self-liking and self-competence as dimensions of global self-esteem: Initial validation of a measure.

Journal: *Journal of Personality*

Assessment, October 1995, *65*(2), 322–342.

■ ■ ■

6931

Test Name: SELF-MASTERY SCALE

Purpose: To measure self-mastery.

Number of Items: 7

Format: 5-point agreement scales. Sample item presented.

Reliability: Alpha was .67.

Authors: Fine, M. A., and Kurdek, L. A.

Article: The adjustment of adolescents in stepfather and stepmother families.

Journal: *Journal of Marriage and the Family*, November 1992, *54*(4), 725–736.

Related Research: Pearlin, L. I., & Schoaler, C. (1978). The structure of coping. *Journal of Health and Social Behavior*, *19*, 2–21.

■ ■ ■

6932

Test Name: SELF-MONITORING SCALE

Purpose: To assess to what extent individuals regulate expressiveness for the sake of public appearances.

Number of Items: 18

Format: True–false format.

Reliability: Alpha was .86.

Authors: Kolligian, J., Jr., and Sternberg, R. J.

Article: Perceived fraudulence in young adults: Is there an "Impostor Syndrome?"

Journal: *Journal of Personality Assessment*, April 1991, *56*(2), 308–326.

Related Research: Snyder, M., & Gangestad, S. (1986). On the

nature of self-monitoring: Matters of assessment, matters of validity. *Journal of Personality and Social Psychology*, *51*, 125–139.

■ ■ ■

6933

Test Name: SELF-MONITORING SCALE

Purpose: To measure self-monitoring.

Number of Items: 25

Reliability: Coefficient alpha was .70.

Validity: Correlations with other variables ranged from -.07 to .16.

Authors: Barber, A. E., et al.

Article: The effects of interview focus on recruitment effectiveness: A field experiment.

Journal: *Journal of Applied Psychology*, December 1994, *79*(6), 886–896.

Related Research: Snyder, M. (1974). Self-monitoring of expressive behavior. *Journal of Personality and Social Psychology*, *30*, 526–537.

■ ■ ■

6934

Test Name: SELF-PERCEPTION PROFILE FOR ADOLESCENTS--NORWEGIAN VERSION

Purpose: To assess self-evaluations.

Number of Items: 35

Format: 4-point scales ranged from 1 (*describes me very poorly*), to 4 (*describes me very well*).

Reliability: Alphas ranged from .56 to .87.

Validity: Correlations with other variables ranged from -.94 to .84. Factorial validity is described.

Author: Wichstrom, L.

Article: Harter's self-perception profile for adolescents: Reliability, validity, and evaluation of the question format.

Journal: *Journal of Personality Assessment*, August 1995, *65*(1), 100–116.

Related Research: Harter, S. (1988). *Manual for the Self-Perception Profile for Adolescents.* Denver, CO: University of Denver.

■ ■ ■

6935

Test Name: SELF-PERCEPTION PROFILE FOR CHILDREN

Purpose: To measure self-concept.

Number of Items: 36

Format: Forced-choice and 2-point rating formats.

Reliability: Alphas ranged from .75 to .80.

Authors: Kishton, J. M., and Dixon, A. C.

Article: Self-perception changes among sports camp participants.

Journal: *The Journal of Social Psychology*, April 1995, *135*(2), 135–141.

Related Research: Harter, S. (1985). *Manual for the Perceived Competence for Children Scale.* Denver, CO: University of Denver.

■ ■ ■

6936

Test Name: SELF-PERCEPTION TEST

Purpose: To enable persons to perceive themselves.

Number of Items: 240

Format: Includes 11 trait scales: Depressed, Crabby, Shy, Wild, Good-Looking, Aggressive, Sociable, Thorough, Logical, Considerate, and Honest.

Reliability: Alpha coefficients ranged from .87 to .94 (*N* = 76).

Validity: Correlations with other variables ranged from -.38 to .40.

Author: Thumin, F. J.

Article: Correlations for a new personality test with age, education, intelligence, and the MMPI-2.

Journal: *Perceptual and Motor Skills*, December 1994, *79*(3) Part 1, 1383–1389.

• • •

6937

Test Name: SELF-REGULATION SCALE

Purpose: To measure self-efficacy and "hardiness."

Number of Items: 105

Format: 6-point Likert format.

Reliability: Alphas ranged from .80 to .90.

Authors: Grossarth-Maticek, R., and Eysenck, H. J.

Article: Alcohol consumption and health: Synergistic interaction with personality.

Journal: *Psychological Reports*, October 1995, *77*(2), 675–687.

Related Research: Eysenck, H. J. (1994). Synergistic interaction between psychosocial and physical factors in the causation of lung cancer. In C. Lewis et al. (Eds.), *The psychopharmacology of human cancer* (pp. 163–178). London: Oxford University Press.

• • •

6938

Test Name: SELF-REPORTED RATING INFLATION MEASURE

Purpose: To measure the self-reported tendency to deliberately inflate performance ratings.

Number of Items: 3

Format: Responses are made on a 7-point Likert-type agree–disagree scale. All items are presented.

Reliability: Alpha coefficients were .67 (*N* = 68) and .78 (*N* = 109).

Validity: Correlations with other variables ranged from -.31 to .30.

Authors: Fried, Y., and Tiegs, R. B.

Article: Supervisors' role conflict and role ambiguity differential relations with performance ratings of subordinates and the moderating effect of screening ability.

Journal: *Journal of Applied Psychology*, April 1995, *80*(2), 282–291.

• • •

6939

Test Name: SELF-STATEMENT INVENTORY

Purpose: To determine patients' cognitions while undergoing a cardiac catherization procedure.

Number of Items: 20

Format: Responses are made on a 5-point Likert scale (1—*hardly ever*; 5—*very often*).

Reliability: Coefficient alpha was .59 for the full scale.

Authors: Ludwick-Rosenthal, R., and Neufeld, R. W. J.

Article: Preparation for undergoing invasive medical procedure: Interacting effects of information and coping style.

Journal: *Journal of Consulting and Clinical Psychology*, February 1993, *61*(1), 156–164.

Related Research: Kendall, P. C., et al. (1979). Cognitive-behavioral and patient education interventions in cardiac catherization procedures: The Palo Alto Medical Psychology Project. *Journal of Consulting*

and Clinical Psychology, *47*, 49–58.

• • •

6940

Test Name: SENSE OF COHERENCE SCALE

Purpose: To measure sense of coherence—the belief that life is comprehensible, manageable, and meaningful.

Number of Items: 13

Format: 7-point frequency scales. Sample items presented.

Reliability: Alphas ranged from .62 to .77 across subscales. Total alpha was .86.

Validity: Correlations with the Interpersonal Support Evaluation List ranged from -.20 to .28.

Authors: Hark, K. E., et al.

Article: Sense of coherence, trait anxiety, and the perceived availability of social support.

Journal: *Journal of Research in Personality*, June 1991, *25*(2), 137–145.

Related Research: Antonovsky, A. (1987). *Unraveling the mystery of health*. San Francisco: Jossey-Bass.

• • •

6941

Test Name: SENSE OF COMPETENCE SCALE

Purpose: To measure sense of competence.

Number of Items: 10

Format: Responses are made on a 7-point Likert scale ranging from 1 (*strongly disagree*) to 7 (*strongly agree*). An example is given.

Reliability: Reliability estimates were .96 and .79.

Validity: Correlations with other variables ranged from -.10 to .48.

Authors: Peluchette, J. V. E.

Article: Subjective career success: The influence of individual difference, family, and organizational variables.

Journal: *Journal of Vocational Behavior*, October 1993, *43*(2), 198–208.

Related Research: Wagner, F., & Morse, J. (1975). A measure of individual sense of competence. *Psychological Reports, 36,* 297–333.

■ ■ ■

6942

Test Name: SENSE OF CONTROL SCALE

Purpose: To assess mastery over the forces that affect one's life.

Number of Items: 6

Format: Likert format. All items presented.

Reliability: Alpha was .70.

Author: Jackson, P. B.

Article: Specifying the buffering hypothesis: Support, strain and depression.

Journal: *Social Psychology Quarterly*, December 1992, *55*(4), 363–378.

Related Research: Pearlin, L. I., & Lieberman, M. A. (1979). Social sources of emotional stress. *Research in Community and Mental Health, 1,* 217–248.

■ ■ ■

6943

Test Name: SENSE OF CONTROL SCALE

Purpose: To measure sense of control without biases resulting from references to only desirable or undesirable outcomes and defensiveness and agreement tendencies.

Number of Items: 8

Format: 5-point agreement scales. All items are presented.

Reliability: Alphas ranged from .57 to .66.

Validity: Correlations with other variables ranged from -.43 to .71. Other validity data presented.

Authors: Mirowsky, J., and Ross, C. E.

Article: Eliminating defense and agreement bias from measures of self-control: A 2 x 2 index.

Journal: *Social Psychology Quarterly*, June 1991, *54*(2), 127–145.

■ ■ ■

6944

Test Name: SHORT INDEX OF SELF-ACTUALIZATION

Purpose: To measure self-actualization.

Number of Items: 15

Format: 4-point Likert format. All items presented.

Reliability: Test–retest was .69. Alpha was .69.

Authors: Tucker, R. K., and Dyson, R.

Article: Factor structure of the Short Form Measure of Self-Actualization in a Black sample.

Journal: *Psychological Reports*, December 1991, *69*(3) Part I, 871–877.

Related Research: Jones, A., & Crandall, R. (1986). Validation of a short index of self-actualization. *Personality and Social Psychology Bulletin, 12,* 63–73.

■ ■ ■

6945

Test Name: SHORT INDEX OF SELF-ACTUALIZATION

Purpose: To measure self-actualization.

Number of Items: 15

Format: 6-point Likert format.

Reliability: Internal consistency ranged from .46 to .75. Test–retest (12 days) was .69.

Author: Sumerlin, J. R.

Article: Adaptation to homelessness: Self-actualization, loneliness, and depression in street homeless men.

Journal: *Psychological Reports*, August 1996, *77*(1), 295–314.

Related Research: Jones, A., & Crondall, R. (1986). Validation of a short index of self-actualization. *Personality and Social Psychology Bulletin, 12,* 63–73.

■ ■ ■

6946

Test Name: SITUATIONAL INVENTORY OF BODY-IMAGE DYSPHORIA

Purpose: To assess negative body-image emotions.

Number of Items: 48

Format: 5-point frequency scales range from 0 (*never*), to 4 (*always or almost always*).

Reliability: Alpha was .90. Stability (1 month) was .86.

Validity: Correlations with other variables ranged from .20 to .43.

Authors: Cash, T. F., and Szymanski, M. L.

Article: The development and validation of the Body-Image Ideals Questionnaire.

Journal: *Journal of Personality Assessment*, June 1995, *64*(3), 466–477.

Related Research: Cash, T. F. (1994). The Situational Inventory of Body-Image Dysphoria: Contexual assessment of a negative body image. *The Behavior Therapist, 17,* 133–134.

6947

Test Name: SIX-FACTOR SELF-CONCEPT SCALE

Purpose: To measure adult self-concepts.

Number of Items: 36

Format: Responses are made on a 7-point rating scale ranging from 1 (*usually not true of me*) to 7 (*always or almost always true of me*). Includes 6 subscales: Likeability, Morality, Task Accomplishment, Giftedness, Power, and Vulnerability.

Reliability: Test–retest (6 weeks) reliability ranged from .68 to .85 ($N = 61$). Test–retest (4 week) reliability ranged from .74 to .88 ($N = 57$). Alpha coefficients ranged from .64 to .86.

Validity: Correlations with other variables ranged from -.38 to .62.

Author: Stake, J. E.

Article: Development and validation of the Six-Factor Self-Concept Scale for Adults.

Journal: *Educational and Psychological Measurement*, Spring 1994, *54*(1), 56–72.

■ ■ ■

6948

Test Name: SMOKING SPECIFIC LOCUS OF CONTROL SCALE

Purpose: To measure locus of control with respect to smoking.

Number of Items: 25

Format: Likert format.

Reliability: Standardized alpha was .75. Unequal length Spearman-Brown split-half reliability was .66.

Validity: Correlation with Rotter I-E Scale was .03 ($p = .40$).

Authors: Bunch, J. M., and Schneider, H. G.

Article: Smoking-specific locus of control.

Journal: *Psychological Reports*, December 1991, *69*(3) Part II, 1075–1081.

Related Research: Donovan, D. M., & O'Leary, M. R. (1978). The Drinking-Related Locus of Control Scale. *Journal of Studies on Alcohol, 39, 759–784.*

■ ■ ■

6949

Test Name: SOURCES OF MATH EFFICACY SCALE

Purpose: To identify sources of math efficacy.

Number of Items: 40

Format: Includes four subscales: Past Performance Accomplishments, Vicarious Learning, Verbal Persuasion, and Emotional Arousal. Examples are presented.

Reliability: Alpha coefficients ranged from .59 to .90.

Validity: Correlations with other variables ranged from -.53 to .65.

Authors: Lopez, F. G., and Lent, R. W.

Article: Sources of mathematics self-efficacy in high school students.

Journal: *The Career Development Quarterly*, September 1992, *41*(1), 3–12.

■ ■ ■

6950

Test Name: STATE SELF-ESTEEM SCALE

Purpose: To measure self-esteem.

Number of Items: 20

Format: 5-point frequency scales. Sample items are presented.

Reliability: Alpha was .88.

Authors: Adams, T., et al.

Article: Principle-centeredness: A values clarification approach to wellness.

Journal: *Measurement and evaluation in counseling and development*, July 1995, *28*(3), 139–147.

Related Research: Heatheron, T. F., & Polivy, J. (1991). Development and validation of a scale for measuring state self-esteem. *Journal of Personality and Social Psychology, 60, 895–910.*

■ ■ ■

6951

Test Name: STATE SPORT CONFIDENCE INVENTORY

Purpose: To measure self-efficacy.

Number of Items: 9

Format: Responses are made on a 9-point scale ranging from 1 (*low confidence*) to 9 (*high confidence*).

Reliability: Alpha coefficients ranged from .82 to .97.

Validity: Correlations with the Situation-Specific Sport-Confidence Inventory were .63 and .54.

Authors: Winfrey, M. L., and Wecks, D. L.

Article: Effects of self-modeling on self-efficacy and balance beam performance.

Journal: *Perceptual and Motor Skills*, December 1993, *77*(3) Part 1, 907–913.

Related Research: Vealey, R. (1986). Conceptualization of sport-confidence and competitive orientation: Preliminary investigation and instrument development. *Journal of Sport Psychology, 8, 221–246.*

6952

Test Name: STEREOTYPE RATING SCALE

Purpose: To measure perceptions of stereotypes of relatives and friends.

Number of Items: 10

Format: 7-point bipolar scales.

Reliability: Alpha was .92.

Author: Somers, M. D.

Article: A comparison of voluntarily childfree adults and parents.

Journal: *Journal of Marriage and the Family*, August 1991, *55*(3), 643–650.

Related Research: Magarick, R. H. (1981*). Social and emotional aspects of voluntary childlessness in vasectomized childless men.* Unpublished doctoral dissertation. University of Maryland, College Park.

■ ■ ■

6953

Test Name: STUDENT–TEACHER RELATIONSHIP SCALE

Purpose: To assess teachers' perceptions of their relationships with an individual student.

Number of Items: 31

Format: Responses are made on a Likert-type format.

Reliability: Coefficient alpha was .90.

Author: Pianta, R. C.

Article: Patterns of relationships between children and kindergarten teachers.

Journal: *Journal of School Psychology*, Spring 1994, *32*(1), 15–31.

Related Research: Pianta, R. C. (1991). *The Student-Teacher Relationship Scale.* Unpublished measure, University of Virginia, Charlottesville.

■ ■ ■

6954

Test Name: SUPERIORITY SCALE

Purpose: To assess how a person views himself or herself in relation to others.

Number of Items: 10

Format: 6-point Likert format.

Reliability: Alphas ranged from .78 to .82. Test–retest reliability was .76 (2 weeks).

Validity: Correlations with other variables ranged from -.10 to .36.

Authors: Multon, K. D., et al.

Article: An Empirical Derivation of Career Decision Subtypes in a High School Sample.

Journal: *Journal of Vocational Behavior*, August 1995, *47*(1), 76–92.

Related Research: Robbins, S. B., & Patton, M. J. (1985). Self-psychology and career development: Construction of the Superiority and Goal Instability Scales. *Journal of Counseling Psychology, 32*, 221–231.

■ ■ ■

6955

Test Name: SUPERVISOR FAIRNESS SCALE

Purpose: To measure the extent salespersons feel that they are fairly treated by their immediate supervisor.

Number of Items: 3

Format: Responses are made on a 7-point scale ranging from 1 (*strongly disagree*) to 7 (*strongly agree*). A sample item is presented.

Reliability: Internal consistency was .86.

Validity: Correlations with other variables ranged from -.12 to .39.

Author: George, J. M.

Article: State or trait: Effects of positive mood or prosocial behaviors at work.

Journal: *Journal of Applied Psychology*, April 1991, *76*(2), 299–307.

■ ■ ■

6956

Test Name: SYMPTOM ATTRIBUTION QUESTIONNAIRE

Purpose: To measure spouse attributions for depressed behavior.

Number of Items: 20

Format: 7-point Likert scales range from 1 (*disagree strongly*) to 7 (*agree strongly*). All items are presented.

Validity: Correlations with other variables ranged from -.81 to -.45.

Authors: Bauserman, S. A. K., et al.

Article: Marital attributions in spouses of depressed patients.

Journal: *Journal of Psychopathology and Behavioral Assessment*, September 1995, *17*(3), 231–249.

Related Research: Fincham, F. D., & Bradbury, T. N. (1992). Assessing attributions in marriage: The Relationship Attribution Measure. *Journal of Personality and Social Psychology, 62*, 457–468.

■ ■ ■

6957

Test Name: TASK LEADERSHIP IDENTITY SCALE

Purpose: To assess a person's self-perceived work identity.

Number of Items: 5

Format: 5-point Likert format. All items are presented.

Reliability: Alpha was .79.

Author: Riley, A., and Burke, P. J.

Article: Identities and self-verification in the small group.

Journal: *Social Psychology Quarterly*, June 1995, *58*(2), 61–73.

Related Research: Burke, P. J. (1971). Task and socio-emotional leadership role performance. *Sociometry*, *34*, 22–40.

■ ■ ■

6958

Test Name: TASK-SPECIFIC SELF-EFFICACY SCALE

Purpose: To assess perceived running self-efficacy.

Number of Items: 14

Format: Includes 2 subscales: Perceived Running Ability and Self-Presentation Self-Confidence. Responses are made on a 7-point scale ranging from *strongly agree* to *strongly disagree*. Examples are given.

Validity: Correlations with other variables ranged from -.38 to -.50.

Authors: LaGuardia, R., and Labbé, E. E.

Article: Self-efficacy and anxiety and their relationship to training and race performance.

Journal: *Perceptual and Motor Skills*, August 1993, *77*(1), 27–34.

Related Research: LaGuardia, R, & Labbé, E. (1990). *Evaluation of self-efficacy beliefs and running performance.* Unpublished manuscript, University of South Alabama, Department of Psychology, Mobile.

6959

Test Name: TEACHER EFFICACY SCALE

Purpose: To access teacher efficacy.

Number of Items: 16

Format: Responses are made on a 6-point Likert-type scale ranging from 1 (*strongly agree*) to 6 (*strongly disagree*).

Reliability: Alpha coefficient was .75.

Authors: Podell, D., and Soodak, L.

Article: Teacher efficacy and bias in special education referrals.

Journal: *Journal of Educational Research*, March/April 1993, *86*(4), 247–253.

Related Research: Gibson, S., & Dembo, M. H. (1984). Teacher efficacy: A construct validation. *Journal of Education of Psychology*, *76*, 569–582.

■ ■ ■

6960

Test Name: TEACHER EFFICACY SCALE

Purpose: To measure teacher efficacy.

Number of Items: 30

Format: Likert-type scale ranging from 1 (*strongly disagree*) to 6 (*strongly agree*). Includes two factors: Personal Efficacy and Teacher Efficacy.

Reliability: Internal consistency coefficients ranged from .75 to .79.

Validity: Convergent validity was .42.

Authors: Agne, K. J., et al.

Article: Relationships between teacher belief systems and teacher effectiveness.

Journal: *Journal of Research and*

Development in Education, Spring 1994, *27*(3), 141–152.

Related Research: Gibson, S., & Dembo, M. (1984). Teacher efficacy: A construct validity. *Journal of Educational Psychology*, 76, 569–582.

■ ■ ■

6961

Test Name: TEACHER EFFICACY SCALE

Purpose: To measure teacher efficacy in classroom management and discipline.

Number of Items: 36

Format: Responses are made on a 6-point Likert-type format ranging from *strongly disagree* to *strongly agree*. Includes 3 factors. All items are presented.

Reliability: Alpha coefficients ranged from .68 to .81. Test-retest correlations ranged from .75 to .86.

Authors: Emmer, E. T., and Hickman, J.

Article: Teacher efficacy in classroom management and discipline.

Journal: *Educational and Psychological Measurement*, Autumn 1991, *51*(3), 755–765.

Related Research: Gibson, S., & Dembo, M. (1984). Teacher efficacy: A construct validation. *Journal of Education Psychology*, 76, 569–582.

■ ■ ■

6962

Test Name: TEACHER INVENTORY OF PROGRAM STANDARDS

Purpose: To assess educators' perception of the *NCATE* (National Council for Accreditation of Teacher Education) *Standards* as program guidelines.

Number of Items: 18

Format: Includes three sections: the 18-items section, a demographic information section, and a section for ranking the value of the five categories of the *NCATE Standards*.

Reliability: KR-20 was .87.

Authors: Moore, K. D., et al.

Article: NCATE accreditation: Visions of excellence.

Journal: *Journal of Research and Development in Education*, Fall 1993, *27*(1), 28–34.

Related Research: Hopkins, W. S., & Moore, K. D. (February, 1991). *NCATE Standards: Restructuring teacher education.* Paper presented at Association of Teacher Educators, New Orleans, Louisiana.

■ ■ ■

6963

Test Name: TEACHER LOCUS OF CONTROL SCALE

Purpose: To measure the internality–externality of the teacher's attributions toward student successes and failures.

Number of Items: 28

Format: Forced-choice format.

Reliability: KR-20 reliabilities were .81 and .71.

Authors: Agne, K. J., et al.

Article: Relationships between teacher belief systems and teacher effectiveness.

Journal: *Journal of Research and Development in Education*, Spring 1994, *27*(3), 141–152.

Related Research: Rose, J., & Medway, F. (1981). Measurement of teachers' beliefs in their control over student outcome. *Journal of Educational Research*, *74*(3), 185–190.

6964

Test Name: TEACHER PERCEPTIONS OF TEACHER EFFICACY SCALE

Purpose: To assess teachers' perception of their own efficacy.

Number of Items: 12

Format: Uses a 5-point Likert-scale ranging from 1 (*strongly disagree*) to 5 to (*strongly agree*).

Reliability: Alpha was .83.

Authors: Hoover, D., et al.

Article: Explorations in parent-school relations.

Journal: *Journal of Educational Research*, May/June 1992, *85*(5), 287–294.

Related Research: Hoover, D. K. V., et al. (1987). Parent involvement contributions of teacher efficacy, school socioeconomic status, and other school characteristics. *American Educational Research Journal 24*, 417–435.

■ ■ ■

6965

Test Name: TEACHERS' PERCEPTIONS OF PARENT AND TEACHER EFFICACY

Purpose: To assess teachers' perceptions of how well parents and teachers help students do well in school.

Number of Items: 19

Format: 5-point Likert format. Sample items are presented.

Reliability: Alphas ranged from .79 to .83 across subscales.

Validity: Correlations with other variables ranged from -.59 to .75.

Authors: Hoover-Dempsey, K. V., et al.

Article: Explorations in parent-school relations.

Journal: *Journal of Educational*

Research, May/June 1992, *85*(5), 287–294.

Related Research: Hoover-Dempsey, K. V., et al. (1987). Parent involvement: Contributions of teacher efficacy, school socioeconomic status, and other school characteristics. *American Educational Research Journal*, *24*, 417–435.

■ ■ ■

6966

Test Name: TEACHER TREATMENT INVENTORY

Purpose: To assess Black and White children's perceptions of teachers' treatment of them.

Number of Items: 30

Time Required: 20 minutes.

Format: 4-point scales range from 4 (*always*) to 1 (*never*). Sample items are presented.

Reliability: Test–retest reliability (2 weeks) was .74.

Authors: Marcus, G., and Gross, S.

Article: Black and White students' perceptions of teacher treatment.

Journal: *Journal of Educational Research*, July/August 1991, *84*(6), 363–367.

Related Research: Weinstein, R. (1984). *Final report: Ecology of student's achievement expectations* (Grant NIE-G-80-0071). Washington, DC: National Institute of Education.

■ ■ ■

6967

Test Name: TEACHING AUTONOMY SCALE

Purpose: To measure perceptions of teaching autonomy.

Number of Items: 18

Format: 4-point Likert format. All items are presented.

Reliability: Alpha was .80 for the total scale. Subscale alphas ranged from .81 to .85 across two subscales.

Validity: The correlation between the subscales was .28.

Authors: Pearson, L. C., and Hall, B. W.

Article: Initial construct validation of the Teaching Autonomy Scale.

Journal: *Journal of Educational Research*, January/February 1993, *86*(3), 172–178.

■ ■ ■

6968

Test Name: TEST OF MISCONCEPTIONS ABOUT PSYCHOLOGY

Purpose: To measure misconceptions about psychology.

Number of Items: 62

Format: Multiple-choice. Sample items presented.

Reliability: Split-half reliability (Spearman-Brown) was .62. Test–retest (6 weeks) was .67.

Validity: Correlations with grades in psychology was .07. Correlation with Test of Common Beliefs was .39.

Author: McCutcheon, L. E.

Article: A new test of misconceptions about psychology.

Journal: *Psychological Reports*, April 1991, *68*(2), 647–653.

Related Research: Holley, J., & Buxton, C. (1950). A factorial study of beliefs. *Educational and Psychological Measurement, 10,* 400–410.

■ ■ ■

6969

Test Name: TEST OF VISUAL IMAGERY CONTROL

Purpose: To measure ability to control images.

Number of Items: 11

Format: Responses are either "Yes" or "No."

Reliability: Coefficient alpha was .80. Split-half reliability was .73.

Author: McKelvie, S. J.

Article: Consistency of interform content for the Gordon Test of Visual Imagery Control.

Journal: *Perceptual and Motor Skills*, June 1992, *74*(3) Part 2, 1107–1112.

Related Research: Gordon, R. (1950). An experiment correlating the nature of imagery with performance on a test of reversal of perspective. *British Journal of Psychology, 41,* 63–67.

■ ■ ■

6970

Test Name: TEXAS SOCIAL BEHAVIOR INVENTORY

Purpose: To measure differences in self-esteem based on interpersonal competence.

Number of Items: 16

Format: 6-point Likert format ranges from 1 (*strongly disagree*) to 6 (*agree strongly*).

Reliability: Alpha was .67.

Authors: Ryckman, R. M., et al.

Article: Personality correlates of the Hypercompetitive Attitude Scale: Validity tests of Horney's theory of neurosis.

Journal: *Journal of Personality Assessment*, February 1994, *62*(1), 84–94.

Related Research: Helmreich, R. L., & Stapp, J. (1974). Short forms of the Texas Social Behavior Inventory (TSBI), an objective measure of self-esteem. *Bulletin of the Psychonomic Society, 4,* 473–475.

6971

Test Name: TEXAS SOCIAL BEHAVIOR INVENTORY

Purpose: To assess social competence and self-esteem.

Number of Items: 32

Format: Responses are made on a 4-point scale ranging from 0 (*not at all characteristic of me*) to 4 (*very characteristic of me*).

Reliability: Test–retest reliability coefficients were .94 (males) and .93 (females).

Validity: Correlations with other variables ranged from -.38 to .20.

Authors: Kenny, M. E., and Donaldson, G. A.

Article: Contributions of parental attachment and family structure to the social and psychological functioning of first-year college students.

Journal: *Journal of Counseling Psychology*, October 1991, *38*(4), 479–486

Related Research: Helmreich, R., et al. (1974). The Texas Social Behavior Inventory (TSBI): An objective measure of self-esteem or social competency. JSAS: *Catalog of Selected Documents in Psychology, 4,* 79 (Ms. No. 861).

■ ■ ■

6972

Test Name: THEORETICAL ORIENTATION TO READING PROFILE

Purpose: To determine orientation to the reading process.

Number of Items: 28

Format: Responses are made on a 5-point Likert scale. An example is presented.

Reliability: Cronbach alpha was .98.

Author: Wham, M. A.

Article: The relationship between undergraduate course work and beliefs about reading instruction.

Journal: *Journal of Research and Development in Education*, Fall 1993, *27*(1), 9–17.

Related Research: DeFord, D. (1979). *A validation of an instrument to determine a teacher's theoretical orientation to reading instruction.* Unpublished doctoral dissertation, Indiana University, Bloomington.

■ ■ ■

6973

Test Name: TOLERANCE FOR AMBIGUITY SCALE

Purpose: To measure tolerance for ambiguity.

Number of Items: 5

Format: 5-point Likert format. Sample items are described.

Reliability: Alpha was .62.

Validity: Correlations with other variables ranged from -.43 to .72.

Authors: Rush, M. C., et al.

Article: Psychological resiliency in the public sector: "Hardiness" and pressure for change.

Journal: *Journal of Vocational Behavior*, February 1995, *46*(1), 1–16.

Related Research: Budner, S. (1962). Intolerance of ambiguity as a personality variable. *Journal of Personality*, *30*, 29–50.

■ ■ ■

6974

Test Name: TRADITIONALITY OF THE HUSBAND SCALE

Purpose: To measure the perceived role of all women in society.

Number of Items: 8

Format: 5-point response alternatives. All items presented.

Reliability: Cronbach's alpha was .76.

Authors: Lange, A., et al.

Article: Status inconsistency, traditionality and marital distress in the Netherlands.

Journal: *Psychological Reports*, June 1991, *68*(3) Part II, 1243–1253.

Related Research: Vandoneren, M. L. van. (1987). *Working young mothers and their well-being.* Paper for the Association of Women With Academic Education, Trinity College, Dublin.

■ ■ ■

6975

Test Name: TRENT ATTRIBUTIONAL PROFILE

Purpose: To measure locus of control.

Number of Items: 12

Format: Each item covers academic, social, and financial life situations. Employs a 5-point Likert scale.

Reliability: Alpha coefficients ranged from .56 to .83.

Validity: Correlations with other variables ranged from -.24 to .51.

Authors: Hyman, G. J., et al.

Article: The relationship between three multidimensional locus of control scales.

Journal: *Educational and Psychological Measurement*, Summer 1991, *51*(2), 403–412.

Related Research: Wong, P. T. P., & Sproule, C. F. (1984). An attributional analysis of the locus of control construct and the Trent Attributional Profile (TAP). In

H. M. Lefcourt (Ed.), *Research with the locus of control construct, Vol. 3.* New York: Academic Press.

■ ■ ■

6976

Test Name: TURNER PERCEIVED OCCUPATIONAL DISCRIMINATION AGAINST WOMEN SCALE

Purpose: To measure perception of gender discrimination in the labor force.

Number of Items: 21

Format: Responses are made to each male occupation indicating to which of 3 levels of openness to women they have.

Reliability: Coefficient alpha was .83.

Authors: Davey, F. H., and Stoppard, J. M.

Article: Some factors affecting the occupational expectations of female adolescents.

Journal: *Journal of Vocational Behavior*, December 1993, *43*(3), 235–250.

Related Research: Turner, B. F., & Turner, C. B. (1975). Race, sex, and perception of the occupational opportunity structure among college students. *Sociological Quarterly*, *16*, 345–360.

■ ■ ■

6977

Test Name: USEFULNESS OF MATHEMATICS SCALE

Purpose: To assess students' perceptions of the relevance of mathematics to their future life and work.

Number of Items: 10

Format: Responses are made on a

5-point scale ranging from 1 (*strongly disagree*) to 5 (*strongly agree*). Examples are presented.

Reliability: Coefficient alpha was .92.

Validity: Correlations with other variables ranged from -.39 to .48.

Authors: Lopez, F. G., and Lent, R. W.

Article: Sources of mathematics self-efficacy in high school students.

Journal: *The Career Development Quarterly*, September 1992, *41*(1), 3–12.

Related Research: Betz, N. E. (1977, August). *Math anxiety: What is it?* Paper presented at the meeting of the American Psychological Association, San Francisco.

■ ■ ■

6978

Test Name: VOCATIONAL RATING SCALE

Purpose: To measure self-concept crystallization with respect to vocationally relevant attributes.

Number of Items: 40

Format: 5-point scales range from 1 (*completely false*) to 5 (*completely true*).

Reliability: Internal consistency was .94. Test–retest reliability (2 weeks) was .76.

Validity: Correlations with other variables ranged from -.81 to .57.

Authors: Brooks, L., et al.

Article: The relation of career-related work or internship experiences to the career development of college seniors.

Journal: *Journal of Vocational Behavior*, June 1995, *46*(3), 332–349.

Related Research: Barrett, T. C., & Tinsley, H. E. A. (1977). Measuring self-concept crystallization. *Journal of Vocational Behavior*, *11*, 305–313.

■ ■ ■

6979

Test Name: WASHINGTON SELF-DESCRIPTION QUESTIONNAIRE

Purpose: To measure general self-esteem.

Number of Items: 14

Format: Responses are made on a 4-point scale ranging from 1 (*not like me*) to 4 (*very much like me*). The entire scale is presented.

Reliability: Alpha coefficients were .80 and .86 (N's were 100 and 123 respectively). Test–retest (6 weeks) reliabilities were .69 and .71.

Validity: Correlations with other variables ranged from .58 to .75.

Authors: Smoll, F. L., et al.

Article: Enhancement of children's self-esteem through social support training for youth sport coaches.

Journal: *Journal of Applied Psychology*, August 1993, *78*(4), 602–610.

Related Research: Wylie, R. C. (1979). *The self-concept* (Vol. 2). Lincoln: University of Nebraska Press.

Rosenberg, M. (1979). *Conceiving the self.* New York: Basic Books.

■ ■ ■

6980

Test Name: WELLNESS ORIENTATION SCALE

Purpose: To assess internally directed wellness.

Number of Items: 30

Format: 5-point Likert format. Sample items are presented.

Reliability: Alphas ranged from .88 to .90.

Author: Adams, T., et al.

Article: Principle-centeredness: A values clarification approach to wellness.

Journal: *Measurement and Evaluation in Counseling and Development*, July 1995, *28*(3), 139–147.

Related Research: Field, L. K., & Steinhardt, M. A. (1992). The relationship of internally directed behaviors to self-reinforcement, self-esteem, and expectancy values for exercise. *American Journal of Health Promotion*, *7*, 21–27.

■ ■ ■

6981

Test Name: WHAT I THINK ABOUT MYSELF

Purpose: To measure self-esteem in children 5 to 13 years of age.

Number of Items: 18

Time Required: 10 minutes (for 25 subjects).

Format: Agree–disagree format. All items are presented.

Reliability: Test–retest reliabilities ranged from .75 to .96 across grade levels.

Authors: Kosmoski, G. J., et al.

Article: Reliability of children's self-esteem assessment: What I think about myself.

Journal: *Psychological Reports*, August 1994, *75*(1) Part I, 83–88.

■ ■ ■

6982

Test Name: "WHAT'S IT LIKE TO BE GIFTED" QUESTIONNAIRE

Purpose: To measure gifted students' perceptions of being gifted.

Number of Items: 96

Format: 6-point response scales ranged from 1 (*not at all*) to 6 (*extremely well*). All items are presented.

Reliability: Internal consistency ranged from .67 to .89.

Authors: Kunkel, M. A., et al.

Article: The experience of giftedness: A concept map.

Journal: *Gifted Child Quarterly*, Summer 1995, *39*(3), 126–134.

Related Research: Robinson, A. (1990). Does that describe me? Adolescents' acceptance of the gifted label. *Journal for the Education of the Gifted, 13*, 245–255.

CHAPTER 17
Personality

6983

Test Name: ACTIVITY PREFERENCE QUESTIONNAIRE

Purpose: To measure fearfulness.

Number of Items: 74

Format: Forced-choice (Thurstone) format.

Reliability: Internal consistency ranged from .82 to .86. Subscale reliabilities ranged from .78 to .84.

Author: Lilienfeld, S. O., et al.

Article: The relations between a self-report honesty test and personality measures in prison and college samples.

Journal: *Journal of Research in Personality*, June 1994, *28*(2), 154–169.

Related Research: Lykken, D. T., et al. (1973). *Manual for the Activity Preference Questionnaire.* Minneapolis: University of Minnesota.

■ ■ ■

6984

Test Name: ADJECTIVE CHECKLIST

Purpose: To measure personality.

Number of Items: 153

Format: Responses are either *all* or *none.*

Reliability: Alpha coefficients across the scales ranged from .76 to .89. Test–retest correlations ranged from .60 to .85.

Author: Strack, S.

Article: Relating Millon's Basic

Personality Styles and Holland's Occupational Types.

Journal: *Journal of Vocational Behavior*, August 1994, *45*(1), 41–54.

Related Research: Strack, S. (1987). Development and validation of an adjective checklist to access the Millon personality types in a normal population. *Journal of Personality Assessment, 51*, 572–587.

■ ■ ■

6985

Test Name: ADOLESCENT EGO IDENTITY SCALE

Purpose: To assess self-identity cohesion.

Number of Items: 38

Format: Likert format. Sample items presented.

Reliability: Alpha was .85.

Authors: Orbach, I., et al.

Article: The impact of subliminal symbiotic vs. identification messages in reducing anxiety.

Journal: *Journal of Research in Personality*, December 1994, *28*(4), 492–504.

Related Research: Tzuriel, D. (1984). Sex-role typing and ego identity in Israeli, Oriental and Western adolescents. *Journal of Personality and Social Psychology, 46*, 440-457.

■ ■ ■

6986

Test Name: ADULT RATING SCALE

Purpose: To assess attention, impulsivity, and hyperactivity.

Number of Items: 25

Format: 4-point rating scales. All items are presented.

Reliability: Test–retest reliability was .80. Alpha was .86.

Validity: Correlation with other variables ranged from .44 to .54.

Authors: Weyandt, L. L., et al.

Article: Reported prevalence of attentional difficulties in a general sample of college students.

Journal: *Journal of Psychopathology and Behavioral Assessment*, September 1995, *17*(3), 293–304.

■ ■ ■

6987

Test Name: AFFECT QUESTIONNAIRE

Purpose: To assess children's affect labeling.

Number of Items: 53 vignettes

Format: Each respondent has 10 chips per vignette. For each vignette they distribute the chips in containers for the four possible emotions (fear, happiness, sadness, anger).

Reliability: Test–retest across the scales ranged from .80 to .66.

Authors: Lochman, J. E., and Dodge, K. A.

Article: Social-cognitive processes of severely violent, moderately aggressive, and nonaggressive boys.

Journal: *Journal of Consulting and*

Clinical Psychology, April 1994, *62*(2), 366–374.

Related Research: Garrison, S. R., & Stolberg, A. L. (1983). Modification of anger in children by affective imagery training. *Journal of Abnormal Child Psychology*, *11*, 115–130.

▪ ▪ ▪

6988

Test Name: AGORAPHOBIC COGNITIONS SCALE

Purpose: To measure the fear of fear among agoraphobic patients.

Number of Items: 10

Format: 5-point scales range from 0 (*no fear*) to 4 (*fear very much*). All items are presented.

Reliability: Interitem correlations range from .12 to .55. Alpha was .80. Test–retest reliability (median 31 days) was .86.

Validity: Correlations with other variables ranged from -.10 to .64 across subscales.

Authors: Hoffart, A., et al.

Article: Assessment of fear of fear among agoraphobic patients: The Agoraphobic Cognitions Scale.

Journal: *Journal of Psychopathology and Behavioral Assessment*, June 1992, *14*(2), 175–187.

Related Research: Chambless, D. L., & Gracely, E. J. (1989). Fear of fear and the anxiety disorders. *Cognitive Therapy and Research*, *13*, 9–20.

▪ ▪ ▪

6989

Test Name: ALTRUISM SCALE

Purpose: To determine degree of altruism.

Number of Items: 23

Format: Responses are made on a

5-point scale ranging from *never* to *very often*.

Reliability: Alpha was .87.

Authors: Eisenberg, N., et al.

Article: Prosocial development in late adolescence: A longitudinal study.

Journal: *Child Development*, August 1995, *66*(4), 1179–1197.

Related Research: Rushton, J. P., et al. *The altruistic personality and the self-report altruism scale: Personality and clinical analysis.* New York: Academic Press.

▪ ▪ ▪

6990

Test Name: AMBIVALENCE OVER EMOTIONAL EXPRESSIVENESS QUESTIONNAIRE

Purpose: To measure emotional expression and regrets on such expression.

Number of Items: 28

Format: 5-point scales.

Reliability: Alpha was .88.

Validity: Correlations with other variables ranged from -.41 to .67.

Authors: King, L. A., et al.

Article: The structure of inhibition.

Journal: *Journal of Research in Personality*, March 1992, *26*(1), 85–102.

Related Research: King, L. A., & Emmons, R. A. (1991). The psychological, physical and interpersonal implications of emotional expression, conflict and control. *European Journal of Personality*, *5*, 131–150.

▪ ▪ ▪

6991

Test Name: AUTOBIOGRAPHICAL COGNITIONS QUESTIONNAIRE

Purpose: To assess the emotional happiness of personal thoughts and memories.

Number of Items: 2

Format: 7-point rating scales range from -3 (*extremely unhappy*) to +3 (*extremely happy*).

Validity: Correlation with Beck Depression Inventory was .54.

Authors: Ruiz-Caballero, J. A., and Bermudez, J.

Article: Neuroticism, mood, and retrieval of negative personal memories.

Journal: *The Journal of General Psychology*, January 1995, *122*(1), 29–35.

Related Research: Clark, D. M., & Teasdale, J. D. (1982). Diurnal variation in clinical depression and accessibility of memories of positive and negative experiences. *Journal of Abnormal Psychology*, *91*, 86–95.

▪ ▪ ▪

6992

Test Name: AUTONOMY SCALE

Purpose: To assess autonomy in adolescents.

Number of Items: 25

Format: True–false format. All items are presented.

Reliability: Alphas ranged from .17 to .47 across subscales. Total alpha was .39.

Authors: Mustaine, B. B., and Wilson, F. R.

Article: An exploration of the internal consistency of the Kurtines Autonomy Scale.

Journal: *Measurement and Evaluation in Counseling and Development*, January 1995, *27*(1), 211–225.

Related Research: Kurtines, W. M. (1978). A measure of autonomy.

Journal of Personality Assessment, 42, 253–257.

■ ■ ■

6993

Test Name: BARRETT IMPULSIVENESS SCALE

Purpose: To measure impulsiveness.

Number of Items: 11

Format: Includes 3 components: motor, cognitive, and nonplanning. Each item has 4 options. Examples are presented.

Reliability: Coefficient alpha was .82.

Validity: Correlations with other variable ranged from -.27 to .76.

Author: Carrillo-de-la-Pena, M. T., et al.

Article: Comparison among various methods of assessment of impulsiveness.

Journal: *Perceptual and Motor Skills,* October 1993, *77*(2), 567–575.

Related Research: Barrett, E. S. (1985). Impulsiveness subtraits, arousal and information process. In J. T. Spence & C. E. Itard (Eds.), *Motivation, emotion and personality* (pp. 137–146). New York: Elsevier North-Holland.

■ ■ ■

6994

Test Name: BELIEF QUESTIONNAIRE

Purpose: To assess personality disorders.

Number of Items: 126

Format: 7-point agreement scales.

Reliability: Alphas ranged from .77 to .93 across subscales. Test–retest reliabilities ranged from .69 to .83.

Validity: Correlations with

corresponding MMPI and PDQ scales ranged from -.04 to .73.

Authors: Trull, T. J., et al.

Article: Psychometric properties of a cognitive measure of personality disorders.

Journal: *Journal of Personality Assessment,* December 1993, *61*(3), 536–546.

Related Research: Beck, A. T. (1990). *Belief Questionnaire.* Unpublished manuscript.

■ ■ ■

6995

Test Name: BELL OBJECT RELATIONS-REALITY TESTING INVENTORY

Purpose: To measure ego functioning and object relations.

Number of Items: 90

Format: Includes two separate measures: Object Relations, which has 4 subscales, and Reality Testing, which has 3 subscales. Responses are true or false.

Reliability: Internal consistency and split-half reliability for Object Relations ranged from .78 to .90. Alpha coefficients for Reality Testing ranged from .82 to .85.

Validity: Correlations with other variables ranged from -.59 to .70.

Authors: Hadley, J. A., et al.

Article: Common aspects of object relations and self-representations in offspring from disparate dysfunctional families.

Journal: *Journal of Counseling Psychology,* July 1993, *40*(3), 348–356.

Related Research: Bell, M., et al. (1985). Scale for the assessment of reality testing: Reliability, validity, and factorial invariance. *Journal of Consulting and Clinical Psychology, 53,* 506–511.

6996

Test Name: BIODATA FORM

Purpose: To assess specific abilities, motivations, and interests using items focused on behaviors and events that actually take place or have taken place.

Number of Items: 25

Format: Responses are made using a multiple-choice format.

Reliability: Test–retest reliability was .79.

Authors: Becker, T. E., and Colquitt, A. L.

Article: Potential vs. actual faking of biodata form: An analysis along several dimensions of item-type.

Journal: *Personnel Psychology,* Summer 1992, *45*(2), 389–406.

Related Research: Childs, A., & Klimoski, R. J. (1986). Successfully predicting career successes: An application of the biographical inventory. *Journal of Applied Psychology, 71,* 3–8.

■ ■ ■

6997

Test Name: BIPOLAR ADJECTIVE SCALE

Purpose: To assess five major personality dimensions.

Number of Items: 80

Format: 7-point bipolar adjective scales.

Reliability: Alphas ranged from .71 to .83 across subscales.

Author: Kosek, R. B.

Article: Measuring prosocial behavior of college students.

Journal: *Psychological Reports,* December 1995, *77*(3) Part I, 739–742.

Related Research: McCrae, R. R., & Costa, P. T., Jr. (1985). Updating Norman's "adequate taxonomy": Intelligence and personality dimensions in natural language and in questionnaires. *Journal of Personality and Social Psychology, 49*, 710–721.

■ ■ ■

6998

Test Name: BUSS-DURKEE HOSTILITY INVENTORY

Purpose: To assess various aspects of hostility.

Number of Items: 75

Format: True–false items along 7 dimensions of hostility: assault, indirect hostility, irritability, negativism, resentment, suspicion, and verbal hostility. There is also a measure of guilt.

Reliability: Test–retest reliability ranged from .64 to .82.

Author: Kopper, B. A.

Article: Role of gender, sex role identity, and Type A behavior in anger expression and mental health functioning.

Journal: *Journal of Counseling Psychology*, April 1993, *40*(2), 232–237.

Related Research: Buss, A. H., & Durkee, A. (1957). An inventory for assessing different kinds of hostility. *Journal of Consulting Psychology, 21*, 343–349.

■ ■ ■

6999

Test Name: CONSUMERS' SUSCEPTIBILITY TO SALESPERSONS' INFLUENCE SCALE

Purpose: To measure susceptibility to a salesperson as a general personality trait.

Number of Items: 6

Format: Summated rating format. All items are presented.

Reliability: Alpha was .70.

Validity: Items were unidimensional.

Authors: Goff, B. G., and Walters, D. L.

Article: Susceptibility to salepersons' influences and consumers' shopping orientations.

Journal: *Psychological Reports*, June 1995, *76*(3) Part I, 915–928.

■ ■ ■

7000

Test Name: DEFENSE MECHANISMS INVENTORY— ADOLESCENT VERSION SHORT FORM

Purpose: To assess the use of defense mechanisms.

Number of Items: 24

Format: Participants respond to four questions for each of six dilemmas in a forced-choice format.

Reliability: Alphas ranged from .61 to .80.

Validity: Correlations between short- and long-form versions ranged from .89 to .95. Correlations with other variables ranged from -.34 to .39.

Authors: Recklitis, C. J., et al.

Article: Development of a short form of the adolescent version of the Defense Mechanisms Inventory.

Journal: *Journal of Personality Assessment*, April 1995, *64*(2), 360–370.

Related Research: Gleser, G. G., & Ihilevich, D. (1969). An objective instrument for measuring defense mechanisms. *Journal of Consulting and Clinical Psychology, 33*, 51–60.

■ ■ ■

7001

Test Name: DEPERSONALIZATION SCALE

Purpose: To assess inauthenticity, self-negation, self-objectification, derealization, and body detachment.

Number of Items: 32

Format: 4-point frequency scales. All items are presented.

Reliability: Alphas ranged from .78 to .84.

Validity: Correlations with the Differential Personality Inventory ranged from -.26 to .58.

Authors: Jacobs, J. R., and Bavasso, G. B.

Article: Toward the clarification of the construct of depersonalization and its association with affective and cognitive dysfunctions.

Journal: *Journal of Personality Assessment*, October 1992, *59*(2), 352–365.

Related Research: Dixon, J. (1963). Depersonalization in a non-clinical sample. *British Journal of Psychiatry, 78*, 235–242.

■ ■ ■

7002

Test Name: EAS TEMPERAMENT SURVEY

Purpose: To measure personality.

Number of Items: 20

Format: Includes subscales of: Emotionality, Activity, and Sociability. Responses are made on a 5-point scale.

Reliability: Alpha coefficients ranged from .57 to .62. Test–retest (2 weeks) reliability coefficients ranged from .81 to .85.

Authors: McGuire, S., et al.

Article: Genetic and environmental influences on perceptions of self-worth and competence in adolescence: A study of twins, full siblings, and step-siblings.

Journal: *Child Development*, June 1994, *65*(3), 785–799.

Related Research: Buss, A. H., & Plomin, R. (1984). *Temperament: Early developing personality traits.* Hillsdale, NJ: Erlbaum.

•••

7003

Test Name: EGO IDENTITY SCALE

Purpose: To measure identity achievement status.

Number of Items: 12

Format: Each item consists of a statement reflecting identity achievement status and a statement reflecting identity diffusion in a forced-choice format. A sample item is presented.

Reliability: Odd–even split correlation was .68.

Validity: Correlation with the Crowne-Marlowe Social Desirability Scale was .14.

Authors: Perosa, S. L., and Perosa, L. M.

Article: Relationships among Minuchin's structural family model: Identity, achievement, and coping style.

Journal: *Journal of Counseling Psychology*, October 1993, *40*(4), 479–489.

Related Research: Tan, A., et al. (1977). A short measure of Eriksonian ego identity. *Journal of Personality Assessment, 41,* 279–284.

•••

7004

Test Name: EGO IDENTITY SCALE

Purpose: To measure ego identity.

Number of Items: 72

Format: Includes 6 subscales.

Reliability: Spearman-Brown split-half reliability was .85.

Authors: Kush, K., and Cochran, L.

Article: Enhancing a sense of agency through career planning.

Journal: *Journal of Counseling Psychology*, October 1993, *40*(4), 434–439.

Related Research: Rasmussen, J. (1964). Relationship of ego identity to psychosocial effectiveness. *Psychological Reports, 15,* 815–825.

•••

7005

Test Name: EGO-INTEGRITY MEASURE

Purpose: To measure ego-integrity as defined by Erickson.

Number of Items: 16

Format: 5-point Likert format.

Reliability: Alpha was .80. Test–retest reliability (6 week) was .70.

Authors: Santor, D. A., and Zuroff, D. C.

Article: Depressive symptoms: Effects of negative affectivity and failing to accept the past.

Journal: *Journal of Personality Assessment*, October 1994, *63*(2), 294–312.

Related Research: Ryff, C. D., & Heincke, S. G. (1983). Subjective organization of personality in adulthood and aging. *Journal of Personality and Social Psychology, 44,* 807–816.

•••

7006

Test Name: EMOTIONAL AUTONOMY SCALE—SHORT VERSION

Purpose: To index emotional autonomy.

Number of Items: 14

Format: Includes 4 aspects: individuation, deidealization of parents, and nondependence on parents.

Reliability: Internal consistency was .82.

Validity: Correlations with other variables ranged from -.46 to .27.

Authors: Lamborn, S. D., and Steinberg, L.

Article: Emotional autonomy redux: Revisiting Ryan and Lynch.

Journal: *Child Development*, August 1993, *64*(2), 483–499.

Related Research: Steinberg, L., & Silverberg, S. (1986). The vicissitudes of autonomy in early adolescence. *Child Development, 57,* 841–851.

•••

7007

Test Name: EMOTIONAL CONTROL QUESTIONNAIRE

Purpose: To measure tendency to inhibit emotional expression.

Number of Items: 40

Format: True–false format.

Reliability: Alphas ranged from .42 to .81 across subscales.

Validity: Correlations with other variables ranged from -.37 to .39.

Authors: King, L. A., et al.

Article: The structure of inhibition.

Journal: *Journal of Research in Personality*, March 1992, *26*(1), 85–102.

Related Research: Rogers, D., & Nesshoever, W. (1987). The construction and preliminary validation of a scale for measuring emotional control. *Personality and Individual Differences, 8,* 527–534.

7008

Test Name: EMOTIONAL EXPRESSIVENESS QUESTIONNAIRE

Purpose: To measure tendency to express emotion.

Number of Items: 16

Format: 7-point rating scale.

Validity: Correlations with other variables ranged from -.53 to .24.

Authors: King, L. A., et al.

Article: The structure of inhibition.

Journal: *Journal of Research in Personality*, March 1992, *26*(1), 85-102.

Related Research: King, L. A., & Emmons, R. A. (1990). Conflict over emotional expression: Psychological and physical correlates. *Journal of Personality and Social Psychology*, *47*, 241–251.

■ ■ ■

7009

Test Name: EMOTIONAL INTENSITY SCALES

Purpose: To enable teachers, aides, and mothers to rate children's emotional intensity.

Number of Items: 5 and 8 item scales.

Format: Includes 5-point and 7-point scales.

Reliability: Alpha coefficients ranged from .62 to .88.

Authors: Eisenberg, N., et al.

Article: The relations of emotionality and regulation to children's anger-related reactions.

Journal: *Child Development*, February 1994, *65*(1), 109–128.

Related Research: Larsen, R. J., & Diener, E. (1987). Affect intensity as an individual difference characteristic: A review.

Journal of Research in Personality, *21*, 1–39.

■ ■ ■

7010

Test Name: EMOTIONALITY SCALE

Purpose: To measure emotionality.

Number of Items: 43

Format: All items are presented.

Reliability: Alpha was .94.

Authors: Basan-Diamond, L. E., et al.

Article: Temperament and a story-telling measure of self-regulation.

Journal: *Journal of Research in Personality*, March 1995, *29*(1), 109–120.

Related Research: Windle, M., & Lerner, R. M. (1986). Reassessing the Dimensions of Temperament Survey (DOTS-R). *Journal of Adolescent Research*, *1*, 213–230.

■ ■ ■

7011

Test Name: EMPLOYMENT CHARACTERISTICS SCALE

Purpose: To identify personal traits that may influence employment potential.

Number of Items: 22

Format: A list of adjectives to which one responds on a 9-point scale. Includes 4 factors: Personality, Power, Competence, and Professionalism. All items are presented.

Reliability: Coefficient alpha was .93.

Authors: Christman, L. A., and Slaten, B. L.

Article: Attitudes toward people with disabilities and judgments of employment potential.

Journal: *Perceptual and Motor Skills*, April 1991, *72*(2), 467–475.

Related Research: Rucker, M., et al. (1985). Effects of similarity and consistency of style dress on impression formation. In M. Solomon (Ed.), *The psychology of fashion* (pp. 309–320). Lexington, MA: Lexington Books.

■ ■ ■

7012

Test Name: EXTENDED OBJECTIVE MEASURE OF EGO-IDENTITY STATUS

Purpose: To assess identity statuses: diffused, foreclosed, moratorium, and achieved.

Number of Items: 64

Format: 6-point Likert format.

Reliability: Median test–retest reliability was .76. Alphas ranged from .44 to .80.

Author: Cramer, P.

Article: Identity, narcissism, and defense mechanisms in late adolescence.

Journal: *Journal of Research in Personality*, September 1995, *29*(3), 341–361.

Related Research: Adams, G. R., et al. (1989). *Objective measure of ego identity status: A reference manual.* Ontario, Canada: University of Guelph.

■ ■ ■

7013

Test Name: FEAR QUESTIONNAIRE—CHINESE VERSION

Purpose: To assess phobic disorders.

Number of Items: 15

Format: All items are presented.

Reliability: Alpha was .83. Item-total correlations ranged from .15 to .59 (mean .45).

Validity: Correlations with other variables ranged from .25 to .44.

Authors: Lee, H. B., and Oei, T. P .S.

Article: Factor structure, validity, and reliability of the Fear Questionnaire in a Hong Kong Chinese population.

Journal: *Journal of Psychopathology and Behavioral Assessment*, September 1994, *16*(3), 189–199.

Related Research: Moyland, A., & Oei, T. P. S. (1992). Is the Fear Questionnaire (FQ) a useful instrument for patients with anxiety disorders? *Behavior Change, 9,* 38–49.

■ ■ ■

7014

Test Name: FEAR SURVEY SCHEDULE

Purpose: To measure fears.

Number of Items: 78

Format: 3-point rating scale.

Reliability: Alpha was .95.

Authors: Moore, S. M., and Gullone, E.

Article: Fear of weight gain: Its correlates among school aged adolescents.

Journal: *Psychological Reports,* June 1995, *76*(3) Part II, 1305–1306.

Related Research: Gullone, E., & King, N. J. (1992). Psychometric evaluation of a fear survey schedule for children and adolescents. *Journal of Child Psychology and Psychiatry, 33,* 987–998.

■ ■ ■

7015

Test Name: HAWAIIAN MIDDLE ADOLESCENT PERSONALITY SCALE

Purpose: To measure the personality of Hawaiian middle adolescents using items from the High School Personality Questionnaire. Items were revised to match the experiences of Hawaiian adolescents.

Number of Items: 185

Format: Dichotomous response categories (Not specified).

Validity: Eight factors were extracted: Ego Strength, Anxiety, Super Ego, Social Activity, Dominance, Dependence, Culture, and Counterculture. Congruence coefficients were greater than .90 and averaged .93.

Authors: Campbell, J. F.

Article: The primary personality factors of Hawaiian middle adolescents.

Journal: *Psychological Reports,* February 1991, *68*(1), 3–26.

Related Research: Cattell, R. B., et al. (1970). Adolescent personality structure in Q-data, checked in the High School Personality Questionnaire. *British Journal of Psychology, 61,* 39–54.

■ ■ ■

7016

Test Name: HOSTILITY SCALE

Purpose: To measure hostility.

Number of Items: 50

Format: True–false format.

Reliability: Alpha was .80. Test–retest (4 years) was .85.

Authors: McGronigle, M. M., et al.

Article: Hostility and nonshared family environment: A study of monozygotic twins.

Journal: *Journal of Research in Personality,* March 1993, *27*(1), 23–34.

Related Research: Cook, W. W., & Medley, D. M. (1954). Proposed hostility and pharisaic-virtue scales for the MMPI. *Journal of Applied Psychology, 38,* 414–418.

■ ■ ■

7017

Test Name: HOSTILITY STRAIN SCALE

Purpose: To assess latent hostility.

Number of Items: 4

Format: Responses are made on a 5-point Likert-type scale. A sample item is presented.

Reliability: Alpha coefficients were .61 and .65.

Validity: Correlations with other variables ranged from -.21 to .56.

Authors: Newton, T., and Keenan, T.

Article: Further analyses of the dispositional argument in organizational behavior.

Journal: *Journal of Applied Psychology,* December 1991, *76*(6), 781–787.

Related Research: West, M., & Rushton, R. (1989). Mismatches in work-role transitions. *Journal of Occupational Psychology, 62,* 271–286.

■ ■ ■

7018

Test Name: HOSTILITY TOWARDS WOMEN SCALE

Purpose: To measure hostility toward women.

Number of Items: 10

Format: True–false format.

Reliability: Alpha was .84.

Authors: Christopher, F. S., et al.

Article: Exploring the darkside of courtship: A test of a model of premarital sexual aggressiveness.

Journal: *Journal of Marriage and the Family*, May 1993, *55*(2), 469–479.

Related Research: Check, J. V., et al. (1985). On hostile ground. *Psychology Today*, *19*(4), 56–61.

•••

7019

Test Name: IMAGINAL PROCESS INVENTORY

Purpose: To assess positive, dysphoric, and distracted daydreaming styles.

Number of Items: 45

Format: 5-point Likert format.

Reliability: Alphas ranged from .79 to .85 across subscales.

Author: Kolligian, J., Jr., and Sternberg, R. J.

Article: Perceived fraudulence in young adults: Is there an "impostor syndrome?"

Journal: *Journal of Personality Assessment*, April 1991, *56*(2), 308–326.

Related Research: Huba, G. J., et al. (1981). Development of scales for three second-order factors of inner experience. *Multivariate Behavioral Research*, *16*, 181–206.

•••

7020

Test Name: IMPULSIVENESS SCALE

Purpose: To measure motor, cognitive, and nonplanning impulsiveness.

Number of Items: 34

Format: 4-point frequency rating scales. Sample items presented.

Reliability: Alphas ranged from .86 to .91.

Validity: Correlations with

boredom proneness ranged from .41 to .56.

Authors: Watt, J. D., and Vodanovich, S. J.

Article: Relationship between boredom proneness and impulsivity.

Journal: *Psychological Reports*, June 1992, *70*(3) Part I, 688–690.

Related Research: Barratt, E. S. (1985). Impulsiveness subtraits: Arousal and information processing. In J. T. Spence & C. E. Izard (Eds.), *Motivation, emotion and personality* (pp. 137–146). Amsterdam: North Holland/Elsevier.

•••

7021

Test Name: INTERNALIZED SHAME SCALE

Purpose: To measure shame that has become an internalized part of a person's identity.

Number of Items: 24

Format: Responses are made on a 5-point Likert-type scale ranging from 1 (*almost always*) to 5 (*never*).

Reliability: Coefficient alpha and test–retest reliabilities were .94 and .71.

Validity: Correlations with other variables ranged from -.65 to .70.

Authors: Hadley, J. A., et al.

Article: Common aspects of object relations and self-representations in offspring from disparate dysfunctional families.

Journal: *Journal of Counseling Psychology*, July 1993, *40*(3), 348–356.

Related Research: Cook, D. R. (1990). *Draft manual: Clinical use of Internalized Shame Scale*. Menomonie: University of Wisconsin-Stout.

7022

Test Name: INVENTORY OF PERSONAL CHARACTERISTICS #7

Purpose: To assess negative emotionality, positive emotionality, conventionality, agreeability, dependability, positive valance, and negative valance.

Number of Items: 161

Format: 4-point scales.

Reliability: Internal consistencies ranged from .83 to .92.

Authors: McCrae, R. R., and Costa, P. T., Jr.

Article: Positive and negative valence within the Five-Factor Model.

Journal: *Journal of Research in Personality*, December 1995, *29*(4), 443–460.

Related Research: Tellegen, A., et al. (1991). *Inventory of Personal Characteristics #7*. Unpublished materials, University of Minnesota.

•••

7023

Test Name: LENIENCY SCALE

Purpose: To measure leniency disposition.

Number of Items: 23

Format: Responses are either "true" or "false."

Validity: Correlations with other variables ranged from .13 to .25.

Author: Highhouse, S.

Article: The Leniency Scale: Is it really independent of ratee behavior?

Journal: *Educational and Psychological Measurement*, Autumn 1992, *52*(3), 781–876.

Related Research: Schriessheim, C. A. (1980). Development and validation of a scale to measure leniency in description of others. Unpublished manuscript, cited in Bannister, B. D., et al. (1987). A new method for the statistical control of rating error in performance ratings. *Educational and Psychological Measurement, 47*, 583–596.

■ ■ ■

7024

Test Name: LEVEL OF EXPRESSED EMOTION SCALE

Purpose: To measure the construct of expressed emotion.

Number of Items: 60

Format: True–false format.

Reliability: KR-20 reliabilities ranged from .84 to .95. Test–retest correlations (6 weeks) ranged from .67 to .82.

Authors: Donat, D. C., et al.

Article: Empirically derived personality subtypes of public psychiatric patients: Effect on self-reported symptom, coping inclinations and evaluation of expressed emotion in caregivers.

Journal: *Journal of Personality Assessment*, February 1992, *58*(1), 36–50.

Related Research: Cole, J. E., & Kazarian, S. S. (1988). The Level of Expressed Emotion Scale: A new measure of expressed emotion. *Journal of Clinical Psychology, 44*, 392–397.

■ ■ ■

7025

Test Name: MAUDSLEY OBSESSIVE COMPULSIVE INVENTORY

Purpose: To assess degree of compulsivity.

Number of Items: 30

Format: True–false format.

Reliability: Alpha was .89. Test–retest reliability was .80.

Validity: Correlations with the Yale-Brown Scale ranged from .07 to .62.

Authors: Frost, R. O., et al.

Article: The relationship of the Yale-Brown Obsessive Compulsive Scale (YBOCS) to other measures of obsessive compulsive symptoms in a nonclinical population.

Journal: *Journal of Personality Assessment*, August 1995, *65*(1), 158–168.

Related Research: Rochman, S., & Hodgson, R. (1980). *Obsessions and compulsions.* Englewood Cliffs, NJ: Prentice-Hall.

■ ■ ■

7026

Test Name: MINI-MARKERS

Purpose: To assess Goldberg's Unipolar Big-Five markers.

Number of Items: 40

Format: All items are presented. 9-point response scales range from 1 (*extremely inaccurate*) to 9 (*extremely accurate*).

Reliability: Alphas ranged from .69 to .86.

Validity: Correlations with full marker sets ranged from .92 to .96.

Author: Saucier, G.

Article: Mini-markers: A brief version of Goldberg's Unipolar Big-Five Markers.

Journal: *Journal of Personality Assessment*, October 1994, *63*(3), 506–516.

Related Research: Goldberg, L. R., & Rosolack, T. K. (1994). The Big-Five factor structure as an integrative framework: An empirical comparison with Eysenck's P-E-N Model. In C. F. Halverson et al. (Eds.), *The developing structure of temperament and personality from*

infancy to adulthood (pp. 7–35). Hillsdale, NJ: Erlbaum.

■ ■ ■

7027

Test Name: MULTIDIMENSIONAL PERSONALITY QUESTIONNAIRE—NEGATIVE EMOTIONALITY

Purpose: To measure negative affectivity.

Number of Items: 14

Format: Items are answered "true" or "false." A sample item is presented.

Reliability: Test–retest (12 weeks) reliability was .72.

Authors: Decker, P. J., and Borgen, F. H.

Article: Dimensions of work appraisal: Stress, strain, coping, job satisfaction, and negative affectivity.

Journal: *Journal of Counseling Psychology*, October 1993, *40*(4), 470–478.

Related Research: Tellegen, A. (1982). *Brief manual for the Differential Personality Questionnaire.* Unpublished manuscript, University of Minnesota, Minneapolis.

■ ■ ■

7028

Test Name: MULTI-TRAIT PERSONALITY INVENTORY

Purpose: To assess clinical personality.

Number of Items: 122

Time Required: 20 minutes.

Format: Adjective rating scale format.

Reliability: Alphas ranged from .53 to .88.

Validity: Congruence coefficients

(across groups) ranged from .33 to .94.

Authors: Cheung, P. C., et al.

Article: Development of the Multi-Trait Personality Inventory (MTPI): Comparison among four Chinese populations.

Journal: *Journal of Personality Assessment*, December 1992, *59*(3), 528–551.

• • •

7029

Test Name: NEED FOR COGNITION SCALE—DUTCH VERSION

Purpose: To measure need for cognition.

Number of Items: 11

Format: 7-point Likert format. Sample items presented.

Reliability: Alpha was .74.

Author: Verplanken, B., et al.

Article: Need for cognition and external information search.

Journal: *Journal of Research in Personality*, June 1992, *26*(2), 128–136.

Related Research: Pieters, R. G. M., et al. (1987). Need for cognition: Relationship with reasoned action. *Nederlands Tijdschrift voor de Psychologie*, *42*, 62-70.

Cacioppo, J. T., et al. (1984). The efficient assessment of need for cognition. *Journal of Personality Assessment*, *48*, 306–307.

• • •

7030

Test Name: NEED FOR COGNITION SCALE

Purpose: To measure an individual's tendency to engage in and enjoy thinking.

Number of Items: 18

Format: Items are scored on a 6-point scale ranging from 0 to 5. Three items are presented.

Reliability: Cronbach's alpha was .88.

Validity: Correlations with other variables ranged from .09 to .27.

Authors: Furlong, P. R.

Article: Personal factors influencing informal reasoning of economic issues and the effect of specific instruction.

Journal: *Journal of Educational Psychology*, March 1993, *85*(1), 171–181.

Related Research: Cacioppo, J. T., & Petty, R. E. (1982). The need for cognition. *Journal of Personality and Social Psychology*, *42*, 116–131.

• • •

7031

Test Name: PERSONAL ATTRIBUTES QUESTIONNAIRE

Purpose: To assess instrumentality and expressiveness.

Number of Items: 24

Format: Consists of bipolar 5-point items.

Reliability: Alpha coefficients were .79 (instrumentality) and .81 (expressiveness).

Authors: Holmbeck, G. N., and Wandrei, M. L.

Article: Individual and relational predictors of adjustment in first-year college students.

Journal: *Journal of Counseling Psychology*, January 1993, *40*(1), 73–78.

Related Research: Spence, J. T., & Helmreich, R. L. (1978). *Masculinity and femininity: Their psychological dimensions, correlates, and antecedents.* Austin: University of Texas Press.

7032

Test Name: PERSONAL CHARACTERISTICS INVENTORY

Purpose: To measure the Big Five personality dimensions.

Number of Items: 132

Format: Includes 5 factors: Extroversion, Agreeableness, Conscientiousness, Emotional Stability, and Openness to Experience.

Reliability: Alpha coefficients ranged from .67 to .89. Test–retest (9 months) reliability coefficients ranged from .07 to .84.

Validity: Correlations with other variables ranged from -.01 to .71.

Authors: Barrick, M. R., et al.

Article: Conscientiousness and performance of sales representatives: Test of the mediating effects of goal setting.

Journal: *Journal of Applied Psychology*, October 1993, *78*(5), 715–722.

Related Research: Barrick, M. R., & Mount, M. K. (1993). Autonomy as a moderator of the relationships between the Big Five personality dimensions and job performance. *Journal of Applied Psychology*, *78*, 111–118.

• • •

7033

Test Name: PERSONAL CHARACTERISTICS INVENTORY

Purpose: To assess the Big Five personality constructs.

Number of Items: 137

Format: Responses are made on a 3-point scale ranging from 1 (*agree*) to 3 (*disagree*). The five personality constructs measured are extroversion, agreeableness, conscientiousness, emotional stability, and openness to experience.

Reliability: Alpha coefficients ranged from .67 to .89. Test–retest (9 months) reliability ranged from .70 to .84 (*N* = 63).

Validity: Correlations with other variables ranged from -.16 to .32 (*N* = 146).

Authors: Barrick, M. R., and Mount, M. K.

Article: Autonomy as a moderater of the relationships between the Big Five personality dimensions and job performance.

Journal: *Journal of Applied Psychology*, February 1993, *78*(2), 111–118.

■ ■ ■

7034

Test Name: PERSONALITY DISORDER EXAMINATION (PDE)

Purpose: To assess personality disorders.

Number of Items: 126

Time Required: 2–3 1/2 hours.

Format: Interviewers rate participants on 3-point scales. An item and the interview process are described.

Validity: Correlations of PDE and MCM-II cluster scores ranged from -.67 to .93.

Authors: Soldz, S., et al.

Article: Diagnostic agreement between the Personality Disorder Examination and the MCMI-II.

Journal: *Journal of Personality Assessment*, June 1993, *60*(3), 486–499.

Related Research: Loranger, A. (1988). *Personality Disorder Examination (PDE) Manual).* Weschester, NY: Cornell University Medical College, Department of Psychiatry.

7035

Test Name: PERSONALITY INVENTORY SCALES

Purpose: To diagnose personality disorders using *DSM* diagnostic criteria stated in everyday language.

Number of Items: 103

Time Required: 15 minutes.

Format: True–false format. All items presented.

Reliability: Split-half ranged from .33 to .77. Test–retest from .62 to .95.

Validity: Correlation with Loranger Personality Disorder examination was .39.

Author: Burgess, J. W.

Article: The Personality Inventory Scales: A self-rating clinical instrument for diagnosis of personality disorder.

Journal: *Psychological Reports*, December 1991, *69*(3) Part II, 1235–1246.

■ ■ ■

7036

Test Name: PREDICTION OF AGGRESSION AND DANGEROUSNESS

Purpose: To measure aggression and dangerousness.

Number of Items: 29

Format: 6 diagnostic rating categories. All items presented.

Reliability: Interrater reliability ranged from .85 to .97.

Author: Bjørkly, S.

Article: Scales for the prediction of aggression and dangerousness in psychiatric patients, an introduction.

Journal: *Psychological Reports*, December 1993, *73*(3) Part II, 1363–1377.

Related Research: Buss, A. H., and Durkee, A. (1957). An inventory for assessing different kinds of hostility. *Journal of Consulting Psychology, 21,* 343–349.

■ ■ ■

7037

Test Name: PRIVATE SELF-CONSCIOUSNESS SCALE

Purpose: To measure the extent to which people tend to their inner thoughts and feelings.

Number of Items: 10

Format: Responses are made on a 5-point scale ranging from 0 (*extremely uncharacteristic*) to 4 (*extremely characteristic*).

Reliability: Test–retest (2 weeks) reliability was .79.

Validity: Correlations with other variables ranged from -.08 to .58.

Authors: Carson, A. D., and Mowsesian, R.

Article: Self-monitoring and private self-consciousness: Relations to Holland's vocational personality types.

Journal: *Journal of Vocational Behavior*, April 1993, *42*(2), 212–222.

Related Research: Fenigstein, A., et al. (1975). Public and private self-consciousness: Assessment and theory. *Journal of Consulting and Clinical Psychology, 43,* 522–527.

■ ■ ■

7038

Test Name: PRIVATE SELF-CONSCIOUSNESS SCALE-ICELANDIC VERSION

Purpose: To measure the tendency to attend to one's own feelings, attitudes, motives, and personality characteristics.

Number of Items: 10

Format: 4-point rating scale

Reliability: Internal consistency was .64.

Validity: Correlations with other variables ranged from .36 to .73.

Author: Smári, J.

Article: Private self-consciousness: Does it influence convergent and discriminant validity of self-reported anxiety and depression?

Journal: *Psychological Reports*, June 1991, *68*(3) Part I, 711–718.

Related Research: Fenigstein, A., et al. (1975). Public and private self-consciousness: Assessment and theory. *Journal of Consulting and Clinical Psychology*, *43*, 522–527.

■ ■ ■

7039

Test Name: PROACTIVE PERSONALITY MEASURE

Purpose: To measure proactive personality.

Number of Items: 17

Format: Responses are made on a 7-point Likert scale ranging from 1 (*strongly disagree*) to 7 (*strongly agree*). Sample items are presented.

Reliability: Alpha coefficients ranged from .87 to .89.

Validity: Correlations with other variables ranged from -.14 to .35.

Author: Crant, J. M.

Article: The Practice Personality Scale and objective job performance among real estate agents.

Journal: *Journal of Applied Psychology*, August 1995, *80*(4), 532–537.

Related Research: Bateman, T. S., & Crant, J. M. (1993). The proactive component of organization behavior. *Journal of Organizational Behavior*, *14*, 103–118.

7040

Test Name: SELF-CONSCIOUSNESS SCALE—REVISED

Purpose: To assess three dimensions of self-consciousness.

Number of Items: 19

Format: Includes 3 dimensions: private self-consciousness, public self-consciousness, and social anxiety.

Validity: Correlations with body-image ranged from -.15 to -.39.

Authors: Theron, W. H., et al.

Article: Relationship between body-image and self-consciousness.

Journal: *Perceptual and Motor Skills*, December 1991, *73*(3) Part 1, 979–983.

Related Research: Mittal, B., & Balasubramanian, S. K. (1987). Testing the dimensionality of the Self-Consciousness Scale. *Journal of Personality Assessment*, *51*, 53–68.

■ ■ ■

7041

Test Name: SELF-CONSCIOUSNESS SCALE

Purpose: To assess individual differences in self-consciousness.

Number of Items: 23

Format: 5-point scales range from 0 (*extremely uncharacteristic*) to 4 (*extremely characteristic*).

Validity: Correlations with other variables ranged from -.43 to .55.

Authors: Edison, J. D., and Adams, H. E.

Article: Depression, self-focus, and social interaction.

Journal: *Journal of Psychopathology and Behavioral Assessment*, March 1992, *14*(1), 1–21.

Related Research: Fenigstein, A., et al. (1975). Public and private self-consciousness: Assessment and theory. *Journal of Consulting and Clinical Psychology*, *43*, 522–527.

■ ■ ■

7042

Test Name: SELF-CONSCIOUSNESS SCALE

Purpose: To measure private and public self-consciousness and social anxiety.

Number of Items: 25

Format: 5-point scales. Sample items presented.

Reliability: Alphas ranged from .69 to .73 across subscales. Test-retest reliabilities ranged from .73 to .84.

Author: Ferrari, J. R.

Article: Procrastinators and perfect behavior: An exploratory factor analysis of self-presentation, self-awareness and self-handicapping components.

Journal: *Journal of Research in Personality*, March 1992, *26*(1), 75–84.

Related Research: Fenigstein, A., et al. (1975). Public and private self-consciousness: Assessment and theory. *Journal of Consulting and Clinical Psychology*, *43*, 522–527.

■ ■ ■

7043

Test Name: SELF-CONSCIOUSNESS SCALE—BRAZILIAN VERSION

Purpose: To measure self-consciousness.

Number of Items: 23

Format: 5-point rating scales (*discordo completamente* to *concordo totalmente*).

Reliability: Alphas ranged from .63 to .74 across subscales. Test–retest reliability ranged from .69 to .89.

Validity: Subscale intercorrelations ranged from -.02 to .40.

Authors: Teixeira, M. A., and Gomes, W. B.

Article: Self-Consciousness Scale: Brazilian version.

Journal: *Psychological Reports*, October 1995, *77*(2), 423–427.

Related Research: Fenigstein, A., et al. (1975). Public and private self-consciousness: Assessment and theory. *Journal of Consulting and Clinical Psychology, 43*, 522–527.

• • •

7044

Test Name: SELF-CONTROL SCHEDULE

Purpose: To assess learned resourcefulness.

Number of Items: 32

Format: 7-point rating scales range from +3 (*very characteristic of me*) to -3 (*very uncharacteristic of me*).

Validity: Correlation with external locus of control was -.40.

Authors: Edwards, D., and Riordan, S.

Article: Learned resourcefulness in Black and White South African university students.

Journal: *The Journal of Social Psychology*, October 1994, *133*(5), 665–675.

Related Research: Rosenbaum, M. (1988). Learned resourcefulness, stress and self-regulation. In S. Fisher and J. Reason (Eds.), *Handbook of life stress cognition and health* (pp. 483–496). Chichester, England: Wiley.

7045

Test Name: SELF-DEFEATING PERSONALITY SCALE

Purpose: To measure the self-defeating personality inventory using the eight *DSM–III–R* criteria.

Number of Items: 48

Format: True–false.

Reliability: Alpha was .68. Test–retest reliabilities ranged from .71 to .75 (3 weeks).

Authors: Schill, T., and Sharp, M.

Article: Self-defeating personality and depression: A closer look.

Journal: *Psychological Reports*, June 1995, *76*(3) Part II, 1167–1170.

Related Research: Schill, T. (1990). A measure of self-defeating personality. *Psychological Reports, 66*, 1343–1346.

• • •

7046

Test Name: SELF-FOCUS SENTENCE COMPLETION

Purpose: To measure egocentricity.

Number of Items: Varies.

Format: Sentence completion format.

Reliability: Interrater reliability ranged from .79 to .90 on 30 protocols following rater training.

Author: Flanagan, R.

Article: Shyness, egocentricity, and psychopathology: Their relationships among non-hospitalized individuals and mental hospital patients.

Journal: *Psychological Reports*, June 1991, *70*(3) Part I, 995–1004.

Related Research: Exner, J. E. (1973). The Self-Focus Sentence

Completion: A study of egocentricity. *Journal of Personality Assessment, 37*, 437–455.

• • •

7047

Test Name: SOCIAL PHOBIA AND ANXIETY INVENTORY

Purpose: To assess the syndrome of social phobia as defined in the *DSM–III–R*.

Number of Items: 44

Format: 7-point Likert format.

Validity: Correlations with other variables ranged from -.47 to .77.

Authors: Herbert, J. D., et al.

Article: Concurrent validity of the Social Phobia and Anxiety Inventory.

Journal: *Journal of Psychopathology and Behavioral Assessment*, December 1991, *13*(4), 357–368.

Related Research: Turner, D., et al. (1989). The Social Phobia and Anxiety Inventory: Construct validity. *Journal of Psychopathology and Behavioral Assessment, 11*, 221–234.

• • •

7048

Test Name: SOCIOTROPY–AUTONOMY SCALE

Purpose: To measure sociotropic and autonomous personality characteristics.

Number of Items: 60

Format: Includes a sociotropic and an autonomy scale. Responses are made on a 5-point scale.

Reliability: Alphas were .80 and .89 for internal consistency.

Validity: Correlations with other variables ranged from .31 to -.35.

Authors: Reynolds, S., and Gilbert, P.

Article: Psychological impact of unemployment: Interactive effects of vulnerability and protective factors on depression.

Journal: *Journal of Counseling Psychology*, January 1991, *38*(1), 76–84.

Related Research: Beck, A. T. (1983). Cognitive theory of depression: New perspectives. In P. Clayton & J. Barrett (Eds.), *Treatment of depression: Old controversies and new approaches* (pp. 265–290). New York: Raven Press.

■ ■ ■

7049

Test Name: SOCIOTROPY– AUTONOMY SCALE

Purpose: To assess sociotropy and autonomy as vulnerability factors in depression.

Number of Items: 93

Format: 5-point frequency scales. All items are presented.

Reliability: Alphas ranged from .76 to .87 across subscales.

Validity: Correlations with other variables ranged from -.36 to .36.

Authors: Clark, D. A., and Beck, A. T.

Article: Personality factors in dysphoria: A psychometric refinement of Beck's Sociotropy-Autonomy Scale.

Journal: *Journal of Psychopathology and Behavioral Assessment*, December 1991, *13*(4), 369–388.

Related Research: Beck, A. T., et al. (1983). *Development of the Sociotropy-Autonomy Scale: A measure of personality factors in psychopathology*. Unpublished manuscript, Center for Cognitive Therapy, University of Pennsylvania Medical School, Philadelphia.

7050

Test Name: S-R INVENTORY OF HOSTILITY

Purpose: To measure respondent frustration and anger.

Number of Items: 14

Format: The responses reported by participants represent the emotional state of anger. Responses are made to situations on a 5-point scale (from *not at all* to *very much*).

Reliability: Coefficient alphas on the scales ranged from .75 to the .90s.

Author: Jaderlund, N. S., and Waldron, H. B.

Article: Mood states associated with induced defensiveness.

Journal: *Journal of College Student Development*, March 1994, *35*(2), 129–134.

Related Research: Endler, N. S., & Hunt, J. M. (1968). S-R inventories of hostility and comparisons of the proportions of variance from persons, responses, and situations for hostility and anxiousness. *Journal of Personality and Social Psychology*, *9*(4), 309–315.

■ ■ ■

7051

Test Name: STOICISM SCALE

Purpose: To measure stoicism.

Number of Items: 20

Format: 5-point Likert format. Sample items are presented.

Reliability: Split-half reliability was .90.

Validity: Correlations with other variables ranged from -.78 to .34.

Authors: Wagstaff, G. F., and Rowledge, A. M.

Article: Stoicism: Its relation to

gender, attitudes toward poverty, and reactions to emotive material.

Journal: *The Journal of Social Psychology*, April 1995, *135*(2), 181–184.

■ ■ ■

7052

Test Name: TASK AND EGO ORIENTATION IN SPORT QUESTIONNAIRE

Purpose: To assess one's proneness for task and ego involvement in tennis.

Number of Items: 13

Format: Responses are made on a 5-point scale ranging from 1 (*strongly disagree*) to 5 (*strongly agree*). Examples are presented.

Reliability: Alpha coefficients were .73 and .82.

Validity: Correlations with Competitive State Anxiety Inventory-2 ranged from -.34 to .20.

Authors: Newton, M., and Duda, J.

Article: Relations of goal orientations and expectations on multidimensional state anxiety.

Journal: *Perceptual and Motor Skills*, December 1995, *81*(3) Part 2, 1107–1112.

Related Research: Duda, J. L. (1992). Motivation in sport settings: A goal perspective approach. In G. Roberts (Ed.), *Motivation in sport and exercise* (pp. 57–92). Champaign, IL: Human Kinetics.

■ ■ ■

7053

Test Name: TENDENCY TO GOSSIP QUESTIONNAIRE

Purpose: To measure the disposition to gossip.

Number of Items: 20

Format: Responses are made on a 7-point scale ranging from 1 (*never*) to 7 (*always*). Includes 4 factors: Physical Appearance, Achievement, Social Information, and Sublimated Gossip. All items are presented except item #4, which did not load strongly on any factor.

Reliability: Coefficient alpha was .87.

Validity: The test correlated with vocational interests in people-oriented professions (.47) and the Social Desirability Questionnaire (-.33).

Authors: Nevo, O., et al.

Article: The development of the Tendency to Gossip Questionnaire: Construct and concurrent validation for a sample of Israeli college students.

Journal: *Educational and Psychological Measurement*, Winter 1993, *53*(4), 973–981.

■ ■ ■

7054

Test Name: THE BIG FIVE

Purpose: To measure each dimension of the Big Five personality structure: extroversion, agreeableness, conscientiousness, emotional stability, and intellect.

Number of Items: 100

Format: 9-point Likert format ranges from 1 (*extremely inaccurate*) to 9 (*extremely accurate*).

Reliability: Internal consistency ranged from .84 to .90.

Validity: Correlations with the NEO Personality Inventory ranged from .46 to .69.

Authors: Heppner, P. P., et al.

Article: Progress in resolving problems: A problem-focused style of coping.

Journal: *Journal of Counseling Psychology*, July 1995, *42*(3), 279–293.

Related Research: Goldberg, L. R. (1992). The development of markers for the Big Five factor structure. *Psychological Assessment, 4*, 26–42.

■ ■ ■

7055

Test Name: THIRD-CULTURE ADOLESCENT QUESTIONNAIRE

Purpose: To determine the characteristics of internationally mobile adolescents.

Number of Items: 70

Format: 57 of the responses are made on a 5-point Likert scale. 13 items require open-ended responses to biographical questions.

Reliability: Cronbach alpha reliability coefficients for the Likert subscales were family relationship .85, peer relationship .46, cultural acceptance .61, travel orientation .66, language acceptance .75, future orientation .71, and stereotyping .85.

Authors: Gerner, M., et al.

Article: Characteristics of internationally mobile adolescents.

Journal: *Journal of School Psychology*, Summer 1992, *30*(2), 197–214.

Related Research: Useem, R. H., & Downie, R. D. (1976, Sept/Oct). Third-culture kids. *Today's Education*, 103–105.

■ ■ ■

7056

Test Name: TORONTO ALEXITHYMIA SCALE

Purpose: To measure alexithymia.

Number of Items: 26

Reliability: Coefficient alpha was .79. Test–retest (7 days) reliability was .82.

Validity: Correlations with other variables ranged from -.55 to .50.

Authors: Mann, L. S., et al.

Article: Alexithymia, affect recognition, and five factors of personality in substance abusers.

Journal: *Perceptual and Motor Skills*, August 1995, *81*(1), 35–40.

Related Research: Taylor, G. J., et al. (1990). Validation of the alexithymia construct: A measurement based approach. *Canadian Journal of Psychiatry, 35*, 290–297.

■ ■ ■

7057

Test Name: TRIDIMENSIONAL PERSONALITY QUESTIONNAIRE

Purpose: To measure three dimensions of temperament: harm avoidance, novelty seeking, and reward dependence.

Number of Items: 100

Format: True–false format.

Validity: Correlations of subscales with MMPI scales ranged from -.64 to .71.

Authors: Wetzel, R. D., et al.

Article: Correlates of Tridimensionality Personality Questionnaire Scales with selected Minnesota Multiphasic Personality Inventory Scales.

Journal: *Psychological Reports*, December 1992, *71*(3) Part II, 1027–1038.

Related Research: Cloninger, C. R., et al. (1991). The Tridimensionality Personality Questionnaire. *Psychological Reports, 69*, 1047–1057.

7058

Test Name: VULNERABILITY SCALE

Purpose: To measure vulnerability.

Number of Items: 30

Format: 7-point Likert format. All items are presented.

Reliability: Alpha was .88. Test–retest (4 weeks) was .81.

Validity: Correlations with other variables ranged from -.23 to .30.

Authors: Glover, H., et al.

Article: Vulnerability Scale: A preliminary report on psychometric properties.

Journal: *Psychological Reports*, December 1994, *75*(3) Part II, 1651–1668.

■ ■ ■

7059

Test Name: YALE–BROWN OBSESSIVE COMPULSIVE SCALE

Purpose: To rate the severity of obsessions and compulsions, interference, distress, resistance, and control.

Number of Items: 10

Format: Responses are made on a 5-point scale from 1 (*none*) to 4 (*extreme*).

Reliability: Interrater reliability was estimated at .95.

Authors: Hiss, H., et al.

Article: Relapse prevention program for treatment of obsessive-compulsive disorder.

Journal: *Journal of Consulting and Clinical Psychology*, August 1994, *62*(4), 801–808.

Related Research: Goodman, W. K., et al. (1989). The Yale-Brown Obsessive-Compulsive Scale (Y-BOCS): Past development, use and reliability. *Archives of General Psychiatry*, *46*, 1006–1016.

CHAPTER 18
Preference

7060

Test Name: APPAREL EVALUATION SCALE

Purpose: To assess importance of brand name, store image, fashionability, and suitability of apparel.

Number of Items: 13

Format: 5-point Likert format.

Reliability: Alphas ranged from .54 to .60 across subscales.

Author: Paek, S.

Article: Employment clothing practices and attitudes of white-collar female workers.

Journal: *Psychological Reports*, December 1992, *71*(3) Part I, 931–938.

Related Research: Cassill, N., & Drake, M. F. (1987). Employment orientation's influence on lifestyle and evaluative criteria for apparel. *Home Economics Research Journal*, *16*, 23–25.

■ ■ ■

7061

Test Name: ATTITUDES TOWARD SEX ROLES SCALE

Purpose: To assess the perception of significant others' attitudes toward women's roles.

Number of Items: 35

Format: Includes five subscales. Responses are made on a 6-point Likert scale ranging from *very strongly agree* to *very strongly disagree*.

Reliability: Internal consistency

estimates ranged from .70 to .93. Test–retest (3 weeks) reliability for the total scale was .86 (N = 79).

Validity: Correlations with other variables ranged from -.09 to .23.

Authors: Tipping, L. M., and Farmer, H. S.

Article: A home-career conflict measure: Career counseling implications.

Journal: *Measurement and Evaluation in Counseling and Development*, October 1991, *24*(3), 111–118.

Related Research: Hawley, P., & Even, B. (1982, December). Work and sex-role attitudes in relation to education and other characteristics. *The Vocational Guidance Quarterly*, 101–108.

■ ■ ■

7062

Test Name: ATTITUDES TOWARD WOMEN SCALE— SHORT FORM

Purpose: To assess sex-role attitudes.

Number of Items: 15

Reliability: Test–retest (3 months) reliability was .86.

Validity: Correlations with other variables ranged from -.18 to .46.

Authors: Long, B. C., et al.

Article: Casual model of stress and coping: Women in management.

Journal: *Journal of Counseling Psychology*, April 1992, *39*(2), 227–239.

Related Research: Spence, J., & Helmreich, R. (1978). *Masculinity and femininity: Their psychological dimensions, correlates and antecedents.* Austin: University of Texas Press.

■ ■ ■

7063

Test Name: ATTITUDES TOWARDS WOMEN SCALE— JAPANESE VERSION

Purpose: To assess sex-role attitudes.

Number of Items: 25

Format: 5-point Likert format.

Reliability: Alpha was .72.

Validity: Correlations with other variables ranged from -.01 to .60.

Authors: Matsui, T., et al.

Article: Women's perceptions of social-sexual behavior: A cross national replication.

Journal: *Journal of Vocational Behavior*, April 1995, *46*(2), 203–215.

Related Research: Spence, J. T., & Helmreich, R. (1972). The Attitudes Towards Women Scale: An objective instrument to measure attitudes toward the rights and roles of women in contemporary society. *JSAS Catalog of Selected Documents in Psychology*, *2*, 66-67 (MS. No. 153).

■ ■ ■

7064

Test Name: BEHAVIORAL SELF-REPORT OF FEMININITY

Purpose: To measure femininity.

Number of Items: 59

Format: 5-point frequency scales. All items are presented.

Reliability: Alpha was .92. Test–retest (2 weeks) was .90.

Validity: Correlations with other variables ranged from .12 to .26.

Authors: Green, K. S., and Gynther, M. D.

Article: Another femininity scale.

Journal: *Psychological Reports*, August 1994, *75*(1) Part I, 163–170.

Related Research: Keisling, B. L., et al. (1993). A behavioral self-report of masculinity: An alternative to trait, attitudinal, and "behavior" questionnaires. *Psychological Reports*, *72*, 835–842.

■ ■ ■

7065

Test Name: BEHAVIORAL SELF-REPORT OF MASCULINITY QUESTIONNAIRE

Purpose: To measure masculinity.

Number of Items: 64

Format: 5-point frequency scales for each behavior. All items presented.

Reliability: Item-total correlations exceeded .30. Alpha was .84. Test–retest (2 weeks) was .88.

Validity: Correlations with other masculinity ranged from .26 to .29 ($p < .05$).

Authors: Keisling, B. L., et al.

Article: A behavioral self-report of masculinity: An alternative to trait, attitudinal and behavioral questionnaires.

Journal: *Psychological Reports*, June 1993, *72*(3) Part I, 385–842.

7066

Test Name: CAREER READING APPRECIATION FORM

Purpose: To assess student appreciation of career literature.

Number of Items: 20

Format: Likert format. Sample items are presented.

Reliability: Alphas ranged from .91 to .94.

Authors: Billups, A., and Peterson, G. W.

Article: The appreciation of career literature in adolescents.

Journal: *The Career Development Quarterly*, March 1994, *42*(3), 229–237.

Related Research: Billups, A., & Peterson, G. W. (1988). *The Career Reading Appreciation Form (CRAF)*. Unpublished manuscript, Florida State University, Tallahassee.

■ ■ ■

7067

Test Name: CLOTHING INTEREST SCALE

Purpose: To measure clothing interest.

Number of Items: 15

Format: Responses are made on a 5-point scale ranging from 1 (*strongly disagree*) to 5 (*strongly agree*). All items are presented.

Reliability: Coefficient alpha was .75.

Validity: Correlations with instructor's characteristics by formality of instructor's dress ranged from -.05 to .21.

Authors: Lukavsky, J., et al.

Article: Perceptions of an instructor: Dress and students' characteristics.

Journal: *Perceptual and Motor Skills*, August 1995, *81*(1), 231–240.

Related Research: Creekmore, A. M. (1971). *Methods of measuring clothing variables*. Michigan Agriculture Experiment Station Project No. 738, Michigan State University.

■ ■ ■

7068

Test Name: COLLEGE CHOICE INFLUENCE SCALE

Purpose: To measure the college choice process.

Number of Items: 25

Format: Responses are made on a Likert-type scale with a 6-category response scale.

Reliability: Overall reliability was .73. Alpha reliability ranged from .66 to .79.

Authors: Martin, N. K., and Dixon, P. N.

Article: Factors influencing students' college choice.

Journal: *Journal of College Student Development*, May 1991, *32*(3), 253–257.

Related Research: Dixon, P. N., & Martin, N. K. (1991). Measuring factors that influence choice. *NASPA Journal*, *29*, 31–36.

■ ■ ■

7069

Test Name: COURSES INTEREST INVENTORY

Purpose: To assess interest in college courses.

Number of Items: 64

Format: Yes–no format.

Reliability: Split-half reliability was .84. Equivalent test reliability was .71.

Author: Meir, E. I.

Article: Comprehensive interests measurement in counseling for congruence.

Journal: *The Career Development Quarterly*, March 1994, *42*(4), 314–325.

Related Research: Meir, E. I., et al. (1994). Congruence and differentiation as predictors of workers' occupational stability and job performance. *Journal of Career Assessment, 2*, 40–54.

■ ■ ■

7070

Test Name: COUNSELOR PREFERENCE QUESTIONNAIRE—REVISED

Purpose: To measure a respondent's level of willingness to see a counselor for each of 19 counseling concerns.

Number of Items: 19

Format: Responses are made on a 7-point Likert Scale ranging from 1 (*definitely not willing to see*) to 7 (*definitely willing to see*). Includes 3 subscales: Personal/Interpersonal, Career, and Sexual Assault/Harassment.

Reliability: Internal consistency reliabilities ranged from .72 to .95.

Authors: Hackett, G., et al.

Article: Reactions of women to nonsexist and feminist counseling: Effects of counselor orientation and mode of information delivery.

Journal: *Journal of Counseling Psychology*, July 1992, *39*(3), 321–330.

Related Research: Enns, C. Z., & Hackett, G. (1990). Comparison of feminist and nonfeminist women's reactions to variants of nonsexist and feminist counseling. *Journal of Counseling Psychology, 37*, 33–40.

7071

Test Name: CUSTOMER SATISFACTION SCALE

Purpose: To measure customer approval of selling arrangement.

Number of Items: 5

Format: 5-point rating scale.

Reliability: Alpha was .76.

Authors: Zemanek, J. E., Jr.

Article: How salespersons' use of a power base can affect customers' satisfaction in a social system: An empirical examination.

Journal: *Psychological Reports*, February 1995, *76*(1), 211–217.

Related Research: Gaski, J. F., & Nevin, J. (1985). The differential effects of exercised and unexercised power sources in a marketing channel. *Journal of Marketing Research, 22*, 130–142.

■ ■ ■

7072

Test Name: DESIRABILITY OF CONTROL SCALE

Purpose: To assess the desire to control events in one's environment.

Number of Items: 20

Format: Responses are made on a 7-point Likert scale (1—*doesn't apply to me*, 7—*always applies to me*).

Reliability: Internal consistency was .80. Test–retest reliability was .75.

Authors: Laudwick-Rosenthal, R., and Neufeld, R. W. J.

Article: Preparation for undergoing invasive medical procedure: Interacting effects of information coping style.

Journal: *Journal of Consulting and Clinical Psychology*, February 1993, *61*(1), 156–164.

Related Research: Burger, J. M., & Cooper, H. M. (1979). The desirability of control. *Motivation and Emotion, 3*, 381–393.

■ ■ ■

7073

Test Name: ENJOYMENT OF MATHEMATICS SCALE

Purpose: To assess enjoyment of mathematics.

Number of Items: 11

Format: 5-point Likert format. A sample item is presented.

Reliability: Alpha is .95.

Authors: Ryckman, R. M., et al.

Article: Personality correlates of the Hypercompetitive Attitude Scale: Validity tests of Horney's theory of neurosis.

Journal: *Journal of Personality Assessment*, February 1994, *62*(1), 84–94.

Related Research: Aiken, L. R. (1974). Two scales of attitude toward mathematics. *Journal for Research in Mathematics Education, 5*, 67–71.

■ ■ ■

7074

Test Name: FEMINISM SCALE

Purpose: To measure feminism.

Number of Items: 6

Format: 5-point scales. All items presented.

Reliability: Alphas ranged from .71 to .84.

Author: Warner, R. L.

Article: Does the sex of your children matter? Support for feminism among women and men in the United States and Canada.

Journal: *Journal of Marriage and the Family*, November 1991, *53*(4), 1051–1056.

Related Research: Carroll, S. J. (1985). *Women as candidates in American politics.* Bloomington: Indiana University Press.

■ ■ ■

7075

Test Name: FEMINIST IDENTITY DEVELOPMENT SCALE

Purpose: To assess feminist identity development.

Number of Items: 39

Format: Includes 5 subscales. Responses are made on a 5-point Likert-type scale ranging from 1 (*strongly disagree*) to 5 (*strongly agree*).

Reliability: Alpha coefficients ranged from .65 to .85.

Authors: Fischer, A. R., and Good, G. E.

Article: Gender, self, and others: Perceptions of the campus environment.

Journal: *Journal of Counseling Psychology*, July 1994, *41*(3), 343–355.

Related Research: Bargad, A., & Hyde, J. S. (1991). Women's studies: A study of feminist identity development in women. *Psychology of Women Quarterly*, *15*, 181–201.

■ ■ ■

7076

Test Name: FEM SCALE

Purpose: To measure attitudes toward feminism.

Number of Items: 20

Format: Responses are made on a 5-point Likert scale ranging from 1 (*strongly disagree*) to 5 (*strongly agree*).

Validity: Correlations with other variables ranged from -.42 to .31.

Authors: Martin, J. K., and Hall, G. C. N.

Article: Thinking Black, thinking internal, thinking feminist.

Journal: *Journal of Counseling Psychology*, October 1992, *39*(4), 509–514.

Related Research: Smith, E. R., et al. (1975). A short scale of attitudes toward feminism. *Representative Research in Social Psychology*, *6*, 51–56.

■ ■ ■

7077

Test Name: GENDER IDENTITY INTERVIEW SCHEDULE

Purpose: To assess gender identity in children.

Number of Items: 12

Format: Multiple-choice. All items are presented.

Validity: Factor analysis extracted an affective and cognitive component. Correlations with other variables ranged from -.34 to .22

Authors: Zucker, K. J., et al.

Article: A gender identity interview for children.

Journal: *Journal of Personality Assessment*, December 1993, *61*(3), 443–456.

Related Research: Meyer-Bahlburg, H. F. L., & Ehrhardt, A. A. (1988). *Gender-Role Assessment Schedule—Child (GRAS-C).* New York: Program of Developmental Psychoendocrinology, New York State Psychiatric Institute.

■ ■ ■

7078

Test Name: GENDER ORIENTATION SCALE

Purpose: To assess androgyny.

Number of Items: 20

Format: Employs a 7-point scale.

Reliability: Alpha coefficients were .93 and .84.

Author: Crawford, C. B.

Article: Effects of sex and sex roles on avoidance of same- and opposite-sex touch.

Journal: *Perceptual and Motor Skills*, August 1994, *79*(1) Part 1, 107–112.

Related Research: Wheeless, L. R., & Wheeless, V. E. (1981). Attribution, gender orientation, and adaptability: Reconceptualization, measurement, and research results. *Communication Quarterly*, *30*, 56–66.

■ ■ ■

7079

Test Name: GENDER ROLE CONFLICT SCALE

Purpose: To measure men's patterns of gender role conflict.

Number of Items: 37

Format: 6-point agreement scales range from 1 (*strongly disagree*) to 6 (*strongly agree*).

Reliability: Internal consistency ranged from .78 to .92. Test–retest (4 weeks) ranged from .72 to .86.

Validity: Correlations with other variables ranged from -.10 to .60.

Authors: Good, G. E., et al.

Article: Male gender role conflict: Psychometric issues and relations to psychological distress.

Journal: *Journal of Counseling Psychology*, January 1995, *42*(1), 3–10.

Related Research: O'Neil, J. M., et al. (1986). Gender Role Conflict Scale: College men's fear of femininity. *Sex Roles*, *14*, 335–350.

7080

Test Name: HANDEDNESS QUESTIONNAIRE

Purpose: To determine handedness.

Number of Items: 13

Format: Responses are "right," "left," or "either."

Reliability: Test–retest reliability was .97 (79 males) and .96 (187 females).

Authors: Ransil, B. S., and Schachter, S. C.

Article: Test-retest reliability of the Edinburgh Handedness Inventory and Global Handedness Preference Measurements, and their correlations.

Journal: *Perceptual and Motor Skills*, December 1994, *79*(3) Part 1, 1355–1372.

Related Research: Chapman, L. J., & Chapman, J. P. (1987). The measurement of handedness. *Brain and Cognition*, *6*, 75–83.

● ● ●

7081

Test Name: HANDEDNESS QUESTIONNAIRE

Purpose: To assess handedness.

Number of Items: 15

Format: Responses are made on a 7-point scale. Response to item 15 is "Yes" or "No." All items are presented.

Reliability: Test–retest reliability coefficients ranged from .62 to .99.

Authors: Jason, D. R., and Lantz, P. E.

Article: The use of next-of-kin in assessing handedness.

Journal: *Perceptual and Motor Skills*, August 1995, *81*(1), 203–208.

Related Research: Oldfield, R. C. (1971). The assessment and

analysis of handedness: The Edinburgh Inventory. *Neuropsychologia*, *9*, 97–113.

● ● ●

7082

Test Name: HARTER'S INTRINSIC/EXTRINSIC ORIENTATION SCALE

Purpose: To measure preference for challenge, curiosity, and independent mastery in regard to school work.

Number of Items: 18

Format: Responses are made on a 4-point scale.

Reliability: Alpha was .71.

Author: Vallerand, R. J., et al.

Article: A comparison of the school intrinsic motivation and perceived competence of gifted and regular students.

Journal: *Gifted Child Quarterly*, Fall 1994, *38*(4), 172–175.

Related Research: Harter, S. (1981). A new self-report scale on intrinsic versus extrinsic orientation in the classroom: Motivational and informational components. *Developmental Psychology*, *17*, 300–312.

● ● ●

7083

Test Name: INNOVATIVENESS SCALE

Purpose: To measure the tendency to adopt a new product such as clothing, food, movies, etc.

Number of Items: 6

Format: Responses are made on a 5-point Likert scale ranging from 1 (*strongly agree*) to 5 (*strongly disagree*). All items are presented.

Reliability: Coefficient alpha was .84.

Validity: Correlations with other variables ranged from .38 to .69.

Authors: Flynn, L. R., and Goldsmith, R. E.

Article: A validation of the Goldsmith and Hofacker Innovativeness Scale.

Journal: *Educational and Psychological Measurement*, Winter 1993, *53*(4), 1105–1116.

Related Research: Goldsmith, R. E., & Hofacker, C. F. (1991). Measuring Consumer innovativeness. *Journal of the Academy of Marketing Science*, *19*, 209–221.

● ● ●

7084

Test Name: INTEREST SURVEY

Purpose: To measure adolescent interest in the mathematics classroom.

Number of Items: 45

Format: Includes 7 scales: Personal Interest, Situational Interest, Meaningfulness, Involvement, Puzzles, Computers, and Group Work. Responses are made on a 6-point Likert scale ranging from 1 (*strongly disagree*) to 6 (*strongly agree*). All items are presented.

Reliability: Alpha coefficients ranged from .77 to .93.

Author: Mitchell, M.

Article: Situational interest: Its multifaceted structure in the secondary school mathematics classroom.

Journal: *Journal of Educational Psychology*, September 1993, *85*(3), 424–436.

Related Research: Mitchell, M. T. (1991). *Formative evaluation report of the Mathematics Achievement Program (MAP)* (Tech. Rep. No. 91-01). Santa Barbara: University of California at Santa Barbara, Office of Instructional Consultation.

7085

Test Name: INTERNATIONAL TRAVEL QUESTIONNAIRE

Purpose: To measure reasons for international travel.

Number of Items: 24

Format: 4-point rating scales.

Reliability: Alphas ranged from .48 to .69.

Validity: Correlations with other variables ranged from -.10 to .24.

Author: Fontaine, G.

Article: Presence seeking and sensation seeking as motives for international travel.

Journal: *Psychological Reports*, December 1994, *75*(3) Part II, 1583–1586.

Related Research: Fontaine, G. (1993). Motivational factors of international travelers. *Psychological Reports, 72*, 1106.

■ ■ ■

7086

Test Name: INTRINSIC SATISFACTION SCALE—SPORT

Purpose: To measure student's intrinsic satisfaction with and interest in sport.

Number of Items: 8

Format: Responses are made on a 5-point Likert-type scale ranging from 1 (*strongly agree*) to 5 (*strongly disagree*). Includes two factors: Satisfaction/Enjoyment and Boredom. All items are presented.

Reliability: Alpha coefficients were .94 and .83.

Authors: Duda, J. L., and Nicholls, J. G.

Article: Dimensions of achievement motivation in school work and sport.

Journal: *Journal of Educational Psychology*, September 1992, *84*(3), 290–299.

Related Research: Nicholls, J. G. (1989). *The competitive ethos and democratic education*. Cambridge, MA: Harvard University Press.

■ ■ ■

7087

Test Name: INVENTORY OF SEX ROLE ORIENTATION SCALE

Purpose: To measure commitment to traditional, feminine gender beliefs.

Number of Items: 16

Format: 5-point agreement scales.

Reliability: Alpha was .84.

Author: Simons, R. L., et al.

Article: Explaining women's double jeopardy: Factors that mediate the association between harsh treatment as a child and violence by a husband.

Journal: *Journal of Marriage and the Family*, August 1993, *55*(3), 713–723.

Related Research: Dreyer, N. A., et al. (1981). ISRO: A scale to measure sex role orientation. *Sex Roles, 7*, 173–182.

■ ■ ■

7088

Test Name: LEISURE ACTIVITIES RATING SCALES

Purpose: To rate leisure activities such as social contacts, traveling, passive activity, the arts, and game-playing.

Number of Items: 38

Format: 4-point Likert formats rated frequency of, fondness for, and evaluation of activities.

Reliability: Mean alpha was .79.

Authors: Fink, B., and Wild, K. P.

Article: Similarities in leisure interests: Effects of selection and socialization in friendships.

Journal: *The Journal of Social Psychology*, August 1995, *135*(4), 471–482.

Related Research: Giegler, H. (1985). Zur sozialwissenschaftlich relevanten semantik von freiheitactivitaten [Semantic of leisure interests in social sciences]. *Angewandte Sozialforschung, 13*, 75–91.

■ ■ ■

7089

Test Name: LEISURE SATISFACTION SCALE—REVISED

Purpose: To measure pleasure or contentment with general leisure experiences and situations.

Number of Items: 24

Format: Responses are made on a 5-point Likert-type scale. Includes 6 subscales: Psychological, Educational, Social, Relaxational, Physiological, and Aesthetic Components of Leisure Satisfaction.

Reliability: Alpha ranged from .53 to .88. Test–retest correlations ranged from .80 to .93.

Authors: Payne, E. C., et al.

Article: Goal directedness and older-adult adjustment.

Journal: *Journal of Counseling Psychology*, July 1991, *38*(3), 302–308.

Related Research: Beard, J. G., & Ragheb, M. G. (1980). Measuring leisure satisfaction. *Journal of Leisure Research, 12*, 20–33.

■ ■ ■

7090

Test Name: LIKING FOR SHORT STORIES SCALE

Purpose: To measure secondary students' liking of short stories.

Number of Items: 26

Format: 4-point Likert format. All items are presented.

Reliability: Alpha was .95.

Validity: Item logit values ranged from -1.87 to 1.72. Five items of the total of 26 had logit values of greater than 1 (absolute value).

Authors: Smith, M. W., and Young, J. W.

Article: Assessing secondary students' liking of short stories.

Journal: *Journal of Educational Research*, September/October 1995, *89*(1), 14–22.

■ ■ ■

7091

Test Name: MALE–FEMALE RELATIONS TEST

Purpose: To identify sex-role behaviors and preferences.

Number of Items: 30

Format: Includes 3 subscales: Social Interaction, Marital Roles, and Preference for Traditional Male Behaviors. Responses are made on a 5-point scale ranging from *strongly agree* to *strongly disagree.*

Reliability: Alpha coefficients ranged from .56 to .85.

Authors: Hock, E., and Schirtzinger, M. B.

Article: Maternal separation anxiety: Its developmental course and relation to maternal mental health.

Journal: *Child Development*, February 1992, *63*(1), 93-102.

Related Research: Spence, J. T., et al. (1980). The Male-Female Relations Questionnaire: A self report inventory of sex-role behavior and preferences and its relationship to masculine and feminine personality traits, sex-

role attitudes, and other measures. *JSAS: Catalog of Selected Documents in Psychology*, *10*, 87.

■ ■ ■

7092

Test Name: MALE ROLE QUALITY QUESTIONNAIRE

Purpose: To assess the rewarding and distressing aspects of men's roles.

Number of Items: 151

Format: 4-point rating scales.

Reliability: Alphas ranged from .86 to .93.

Authors: Barnett, R. C., et al.

Article: Men's multiple roles and their relationships to men's psychological stress.

Journal: *Journal of Marriage and the Family*, May 1991, *54*(2), 358–367.

Related Research: Barnett, R. C., et al. (1991). Adult daughter-parent relationships and their associations with daughters' subjective well-being and psychological distress. *Journal of Marriage and the Family*, *53*, 29–42.

■ ■ ■

7093

Test Name: MANAGERIAL FRAMES OF MIND SURVEY— REVISED

Purpose: To provide a measure of school and business executives' frames of reference preferences.

Number of Items: 37

Format: Responses are made on a scale ranging from *strongly disagree* to *strongly agree.*

Reliability: Alpha coefficients ranged from .73 to .82.

Authors: Epps, P. D. V., and Thompson, B.

Article: Validity of a measure of the frames of reference preferences of school and business executives.

Journal: *Educational and Psychological Measurement*, Winter 1991, *51*(4), 999–1008.

Related Research: Roussel, D. M. (1989). Managerial frames of mind among school principals: A construct validation study. *Dissertation Abstracts International*, *50*, 1887A. (University Microfilms No. 89-24, 107)

■ ■ ■

7094

Test Name: MASCULINITY SCALE

Purpose: To assess degree of endorsement of the traditional North American male gender role.

Number of Items: 58

Format: 7-point agreement scales range from 1 (*strongly disagree*) to 7 (*strongly agree*).

Reliability: Alpha was .92.

Authors: Good, G. E., et al.

Article: Male gender role conflict: Psychometric issues and relations to psychological distress.

Journal: *Journal of Counseling Psychology*, January 1995, *42*(1), 3–10.

Related Research: Bannon, R., & Juni, S. (1984). A scale for measuring attitudes about masculinity. *Psychological Documents*, *14*, 2612.

■ ■ ■

7095

Test Name: MATHEMATICS COURSE INTERESTS SCALE

Purpose: To measure degree of interest in mathematics-related courses.

Number of Items: 15

Format: Responses are made on a 10-point scale ranging from 0 (*strongly disinterested*) to 9 (*strongly interested*).

Reliability: Coefficient alpha was .86. Test–retest (2 weeks) reliability was .72.

Validity: Correlations with other variables ranged from -.27 to .68.

Authors: Lent, R. W., et al.

Article: Predicting mathematics-related choice and success behavior: Test of an expanded social cognitive model.

Journal: *Journal of Vocational Behavior*, April 1993, *42*(2), 223–236.

Related Research: Lent, R. W., et al. (1991). Mathematics self-efficacy: Sources and relation to science-based career choice. *Journal of Counseling Psychology*, *38*, 424–430.

■ ■ ■

7096

Test Name: MATH/SCIENCE INTERESTS FORM

Purpose: To identify students' interest in math/science-related activities.

Number of Items: 20

Format: Responses are either *like, indifferent,* or *dislike.*

Reliability: Coefficient alpha was .91.

Validity: Correlations with other variables ranged from -.29 to .51.

Authors: Lopez, F. G., and Lent, R. W.

Article: Sources of mathematics self-efficacy in high school students.

Journal: *The Career Development Quarterly*, September 1992, *41*(1), 3–12.

7097

Test Name: MENTAL RETARDATION PREFERENCE SCALE

Purpose: To assess counseling psychologists' preference for counseling clients who have mental retardation.

Number of Items: 6

Format: Responses are made on a 9-point scale ranging from 1 (*dislike*) to 9 (*like*).

Reliability: Coefficient alpha was .99.

Author: Spengler, P. M., and Strohmer, D. C.

Article: Clinical judgmental biases: The moderating roles of counselor cognitive complexity and counselor client preferences.

Journal: *Journal of Counseling Psychology*, January 1994, *41*(1), 8–17.

Related Research: Spengler, P. M., et al. (1990). Diagnostic and treatment overshadowing of career problems by personal problems. *Journal of Counseling Psychology*, *37*, 372–381.

■ ■ ■

7098

Test Name: ORGANICISM–MECHANISM PARADIGM INVENTORY

Purpose: To measure preferences for factual or creative approaches to management.

Number of Items: 26

Format: Forced-choice statement pairs. A sample item is presented.

Reliability: Alpha was .76. Split-half was .86. Test–retest was .77 (3 weeks).

Author: White, J.

Article: Individual characteristics

and social knowledge in ethical reasoning.

Journal: *Psychological Reports*, August 1994, *75*(1) Part II, 627–649.

Related Research: Germer, C. K., et al. (1982). *The Organicism-Mechanism Paradigm Inventory*. Arlington, MA: Authors.

■ ■ ■

7099

Test Name: PERSONAL ATTRIBUTES QUESTIONNAIRE—SHORT FORM

Purpose: To assess gender role.

Number of Items: 24

Format: Items are bipolar. Responses are made on a 5-point scale.

Reliability: Test–retest (13 weeks) reliability was .80 (men) and .91 (women). Alpha coefficients were .73 (men) and .91 (women).

Validity: Correlations with the BEM Sex Role Inventory ranged from .57 to .75.

Authors: Fassinger, R. E., and Richie, B. S.

Article: Being the best: Preliminary results from a national study of the achievement of prominent Black and White women.

Journal: *Journal of Counseling Psychology*, April 1994, *41*(2), 191–204.

Related Research: Spence, J. T., & Helmrich, R. L. (1978). *Masculinity and femininity: Their psychological dimensions, correlates, and antecedents.* Austin, TX: University of Texas Press.

■ ■ ■

7100

Test Name: PERSONAL INVOLVEMENT INVENTORY

Purpose: To measure product category involvement.

Number of Items: 10

Format: Items consist of bipolar adjective pairs measuring interest, enthusiasm, and involvement with a product.

Reliability: Coefficient alpha was .96.

Validity: Correlations with other variables ranged from .24 to .60.

Authors: Flynn, L. R., and Goldsmith, R. E.

Article: A validation of the Goldsmith and Hofacker Innovativeness Scale.

Journal: *Educational and Psychological Measurement*, Winter 1993, *53*(4), 1105–1116.

Related Research: Zaichkowsky, J. L. (1987). *The Personal Involvement Inventory: Reduction, revision and application to advertising.* Discussion Paper 87-08-08, Faculty of Business Administration, Simon Fraser University, Bernaby, British Columbia.

• • •

7101

Test Name: PREFERENCE FOR NUMERICAL INFORMATION SCALE

Purpose: To identify one's productivity or preference for numerical information.

Number of Items: 20

Format: Responses are made on a 7-point scale ranging from 1 (*strongly disagree*) to 7 (*strongly agree*). All items are presented.

Reliability: Alpha coefficients ranged from .87 to 94.

Validity: Correlations with other variables ranged from -.05 to .74.

Author: Viswanathan, M.

Article: Measurement of individual difference in preference for numerical information.

Journal: *Journal of Applied Psychology*, October 1993, *78*(5), 741–752.

• • •

7102

Test Name: PREFERENCE FOR SOLITUDE SCALE

Purpose: To assess individual differences in preference for solitude.

Number of Items: 12

Format: Respondents choose 1 of 2 statements in each of 12 pairs.

Reliability: KR-20 reliability was .70. Test–retest reliability was .72.

Validity: Correlations with other variables ranged from -.56 to .49.

Author: Burger, J. M.

Article: Individual differences in preference for solitude.

Journal: *Journal of Research in Personality*, March 1995, *29*(1), 85–108.

• • •

7103

Test Name: PRIMARY APPRAISAL OF SMOKING CESSATION INVENTORY

Purpose: To measure smokers' primary appraisal of what they stand to gain and to lose by quitting smoking.

Number of Items: 24

Format: Responses are made on a 4-point Likert scale.

Reliability: Internal reliability coefficient alpha was .84. Test–retest was .83.

Author : Carey, M. P., et al.

Article: Stress and unaided smoking cessation: A prospective investigation.

Journal: *Journal of Consulting and Clinical Psychology*, October 1993, *61*(5), 831–838.

Related Research: Kalra, D. L., et al. (1992). *Development and psychometric evaluation of the Primary Appraisal of Smoking Cessation Inventory.*

• • •

7104

Test Name: REVISED PERSONAL INVOLVEMENT INVENTORY—SERVICES

Purpose: To measure the importance, risk, pleasure, and symbolic value an individual attaches to a particular service.

Number of Items: 14

Format: 7-point semantic differential.

Reliability: Alphas ranged from .76 to .82 across subscales.

Validity: Subscale correlations ranged from .45 to .58. Correlations with other variables ranged from -.12 to .39.

Authors: Celuch, K .G., and Longfellow, T. A.

Article: Consumers' service involvement: An exploratory examination.

Journal: *Psychological Reports*, December 1992, *71*(3) Part I, 959–970.

Related Research: McQuarrie, E. F., & Munson, J. M. (1987). *A multidimensional, arousal-based measure of consumer involvement.* (Unpublished working paper, Department of Marketing, Santa Clara University, Santa Clara, CA)

7105

Test Name: SCIENTIFIC ORIENTATION SCALE

Purpose: To assess endorsement of a scientific viewpoint in personal and professional life.

Number of Items: 10

Format: All items presented. 5-point Likert format.

Reliability: Cronbach's alpha was .70.

Validity: Correlation with a religiosity scale was -.50 ($p < .001$) and with a religious ideology scale was -.58 ($p < .001$).

Authors: Eckhardt, C. I., et al.

Article: Religious beliefs and scientific ideology in psychologists: Conflicting or coexisting systems.

Journal: *Psychological Reports*, August 1992, *71*(1), 131–145.

■ ■ ■

7106

Test Name: SELF-REPORT HANDEDNESS INVENTORY

Purpose: To identify handedness.

Number of Items: 12

Format: Participant indicates left, right, or either hand. All items are presented.

Validity: Correlation with a 4-item version was .95.

Author: Coren, S.

Article: Measurement of handedness via self-report: The relationship between brief and extended inventories.

Journal: *Perceptual and Motor Skills*, June 1993, *76*(3) Part 1, 1035–1042.

Related Research: Coren, S. (1992). *The left-hander syndrome: The causes and consequences of left-handedness.* New York: Free Press.

7107

Test Name: SEX ROLE ATTITUDES SCALE

Purpose: To assess attitudes about male and female roles.

Number of Items: 17

Format: Likert format. Sample items presented.

Reliability: Alphas ranged from .75 to .84.

Validity: Correlations with communal orientation ranged from -.24 to -.25.

Authors: Vanyperen, N. W., and Buunk, B. P.

Article: Equity theory and exchange and communal orientation from a cross-national perspective.

Journal: *The Journal of Social Psychology*, February 1991, *131*(1), 5–20.

■ ■ ■

7108

Test Name: SEX ROLE CAREER INDECISION SCALE FOR WOMEN

Purpose: To measure career indecision in women undergraduates.

Number of Items: 30

Reliability: Alpha was .84.

Validity: The scale discriminates between men and women, but not between freshmen and senior women.

Authors: Sutherland, V., et al.

Article: Validating sex-role-related items designed to measure career indecision.

Journal: *Psychological Reports*, April 1993, *72*(2), 531–536.

Related Research: Slaney, R. B., & Dickson, R. D. (1985).

Relation of career indecision to career exploration with re-entry women: A treatment and follow-up study. *Journal of Counseling Psychology*, *32*, 355–362.

■ ■ ■

7109

Test Name: SEX-ROLE EGALITARIAN SCALE

Purpose: To measure gender-role attitudes.

Number of Items: 25

Format: 5-point Likert format.

Reliability: Alpha was .94. Test–retest (3 weeks) was .88.

Author: Fischer, A. R.

Article: Income and gender-role egalitarianism

Journal: *Psychological Reports*, October 1993, *73*(2), 699–702.

Related Research: King, L. A., & King, D. W. (1990). Abbreviated measures of sex role egalitarian attitudes. *Sex Roles*, *23*, 659–673.

■ ■ ■

7110

Test Name: SEX-ROLE IDEOLOGY SCALE

Purpose: To measure sex-role ideology along a traditionalist–feminist dimension.

Number of Items: 30

Format: Responses are made on a 7-point scale.

Reliability: Split-half reliability coefficients ranged from .57 to .91. Coefficient alpha was .88 ($N = 184$).

Validity: Correlation with the Women in the Military Scale was .36.

Authors: Hurrell, R. M., and Lukens, J. H.

Article: Attitudes toward women in the military during the Persian Gulf War.

Journal: *Perceptual and Motor Skills*, February 1994, *78*(1), 99–104.

Related Research: Kalin, R., & Tilby, P. J. (1978). Development and validation of a sex-role ideology scale. *Psychological Reports*, *42*, 731–738.

• • •

7111

Test Name: SEX ROLE SCALE

Purpose: To measure traditional sex roles.

Number of Items: 9

Format: 7-point Likert scales range from 1 (*strongly disagree*) to 7 (*strongly agree*). Sample items are presented.

Reliability: Alpha was .69.

Authors: Rosenthal, E. H., et al.

Article: Changing the rape-supportive attitudes of traditional and non-traditional male and female college students.

Journal: *Journal of Counseling Psychology*, April 1995, *42*(2), 171–177.

Related Research: Burt, M. R. (1980). Cultural myths and support for rape. *Journal of Personality and Social Psychology*, *38*, 217–230.

• • •

7112

Test Name: SHOPPING INVOLVEMENT SCALE

Purpose: To measure shopping in four dimensions: leisure, economic, social, apathetic.

Number of Items: 18

Format: 6-point Likert format. All items are presented.

Reliability: Alphas ranged from .77 to .90 across subscales.

Authors: Bergadaá, M., et al.

Article: Enduring involvement with shopping.

Journal: *The Journal of Social Psychology*, February 1995, *135*(1), 17–25.

Related Research: Moschis, G. P. (1976). Shopping orientations and consumer use of information. *Journal of Retailing*, *52*, 61–70.

• • •

7113

Test Name: SHOPPING ORIENTATION SCALES

Purpose: To measure shopping orientation including esteem enhancement, enjoyment, affiliation, variety, role enactment, and negotiation.

Number of Items: 34

Format: Varied Likert formats. Sample items are presented.

Reliability: Alphas ranged from .69 to .93 across subscales.

Authors: Goff, B. G., and Walters, D. L.

Article: Susceptibility to salepersons' influences and consumers' shopping orientations.

Journal: *Psychological Reports*, June 1995, *76*(3) Part I, 915–928.

Related Research: Westbrook, R. A., & Black, W. C. (1985). A motivation-based shopper typology. *Journal of Retailing*, *61*, *78-103*.

• • •

7114

Test Name: WILDERNESS PURISM SCALE

Purpose: To differentiate between types of wilderness users.

Number of Items: 14

Format: Semantic differential format. All items are presented.

Reliability: Alpha was .86. Spearman-Brown split-half was .81.

Authors: Jaakson, R., and Shin, W. S.

Article: Purism and wilderness campers.

Journal: *The Journal of Social Psychology*, August 1993, *133*(4), 489–493.

Related Research: Stanley, G. H. (1973). *Visitor perception of wilderness recreation carrying capacity*. USDA Forest Service Research Paper INT-142.

• • •

7115

Test Name: WOMEN'S ROLE QUALITY SCALE

Purpose: To measure the rewarding and distressing aspects of women's roles as worker, spouse, and parent.

Number of Items: 111

Format: 4-point rating scales.

Reliability: Test–retest reliabilities (3 months) ranged from .68 to .95. Alphas ranged from .87 to .93.

Author: Barnett, R. C.

Article: Home-to-work spillover revisited: A study of full-time employed women in dual earner couples.

Journal: *Journal of Marriage and the Family*, August 1994, *56*(3), 647–656.

Related Research: Barnett, R. C., et al. (1991). Adult daughter-parent relationships and their associations with daughters' subjective well-being and psychological distress. *Journal of Marriage and the Family*, *53*, 29–42.

■ ■ ■

7116

Test Name: WRITING ATTITUDE SURVEY FOR CHILDREN

Purpose: To measure how positively children regard reading.

Number of Items: 19

Time Required: 30 minutes.

Format: Likert format ranging from 1 (*almost always*) to 5 (*almost never*).

Validity: Group difference tests showed that girls had more positive attitudes than boys and that scores increased in a positive direction with grade in school ($p \leq .05$).

Author: Knudson, R. E.

Article: Effects of ethnicity in attitudes toward writing.

Journal: *Psychological Reports*, February 1993, *72*(1), 39–45.

Related Research: Knudson, R. E. (1991). Development and use of a writing attitude survey in Grades 4 to 8. *Psychological Reports*, *68*, 807–816.

CHAPTER 19
Problem-Solving and Reasoning

7117

Test Name: ACTIVE ENGAGEMENT SCALE

Purpose: To assess students' reported use of cognitive strategies indicative of self-regulated learning.

Number of Items: 8

Format: Responses are made on a 3-point scale ranging from 1 (*not like me*) to 3 (*a lot like me*). Examples are presented.

Reliability: Cronbach alpha was .79.

Validity: Correlations with other variables ranged from -.34 to .14.

Authors: Meece, J. L., and Holt, K.

Article: A pattern analysis of students' achievement goals.

Journal: *Journal of Educational Psychology,* December 1993, *85*(4), 582-590.

Related Research: Meece, J. L., et al. (1988). Students' goal orientations and cognitive engagement in classroom activities. *Journal of Educational Psychology, 80,* 514-523.

•••

7118

Test Name: ADAPTATION-INNOVATION INVENTORY

Purpose: To measure adapted and innovative predispositions.

Number of Items: 32

Reliability: Alphas ranged between .85 and .90. Test–retest (up to 17

months) ranged between .82 and .86.

Validity: Correlations with demographic variables ranged from -.02 to .54.

Author: Clapp, R. G.

Article: Stability of cognitive style in adults and some implications, a longitudinal study of the Kirton Adaptation-Innovation Inventory.

Journal: *Psychological Reports,* December 1993, *73*(3) Part II, 1235-1245.

Related Research: Kirton, M. J. (1987). *Adaptation Innovation Inventory (KAI)—Manual* (2nd ed.). Occupational Research Centre, Hatfield, Hertfordshire, England.

•••

7119

Test Name: CHILDREN'S PACED AUDITORY SERIAL ADDITION TASK

Purpose: To assess auditory–verbal attention.

Number of Items: 61 random single-digit numbers.

Format: Five trials of the numbers are given by prerecorded audiocassette taped instructions.

Reliability: Split-half reliability coefficient was .92. Test-retest reliability coefficients ranged from .77 to .90 (*N* = 70).

Validity: Correlations with arithmetic and digit span were .38 and .35, respectively.

Authors: Dyche, G. M., and Johnson, D. A.

Article: Development and evaluation of CHIPASAT, an attention test for children: II. Test-retest reliability and practice effect for a normal sample.

Journal: *Perceptual and Motor Skills,* April 1991, *72*(2), 563-572.

Related Research: Johnson, D. A., et al. (1988). Development and evaluation of an attention test for head-injured children: I. Information processing capacity in a normal sample. *Journal of Child Psychology and Psychiatry, 29,* 199-208.

•••

7120

Test Name: CLASSROOM TEST OF FORMAL REASONING

Purpose: To assess formal reasoning.

Number of Items: 15

Format: Items measure conservation of weight and volume, proportional reasoning, controlling variables, combinatorial reasoning, and probability.

Reliability: Coefficient alpha was .86.

Authors: Billups, A., and Peterson, G. W.

Article: The application of career literature in adolescents.

Journal: *The Career Development Quarterly,* March 1994, *42*(3), 229-237.

Related Research: Lawson, A. E. (1978). The development and validation of a classroom test of formal reasoning. *Journal of Research in Science Teaching, 15,* 11–24.

•••

7121

Test Name: CONSTRUCTIVE THINKING SCALE

Purpose: To assess patterns of habitual everyday thoughts.

Number of Items: 108

Format: 5-point response scales range from 1 (*definitely false*) to 5 (*definitely true*).

Reliability: Alphas ranged from .65 to .92 across subscales.

Authors: Spirrison, C. L., and Gordy, C. C.

Article: Nonintellectual intelligence and personality: Variance shared by the Constructive Thinking Inventory and the Myers-Briggs Type Indicator.

Journal: *Journal of Personality Assessment,* April 1994, *62*(2), 352–363.

Related Research: Epstein, S., & Meier, P. (1989). Constructive thinking: A broad coping variable with specific components. *Journal of Personality and Social Psychology, 57,* 332–350.

•••

7122

Test Name: DECISION-MAKING AUTHORITY SCALE

Purpose: To measure the degree of decision-making authority.

Number of Items: 5

Format: Examples are presented.

Reliability: Coefficient alpha was .91.

Validity: Correlations with other variables ranged from -.56 to .50.

Authors: Mossholder, K. W., et al.

Article: Confounding constructs

and levels of construct in affectivity measurement: An empirical investigation.

Journal: *Educational and Psychological Measurement,* Summer 1994, *54*(2), 336–349.

Related Research: Price, J. L., & Mueller, C. W. (1986). *Handbook of organizational measurement.* Marshfield, MA: Pitman.

•••

7123

Test Name: DECISION-MAKING QUESTIONNAIRE

Purpose: To assess individuals' effectiveness and confidence in making both tactical and strategic organizational decisions.

Number of Items: 10

Format: Items include 5 tactical and 5 strategic scenarios. An example is presented.

Validity: Correlations with other variables ranged from -.28 to .67.

Author: Kline, T. J. B.

Article: Measurement of tactical and strategic decision making.

Journal: *Educational and Psychological Measurement,* Fall 1994, *54*(3), 745–756.

Related Research: Kline, T. J. B. (1990). *Tactical and strategic decision-making.* Unpublished doctoral dissertation, University of Calgary.

•••

7124

Test Name: GENERAL DECISION-MAKING STYLE

Purpose: To assess decision-making style.

Number of Items: 25

Format: Includes 5 factors: Rational, Intuitive, Dependent, Spontaneous, and Avoidant.

Responses are made on a 5-point scale ranging from *strongly disagree* to *strongly agree.* All but one item are presented.

Reliability: Alpha coefficients ranged from .68 to .94.

Validity: Correlations with other variables ranged from -.38 to .36.

Authors: Scott, S. G., and Bruce, R. A.

Article: Decision-making style: The development and assessment of a new measure.

Journal: *Educational and Psychological Measurement,* October 1995, *55*(5), 818–831.

•••

7125

Test Name: HIGH SCHOOL STUDY HABITS SCALE

Purpose: To measure note-taking, test-taking, test preparation, reading, writing, and learning strategies.

Number of Items: 23

Format: 4-point rating scale (*hardly ever* to *most always*).

Reliability: Alpha was .85.

Authors: Matt, G. E., et al.

Article: High school study habits and early college achievement.

Journal: *Psychological Reports,* August 1991, *69*(1), 91–96.

Related Research: Devine, T. (1981). *Teaching study skill: A guide for teachers.* Boston: Allyn & Bacon.

•••

7126

Test Name: INDIVIDUAL DIFFERENCES QUESTIONNAIRE

Purpose: To measure imaginal and verbal thinking habits and skills.

Number of Items: 86

Format: Responses are *true* or *false*. There are verbal and imagery scores and 6 factors. Examples are presented.

Validity: Correlations with other variables ranged from -.10 to .47.

Author: Cullari, S.

Article: Use of Individual Differences Questionnaire with psychiatric inpatients.

Journal: *Perceptual and Motor Skills*, February 1995, *80*(1), 128–130.

Related Research: Paivio, A., & Harshman, R. (1983). Factor analysis of a questionnaire on imagery and verbal habits and skills. *Canadian Journal of Psychology*, *37*, 461–483.

■ ■ ■

7127

Test Name: INVENTED SPELLING TEST

Purpose: To assess ability to associate letter and sound units systematically.

Number of Items: 10

Format: Respondent is asked to individually spell 10 predetermined words by choosing plastic letters.

Reliability: Interrater reliability was .96.

Author: Cannella, G.

Article: Effects of social interaction on the creation of a sound/symbol system by kindergarten children.

Journal: *Child Study Journal*, June 1991, *21*(2), 117–133.

Related Research: Richgels, D. (1986). Beginning first graders' "invented spelling" ability and their performance in functional classroom writing activities. *Early Childhood Quarterly*, *1*, 85–97.

7128

Test Name: INVENTORY OF LEARNING PROCESSES

Purpose: To assess information-processing activities used in learning academic material.

Number of Items: 62

Format: True–false format. Sample items are presented.

Reliability: Alphas ranged from .56 to .82. Test–retest ranged from .68 to .88.

Validity: Interscale correlations ranged from .15 to .42. Correlation with GPA ranged from .09 to .39.

Author: Albaili, M. A.

Article: Psychometric properties of the Inventory of Learning Processes: Evidence from United Arab Emeritus college students.

Journal: *Psychological Reports*, June 1993, *72*(3) Part II, 1331–1336.

Related Research: Schmeck, R. R., et al. (1977). Development of a self-report inventory for assessing individual learning differences in learning process. *Applied Psychological Measurement*, *1*, 413–431.

■ ■ ■

7129

Test Name: LEARNING STRATEGY SCALE

Purpose: To assess the likelihood of using various learning strategies.

Number of Items: 16

Format: 5-point scales ranged from *not at all* to *a lot*. Sample items are presented.

Reliability: Alpha was .74.

Author: Bergin, D. A.

Article: Effects of a mastery versus competitive motivation situation on learning.

Journal: *Journal of Experimental Education*, Summer 1995, *63*(4), 281–299.

Related Research: Weinstein, C. E., et al. (1985). College and university students' study skills in the USA: The LASSI. In G. d'Ydewalle (Ed.), *Cognition information processing, and motivation* (pp. 703–726). Amsterdam: Elsevier.

■ ■ ■

7130

Test Name: LEARNING STYLE INVENTORY—KOREAN VERSION

Purpose: To measure a child's learning style.

Number of Items: 104

Format: 5-point agreement scales.

Reliability: Internal consistency (Korean version) was .77.

Authors: Hong, E., et al.

Article: Homework style and homework behavior of Korean and American children.

Journal: *Journal of Research and Development in Education*, Summer 1995, *28*(4), 197–207.

Related Research: Dunn, R., et al. (1987). *Learning Style Inventory*. Lawrence, KS: Price Systems.

■ ■ ■

7131

Test Name: LEARNING STYLE SCALE

Purpose: To measure learning styles.

Number of Items: 14

Format: Includes two factors: Concreteness/Abstractness and Reflection/Action. Responses are made on a 6-point scale. All items are presented.

Reliability: Coefficient alpha ranged from .78 to .86. Test–retest reliabilities were .73 to .75.

Authors: Romero, J. E., et al.

Article: Development and validation of new scales to measure Kolb's (1985) learning style dimensions.

Journal: *Educational and Psychological Measurement*, Spring 1992, *52*(1), 171–180.

Related Research: Highhouse, S., & Doverspike, D. (1987). The validity of the Learning Style Inventory 1985 as a predictor of cognitive style and occupational preference. *Educational and Psychological Measurement, 47*, 749–753.

■ ■ ■

7132

Test Name: LIBRARY RESEARCH STRATEGIES QUESTIONNAIRE

Purpose: To measure how students use the library.

Number of Items: 33

Format: Multiple-choice format. All items are presented.

Reliability: Alpha was .89.

Validity: Correlations among subscales ranged from .31 to .44. Correlations with other variables ranged from -.38 to .36.

Authors: Landrum, R. E., and Muench, D. M.

Article: Assessing students' library skills and knowledge: The Library Research Strategies Questionnaire.

Journal: *Psychological Reports*, December 1994, *75*(3) Part II, 1619–1628.

■ ■ ■

7133

Test Name: LOGICAL THINKING ABILITY TEST

Purpose: To test for ability to think logically.

Number of Items: 10

Format: Open-ended questions related to identifying and controlling variables and to proportional, correlational, probabilistic, and combinatorial reasonings.

Reliability: Coefficient was .77.

Authors: Geben, O., et al.

Article: Effects of computer simulations and problem-solving approaches on high school students.

Journal: *Journal of Educational Research*, Sept./Oct. 1992, *86*(1), 5–10.

Related Research: Tobin, K., & Capie, W. (1981). *Test of Logical Thinking.* (Available from Dr. Kenneth G. Tobin and Dr. William Capie, Department of Science Education, University of Georgia, Athens, GA 30602.)

■ ■ ■

7134

Test Name: MODES OF PROBLEM-SOLVING SCALE

Purpose: To measure modes of problem solving.

Number of Items: 19

Format: Includes two categories: Associative Dimension and Bisociative Dimension. Responses are made on a 7-point scale ranging from *unlikely to enjoy* to *likely to enjoy.* All items are presented.

Reliability: Alpha coefficients ranged from .80 to .87. Test–retest (2 weeks) reliabilities were .77 and .83.

Validity: Correlations with other variables ranged from .41 to .94.

Author: Jabri, M. M.

Article: The development of

conceptually independent subscales in the measurement of modes of problem solving.

Journal: *Educational and Psychological Measurement*, Winter, 1991, *51*(4), 975–993.

Related Research: Koestler, A. (1964). *The act of creation.* London: Hutchinson.

■ ■ ■

7135

Test Name: PARTICIPATIVE DECISION-MAKING SCALE

Purpose: To measure participative decision-making.

Number of Items: 4

Format: 5-point scale ranging from *very little* to *very much.* All items presented.

Reliability: Reliability was .81.

Validity: Correlations with work values ranged from .18 to .65.

Author: Knoop, R.

Article: Achievement of work values and participative decision-making.

Journal: *Psychological Reports*, June 1991, *68*(3) Part I, 775–781.

Related Research: Siegel, A., & Ruh, R. (1973). Job involvement, participation in decision-making, personal background, and job behavior. *Organizational Behavior and Human Performance, 9*, 318–327.

■ ■ ■

7136

Test Name: PROBLEM-SOLVING INVENTORY

Purpose: To measure a person's perception of his or her problem-solving ability.

Number of Items: 35

Format: 6-point Likert format.

Reliability: Alpha was .90. Test–retest reliability (2 weeks) was .89.

Validity: Correlations with other variables ranged from -.21 to .67 across subscales.

Authors: Clum, G. A., and Febbraro, G. A. R.

Article: Stress, social support, and problem-solving appraisal/skills: Prediction of suicide severity within a college population.

Journal: *Journal of Psychopathology and Behavioral Assessment*, March 1994, *16*(1), 69–83.

Related Research: Heppner, P. P. (1986). *Manual for the Problem-Solving Inventory (PSI)*. Paper presented at the annual meeting of the American Psychological Association, Washington, DC.

■ ■ ■

7137

Test Name: PROBLEM SOLVING STYLE QUESTIONNAIRE

Purpose: To measure learning style.

Number of Items: 14

Format: Includes two subscales: Abstract Conceptualization/ Concrete Experience and Active Experimentation/Reflective Observation.

Reliability: Alpha coefficients were .76 and .74.

Validity: Correlations with other variables ranged from -.37 to .35 (*N* = 227).

Authors: Tepper, B. J., et al.

Article: Discriminant and convergent Validity of the Problem Solving Style Questionnaire.

Journal: *Educational and Psychological Measurement*, Summer 1993, *53*(2), 437–444.

Related Research: Romero, J. E., et al. (1992). Development and

preliminary validation of new measures of Kolb's learning style dimensions. *Educational and Psychological Measurement, 52*, 171–180.

■ ■ ■

7138

Test Name: PROBLEM-SOLVING TASK INVENTORY

Purpose: To measure the quality of choices made by participants in a problem situation.

Number of Items: 11

Format: 5-point rating scales.

Reliability: Test–retest was .68.

Validity: Construct validity ranged from .70 to .78.

Authors: Wege, J. W., and Moeller, A. T.

Article: Effectiveness of a problem-solving training program.

Journal: *Psychological Reports*, April 1995, *76*(2), 495–503.

Related Research: Wege, J. W. (1988). *Effectiveness of a problem-solving training program.* Unpublished master's thesis, Stellenbosch University, South Africa.

■ ■ ■

7139

Test Name: QUESTIONING SKILL INSTRUMENT

Purpose: To assess questioning skills.

Number of Items: 2

Format: Involves a picture and a short story. Pupils look at the picture and write questions about it, then read the story and do the same.

Reliability: Coefficient was .88.

Authors: Mevarech, Z., and Susak, Z.

Article: Effects of learning with

cooperative-mastery method on elementary students.

Journal: *Journal of Educational Research*, March/April 1993, *86*(4), 197–205.

Related Research: Berlyne, D. E., & Frommer, F. D. (1966). Some determinants of the incidence and content of children's questions. *Child Development, 37*, 177–189.

■ ■ ■

7140

Test Name: REFLECTIVE JUDGMENT SCALE

Purpose: To measure assumptions of knowledge and justification of knowledge in seven levels from dualistic to relativistic.

Number of Items: 9

Format: Open-ended format. All items and sample issues presented.

Reliability: Interrater reliabilities ranged from .92 to .98.

Authors: Pape, S. L., and Kelly, F. J.

Article: Reflective judgment: A cross-sectional study of undergraduate education majors.

Journal: *Psychological Reports*, April 1991, *68*(2), 387–395.

Related Research: Kitchener, K. S., & King, P. M. (1985). *Reflective judgment scoring rules.* Unpublished Manuscript, University of Minnesota.

■ ■ ■

7141

Test Name: SCIENCE PROCESS SKILL TEST

Purpose: To test for problem-solving abilities in science.

Number of Items: 36

Format: Includes five subsets: identification, defining, graphing, and interpretation of science information.

Reliability: Coefficient was .81.

Authors: Geben, O., et al.

Article: Effects of computer simulations and problem-solving approaches on high school students.

Journal: *Journal of Educational Research*, Sept./Oct. 1992, *86*(21), 5–10.

Related Research: Okey, J. R., et al. (1982). *Integrated Process Skill Test-2.* (Available from James Okey, Dept. of Science Ed., University of Georgia, Athens, GA 30602.)

■ ■ ■

7142

Test Name: SPEED OF THINKING TEST

Purpose: To measure cognitive speed.

Number of Items: 180

Time Required: Entire testing process takes about 8 minutes.

Format: For each item the respondent indicates whether a pair of letters are the same or different. Sample items are presented.

Reliability: Test–retest reliability coefficient was .80.

Validity: Correlations with other variables ranged from .03 to .60.

Author: Carver, R. P.

Article: Reliability and validity of the Speed of Thinking Test.

Journal: *Educational and Psychological Measurement*, Spring 1992, *52*(1), 125–134.

Related Research: Posner, M. I., et al. (1969). Retention of visual and name codes of single letters. *Journal of Experimental Psychology Monograph*, *79*(1) Part 2, 1–16.

7143

Test Name: STUDY PROCESS QUESTIONNAIRE—ARABIC VERSION

Purpose: To assess the study process in three dimensions: surface, deep, and achieving.

Number of Items: 42

Format: 5-point scales (*never or only rarely true of me* to *always or almost always true of me*).

Reliability: Alphas ranged from .49 to .73 across subscales. Test–retest reliability (4 weeks) ranged from .63 to .76.

Validity: Correlations with GPA ranged from -.25 to .36.

Author: Albaili, M. A.

Article: An Arabic version of the Study Process Questionnaire: Reliability and validity.

Journal: *Psychological Reports*, December 1995, *77*(3) Part II, 1083–1089.

Related Research: Biggs, J. B. (1987). *The Study Process Questionnaire manual.* Hawthorn, Victoria: Australian Council for Educational Research.

■ ■ ■

7144

Test Name: SUPERFICIAL ENGAGEMENT SCALE

Purpose: To assess children's use of work strategies that minimize effort expenditures.

Number of Items: 5

Format: Responses are made on a 3-point scale ranging from 1 (*not like me*) to 3 *(a lot like me).* Examples are given.

Reliability: Cronbach alpha was .85.

Validity: Correlations with other variables ranged from -.22 to -.34.

Authors: Meece, J. L., and Holt, K.

Article: A pattern analysis of students' achievement goals.

Journal: *Journal of Educational Psychology*, December 1993, *85*(4), 582–590.

Related Research: Meece, J. L., et al. (1988). Students' goal orientations and cognitive engagement in classroom activities. *Journal of Educational Psychology*, *80*, 514–523.

■ ■ ■

7145

Test Name: TEST OF ANALOGICAL REASONING IN CHILDREN

Purpose: To assess cognitive abilities in young children.

Number of Items: 16

Time Required: 25 minutes

Format: Form A—(Game)— analogy problems are solved by selecting a solution block. Form E—(Paper and Pencil)—Analogy problems on cards are solved by marking a selected option.

Authors: Caropreso, E., and White, C. S.

Article: Analogical reasoning and giftedness: A comparison between identified gifted and nonidentified children.

Journal: *Journal of Educational Research*, May/June 1994, *87*(5), 271–278.

Related Research: Alexander, P. A., et al. (1987). Analogical reasoning in young children. *Journal of Educational Psychology*, *79*, 401–408.

■ ■ ■

7146

Test Name: THINKING ORIENTATION QUESTIONNAIRE

Purpose: To assess teachers' theoretical orientations toward teaching thinking.

Number of Items: 20

Format: 5-point Likert format. All items are presented.

Reliability: Alphas were .76 (content orientation) and .78 (skill orientation).

Author: Yilirim, A.

Article: Teachers' theoretical orientations toward teaching thinking.

Journal: *Journal of Educational Research*, September/October 1994, *88*(1), 28–35.

Related Research: Glaser, R. (1984). Education and thinking: The scale of knowledge. *American Psychologist*, *39*, 93–104.

■ ■ ■

7147

Test Name: YOUR STYLE OF LEARNING AND THINKING

Purpose: To measure cerebral dominance.

Number of Items: 41

Reliability: Alphas ranged from .26 to .61 across subscales. Test–retest reliabilities ranged from .62 to .77 across subscales.

Validity: Correlations with localization of brain injury ranged from -.13 to .05.

Authors: Zalewski, L. J., et al.

Article: Using cerebrum dominance for education programs.

Journal: *The Journal of General Psychology*, January 1992, *119*(1), 45–57.

Related Research: Torrence, E. P., et al. (1977). Your Style of Learning and Thinking, Forms A and B: Preliminary norms, abbreviated technical notes, scoring keys, and selected references. *Gifted Child Quarterly*, *21*, 563–573.

...
CHAPTER 20
Status

7148

Test Name: TREATMENT OF ADVANCING MINORITIES SCALES

Purpose: To assess problems and issues that arise if a company becomes concerned for visible minorities, actions taken on behalf of minorities, and perceived experiences of minorities.

Number of Items: 36

Format: Varies. Sample items are presented.

Reliability: Ranged from .63 to .92.

Author: Burke, R. J.

Article: Organizational treatment of minority managers and professionals: Costs to the majority?

Journal: *Psychological Reports*, April 1991, *68*(2), 439–449.

Related Research: Fernandez, J. P. (1981). *Racism and sexism in corporate life.* Lexington, MA: Lexington Books.

Zuriek, E. (1983). *The experience of visible minorities in the work world: The case of MBA graduates.* Report submitted to the Race Relations Subdivision at the Ontario Human Rights Commission, Ministry of Labour, Toronto.

CHAPTER 21
Trait Measurement

7149

Test Name: AGGRESSION INVENTORY

Purpose: To measure trait aggressive behavior by self-report.

Number of Items: 28

Format: 5-point scale (1—*does not apply to me at all* to 5—*applies exactly to me*).

Reliability: Alphas ranged from .65 to .82 across subscales.

Validity: Men generally score significantly higher than women do.

Author: Gladue, B. A.

Article: Qualitative and quantitative sex differences in self-reported aggressive behavioral characteristics.

Journal: *Psychological Reports*, April 1991, *68*(2), 675–684.

Related Research: Olweus, D. (1986). Aggression and hormones: Behavioral relationship with testosterone and adrenaline. In D. Olweus et al. (Eds.), *Development of antisocial and prosocial behavior* (pp. 51–72). New York: Academic Press.

■ ■ ■

7150

Test Name: AGGRESSIVE ORIENTATION SCALE

Purpose: To measure aggression.

Number of Items: 7

Format: Responses are made on 5-point scales. Some items presented.

Reliability: Alpha was .80.

Authors: Simons, R. L., et al.

Article: The impact of mothers' parenting, involvement by nonresidential fathers, and parental conflict on the adjustment of adolescent children.

Journal: *Journal of Marriage and the Family*, May 1994, *56*(2), 356–374.

Related Research: Velicer, W. R., et al. (1985). Item format and the structure of the Buss-Durkee hostility inventory. *Aggressive Behavior*, *11*, 65–82.

■ ■ ■

7151

Test Name: AMBIGUITY TOLERANCE SCALE

Purpose: To measure ambiguity tolerance.

Number of Items: 8

Reliability: Alpha coefficient was .71.

Validity: Correlations with other variables ranged from -.19 to .58 ($N = 148$).

Author: McLain, D. L.

Article: The MSTAT-1: A new measure of an individual's tolerance for ambiguity.

Journal: *Educational and Psychological Measurement*, Spring 1993, *53*(1), 183–189.

Related Research: Storey, R. G., & Aldag, R. J. (1983). *Perceived environmental uncertainty: A test of an integrated explanatory model.* Paper presented at the 43rd annual meeting of the

National Academy of Management.

■ ■ ■

7152

Test Name: AMBIGUITY TOLERANCE SCALE

Purpose: To measure ambiguity tolerance.

Number of Items: 16

Reliability: Alpha coefficient was .60.

Validity: Correlations with other variables ranged from -.25 to .37 ($N = 148$).

Author: McLain, D. L.

Article: The MSTAT-1: A New Measure of an Individual's Tolerance for Ambiguity.

Journal: *Educational and Psychological Measurement*, Spring 1993, *53*(1), 183–189.

Related Research: Budner, J. (1962). Tolerance of ambiguity as a personality variable. *Journal of Personality*, *30*, 29–40.

■ ■ ■

7153

Test Name: AMBIGUITY TOLERANCE SCALE

Purpose: To measure ambiguity tolerance.

Number of Items: 20

Reliability: Alpha coefficient was .58.

Validity: Correlations with other variables ranged from -.45 to .33 ($N = 148$).

Author: McLain, D. L.

Article: The MSTAT-1: A new measure of an individual's tolerance for ambiguity.

Journal: *Educational and Psychological Measurement*, Spring 1993, *53*(1), 183–189.

Related Research: MacDonald, A. P. (1970). Revised Scale for ambiguity tolerance: Reliability and validity. *Psychological Reports*, *26*, 791–798.

■ ■ ■

7154

Test Name: ANGER/ AGGRESSION QUESTIONNAIRE

Purpose: To measure anger.

Number of Items: 17

Format: 3-point response scales.

Reliability: Cronbach's alpha was .79.

Author: Harris, M. B.

Article: Beliefs about reducing anger.

Journal: *Psychological Reports*, February 1992, *70*(1), 203–210.

Related Research: Harris, M. B., & Siebel, C. E. (1975). Affect, aggression and altruism. *Developmental Psychology*, *11*, 623–627.

■ ■ ■

7155

Test Name: ANGER DISCOMFORT SCALE

Purpose: To measure discomfort with one's own anger.

Number of Items: 15

Format: Items are rated on a 4-point Likert-type scale ranging from *almost never* to *almost always*. All items are presented.

Reliability: Alpha was .81. Test–retest coefficient was .87.

Validity: Correlations with other

variables ranged from -.16 to .51.

Authors: Sharkin, B. S., and Gelso, C. J.

Article: The Anger Discomfort Scale: Beginning reliability and validity data.

Journal: *Measurement and Evaluation in Counseling and Development*, July 1991, *24*(2), 61–68.

■ ■ ■

7156

Test Name: ANGER EXPRESSION SCALE

Purpose: To measure anger expression.

Number of Items: 24

Format: Provides 4 scores: Anger-In, Anger-Out, Anger-Control, and a total score. Examples are presented.

Reliability: Alpha reliabilities ranged from .73 to .85.

Validity: Correlations with the Anger Discomfort Scale ranged from -.16 to .34.

Authors: Sharkin, B. S., and Gelso, C. J.

Article: The Anger Discomfort Scale: Beginning reliability and validity data.

Journal: *Measurement and Evaluation in Counseling and Development*, July 1991, *24*(2), 61–68.

Related Research: Spielberger, C. D., et al. (1988). The experience, expression and control of anger. In M. P. Janisse (Ed.), *Individual differences, stress, and health psychology* (pp. 89–108). New York: Springer Verlag.

■ ■ ■

7157

Test Name: ANGER SCALES

Purpose: To measure anger

arousal and anger turned inward.

Number of Items: 13

Format: 5-point Likert format.

Reliability: Alphas ranged from .69 (inward) and .86 (arousal).

Authors: Christopher, F. S., et al.

Article: Exploring the darkside of courtship: A test of a model of premarital sexual aggressiveness.

Journal: *Journal of Marriage and the Family*, May 1993, *55*(2), 469–479.

Related Research: Siegel, J. M. (1986). The multidimensional anger inventory. *Journal of Personality and Social Psychology*, *51*, 191–200.

■ ■ ■

7158

Test Name: ANGER STRAIN SCALE

Purpose: To assess feelings of annoyance and irritability.

Number of Items: 3

Format: Responses are made on a 5-point Likert-type scale. An example is presented.

Reliability: Alpha coefficients were .76 and .79.

Validity: Correlations with other variables ranged from -.56 to .59.

Authors: Newton, T., and Keenan, T.

Article: Further analyses of the dispositional argument in organizational behavior.

Journal: *Journal of Applied Psychology*, December 1991, *76*(6), 781–787.

Related Research: Keenan, A., & Newton, T. J. (1984). Frustration in organizations: Relationships to role stress, climate and psychological strain. *Journal of Occupational Psychology*, *57*, 57–65.

7159

Test Name:
ARGUMENTATIVENESS
SCALES

Purpose: To assess tendency to approach or tendency to avoid arguments.

Number of Items: 20

Format: 5-point scales (*almost never true* to *almost always true*).

Reliability: Alpha was .86. Test–retest ranged from .82 to .86.

Validity: Correlations with other variables ranged from -.76 to .63.

Author: Blickle, G.

Article: Conceptualization and measurement of argumentativeness: A decade later.

Journal: *Psychological Reports*, August 1995, *77*(1), 99–110.

Related Research: Infante, D. A., & Rancer, A. S. (1982). A conceptualization and measurement of argumentativeness. *Journal of Personality Assessment*, *46*, 72–80.

● ● ●

7160

Test Name: ASSERTIVE JOB HUNTING SURVEY

Purpose: To assess assertiveness in job-hunting behaviors.

Number of Items: 25

Format: Responses are made on a 6-point Likert scale ranging from *very unlikely* to *very likely*.

Reliability: Alpha coefficient was .82. Test–retest was .77.

Authors: Schmit, M. J., et al.

Article: Self-reported assertive job-seeking behaviors of minimally educated job hunters.

Journal: *Personnel Psychology*, Spring 1993, *46*(1), 105–124.

Related Research: Becker, H. A. (1980). The Assertive Job-Hunting Survey. *Measurement and Evaluation in Guidance*, *13*, 43–48.

● ● ●

7161

Test Name: ASSERTIVENESS INVENTORY

Purpose: To measure assertiveness in adolescents.

Number of Items: 18

Format: 5-point scales (*never* to *always*). All items are presented.

Validity: Five assertiveness factors extracted: Substance, Mastery of Cognitive Skills, Individual Rights, Dating and Social.

Authors: Golberg, C. J., and Botvin, G. J.

Article: Assertiveness in Hispanic adolescents: Relationship to alcohol use and abuse.

Journal: *Psychological Reports*, August 1993, *73*(1), 227–238.

Related Research: Gambrill, E., & Richey, C. (1975). An assertion inventory for use in assessment and research. *Behavior Therapy*, *6*, 550–561.

● ● ●

7162

Test Name: ASSERTIVENESS SCHEDULE

Purpose: To measure assertiveness.

Number of Items: 30

Format: 6-point scales ranged from -3 (*very characteristic of me*) to +3 (*very uncharacteristic of me*). Sample items are presented.

Reliability: Alpha was .74. Test–retest was .78. Split-half reliability was .77.

Validity: Correlations with other variables ranged from -.62 to .52.

Authors: Solberg, V. S., et al.

Article: Career decision-making and career search activity: Relative effects of career search self-efficacy and human agency.

Journal: *Journal of Counseling Psychology*, October 1995, *42*(4), 448–455.

Related Research: Rathus, S. A. (1973). A 30-item schedule for assessing assertive behavior. *Behavior Therapy*, *4*, 398–406.

● ● ●

7163

Test Name:
AUTHORITARIANISM SCALE

Purpose: To measure authoritarianism.

Number of Items: 24

Format: 5-point format. All items presented.

Reliability: Alpha was .40. Spearman-Brown was .29.

Authors: Ahmed, S. M. S., et al.

Article: Factor analysis of Authority Behavior Inventory.

Journal: *Psychological Reports*, August 1991, *69*(1), 168–170.

Related Research: Rigby, K. (1987). An authority behavior inventory. *Journal of Personality Assessment*, *51*, 615–625.

● ● ●

7164

Test Name: BATTERY OF INTERPERSONAL CAPABILITIES

Purpose: To measure flexibility.

Number of Items: 80 (long form) and 16 (short form).

Format: 7-point scale (1—*disagree very much* to 7—*agree very much*).

Reliability: Alpha was .81 (long) and .74 (short).

Validity: Correlation of long form with Dogmatism Scale was -.25 ($p < .01$). Correlation of short form was -.14 ($p = .08$).

Authors: Goldman, B. A., and Flake, W. L.

Article: The Battery of Interpersonal Capabilities and Rokeach's Dogmatism Scale.

Journal: *Psychological Reports*, August 1992, *71*(1), 104–106.

Related Research: Paulhus, D. L., & Martin, C. L. (1988). Functional flexibility: A new conception of interpersonal flexibility. *Journal of Personality and Social Psychology, 55,* 88–101.

■ ■ ■

7165

Test Name: BORTNER RATING SCALE

Purpose: To assess Type A behavior.

Number of Items: 14

Format: Participant indicates his or her place on a continuum.

Reliability: Test–retest reliability (4 months) was .80.

Validity: Correlations with other variables ranged from .25 to .42.

Authors: Ohman, A., et al.

Article: Decomposing coronary-prone behavior: Dimensions of Type A behavior in the Videotaped Structured Interview.

Journal: *Journal of Psychopathology and Behavioral Assessment*, March 1992, *14*(1), 21–54.

Related Research: Bortner, R. W. (1969). A short rating scale as a potential measure of Pattern A behavior. *Journal of Chronic Diseases, 22,* 878–891.

7166

Test Name: CIRCADIAN TYPE SCALES

Purpose: To measure circadian type.

Number of Items: 18

Format: Includes two subscales: Flexibility and Languidity.

Reliability: Coefficient alpha was .79.

Author: Barton, J.

Article: Choosing to work at night: A moderating influence on individual tolerance to shift work.

Journal: *Journal of Applied Psychology*, June 1994, *79*(3), 449–454.

Related Research: Folkard, S., et al. (1979). Towards a predictive test of adjustment to shift work. *Ergonomics, 22,* 79–91.

■ ■ ■

7167

Test Name: COGNITIVE FLEXIBILITY SCALE

Purpose: To measure cognitive flexibility.

Number of Items: 12

Format: 6-point Likert format. All items are presented.

Reliability: Test–retest was .83 (1 week).

Validity: Correlations with other variables ranged from -.57 to .63.

Authors: Martin, M. M., and Rubin, R. B.

Article: A new measure of cognitive flexibility.

Journal: *Psychological Reports*, April 1995, *76*(2), 623–626.

■ ■ ■

7168

Test Name: COLLEGE SELF-EXPRESSION SCALE

Purpose: To measure assertiveness.

Number of Items: 96

Format: Responses are made on a scale ranging from 1 (*strongly agree*) to 5 (*strongly disagree*).

Reliability: Rate–rerate reliability was .89.

Authors: Howard, G. S., et al.

Article: In stories we trust: Studies of the validity of autobiographies.

Journal: *Journal of Counseling Psychology*, July 1992, *39*(3), 398–405.

Related Research: Galassi, J., et al. (1974). The College Self-Expression scale: A measure of assertiveness. *Behavior Therapist, 5,* 165–175.

■ ■ ■

7169

Test Name: COMPETITIVENESS INDEX

Purpose: To measure competitiveness.

Number of Items: 20

Format: Includes 3 factors: Emotion, Argument, and Games. All items are presented.

Reliability: Alpha coefficient was .90.

Validity: Correlations with other variables ranged from .17 to .61.

Authors: Smither, R. D., and Houston, J. M.

Article: The nature of competitiveness: The development and validation of the Competitiveness Index.

Journal: *Educational and Psychological Measurement*, Summer 1992, *52*(2), 407–418

■ ■ ■

7170

Test Name: DATING AND ASSERTION QUESTIONNAIRE

Purpose: To measure assertion.

Number of Items: 9

Format: 5-point rating scales.

Reliability: Alpha was .85.

Authors: Bruch, M. A., et al.

Article: Type A behavior and processing social conflict information.

Journal: *Journal of Research in Personality*, December 1991, *25*(4), 434–444.

Related Research: Levenson, R. W., & Gottman, J. M. (1978). Toward the assessment of social competence. *Journal of Consulting and Clinical Psychology, 46*, 453–462.

■ ■ ■

7171

Test Name: DOGMATISM SCALE

Purpose: To measure rigid thinking.

Number of Items: 20

Format: 7-point agreement scales.

Reliability: Reliability was .79.

Validity: Correlations with Battery of Interpersonal Capabilities ranged from -.14 (ns) to -.25 (*p* < .01) for short and long forms, respectively.

Authors: Goldman, B. A., and Flake, W. L.

Article: The Battery of Interpersonal Capabilities and Rokeach's Dogmatism Scale.

Journal: *Psychological Reports*, August 1992, *71*(1), 104–106.

Related Research: Trudahl, V. C., & Powell, F. A. (1965). A short-form dogmatism scale for use in field studies. *Social Forces, 44*, 211–214.

■ ■ ■

7172

Test Name: EMPATHIC CONCERN SCALE

Purpose: To assess empathy.

Number of Items: 7

Format: Responses are made on a 5-point scale ranging from 1 (*does not describe me well*) to 5 (*describes me very well*).

Reliability: Internal consistency ranged from .71 to .77. Test–retest reliabilities ranged from .62 to .71.

Validity: Correlations with other variables ranged from -.19 to .23.

Authors: McNeely, B. L., and Meglino, B. M.

Article: The role of dispositional and situational antecedents in prosocial organizational behavior: An examination of the intended beneficiaries of prosocial behavior.

Journal: *Journal of Applied Psychology*, December 1994, *79*(6), 836–844.

Related Research: Davis, M. H. (1980). A multidimensional approach to individual differences in empathy. *JSAS Catalog of Selected Documents in Psychology, 10*, 85.

■ ■ ■

7173

Test Name: EMPATHY SCALE

Purpose: To measure empathy.

Number of Items: 23

Format: Responses are made on a 5-point scale ranging from 1 (*do not agree at all*) to 5 (*agree very much*).

Validity: Correlations with other variables ranged from -.56 to .54.

Author: Trommsdorff, G.

Article: Child-rearing and children's empathy.

Journal: *Perceptual and Motor Skills*, April 1991, *72*(2), 387–390.

Related Research: Mehrabian, A.,

& Epstein, N. A. (1972). A measure of emotional empathy. *Journal of Personality, 40*, 525–543.

■ ■ ■

7174

Test Name: EMPATHY SCALE

Purpose: To measure emotional empathy.

Number of Items: 33

Format: Scoring range for each item ranges from +4 to -4.

Reliability: Split-half was .84. Alpha was .79.

Author: Kalliopusa, M.

Article: Creative way of living

Journal: *Psychological Reports*, February 1992, *70*(1), 11–14.

Related Research: Mehrabian, A., & Epstein, N. (1972). A measure of emotional empathy. *Journal of Personality, 40*, 525–543.

■ ■ ■

7175

Test Name: FRAMINGHAM TYPE A SCALE

Purpose: To measure Type A personality.

Number of Items: 10

Format: 4-point Likert format.

Reliability: Alpha was .70.

Author: Westra, H. A., and Kuiper, N. A.

Article: Type A, irrational cognitions, and situational factors relating to stress.

Journal: *Journal of Research in Personality*, March 1992, *26*(1), 1–20.

Related Research: Haynes, S. G., et al. (1978). The relationship of psychosocial factors to coronary heart disease in the Framingham study: I. Methods and risk factors. *American Journal of Epidemiology*, *109*, 362–383.

■ ■ ■

7176

Test Name: GAMBRILL-RICHEY ASSERTION INVENTORY

Purpose: To assess the probability of participants responding in an assertive manner and the degree of discomfort in acting in an assertive manner.

Number of Items: 40

Format: Responses are made on a 5-point scale ranging from 1 (*always do it*) to 5 (*never do it*). Examples are presented.

Reliability: Test–retest reliabilities were .81 (probability) and .87 (discomfort).

Validity: Correlations with other variables ranged from -.15 to .47.

Authors: Ernst, J. M., and Heesacker, M.

Article: Application of the elaboration likelihood model of attitude change to assertion training.

Journal: *Journal of Counseling Psychology*, January 1993, *40*(1), 37–45.

Related Research: Gambrill, E. D., & Richey, C. A. (1975). An assertion inventory for use in assessment and research. *Behavior Therapy*, *6*, 550–561.

■ ■ ■

7177

Test Name: GUILT INVENTORY

Purpose: To assess trait guilt, state guilt, and degree of subscription to a set of moral standards.

Number of Items: 45

Format: 5-point Likert format.

Reliability: Internal reliabilities ranged from .79 to .89. Test–

retest reliabilities (10 and 36 weeks) ranged, respectively, between .56 and .81 and from .58 to .77.

Validity: Correlations with other variables ranged from -.38 to .59.

Authors: Jones, W. H., and Kugler, K.

Article: Interpersonal correlates of the Guilt Inventory.

Journal: *Journal of Personality Assessment*, October 1993, *61*(2), 246–258.

Related Research: Kugler, K., & Jones, W. H. (1992). On conceptualizing and assessing guilt. *Journal of Personality and Social Psychology*, *62*, 315–327.

■ ■ ■

7178

Test Name: HOGAN EMPATHY SCALE

Purpose: To measure empathy.

Number of Items: 38

Format: True–false format.

Reliability: Internal consistency was .71. Test–retest reliability was .85.

Authors: Brems, C., et al.

Article: Group modification of empathic verbalizations and self-disclosure.

Journal: *The Journal of Social Psychology*, April 1992, *132*(2), 189–200.

Related Research: Hogan, R. (1969). Development of an empathy scale. *Journal of Consulting and Clinical Psychology*, *33*, 307–316.

■ ■ ■

7179

Test Name: INTERPERSONAL FACILITY SCALE

Purpose: To measure shyness.

Number of Items: 28

Format: 5-point Likert format. Sample items are presented.

Reliability: Total alpha was .95. Subscale alphas ranged from .88 to .93.

Validity: Correlations with other variables ranged from -62 to .18.

Authors: Solberg, V. S., et al.

Article: Career decision-making and career search activity: Relative effects of career search self-efficacy and human agency.

Journal: *Journal of Counseling Psychology*, October 1995, *42*(4), 448–455.

Related Research: Jones, W. H., et al. (1986). Shyness: Conceptualization and measurement. *Journal of Personality and Social Psychology*, *51*, 629–239.

■ ■ ■

7180

Test Name: INTOLERANCE OF AMBIGUITY SCALE

Purpose: To assess the tendency to perceive ambiguous situations as sources of threat.

Number of Items: 16

Format: 7-point agreement format.

Reliability: Test–retest ranged from .73 to .85. Alphas ranged from .52 to .62.

Validity: Correlations with other variables ranged from .36 to .54.

Authors: Sobal, J., and DeForge, B. R.

Article: Reliability of Budner's Intolerance of Ambiguity Scale in medical students.

Journal: *Psychological Reports*, August 1992, *71*(1), 15–18.

Related Research: Budner, S.

(1962). Intolerance of ambiguity as a personality variable. *Journal of Personality*, *30*, 29–50.

•••

7181

Test Name: JUROR BIAS SCALE

Purpose: To measure juror bias. May also measure legal authoritarianism.

Number of Items: 21

Format: Includes two subscales: Probability of Commission and Reasonable Doubt. Examples are given.

Reliability: Split-half reliability was .81. Test–retest (5 weeks) reliability was .67.

Authors: Narby, D. J., et al.

Article: A meta-analysis of the association between authoritarianism and jurors' perceptions of defendant culpability.

Journal: *Journal of Applied Psychology*, February 1993, *78*(1), 34–42.

Related Research: Kassin, S. M., & Wrightsman, L. S. (1983). The construction and validation of a juror bias scale. *Journal of Research in Personality*, *17*, 423–442.

•••

7182

Test Name: MACH V SCALE

Purpose: To measure Machiavellianism.

Number of Items: 20

Format: Respondents indicate which of three statements they most and least agree with. These responses are then converted to a 1–7 scale.

Reliability: Alpha coefficients were .58 and .56.

Validity: Correlations with other variables ranged from -.04 to -.28.

Authors: King, W. C., Jr., and Miles, E. W.

Article: A quasi-experimental assessment of the effect of computerizing noncognitive paper-and-pencil measurements: A test of measurement equivalence.

Journal: *Journal of Applied Psychology*, December 1995, *80*(6), 643–651.

Related Research: Christie, R., & Geis, F. L. (1970). *Studies in Machiavellianism*. New York: Academic Press.

•••

7183

Test Name: MORNINGNESS SCALE

Purpose: To assess morningness.

Number of Items: 13

Format: Scores ranged from 13 to 55.

Reliability: Coefficient alpha was .90.

Validity: Correlations with other variables ranged from -.66 to .57.

Authors: Guthrie, J. P., et al.

Article: Additional validity evidence for a measure of *morningness*.

Journal: *Journal of Applied Psychology*, February 1995, *80*(1), 186–190.

Related Research: Smith, C. S., et al. (1989). Evaluation of three circadian rhythm questionnaires with suggestions for an improved measure of morningness. *Journal of Applied Psychology*, *74*, 728–738.

•••

7184

Test Name: MORNINGNESS SCALE

Purpose: To measure circadian rhythms.

Number of Items: 19

Format: All items are presented.

Reliability: Reliability coefficients were .80 and .82.

Authors: Smith, C. S., et al.

Article: Psychometric equivalence of a translated circadian rhythm questionnaire: Implications for between- and within-population assessments.

Journal: *Journal of Applied Psychology*, October 1991, *76*(5), 628–636.

Related Research: Horne, J., & Osterberg, O. (1976). A self-assessment questionnaire to determine morningness-eveningness in human circadian rhythms. *International Journal of Chronobiology*, *4*, 97–110.

•••

7185

Test Name: MULTIDIMENSIONAL ANGER INVENTORY

Purpose: To measure anger.

Number of Items: 38

Format: Includes two factors: Anger-Arousal/Experience and Range of Interpersonal Anger-Eliciting Situations. All items are presented.

Reliability: Alpha coefficients ranged from .85 to .93.

Validity: Correlation with age was -.07.

Authors: Kroner, D. G., et al.

Article: The Multidimensional Anger Inventory: Reliability and factor structure in an inmate sample.

Journal: *Educational and Psychological Measurement*, Autumn 1992, *52*(3), 687–693.

Related Research: Siegel, J. M. (1986). The Multidimensional Anger Inventory. *Journal of Personality and Social Psychology, 51,* 191–200.

■ ■ ■

7186

Test Name:
MULTIDIMENSIONAL
PERFECTIONISM SCALE

Purpose: To measure perfectionism as concern over mistakes, personal standards, parental expectations, parental criticism, doubting of actions, and organization.

Number of Items: 35

Reliability: Alphas ranged from .78 to .92.

Validity: Correlations with other variables ranged from -.11 to .61.

Authors: Flett, G. L., et al.

Article: Dimensions of perfectionism and goal commitment: A further comparison of two perfectionism measures.

Journal: *Journal of Psychopathology and Behavioral Assessment,* June 1995, *17*(2), 111–124.

Related Research: Frost, R., et al. (1990). The dimensions of perfectionism. *Cognitive Therapy and Research, 14,* 449–468.

Parker, W. D., et al. (1995). A psychometric examination of the Multidimensional Perfectionism Scale. *Journal of Psychopathology and Behavioral Assessment, 17,* 323–333.

■ ■ ■

7187

Test Name:
MULTIDIMENSIONAL
PERFECTIONISM SCALE

Purpose: To measure perfectionism as a self-oriented,

other-oriented, and social prescribed phenomenon.

Number of Items: 45

Format: 7-point rating scales. Sample items are presented.

Reliability: Alphas ranged from .79 to .89 across subscales. Test–retest reliabilities exceeded .74.

Validity: Correlations with other variables ranged from .02 to .61.

Authors: Flett, G. L., et al.

Article: Dimensions of perfectionism and goal commitment: A further comparison of two perfectionism measures.

Journal: *Journal of Psychopathology and Behavioral Assessment,* June 1995, *17*(2), 111–124.

Related Research: Hewitt, P., & Flett, G. (1991). Perfectionism in the self and social contexts: Conceptualization, assessment, and association with psychopathology. *Journal of Personality and Social Psychology, 60,* 456–470.

■ ■ ■

7188

Test Name: MULTIPLE
STIMULUS TYPES AMBIGUITY
TOLERANCE—1

Purpose: To measure one's tolerance for ambiguity.

Number of Items: 22

Format: Responses are made on a 7-point Likert scale ranging from 1 (*strongly disagree*) to 7 (*strongly agree*). All items are presented.

Reliability: Alpha coefficient was .86.

Validity: Correlations with other variables ranged from -.34 to .58 (*N* = 148).

Author: McLain, D. L.

Article: The MSTAT-1: A new

measure of an individual's tolerance for ambiguity.

Journal: *Educational and Psychological Measurement,* Spring 1993, *53*(1), 183–189.

■ ■ ■

7189

Test Name: NARCISSISTIC
INJURY SCALE

Purpose: To assess narcissistic injury.

Number of Items: 50

Format: Responses are made on a 6-point Likert scale ranging from 1 (*definitely most uncharacteristic of you*) to 6 (*definitely most characteristic of you*). All items are presented.

Reliability: Coefficient alpha was .94.

Validity: Correlations with other variables ranged from -.58 to .64.

Authors: Zamostny, K. P., et al.

Article: Narcissistic injury and its relationship to early trauma, early resources, and adjustment to college.

Journal: *Journal of Counseling Psychology,* October 1993, *40*(4), 501–510.

Related Research: Slyter, S. L. (1991). *Narcissistic Injury Scale* (Rev. version). Unpublished instrument.

■ ■ ■

7190

Test Name: NARCISSISTIC
PERSONALITY INVENTORY

Purpose: To measure extreme and less extreme forms of narcissism.

Number of Items: 37

Format: True–false format.

Validity: Correlations with other variables ranged from -.27 to .46.

Authors: Rhodewalt, F., and Morf, C. C.

Article: Self and interpersonal correlates of the Narcissistic Personality Inventory: A review and new findings.

Journal: *Journal of Research in Personality*, March 1995, *29*(1), 1–23.

Related Research: Raskin, R., & Terry, H. (1988). A principal-components analysis of the Narcissistic Personality Inventory and further evidence of its construct validity. *Journal of Personality and Social Psychology, 54,* 890–902.

■ ■ ■

7191

Test Name: NARCISSISTIC PERSONALITY INVENTORY

Purpose: To measure narcissism.

Number of Items: 54

Format: Forced-choice format.

Reliability: Split-half was .80.

Authors: Ramanaiah, N. V., et al.

Article: Revised NEO Personality inventory profiles of narcissistic and nonnarcissistic people.

Journal: *Psychological Reports*, August 1994, *75*(1) Part II, 512–514.

Related Research: Raskin, R. N., & Hall, C. S. (1979). A narcissistic personality inventory. *Psychological Reports, 45,* 590.

■ ■ ■

7192

Test Name: PENN STATE WORRY QUESTIONNAIRE

Purpose: To measure the trait of worry.

Number of Items: 16

Format: Responses are made on a 5-point scale.

Reliability: Alpha coefficients ranged from .91 to .95. Test–retest (2 to 10 weeks) reliability ranged from .74 to .93.

Authors: Hill, C. E., et al.

Article: Methodological examination of videotape-assisted reviews in brief therapy: Helpfulness ratings, therapist intentions, client reactions, mood, and session evaluation.

Journal: *Journal of Counseling Psychology*, April 1994, *41*(2), 236–247.

Related Research: Meyer, T. J., et al. (1990). Development and validation of the Penn State Worry Questionnaire. *Behavior Research and Therapy, 28,* 487–495.

■ ■ ■

7193

Test Name: PERFECTIONISM SCALE

Purpose: To self-rate perceived perfectionism.

Number of Items: 10

Format: 5-point scales. Sample item presented.

Reliability: Alphas ranged from .70 to .78. Test–retest reliabilities ranged from .78 (6 weeks) to .63 (2 months).

Author: Ferrari, J. R.

Article: Procrastinators and perfect behavior: An exploratory factor analysis of self-presentation, self-awareness and self-handicapping components.

Journal: *Journal of Research in Personality*, March 1992, *26*(1), 75–84.

Related Research: Burns, D. D. (1980, November). The perfectionist's script for self-defeat. *Psychology Today*, 34–52.

7194

Test Name: PERSPECTIVE TAKING EMPATHIC CONCERN AND PERSONAL DISTRESS SCALE

Purpose: To measure empathy.

Number of Items: 7

Format: 5-point Likert format.

Reliability: Alphas were .74 (perspective taking), .76 (empathic concern), and .70 (personal distress).

Authors: Christopher, F. S., et al.

Article: Exploring the darkside of courtship: A test of a model of premarital sexual aggression.

Journal: *Journal of Marriage and the Family*, May 1993, *55*(2), 469–479.

Related Research: Davis, M. H. (1980). A multidimensional approach to individual differences in empathy. *Catalog of Selected Documents in Psychology, 10*(4), 85.

■ ■ ■

7195

Test Name: RATHUS ASSERTIVENESS SCALE– SWEDISH VERSION

Purpose: To measure assertiveness.

Number of Items: 30 (24).

Reliability: Cronbach's alpha was .82. Split-half was .85. Alpha for the 24-item scale was .84.

Validity: Correlations with other related variables ranged from .24 to .52. Correlations with "irrelevant" scales ranged from .06 to .16.

Author: Gustafson, R.

Article: A Swedish psychometric test of the Rathus Assertiveness Scale.

Journal: *Psychological Reports*, October 1992, *71*(2), 479–482.

Related Research: Rathus, S. A. (1973). A 30-item scale for assessing assertive behavior. *Behavior Therapy*, *4*, 398–406.

■ ■ ■

7196

Test Name: REVISED CHILDREN'S MANIFEST ANXIETY SCALE

Purpose: To assess trait anxiety.

Number of Items: 27

Format: *Yes* or *No* is circled.

Reliability: Coefficient alpha was .83.

Authors: Grych, J. H., et al.

Article: Assessing marital conflict from the child's perspective: The children's perception of Interpersonal Conflict Scale.

Journal: *Child Development*, June 1992, *63*(3), 558–572.

Related Research: Reynolds, C. R., & Richmond, B. O. (1978). What I think and feel: A revised measure of children's anxiety. *Journal of Abnormal Child Psychology*, *6*, 271–280.

■ ■ ■

7197

Test Name: RIGHT-WING AUTHORITARIANISM SCALE

Purpose: To measure authoritarianism.

Number of Items: 30

Reliability: Alphas ranged from .75 to .95 across subscales.

Validity: Correlations with other variables ranged from -.63 to .69.

Author: Duckitt, J.

Article: Right-wing authoritarianism among White South African students: Its measurement and correlates.

Journal: *The Journal of Social Psychology*, August 1993, *133*(4), 553–563.

Related Research: Altemeyer, B. (1981). *Right-wing authoritarianism*. Winnipeg: University of Manitoba Press.

■ ■ ■

7198

Test Name: ROKEACH DOGMATISM SCALE—SHORT FORM

Purpose: To assess counselor dogmatism.

Number of Items: 20

Format: Items are rated on a 6-point Likert-type scale ranging from 1 (*agree a little*) to 6 (*disagree very much*).

Validity: Cross-validation coefficients for the scale ranged from .94 to .95.

Reliability: Split-half reliability was .79.

Authors: Wade, P., and Bernstein, B. L.

Article: Culture sensitivity training and counselor's race: Effects on Black female client's perceptions and attrition.

Journal: *Journal of Counseling Psychology*, January 1991, *38*(1), 9–15.

Related Research: Troldahl, V. C., & Powell, F. A. (1965). A short-form dogmatism scale for use in field studies. *Social Forces*, *44*, 211–215.

■ ■ ■

7199

Test Name: SHORT BALANCED F SCALE

Purpose: To assess authoritarianism.

Number of Items: 14

Format: 5-point Likert format.

Reliability: Alpha was .80.

Authors: Gold, B. T., and Ziegler, M.

Article: Measuring environmental/biological attribution: A fundamental dimension.

Journal: *The Journal of Social Psychology*, December 1994, *133*(6), 837–845.

Related Research: Ray, J. J. (1979). A short balanced F scale. *The Journal of Social Psychology*, *109*, 309–310.

■ ■ ■

7200

Test Name: SHORT FORM DOGMATISM SCALE

Purpose: To measure dogmatism.

Number of Items: 10

Reliability: Alpha coefficient was .68.

Validity: Correlations with other variables ranged from -.06 to -.45 (*N* = 148).

Author: McLain, D. L.

Article: The MSTAT-1: A new measure of an individual's tolerance for ambiguity.

Journal: *Educational and Psychological Measurement*, Spring 1993, *53*(1), 183–189.

Related Research: Troldahl, V., & Powell, F. (1965). A short form dogmatism scale for use in field studies. *Social Forces*, *44*, 211–214.

■ ■ ■

7201

Test Name: SHYNESS SCALE

Purpose: To measure shyness.

Number of Items: 13

Format: 5-point rating scales. Sample items presented.

Reliability: Alphas ranged from .87

to .90. Test–retest reliability (45 days) was .88.

Authors: Bruch, M. A., et al.

Article: Shyness, alcohol expectancies, and alcohol use: Discovery of a suppressor effect.

Journal: *Journal of Research in Personality*, June 1992, *26*(2), 137–149.

Related Research: Cheek, J. M., & Buss, A. H. (1981). Shyness and sociability. *Journal of Personality and Social Psychology, 41,* 330–339.

■ ■ ■

7202

Test Name: SOCIAL RETICENCE SCALE

Purpose: To measure shyness.

Number of Items: 21

Format: 5-point Likert format.

Reliability: Alpha was .91. Test–retest (8 weeks) ranged from .88 to (12 weeks) .78.

Validity: Correlation with a single self-descriptive item was .56.

Author: Flanagan, R.

Article: Shyness, egocentricity, and psychopathology: Their relationships among non-hospitalized individuals and mental hospital patients.

Journal: *Psychological Reports*, June 1991, *70*(3) Part I, 995–1004.

Related Research: Jones, W. H., & Russell, D. R. (1982). The Social Reticence Scale: An objective instrument to measure shyness. *Journal of Personality Assessment, 46,* 629–630.

■ ■ ■

7203

Test Name: STUDENT JENKINS ACTIVITY SURVEY

Purpose: To measure Type A

behavior in college undergraduates.

Number of Items: 21

Reliability: Alphas ranged from .66 to .88 across various factor models.

Validity: Correlations between factors ranged from .20 to .94.

Authors: Bryant, F. B., and Yarnold, P. R.

Article: Comparing five alternative factor-models of the Student Jenkins Activity Survey: Separating the wheat from the chaff.

Journal: *Journal of Personality Assessment*, February 1995, *64*(1), 145–158.

Related Research: Yarnold, P. R., et al. (1987). Comparing the long and short forms of the Student Jenkins Activity Survey. *Journal of Behavioral Medicine, 10,* 75–90.

■ ■ ■

7204

Test Name: SUPERIORITY SCALE

Purpose: To provide a measure of narcissistic behaviors associated with the grandiose–exhibitionistic line of development.

Number of Items: 10

Format: A 6-point Likert scale is used.

Reliability: Test–retest reliability was .80. Internal consistency was .76.

Validity: Correlations with other variables ranged from -.15 to .40.

Authors: Robbins, S. B., and Dupont, P.

Article: Narcissistic needs of the self and perceptions of interpersonal behavior.

Journal: *Journal of Counseling Psychology*, October 1992, *39*(4), 462–467.

Related Research: Robbins, S. B., & Patton, M. J. (1985). Self-psychology and career development: Construction of the Superiority and Goal Instability scales. *Journal of Counseling Psychology, 32,* 221–231.

■ ■ ■

7205

Test Name: TAYLOR MANIFEST ANXIETY SCALE

Purpose: To assess trait anxiety.

Number of Items: 44

Reliability: Coefficient alpha was .83.

Validity: Correlations with other variables ranged from -.17 to .14.

Authors: Barber, A. E., et al.

Article: The effects of interview focus on recruitment effectiveness: A field experiment.

Journal: *Journal of Applied Psychology*, December 1994, *9*(6), 886–896.

Related Research: Taylor, J. (1953). A personality scale of manifest anxiety. *Journal of Abnormal and Social Psychology, 48,* 285–290.

■ ■ ■

7206

Test Name: TYPE A SELF-RATING INVENTORY

Purpose: To measure Type A traits and Type B traits.

Number of Items: 38

Format: 7-point Likert format.

Reliability: Alphas ranged from .67 to .84.

Authors: Yarnold, P. R., and Bryant, F. B.

Article: A measurement model for the Type A Self-Rating Inventory.

Journal: *Journal of Personality*

Assessment, February 1994, *62*(1), 102–115.

Related Research: Herman, S., et al. (1986). Type As who think they are Type Bs: Discrepancies between self-ratings and interview ratings of the Type A (coronary-prone) behavior pattern. *British Journal of Medical Psychology*, *59*, 83–88.

■ ■ ■

7207

Test Name: USE OF POWER SCALE

Purpose: To measure use of class master's power.

Number of Items: 15

Format: Includes five areas: position power, reward power, coercive power, expert power, and personal power. Responses are made on a 5-point scale. Sample items are presented.

Reliability: Coefficient alphas ranged from .57 to .78.

Validity: Correlations with other variables ranged from -.45 to .64.

Author: Cheng, Y. C.

Article: Classroom environment and student affective performance: An effective profile.

Journal: *Journal of Experimental Education*, Spring 1994, *62*(3), 221–239.

Related Research: Cheng, Y. C. (1992, July). *Teachers' professional ethics as related to students' educational outcomes and organizational characteristics.* Paper presented to the World Assembly of the International Council on Education for Teaching, Paris, France.

■ ■ ■

7208

Test Name: WAY OF LIFE SCALE

Purpose: To measure the coronary prone/Type A behavior pattern subcomponent of exaggerated interpersonal control.

Number of Items: 43

Format: Includes 21 items and 22 filler items. Involves forced-choice pairs. All items are presented.

Reliability: Coefficient alpha was .73 (N= 80). Test–retest (2 weeks) reliability was .78 (N= 40).

Authors: Wright, L., et al.

Article: A more bias-proof measure for the Type A subcomponent of exaggerated interpersonal control.

Journal: *Educational and Psychological Measurement*, Spring 1994, *54*(1), 146–154.

Related Research: Wright, L., et al. (1991). Exaggerated social control and its relationship to the Type A behavior pattern as

measured by the structured interview. *Journal of Research in Personality*, *25*, 135–136.

■ ■ ■

7209

Test Name: WOLPE-LAZARUS ASSERTIVENESS INVENTORY

Purpose: To assess assertiveness in older adults.

Number of Items: 30

Format: Yes–no format. Sample items are presented.

Reliability: Alphas ranged from .74 to .77. Test–retest reliability (3 weeks) was .84; after (4 weeks) it was .82.

Validity: Mean assertiveness levels were significantly different by race (Whites highest) and socioeconomic status (high socioeconomic status highest).

Authors: Kogan, E. S., et al.

Article: Psychometric properties of the Wolpe-Lazarus Assertiveness Scale with community dwelling older adults.

Journal: *Journal of Psychopathology and Behavioral Assessment*, June 1995, *17*(2), 97–109.

Related Research: Wolpe, J., & Lazarus, A. A. (1966). *Behavior therapy techniques: A guide to the treatment of neurosis.* New York: Pergamon Press.

CHAPTER 22
Values

7210

Test Name: ATTITUDES TOWARD WOMEN SCALE

Purpose: To assess participants' liberal sex role values.

Number of Items: 10

Format: Responses are made on a 5-point Likert-type scale ranging from 1 (*strongly disagreeable*) to 5 (*strongly agreeable*).

Reliability: Coefficient alpha was .83.

Validity: Correlations with other variables ranged from -.16 to .40.

Authors: Matsui, T., et al.

Article: Personality and career commitment among Japanese female clerical employees.

Journal: *Journal of Vocational Behavior*, June 1991. *38*(3), 351–360.

Related Research: Spence, J. T., & Helmreich, R. L. (1972). The Attitudes Toward Women Scale: An objective instrument to measure attitudes toward the rights and roles of women in contemporary society. *JSAS Catalog of Selected Documents in Psychology, 2*, 66–67.

• • •

7211

Test Name: ATTITUDE TOWARD PHYSICAL ACTIVITY INVENTORY

Purpose: To measure values for participation in physical activity.

Number of Items: 59 (men); 54 (women).

Format: Includes 6 dimensions: social experience, health and fitness, pursuit of vertigo, aesthetic experience, catharsis, and ascetic experience. Responses are made on a 7-point Likert format ranging from 1 (*very strongly disagree*) to 7 (*very strongly agree*).

Reliability: Internal consistency reliabilities ranged from .68 to .89.

Authors: Moode, F. M., and Finkenberg, M. E.

Article: Participation in a wellness course and attitude toward physical education.

Journal: *Perceptual and Motor Skills*, October 1994, *79*(2), 767–770.

Related Research: Kenyon, G. S. (1968). Six scales for assessing attitudes toward physical activity. *Research Quarterly, 39*, 566–574.

• • •

7212

Test Name: ATTITUDES TOWARDS CHRISTIANITY SCALE

Purpose: To measure attitudes toward Christianity.

Number of Items: 7

Format: All items presented (agreement scales implied).

Reliability: Alpha was .98.

Validity: Correlations with long parent scale was .98.

Author: Francis, L. J.

Article: Reliability and validity of a short scale of attitudes towards Christianity among adults.

Journal: *Psychological Reports*, April 1993, *72*(2), 615–618.

• • •

7213

Test Name: ATTITUDE TOWARDS CHRISTIANITY

Purpose: To measure attitudes toward Christianity.

Number of Items: 24

Format: 5-point Likert format. All items are presented.

Reliability: Alphas ranged from .97 to .98.

Validity: Correlations with other variables ranged from -.05 to .88.

Authors: Lewis, C. A., and Maltby, J.

Article: Reliability and validity of the Francis Scale of Attitude Towards Christianity among U.S. adults.

Journal: *Psychological Reports*, June 1995, *76*(3) Part II, 1243–1247.

Related Research: Francis, L. J., & Stubbs, M. T. (1987). Measuring attitudes towards Christianity: From childhood to adulthood. *Personality and Individual Differences, 8*, 741–743.

• • •

7214

Test Name: AUSTRALIAN WORK ETHIC SCALE

Purpose: To measure commitment to the Protestant work ethic.

Number of Items: 7

Format: 4-point Likert format. Sample items are presented.

Reliability: Alphas ranged from .71 to .84.

Validity: Factor structure differed between Australia and Sri Lanka.

Author: Niles, F. S.

Article: The work ethic in Australia and Sri Lanka.

Journal: *The Journal of Social Psychology*, February 1994, *134*(1), 55–59.

Related Research: Ho, R., & Lloyd, J. L. (1984). Development of an Australian work ethic scale. *Australian Psychologist*, *19*, 321–332.

■ ■ ■

7215

Test Name: BELIEFS ABOUT ATTRACTIVENESS QUESTIONNAIRE

Purpose: To measure degree of endorsement of U.S. values regarding attractiveness and thinness.

Number of Items: 12

Format: 7-point Likert format. Sample items are presented.

Reliability: Alpha was .65.

Authors: Lester, R., and Petrie, T. A.

Article: Personality and physical correlates of bulimic symptomatology among Mexican American female college students.

Journal: *Journal of Counseling Psychology*, April 1995, *42*(2), 199–203.

Related Research: Mintz, L. B., & Betz, N. E. (1988). Prevalence and correlates of eating disordered behaviors among undergraduate women. *Journal of Counseling Psychology*, *35*, 463–471.

7216

Test Name: CHRISTIANITY ORTHODOXY SCALE

Purpose: To measure the acceptance of the central tenants of Christianity.

Number of Items: 24

Reliability: Alphas ranged from .97 to .98 across Christian samples (Catholic, Greek Orthodox, and Protestant).

Validity: Correlations with Christian Orientation Scales ranged from .04 to .66.

Authors: Johnson, R. W., et al.

Article: The Christian Orthodoxy Scale: A validity study.

Journal: *Psychological Reports*, April 1993, *72*(2), 537–538.

Related Research: Fullerton, J. T., & Hunsberger, B. E. (1982). A unidimensional measure of Christian Orthodoxy. *Journal for the Scientific Study of Religion*, *21*, 317–326.

■ ■ ■

7217

Test Name: CONFUCIAN ETHICS SCALE

Purpose: To measure Confucian ethics regarding family relations, child-rearing, and morality.

Number of Items: 13

Format: All items are presented.

Reliability: Alpha was .76.

Authors: Ma, L. C., and Smith, K.

Article: Social correlates of Confucian ethics in Taiwan.

Journal: *The Journal of Social Psychology*, October 1992, *132*(5), 655–659.

Related Research: Ma, L. C., & Smith, K. B. (1990). Social class, parental values and child-rearing practices in Taiwan. *Sociological Spectrum*, *10*, 577–586.

7218

Test Name: CONTEMPORARY WORK ETHIC SCALE

Purpose: To assess the degree to which people believe that work is a source of independence and fulfillment and is achieved through commitment and a desire to improve the community.

Number of Items: 24

Format: 5-point Likert format.

Reliability: Alpha was .76.

Authors: Ali, A. S., and Azim, A.

Article: Work ethic and loyalty in Canada.

Journal: *The Journal of Social Psychology*, February 1995, *135*(1), 31–37.

Related Research: Ali, S. (1988). Scaling an Islamic work ethic. *The Journal of Social Psychology*, *128*, 575–583.

■ ■ ■

7219

Test Name: COUNSELING AND RELIGION OPINION SURVEY

Purpose: To assess views about counseling and religion.

Number of Items: 11

Format: 5-point Likert format.

Reliability: Test–retest ranged from .50 to .86 across items.

Authors: Privette, G., et al.

Article: Preferences for religious or ronreligious counseling and psychotherapy.

Journal: *Psychological Reports*, August 1995, *74*(1) Part II, 539–546.

Related Research: Quackenbos, S. (1983). *Psychotherapy: Sacred or secular?* Unpublished Master's Thesis. The University of West Florida, Pensecola.

7220

Test Name: CURRENT LIFE ORIENTATION SCALE

Purpose: To measure the scored personal values including spirituality, validity, love, talent, and finance.

Number of Items: 90 (18 per value)

Format: Multiple choice format. Sample items presented.

Reliability: Alphas ranged from .70 to .92 across subscales. Split-half ranged from .60 to .86.

Validity: Correlations with other variables ranged from -.36 to .62.

Author: Madhere, S.

Article: The development and validation of the Current Life Orientation Scale.

Journal: *Psychological Reports*, April 1993, *72*(2), 467–472.

• • •

7221

Test Name: DISTRIBUTIVE JUSTICE EVALUATIONS SCALE

Purpose: To measure the evaluation of the rewards of status, security, opportunity for friendship, opportunity for self-actualization, and opportunity for altruism.

Number of Items: Varies by reward.

Format: Sample items are presented. Two 7-point scales (*minimum* to *maximum*) for actual rewards and how many rewards there should be.

Reliability: Reported alphas ranged from .72 to .74.

Authors: Randall, C. R., and Mueller, C. W.

Article: Extensions of justice theory: Justice evaluations and

employees' reactions in a natural setting.

Journal: *Social Psychology Quarterly*, September 1995, *58*(3), 178–194.

Related Research: Jasso, G. (1978). On the justice of earnings: A new specification of the justice evaluation function. *American Journal of Sociology*, *83*, 1398–1419.

• • •

7222

Test Name: DISTRIBUTIVE JUSTICE SCALE

Purpose: To measure distributive justice.

Number of Items: 6

Format: Examples are presented.

Reliability: Coefficient alpha was .96.

Validity: Correlations with other variables ranged from -.34 to .29.

Authors: Mossholder, K. W., et al.

Article: Confounding constructs and levels of construct in affectivity measurement: An empirical investigation.

Journal: *Educational and Psychological Measurement*, Summer 1994, *54*(2), 336–349.

Related Research: Price, J. L., & Mueller, C. W. (1986). *Handbook of organizational measurement*. Marshfield, MA: Pitman.

• • •

7223

Test Name: EQUITY SENSITIVITY INSTRUMENT

Purpose: To assess an individual's sensitivity to equity.

Number of Items: 5

Format: Responses are made on a 10-point scale.

Reliability: Alpha coefficients ranged from .77 to .83.

Authors: Patrick, S. L., and Jackson, J. J.

Article: Further examination of the equity sensitivity construct.

Journal: *Perceptual and Motor Skills*, December 1991, *73*(3) Part 2, 1091–1106.

Related Research: Huseman, R. C., et al. (1985). Test for individual perceptions of job equity: Some preliminary findings. *Perceptual and Motor Skills*, *61*, 1055–1064.

• • •

7224

Test Name: FUTURE TIME ORIENTATION SCALE

Purpose: To measure general concern, occupation, and involvement in the future.

Number of Items: 14

Format: Responses are made on a 4-point scale ranging from 4 (*is very true of me*) to 1 (*is not at all true of me*). Includes 4 dimensions: involvement, occupation, anticipation, and speed. Examples are presented.

Reliability: Coefficient alpha was .67.

Validity: Correlations with other variables ranged from -.30 to .27.

Author: Halvari, H.

Article: Maximal aerobic power as a function of achievement motives, future time orientation, and perceived intrinsic instrumentality of physical tasks for future goals among males.

Journal: *Perceptual and Motor Skills*, April 1991, *72*(2), 367–381.

Related Research: Gjesme, T. (1979). Future time orientation as a function of achievement motives, ability, delay of gratification, and sex. *Journal of Psychology, 101,* 173–188.

■ ■ ■

7225

Test Name: HELP-SEEKING ATTITUDE SCALE

Purpose: To reflect non-White cultural values or beliefs.

Number of Items: 40

Format: Responses are made on a 4-point Likert-type scale ranging from 1 (*strongly agree*) to 4 (*strongly disagree*).

Reliability: K-R 20 internal reliability estimate was .87.

Validity: Correlations with other variables ranged from -.32 to .49.

Authors: Nickerson, K. J., et al.

Article: Cultural mistrust, opinions about mental illness, and Black students' attitudes toward seeking psychological help from White counselors.

Journal: *Journal of Counseling Psychology,* July 1994, *41*(3), 378–385.

Related Research: Plotkin, R. (1983). *Measurement of help-seeking attitudes and expectations concerning psychotherapy.* Unpublished manuscript. University of North Texas, Department of Psychology, Denton.

■ ■ ■

7226

Test Name: HUMANISTIC WORK BELIEF

Purpose: To assess children's work beliefs.

Number of Items: 10

Format: Examples are presented.

Reliability: Coefficient alpha was .87.

Validity: Correlations with other variables ranged from -.06 to .26.

Authors: Barling, J., et al.

Article: Preemployment predictors of union attitudes: The role of family socialization and work beliefs.

Journal: *Journal of Applied Psychology,* October 1991, *76*(5), 725–731.

Related Research: Buchholz, R. A. (1978). An empirical study of contemporary beliefs about work in American society. *Journal of Applied Psychology, 63,* 219–227.

■ ■ ■

7227

Test Name: INDIVIDUAL BELIEFS ABOUT ORGANIZATIONAL ETHICS SCALE

Purpose: To identify the perceptions of employees' beliefs about ethical behavior within an organizational setting.

Number of Items: 10

Format: Responses are made on a 7-point Likert-type scale ranging from *1 (strongly agree)* to 7 (*strongly disagree*). All items are presented.

Reliability: Internal consistency estimate was .89.

Validity: Correlations with other variables ranged from .09 to .13.

Authors: Froelich, K. S., and Kottke, J. L.

Article: Measuring individual beliefs about organizational ethics.

Journal: *Educational and Psychological Measurement,* Summer 1991, *51*(2), 377–383.

Related Research: Brenner, S. N., & Molander, E. A. (1977, January/February). Is the ethics of business changing? *Harvard Business Review, 55,* 57–71.

Clinard, M. B., & Yeager, P .C. (1980). *Corporate crime.* New York: Free Press.

■ ■ ■

7228

Test Name: INDIVIDUALISM– COLLECTIVISM SCALE— SHORT FORM

Purpose: To measure the individualism–collectivism continuum.

Number of Items: 33

Format: All items presented.

Reliability: Alphas ranged from .38 to .73 on lower order scales and from .59 to .63 on two higher order scales.

Validity: Correlations between lower order scales ranged from -.08 to .32. The two higher order scales were not correlated.

Authors: Hui, C. H., and Yee, C.

Article: The shortened Individualism-Collectivism Scale: Its relationship to demographic and work related variables.

Journal: *Journal of Research in Personality,* December 1994, *28*(4), 409–424.

■ ■ ■

7229

Test Name: INDIVIDUALISM SCALE

Purpose: To measure individualism.

Number of Items: 7

Format: 5-point Likert format.

Reliability: Alpha was .60.

Authors: Ali, A. S., and Azim, A.

Article: Work ethic and loyalty in Canada.

Journal: *The Journal of Social Psychology,* February 1995, *135*(1), 31–37.

Related Research: Triandis, H.

(1990). *Individualism and collectivism manual.* Champaign, IL: University of Illinois.

■ ■ ■

7230

Test Name: INSTRUMENTAL NORMATIVE VALUES SCALES

Purpose: To measure instrumental normative work values.

Number of Items: 10

Format: Includes two scales: Instrumental Values and Normative Values. Responses are made on a 5-point scale ranging from 1 (*not important at all*) to 5 (*very important*). All items are presented.

Reliability: Alpha coefficients were .66 and .88.

Validity: Correlations with the Marlowe-Crown Scale (Hebrew version) were .20 and .22.

Author: Popper, M., and Lipshitz, R.

Article: "Ask not what your country can do for you": The normative basis of organizational commitment.

Journal: *Journal of Vocational Behavior*, August 1992, *41*(1), 1–12.

■ ■ ■

7231

Test Name: ISSUE INVOLVEMENT SCALE

Purpose: To assess an individual's involvement with nuclear energy as a source of electricity and with coal as a source of electricity.

Number of Items: 5

Format: Responses to each item are made on a 5-point scale ranging from 0 to 5. All items are presented.

Validity: Correlations with other variables ranged from -.02 to .38.

Author: Furlong, P. R.

Article: Personal factors influencing informal reasoning of economic issues and the effect of specific instructions.

Journal: *Journal of Educational Psychology*, March 1993, *85*(1), 171–181.

Related Research: Verplanken, B. (1989). Involvement and need for cognition as moderators of beliefs-attitude-intention consistency. *British Journal of Social Psychology*, *28*, 115–122.

■ ■ ■

7232

Test Name: JUST WORLD SCALE

Purpose: To measure the belief that good things happen to good people.

Number of Items: 20

Format: All items presented.

Reliability: Total alpha was .72. Item-total correlations ranged from -.10 to .38. Alphas for subscales ranged from .42 to .59.

Validity: Confirmatory factor analysis did not represent a good fit with prior solutions.

Author: Caputi, P.

Article: Factor structure of the Just World Scale among Australian undergraduates.

Journal: *The Journal of Social Psychology*, August 1994, *133*(4), 475–482.

Related Research: Rubin, Z., & Peplau, A. (1973). Belief in a just world and reactions to another's lot: A study of participants in the national draft lottery. *Journal of Social Issues*, *29*, 73–93.

Janof-Bulman, R. (1989). Assumptive worlds and the stress of traumatic events: Application of the schema construct. *Social Cognition*, *7*, 113–136.

7233

Test Name: MARXIST WORK BELIEFS SCALE

Purpose: To measure Marxist work beliefs.

Number of Items: 10

Reliability: Alpha coefficients were .70 (students) and .81 (parents).

Validity: Correlations with other variables ranged from .09 to .34 ($N = 69$).

Authors: Kelloway, E. K., and Watts, L.

Article: Preemployment predictors of union attitudes: Replication and extension.

Journal: *Journal of Applied Psychology*, August 1994, *79*(4), 631–634.

Related Research: Buchholz, R. A. (1978). An empirical study of contemporary beliefs about work in American society. *Journal of Applied Psychology*, *63*, 219–227.

■ ■ ■

7234

Test Name: MARXIST WORK BELIEF

Purpose: To assess children's work beliefs.

Number of Items: 11

Format: An example is presented.

Reliability: Coefficient alpha was .76.

Validity: Correlations with other variables ranged from -.02 to .47.

Authors: Barling, J., et al.

Article: Pre-employment predictors of union attitudes: The role of family socialization and work beliefs.

Journal: *Journal of Applied Psychology*, October 1991, *76*(5), 725–731.

Related Research: Buchholz, R. A.

(1978). An empirical study of contemporary beliefs about work in American society. *Journal of Applied Psychology, 63*, 219–227.

■ ■ ■

7235

Test Name: MATH–SCIENCE UTILITY SCALE

Purpose: To assess values a person holds about math and science.

Number of Items: 10

Format: 5-point Likert format.

Reliability: Alpha was .88.

Authors: Farmer, H. S., et al.

Article: Women's career choices: Focus on science, math and technology careers.

Journal: *Journal of Counseling Psychology*, April 1995, *42*(2), 155–170.

Related Research: Eccles, J., et al. (1984). Sex differences in achievement: A test of alternate theories. *Journal of Personality and Social Psychology, 46*, 26–43.

■ ■ ■

7236

Test Name: MENTAL HEALTH VALUES QUESTIONNAIRE

Purpose: To measure mental health values.

Number of Items: 99

Format: 5-point Likert format.

Reliability: Reliability ranged from .76 to .88 across subscales.

Authors: Langston, M. G., et al.

Article: Mental health values of clergy: Effects of open-mindedness, religious affiliation, and education in counseling.

Journal: *Psychological Reports*, August 1994, *75*(1) Part II, 499–506.

Related Research: Tyler, J., et al. (1983). Measuring mental health

values. *Counseling and Values, 28*, 20–30.

■ ■ ■

7237

Test Name: MORAL ORIENTATION QUESTIONNAIRE

Purpose: To measure communitarian or consequentialist moral orientations.

Number of Items: 16

Format: Forced-choice format. A sample item is presented.

Reliability: Alpha was .58.

Author: White, J.

Article: Individual characteristics and social knowledge in ethical reasoning.

Journal: *Psychological Reports*, August 1994, *75*(1) Part II, 627–649.

Related Research: White, J. A. (1992). *The role of individual characteristics and structures of social knowledge in ethical reasoning using an experiential learning framework.* Unpublished doctoral dissertation, Case Western Reserve University, Cleveland, Ohio.

■ ■ ■

7238

Test Name: NONPROTESTANT ETHIC SCALE

Purpose: To measure Protestant ethic attitudes.

Number of Items: 4

Format: All items are presented.

Reliability: Coefficient alpha was .44.

Validity: Correlations with other variables ranged from -.35 to .33.

Authors: Waters, L. K., and Zakrajsek, T.

Article: The construct validity of

four Protestant ethic attitude scales.

Journal: *Educational and Psychological Measurement*, Spring 1991, *51*(1), 117–122.

Related Research: Blood, M. R. (1969). Work values and job satisfaction. *Journal of Applied Psychology, 53*, 456–459.

■ ■ ■

7239

Test Name: ORGANIZATIONAL VALUE ORIENTATION QUESTIONNAIRE

Purpose: To measure organizational value orientation in two dimensions: normative and utilitarian.

Number of Items: 10

Format: 5-point Likert format.

Reliability: Reliabilities ranged from .85 to .91.

Validity: Correlations with other variables ranged from -.08 to .28.

Authors: Shaw, J., and Reyes, P.

Article: School cultures: Organizational value orientation and commitment.

Journal: *Journal of Educational Research*, May/June 1992, *85*(5), 295–302.

Related Research: Reyes, P. (1990). Individual work orientation and teacher outcomes. *Journal of Educational Research, 83*, 327–335.

■ ■ ■

7240

Test Name: PERSONAL BELIEFS SCALE

Purpose: To measure the relative influence of six mind–body positions in the thinking of the ordinary person.

Number of Items: 66

Format: 7-point Likert format. All items presented.

Reliability: Split-half was .83 or greater across subscales.

Validity: Subscale intercorrelations ranged from -.34 to .72.

Authors: Embree, R. A., and Embree, M. C.

Article: The Personal Beliefs Scale: A measure of individual differences in commitment to mind-body beliefs proposed by F. F. Centore.

Journal: *Psychological Reports*, October 1993, *73*(2), 411–428.

■ ■ ■

7241

Test Name: PERSONAL RELIGIOSITY INVENTORY

Purpose: To assess nine dimensions of religion.

Number of Items: 45

Format: Responses are made to 36 of the questions on a 6-point Likert scale ranging from *strongly agree* to *strongly disagree*. Nine questions are presented in a multiple-choice, yes–no format.

Reliability: Test–retest reliability coefficients ranged from .83 to .97 across the 9 scales. Internal consistency of the scales ranged from .75 to .97.

Authors: Low, C. A., and Handal, P. J.

Article: The relationship between religion and adjustment to college.

Journal: *Journal of College Student Development*, September/ October 1995, *36*(5), 406–412.

Related Research: Lipsmeyer, M. E. (1984). *The measurement of religion and its relationship to mental health impairment.* Unpublished doctoral dissertation, St. Louis University, St. Louis, Missouri.

7242

Test Name: POLARITY SCALE

Purpose: To assess humanist and normative orientations.

Number of Items: 59

Format: Items are two polar choices. A sample item is described.

Reliability: Total alpha was .77. Humanist alpha was .78. Normative alpha was .81.

Validity: Correlations with other variables ranged from -.28 to .23.

Authors: Farre, B., and Duckitt, J.

Article: The validity of Tomkin's Polarity Scale among White South Africans.

Journal: *The Journal of Social Psychology*, June 1994, *133*(3), 287–296.

■ ■ ■

7243

Test Name: PRINCIPLE-CENTERED LIVING SURVEY

Purpose: To measure principle centeredness.

Number of Items: 26

Format: 6-point Likert format. All items are presented.

Reliability: Alpha was .80. Item-total correlations ranged from .33 to .55.

Validity: Correlations with other variables ranged from .15 to .48.

Authors: Adams, T., et al.

Article: Principle-centeredness: A values clarification approach to wellness.

Journal: *Measurement and Evaluation in Counseling and Development*, October 1995, *28*(3), 139–147.

Related Research: *Seven habits*

personal profile. (1995). Covey Leadership Center.

■ ■ ■

7244

Test Name: PROPROTESTANT ETHIC SCALE

Purpose: To measure Protestant ethic attitudes.

Number of Items: 4

Format: All items are presented.

Reliability: Coefficient alpha was .68.

Validity: Correlations with other variables ranged from .11 to .60.

Authors: Waters, L. K., and Zakarajsek, T.

Article: The construct validity of four Protestant ethic attitude scales.

Journal: *Educational and Psychological Measurement*, Spring 1991, *51*(1), 117–122.

Related Research: Blood, M. R. (1969). Work values and job satisfaction. *Journal of Applied Psychology*, *53*, 456–459.

■ ■ ■

7245

Test Name: PROTESTANT WORK ETHIC QUESTIONNAIRE

Purpose: To assess the dimensionality of several Protestant work ethic scales.

Number of Items: 77

Format: Various agree–disagree formats.

Reliability: Alphas ranged from .67 to .82 across scales.

Validity: Correlations between scales ranged from -.40 to .47. Correlations with other variables ranged from -.15 to .12.

Author: Furnham, A.

Article: The Protestant work ethic in Barbados.

Journal: *The Journal of Social Psychology*, February 1991, *131*(1), 29–43.

■ ■ ■

7246

Test Name: PROTESTANT WORK ETHIC SCALE

Purpose: To measure Protestant work ethic beliefs.

Number of Items: Varied from 4 to 19 across forms administered cross-culturally.

Reliability: Alphas ranged from .67 to .82.

Validity: Correlations with other variables ranged from -.57 to .91.

Authors: Furnham, A., et al.

Article: A comparison of Protestant work ethic beliefs in thirteen nations.

Journal: *The Journal of Social Psychology*, April 1993, *133*(2), 185–197.

Related Research: Furnham, A. (1990). A content correlational and factor analytic study of seven questionnaire measures of the Protestant work ethic. *Human Relations*, *43*, 383–399.

■ ■ ■

7247

Test Name: PROTESTANT WORK ETHIC SCALE

Purpose: To measure the Protestant work ethic.

Number of Items: 19

Format: 5-point Likert format.

Reliability: Alpha was .72.

Authors: Ali, A. S., and Azim, A.

Article: Work ethic and loyalty in Canada.

Journal: *The Journal of Social*

Psychology, February 1995, *135*(1), 31–37.

Related Research: Mirels, H., & Garret, J. (1971). Protestant ethic as a personality variable. *Journal of Consulting and Clinical Psychology*, *69*, 40–44.

■ ■ ■

7248

Test Name: RELIGION–SCIENCE CONFLICT SCALE

Purpose: To measure perceived conflict between endorsing religious and scientific principles.

Number of Items: 9

Format: 5-point Likert format. All items presented.

Reliability: Cronbach's Alpha was .70.

Validity: Correlation with religious ideology was .23 and with religiosity was .26 (both $p < .01$).

Authors: Eckardt, C.I., et al.

Article: Religious beliefs and scientific ideology in psychologists: Conflicting or coexisting systems.

Journal: *Psychological Reports*, August 1992, *71*(1), 131–145.

■ ■ ■

7249

Test Name: RELIGIOSITY SCALE

Purpose: To measure degree of religiosity based on good works, ritual, beliefs, and emotional experience.

Number of Items: 8

Reliability: Alpha was .90.

Validity: Correlation with religious involvement was .80.

Authors: Sazer, L., and Kassinove, H.

Article: Effects of counselor's profanity and subject's religiosity on content acquisition of a

counseling lecture and behavioral compliance.

Journal: *Psychological Reports*, December 1991, *69*(3) Part II, 1059–1070.

Related Research: Rohrbough, J., & Jessor, R. (1975). Religiosity in youth: A personal control against deviant behavior. *Journal of Personality*, *43*, 136–155.

■ ■ ■

7250

Test Name: RELIGIOUS IDEOLOGY SCALE

Purpose: To assess endorsement of a religious point of view.

Number of Items: 10

Format: 5-point Likert format. All items presented.

Reliability: Cronbach's alpha was .93.

Validity: Correlations with a religiosity scale was .89 ($p < .001$).

Authors: Eckhardt, C. I., et al.

Article: Religious beliefs and scientific ideology in psychologists: Conflicting or coexisting systems.

Journal: *Psychological Reports*, August 1992, *71*(1), 131–145.

Related Research: Kassinove, H., & Uecke, C. I. (1991). Religious involvement and behavior therapy training: Student conflicts and ethical concerns. *The Behavior Therapist*, *14*, 148–150.

■ ■ ■

7251

Test Name: RELIGIOUS ORIENTATION SCALE

Purpose: To measure two orientations toward religion.

Format: Includes two orientations scored on a fourfold typology system.

Reliability: Reliabilities ranged from .69 to .93.

Validity: Correlations with other variables ranged from -.29 to .77.

Author: Richards, P. S.

Article: Religious devoutness in college students: Relations with emotional adjustment and psychological separation from parents.

Journal: *Journal of Counseling Psychology*, April 1991, *38*(2), 189–196.

Related Research: Donahue, M. J. (1985). Intrinsic and extrinsic religiousness: The empirical research. *Journal for the Scientific Study of Religion, 24,* 418–432.

■ ■ ■

7252

Test Name: RELIGIOUS ORIENTATION SCALE— REVISED

Purpose: To measure both intrinsic and extrinsic religious orientation.

Number of Items: 20

Format: Responses are made on a 5-point scale. Four factors have been identified: Intrinsic–Ethical, Intrinsic–Intellectual, Extrinsic–Personal, and Extrinsic–Social. All items are presented.

Reliability: Alpha coefficients ranged from .64 to .86.

Validity: Correlations with the Derogatis Sexual Functioning Inventory ranged from -.52 to .26.

Authors: Reed, L. A., and Meyers, L. S.

Article: A structural analysis of religious orientation and its relation to sexual attitudes.

Journal: *Educational and Psychological Measurement,* Winter 1991, *51*(4), 943–952.

Related Research: Allport, G. W., & Ross, J. M. (1967). Personal religious orientation and

prejudice. *Journal of Personality and Social Psychology, 5,* 432–443.

Gorsuch, R. L., & McPherson, S. (1989). Intrinsic/extrinsic measurement: I/E-revised and single-item scales. *Journal for the Scientific Study of Religion, 28,* 348–354.

■ ■ ■

7253

Test Name: ROKEACH VALUE SURVEY

Purpose: To measure terminal and instrumental values.

Number of Items: 36 (18 terminal, 18 instrumental).

Format: Respondents rank each set of 18 values from *most* to *least important.*

Reliability: Test–retest ranged from .45 to .80.

Author: Glover, R.

Article: Value selection in relation to grade in school and stage of moral reasoning.

Journal: *Psychological Reports,* June 1991, *68*(3) Part I, 931–937.

Related Research: Rokeach, M. (1973). *The nature of human values.* New York: Free Press.

■ ■ ■

7254

Test Name: SCALE TO ASSESS WORLD VIEWS (MODIFIED)

Purpose: To assess world views.

Number of Items: 20

Format: Responses are made on a 6-point scale (ranging from *do not believe at all* to *believe strongly*).

Reliability: Full scale alpha was .77.

Authors: Kwan, K. L., et al.

Article: Worldviews of Chinese

international students: An extension and new findings.

Journal: *Journal of College Student Development*, May 1994, *35*(3), 190–197.

Related Research: Ibrahim, F., and Kahn, H. (1987). Assessment of world views. *Psychological Reports, 60,* 163–176.

■ ■ ■

7255

Test Name: SOCIAL REFLECTION MEASURE— SHORT FORM

Purpose: To assess moral values.

Number of Items: 11

Format: 3-point importance scales. A sample item is presented.

Reliability: Alphas ranged from .79 to .80.

Validity: Differentiates between adolescents and adults (p < .0001).

Authors: Comunian, A. L., and Gielen, U. P.

Article: Moral reasoning and prosocial action in Italian culture.

Journal: *The Journal of Social Psychology*, December 1995, *135*(6), 699–706.

Related Research: Gibbs, J. C., et al. (1992). Construction and validation of a simplified group-administrable equivalent to the Moral Judgment Interview. *Child Development, 53,* 875–910.

■ ■ ■

7256

Test Name: STRESSFUL EVENTS/APPRAISAL FORM

Purpose: To measure the degree to which various issues are important to an individual.

Number of Items: 134

Format: Responses are made on an 8-point Likert scale ranging from *not at all* to *extremely*.

Reliability: Internal consistency ranged from .95 to .98.

Authors: Santiago-Rivera, A. L., et al.

Article: The importance of achievement and the appraisal of stressful events as predictors of coping.

Journal: *Journal of College Student Development*, July/August 1995, *36*(4), 374–383.

Related Research: Berenstein, B. L., et al. (1989, August). *Development and preliminary validation of the Scale of Central Issues.* Paper presented at the annual meeting of the American Psychological Association, New Orleans, Louisiana.

■ ■ ■

7257

Test Name: STUDENT RELIGIOSITY QUESTIONNAIRE

Purpose: To measure high school students' religiosity.

Number of Items: 20

Format: Includes two factors: Religious Principles and Religious Practices. Responses are made on a 5-point scale ranging from 1 (*minimal agreement*) to 5 (*maximal agreement*).

Reliability: Alpha coefficients ranged from .83 to .91.

Authors: Katz, Y. J., and Schneida, M.

Article: Validation of the Student Religiosity Questionnaire.

Journal: *Educational and Psychological Measurement*, Summer 1992, *52*(2), 353–356.

Related Research: Katz, Y. J. (1988). The relationship between intelligence and attitude in a bilingual society: The case of White South Africa. *Journal of Social Psychology, 128*, 65–74.

7258

Test Name: TEACHER BELIEF INVENTORY

Purpose: To measure reflectivity.

Number of Items: 7

Format: The items concern assertions about teaching and are grouped under six areas: control, diversity, learning, teacher's role, school and society, and knowledge. Responses are made on a 4-point Likert scale ranging from 1 (*strongly disagree*) to 4 (*strongly agree*).

Reliability: Test–retest reliability was .73.

Authors: Wedman, J. M., and Martin, M. W.

Article: The influence of a reflective student teaching program: An evaluation study.

Journal: *Journal of Research and Development in Education*, Winter 1990, *24*(2), 33–40.

Related Research: Posner, G. (1985). *Field experience: A guide to reflective teaching.* New York: Longman.

■ ■ ■

7259

Test Name: TRUST EXPECTANCY QUESTIONNAIRE

Purpose: To assess children's judgments about promise keeping, secret keeping, and telling the truth.

Number of Items: 12

Format: 5-point rating scales range from 1 (*not at all*) to 5 (*very much*). Sample items are presented.

Reliability: Alphas ranged from .71 to .85.

Authors: Rotenberg, K. J., and Cerda, C.

Article: Racially based trust

expectancies of Native American and Caucasian children.

Journal: *The Journal of Social Psychology*, October 1994, *133*(5), 621–631.

Related Research: Johnson-George, C., & Swop, W. C. (1982). Measurement of specific interpersonal trust: Construction and validation of a scale to assess trust in a specific other. *Journal of Personality and Social Psychology, 43*, 1306–1317.

■ ■ ■

7260

Test Name: VALUE ORIENTATION INVENTORY

Purpose: To examine teachers' educational belief structures.

Number of Items: 75

Format: Includes 5 value orientations: disciplinary mastery, ecological integration, social reconstruction, learning process, and self-actualization.

Reliability: Alpha coefficients ranged from .77 to .91.

Authors: Ennis, C. D., and Chen, A.

Article: Educational value orientations as a theoretical framework for experienced urban teachers' curricular decision making.

Journal: *Journal of Research and Development in Education*, Spring 1992, *25*(3), 156–164.

Related Research: Ennis, C. D., & Hooper, L. M. (1988). Development of an instrument for assessing educational value orientation. *Journal of Curriculum Studies, 20*, 277–280.

■ ■ ■

7261

Test Name: VALUE ORIENTATION SCALE

Purpose: To estimate health value orientations.

Number of Items: 47

Format: Includes 4 fundamental value orientations: time, activity, relational, and human nature. Responses are made on a 6-point scale ranging from 1 (*strongly disagree*) to 6 (*strongly agree*).

Validity: Correlations with other variables ranged from -.35 to .36.

Authors: Keller, C., and Bergstrom, D.

Article: Value orientations in African-American women.

Journal: *Perceptual and Motor Skills*, February 1993, *76*(1), 319–322.

Related Research: Murdaugh, C. L. (1982). *Instrument development to assess specific psychological variables explaining individual differences in preventive behaviors for coronary heart disease.* Doctoral dissertation, University of Arizona, Tucson. (University Microfilms No. 8417442).

• • •

7262

Test Name: VALUE SCALE

Purpose: To measure the intrinsic value, interest, and importance that students attribute to academic schoolwork.

Number of Items: 6

Format: Responses are made on a 5-point Likert-type scale ranging from 1 (*not at all true*) to 5 (*completely true*).

Reliability: Alpha was .81.

Validity: Correlations with other variables ranged from .31 to .55.

Authors: Goodenow, C., and Grady, K. E.

Article: The relationship of school

belonging and friends' values to academic motivation among urban adolescent students.

Journal: *Journal of Experimental Education*, Fall 1993, *62*(1), 60–71.

Related Research: Pintrich, P., & DeGroot, E. (1990). Motivational and self-regulated learning components of classroom academic performance. *Journal of Educational Psychology*, *82*, 33–40.

• • •

7263

Test Name: VALUE SURVEY

Purpose: To measure 56 values that are recognized across cultures.

Number of Items: 56

Format: 9-point importance scales. All items are presented.

Reliability: Alphas ranged from .50 to .80 across subscales.

Authors: Schwartz, S. H., and Huismans, S.

Article: Value priorities and religiosity in four Western religions.

Journal: *Social Psychology Quarterly*, June 1995, *58*(2), 88–107.

Related Research: Schwartz, S. H. (1992). Universals in the content and structure of values: Theoretical advances and empirical tests in 20 countries. In M. P. Zanna, (Ed.), *Advances in experimental social psychology, Vol. 25* (pp. 1–65). Orlando, FL: Academic Press.

• • •

7264

Test Name: WORK COMMITMENT SCALE

Purpose: To assess the centrality of work to the self.

Number of Items: 17

Format: 6-point agreement scales. Sample items presented.

Reliability: Alphas ranged from .78 to .83.

Authors: O'Neil, R., and Greenberger, E.

Article: Patterns of commitment to work and parenting: Implications for role strain.

Journal: *Journal of Marriage and the Family*, February 1994, *56*(1), 101–118.

Related Research: Safilios-Rothschild, C. (1971). Towards the conceptualization and measurement of work commitment. *Human Relations*, *42*, 489–493.

• • •

7265

Test Name: WORK SITUATIONS QUESTIONNAIRE

Purpose: To assess the intrinsic and extrinsic aspects of the obligation to work.

Number of Items: 15

Format: 5-point rating scales. All items are presented.

Reliability: Alphas ranged from .60 to .81 across two subscales. Total alpha was .82.

Author: Sagie, A.

Article: Measurement of religiosity and work obligations among Israeli youth.

Journal: *The Journal of Social Psychology*, August 1993, *133*(4), 529–537.

Related Research: Tittle, C., & Welch, M. (1983). Religiosity and deviance: Toward a contingency theory of constraining effects. *Social Forces*, *61*, 653–682.

7266

Test Name: WORK VALUES SCALE

Purpose: To measure intrinsic and extrinsic work values.

Number of Items: 11

Reliability: Alphas ranged from .44 to .66.

Validity: Correlations with other variables ranged from -.09 to .43.

Authors: Feij, J. A., et al.

Article: The development of career-enhancing strategies and content innovation: A longitudinal study of new workers.

Journal: *Journal of Vocational Behavior*, June 1995, *46*(3), 231–256.

Related Research: MOW International Research Team. (1987). *The meaning of work*. New York: The Academic Press.

CHAPTER 23
Vocational Evaluation

7267

Test Name: ATTACHMENT INTERVIEW Q-SET

Purpose: To rate interviews.

Number of Items: 100

Format: Items are sorted into 9 categories ranging from *least characteristic* to *most characteristic*.

Reliability: Spearman-Brown reliability coefficients ranged from .60 to .91.

Authors: Dozier, M., and Kobak, R. R.

Article: Psychophysiology in attachment interviews: Converging evidence for deactivating strategies.

Journal: *Child Development*, December 1992, *63*(6), 1473–1480.

Related Research: Kobak, R. R. (1989). *The Attachment Interview Q-Set.* Unpublished document, University of Delaware.

• • •

7268

Test Name: ATTRIBUTE RATING SCALE

Purpose: To assess different characteristics of supervisory interventions.

Number of Items: 10

Format: A 9-point Likert format was used. All positive poles for the 10 items are given.

Reliability: Alpha coefficients ranged from .85 to .94.

Authors: Heppner, P. P., et al.

Article: Dimensions that characterize supervisor interventions delivered in the context of live supervision of practicum counselors.

Journal: *Journal of Counseling Psychology*, April 1994, *41*(2), 227–235.

Related Research: Ellis, M. V., & Dell, D. M. (1986). Dimensionality of supervisor roles: Supervisor's perceptions of supervision. *Journal of Counseling Psychology, 33*, 282–291.

• • •

7269

Test Name: BARRETT-LENNARD RELATIONSHIP INVENTORY

Purpose: To assess counselor or client perceptions of the helping relationship.

Number of Items: 64

Format: Includes 4 subscales: Empathic Understanding, Congruence, Level of Regard, and Unconditionality of Regard.

Reliability: Split-half reliability ranged from .75 to .94; Test–retest reliability estimates ranged from .86 to .92.

Authors: Heppner, P. P., et al.

Article: Three methods in measuring the therapeutic process: Clients' and counselors' constructions of the therapeutic process versus actual therapeutic events.

Journal: *Journal of Counseling Psychology*, January 1992, *39*(1), 20–31.

Related Research: Barrett-Lennard, B. T. (1962). Dimensions of therapist response as causal factors in therapeutic change. *Psychological Monographs, 76* (43, Whole No. 562).

• • •

7270

Test Name: BARRETT-LENNARD RELATIONSHIP INVENTORY–REVISED

Purpose: To assess the client's perceptions of the counseling process.

Number of Items: 24

Format: Responses are made on a 7-point scale ranging from 1 (*disagree*) to 7 (*agree*).

Reliability: Consistency of subscales ranged from .53 to .82.

Authors: Wade, P., and Bernstein, B. L.

Article: Culture sensitivity training and counselor's race: Effects on Black female clients' perceptions and attrition.

Journal: *Journal of Counseling Psychology*, January 1991, *38*(1), 9–15.

Related Research: Strong, S. R., et al. (1979). Motivational and equipping functions of interpretation in counseling. *Journal of Counseling Psychology, 26*, 98–107.

7271

Test Name: BEHAVIORAL SURVEY OF MENTOR BEHAVIOR.

Purpose: To assess mentor behavior in the mentor–protegé relationship.

Number of Items: 195

Time Required: 1 hour.

Format: Yes–no format followed by 5-point Likert format with ranging from 1 (*not very often*) to 5 (*very often*).

Reliability: Alphas ranged from .72 to .90 across factorially derived subscales.

Validity: Correlations with other variables ranged from .12 to .47.

Author: Pollock, R.

Article: A test of conceptual models depicting the developmental course of informal mentor-protegé relationships in the work place.

Journal: *Journal of Vocational Behavior*, April 1995, *46*(2), 144–162.

■ ■ ■

7272

Test Name: CAREER COUNSELOR WORK ACTIVITY QUESTIONNAIRE

Purpose: To determine whether career counselors engage in certain activities and also to determine whether they should engage in these activities.

Number of Items: 40

Format: Two versions: Student and Counselor. Responses are either *Yes, No,* or *I don't know.* All items are presented.

Reliability: Alpha coefficients were .86 and .83. KR-20 (for questions 1 and 2) correlations were .86 and .83.

Authors: Olson, T. F., and Matkin, R. E.

Article: Student and counselor perceptions of career counselor work activities in a community college.

Journal: *The Career Development Quarterly*, June 1994, *40*(4), 324–333.

Related Research: Herr, E. L., & Cramer, S. H. (1988). *Career guidance and counseling through the life span* (3rd ed.). Boston: Little, Brown.

Nyre, G. F., & Reilly, K. C. (1987). *A study of career/ vocational counseling in California community colleges.* Santa Clara, CA: C/VEG Publications.

■ ■ ■

7273

Test Name: CAREER SUPPORT SCALE—MODIFIED.

Purpose: To measure mentoring.

Number of Items: 24

Format: 5-point Likert format.

Reliability: Subscale alphas exceeded .80.

Validity: Correlations with other variables ranged from .12 to .47.

Author: Pollock, R.

Article: A test of conceptual models depicting the developmental course of informal mentor-protegé relationships in the work place.

Journal: *Journal of Vocational Behavior*, April 1995, *46*(2), 144–162.

Related Research: Riley, S., & Wrench, D. (1985). Mentoring among women lawyers. *Journal of Applied Social Psychology*, 15, 374–386.

■ ■ ■

7274

Test Name: CAREGIVER SUPPORTIVE BEHAVIOR

Purpose: To measure how likely

one's child's caregiver would be to help out.

Number of Items: 45

Format: Includes 5 subscales: Emotional Support, Socializing, Practical Assistance, Financial Assistance, and Advice/Guidance. All items are presented.

Reliability: Coefficient alphas ranged from .93 to .98. Test–retest (3 weeks) reliability coefficients ranged from .87 to .92.

Validity: Correlations with other variables ranged from .23 to .50.

Author: Caruso, G.-A. L.

Article: The development of three scales to measure the supportiveness of relationships between parents and child care providers.

Journal: *Educational and Psychological Measurement*, Spring 1992, *52*(1), 149–160.

Related Research: Vaux, A., et al. (1987). Modes of social support: The social support behaviors (SS-B) scale. *American Journal of Community Psychology*, *15*, 209–237.

■ ■ ■

7275

Test Name: CLASSROOM PROCEDURES EVALUATION FORM

Purpose: To enable student teaching supervisors to rate student teachers' classroom behavior.

Number of Items: 40

Format: Responses are made on a 5-point Likert scale. All items are presented.

Reliability: KR-21 coefficient was .83.

Validity: Selected item correlations with the Myers-Briggs Type Indicator ranged from –.56 to .31.

Authors: McCutcheon, J. W., et al.

Article: Relationships among selected personality variables, academic achievement and student teaching behavior.

Journal: *Journal of Research and Development in Education*, Spring 1991, *24*(3), 38–44.

• • •

7276

Test Name: CLIENT ATTACHMENT TO THERAPIST SCALE

Purpose: To measure psychotherapy relationships.

Number of Items: 36

Format: 6-point Likert format. All items are presented.

Reliability: Alphas ranged from .64 to .81 across subscales. Test–retest reliabilities ranged from .72 to .86.

Validity: Correlations with other variables ranged from -.71 to .82.

Authors: Mallinckrodt, B., et al.

Article: Attachment patterns in the psychotherapy relationship: Development of the Client Attachment to Therapist Scale.

Journal: *Journal of Counseling Psychology*, July 1995, *42*(3), 307–317.

• • •

7277

Test Name: CLIENT CHANGE INVENTORY

Purpose: To assess counseling outcome.

Number of Items: 30

Format: Includes 8 subscales: Life Adjustment, Self-Concept, Communication Skills, Interpersonal Relationships, Attitudes Toward Therapy, Client–Therapist Relationship, Client Insight, and Time-Limited

Therapy. Responses are made on a 7-point scale ranging from 1 (*strongly disagree*) to 7 (*strongly agree*).

Reliability: Test–retest reliabilities ranged from .70 to .94.

Authors: Hoyt, W. T., et al.

Article: Interpersonal influence in a single case of brief counseling: An analytic strategy and a comparison of two indexes of influence.

Journal: *Journal of Counseling Psychology*, April 1993, *40*(2), 166–181.

Related Research: Adelstein, D. M., et al. (1983). The change process following time-limited therapy. In C. J. Gelso & D. H. Johnson (Eds.), *Explorations in time-limited counseling and psychotherapy* (pp. 63–81). New York: Teachers College Press.

• • •

7278

Test Name: CLIENT EVALUATION OF COUNSELOR SCALE

Purpose: To enable clients to evaluate counselors.

Number of Items: 10

Format: Uses a 5-point scale.

Reliability: Alpha coefficients ranged from .91 to .94.

Authors: Dansereau, D. F., et al.

Article: Node-link mapping: A visual representation strategy for enhancing drug abuse counseling.

Journal: *Journal of Counseling Psychology*, October 1993, *40*(4), 385–395.

Related Research: Corrigan, J. D., et al. (1980). Counseling as a social influence process: A review [Monograph]. *Journal of Counseling Psychology*, 27, 395–441.

7279

Test Name: CLIENT RESISTANCE SCALE

Purpose: To measure client resistance.

Number of Items: 35

Format: Includes 5 subscales: Opposing Expression of Painful Affect, Opposing Recollection of Material, Opposing Therapist, Opposing Change, and Opposing Insight. All items are presented.

Reliability: The range of reliabilities for the individual sessions ranged from a mean of .55 to a mean of .96.

Author: Mahalik, J. R.

Article: Development of the Client Resistance Scale.

Journal: *Journal of Counseling Psychology*, January 1994, *41*(1), 58–68.

Related Research: Mahalik, J. R. (1992). *Manual for the Client Resistance Scale.* Unpublished manuscript, Boston College, Chestnut Hill, Massachusetts.

• • •

7280

Test Name: COMPLUTENSE UNIVERSITY TEACHERS EVALUATION QUESTIONNAIRE

Purpose: To measure two fundamental dimensions of teaching quality.

Number of Items: 22

Format: Includes 2 factors: Teaching Competence and Motivational Skills. All items are presented.

Reliability: Alpha coefficients ranged from .93 to .98.

Authors: Fernandez, J., and Mateo, M. A.

Article: Students' evaluation of university teaching quality:

Analysis of a questionnaire for a sample of university students in Spain.

Journal: *Educational and Psychological Measurement*, Autumn 1992, *52*(3), 675–686.

Related Research: Angulo, F., et al. (1987). *La evaluación de la enseñanza universitaria.* Madrid: Instituto de Ciencias de la Educación.

* * *

7281

Test Name: COMPUTER RATING FORM

Purpose: To assess perceptions of counselor behavior in a variety of conditions and contexts.

Number of Items: 36

Format: Includes 3 scales: Expertness, Attractiveness, and Trustworthiness.

Reliability: Split-half reliability coefficients ranged from .85 to .91.

Authors: Sampson, J. P., Jr., et al.

Article: The social influence of two computer-assisted career guidance systems: Discover and SIGI.

Journal: *The Career Development Quarterly*, September 1992, *41*(1), 75–83.

Related Research: LaCrosse, M. B., & Barak, A. (1976). Differential perception of counselor behavior. *Journal of Counseling Psychology*, *23*, 170–172.

* * *

7282

Test Name: CONSULTANT EVALUATION FORM.

Purpose: To gather consultees' perceptions of consultation outcomes.

Number of Items: 12

Format: Responses are made on a 7-point Likert scale, 1 representing *strongly disagree* and 7 representing *strongly agree*.

Reliability: Coefficient alpha was .95.

Authors: Hughes, J. N., and Deforest, P.

Article: Consultant directiveness and support as predictors of consultation outcomes.

Journal: *Journal of School Psychology*, Fall 1993, *31*(3), 355–373.

Related Research: Erchul, W. P. (1987). A relational communication analysis of control in school consultation. *Professional School Psychology*, 113–124.

* * *

7283

Test Name: COUNSELING EVALUATION INVENTORY

Purpose: To rate counselors.

Number of Items: 68

Format: Employs a 5-point Likert scale ranging from 1 (*never*) to 5 (*always*). A sample item is presented.

Reliability: Median test–retest reliability coefficient was .83.

Author: Freund, R. D., et al.

Article: Influence of length of delay between intake session and initial counseling session on client perception of counselor's and counseling outcomes.

Journal: *Journal of Counseling Psychology*, January 1991, *38*(1), 3–8.

Related Research: Linden, J. D., et al. (1965). Development and evaluation of an inventory for rating counseling. *Personnel and Guidance Journal*, *44*, 267–276.

7284

Test Name: COUNSELING OUTCOME QUESTIONNAIRE

Purpose: To measure the therapist's perceptions concerning client's changes in feelings, behavior, insight, and overall change made during counseling.

Number of Items: 4

Format: Likert-type scale ranging from 1 (*much worse*) to 7 (*much improved*).

Reliability: Test–retest (2–3 weeks) reliability ranged from .63 to .81.

Validity: Correlations of counselors' and clients' ratings ranged from .14 to .50.

Authors: Quintana, S. M., and Holahan, W.

Article: Termination in short-term counseling: Comparison of successful and unsuccessful cases.

Journal: *Journal of Counseling Psychology*, July 1992, *39*(3), 299–305.

Related Research: Adelstein, D. M., et al. (1983). The change process following time-limited therapy. In C. J. Gelso & D. H. Johnson (Eds.), *Explorations in time-limited counseling and psychotherapy.* New York: Teachers College, Columbia University.

* * *

7285

Test Name: COUNSELOR COMPETENCE SCALE

Purpose: To assess counselor competence.

Number of Items: 5

Format: Each of the 5 items is noted on a 7-point scale.

Reliability: Coefficient alpha was .88.

Author: Schneider, L. J.

Article: Effects of counselors' smoking behavior and the intimacy level of clients' presenting concerns on nonsmokers' perceptions of counselors.

Journal: *Journal of Counseling Psychology*, July 1992, *39*(3), 313–316.

Related Research: Dowd, E. T., & Boroto, D. R. (1982). Differential effects of counselor self-disclosure, self-involving statements, and interpretations. *Journal of Counseling Psychology, 29*, 8–13.

■ ■ ■

7286

Test Name: COUNSELOR EFFECTIVENESS RATING SCALE–MODIFIED

Purpose: To measure counselor effectiveness.

Number of Items: 10

Format: Items measured: Expertness, Attractiveness, Trustworthiness, and Counselor Utility. Items are in the semantic differential format. Items are rated on a scale from 1 (*bad*) to 7 (*good*).

Validity: Correlation with the Counselor Rating Form was .80.

Authors: Merta, R. J., et al.

Article: Comparing the effectiveness of two directive styles in the academic counseling of foreign students.

Journal: *Journal of Counseling Psychology*, April 1992, *39*(2), 214–218.

Related Research: Atkinson, D. R., & Wampold, B. E. (1982). A comparison of the Counseling Rating Form and Counselor Effectiveness Rating Scale. *Counselor Education and Supervision, 22*, 25–36.

7287

Test Name: COUNSELOR EFFECTIVENESS SCALE

Purpose: To measure the client's overall satisfaction with counseling.

Number of Items: 21

Format: Items are rated on a 5-point Likert type scale ranging from 1 (*always*) to 5 (*never*). Three dimensions are measured: counseling climate, counselor comfort, and client satisfaction.

Reliability: Test–retest reliability was .74.

Authors: Wade, P., and Bernstein, B. L.

Article: Culture sensitivity training and counselor's race: effects on Black female client's perceptions and attrition.

Journal: *Journal of Counseling Psychology*, January 1991, *38*(1), 9–15.

Related Research: Linden, J. D., et al. (1965). Development and evaluation of an inventory for rating counseling. *Personnel and Guidance Journal, 44*, 267–276.

■ ■ ■

7288

Test Name: COUNSELOR EVALUATION OF SUPERVISOR FORM—MODIFIED

Purpose: To evaluate both the supervisor trainees and the trainer.

Number of Items: 41

Format: Responses are made on a 9-point scale ranging from 1 (*strongly disagree)* to 9 (*strongly agree*).

Reliability: Alpha was .96.

Authors: Ellis, M. V.

Article: Critical incidents in clinical supervision and in supervisor

supervision: Assessing supervisory issues.

Journal: *Journal of Counseling Psychology*, July 1991, *38*(3), 342–349

Related Research: Borders, L. D., & Leddick, G. R. (1987). *Handbook of counseling supervision.* Alexandria, VA: American Association for Counseling and Development.

■ ■ ■

7289

Test Name: COUNSELOR EVALUATION RATING SCALE

Purpose: To assess the performance and progress of trainees in counseling and supervision.

Number of Items: 26

Format: Responses are made on a 7-point Likert Scale.

Reliability: Test–retest reliability was .94. A split-half coefficient was .95.

Authors: Newman, J. L., and Fuqua, D. R.

Article: Effects of order of presentation on perceptions of the counselor.

Journal: *Journal of Counseling Psychology*, October 1992, *39*(1), 550–554.

Related Research: Myrick, R. D., & Kelly, F. D. (1971). A scale for evaluating practicum students in counseling and supervision. *Counselor Education and Supervision, 10*, 330–336.

■ ■ ■

7290

Test Name: COUNSELOR PREFERENCE INVENTORY

Purpose: To identify counselor preference.

Number of Items: 10

Format: The respondents address

each problem by providing a rating on each of 6 preferences. A 5-point Likert scale ranging from 1 (*strongly disagree*) to 5 (*strongly agree*) is used. An example is presented.

Reliability: Alpha coefficients ranged from .79 to .90.

Authors: Helms, J. E., and Carter, R. T.

Article: Relationships of White and Black racial identity attitudes and demographic similarity to counselor preferences.

Journal: *Journal of Counseling Psychology*, October 1991, *38*(4), 446–457

Related Research: Parham, T. A., & Helms, J. E. (1981). The influence of Black students' racial identity attitudes on preferences for counselor's race. *Journal of Counseling Psychology*, *28*, 250–257.

Westbrook, F. D., et al. (1978). Perceived problem areas by Black and White students and hints about comparative counseling needs. *Journal of Counseling Psychology*, *25*, 119–123.

■ ■ ■

7291

Test Name: COUNSELOR RATING FORM

Purpose: To rate the counselor.

Number of Items: 36

Format: Items are bipolar adjective pairs that describe counselor behavior. Employs a 7-point Likert-type scale. Includes three subscales: Counselor Expertness, Attractiveness, and Trustworthiness.

Reliability: Split-half reliabilities ranged from .85 to .91.

Authors: Freund, R. D., et al.

Article: Influence of length of delay between intake session and initial

counseling session on client perceptions of counselors and counseling outcomes.

Journal: *Journal of Counseling Psychology*, January 1991, *38*(1), 3–8.

Related Research: Heppner, P. P., & Claiborn, C. D. (1989). Social influence research in counseling: A review and critique. *Journal of Counseling Psychology*, *36*, 365–387.

■ ■ ■

7292

Test Name: COUNSELING RATING FORM—SHORT FORM

Purpose: To rate counselor characteristics including expertness, attractiveness, and trustworthiness.

Number of Items: 12

Format: 7-point summed rating scales for each of 12 descriptive adjectives.

Reliability: Split-half reliabilities ranged from .87 to .91.

Validity: Correlations between subscales ranged from .48 to .72.

Authors: Glidden-Tracey, C. E., and Wagner, L.

Article: Gender Salient Attribute x Treatment interaction effects on ratings of two analogue counselors.

Journal: *Journal of Counseling Psychology*, April 1995, *42*(2), 223–231.

Related Research: Corrigan, J. D., & Schmidt, L. D. (1983). Development and validation of revisions in the Counselor Rating Form. *Journal of Counseling Psychology*, *30*, 64–75.

■ ■ ■

7293

Test Name: COUNSELOR RATING FORM

Purpose: To measure perceptions of a counselor in three dimensions: Expertness, Attractiveness, and Trustworthiness.

Number of Items: 36

Format: 7-point semantic differential format.

Reliability: Reliabilities ranged from .85 to .91.

Validity: Correlations with other variables ranged from .53 to .57.

Authors: Miller, M. J., et al.

Article: Effects of structuring on students' perceptions of career counseling.

Journal: *The Career Development Quarterly*, March 1995, *43*(3), 233–239.

Related Research: LaCrosse, M. F. (1980). Perceived counselor social influence and counseling outcomes: Validity of the counselor rating form. *Journal of Counseling Psychology*, *27*, 320–327.

■ ■ ■

7294

Test Name: COUNTERTRANSFERENCE FACTORS INVENTORY— MODIFIED

Purpose: To measure countertransference management ability.

Number of Items: 21

Format: 5-point importance scales.

Reliability: Alphas ranged from .71 to .92 across subscales. Total alpha was .93.

Authors: Gelso, C. J., et al.

Article: Countertransference reaction in lesbian clients: The role of homophobia, counselor gender and countertransference management.

Journal: *Journal of Counseling Psychology*, July 1995, *42*(3), 356–364.

Related Research: Hayes, J. A., et al. (1991). Managing countertransference: What the experts think. *Psychological Reports*, *69*, 139–148.

■ ■ ■

7295

Test Name: COUNTERTRANSFERENCE FACTOR INVENTORY

Purpose: To measure factors important in a therapists' management of countertransference reactions: self-integration, anxiety management, conceptualizing skills, empathy, and self-insight.

Number of Items: 50

Format: 5-point Likert format. All items presented.

Reliability: Alphas ranged from .88 to .97 across subscales.

Authors: Hayes, J. A., et al.

Article: Managing countertransference: What the experts think.

Journal: *Psychological Reports*, August 1991, *69*(1), 139–148.

Related Research: Cutler, R. L. (1958). Countertransference effects in psychotherapy. *Journal of Consulting Psychology*, *22*, 349–356.

■ ■ ■

7296

Test Name: COURSE EVALUATION QUESTIONNAIRE

Purpose: To evaluate instructor and course.

Number of Items: 15

Format: Likert format. All items presented.

Reliability: Alpha was .91.

Author: Rohde, R. I.

Article: Effect of word processing on student grades and evaluation of instruction in freshman composition.

Journal: *Psychological Reports*, June 1993, *72*(3) Part II, 1259–1274.

Related Research: Chase, C. I., & Keene, J. M. (1979). *Validity of student ratings of faculty* (Tech. Rep. No. 40). Bloomington: Indiana University, Indiana Studies of Higher Education.

■ ■ ■

7297

Test Name: CROSS-CULTURAL COUNSELING INVENTORY— REVISED

Purpose: To assess respondents' perceptions of a counselor's cultural competence.

Number of Items: 20

Format: Responses are made on a 6-point bipolar scale ranging from 1 (*strongly disagree*) to 6 (*strongly agree*). Examples are presented.

Reliability: Alpha coefficients were .78 and .95.

Authors: Atkinson, D. R., et al.

Article: Mexican-American acculturation, counselor ethnicity and cultural sensitivity, and perceived counselor competence.

Journal: *Journal of Counseling Psychology*, October 1992, *39*(4), 515–520.

Related Research: LaFromboise, T. D., et al. (1991). Development and factor structure of the cross-cultural counseling inventory-revised. *Professional Psychology: Research and Practice*, *22*, 380-388.

7298

Test Name: DISTRIBUTIONAL RATING SCALE

Purpose: To indicate the percentage of lecturing time for each performance level.

Number of Items: 10

Format: Responses are made on a 7-point scale.

Reliability: Internal consistency was .89.

Authors: Steiner, D. D., et al.

Article: Distributional ratings of performance: Further examination of a new rating format.

Journal: *Journal of Applied Psychology*, June 1993, *78*(3), 438–442.

Related Research: Jako, R. A., & Murphy, K. R. (1990). Distributional ratings, judgment decomposition, and their impact on interrater agreement and rating accuracy. *Journal of Applied Psychology*, *75*, 500–505.

■ ■ ■

7299

Test Name: EXCHANGE APPROVAL SCALE

Purpose: To assess distribution satisfaction with salespersons.

Number of Items: 5

Format: 5-point rating scale.

Reliability: Alpha ranged from .76 to .91.

Authors: Zemanek, J. E., and McIntyre, R. P.

Article: Power, dependence and satisfaction in a marketing system.

Journal: *Psychological Reports*, December 1995, *77*(3) Part II, 1155–1158.

Related Research: Gaski, J. F., & Nevin, J. (1985). The differential effects of exercised and unexercised power sources in a marketing channel. *Journal of Marketing Research, 22,* 130–142.

■ ■ ■

7300

Test Name: FACILITATIVE RELATIONSHIP INDICATORS CHECKLIST

Purpose: To measure counselor behavior.

Number of Items: 13

Format: Checklist format for eight nonverbal behaviors and five verbal behaviors.

Reliability: Interrater agreement was .96.

Author: Neidigh, L. W.

Article: An experimental analogue examining effects of facilitative behaviors and subjects' warmth on students' perceptions of a counseling relationship.

Journal: *Psychological Reports,* June 1991, *68*(3) Part II, 1099–1106.

Related Research: Barker, K., & Neidigh, L. W. (1990). *Development of the Facilitative Relationship Indicators Checklist.* Paper presented at the meeting of the 36th Annual Southeastern Psychological Association, Atlanta, Georgia.

■ ■ ■

7301

Test Name: HIREES ADJECTIVAL CHARACTERIZATIONS SCALES

Purpose: To discuss characterizations of hirees.

Number of Items: 11

Format: Contains 9-point bipolar adjectives describing hiree's activity, potency, and

interpersonal characteristics. All items are presented.

Reliability: Alpha coefficients ranged from .82 to .88.

Validity: Correlations with presumed role of affirmative action in hiring decisions ranged from -.81 to .03.

Authors: Heilman, M. E., et al.

Articles: Presumed incompetent? Stigmatization and affirmative action efforts.

Journal: *Journal of Applied Psychology,* August 1992, *77*(4), 536–544.

■ ■ ■

7302

Test Name: IMPORTANT EVENTS QUESTIONNAIRE

Purpose: To identify important events relative to the counseling session.

Number of Items: 5

Format: Five categories of responses are identified. All questions are presented.

Reliability: Interjudge agreement coefficients ranged from .80 to .89.

Authors: Cummings, A. L., et al.

Article: Session evaluation and recall of important events as a function of counselor experience.

Journal: *Journal of Counseling Psychology,* April 1993, *40*(2), 156–165.

Related Research: Cummings, A. L., et al. (1992). Memory for therapeutic events, session effectiveness, and working alliance in short-term counseling. *Journal of Counseling Psychology, 39,* 306–312.

■ ■ ■

7303

Test Name: INDEX OF INTERVIEWER CREDIBILITY

Purpose: To evaluate three aspects of the interviewer's image.

Number of Items: 6

Format: Items contain bipolar pairs of adjectives rated on a 7-point scale. The three aspects of interviewer's image are trustworthiness, qualification, and dynamism. All adjective pairs are presented.

Reliability: Alpha coefficients ranged from .76 to .89.

Author: Schneider, L. J.

Article: Effects of counselors' smoking behavior and the intimacy level of clients' presenting concerns on nonsmokers' perceptions of counselors.

Journal: *Journal of Counseling Psychology,* July 1992, *39*(3), 313–316.

Related Research: Berlo, D. K., et al. (1969–1970). Dimensions for evaluating the acceptability of message sources. *Public Opinion Quarterly, 33,* 563–576.

■ ■ ■

7304

Test Name: JOB PERFORMANCE RATING SCALE

Purpose: To enable supervisors to rate job performance.

Number of Items: 33

Format: Includes 11 dimensions: job knowledge, quality of work, quantity of work, initiative, customer communications, organizational commitment, job commitment, planning and allocation, interpersonal orientation, self-development, and account management. Responses are made on a 5-point scale ranging from 5 (*consistently exceeds job requirements*) to 1 (*somewhat below job requirements*).

Reliability: Coefficient alpha was

.75. Average interrater reliability was .50.

Validity: Correlations with other variables ranged from -.09 to .34.

Authors: Barrick, M. R., et al.

Article: Conscientiousness and performance of sales representatives: Test of the mediating effects of goal setting.

Journal: *Journal of Applied Psychology*, October 1993, *78*(5), 715–722.

■ ■ ■

7305

Test Name: JOB PERFORMANCE SCALE

Purpose: To measure job performance.

Number of Items: 11

Format: Responses are made on a 5-point Likert scale (*consistently exceeds job requirements* to *somewhat below job requirements*).

Reliability: Alpha coefficient was .86.

Authors: Barrick, M. R., et al.

Article: Antecedents of involuntary turnover due to a reduction in force.

Journal: *Personnel Psychology*, Autumn 1994, *47*(3), 515–535.

Related Research: Barrick, M. R., et al. (1993). Conscientiousness and performance of sales representatives: A test of the mediating effects of goal setting. *Journal of Applied Psychology*, *78*, 715–722.

■ ■ ■

7306

Test Name: LOGIC OF CONFIDENCE QUESTIONNAIRE

Purpose: To determine the

teachers' perceptions of their principal's logic of confidence.

Number of Items: 29

Format: Responses are made on a 6-point scale ranging from *disagree strongly* to *agree strongly*. Includes three dimensions: professionalism, avoidance, and overlooking.

Reliability: Alpha coefficients ranged from .71 to .81.

Authors: Okeafor K. R., and Frere, R. M.

Article: Administrators' confidence in teachers, leader consideration, and coupling in schools.

Journal: *Journal of Research and Development in Education*, Summer 1992, *25*(4), 204–212.

Related Research: Okeafor, K., et al. (1987). Toward an operational definition of the logic of confidence. *The Journal of Experimental Education*, *56*(1), 47–54.

■ ■ ■

7307

Test Name: MENTORING FUNCTIONS SCALE

Purpose: To assess mentoring functions.

Number of Items: 15

Format: Includes 3 factors: Psycho-Social Support, Career Development, and Role Modeling. All items are presented.

Reliability: Alpha coefficients ranged from .70 to .81.

Validity: Correlations with other variables ranged from -.07 to .18.

Authors: Scandura, T. A., and Ragins, B. R.

Article: The effects of sex and gender role orientation on mentorship in male-dominated occupations.

Journal: *Journal of Vocational*

Behavior, December 1993, *43*(3), 251–265.

Related Research: Scandura, T. A. (1992). Mentorship and career mobility: An empirical investigation. *Journal of Organizational Behavior*, *13*, 169–174.

■ ■ ■

7308

Test Name: MENTOR–PROTEGE RELATIONSHIP QUESTIONNAIRE

Purpose: To measure mentor–protégé relationships.

Number of Items: 18

Format: Includes 3 dimensions: career functions, role modeling, and psychosocial. Responses are made on a 5-point scale ranging from 1 (*not at all*) to *5 (to a very great extent*). Sample items are presented.

Reliability: Alpha coefficients ranged from .72 to .90.

Author: Fagenson, E. A.

Article: Mentoring—Who needs it? A comparison of protegés' and nonprotcgés' needs for power, achievement, affiliation, and autonomy.

Journal: *Journal of Vocational Behavior*, August 1992, *41*(1), 48–60.

Related Research: Scandura, T. A., & Katterberg, R. J. (1988). *Much ado about mentors and little ado about measurement: Development of an instrument.* Paper presented at the Academy of Management Conference, Anaheim, California.

■ ■ ■

7309

Test Name: MENTOR SCALE

Purpose: To measure respondents' perceptions of mentor functions.

Number of Items: 21

Format: Responses are made on a 5-point Likert scale.

Reliability: Coefficient alphas for the two scales were .84 (psychosocial) and .79 (career-related).

Authors: Chao, G. T., et al.

Article: Formal and informal mentorships: A comparison on mentoring functions and contrast with nonmentored counterparts.

Journal: *Personnel Psychology*, Fall 1992, *45*(3), 619–636.

Related Research: Noe, R. A. (1988). An investigation of the determinants of successful assigned mentoring relationships. *Personnel Psychology*, *41*, 457–479.

■ ■ ■

7310

Test Name: MENTORSHIP VS. SUPERVISORY RELATIONSHIP SCALES

Purpose: To assess mentorship and supervisory relationships.

Number of Items: 165

Format: Varied. Unspecified.

Reliability: Reliabilities ranged from .15 to .92 across subscales. Reliabilities of six scales derived from factor analysis ranged from .54 to .89.

Authors: Burke, R. J., et al.

Article: How do mentorships differ from typically supervisory relationships?

Journal: *Psychological Reports*, April 1991, *68*(2), 459–466.

Related Research: Lindholm, J. (1985). *A comparison of mentoring relationships and typical subordinates: The mentor's perspective*. Paper presented at the annual meeting of the American Academy of

Management, San Diego, California.

■ ■ ■

7311

Test Name: MULTICULTURAL COUNSELING INVENTORY

Purpose: To measure multicultural counseling competencies.

Number of Items: 40

Format: Includes 4 factors: Multicultural Counseling Skills, Multicultural Awareness, Multicultural Counseling Relationship, and Multicultural Knowledge. Responses are made on a 4-point scale ranging from 4 (*very accurate*) to 1 (*very inaccurate*).

Reliability: Alpha coefficients ranged from .67 to .86.

Authors: Sodowsky, G. R., et al.

Article: Development of the Multicultural Counseling Inventory: A self-report measure of multicultural competencies.

Journal: *Journal of Counseling Psychology*, April 1994, *41*, 137–148.

Related Research: Sue, D. W., et al. (1992). Multicultural competencies and standards: A call to the professional. *Journal of Counseling and Development*, *70*, 477–486.

■ ■ ■

7312

Test Name: NORMATIVE PATTERNS SCALES

Purpose: To assess normative patterns in college teaching.

Number of Items: 21

Format: 5-point scales. All items are presented.

Reliability: Alphas ranged from .52 to .85 across subscales and across samples of faculty and teaching assistants.

Authors: Braxton, J. M., et al.

Article: Anticipatory socialization of undergraduate teaching norms by entering graduate teaching assistants.

Journal: *Research in Higher Education*, December 1995, *36*(6), 671–686.

Related Research: Braxton, J. M., et al. (1992). Teaching performance norms in academia. *Research in Higher Education*, *33*, 533–569.

■ ■ ■

7313

Test Name: PEER COUNSELING CONSUMER SATISFACTION QUESTIONNAIRE

Purpose: To measure the overall client satisfaction with peer counselors.

Format: Uses a 5-point Likert Scale format. Scores range from 4 to 20.

Reliability: Coefficient alpha was .94.

Authors: Morey, R., and Miller, C.

Article: High school peer counseling: The relationship between student satisfaction and peer counselors' style of helping.

Journal: *The School Counselor*, January 1993, *40*(3), 293–300.

Related Research: Morey, R., & Miller, C. (1987). *Peer Counseling Consumer Satisfaction Questionnaire*. Atascedero, CA: Author.

■ ■ ■

7314

Test Name: PERCEIVED CONTROL SCALE

Purpose: To provide an indication of the perceived control that the client and the therapist had.

Number of Items: 8

Format: Responses are made on a 7-point scale ranging from 1 (*very strongly disagree*) to 7 (*very strongly agree*).

Reliability: Alpha coefficients ranged from .64 to .88; interrater reliability coefficients ranged from .45 to .97.

Validity: Correlations with other variables ranged from -.23 to .62.

Author: Tracey, T. J.

Article: The structure of control and influence in counseling and psychotherapy: A comparison of several definitions and measures.

Journal: *Journal of Counseling Psychology*, July 1991, *38*(3), 265–278.

■ ■ ■

7315

Test Name: PERFORMANCE JUDGMENT SCALE

Purpose: To judge the lecturer's performance in 8 areas.

Number of Items: 8

Format: Responses are made on a 5-point scale ranging from 1 (*very bad*) to 5 (*very good*).

Reliability: Test–retest reliability ranged from .18 to .43.

Validity: Correlations with the Behavior Rating Scale ranged from .06 to .70.

Authors: Murphy, K. R., and Anhalt, R. L.

Article: Is halo error a property of the rater, ratees, or the specific behaviors observed?

Journal: *Journal of Applied Psychology*, August 1992, *77*(4), 494–500.

Related Research: Murphy, K. R., & Reynolds, D. H. (1988). Does true halo affect observed halo? *Journal of Applied Psychology*, *73*, 1–4.

7316

Test Name: PRIMARY GRADE PUPIL REPORT

Purpose: To allow primary children to rate teacher effectiveness.

Number of Items: 11

Format: Respondents mark "smile" faces if the statement read was like their teacher and "frown" faces of the statement read was unlike their teacher.

Reliability: Test–retest using Scott's pi was .92. Kuder-Richardson internal consistency reliability estimate was .81.

Author: Follman, J.

Article: Elementary public school pupil rating of teacher effectiveness.

Journal: *Child Study Journal*, March 1995, *25*(1), 57–78.

Related Research: Driscoll, A., et al. (1985). Student reports for primary teacher evaluation. *Educational Research Quarterly*, *9*, 43–50.

■ ■ ■

7317

Test Name: PROCESS OF CHANGE QUESTIONNAIRE

Purpose: To measure 10 processes of change.

Number of Items: 40

Format: 5-point Likert format.

Reliability: Internal consistency ranged from .78 to .91.

Authors: Smith, K. J., et al.

Article: The transtheoretical model's stages and processes of change and their relation to premature termination.

Journal: *Journal of Counseling Psychology*, January 1995, *42*(1), 34–39.

Related Research: Prochaska, J.

O., et al. (1988). Measuring processes of change: Applications to the cessation of smoking. *Journal of Consulting and Clinical Psychology*, *56*, 520–528.

■ ■ ■

7318

Test Name: PRODUCTIVITY GAIN MEASURE

Purpose: To measure productivity gain.

Number of Items: 5

Format: Items require of supervisors to respond. All items are presented.

Reliability: Internal consistency reliability was .78.

Validity: Correlations with other variables ranged from -.31 to .65.

Author: Campion, M. A.

Article: Meaning and measurement of turnover: Comparison of alternative measures and recommendations for research.

Journal: *Journal of Applied Psychology*, April 1991, *76*(2), 199–212.

■ ■ ■

7319

Test Name: PSYCHOTHERAPY PROCESS Q-SORT

Purpose: To provide a standard language and rating procedure for the therapy process.

Number of Items: 100

Format: Includes 3 types of items: those describing patient attitude and behavior or experience, those reflecting the therapist's actions and attitudes, and those attempting to capture the nature of the interaction in the dyad or the climate or atmosphere of the encounter.

Reliability: Interrater reliability ranged from .68 to .90.

Authors: Kivlighan, D. M., Jr., and Schmitz, P. J.

Article: Counselor technical activity in cases with improving working alliances and continuing-poor working alliances.

Journal: *Journal of Counseling Psychology*, January 1992, *39*(1), 32–38.

Related Research: Jones, E. E. (1985). *Manual for the Psychotherapy Process Q-Sort.* Unpublished manuscript, University of California, Berkeley.

■■■

7320

Test Name: SELLING ORIENTATION CUSTOMER MEASURE

Purpose: To measure salespersons' orientations.

Number of Items: 12

Format: 6-point scales. Sample items are presented.

Reliability: Alphas ranged from .69 to .88 across subscales.

Authors: Pilling, B. K., et al.

Article: Comparing projective with self-rating measurement scales: An application to customer-orientation measures.

Journal: *Psychological Reports*, April 1994, *74*(2), 427-434.

Related Research: Michaels, R. E., & Day, R. L. (1985). Measuring customer orientation of salespeople: A replication with industrial buyers. *Journal of Marketing Research*, *22*, 443–446.

■■■

7321

Test Name: SESSION EVALUATION QUESTIONNAIRE

Purpose: To measure the impact of counseling sessions.

Number of Items: 11

Format: Bipolar-item scales are presented in a 7-point differential format.

Reliability: Test–retest reliability was .80 or greater.

Author: Kivlighan, D. M., Jr., and Angelone, E. O.

Article: Helpee introversion, novice counselor intention use, and helpee-rated session impact.

Journal: *Journal of Counseling Psychology*, January 1991, *38*(1), 25–29.

Related Research: Stiles, W. B., & Snow, J. S. (1984). Counseling session impact as viewed by novice counselors and their clients. *Journal of Counseling Psychology*, *31*, 3–12.

■■■

7322

Test Name: SESSION EVALUATION QUESTIONNAIRE

Purpose: To evaluate counseling sessions.

Number of Items: 12

Format: Consists of two factors: Depth (quality) and Smoothness (comfort). Items are bipolar adjectives employing a 7-point semantic differential format.

Reliability: Internal consistency ranged from .87 to .93.

Authors: Regan, A. M., and Hill, C. E.

Article: Investigation of what clients and counselors do not say in brief therapy.

Journal: *Journal of Counseling Psychology*, April 1992, *39*(2), 168–174.

Related Research: Stiles, W. B., & Snow, J. S. (1984). Counseling session impact as viewed by novice counselors and their clients.

Journal of Counseling Psychology, 31, 3–12.

■■■

7323

Test Name: SESSION EVALUATION QUESTIONNAIRE

Purpose: To measure session impact.

Number of Items: 27

Format: Includes 3 sections: session evaluation, postsession mood, and therapist evaluation. Items consist of 7-point bipolar adjectives.

Reliability: Alpha coefficients ranged from .77 to .92.

Validity: Correlations with other variables ranged from -.39 to .72.

Authors: Stiles, W. B., et al.

Article: Evaluation and description of psychotherapy sessions by clients using the Session Evaluation Questionnaire and the Session Impact Scale.

Journal: *Journal of Counseling Psychology*, April 1994, *41*(2), 175-185.

Related Research: Stiles, W. B., & Snow, J. S. (1984). Dimensions of psychotherapy session impact across sessions and across clients. *British Journal of Clinical Psychology*, *23*, 59–63.

■■■

7324

Test Name: SESSION EVALUATION QUESTIONNAIRE

Purpose: To assess participants' perceptions of counseling session impact and effectiveness.

Number of Items: 48

Format: Items are 7-point bipolar adjective pairs. Includes two parts: self-perspective and other perspective. Contains 4 factors:

Depth, Smoothness, Positivity, and Arousal.

Reliability: Alpha coefficients ranged from .78 to .93.

Authors: Cummings, A. L., et al.

Article: Memory for therapeutic events, session effectiveness, and working alliance in short-term counseling.

Journal: *Journal of Counseling Psychology*, July 1992, *39*(3), 306–312.

Related Research: Stiles, W. B., & Snow, J. S. (1984). Counseling session impact as viewed by novice counselors and their clients. *Journal of Counseling Psychology*, *31*, 3–12.

Dill-Standiford, T. J., et al. (1988). Counselor-client agreement on session impact. *Journal of Counseling Psychology*, *35*, 47–55.

■ ■ ■

7325

Test Name: SESSION EVALUATION QUESTIONNAIRE—FORM 4

Purpose: To evaluate a therapy session from the therapist's and client's perspective.

Number of Items: 24

Format: Uses bipolar adjectives. Includes 4 subscales: Depth, Smoothness, Positivity, and Arousal.

Reliability: Alphas ranged from .78 to .93.

Author: Hill, C. E., et al.

Article: Methodological Examination of Videotape-Assisted Reviews in Brief Therapy: Helpfulness Ratings, Therapist Intentions, Client Reactions, Mood and Session Evaluation.

Journal: *Journal of Counseling Psychology*, April 1994, *41*(2), 236–247.

Related Research: Stiles, W. B., & Snow, J. S. (1984). Counseling session impact as viewed by novice counselors and their clients. *Journal of Counseling Psychology*, *31*, 3–12.

■ ■ ■

7326

Test Name: SESSION IMPACTS SCALE

Purpose: To measure session impact.

Number of Items: 17

Format: Items consist of a label and short paragraph description. All labels are presented. Responses are made on a 5-point scale ranging from 1 (*not at all*) to 5 (*very much*). There is also one open-ended item. Includes 5 factors.

Reliability: Alpha coefficients ranged from .78 to .90.

Validity: Correlations with other variables ranged from -.46 to .70.

Authors: Stiles, W. B., et al.

Article: Evaluation and description of psychotherapy sessions by clients using the Session Evaluation Questionnaire and the Session Impact Scale.

Journal: *Journal of Counseling Psychology*, April 1994, *41*(2), 175–185.

Related Research: Elliott, R., & Wexler, M. M. (1994). Measuring the impact of sessions in process-experiential therapy of depression: The Session Impact Scale. *The Journal of Counseling Psychology*, *41*, 166–174.

■ ■ ■

7327

Test Name: SIMULATION OF INTERACTIVE DECISION-MAKING: VERSION 1

Purpose: To test for teacher

competence in the classroom.

Number of Items: 65

Time Required: 1 1\2 hours.

Format: Involves descriptive problems accompanied by four different responses that a teacher could make. Each response is evaluated by the teacher as being *appropriate* or *inappropriate*.

Reliability: Coefficient was .89.

Authors: Shannon, D., et al.

Article: Construct validity of a simulation of interactive decision-making.

Journal: *Journal of Educational Research*, Jan./Feb. 1993, *86*(3), 180–183.

Related Research: Hays, L. *A simulation test of interactive teaching competencies.* Unpublished doctoral dissertation, University of Virginia, Charlottesville.

■ ■ ■

7328

Test Name: SIMULATION OF INTERACTIVE DECISION MAKING

Purpose: To identify teachers in 11 competency areas.

Number of Items: 125

Time Required: 45 minutes.

Format: Examiners view teaching problem on a video tape and select and rate each of four solutions as *appropriate* or *inappropriate*.

Reliability: Alpha was .92.

Validity: Known-group differences are presented.

Authors: Shannon, D. M., et al.

Article: Construct validity of a simulation of interactive decision making.

Journal: *Journal of Educational*

Research, January/February 1993, *86*(3), 180–183.

• • •

7329

Test Name: STAGE OF CHANGE SCALE

Purpose: To measure stages of change: precontemplation, contemplation, action, and maintenance.

Number of Items: 32

Format: 5-point Likert format.

Reliability: Internal consistency was .79. Correlations between subscales ranged from .52 to .53.

Authors: Smith, K. J., et al.

Article: The transtheoretical model's stages and processes of change and their relation to premature termination.

Journal: *Journal of Counseling Psychology*, January 1995, *42*(1), 34–39.

Related Research: McCommaughy, E. A., et al. (1983). Stages of change in psychotherapy: Measurement and sample profiles. *Psychotherapy*, *20*, 368–375.

• • •

7330

Test Name: STRUCTURE, CLIMATE AND MENTORING SCALES

Purpose: To assess the structure and mentoring of graduate students and the climate of the department.

Number of Items: 42

Format: All items are presented.

Reliability: Alphas ranged from .62 to .87.

Authors: Anderson, M. S., and Louis, K. S.

Article: The graduate student experience and subscription to the norms of science.

Journal: *Research in Higher Education*, June 1995, *35*(3), 273–299.

• • •

7331

Test Name: STUDENTS' EVALUATIONS OF EDUCATIONAL QUALITY

Purpose: To evaluate teaching effectiveness.

Number of Items: 34

Format: Includes 9 factors: Learning/Value, Instructor Enthusiasm, Organization/Clarity, Group Interactions/Grading, Assignment/Readings, and Workload/Difficulty.

Reliability: Alpha coefficients ranged from .85 to .97.

Authors: Watkins, D., and Gerong, A.

Article: Evaluating undergraduate college teaching: A Filipino investigation.

Journal: *Educational and Psychological Measurement*, Autumn 1992, *52*(3), 727–734.

Related Research: Marsh, H. W. (1987). Students' evaluations of university teaching: Research findings, methodological issues, and directions for future research. *International Journal of Educational Research*, *11*, 253–388.

• • •

7332

Test Name: SUPERVISING PETTY OFFICER QUESTIONNAIRE

Purpose: To assess personality patterns: anxiety, job involvement, self-esteem, rigidity, achievement motivation, impulsiveness, and internal locus of control.

Number of Items: Subscales range from 5 to 13 items.

Format: 5-point response scales.

Reliability: Alphas ranged from .73 to .85 across subscales.

Authors: Gustafson, S. B., and Mumford, M. D.

Article: Personal style and person-environment fit: A pattern approach.

Journal: *Journal of Vocational Behavior*, April 1995, *46*(2), 163–188.

Related Research: Jones, A. P., & James, L. R. (1979). Psychological climate: Dimensions and relationships of individual and aggregated work environment perceptions. *Organizational Behavior and Human Performance*, *23*, 201–250.

• • •

7333

Test Name: SUPERVISOR EVALUATION RATINGS

Purpose: To enable counselors and supervisor trainees to rate the effectiveness of the supervision they received.

Number of Items: 3

Format: Uses 7-point scales. Items deal with satisfaction with and competence of the supervisor, and impact of interaction with the supervisor on improving their counseling or supervision ability.

Reliability: Alpha was .83.

Author: Ellis, M. V.

Article: Critical incidents in clinical supervision and in supervisor supervision: Assessing supervisory issues.

Journal: *Journal of Counseling Psychology*, July 1991, *38*(3), 342–349.

Related Research: Worthington, E. J., Jr., & Roehlke, H. J. (1979). Effective supervision as perceived by beginning counselors-in-training. *Journal of Counseling Psychology, 26,* 64–73.

• • •

7334

Test Name: SUPERVISOR SUPPORT SCALE

Purpose: To measure supervisor support.

Number of Items: 9

Format: Responses are made on a 5-point scale ranging from 1 (*strongly disagree*) to 5 (*strongly agree*).

Reliability: Alpha coefficients were .93 and .94.

Validity: Correlations with other variables ranged from -.33 to .48.

Author: Aryee, S., et al.

Article: An investigation of the predictors and outcomes of career commitment in three career stages.

Journal: *Journal of Vocational Behavior,* February 1994, *44*(1), 1–16.

Related Research: Greenhaus, J., et al. (1990). Effects of race on organizational experience, job performance, evaluation and career outcomes. *Academy of Management Journal, 33,* 64–86.

• • •

7335

Test Name: SUPERVISOR SUPPORT SCALE

Purpose: To assess supervisor support.

Number of Items: 9

Format: Responses are made on a 5-point scale ranging from 1 (*never*) to 5 (*very often*). All items are presented.

Reliability: Coefficient alpha was .83.

Validity: Correlation with other variables ranged from -.35 to .33 (*N* = 398).

Authors: Thomas, L. T., and Ganster, D. L.

Article: Impact of family-supportive work variables on work-family conflict and strain: A control perspective.

Journal: *Journal of Applied Psychology,* February 1995, *80*(1), 6–15.

Related Research: Shinn, M., et al. (1989). Promoting the well-being of working parents: Cooperating, social support, and flexible job schedules. *American Journal of Community Psychology, 17,* 31–55.

• • •

7336

Test Name: SUPERVISORY STYLES INVENTORY

Purpose: To assess the supervisor trainees' supervisory styles.

Number of Items: 33

Format: Items are unipolar adjectives rated along a 7-point scale ranging from 1 (*not very descriptive*) to 7 (*very descriptive*).

Reliability: Alphas ranged from .76 to .93; test-related reliability coefficients ranged from .78 to .94.

Author: Ellis, M. V.

Article: Critical incidents in clinical supervision and in supervisor supervision: Assessing supervisory issues.

Journal: *Journal of Counseling Psychology,* July 1991, *38*(3), 342–349.

Related Research: Friedlander, M. L., & Ward, L. G. (1984). Development and validation of the Supervisory Styles Inventory. *Journal of Counseling Psychology, 31,* 541–557.

7337

Test Name: TEACHER EFFECTIVENESS SCALE

Purpose: To allow students to rate teacher effectiveness.

Number of Items: 50

Format: Responses are made on a yes–no format.

Reliability: Odd–even reliability estimate was .94.

Author: Follman, J.

Article: Elementary public school pupil rating of teacher effectiveness.

Journal: *Child Study Journal,* March 1995, *25*(1), 57–78.

Related Research: Cook, W., & Leeds, C. H. (1947). Measuring the teacher personality. *Educational and Psychological Measurement, 7,* 399–409.

• • •

7338

Test Name: TEACHER EFFECTIVENESS SURVEY

Purpose: To assess teacher education program graduates' teaching effectiveness.

Number of Items: 28

Format: Includes 3 factors: Instruction, Interpersonal/Professional, and Leadership. All items are presented.

Reliability: Alpha coefficients were .92 and .96.

Authors: Barton, R. M., et al.

Article: Factorial validity and reliability of a survey to assess the teaching effectiveness of graduates of teacher education programs.

Journal: *Educational and Psychological Measurement,* Spring 1994, *54*(1), 218–226.

Related Research: Gable, R. (1989). *The University of Connecticut survey of graduates.*

Unpublished instrument, University of Connecticut, Storrs.

Streifer, P. A., & Iwanicki, E. F. (1987). The validation of beginning teacher competencies in Connecticut. *Journal of Personnel Evaluation in Education, 1,* 33–55.

■ ■ ■

7339

Test Name: TEACHER OBSERVATION FORM

Purpose: To assess teaching skills.

Number of Items: 12

Format: Responses are made on a 5-point scale ranging from 1 (*not satisfactory*) to 5 (*outstanding*).

Reliability: Interrater agreement was 88.7%.

Authors: Hansen, J. B., et al.

Article: Comparison of trained and untrained teachers of gifted students.

Journal: *Gifted Child Quarterly,* Summer 1994, *38*(3), 115–121.

Related Research: Feldhusen, J. F., & Huffman, L. (1988). Practicum experiences in an educational program for teachers of the gifted. *Journal for the Education of the Gifted, 12,* 34–45.

■ ■ ■

7340

Test Name: TEACHING RATING SCALE

Purpose: To rate music instructors.

Number of Items: 36

Format: Employs a Likert scale.

Reliability: Test–retest reliability was .82.

Authors: Schmidt, C. P., and Stephens, R.

Article: Locus of control and field dependence as factors in students' evaluations of applied music instruction.

Journal: *Perceptual and Motor Skills,* August 1991, *73*(1), 131–136.

Related Research: Abeles, H. F. (1975). Student perceptions of characteristics of effective applied music instructors. *Journal of Research in Music Education, 23,* 147–154.

■ ■ ■

7341

Test Name: TEACHER SUPPORT BEHAVIOR SURVEY

Purpose: To measure mentoring and other social support behaviors related to teaching careers.

Number of Items: 33

Format: Likert format.

Reliability: Alpha was .91.

Authors: Bainer, D. L., and Didham, C.

Article: Mentoring and other support behaviors in elementary schools.

Journal: *Journal of Educational Research,* March/April 1994, *87*(4), 240–247.

Related Research: Hill, S. E. K., et al. (1989). Mentoring and other communication support in the academic setting. *Group and Organizational Studies, 14,* 355–368.

■ ■ ■

7342

Test Name: TEACHING EVALUATION QUESTIONNAIRE

Purpose: To provide for teacher evaluation.

Format: Includes 8 dimensions:

organized, participative, evaluation, availability, personal style, amount learned, recommend the class to other, and overall evaluation. Examples are presented.

Reliability: Alpha coefficients ranged from .83 to .98.

Validity: Correlations with other variables ranged from -.08 to .50.

Authors: Schneider, B., et al.

Article: Do customer service perceptions generalize? The case of student and chair ratings of faculty effectiveness.

Journal: *Journal of Applied Psychology,* October 1994, *79*(5), 685–690.

Related Research: Hanges, P. J., et al. (1990). Stability of performance: The interactionist perspective. *Journal of Applied Psychology, 75*(5), 658–667.

■ ■ ■

7343

Test Name: THERAPIST ACTIVITY RATING SCALE

Purpose: To measure therapist's activity.

Number of Items: 61

Format: 3-point rating scale (*not at all* to *a lot*). All items presented.

Reliability: Interrater reliability ranged from .41 to .50. Intraclass correlations ranged from .80 to .89.

Validity: Correlations between scale profiles from five therapists ranged from .23 to .86.

Authors: Conte, H. R., et al.

Article: Development of a therapist activity rating scale: Preliminary findings.

Journal: *Psychological Reports,* June 1993, *72*(3) Part II, 1139–1144.

7344

Test Name: TREATMENT ACCEPTABILITY QUESTIONNAIRE

Purpose: To measure treatment acceptability.

Number of Items: 6

Format: Responses are made on a 7-point Likert scale. Items focus on acceptability, ethics, effectiveness, negative side effects, the psychologist's knowledge, and the psychologist's trustworthiness.

Reliability: Alpha coefficients ranged from .74 to .81. Test–retest (3 weeks) reliability was .78.

Validity: Correlation with the Treatment Evaluation Inventory was .87.

Author: Hunsley, J.

Article: Treatment acceptability of symptom prescription techniques.

Journal: *Journal of Counseling Psychology*, April 1993, *40*(2), 139–143.

Related Research: Hunsley, J. (1992). Development of the Treatment Acceptability Questionnaire. *Journal of Psychopathology and Behavioral Assessment, 14*, 55–64.

■ ■ ■

7345

Test Name: VANDERBILT THERAPEUTIC STRATEGIES SCALE

Purpose: To determine general interviewing behaviors and specific strategies.

Number of Items: 21

Format: Responses are made on a 5-point Likert scale.

Reliability: Interrater reliability was .74 (interviewing style) and .91 for specific strategies.

Authors: Henry, W. P., et al.

Article: Effects of training in time-limited dynamic psychotherapy: Changes in therapist behavior.

Journal: *Journal of Consulting and Clinical Psychology*, June 1993, *61*(3), 434–440.

Related Research: Butler, S. F., et al. (1992). *Measuring adherence and skill in time-limited dynamic psychotherapy*. Unpublished manuscript.

■ ■ ■

7346

Test Name: WORK ACTIVITY QUESTIONNAIRE

Purpose: To measure the actual and desirable job characteristics of career counselors.

Number of Items: 40

Format: Yes–No–I Don't Know format. All items are presented.

Reliability: Alphas ranged from .83 to .86. KR-20 reliabilities ranged from .83 to .86.

Authors: Olson, T. F., and Matkin, R. E.

Article: Student and counselor perceptions of career counselor work activities in a community college.

Journal: *The Career Development Quarterly*, June 1992, *40*(4), 324–333.

Related Research: Herr, E. L., & Cramer, S. H. (1988). *Career guidance and counseling through the life span* (3rd ed.). Boston: Little, Brown.

■ ■ ■

7347

Test Name: WORKING ALLIANCE INVENTORY

Purpose: To measure the working alliance.

Number of Items: 36

Format: Two forms: One for clients and one for counselors. Includes three scales: Congruence on Goals, Tasks, and Emotional Bond Between Participants.

Reliability: Alpha coefficients ranged from .88 to .93.

Authors: Al-Darmaki, F., and Kivlighan, D. M., Jr.

Article: Congruence in client-counselor expectations for relationship and the working alliance.

Journal: *Journal of Counseling Psychology*, October 1993, *40*(4), 379–384.

Related Research: Horvath, A. O., & Greenberg, L. (1989). Development and validation of the Working Alliance Inventory. *Journal of Counseling Psychology, 36*, 223–232.

■ ■ ■

7348

Test Name: WORKING ALLIANCE INVENTORY— SHORT VERSION

Purpose: To assess the working alliance of counselors and of clients.

Number of Items: 12

Format: Includes three subscales: Bond, Task, and Goal. Each item is rated on a 7-point scale ranging from 1 (*never*) to 7 (*always*).

Reliability: Alpha coefficients were .98 (clients) and .95 (counselor). $N = 124$.

Authors: Tryon, G. S., and Kane, A. S.

Article: Relationship of working alliance to mutual and unilateral termination.

Journal: *Journal of Counseling Psychology*, January 1993, *40*(1), 33–36.

Related Research: Tracey, T. J., & Kokotovic, A. M. (1989). Factor structure of the Working

Alliance Inventory. *Psychological Assessment: A Journal of Consulting and Clinical Psychology, 1,* 207–210.

. . .

7349

Test Name: WORK PERFORMANCE RATING SCALE

Purpose: To measure job performance.

Number of Items: 12

Format: Responses are made on a 5-point Likert scale.

Reliability: Cronbach's alphas for the four dimensions ranged from .80 to .89.

Authors: Farh, J. L., et al.

Article: Cultural relativity in action: a Comparison of self-ratings made by Chinese and US workers.

Journal: *Personnel Psychology,* Spring 1991, *44*(1), 129–147.

Related Research: Chang, B. S. (1985). *Task-oriented leadership behavior and subordinate performance: A supplementary model and its validation.* Unpublished doctoral dissertation, National Taiwan University, Taiwan (in Chinese).

CHAPTER 24
Vocational Interest

7350

Test Name: AFFECTIVE AND CONTINUANCE COMMITMENT SCALE

Purpose: To assess affective and continuance commitment.

Number of Items: 16

Format: Responses were made on a 5-point scale ranging from 1 (*strongly disagree*) to 5 (*strongly agree*).

Reliability: Alpha coefficients were .88 (affective commitment) and .82 (continuance commitment).

Validity: Correlations with other variables ranged from -.20 to .64.

Authors: Shore, L. M., and Wayne, S. J.

Article: Commitment and employee behavior: Comparison of affective commitment and continuance commitment with perceived organizational support.

Journal: *Journal of Applied Psychology*, October 1993, *78*(5), 774–780.

Related Research: Meyer, J. P., & Allen, N. J. (1984). Testing the "side-bet theory" of organizational commitment: Some methodological considerations. *Journal of Applied Psychology*, *69*, 372–378.

■ ■ ■

7351

Test Name: AFFECTIVE COMMITMENT SCALE

Purpose: To measure commitment.

Number of Items: 8

Format: Responses are made on a 7-point agree–disagree scale.

Reliability: Alpha coefficients were .83 and .86.

Authors: Irving, P. G., and Meyer, J. P.

Article: Reexamination of the met-expectations hypothesis: A longitudinal analysis.

Journal: *Journal of Applied Psychology*, December 1994, *79*(6), 937–949.

Related Research: Allen, N. J., & Meyer, J. P. (1990). The measurement and antecedents of affective, continuance and normative commitment. *Journal of Occupational Psychology*, *63*, 1–18.

■ ■ ■

7352

Test Name: AFFECTIVE ORGANIZATIONAL COMMITMENT SCALE

Purpose: To measure affective organizational commitment.

Number of Items: 8

Format: Responses are made on a 5-point scale ranging from 1 (*strongly disagree*) to 5 (*strongly agree*). Examples are presented.

Reliability: Coefficient alpha was .89.

Validity: Correlations with other variables ranged from -.60 to .52.

Authors: Carson, K. D., and Bedeian, A. G.

Article: Career commitment:

Construction of a measure and examination of its psychometric properties.

Journal: *Journal of Vocational Behavior*, June 1994, *44*(3), 237–262.

Related Research: Meyer, J. P., & Allen, N. J. (1984). Testing the "side bet theory" of organizational commitment: Some methodological considerations. *Journal of Applied Psychology*, *69*, 372–378.

■ ■ ■

7353

Test Name: AFFECTIVE SCALE

Purpose: To measure organizational commitment.

Number of Items: 8

Format: Responses are made on a 6-point scale ranging from 1 (*strongly disagree*) to 6 (*strongly agree*).

Reliability: Alpha coefficients were .85 and .88.

Validity: Correlations with other variables ranged from -.24 to .41.

Author: Blau, G.

Article: Developing and testing a taxonomy of lateness behavior.

Journal: *Journal of Applied Psychology*, December 1994, *79*(6), 959–970.

Related Research: Meyer, J., & Allen, N. (1984). Testing the "side bet theory" of organizational commitment: Some methodological considerations. *Journal of Applied Psychology*, *69*, 372–378.

7354

Test Name: AMOUNT OF INFORMATION OBTAINED SCALE

Purpose: To determine amount of information obtained in career exploration.

Number of Items: 3

Format: A sample item is presented.

Reliability: Internal consistency was .87.

Validity: Correlations with other variables ranged from -.70 to .56.

Authors: Blustein, D. L., et al.

Article: Relation between exploratory and choice factors and decisional progress.

Journal: *Journal of Vocational Behavior*, February 1994, *44*(1), 75–90.

Related Research: Kidney, B. A. (1992). *Career exploration considered from the perceptive of the person-environment fit model.* Unpublished doctoral dissertation, State University of New York, Albany.

■ ■ ■

7355

Test Name: ATTITUDE TOWARD TEACHING AS A CAREER SCALE

Purpose: To measure attitudes toward teaching.

Number of Items: 11

Format: Responses are made on a 6-point scale ranging from 1 (*strongly disagree*) to 6 (*strongly agree*).

Reliability: Test–retest reliability was .79.

Authors: Pigge, F. L., and Marso, R. N.

Article: A longitudinal comparison of the academic, affective, and personal characteristics of persisters and nonpersisters in teacher preparation.

Journal: *Journal of Experimental Education*, Fall 1992, *61*(1), 19–26.

Related Research: Merwin, J. C., & Divesta, F. J. (1959). The study of need theory and career choice. *Journal of Counseling Psychology, 6,* 302–308.

■ ■ ■

7356

Test Name: CAREER COMMITMENT MEASURE

Purpose: To measure career commitment.

Number of Items: 12

Format: Includes 3 dimensions: career identity, career planning, and career resilience.

Reliability: Alpha coefficients ranged from .79 to .85.

Validity: Correlations with other variables ranged from -.54 to .73.

Authors: Carson, K. D., and Bedeian, A. G.

Article: Career commitment: Construction of a measure and examination of its psychometric properties.

Journal: *Journal of Vocational Behavior*, June 1994, *44*(3), 237–262.

■ ■ ■

7357

Test Name: CAREER COMMITMENT SCALE

Purpose: To determine the importance people place on continuing research in their future careers.

Number of Items: 6

Format: Responses are made on a 5-point scale ranging from 1 (*strongly disagree*) to 5 (*strongly agree*). Examples are presented.

Reliability: Coefficient alpha was .77 (*N* = 193).

Validity: Correlations with other variables ranged from -.24 to .81 (*N* = 193).

Authors: Bauer, T. N., and Green, S. G.

Article: Effect of newcomer involvement in work-related activities: Aa longitudinal study of socialization.

Journal: *Journal of Applied Psychology*, April 1994, *79*(2), 211–223.

■ ■ ■

7358

Test Name: CAREER COMMITMENT SCALE

Purpose: To measure career commitment.

Number of Items: 7

Format: Responses are made on a 5-point scale ranging from 1 (*strongly disagree*) to 5 (*strongly agree*). Examples are presented.

Reliability: Internal consistency was .87 and .85. Test–retest (7 months) reliability was .67.

Validity: Correlations with other variables ranged from -.57 to .42.

Authors: Aryee, S., et al.

Article: An investigation of the predictors and outcomes of career commitment in three career stages.

Journal: *Journal of Vocational Behavior*, February 1994, *44*(1), 1–16.

Related Research: Blau, G. (1988). Further exploring the meaning and measurement of career commitment. *Journal of Vocational Behavior, 32,* 284–297.

■ ■ ■

7359

Test Name: CAREER COMMITMENT SCALE

Purpose: To measure career commitment.

Number of Items: 10

Format: Responses are made on a 5-point scale ranging from 1 (*entirely inapplicable*) to 5 (*highly applicable*). Examples are presented.

Reliability: Coefficient alpha was .91.

Validity: Correlations with other variables ranged from -.24 to .40.

Authors: Matsui, T., et al.

Article: Personality and career commitment among Japanese female clerical employees.

Journal: *Journal of Vocational Behavior*, June 1991, *38*(3), 351–360.

• • •

7360

Test Name: CAREER COUNSELING DIAGNOSTIC INVENTORY

Purpose: To identify psychological conflicts and developmental crises that interfere with career decision making.

Number of Items: 42

Format: Includes three 14-item scales. Items are rated on a 5-point Likert scale ranging from *strongly disagree* to *strongly agree.*

Reliability: Alpha coefficients ranged from .55 to .73.

Author: Tinsley, D. J.

Article: A construct validation study of the Expectations About Counseling-Brief Form: Factorial validity.

Journal: *Measurement and Evaluation in Counseling and Development*, October 1991, *24*(3), 101–110.

Related Research: Arnold, R. A. (1985, March). Career decision-

making difficulties as a result of cognitive, social and emotional deficits: A conceptual model. In H. E. A. Tinsley (Chair), *Assessment of career development constructs.* Symposium presented at the meeting of the American College Personnel Association, Boston.

• • •

7361

Test Name: CAREER DECISION PROFILE

Purpose: To assess clarity of career decision making.

Number of Items: 6

Format: 8-point scales range from 1 (*strongly disagree*) to 8 (*strongly agree*). Sample items are presented.

Reliability: Alpha was .84.

Authors: Solberg, V. S., et al.

Article: Career decision-making and career search activity: Relative effects of career search self-efficacy and human agency.

Journal: *Journal of Counseling Psychology*, October 1995, *42*(4), 448–455.

Related Research: Jones, L. (1989). Measuring a three-dimensional construct of career indecision among college students: A revision of the Vocational Decision Scale—The Career Decision Profile. *Journal of Counseling Psychology, 51,* 629–239.

• • •

7362

Test Name: CAREER DECISION PROFILE

Purpose: To assess career decidedness including self-clarity, knowledge about occupations, training, and career choice importance and comfort.

Number of Items: 16

Format: 8-point Likert format ranges from 1 (*strongly disagree*) to 8 (*strongly agree*).

Reliability: Internal consistency ranged from .66 to .85. Test–retest reliabilities ranged from .66 to .80 over 3 weeks.

Validity: Correlations with other variables ranged from -.49 to .50.

Authors: Multon, K. D., et al.

Article: An empirical derivation of career decision subtypes in a high school sample.

Journal: *Journal of Vocational Behavior*, August 1995, *47*(1), 76–92.

Related Research: Jones, L. K. (1988). *The Career Decision Profile.* (Available from L. K. Jones, North Carolina State University, Department of Counselor Education, Box 7801, Raleigh, NC 27695.)

• • •

7363

Test Name: CAREER DECISION SCALE

Purpose: To measure the antecedents of career indecision.

Number of Items: 16

Reliability: Alpha was .85.

Validity: Coefficients of congruence with other factor analyses ranged from -.13 to .95 across factors.

Authors: Watson, M. B., et al.

Article: Factor analysis of the Career Decision Scale on South African high school students.

Journal: *Psychological Reports*, December 1991, *69*(3) Part II, 1083–1088.

Related Research: Hartman, B. W., & Hartman, P. T. (1982). The concurrent and predictive validity of the Career Decision Scale adapted for high school students. *Journal of Vocational Behavior, 20,* 244–252.

• • •

7364

Test Name: CAREER-ENHANCING STRATEGIES SCALE

Purpose: To assess how individuals attempt to plan their careers.

Number of Items: 14

Format: 5-point scales.

Reliability: Alphas ranged from .65 to .68 across subscales.

Validity: Correlations with other variables ranged from .00 to .20.

Authors: Feij, J. A., et al.

Article: The development of career-enhancing strategies and content innovation: A longitudinal study of new workers.

Journal: *Journal of Vocational Behavior,* June 1995, *46*(3), 231–256.

Related Research: Penley, L., & Gould, S. (1981). *Measuring career strategies: The psychometric characteristics of the Career Strategies Inventory.* San Antonio: Center for Studies in Business Economics and Human Resources, University of Texas.

• • •

7365

Test Name: CAREER EXPLORATION SCALE

Purpose: To evaluate one's career exploration.

Number of Items: 11

Format: Responses are made on a 5-point scale ranging from 1 (*strongly disagree*) to 5 (*strongly agree*). A sample item is presented.

Reliability: Internal consistency was .78.

Authors: Noe, R. A., and Wilk, S. L.

Article: Investigation of the factors that influence employees' participation in development activities.

Journal: *Journal of Applied Psychology,* April 1993, *78*(2), 291–302.

Related Research: Stumpf, S. A., et al. (1983). Development of the Career Exploration Survey (CES). *Journal of Vocational Behavior, 22,* 191–226.

• • •

7366

Test Name: CAREER EXPLORATION SURVEY

Purpose: To provide a self-report measure of career exploration.

Number of Items: 59

Format: Includes 3 domains: exploration process, reactions to exploration, and beliefs about exploration.

Reliability: Internal consistency ranged from .67 to .88.

Authors: Kirschner, T., et al.

Article: Case study of the process and outcome of career counseling.

Journal: *Journal of Counseling Psychology,* April 1994, *41*(2), 216–226.

Related Research: Stumpf, S. A., et al. (1983). Development of the Career Exploration Survey (CES). *Journal of Vocational Behavior, 22,* 191–226.

• • •

7367

Test Name: CAREER FACTORS INVENTORY

Purpose: To measure career choice anxiety, generalized

indecisiveness, need for career information, and need for self-knowledge.

Number of Items: 21

Format: 5-point Likert format. Sample items are presented.

Reliability: Internal consistency ranged from .86 to .91. Test–retest reliabilities (2 weeks) ranged from .79 to .84.

Validity: Interscale correlations ranged from .30 to .65.

Authors: Cohen, C. R., et al.

Article: Relationships between career indecision subtypes and ego identity development.

Journal: *Journal of Counseling Psychology,* October 1995, *42*(4), 440–447.

Related Research: Chartrand, J. M., et al. (1990). Development and validation of the Career Factors Inventory. *Journal of Counseling Psychology, 37,* 491–501.

• • •

7368

Test Name: CAREER IMPORTANCE SCALE

Purpose: To measure career importance.

Number of Items: 13

Format: 5-point Likert format.

Reliability: Alphas ranged from .83 to .89.

Authors: Farmer, H. S., et al.

Article: Women's career choices: Focus on science, math and technology careers.

Journal: *Journal of Counseling Psychology,* April 1995, *42*(2), 155–170.

Related Research: Super, D., & Culha, M. (1976). *Work Salience Inventory.* (Available from Helen S. Farmer, 210 Department of

Educational Psychology, University of Illinois, 1310 S. 6th Street, Champaign, IL 61820.)

● ● ●

7369

Test Name: CAREER MOTIVATION STUDY

Purpose: To assess career resilience, career insight, and career identity.

Number of Items: 26

Format: 5-point scales range from 1 (*to a very slight extent*) to 5 (*to a very large extent*). Sample items are described.

Reliability: Alphas ranged from .74 to .80 across subscales.

Validity: Correlations of total scores with other variables ranged from -.12 to .27.

Authors: Wolf, G., et al.

Article: Career experience and motivation as predictors of training behaviors and outcomes for displaced engineers.

Journal: *Journal of Vocational Behavior*, December 1995, *47*(3), 316–331.

Related Research: Noe, R. A., et al. (1990). Correlates of career motivation. *Journal of Vocational Behavior*, *37*, 340–356.

● ● ●

7370

Test Name: CAREER WITHDRAWAL COGNITIONS SCALE

Purpose: To measure career withdrawal cognition.

Number of Items: 3

Reliability: Coefficient alpha was .82.

Validity: Correlations with other variables ranged from -.73 to .63.

Authors: Carson, K. D., and Bedeian, A. G.

Article: Career commitment: Construction of a measure and examination of its psychometric properties.

Journal: *Journal of Vocational Behavior*, June 1994, *44*(3), 237–262.

Related Research: Michaels, C., & Spector, P. (1982). Causes of employee turnover: A test of the Mobley, Griffeth, Hand and Meglino model. *Journal of Applied Psychology*, *67*, 53–59.

● ● ●

7371

Test Name: COMMITMENT TO CAREER CHOICES SCALE

Purpose: To assess vocational commitment and the tendency to foreclose.

Number of Items: 28

Format: 7-point scales range from 1 (*never true about me*) to 7 (*always true about me*).

Reliability: Alphas ranged from .78 to .82 across subscales. Test–retest (2 weeks) reliabilities ranged from .82 to .92.

Validity: Correlations with other variables ranged from -.81 to .19.

Authors: Brooks, L., et al.

Article: The relation of career-related work or internship experiences to the career development of college seniors.

Journal: *Journal of Vocational Behavior*, June 1995, *46*(3), 332–349.

Related Research: Blustein, D. L., et al. (1989). The development and validation of a two-dimensional model of the commitment to career choices process. *Journal of Vocational Behavior*, *35*, 342–378.

7372

Test Name: COMMITMENT TO THE UNION SCALE

Purpose: To assess union commitment.

Number of Items: 21

Format: Includes 4 dimensions: loyalty, responsibility, willingness to work, and belief in unionism. Responses are made on a 7-point scale ranging from 1 (*strongly disagree*) to 7 (*strongly agree*).

Reliability: Alpha coefficients ranged from .77 to .93.

Validity: Correlations with other variables ranged from -.42 to .23.

Authors: Mellor, S., et al.

Article: Cross-level analysis of the influence of local union structure on women's and men's union commitment.

Journal: *Journal of Applied Psychology*, April 1994, *79*(2), 203–210.

Related Research: Gordon, M. E., et al. (1980). Commitment to the union: Development of a measure and an examination of its correlates. *Journal of Applied Psychology*, *65*, 479–499.

● ● ●

7373

Test Name: CONTINUANCE COMMITMENT SCALE

Purpose: To measure continuance commitment.

Number of Items: 4

Reliability: Internal reliability was .89.

Validity: Correlations with other variables -.37 to .93.

Authors: Huselid, M. A., and Day, N. E.

Article: Organizational commitment, job involvement, and turnover: A substantive and methodological analysis.

Journal: *Journal of Applied Psychology*, June 1991, *76*(3), 380–391.

Related Research: Alutto, J. A., et al. (1973). On operationalizing the concept of commitment. *Social Forces, 51,* 448–454.

■ ■ ■

7374

Test Name: CONTINUANCE COMMITMENT SCALE

Purpose: To measure continuance commitments.

Number of Items: 8

Format: Responses are made on a 5-point scale ranging from 1 (*strongly disagree*) to 5 (*strongly agree*). Examples are presented.

Reliability: Coefficient alpha was .88 (N= 193).

Validity: Correlations with other variables ranged from -.25 to .52 (N= 193).

Authors: Bauer, T. N., and Green, S. G.

Article: Effect of newcomer involvement in work-related activities: A longitudinal study of socialization.

Journal: *Journal of Applied Psychology*, April 1994, *79*(2), 211–223.

Related Research: McGee, G. W., & Ford, R. C. (1987). Two (or more?) dimensions of organizational commitment: Reexamination of the affective and continuance commitment scales. *Journal of Applied Psychology, 72,* 638–641.

■ ■ ■

7375

Test Name: DEPARTMENTAL COMMITMENT QUESTIONNAIRE

Purpose: To measure departmental commitment.

Number of Items: 9

Format: Responses are made on a 5-point scale ranging from 1 (*strongly disagree*) to 5 (*strongly agree*).

Reliability: Internal consistency coefficients were .87 and .73. Stability coefficient was .67.

Authors: Vandenberg, R. J., and Scarpello, V.

Article: Multitrait-multimethod validation of the Satisfaction With My Supervisor Scale.

Journal: *Educational and Psychological Measurement*, Spring 1992, *52*(1), 203–212.

Related Research: Mowday, R. T., et al. (1979). The measurement of organizational commitment. *Journal of Vocational Behavior, 14,* 224–247.

■ ■ ■

7376

Test Name: DESIRED JOB CHARACTERISTICS SCALE

Purpose: To measure how much a job fosters a career, a comfortable environment, self-actualization, and autonomy.

Number of Items: 25

Format: Sample items are presented.

Reliability: Alphas ranged from .58 to .63 across subscales.

Author: Burke, R. J.

Article: Career and life values and expectations of university business students.

Journal: *Psychological Reports*, August 1994, *75*(1) Part I, 147–160.

Related Research: Manhardt, P. J. (1972). Job orientation of male and female college graduates in business. *Personnel Psychology, 25,* 361–368.

■ ■ ■

7377

Test Name: ENGINEERING INTEREST SCALE

Purpose: To determine interest in engineering-related occupations

Number of Items: 18

Format: Degree of interest was recorded on a 10-point scale ranging from 0 (*strongly dislike*) to 9 (*strongly like*).

Reliability: Coefficient alpha was .79.

Validity: Correlations with other variables ranged from -.10 to .39.

Authors: Hackett, G., et al.

Article: Gender, ethnicity, and social cognitive factors predicting the academic achievement of students in engineering.

Journal: *Journal of Counseling Psychology*, October 1992, *39*(4), 527–538.

Related Research: Lent, R. W., et al. (1986). Self-efficacy in the prediction of academic performance and perceived career options. *Journal of Counseling Psychology, 33,* 265–269.

■ ■ ■

7378

Test Name: EXCHANGE VARIABLES SCALE

Purpose: To measure job commitment.

Number of Items: 18

Format: Includes rewards, costs, side-bets, attractive alternatives, comparison to other's rewards, and comparison to others' costs. All items are presented.

Reliability: Alpha coefficients ranged from .56 to .75.

Validity: Correlation with other variables ranged from -.50 to .46.

Author: Whitener, E. M., and Walz, P. M.

Article: Exchange theory determinants of affective and continuance commitment and turnover.

Journal: *Journal of Vocational Behavior*, June 1993, *42*(3), 265–281.

Related Research: Rusbutt, C. E., & Farrell, D. (1983). A longitudinal test of the investment model: The impact on job satisfaction, job commitment, and turnover of variations in rewards, costs, alternatives, and investments. *Journal of Applied Psychology*, *68*, 429–438.

■ ■ ■

7379

Test Name: EXPECTED UTILITY OF PRESENT JOB SCALE

Purpose: To assess use of one's present job for attainment of valued career outcomes.

Number of Items: 4

Format: Responses are made on a 5-point scale ranging from 1 (*strongly disagree*) to 5 (*strongly agree*). Sample items are presented.

Reliability: Alpha coefficients were .77 and .87.

Validity: Correlations with other variables ranged from -.42 to .49.

Authors: Aryee, S., et al.

Article: An investigation of the predictors and outcomes of career commitment in three career stages.

Journal: *Journal of Vocational Behavior*, February 1994, *44*(1), 1–16

Related Research: Bedeian, A., et al. (1991). The measurement and

conceptualization of career stages. *Journal of Career Development*, *17*, 153–166.

■ ■ ■

7380

Test Name: EXPLORATION PROCESS SCALE

Purpose: To measure the dynamics of career-information-seeking activity.

Number of Items: 14

Format: Each item is rated on a scale ranging from 1 (*little*) to 5 (*a great deal*). Examples are presented.

Reliability: Internal consistency was .87.

Author: Robbins, S.B., et al.

Article: Efficacy of leader-led and self-directed career workshops for middle-aged and older adults.

Journal: *Journal of Counseling Psychology*, January 1994, *41*(1), 83-90.

Related Research: Stumpf, S. A., et al. (1983). Development of the Career Exploration Survey (CES). *Journal of Vocational Behavior*, *22*, 191–226.

■ ■ ■

7381

Test Name: EXTENT OF CONSIDERATION QUESTIONNAIRE

Purpose: To assess students' willingness to consider 31 occupations and their range of occupational consideration.

Number of Items: 31

Format: Students rate on a 6-point scale ranging from 1 (*not at all*) to 6 (*very much*) how much they would consider choosing each of 31 occupations. All occupations are indicated.

Reliability: Coefficient alpha was .90. Test-rated reliabilities were .80 and .83.

Validity: Correlations with other variables ranged from .06 to .58.

Authors: Church, A. T., et al.

Article: Self-efficacy for careers and occupational consideration in minority high school equivalency students.

Journal: *Journal of Counseling Psychology*, October 1992, *39*(4), 498–508.

Related Research: Teresa, J. S. (1991). *Increasing self-efficacy for careers in young adults from migrant farm workers backgrounds.* Unpublished doctoral dissertation, Washington State University, Pullman.

■ ■ ■

7382

Test Name: FOCUS SCALE

Purpose: To assess students' preparedness to implement their career choices.

Number of Items: 5

Format: Responses are made on a 5-point Likert-type scale.

Reliability: Coefficient alpha was .92.

Validity: Correlations with other variables ranged from -.62 to .70.

Authors: Blustein, D. L., et al.

Article: Relation between exploratory and choice factors and decisional progress.

Journal: *Journal of Vocational Behavior*, February 1994, *44*(1), 75–90.

Related Research: Stumpf, S. A., et al. (1983). Development of the Career Exploration Survey (CES). *Journal of Vocational Behavior*, *23*, 191–226.

7383

Test Name: INTENDED SYSTEMATIC EXPLORATION SCALE

Purpose: To assess variations in students' approach to career exploration.

Number of Items: 3

Format: Responses are made on a 5-point Likert scale.

Reliability: Internal consistency was .78.

Authors: Blustein, D. L., et al.

Article: Relation between exploratory and choice factors and decisional progress.

Journal: *Journal of Vocational Behavior*, February 1994, *44*(1), 75–90.

Related Research: Stumpf, S. A., et al. (1983). Development of the Career Exploration Survey (CES). *Journal of Vocational Behavior*, *23*, 191–226.

■ ■ ■

7384

Test Name: INTENTION TO SEARCH SCALE

Purpose: To assess one's intention to search for a job and for financial and educational opportunities in a field other than teaching.

Number of Items: 3

Format: Responses are made on a 5-point scale.

Reliability: Coefficient alpha was .92.

Authors: Rhodes, S. R., and Doering, M. M.

Article: Intention to change careers: Determinants and process.

Journal: *The Career Development Quarterly*, September 1993, *42*(1), 76–92.

Related Research: Spencer, D. G., et al. (1983). An empirical test of the inclusion of job search linkages into Mobley's model of the turnover decision process. *Journal of Occupational Psychology*, *56*, 137–144.

■ ■ ■

7385

Test Name: INTEREST QUESTIONNAIRE

Purpose: To assess students' interest in 31 occupations as well as their range of interests.

Number of Items: 31

Format: Students rate on a 3-point scale ranging from 1 (*dislike*) to 3 (*like*) their interest in each of 31 occupations. All occupations are indicated.

Reliability: Coefficient data was .86. Test–retest (8 days) reliability was .76 for specific occupations and .81 for the range of interest.

Validity: Correlations with other variables ranged from -.01 to .68.

Authors: Church, A. T., et al.

Article: Self-efficacy for careers and occupational consideration in minority high school equivalency students.

Journal: *Journal of Counseling Psychology*, October 1992, *39*(4), 498–508.

Related Research: Lent, R. W., et al. (1989). Relation of self-efficacy to inventoried vocational interests. *Journal of Vocational Behavior*, *34*, 279–288.

■ ■ ■

7386

Test Name: JOB INVESTMENT SCALE

Purpose: To assess how much a person has invested in a job.

Number of Items: 5

Format: Varies by item. All items presented.

Reliability: Alphas ranged from .63 to .86.

Authors: Pierce, L. G., and Geyer, P. D.

Article: Combining intention with investment to predict withdrawal behavior.

Journal: *The Journal of Social Psychology*, February 1991, *131*(1), 117–124.

Related Research: Koslowsky, M., et al. (1987). Predicting behaviors: Combining intention with investment. *Journal of Applied Psychology*, *73*, 102–106.

■ ■ ■

7387

Test Name: JOB INVOLVEMENT SCALE

Purpose: To measure job involvement.

Number of Items: 3

Format: Responses are made on a 5-point scale ranging from 5 (*strongly agree*) to 1 (*strongly disagree*).

Reliability: Coefficient alpha was .53.

Validity: Correlations with other variables ranged from .07 to .28.

Authors: Maurer, T. J., and Tarulli, B. A.

Article: Investigation of perceived environment, perceived outcome, and person variables in relationship to voluntary development activity by employees.

Journal: *Journal of Applied Psychology*, February 1994, *79*(1), 3–14.

Related Research: Kanungo, R. (1979). The concepts of alienation and involvement revisited.

Psychological Bulletin, 86,
119–138.

• • •

7388

Test Name: JOB INVOLVEMENT
SCALE

Purpose: To measure job
involvement.

Number of Items: 5

Format: Examples are presented.

Reliability: Coefficient alpha
was .82.

Validity: Correlations with other
variables ranged from -.22 to .35.

Authors: Mossholder, K. W., et al.

Article: Confounding constructs
and levels of constructs in
affectivity measurement: An
empirical investigation.

Journal: *Educational and
Psychological Measurement,*
Summer 1994, *54*(2), 336–349.

Related Research: Kanungo, R. N.
(1982). Measurement of job and
work involvement. *Journal of
Applied Psychology, 67,* 341–349.

• • •

7389

Test Name: JOB INVOLVEMENT
SCALE

Purpose: To measure job
involvement.

Number of Items: 9

Format: Responses are made on a
6-point scale ranging from 1
(*strongly disagree*) to 6 (*strongly
agree*).

Reliability: Alpha coefficients were
.84 and .77.

Validity: Correlations with other
variables ranged from -.38 to .41.

Author: Blau, G.

Article: Developing and testing a
taxonomy of lateness behavior.

Journal: *Journal of Applied
Psychology*, December 1994,
79(6), 959–970.

Related Research: Kanungo, R.
(1982). Measurement of job and
work involvement. *Journal of
Applied Psychology, 67,* 341–349.

• • •

7390

Test Name: JOB INVOLVEMENT
SCALE

Purpose: To measure job
involvement.

Number of Items: 10

Format: Responses are made on a
5-point scale ranging from 1
(*strongly disagree*) to 5 (*strongly
agree*). A sample item is
presented.

Reliability: Coefficient alpha
was .87.

Validity: Correlations with other
variables ranged from -.35 to .49.

Authors: Carson, K. D., and
Bedeian, A. G.

Article: Career commitment:
Construction of a measure and
examination of its psychometric
properties.

Journal: *Journal of Vocational
Behavior*, June 1994, *44*(3),
237–262.

Related Research: Kanungo, R.
(1982). Measurement of job and
work involvement. *Journal of
Applied Psychology, 67,* 341–349.

• • •

7391

Test Name: JOB INVOLVEMENT
SCALE—SHORT FORM

Purpose: To assess job
involvement.

Number of Items: 6

Format: 5-point Likert format.

Reliability: Alpha was .67.

Validity: Correlations with other
variables ranged from -.17 to .43.

Authors: Rosin, H., and
Korabik, K.

Article: Organizational experiences
and propensity to leave: A
multivariate study of men and
women managers.

Journal: *Journal of Vocational
Behavior*, February 1995, *46*(1),
1–16.

Related Research: Lodahl, T., &
Kejner, M. (1965). The definition
and measurement of job
involvement. *Journal of Applied
Psychology, 49,* 24–33.

• • •

7392

Test Name: JOB SEARCH
BEHAVIOR INDEX

Purpose: To determine job search
activities.

Number of Items: 10

Format: Responses are made using
a yes–no format.

Reliability: Internal consistency
was .86.

Authors: Bretz, R. D., et al.

Article: Job search behavior of
employed managers.

Journal: *Personnel Psychology*,
Summer 1994, *47*(2), 275–301.

Related Research: Kopelman, R.,
et al. (1992). Rationale and
construct validity evidence for the
Job Search Behavior Index:
Because intentions (and New
Year's resolutions) often come to
naught. *Journal of Vocational
Behavior, 40,* 269–287.

• • •

7393

Test Name: JOB WITHDRAWAL
COGNITIONS SCALE

Purpose: To measure job
withdrawal cognitions.

Number of Items: 3

Format: Sample items are presented.

Reliability: Internal consistency correlations were .70 and .73. Test–retest reliability was .60.

Validity: Correlations with other variables ranged from -.60 to .63.

Authors: Carson, K. D., and Bedeian, A. G.

Article: Career commitment: Construction of a measure and examination of its psychometric properties.

Journal: *Journal of Vocational Behavior*, June 1994, *44*(3), 237–262.

Related Research: Michaels, C., & Spector, P. (1982). Causes of employee turnover: A test of the Mobley, Griffith, Hand and Meglino model. *Journal of Applied Psychology, 67*, 53–59.

• • •

7394

Test Name: LOYALTY SCALE

Purpose: To measure personal and organizational loyalty.

Number of Items: 9

Format: 5-point importance scales.

Reliability: Alpha was .74.

Authors: Ali, A. S., and Azim, A.

Article: Work ethic and loyalty in Canada.

Journal: *The Journal of Social Psychology*, February 1995, *135*(1), 31–37.

Related Research: Ali, A. (1988). Scaling an Islamic work ethic. *The Journal of Social Psychology, 128*, 575–583.

• • •

7395

Test Name: MEASURE OF PERCEIVED UNION INSTRUMENTALITY

Purpose: To measure perceived union instrumentality.

Number of Items: 7

Reliability: Coefficient alpha was .79.

Validity: Correlations with other variables ranged from .06 to .55.

Authors: Kelloway, E. K., and Barling, J.

Article: Members' participation in local union activities: Measurement, prediction, and replication.

Journal: *Journal of Applied Psychology*, April 1993, *78*(2), 262–279.

Related Research: Chacko, T. J. (1985). Member participation in union activities: Perceptions of union priorities, performance, and satisfaction. *Journal of Labor Research, 4*, 363–373.

• • •

7396

Test Name: NURSING COMMITMENT SCALE

Purpose: To measure nursing commitment.

Number of Items: 31

Format: Includes 4 areas of commitment: career, affective, continuance, and normative. Responses are made on a 5-point scale ranging from 1 (*strongly agree*) to 5 (*strongly disagree*). All items are presented.

Reliability: Alpha coefficients ranged from .67 to .91.

Authors: Reilly, N. P., and Orsak, C. L.

Article: A career stage analysis of career and organizational commitment in nursing.

Journal: *Journal of Vocational Behavior*, December 1991, *39*(3), 311–330.

Related Research: Blau, G. J.

(1988). Further exploring the meaning and measurement of career commitment. *Journal of Vocational Behavior, 32*, 284–297.

McGee, G. W., & Ford, R. C. (1987). Two (or more?) dimensions of organizational commitment: Reexamination of the affective and continuance commitment scales. *Journal of Applied Psychology, 72*, 638–642.

• • •

7397

Test Name: OCCUPATIONAL ALTERNATIVES QUESTIONNAIRE

Purpose: To assess career decidedness.

Number of Items: 2

Format: Respondents list occupations and indicate their first choice. Scoring rules are presented. All items are presented.

Reliability: Test–retest reliability was .93.

Validity: Correlations with other variables ranged from -.55 to .31.

Authors: Brooks, L., et al.

Article: The relation of career-related work or internship experiences to the career development of college seniors.

Journal: *Journal of Vocational Behavior*, June 1995, *46*(3), 332–349.

Related Research: Zener, T. B., & Schnuelle, L. (1972). *An evaluation of the self-directed search* (Center for Social Organization of Schools, Report No. 124). Baltimore: Johns Hopkins University.

• • •

7398

Test Name: OCCUPATIONAL NEEDS AND VALUES QUESTIONNAIRE

Purpose: To assess which of 69 occupations are perceived by students as satisfying their most important occupational incentive or value and also to provide the students' range of incentives satisfaction.

Number of Items: 69

Format: Includes 19 incentive labels.

Reliability: Test–retest reliability was .64 for incentives satisfaction ratings and .91 for the range of consideration score.

Validity: Correlations with other variables ranged from .01 to .43.

Authors: Church, A. T., et al.

Article: Self-efficacy for careers and occupational consideration in minority high school equivalency students.

Journal: *Journal of Counseling Psychology*, October 1992, *39*(4), 498–508.

Related Research: Bores-Rangel, E., et al. (1990). Self-efficacy in relation to occupational consideration and academic performance in high school equivalency students. *Journal of Counseling Psychology, 37,* 407–418.

■ ■ ■

7399

Test Name: OCCUPATIONAL VALUE COMMITMENT SCALE

Purpose: To measure commitment to the occupation.

Number of Items: 8

Format: Responses are made on a 5-point scale ranging from 1 (*strongly disagree*) to 5 (*strongly agree*).

Reliability: Internal consistency coefficients were .69 to .61. Stability coefficient was .57.

Authors: Vandenberg, R. J., and Scarpello, V.

Article: Multitrait-multimethod validation of the Satisfaction With My Supervisor Scale.

Journal: *Educational and Psychological Measurement,* Spring 1992, *52*(1), 203–212.

Related Research: Mowday, R. T., et al. (1979). The measurement of organizational commitment. *Journal of Vocational Behavior, 14,* 224–247.

■ ■ ■

7400

Test Name: ORGANIZATIONAL COMMITMENT AND SATISFACTION INVENTORY

Purpose: To measure organizational commitment and satisfaction.

Number of Items: 78

Format: 5-point Likert format.

Reliability: Alphas ranged from .54 to .82 across subscales.

Author: Cramer, D.

Article: Tenure, commitment, and satisfaction of college graduates in an engineering firm.

Journal: *The Journal of Social Psychology,* December 1993, *133*(6), 791–796.

Related Research: Farkas, A. J., & Tetrick, L. E. (1989). A three-wave longitudinal analysis of the causal ordering of satisfaction and commitment on turnover decisions. *Journal of Applied Psychology, 74,* 855–868.

■ ■ ■

7401

Test Name: ORGANIZATIONAL COMMITMENT QUESTIONNAIRE

Purpose: To assess the strength of one's identification with and involvement in an organization.

Number of Items: 12

Format: Responses are made on a 5-point scale. Includes 3 factors: Goal/Value Acceptance, Intent to Stay, and Willingness to Work. All items are presented.

Reliability: Alpha coefficients ranged from .48 to .88.

Authors: White, M. M., et al.

Article: Validity of evidence for the Organizational Commitment Questionnaire in the Japanese corporate culture.

Journal: *Educational and Psychological Measurement*, April 1995, *55*(2), 278–290.

Related Research: Porter, L. W., et al. (1974). Organizational commitment, job satisfaction, and turnover among psychiatric technicians. *Journal of Applied Psychology, 59,* 603–609.

■ ■ ■

7402

Test Name: ORGANIZATIONAL COMMITMENT QUESTIONNAIRE

Purpose: To measure organizational commitment.

Number of Items: 14

Format: Responses are made on a 5-point Likert scale ranging from 5 (*strongly agree*) to 1 (*strongly disagree*).

Reliability: Alpha coefficients were .90 and .88. Test–retest (3–6 weeks) reliabilities ranged from .53 to .75.

Validity: Convergent validities with theoretically relevant constructs ranged from .31 to .74.

Authors: Lee, T. W., and Johnson, D. R.

Article: The effects of work schedule and employment status on the organizational commitment and job satisfaction of full versus part time employees.

Journal: *Journal of Vocational Behavior*, April 1991, *38*(2), 208–224.

Related Research: Mowday, R. T., et al. (1979). The measurement of organizational commitment. *Journal of Vocational Behavior*, *14*, 224–247.

• • •

7403

Test Name: ORGANIZATIONAL COMMITMENT QUESTIONNAIRE

Purpose: To measure organizational commitment.

Number of Items: 15

Format: 5-point Likert format.

Reliability: Alpha was .89.

Authors: Aryee, S., et al.

Article: Antecedents of organizational commitment and turnover intentions among professional accountants in differing employment settings in Singapore.

Journal: *The Journal of Social Psychology*, August 1991, *131*(4), 545–556.

Related Research: Porter, L., et al. (1974). Organizational commitment, job satisfaction and turnover among psychiatric technicians. *Journal of Applied Psychology*, *59*, 603–609.

• • •

7404

Test Name: ORGANIZATIONAL COMMITMENT QUESTIONNAIRE

Purpose: To measure off-job satisfaction.

Number of Items: 15

Format: Responses were made on a 6-point agree–disagree scale.

Reliability: Internal consistencies ranged from .82 to .92. Test–retest reliabilities ranged from .53 to .75.

Validity: Correlations with other variables ranged from -.28 to .76.

Authors: O'Driscoll, M. P., et al.

Article: Time devoted to job and off-job activities, interrole conflict, and affective experiences.

Journal: *Journal of Applied Psychology*, June 1992, *77*(3), 272–279.

Related Research: Mowday, R., et al. (1979). The measurement of organizational commitment. *Journal of Vocational Behavior*, *17*, 50–57.

• • •

7405

Test Name: ORGANIZATIONAL COMMITMENT QUESTIONNAIRE

Purpose: To measure organizational commitment.

Number of Items: 15

Format: Responses are made on a 7-point agree–disagree scale. An example is presented.

Validity: Correlations with other variables ranged from -.05 to .23.

Authors: Campbell, K. M., and Campbell, D. J.

Article: Psychometric properties of the life role salience scales: Some construct validation evidence from a sample of nonprofessional women.

Journal: *Educational and Psychological Measurement*, April 1995, *55*(2), 317–328.

Related Research: Mowday, R., et al. (1979). The measurement of organizational commitment. *Journal of Vocational Behavior*, *14*, 224–247.

7406

Test Name: ORGANIZATIONAL COMMITMENT QUESTIONNAIRE–ADAPTED

Purpose: To measure commitment to the organization.

Number of Items: 4

Format: Responses are made on a 7-point scale ranging from 1 (*disagree strongly*) to 7 (*agree strongly*). All items are presented.

Reliability: Coefficient alpha was .76.

Validity: Correlations with other variables ranged from -.56 to .46.

Authors: Schaubroeck, J., et al.

Article: Procedural justice explanations and employee reactions to economic hardship: A field experiment.

Journal: *Journal of Applied Psychology*, June 1994, *79*(3), 455–460.

Related Research: Mowday, R. T., et al. (1979). The measurement of organizational commitment. *Journal of Vocational Behavior*, *14*, 224–247.

• • •

7407

Test Name: ORGANIZATIONAL COMMITMENT SCALE

Purpose: To measure organizational commitment.

Number of Items: 4

Reliability: Coefficient alpha was .85.

Validity: Correlations with other variables ranged from -.58 to .65.

Authors: Nye, L. G., and Witt, L. A.

Article: Dimensionality and construct validity of the Perceptions of Organizational Politics Scale (POPS).

Journal: *Educational and*

Psychological Measurement, Autumn 1993, *53*(3), 821–829.

Related Research: Hrebiniak, L. G., & Alutto, J. A. (1972). Personal and role-related factors in the development of organizational commitment. *Administrative Science Quarterly, 17,* 555–572.

■ ■ ■

7408

Test Name: ORGANIZATIONAL COMMITMENT SCALE

Purpose: To measure organizational commitment.

Number of Items: 5

Format: Responses were made on a 7-point Likert-type scale ranging from 1 (*strongly disagree*) to 7 (*strongly agree*). Examples are presented.

Reliability: Coefficient alpha was .89.

Validity: Correlations with other variables ranged from -.71 to .77.

Author: Saks, A. M.

Article: Longitudinal field investigation of the moderating and mediating effects of self-efficacy on the relationship between training and newcomer adjustment.

Journal: *Journal of Applied Psychology,* April 1995, *80*(2), 211–225.

Related Research: Mowday, R. T., et al. (1979). The measurement of organizational commitment. *Journal of Vocational Behavior, 14,* 224–247.

■ ■ ■

7409

Test Name: ORGANIZATIONAL COMMITMENT SCALE

Purpose: To measure affective,

normative, and continuance commitment.

Number of Items: 7

Format: 7-point agreement scales. All items are presented.

Reliability: Alphas ranged from .65 to .87 across subscales.

Author: Shouksmith, G.

Article: Variables related to organizational commitment in health professionals.

Journal: *Psychological Reports,* June 1994, *74*(3) Part I, 707–711.

Related Research: Mowday, R., et al. (1979). The measurement of organizational commitment. *Journal of Vocational Behavior, 14,* 224–247.

■ ■ ■

7410

Test Name: ORGANIZATIONAL COMMITMENT SCALE

Purpose: To measure organizational commitment.

Number of Items: 8

Format: Responses are made on a 5-point scale ranging from 1 (*strongly disagree*) to 5 (*strongly agree*).

Reliability: Coefficient alpha was .87.

Authors: Major, D. A., et al.

Article: A longitudinal investigation of newcomer expectations, early socialization outcomes, and the moderating effects of role development factors.

Journal: *Journal of Applied Psychology,* June 1995, *80*(3), 418–431.

Related Research: Ostroff, C., & Kozlowski, S. W. J. (1992). Organizational socialization as a learning process: The role of information acquisition. *Personnel Psychology, 45,* 849–874.

7411

Test Name: ORGANIZATIONAL COMMITMENT SCALE

Purpose: To measure organizational commitment.

Number of Items: 9

Reliability: Coefficient alpha was .80.

Validity: Correlations with other variables ranged from -.29 to .60.

Authors: Lehman, W. E. K., and Simpson, D. D.

Article: Employee substance use and on-the-job behaviors.

Journal: *Journal of Applied Psychology,* June 1992, *77*(3), 309–321.

Related Research: Cook, J., & Wall, T. D. (1980). New work attitude measures of trust, organizational commitment and personal need non-fulfillment. *Journal of Occupational Psychology, 53,* 39–52.

■ ■ ■

7412

Test Name: ORGANIZATIONAL COMMITMENT SCALE

Purpose: To measure organizational commitment.

Number of Items: 9

Format: Responses are made on a 5-point scale ranging from 1 (*strongly disagree*) to 5 (*strongly agree*). Examples are presented.

Reliability: Alpha coefficients ranged from .82 to .93.

Validity: Correlations with other variables ranged from -.33 to .49.

Authors: Aryee, S., et al.

Article: An investigation of the predictors and outcomes of career commitment in three career stages.

Journal: *Journal of Vocational*

Behavior, February 1994, *44*(1), 1–16.

Related Research: Mowday, R. T., et al. (1979). The measurement of organizational commitment. *Journal of Vocational Behavior*, *14*, 224–247.

■ ■ ■

7413

Test Name: ORGANIZATIONAL COMMITMENT SCALE

Purpose: To measure attitude involvement and identification with school.

Number of Items: 9

Format: Responses are made on a scale ranging from 0 (*strongly disagree*) to 4 (*strongly agree*).

Reliability: Internal consistency was .83 (*N* = 11,633).

Validity: Correlations with other variables ranged from -.47 to .74 (*N* = 11,633).

Authors: Vancouver, J B., et al.

Article: Multilevel analysis of organizational goal congruence.

Journal: *Journal of Applied Psychology*, October 1994, *79*(5), 669–679.

Related Research: Schmitt, N., & Ostroff, C. (1987). *Pilot study of measurement and model linkage issues for the comprehensive assessment of school environments.* Reston, VA: National Association for Secondary School Principles.

■ ■ ■

7414

Test Name: ORGANIZATIONAL COMMITMENT SCALE

Purpose: To assess organizational commitment.

Number of Items: 11

Format: Responses are made on a

7-point Likert-type scale ranging from 1 (*strongly disagree*) to 7 (*strongly agree*). An example is presented.

Reliability: Alpha coefficients were .82 and .83.

Validity: Correlations with other variables ranged from -.16 to .53.

Authors: Tannenbaum, S. I., et al.

Article: Meeting trainees' expectations: The influence of training fulfillment on the development of commitment, self-efficacy, and motivation.

Journal: *Journal of Applied Psychology*, December 1991, *76*(6), 759–769.

Related Research: Mowday, R. J., et al. (1982). *Employee-organization linkages: The psychology of commitment, absenteeism, and turnover.* San Diego, CA: Academic Press.

■ ■ ■

7415

Test Name: ORGANIZATIONAL COMMITMENT SCALE

Purpose: To measure organizational commitment.

Number of Items: 12

Format: Includes two factors: (a) Internalization and Identification and (b) Compliance. All items are presented.

Reliability: Alpha coefficients were .91 and .54.

Authors: Sutton, C. D., and Harrison, A. W.

Article: Validity assessment of compliance, identification, and internalization as dimensions of organizational commitment.

Journal: *Educational and Psychological Measurement*, Spring 1993, *53*(1), 217–223.

Related Research: O'Reilly, C., & Chatman, J. (1986).

Organizational commitment and psychological attachment: The effects of compliance, identification, and internalization on prosocial behavior. *Journal of Applied Psychology*, 71, 492–499.

■ ■ ■

7416

Test Name: ORGANIZATIONAL COMMITMENT SCALE

Purpose: To measure organizational commitment.

Number of Items: 18

Format: Includes 3 factors: Affective, Continuous, and Normative. Responses are made on a 7-point scale ranging from 1 (*strongly disagree*) to 7 (*strongly agree*). All items are presented.

Reliability: Alpha coefficients ranged from .74 to .83.

Validity: Correlations with other variables ranged from -.45 to .74.

Authors: Meyer, J. P., et al.

Article: Commitment to organizations and occupations: Extensions and test of a three-component conceptualization.

Journal: *Journal of Applied Psychology*, August 1993, *78*(4), 538–551.

■ ■ ■

7417

Test Name: ORGANIZATIONAL COMMITMENT SCALE

Purpose: To measure organizational commitment.

Number of Items: 24

Format: Sample items are presented. 7-point scales.

Reliability: Alphas ranged from .65 to .86 across subscales and samples.

Validity: Correlations with other variables ranged from -.23 to .26.

Authors: Cohen, A., and Kirchmeyer, C.

Article: A multidimensional approach to the relation between organizational commitment and nonwork participation.

Journal: *Journal of Vocational Behavior*, April 1995, *46*(2), 189–202.

Related Research: Allen, N. J., & Meyer, J. P. (1990). The measurement and antecedents of affective, continuance, and normative commitment to the organization. *Journal of Occupational Psychology, 63,* 1–18.

•••

7418

Test Name: ORGANIZATIONAL COMMITMENT QUESTIONNAIRE—SHORT FORM

Purpose: To measure organizational commitment.

Number of Items: 9

Format: Responses are made on a 7-point Likert scale ranging from 1 (*strongly disagree*) to 7 (*strongly agree*).

Reliability: Coefficient alpha was .91.

Validity: Correlations with other variables ranged from -.45 to .48.

Authors: Morrow, P. C., et al.

Article: Sexual harassment behaviors and work related perceptions and attitudes.

Journal: *Journal of Vocational Behavior*, December 1994, *45*(3), 295–309.

Related Research: Mowday, R. T., et al. (1979). The measurement of organizational commitment. *Journal of Vocational Behavior, 14,* 224–247.

7419

Test Name: ORGANIZATIONAL IDENTIFICATION SCALE

Purpose: To identify one's sense of organizational identification.

Number of Items: 6

Format: Responses are made on a 5-point agree–disagree scale.

Reliability: Reliabilities ranged from .83 to .93.

Authors: Vandenberg, R. J., and Self, R. M.

Article: Assessing newcomers' changing commitments to the organization during the first 6 months of work.

Journal: *Journal of Applied Psychology*, August 1993, *78*(4), 557–568.

Related Research: Mael, F. (1988). *Organizational identification: Construct redefinition and field application with organizational alumni.* Unpublished doctoral dissertation, Wayne State University, Detroit, Michigan.

•••

7420

Test Name: PORTER COMMITMENT SCALE

Purpose: To measure organizational commitment.

Number of Items: 15

Reliability: Coefficient alpha was .89.

Validity: Correlations with other variables ranged from -.06 to .42.

Authors: Dalton, D. R., and Mesch, D. J.

Article: On the extent and reduction of avoidable absenteeism: An assessment of absence policy provisions.

Journal: *Journal of Applied*

Psychology, December 1991, *76*(6), 810–817.

Related Research: Mowday, R. T., et al. (1979). The measurement of organizational commitment. *Journal of Vocational Behavior, 14,* 224–247.

•••

7421

Test Name: PORTUGUESE VOCATIONAL INTEREST INVENTORY

Purpose: To assess vocational interest based on Holland types.

Number of Items: 174

Format: 3-point scales (*like, indifferent, dislike*).

Reliability: Alphas ranged from .88 to .92 across six subscales.

Validity: Correlations between scales in the Portuguese sample were similar to between-scale correlations in a Holland-type inventory in the United States. Exceptions to the U.S. pattern are noted.

Authors: Armando, J., and Ferreira, A.

Article: The development and validation of a Holland-type Portuguese Vocational Interest Inventory.

Journal: *Journal of Vocational Behavior*, April 1995, *46*(2), 119–130.

Related Research: Holland, J. L. (1966). A psychological classification scheme for vocations and major field. *Journal of Counseling Psychology, 13,* 278–288.

•••

7422

Test Name: PROFESSIONAL COMMITMENT SCALE

Purpose: To measure commitment to the profession.

Number of Items: 5

Format: Responses were made on a 7-point Likert-type scale ranging from 1 (*strongly disagree*) to 7 (*strongly agree*). Sample items are presented.

Reliability: Coefficient alpha was .85.

Validity: Correlations with other variables ranged from -.57 to .61.

Author: Saks, A. M.

Article: Longitudinal field investigation of the moderating and mediating effects of self-efficacy on the relationship between training and newcomer adjustment.

Journal: *Journal of Applied Psychology*, April 1995, *80*(2), 211–225.

Related Research: Mowday, R. T., et al. (1979). The measurement of organizational commitment. *Journal of Vocational Behavior*, *14*, 224–247.

■ ■ ■

7423

Test Name: PROFESSIONAL COMMITMENT SCALE

Purpose: To measure professional commitment.

Number of Items: 10

Format: Responses are made on a 7-point scale ranging from *strongly disagree* to *strongly agree*.

Reliability: Coefficient alpha was .91.

Validity: Correlations with other variables ranged from -.21 to .43.

Authors: Grover, S. L.

Article: The effect of increasing education on individual professional behavior and commitment.

Journal: *Journal of Vocational Behavior*, February 1992, *40*(1), 1–13.

Related Research: Morrow, P. C., & Wirth, R. E. (1989). Work commitment among salaried professionals. *Journal of Vocational Behavior*, *34*, 40–56.

■ ■ ■

7424

Test Name: PROFESSIONAL INVOLVEMENT SCALE

Purpose: To measure professional involvement.

Number of Items: 6

Format: Responses are either 1 (*yes*) or 0 (*no*).

Validity: Correlations with other variables ranged from -.31 to .39 ($N = 193$).

Authors: Bauer, T. N., and Green, S. G.

Article: Effect of newcomer involvement in work-related activities: A longitudinal study of socialization.

Journal: *Journal of Applied Psychology*, April 1994, *79*(2), 211–223.

Related Research: Girves, J. E., & Wemmerus, V. (1988). Developing models of graduate student degree progress. *Journal of Higher Education*, *59*, 163–189.

■ ■ ■

7425

Test Name: PROPENSITY TO STRIKE SCALE

Purpose: To assess the willingness and propensity to strike.

Number of Items: 9

Format: 5-point scales ranging from 1 (*likely to strike*) to 5 (*highly unlikely to strike*). Items are described.

Reliability: Alpha was .93.

Author: Barling, J., et al.

Article: Union loyalty and strike propensity.

Journal: *The Journal of Social Psychology*, October 1992, *132*(5), 581–590.

Related Research: Martin, J. E. (1986). Predictors of individual propensity to strike. *Industrial and Labor Relations Review*, *39*, 214–227.

■ ■ ■

7426

Test Name: RAMAK INTEREST INVENTORY

Purpose: To measure occupational interest.

Number of Items: 72

Format: Yes–?–No format.

Reliability: Test–retest reliability (7 years) was .41. Equivalent test reliability was .76.

Validity: Correlations with other variables ranged from .28 to .40.

Author: Meir, E. I.

Article: Comprehensive interests measurement in counseling for congruence.

Journal: *The Career Development Quarterly*, June 1994, *42*(4), 314–325.

Related Research: Barak, A., & Meir, E. I. (1974). The predictive validity of a vocational interest inventory—RAMAK: Seven year follow-up. *Journal of Vocational Behavior*, *4*, 377–387.

■ ■ ■

7427

Test Name: REACTION TO EXPLORATION SCALE

Purpose: To measure the dynamics of career-information-seeking activity.

Number of Items: 6

Format: Each item is rated on a

scale ranging from 1 (*little*) to 5 (*a great deal*).

Reliability: Internal consistency was .92.

Authors: Robbins, S. B., et al.

Article: Efficacy of leader-led and self-directed career workshops for middle-aged and older adults.

Journal: *Journal of Counseling Psychology*, January 1994, *41*(1), 83–90.

Related Research: Stumpf, S. A., et al. (1983). Development of the Career Exploration Survey (CES). *Journal of Vocational Behavior*, *22*, 191–226.

■ ■ ■

7428

Test Name: SATISFACTION OPINIONNAIRE

Purpose: To learn about suitable occupations and choosing a career.

Number of Items: 10

Format: Uses a 5-point scale for each item that runs from 1 (*strongly disagree*) to 5 (*strongly agree*).

Reliability: Coefficient alpha was .96.

Authors: Zener, T., and Schnuelle, L.

Article: Two career guidance instruments: Their helpfulness to students and effect on students' career exploration.

Journal: *The School Counselor*, January 1993, *40*(3), 191–200.

Related Research: Zener, T., & Schnuelle, L. (1972). *An evaluation of the self-directed search* (Research Report No. 24). Baltimore: Johns Hopkins University, Center for Social Organization of Schools (ED 061458).

7429

Test Name: SCIENTIST–PRACTITIONER INVENTORY

Purpose: To measure career specialty interests of psychology students.

Number of Items: 42

Format: Includes two scales: Practitioner scale and Scientist scale. All items are presented.

Reliability: Coefficient alpha was .92 (Scientist scale) and .94 (Practitioner scale).

Validity: Correlations with the Vocational Preference Inventory ranged from -.43 to .62

Authors: Leong, F. T. L., and Zachar, P.

Article: Development and validation of the Scientist-Practitioner Inventory for Psychology.

Journal: *Journal of Counseling Psychology*, July 1991, *38*(3), 331–341.

■ ■ ■

7430

Test Name: SPORTS ORIENTATION QUESTIONNAIRE

Purpose: To measure three dimensions of sports orientation: compete, win, goal.

Number of Items: 25

Format: Likert format. Sample items presented.

Reliability: Internal reliability ranged from .79 to .95; test–retest ranged from .73 to .95.

Authors: Green, A. F., et al.

Article: Anger and sports participation.

Journal: *Psychological Reports*, April 1993, *72*(2), 523–529.

Related Research: Mill, D. L., & Deetes, T. E. (1988).

Development of Sport Orientation Questionnaire. *Research Quarterly for Exercise and Sports*, *59*, 191–202.

■ ■ ■

7431

Test Name: UNION ACTIVITY PARTICIPATION SCALE

Purpose: To assess the extent of union participation.

Number of Items: 11

Format: Consists of a checklist of dichotomous items. Includes items measuring informal and formal participation.

Reliability: Alpha coefficients were .84 (informal) and .89 (formal).

Validity: Correlations with other variables ranged from -.08 to .40.

Authors: Fullagar, C. J. A., et al.

Article: Impact of early socialization on union commitment and participation: A longitudinal study.

Journal: *Journal of Applied Psychology*, February 1995, *80*(1), 147–157.

Related Research: Fullagar, C., & Marling, J. (1989). A longitudinal test of a model of the antecedents and consequences of union loyalty. *Journal of Applied Psychology*, *74*, 213–227.

■ ■ ■

7432

Test Name: UNION COMMITMENT SCALE

Purpose: To measure union commitment.

Number of Items: 13

Format: Includes 3 factors: Union Loyalty, Responsibility to the Union, and Willingness to Participate in Union Activities. Examples are presented.

Reliability: Alpha coefficients ranged from .75 to .90.

Validity: Correlations with other variables ranged from -.03 to .43.

Authors: Fullagar, C. J. A., et al.

Article: Impact of early socialization on union commitment and participation: A longitudinal study.

Journal: *Journal of Applied Psychology*, February 1995, *80*(1), 147–157.

Related Research: Kelloway, E. K., et al. (1992). The construct validity of union commitment: Development and dimensionality of a shorter scale. *Journal of Occupational and Organizational Psychology*, *65*, 197–212.

▪ ▪ ▪

7433

Test Name: UNION COMMITMENT SCALE

Purpose: To measure union commitment.

Number of Items: 19

Format: Includes three dimensions: union loyalty, responsibility to the union, and willingness to work for the union.

Reliability: Alpha coefficients ranged from .79 to .85.

Validity: Correlations with other variables ranged from -.06 to .72

Authors: Kelloway, E. K., and Barling, J.

Article: Members' participation in local union activities: Measurement, prediction, and replication.

Journal: *Journal of Applied Psychology*, April 1993, *78*(2), 262–279.

Related Research: Kelloway, E. K., et al. (1992). Construct validity of union commitment: Development and dimensionality of a shorter scale. *Journal of Occupational and Organizational*

Psychology, *65*, 197–211.

Gordon, M. E., et al. (1980). Commitment to the union: Development of a measure and an examination of its correlates. *Journal of Applied Psychology*, *65*, 474–499.

▪ ▪ ▪

7434

Test Name: UNION COMMITMENT SCALE—REVISED

Purpose: To measure union commitment.

Number of Items: 18

Format: Includes three dimensions: union loyalty, responsibility to the union, and willingness to work for the union.

Reliability: Alpha coefficients ranged from .71 to .93.

Validity: Correlations with other variables ranged from -.12 to .81.

Authors: Kelloway, E. K., and Barling, J.

Article: Members' participation in local union activities: Measurement, prediction, and replication.

Journal: *Journal of Applied Psychology*, April 1993, *78*(2), 262–279.

Related Research: Ladd, R. T., et al. (1982). Union commitment: Replication and extension. *Journal of Applied Psychology*, *67*, 640–644.

▪ ▪ ▪

7435

Test Name: UNION COMMITMENT SCALE

Purpose: To assess union commitment.

Number of Items: 22

Format: Responses are made on a

5-point scale ranging from 1 (*strongly disagree*) to 5 (*strongly agree*). Includes 4 dimensions: union loyalty, responsibility for the union, willingness to work for the union, and belief in unionism.

Reliability: Alpha coefficients ranged from .71 to .89.

Validity: Correlations with other variables ranged from .33 to .87.

Authors: Shore, L. M., et al.

Article: Validation of a measure of perceived union support.

Journal: *Journal of Applied Psychology*, December 1994, *79*(6), 971–977.

Related Research: Gordon, M. E., et al. (1980). Commitment to the union: Development of a measure and an examination of its correlates. *Journal of Applied Psychology*, *65*, 479–499.

▪ ▪ ▪

7436

Test Name: UNION SATISFACTION MEASURE

Purpose: To measure union satisfaction.

Number of Items: 6

Reliability: Coefficient alpha was .79.

Validity: Correlations with other variables ranged from -.01 to .72.

Authors: Kelloway, E. K., and Barling, J.

Article: Members' participation in local union activities: Measurement, prediction, and replication.

Journal: *Journal of Applied Psychology*, April 1993, *78*(2), 262–279.

Related Research: Glick, W., et al. (1977). Union satisfaction and participation. *Industrial Relations*, *16*, 145–151.

7437

Test Name: UNION SATISFACTION SCALE

Purpose: To measure union satisfaction.

Number of Items: 2

Reliability: Interitem correlation was .57.

Validity: Correlation with other variables ranged from -.08 to .62.

Authors: Kelloway, E. K., and Barling, J.

Article: Members' participation in local union activities: Measurement, prediction, and replication.

Journal: *Journal of Applied Psychology*, April 1993, *78*(2), 262–279.

Related Research: Glick, W., et al. (1977). Union satisfaction and participation. *Industrial Relations, 16*, 145–151.

■ ■ ■

7438

Test Name: VOCATIONAL DECISION MAKING DIFFICULTIES SCALE

Purpose: To measure indecision.

Number of Items: 13

Format: True–false format. Items deal with lack of confidence about decisional skill and lack of information about self and occupations.

Reliability: KR-20 reliability coefficients ranged from .63 to .86.

Authors: Savickas, M. L., and Jarjoura, D.

Article: The Career Decision Scale as a type indicator.

Journal: *Journal of Counseling Psychology*, January 1991, *38*(1), 85–90.

Related Research: Holland, J. L., et al. (1973). *A diagnostic scheme for specifying vocational assistance* (Rep. No. 164). Baltimore: Johns Hopkins University, Center for Social Organization of Schools.

■ ■ ■

7439

Test Name: VOCATIONAL EXPLORATION AND COMMITMENT SCALE

Purpose: To assess progress in the commitment to career choices process.

Number of Items: 19

Format: Responses are made on a 7-point Likert type scale.

Reliability: Test–retest (2 weeks) reliability was .92 and for 4 weeks reliability was .92. Coefficient alpha was .92.

Validity: Correlations with other variables ranged from -.68 to .12.

Authors: Blustein, D. L., et al.

Article: Relation between exploratory and choice factors and decisional progress.

Journal: *Journal of Vocational Behavior*, February 1994, *44*(1), 75-90.

Related Research: Blustein, D. L., et al. (1989). The development and validation of a two-dimensional model of the commitment to career choices process [Monograph]. *Journal of Vocational Behavior, 35*, 342–378.

■ ■ ■

7440

Test Name: VOCATIONAL RATING SCALE

Purpose: To assess progress in the formation of the vocational self-concept.

Number of Items: 40

Format: Responses are made on a 5-point Likert scale. A sample item is presented.

Reliability: Test–retest (2 weeks) reliability was .76. Internal consistency was .94.

Validity: Correlations with other variables ranged from -.81 to .69.

Authors: Blustein, D. L., et al.

Article: Relation between exploratory and choice factors and decisional progress.

Journal: *Journal of Vocational Behavior*, February 1994, *44*(1), 75–90.

Related Research: Barrett, T. C., & Tinsley, H. E. (1977). Measuring vocational self-concept crystallization. *Journal of Vocational Behavior, 11*, 305–313.

■ ■ ■

7441

Test Name: WORK QUALITY SCALE

Purpose: To measure work quality.

Number of Items: 4

Format: Responses are made on a 5-point scale ranging from 1 (*very inaccurate*) to 5 (*very accurate*). Sample items are presented.

Reliability: Coefficient alpha was .81.

Authors: Aryee, S., and Tan, K.

Article: Antecedents and outcomes of career commitment.

Journal: *Journal of Vocational Behavior*, June 1992, *40*(3), 288–305.

Related Research: Randall, D., et al. (1990). The behavioral expression of organizational commitment. *Journal of Vocational Behavior, 36*, 210–224.

Author Index

All numbers refer to test numbers for the current volume.

Boudewyn, A. C., 6217
Bouvard, M., 5604
Bowers, D., 6644
Bowers, D. G., 5960, 6254, 6610
Bowman, G. D., 5679, 5982, 6037
Boyd, C., 6467
Boyer, S. P., 5614, 6330
Boyum, L. A., 6216, 6419
Brack, G., 5636, 6451
Bradburn, N. M., 5452
Bradbury, T. N., 6956
Bradford, E., 5687
Braiker, H., 6450
Braiker, H. B., 6744
Brand, H. J., 6436
Braunstein, D. N., 6627, 6653, 6657
Braxton, J. M., 6750, 7312
Bray, J. H., 6445, 6597
Brayfield, A. H., 5967
Brems, C., 5773, 6094, 6686, 7178
Brennan, T., 6264
Brenner, S. N., 7227
Bretherton, I., 5404
Brett, J. M., 6152, 6186
Bretz, R. D., 7392
Bretz, R. D., Jr., 5601
Breznitz, S., 6553
Brief, A. P., 5563
Briem, H., 6078
Bringle, R. G., 6496, 6851
Brink, T. L., 5535
Brody, G. H., 5476, 6446, 6471, 6900
Brookover, W. B., 6897
Brooks, J. H., 5450
Brooks, L., 6565, 6730, 6978, 7371, 7397
Brost, L., 6510
Brown, K. A., 6620
Brown, L. G., 5554
Brown, P. J., 5790
Brown, R. A., 5840
Brown, S., 5870
Brown, S. A., 6690, 6691, 6692
Bruce, D. J., 5398
Bruce, R. A., 7124
Bruch, M. A., 6375, 6391, 6690, 7170, 7201
Bryant, F. B., 7203, 7206
Brynes, D., 6141
Brynes, D. A., 5864, 6167
Buchholz, R. A., 7226, 7233, 7234
Buckley, R. M., 6209
Buczynski, P. L., 6364, 6374, 6378
Budner, J., 7152
Budner, S., 6973, 7180

Buehler, C., 5452, 5498, 6891
Bunch, J. M., 6948
Bunker, B. B., 5577
Buntzman, G. F., 6222
Burbach, H. J., 5443, 5890
Burger, J. M., 7072, 7102
Burgess, J. W., 7035
Buri, J. R., 6435, 6477, 6478, 6481, 6489
Burke, P. J., 6321, 6957
Burke, R. J., 5906, 6042, 6456, 7148, 7310, 7376
Burley, K. A., 6410, 6433, 6448, 6525
Burns, A., 6392
Burns, D. D., 7193
Burr, R., 6705
Burrell, B., 6495
Burt, M. R., 6061, 6063, 6064, 6159, 7111
Burt, S. L., 6156
Buss, A. H., 6192, 6998, 7002, 7036, 7201
Busse, W. M. O., 5735
Butcher, J., 5383
Butler, J. K., Jr., 6647
Butler, M. C., 6044
Butler, S. F., 7345
Buunk, B. P., 5509, 5542, 5754, 5833, 5836, 5899, 6010, 6164, 7107
Buxton, C., 6968
Bylski, N. C., 5523

■ ■ ■

Cacioppo, J. T., 7029, 7030
Calder, P., 6091, 6442
Calloni, J. C., 6452
Caltabiano, M. L., 6236
Caltabiano, N. J., 6236
Camarigg, V., 6571
Cammann, C., 5929, 5940, 5980, 6612, 6646
Camp, C. C., 5403
Campbell, D. J., 6142, 7405
Campbell, J. F., 7015
Campbell, K. M., 6142, 7405
Campbell, L., 5640
Campion, M. A., 5962, 6202, 6333, 6579, 7317
Campos, A., 6704
Candler-Lotven, A. C., 6287
Canfield, K. R., 6510
Cannella, G., 7127

Cantanzaro, S. J., 5502, 5599
Capie, W., 7133
Caplan, R. D., 5608, 5624, 5625, 5671, 5672, 5968, 6019, 6047, 6048
Caputi, P., 7232
Cardinal, B. J., 6256
Cardinal, M. K., 6256
Carey, L. M., 6532
Carey, M. P., 7103
Caropreso, E., 7145
Carracher, S. M., 5991
Carrere, 6569
Carrick, D. A., 6160
Carrillo-de-la-Pena, 6237, 6993
Carroll, S. J., 7074
Carson, A. D., 6874, 7037
Carson, D. K., 5540
Carson, K. D., 7352, 7356, 7370, 7390, 7393
Carter, C., 6663
Carter, R. T., 5892, 7290
Caruer, C. S., 5571
Caruso, G. A. L., 5867, 6392, 6393
Carver, C. S., 5492, 5572, 5574, 5633, 6862, 6899
Carver, R. P., 7142
Casey, T. A., 6808
Cash, T. F., 5619, 6645, 6667, 6711, 6712, 6717, 6806, 6946
Cassidy, J., 6216, 6419
Cassill, N., 7060
Catanzaro, S. J., 5512
Cattell, R. B., 7015
Causo, G. A. L., 7274
Cegala, D. J., 6343
Celano, M. P., 5722
Celuch, K. G., 7104
Cerda, C., 7259
Chacko, T. J., 7396
Chamberlain, P., 6268
Chambless, D. L., 6988
Chan, L. K. S., 6826
Chance, P. R., 6770
Chang, B. S., 7349
Chang, L. W., 6454, 6459
Chantal, Y., 6636
Chao, G. T., 5987, 7309
Chapman, D. W., 6362
Chapman, J. P., 7080
Chapman, J. W., 6869
Chapman, L. J., 5848, 7080
Chartrand, J. M., 5403, 7368
Chase, C. I., 7296
Chase-Lansdale, P. L., 5584, 6212
Chastain, R. L., 6292

Daly, J. A., 6173
Dance, K. A., 6120
Dangoor, N., 5587, 5606, 6416
Dangour, W., 6269
Daniel, L. G., 6188, 6189
Dansereau, D. F., 7278
Darkes, J., 6746
Das Eiden, R., 6390
Das-Smaal, E. A., 6198
Davey, F. H., 6853, 6976
Davidson, B., 6335
Davidson, W., 5844
Davidson, W. B., 5844
Davies, A. R., 5645
Daville, D. M., 5681
Davis, G. A., 6367
Davis, M. H., 5773, 7172, 7194
Davis, S., 6421, 6425
Dawling, D. M., 5381
Dawson, S., 6097
Day, D. V., 5960, 5973, 6610, 6782, 6883
Day, N. E., 7373
Day, R. L., 7320
De Baryshe, B. D., 6151
de Beurs, E., 5596
Dean, D. G., 5712, 5839
Deaner, S. I., 5662
Deanne, K. E., 5404, 6390
DeBerard, M. S., 5688
Decker, D., 6830
Decker, P. J., 7027
DeCotiis, T. A., 5683, 6621
Deeter, T. E., 6312
Deetes, T. E., 7430
Deffenbacher, J. L., 5428, 6232
DeFord, D., 6972
Deforest, P., 7282
DeForge, B. R., 7180
DeGenova, M. K., 5549
DeGroot, E., 6747, 7262
DeJong, P. F., 6198, 6324
deJong-Gierveld, J., 5793
Delamater, J. D., 6100
Delbecg, A. L., 6025
Delcourt, M. A. B., 6062, 6908
Delin, C. R., 5516
Delin, P. S., 5516
Dell, D. M., 5830, 7268
Delongis, A., 5538
Deluca, V. M., 6560
Delworth, U., 6374
Dembo, M., 6960, 6961
Dembo, M. H., 6959
DeMoja, C. A., 5738
Denton, S., 6380

Der-Karabetian, A., 5753, 6118
Derogatis, L., 5555, 5687
Derogatis, L. R., 5472, 5513, 5611
Descutner, C. J., 5755
Detommaso, L., 6190
Devereaux, E. C., 6493
Devine, T., 7125
Dewar, R. D., 6585
Diaz-Veizades, J., 6136
Dicker, R., 5774
Dickson, R. D., 7108
DiClemente, R. J., 5365
Didham, C., 7341
Diener, E., 5653, 5654, 7009
Diever, E. R., 5579
Dill, D., 6309
Dill-Standiford, T. J., 7324
Dillon, K. M., 5447
Dillon, W. R., 5426
Dinning, R. E., 6286
DiPaola, M. F., 6001, 6102, 6112
Dishman, R. K., 6670
DiVesta, F. J., 5372, 7356
Dixon, A. C., 6935
Dixon, J., 7001
Dixon, P. N., 6774, 7068
Dixon, W. A., 5539, 5550, 5570, 5591, 5655
Doan, G. H., 5590
Dodd, D. K., 6395
Dodge, K. A., 6987
Doering, M. M., 5903, 7385
Dohrenwend, B. P., 5639
Dominico, D., 6455
Donahue, M. J., 7251
Donaldson, G. A., 5421, 5555, 6431, 6971
Donat, D. C., 7024
Donnelly, D., 6493
Donovan, D. M., 6948
Doverspike, D., 7131
Dow, T., 5615, 5684
Dowd, E. T., 6329, 7285
Dowell, K. A., 6689
Downie, R. D., 7055
Dozier, M., 7267
Drake, M. F., 7060
Dreger, R. M., 6286
Dreyer, N. A., 7087
Driscoll, A., 7316
Dubinsky, A. J., 6140, 6357
DuBois, D. L., 5450, 5501, 5565, 5815, 6896
Dubow, E. F., 5865, 5866
DuBrin, A. J., 6275
Duckitt, J., 5715, 5717, 5823, 7197,

7242
Duckitt, J. H ., 5715
Duda, J., 7052
Duda, J. L., 6107, 6108, 6640, 6664, 6761, 6824, 6845, 7052, 7086
Duke, M. P., 6685, 6693, 6788
Dunbar, E., 5716
Dunham, R. B., 6601
Dunlop, R., 6392
Dunn, A., 5388
Dunn, R., 7130
Dunnell, P. A., 6361
Dunson, R. M., 6139
Dunst, C., 5868
Dunst, C. J., 6421
Dunst, R., 6016
Dupont, P., 5732, 7204
Dupras, A., 5594, 6134
Duran, R. L., 6338
Durand, V. M., 6654
Durgunoglu, A. Y., 6057
Durkee, A., 6998, 7036
Dush, D. M., 5544
Duttweiler, P. C., 6773, 6785
Duveen, G., 6210
Dvir, T., 6616
Dweck, C. S., 6633
Dwinell, P. L., 5792
Dwyer, J. J. M., 6661
Dyche, G. M., 7119
Dyson, R., 6944

∎∎∎

Eagleston, J. R., 5660
Eagly, A. H., 6777
Earls, F., 6476, 6504
East, P. L., 6674
Easterbrook, A., 6411
Easterbrooks, M., 6476
Eccles, J., 7235
Eckert, T. L., 6536
Eckhardt, C. I., 7105, 7248, 7250
Edelbrock, C. S., 6215
Eden, D., 6254, 6616
Eden, E., 6758
Edgerton, M., 6512
Edgerton, S. M., 5720
Edison, J. D., 7041
Edwards, D., 7044
Edwards, J. N., 6461
Edwards, J. R., 5693, 6004, 6549
Eells, T. D., 5933
Ehlers, A., 5562
Ehrhardt, A. A., 7077

Frauenknecht, M., 5860
Frederick, C. J., 5694
Freeston, M. H., 5559
French, J. R. P., 5970
French, Jr., 6549
Frentz, C., 6289, 6293
Frere, R. M., 7306
Fretz, B. R., 5530
Freudiger, P., 6506
Freund, R. D., 7283, 7291
Frey, D. K., 5907
Fried, Y., 5387, 6023, 6609, 6878, 6889, 6938
Fried-Buchalter, S., 5526, 6770
Friedland, N., 6873
Friedlander, M. L., 6027, 7336
Friedman, I. A., 5926, 6283
Friend, R., 5524, 6692
Frieze, I. H., 6702
Frith, S., 6896
Froelich, K. S., 7227
Froman, R. D., 6065
Froming, W. J., 5592
Frommer, F. D., 7139
Frone, M. R., 5477, 5642, 5946, 6423, 6430
Frost, R., 7186
Frost, R. O., 5604, 7025
Frost, S. H., 6531
Frum, J., 5735
Fry, P. S., 5535
Fukada, H., 5432, 5877
Fullagar, C., 6621, 7431
Fullagar, C. J. A., 7431, 7432
Fuller, G. B., 5590
Fullerton, J. T., 7216
Funtowicz, M. N., 5849
Fuqua, D. R., 7289
Furlong, M., 5864, 6167
Furlong, P. R., 7030, 7231
Furnham, A., 5947, 7245, 7246
Furstenburg, F. F., 6503

■ ■ ■

Gable, R., 7337
Gadzella, B. M., 5437, 6783
Galagan, P. A., 6584
Galambos, N. L., 6453
Galassi, J., 7168
Gallagher, R. P., 5438
Galvin, S. L., 6310
Gambrill, E., 7161
Gambrill, E. D., 7176
Gangstad, S., 6932
Gannon, L., 5628
Ganster, D. C., 5945

Ganster, D. L., 5508, 6406, 6523, 6524, 7335
Garber, J., 5480
Garcia, R. E., 6492
Garden, A. M., 5919
Garden, R. A., 6144
Gardner, W. M., 6073
Garfinkel, P. E., 6234
Garner, D. M., 6234, 6235
Garret, J., 7247
Garrison, S. R., 6987
Garthoeffner, J. L., 5801
Gaski, J. F., 6665, 7071, 7299
Gattiker, U., 6021
Gavazzi, S. M., 6497
Gayer, P. D., 6031
Gaynor, J. L. R., 6369
Geben, O., 7133, 7141
Geehr, J. L., 6122, 6284
Gehlauf, D. N., 6251
Geis, F. L., 7182
Geissler, T., 6806
Gelfand, M. J., 6305
Gelso, C. J., 5614, 6133, 6327, 7155, 7156, 7294
Gelson, C. J., 6072
Genereux, R. L., 6214
George, J. M., 5989, 6546, 6608, 6955
Germer, C. K., 7098
Gerner, M., 7055
Gerong, A., 7331
Gerrity, M. S., 5997
Getman, J. G., 6128
Gettinger, M., 6421, 6425
Geyer, P. D., 6846, 7387
Ghiselli, E., 6903
Gibbs, J. C., 7255
Gibson, D. B., 5737
Gibson, S., 6959, 6960, 6961
Gibson, S. G., 6737
Giegler, H., 7088
Gielen, U. P., 7255
Gierl, M. J., 6146
Gilbert, L. A., 5498, 5522
Gilbert, P., 5871, 7048
Gill, D. L., 6312, 6661
Gilliland, S. W., 6555, 6558
Gimbel, C., 6221
Ginter, E. J., 5792
Giordano, P. L., 6494
Girlin-Butcher, S., 6599
Girves, J. E., 7424
Gist, M., 6911
Gjesme, T., 6628, 7224
Gladue, B. A., 7149

Glamser, F. D., 6053
Glaser, R., 7146
Glass, C. R., 5424, 5857
Glass, D., 5992
Glass, J., 6571
Glencross, M. J., 6169
Gleser, G. G., 7000
Glick, W., 7436, 7437
Glidden-Tracey, C. E., 7292
Glover, H., 5695, 7058
Glover, R., 7253
Glynn, M. A., 6197
Goddard, H. W., 6830
Goff, B. G., 6830, 6999, 7113
Goh, D. S., 6087
Goh, S. C., 6580
Golberg, C. J., 7161
Gold, B. T., 5800, 6677, 6743, 7199
Goldberg, L. R., 7026, 7054
Goldberg, S., 6411
Goldberg, W., 6476, 6504
Goldfine, D. C., 5768
Goldman, B. A., 7164, 7171
Goldman, M. S., 6746
Goldsmith, R. E., 6265, 6839, 7083, 7100
Gomes, W. B., 7043
Gomez, M. J., 5724
Gonzalez, M. A., 6704
Good, G. E., 5755, 6539, 7075, 7079, 7094
Good, L. R., 5525
Goodenow, C., 5420, 6669, 6747, 7262
Goodglass, H., 6359
Goodman, W. K., 7059
Gordon, M. E., 7372, 7433, 7435
Gordon, R., 6969
Gordy, C. C., 7121
Gorsuch, R. L., 6281, 7252
Goswick, R. A., 5843
Gotlieb, J. B., 6140, 6204, 6357, 6559, 6593
Gottlieb, B. H., 5730
Gottman, J. M., 5741, 7170
Gould, R. P., 5614
Gould, S., 5903, 7364
Gracely, E. J., 6988
Grady, K. E., 5420, 6669, 6747, 7262
Graen, G. B., 6346, 6349
Graham, S., 6321, 6868
Grandbois, G. H., 5712
Grasha, A. F., 5828
Gray, J. J., 6710
Gray-Toft, P. A., 5982

Kin, U., 5703
King, D. W., 7109
King, L. A., 5837, 6902, 6990, 7007, 7008, 7109
King, N. J., 7014
King, P. M., 7140
King, W. C., 5751
King, W. C. , Jr., 5721, 5751, 6925, 7182
Kinicki, A. J., 6751
Kinicki, A. V., 5578
Kininmonth, L. A., 5835
Kinzer, C. K., 6109, 6160
Kinzie, M. B., 6908
Kirby, P. C., 6287
Kirchmeyer, C., 5617, 5750, 6046, 7418
Kirschner, T., 7366
Kirton, M. J., 7118
Kishton, J. M., 6935
Kisler, V., 5616, 5729
Kitchener, K. S., 7140
Kivlighan, D., 5762, 6766
Kivlighan, D. M., 6360
Kivlighan, D. M., Jr., 5759, 5768, 5776, 5777, 5778, 5784, 6331, 6872, 7319, 7321, 7347
Klebanov, P. K., 5541
Kleijn, W. C., 6059
Kleinke, C. L., 5838
Kleinknecht, R. A., 5688
Kleinpenning, G., 5831
Klen, T., 6684
Klimoski, R. J., 6996
Kline, C. A., 6428
Kline, M., 6500
Kline, T. J. B., 6219, 7123
Knight, G. P., 6398, 6414, 6473, 6759
Knoop, R., 5690, 5944, 7135
Knox, D. H., 5840
Knudson, R. E., 6173, 6184, 6185, 7116
Kobak, R. R., 7267
Kobasa, S. C., 5650
Koch, J. L., 5921
Koenig, L. J., 5745, 5869
Koeske, G. F., 5435, 5436
Koeske, R. D., 5435, 5436
Koestler, A., 7134
Kogan, E. S., 5534, 7209
Kohn, P. M., 5408
Kokdemir, D., 5824
Kokotovic, A. M., 7348
Kolb, K. J., 5470, 5918
Kolligian, J., Jr., 5756, 6833, 6932,

7019
Kolloff, M. B., 6803
Komives, S., 6261
Konopak, B., 6109
Konopak, B. C., 6160
Konovsky, M. A., 6029
Konvsky, M. A., 6035
Kopelman, R., 5595, 6526, 7392
Kopelman, R. E., 6433, 6448, 6523
Kopper, B. A., 6998
Korabik, K., 5979, 6008, 7391
Korkman, M., 6337
Korman, J. J., 6339
Kosek, R. B., 6997
Koslowksy, M., 6235
Koslowsky, M., 6714, 7386
Kosmoski, G. J., 6981
Koss, M. P., 6307
Kosterman, R., 6101
Kottke, J. L., 7227
Koufteros, X., 6739
Kovacs, M., 5478
Kowalewski, B. M., 6207
Kowalski, R. M., 5766
Kozlowski, S. W. J., 6032, 7410
Kraska, M. F., 6800
Kratochwill, T. R., 6536
Kristof, A. L., 6199
Kroner, D. G., 7185
Kubany, E. S., 6070
Kugler, K., 7177
Kuhl, J., 6276
Kuhlman, E., 6001, 6112
Kuhlman, T., 5536
Kuiper, N. A., 6120, 7175
Kumar, A., 5426
Kumar, K., 5977
Kumar, V. K., 6365
Kunkel, M. A., 6982
Kupersmith, W. J., 5922, 5923, 5924
Kurdek, L. A., 5579, 6403, 6443, 6489, 6931
Kurder, L. A., 6514
Kuriloff, P. J., 5845
Kurtines, W. M., 6992
Kurtz, J. E., 5809
Kush, K., 5713, 5901, 6732, 7004
Kuvlesky, W. P., 5752
Kwan, K. L., 7254
Kyes, K. B., 5366, 6080, 6092
Kyriacou, C., 6622

■ ■ ■

Labbe, E., 6958
Labbe, E. E., 6958

Labouvie, E. W., 6187
Labrosse, D., 5846
LaCrosse, M. B., 7281
LaCrosse, M. F., 7293
Ladd, R. T., 7434
Lafreniere, P. J., 5811
LaFromboise, T. D., 7297
Lagace, R. R., 6014
LaGaipa, J., 5733
LaGuardia, R., 6958
Lagunes, I. R., 5703
Lai, J. C. L., 5408, 5626, 5633
Laitinen, M., 5747
Lakey, B., 5489
Lam, P., 6622
Lambert, M. J., 5607
Lamborn, S., 6385, 6517
Lamborn, S. D., 7006
Lampert, M., 6792
Lamude, K. G., 5906, 6890
Landrum, R. E., 7132
Landy, F. J., 5673, 5693
Lane, A., 5634
Lang, M., 5479
Lange, A., 6444, 6974
Langston, M. G., 7236
Lantz, P. E., 7081
Larose, S., 5422
Larrance, D. T., 5814
Larsen, D. L., 6541
Larsen, K. S., 6084, 6098
Larsen, R. J., 5453, 7009
Larson, D. C., 6292
Larson, L. M., 6741
Larwood, L., 6021
Lasswell, M. E., 5841
Lasswell, T. E., 5841
Latack, J. C., 5496, 5578
Lathom, G. P., 6206
Laube, J., 5694
Laudwick-Rosenthal, R., 7072
Lawler, E. E., 6042, 6635
Lawler, E. G., III, 5952
Lawless, K. A., 6177
Lawson, A. E., 7120
Lawson, M. B., 5916
Lawton, M. P., 5661
Lay, C., 6279
Lay, C. H., 6241, 6279
Lay, C. L., 6296
Lazarus, A. A., 7209
Lazarus, R. S., 5696, 5700
Le Clere, F. B., 6207
Leak, G. K., 5848
Leana, C. R., 6778
Leary, M. K., 5756

Martin, C. L., 7164
Martin, C. M., 6691
Martin, H. J., 6036
Martin, J. E., 7425
Martin, J. K., 7076
Martin, J. L., 5711
Martin, M. M., 7167
Martin, M. W., 7258
Martin, N. K., 6774, 7068
Martin, R. A., 5493, 5662, 5669
Martin, T. N., 5935
Martinez-Pons, M., 6301
Martocchio, J. J., 5909, 6223
Marx, J. A., 5614, 6327
Massaro, A. V., 5409
Matby, J., 7213
Mateo, M. A., 6533, 7280
Mathews, A. M., 5527
Mathieu, J. E., 5449, 5928, 5964, 5972, 6012, 6573, 6574, 6617, 6627, 6892
Matkin, R. E., 7272, 7346
Matsui, T., 5675, 5898, 5985, 6722, 6729, 6849, 6909, 7063, 7210, 7359
Matt, G. E., 7125
Matteson, M. T., 5970, 5971
Mattsson, N. B., 5554
Matusi, T., 5605, 6441, 6527
Maurer, T. J., 6209, 6725, 6843, 6911, 7387
Mawson, D. L., 5762, 6766
Maxwell, S., 6362
May, B. A., 5772
May, K. M., 6170, 6214, 6756
May, R., 5523
Mayer, J. D., 5589
Mboya, M. M., 6271, 6897, 6904, 6905
McBain, B., 5939
McBain, G. D. M., 5460
McBride-Chang, C., 6056
McCarthy, B., 6162
McClain, E. W., 6379
McClanahan, G., 6412, 6482, 6926
McClelland, C. L., 5962, 6579
McCloskey, J., 5939, 6011
McCloskey, L. A., 6491
McCoard, D., 6264
McCommaughy, E. A., 7329
McConahay, J. B., 5800, 6006, 6147
McConatha, J. T., 5662
McConnaughy, E. A., 6505
McCormack, W. A., 5771, 5889
McCown, W., 5376, 6196
McCrae, R. R., 6997, 7022

McCrosby, J., 6351
McCroskery, J. H., 5673
McCroskey, J. C., 6348, 6631
McCroskey, L. L., 6631
McCubbin, H., 6386
McCubbin, H. I., 6410, 6416
McCutcheon, J. W., 7275
McCutcheon, L. E., 6968
McCutcheon, S. M., 5565
McDermott, D., 5992
McElroy, J. C., 6560
McEwen, M. K., 5726
McGee, C. R., 6187
McGee, G., 6537
McGee, G. W., 5454, 7374, 7396
McGiboney, G. W., 6663
McGreal, R., 5505
McGronigle, M. M., 7016
McGuire, J., 6476, 6504
McGuire, S., 7002
McHale, S. M., 5478, 6389, 6512
McIntire, S. M., 6681, 6859
McIntyre, R. P., 7299
McKee, I. R., 6175
McKelvie, S. J., 6969
McKenry, P. C., 5568, 5720
McKenzie, B. J., 6091, 6442
McKinney, J., 5564
McLain, D. L., 6601, 7151, 7152, 7153, 7188, 7200
Mclamed, S., 5983
McLeod, B. A., 6214
McNamara, P., 6229
McNeely, B. L., 6228, 6281, 7172
McNichols, C., 5934
McPherson, S., 7252
McQuarrie, E. F., 7104
McRobbie, C. J., 6606
McShane, S., 6128
McSheffrey, R., 6291
Mearns, J., 5599
Medley, D. M., 7016
Medora, N. P., 5791, 5839, 6927
Medway, F., 6963
Meece, J. L., 7117, 7144
Meglino, B. M., 6228, 6281, 7172
Mehrabian, A., 5387, 6629, 6632, 7173, 7174
Meier, P., 7121
Meile, R. L., 5682
Meir, E. I., 5672, 5897, 5983, 6019, 7069, 7426
Meirs, T. C., 6220
Melancon, J. G., 6123
Melburg, U., 6199
Melchior, L. A., 5474, 5475

Melisaratos, N., 5472
Mellor, S., 6520, 6576, 7372
Melnick, M. J., 6707
Melvin, K. B., 6073
Menchaca, V. D., 6629
Mendelson, M., 6714
Mendozo, P., 5430, 5677
Menec, Y. H., 6276
Merrill, J. M., 5796
Merriman, W. J., 5821, 6274
Merta, R. J., 7286
Merwin, J. C., 7355
Merwin, M. M., 5659
Mesch, D. J., 7420
Metzer, J., 6118
Mevarech, Z., 7139
Meyer, J., 7353
Meyer, J. P., 5455, 5916, 5954, 7350, 7351, 7352, 7416, 7417
Meyer, T. J., 7192
Meyer-Bahlburg, H. F. L., 7077
Meyers, L. S., 7252
Michaels, C., 7370, 7393
Michaels, R. E., 7320
Mickelson, R., 5433
Milani, K. R., 5953
Miles, E. W., 5721, 5751, 6925, 7182
Milgram, N. A., 5442, 6269
Milgram, R. M., 6245, 6326
Mill, D. L., 7430
Miller, C., 6823, 7313
Miller, I. W., 5591
Miller, J. D., 5371
Miller, J. L., 6547
Miller, L., 6585
Miller, M. D., 5381, 6173, 6796
Miller, M. J., 6733, 7293
Miller, R. S., 5798, 5858
Miller, T. R., 5886
Miller, W. B., 6506
Miller-Johnson, S., 6485
Minatoya, L. Y., 6161
Mines, R. A., 5799
Mintz, L. B., 6285, 6715, 7215
Mirels, H., 7247
Mirowsky, J., 5996, 6831, 6943
Mitchell, M., 7084
Mitchell, M. T., 7084
Mitchell, S. L., 5830
Mitchell, T. R., 6620
Mittal, B., 6105, 7040
Mobley, W. H., 5896, 6038
Moeller, A. T., 5862, 7138
Mohr, P. B., 6157
Moilanen, D. L., 5518

Roedcl, T. D., 5423, 6641, 6701
Roehlke, H. J., 7333
Rogers, D., 7007
Rogers, S. U., 5913
Rohde, R. I., 7296
Rohner, R. P., 5618, 6474
Rohrbough, J., 7249
Roid, G. H., 6510
Roig, M., 5414, 5758, 6073, 6190
Rokeach, M., 7253
Romano, J. L., 6724
Romans, J. S., 6870
Romero, J. E., 7131, 7137
Rompa, D., 6659, 6675, 6676
Rook, K., 5639
Rooney, R. A., 6816
Roopnarne, J. L., 5868, 6480
Roosa, M. W., 6395
Rose, J., 6963
Rosen, H., 6013
Rosen, J. C., 6711
Rosenbaum, M., 6294, 7044
Rosenberg, M., 6922, 6923, 6925, 6979
Rosenberg, S. D., 6768
Rosenfeld, P., 6263
Rosenthal, E. H., 6061, 6064, 6159, 7111
Roshin, H., 6008
Rosin, H., 5979, 7391
Rosolack, T. K., 7026
Ross, C. E., 6831, 6943
Ross, J. M., 7252
Rosse, J., 6547
Rosse, J. G., 6547
Rotberg, H., 6732
Rotenberg, K. J., 7259
Roth, W. M., 5427
Rothbaum, B. O., 6314
Rothblum, E. D., 5401, 5402
Rothe, H. F., 5967
Rotter, G. S., 6774
Rotter, J. B., 5782, 6784, 6893, 6894
Roussel, D. M., 7093
Rowland, V. T., 6495
Rowledge, A. M., 7051
Rowlinson, R. T., 5501
Roy, R., 5422
Roychoudhury, A., 5427
Rubin, A. M., 5842
Rubin, R. B., 5842, 7167
Rubin, Z., 7232
Rucker, C. N., 6079
Rucker, M., 7011
Rudd, M. D., 5569

Rudisill, M. E., 6805
Ruh, R., 7135
Ruiz-Caballero, J. A., 6991
Runco, M. A., 6369
Rusbutt, C. E., 7378
Rush, M. C., 5496, 5957, 5971, 6038, 6973
Rushton, J. P., 6989
Rushton, R., 7017
Russell, D., 5885, 5886, 5887, 5888, 5889
Russell, D. R., 7202
Russell, D. W., 5729, 5861
Russo, M. F., 6672
Rustemli, A., 5824
Rutter, M., 5584
Ryan, A. M., 6179
Ryan, B. A., 6427
Ryan, L. B., 6079
Ryan, R. M., 6300
Ryckman, R. M., 6137, 6744, 6837, 6860, 6970, 7073
Ryff, C. D., 5646, 6376, 7005

● ● ●

Saad, I. A., 5952
Saavedra, R., 5783, 6342
Sabnani, H. B., 6147, 6688
Sabo, D. J., 6581
Sabourin, S., 5686
Sachs, R., 6085
Sackeim, H. A., 6902
Safilios-Rothschild, C., 7264
Sagi, A., 6247, 6465
Sagie, A., 7265
Saks, A. M., 5395, 5445, 5937, 5938, 6049, 6771, 6914, 7408, 7422
Salminen, S., 6684
Salt, R., 5884
Salt, R. E., 5884
Sameroff, A. J., 6371
Sampson, J. P., Jr., 7281
Sanders, V. L., 5802
Sandhu, D. S., 5705
Sandler, I. N., 5489
Sandman, B. A., 5970
Sandor, J. A., 6531
Santiago-Rivera, A. L., 7256
Santor, D. A., 5560, 7005
Santor, D. M., 6683
Sapp, S. G., 6789
Sarason, I., 5568, 5569, 5570
Sarason, I. G., 5423, 5442, 5487,

5565, 5567, 5692, 5873, 5874
Sarason, S. B., 5441
Sardo-Brown, D., 6176
Satterfield, W. A., 6749
Saucier, G., 7026
Savage, M. P., 6734
Savickas, M. L., 5984, 6625, 6651, 7438
Sawilowsky, S. S., 6187
Sawyer, J. E., 6880
Sazer, L., 7249
Scalise, J. J., 5792
Scandura, T. A., 6346, 6349, 7307, 7308
Scarpello, V., 6015, 7375, 7399
Schachter, S. C., 7080
Schadt, D., 5712
Schaefer, E. S., 5720, 6218, 6398
Schaeffer, A. M., 6086
Schaeffer, E., 6512
Schalling, D., 6643
Schau, C., 6083, 6174
Schaubroeck, J., 5510, 5625, 5931, 5990, 6030, 6879, 6885, 7406
Schechter, J. O., 6285
Scheehan, M. K., 6153
Scheer, S. D., 6515, 6530
Scheier, M., 5571, 5572
Scheier, M. F., 5573, 5574, 5633, 6899
Schell, B. H., 6560
Scherer, M., 6666, 6757
Scherer, R. F., 5676
Scheuring, S. B., 5438
Schill, T., 5481, 5488, 5708, 5767, 7045
Schirtzinger, M. B., 5586, 7091
Schlein, S., 5801
Schlein, S. P., 5775
Schlenker, B. R., 6199
Schmeck, R. R., 7128
Schmidt, C. P., 7340
Schmidt, L. D., 7292
Schmidt, N., 5747
Schmit, M. J., 6179, 7160
Schmitt, N., 5961, 6648, 6655, 7413
Schmitz, P. J., 7319
Schnake, M., 5963
Schneida, M., 7257
Schneider, B., 6607, 7342
Schneider, H. G., 6948
Schneider, L. J., 7285, 7303
Schneider, N. G., 6238
Schneider, W. J., 5451
Schnittger, M. H., 5498
Schnuelle, L., 7397, 7428

Souliere, M. D., 5826, 5846
South, R., 6505
Southern, W. T., 6104
Sowa, C. J., 5623, 6756, 6813
Spanier, G., 6460
Spector, J. E., 5398
Spector, P., 5947, 7370, 7393
Spector, P. E., 5769, 5994, 6017, 6045, 6887
Speight, J. D., 6801
Spence, J., 6094, 6522, 7062
Spence, J. T., 5543, 6041, 6085, 6086, 6092, 6093, 6853, 6854, 7031, 7063, 7091, 7099, 7210
Spencer, D. G., 7384
Spengler, P. M., 7097
Sperling, M. B., 5461, 5746
Spielberger, C. D., 5565, 7156
Spirrison, C. L., 6619, 7121
Spitzberg, B. H., 5832
Spivack, G., 6317
Spokane, A. R., 5675, 6863
Sporakowski, M. J., 5840
Spoth, R. L., 5544
Sprecher, S., 5812, 5838
Sproule, C. F., 6975
St. Lawrence, J. S., 5368
Stager, S. F., 6150
Stahl, M. J., 6647
Stahl, S. A., 6363
Stains, G., 6036
Stake, J. E., 6694, 6851, 6947
Stamp, C., 5610
Stanley, G. H., 7114
Stanley, S. M., 6401
Stanovich, K. E., 5369, 5373, 5379, 5382, 5384, 5392, 5393, 5394
Staples, C. L., 6924
Stapp, J., 6970
Stark, J. S., 6650
Stead, G. B., 6727
Steenkamp, J. B. E. M., 6632, 6660, 6673
Steers, R., 6653
Steers, R. M., 6627, 6657
Steffy, B., 6439
Stein, R., 6466
Steinberg, L., 6385, 6412, 6517, 7006
Steinberg, S., 5716
Steiner, D. D., 6206, 7298
Steinhardt, M. A., 6861, 6980
Stephens, R., 7340
Stern, M., 5679, 5982, 6037
Stern, P. C., 6236
Stern, R. M., 5673

Sternberg, R. J., 5756, 6113, 6698, 6833, 6932, 7019
Stets, J. E., 5742, 5743, 5744, 5820
Stevens, A. A., 5589
Stevens, C. K., 6199, 6829
Stevens, G. E., 6111, 6132
Stevens, H. B., 6310
Stevens, M. J., 6294
Stever, G. S., 5731
Steward, R. J., 5443, 6240, 6836
Stewart, A.L., 5532
Stickel, S. A., 6721
Stiles, W. B., 7321, 7322, 7323, 7324, 7325, 7326
Stinnett, J. L., 6285
Stith, S. M., 5699
Stockdale, M. S., 6306
Stolberg, A. L., 6987
Stoppard, J. M., 6853, 6976
Storey, R. G., 7151
Stott, D. H., 6212
Strack, S., 6984
Street, E. M., 5704
Streifer, P. A., 7338
Strickland, B. R., 6814
Stringer, R. A., Jr., 6782
Stringfield, S., 6210
Strohmer, D. C., 7097
Strong, S. R., 7270
Strube, M. J., 6295
Struening, E. L., 6149
Strutton, D., 5571, 5696, 6014, 6598
Stubbs, M. T., 7213
Stumpf, S. A., 7365, 7366, 7380, 7382, 7383, 7427
Stunkard, A., 6714
Subich, L. M., 6910
Suchet, M., 6513
Sudhir, M. A., 6366
Sue, D. W., 7311
Sugar, F., 6054
Suinn, R., 5880
Sujan, H., 6668
Sumerlin, J. R., 6860, 6945
Sun, A., 5433
Sundberg, N. D., 5469
Super, D., 6400, 7368
Susak, Z., 7139
Sutherland, V., 7108
Sutton, C. D., 7415
Svebak, S., 5662
Swann, W. B., Jr., 6930
Swiatek, M. A., 5670
Swift, M. S., 6316
Swop, W. C., 7259

Syrik, B., 5403
Szajna, B., 5908, 5911
Szapocznik, J., 5722
Szymanski, M. L., 6711, 6712, 6946

• • •

Tafarodi, R. W., 6930
Takagi, H., 5787
Tan, A., 7003
Tan, K., 5975, 6043, 6050, 6381, 6439, 6513, 6586, 7442
Tanaka, K., 5605
Tangel, D. M., 6363
Tannenbaum, A. S., 6828
Tannenbaum, S. I., 6635, 6681, 6859, 7414
Tantleff, S., 6710
Tappe, M. K., 6664
Tarenzini, P. T., 5444
Tarter, C. J., 5924
Tarulli, B. A., 6725, 6843, 7387
Tarullin, B. A., 6911
Tata, S. P., 5765
Taub, D., 5799, 5806
Taub, D. J., 5726
Taylor, G. J., 7056
Taylor, J., 6380, 7205
Taylor, J. A., 5585
Taylor, J. C., 5960, 6610
Taylor, K. M., 6722, 6723, 6724
Taylor, M. S., 6914
Teasdale, J. D., 6991
Teddlie, C., 6287
Tedeschi, J., 6199
Tegano, D. W., 6367
Teixeira, M. A., 7043
Tellegen, A., 7022, 7027
Telljohann, S. K., 6090
Templar, D. I., 5503, 5691
Temple, L. E., 6847
Tennen, H., 6700
Tepper, B. J., 7137
ter Kuile, M. M., 6810
Terenzini, P. T., 5410
Teresa, J. S., 6815, 7381
Terrell, F., 5739
Terrell, S. L., 5739
Terry, H., 7190
Terry, P. C., 5491
Terwilliger, J. S., 6099
Tesch, B., 5364
Tetrick, L. E., 5763, 6594, 7400
Thauberger, P. C., 5465
Thayer, R. E., 5447

Subject Index

All numbers refer to test numbers. Numbers 1 through 339 refer to entries in Volume 1, numbers 340 through 1034 refer to entries in Volume 2, numbers 1035 through 1595 refer to entries in Volume 3, numbers 1596 through 2369 refer to entries in Volume 4, numbers 2370 through 3665 refer to entries in Volume 5, numbers 3666 through 5363 refer to entries in Volume 6, and numbers 5364 through 7441 refer to entries in Volume 7.

Abasement, 1720

Aberration, perceptual, 3266

Abidingness, law, 287

Abilit(ies)(y): 6996; academic, 766, 6824; analytic, 661; cognitive, 2678; conclusions, 2217; confidence, 6018; cope, stress, 1677; coping, 5445; discrimination, 1041, 1249; general reasoning, 2220; human relation, 1714; inductive reasoning, 2209, 2221; information-transformation, 110; intuitive, 3430; letter formation, 1052; learning, 6054; lipreading, 5386; mental, 138; occupational, 305; perceptual motor, 2213; performance, 6; problem solving, 1468, 2226; reasoning, 2204; screening, 5387; self-concept, 1850; self-estimates, 305, 766, 1428, 1429; sports, perceived, 6845; supervisor(y), 1019, 2265; verbal, quantitative, 2213; visual-spatial, 6053; work, 1033

Abortion, attitude toward, 1131, 4229, 4318

Abrasiveness, self-rated, 749

Absenteeism: attitude toward, 4230; consequences of, 4118; group influence, 4148; self-reported, 6302, 6303; student, 3698

Abstract(ness): conceptualization, 2216; concreteness, 2200; reasoning, 2201, 2202, 3424

Academic(ally)(s), 388, 621, 675, 2191: ability, 766, 6824; ability, confidence, 2147; ability, self-concept, 2128; acceleration,

6104; achievement, 477, 1337; achievement accountability, 467; achievement motivation, 1987; achievement orientation, 228; achievement predictor, 2683, 2684; achievement, university residence, 704; adequacy, peer counseling, 1973; adjustment, 22; advising, 1959, 6531; advisors, undergraduates, 992; anxiety, 400, 2404; assistant, evaluation, 992; attitudes, 1126, 6060, 7262; attribution, 3327, 5399,5439; autonomy, 5400; barriers to women, 5894; climate, 1335; competence, 2421, 5391; constraints, 6534; course evaluation, 6532; curiosity, 1984; environment, attitude, 1126; factors, 527; integration, 2399; locus of control, 3222; misconduct, 6188, 6189, 6190; motivation, 578, 1985, 3123, 6532, 6624; orientation, 228; performance, 471, 5430; prediction, 231, 6059; procrastination, 5401, 5402; progress assessment, 5405; self-concept, 1395, 2030, 2056, 3153, 3301, 3303, 6679, 6680, 6852; self-concept, elementary school, 2147; self-efficacy, 6681, 6682; self-esteem, 2031, 3154, 3155, 3278; skills, 400; status, college freshmen, 904; stress, 5430, 5446; success, correlates, 95, 6291; success, fear of, 2410; support for achievement, 6550; talented elementary students, 1606

Acceptance, 583, 645, 655, 659: among children, 3965; of authority, 4352, 4353; blame, 907; of career stagnation, 4128; disability, 1636; father, 645; interpersonal, 5772; group, perceived, 5702; loss, 1636; of generalized other, 4065; peer, 5774; of past, 6683; perceived maternal, 759; school, 1070; self, 249, 759, 831, 1105, 1425, 4065, 4832; social, 1104, 2593

Access, social, 1452

Accidents, 6273: locus of control, 6684; pilot, 478

Accountability, academic achievement, 467, 1367

Accounting: attitude toward, 4240; job satisfaction, 4146; self-efficacy, 6771

Acculturation, 1696, 5714, 5752, 5761: Asian(-American), 4100, 5880; attitudes, 5703;behavioral, 5722; Mexican-Americans, 2547, 3519, 3966; Puerto Rican, 3967; Vietnamese, 5722

Achievement, 1-21, 218, 340–386, 949, 1035–1066, 1596–1624: academic, 477, 1337; academic accountability, 467, 1367; academic, locus of control, 3196; anxiety, 23, 908, 1625, 2433, 2439; artistic and sex role, 877; athletic and sex role, 877; attitudes toward, 6175; attribution, 3157, 3253; college, 480; competitive, 989; controlled, 989; dynamics, 1631; excellence, 861; expectations, 6625; first grade, 469, 474; identity, 271, 628,

satisfaction, 182, 999, 2335, 3059, 4635–4637, 4684, 5261, 5265, 5266; self-rating, 310; therapist, 2903; verbal behavior system, 587

Climate: bank, 3054; classroom, 3100, 6580; counseling, 999; job, 1967; learning, 1323; organization, 1308, 3050, 3097–3099, 3102, 6581, 6598, 6610; perceptions, 6782; school, 3108; work, 6622

Closed-mindedness, 413, 2292

Closure, speed, 1612, 1617

Clothing, 7060, 7067: deprivation, perception of, 4894, 5224; orientation, 875; values, 5224

Coding, 2215

Coffee, 1122

Cognit(ion)(ive), 3, 1255: ability, 2678, 2961; affect, 404; agoraphobic, 2438; anxiety assessment, 3787, 5457, 5485, 5486, 5490; assessment, children, 2405, 7145; automatic thoughts, 5119, 5463, 5464; Beck's cognitive triad, 3788; behavioral changes, 572; behavior, infant, 1287; behavior, student, 568; belief systems, 4492; career decision-making, 5118; catastrophic, 5473; child critical thinking strategies, 5157; child problem-solving skills, 5120; in claustrophobic situations, 5482; coherence in daily living, 3931;competence, 6835; complexity, 47, 1279, 1465, 1913, 2229, 3408, 3421; complexity, children, 2203; complexity, interpersonal, 433; complexity, simplicity, 433; complexity, vocational, 707; components, 1209; conceptual level, 4492, 4493; control, 913, 924, 1506, 2289; couple functioning, 4533; dealing with strangers, 4097; decision-making needs, 4702; in depression, 3784, 5488; development, 623, 627, 635, 4515, 5149, 6378; differentiation, 2230; difficulty, 1670; distortion avoidance, 3811; distortion in rheumatoid

arthritis, 3786; educational objectives, 5138; egocentricism, 1491; emotional autonomy, 4000, 4001; error, 3192, 5028, 6735; evaluation of display formats, 285; flexibility, 923, 7167; functioning, 260, 1121, 2213; functioning, adolescents, 605; functioning, preschool, 59; future expectation, 3845–3847, 4922; hemisphere specialization, 5129, 5160; home environment, 642; hope, 3844; impairment, 2681; individual differences, 5142; information processing style, 5106, 5116, 5128, 5159; inner speech, 6250; intellectual development, 4506; intelligent vs. unintelligent behavior, 4397; intention to quit job, 4141, 4212, 4215; intrusive thoughts, 5122, 5487; irrational thinking, 5125, 5154; job outcomes appraisal, 4144; knowledge of, 3669; lapses in control, 5121; learning, 175, 5131–5133, 5135–5137, 5153; level, children, 2224; logic of confidence, 4029; logical thinking, 5158; mental states, 5590; metacognitive awareness, 6056; moral reasoning, 5126, 5140, 5232; need, 3367, 4725–4727, 7029, 7030; objectivism, 5058; obsessive-compulsive, 3893; optimism, 4863; in oral examination, 5424; pessimism, 3834; predisposition to depression, 3813; preference, 2179, 3391, 3410; problem solving styles, 5134; process, 265, 3193, 3423; processing, children, 1905; propositional logic, 5147; proverb interpretation, 5148; quick assessment in patient-care setting, 5123; rational thinking in children, 5124; reflective judgment, 5149, 5150; regulation 3669; rigidity, 5175, 5176, 5184, 5206; schizotypal, 6220; sense of coherence, 6940; skills assessment, 5372; social studies strategies, 5151; speed, 7142; structure, 218; student

strategies, 7117; style, 1479, 1498, 3369; style, field dependence, 815; style, flexibility, 939; style, fourth-sixth graders, 939; subjectivism, 5076; suicidal ideation, 3917, 3925, 3942; during surgery, 6939; teacher decision-making, 5152; tempo, 603, 942; temporal lobe signs, 5143, 5155; testwiseness, 5127; vocational maturity, 1040, 1938

Cohabitation, off campus, 181

Cohesion: gross, 1710; group, 1710, 1711, 2569

Colleagues, evaluation, 1009

Collective: bargaining, 1773, 6542; negotiations, 538

Collectivism, 5225, 5765, 7228

College/University: absenteeism, 3698; achievement, 480; achievement motivation, 4695; activities, 683; adjustment, 22, 2401, 3695, 3696, 3701, 3703, 3709, 3735, 5403, 5408, 5421, 5432, 6482; adaptation, 5422, 5431; admissions assistance, 660; alienation, 5443; application, 553; aptitude, 1120; assertiveness, 3467–3469, 5166, 7168; attendance, goals and purposes, 719; business major curriculum objectives, 661; campus dissent, 1098; characteristics, 117, 180; choice, 7068; classes, teacher effect, 333; classroom and social involvement, 3699; commitment, 206; community, sense of, 4674; counseling center effectiveness, 4638; counseling needs, 4999; courses, attitude toward, 151, 7069; course evaluation, 1024, 1540, 3064; departments, 3067; environment, 165, 172, 177, 179, 184, 187, 212, 672, 675, 683, 1311, 4633, 4686; equal opportunity climate, 4675; expectations, 662, 6750; experience, 675; extent of sexual harassment, 4676; freshmen, 353, 364, 441, 632, 662; freshmen, academic status, 904; freshmen adjustment, 2420; freshmen, attitudes, 1135;

nurses, 4478; organization(al), 1898, 1901, 2919; pantomime, 6359; parent-child, 103, 640, 1295, 1297, 2897; patterns, 597; principal teacher, 688; referential, 2923; respect, 2344; satisfaction, 2904, 5842, 6344, 6354; self-disclosure, 4486–4490, 6355; self-evaluation, 6356; skills, 175, 2913, 6353; suggestion, 2902; supervisors, 1023, 2915, 2916, 2926; teacher-student, 2911; team, 6358; verbal-nonverbal, 2921; workplace, 4479

Community college: aptitude, 75; articulation, 3163; counselor training, 664; faculty attitudes, 1159; freshmen, 472; public, 508; sex role, 3389

Community: employee commitment, 1996; judgment, 1312; participation, 1454; satisfaction, 3060; sense of, 5844

Companion, imaginary, 1397

Comparing, 2215

Compensation, 663

Competenc(e)(y), 659, 3317, 6737: academic, 2421, 5391; adolescents' interpersonal, 3698; behavior, 432; children, 2593, 3260, 3685; children, young, 4052; children's self-concept, 4917; children's social skills self-assessment, 3980; cognitive, 6825; communicative, 2922, 2924, 6338; consumer, 3681; counselor, 3571; daily living, 3672, 3681, 3791, 3926, 4367; dating, 3992, 3997, 5741; educational, 767; female professional, 975, 3243; general social, 636; hockey, 6765; interpersonal, 446, 1724, 6970; language, 380, 384; leader, 1555; managerial, 3586; motor, 6805; occupational, 4123; parenting, 4608; perceived, 6836; perception of, in children, 4895; personal, 1105; physical, 6837; premorbid, 2594; presenter, 3591; problem solving, 3681; self-efficacy beliefs, 4986, 4989; self-perception, 6826, 6970, 6971;

sense of, 2070, 6941; social, 2567, 6971; social, teacher rated, 4077; students', 2349, 6762; students' social, 5010; teacher, 7327, 7328; teaching, 1015, 1025; therapist, 5262

Competit(ion)(ive), 713, 1775, 1802, 2826, 3412, 5738: anxiety, 3790, 5212, 5491; athletic, attitude toward, 4339; attitude toward, 4286; knowledge, 2928; in sports, 6312; trait self-confidence, 5217

Competitive(ness), 1720, 4700, 5183, 6219, 7169: achievement, 989; hypercompetitiveness, 4711, 6318

Complexity, 614: cognitive, 1279, 3408; conceptual, 120, 1421, 1499, 1509; interpersonal, 47; perceptions, 768; sentence, 7; tolerance, 612; work, 268; vocational, 336

Compliance, 6222: smoking ban, 5896; supervisors, 1005

Composition: ability, 370; evaluation, 1031; written, 370

Comprehension, 5, 15, 349, 355, 1735, 5374: age four, 134; anaphora, 5, 2370; counselors, 380, 384; humor, 2378; inferential reading, 1605; languages, 355; listening, 2688; literal reading, 1609; moral, 3556; oral, 365; reading, 14, 20, 1055, 1062, 2688; reading, college students, 1615; sentence, 5; social-moral(s) concepts, 1599, 2308; syntactic, 383; verbal, 1904, 1912, 1915; vocabulary, 365

Compulsiveness, 3493, 3497, 7025

Computer science, 2679

Computer(s): anxiety, 3705, 3774, 3792–3797, 5908–5911; aptitude, 4224, 4225; attitude toward, 115, 152, 2724, 2726–2729, 4278, 4280–4285, 4287, 5907, 6062, 6116; concerns, 5914; operational hassles, 3796, 3797; perceived self-efficacy, 4800, 6739, 6740; perceptions about, 4830, 4831; playfulness, 6223; stress, 5912, 5913

Concentration, 645

Concept(s): anthropological, 1269;

attainment, 2924; educational research, 1746; formation, 120, 2213; identification, 884, 2928; justice, 381; masculine-feminine, 114; meaning, 106–125, 602–605, 1269–1279, 1903–1919, 2930; number, 2939; occupational, 1909; people, 502; relationships, 2936; social work, 1277; task, multiplecategory, 358–363; unpleasant, 35

Conceptual: complexity, 120, 1499, 1509, 2934; development, 135; differentiation, 1273; flexibility, 923; set, 1068; structure, 122, 604; style, 603, 1272, 1906; style, children, 1905; tempo, 604, 1919, 2211

Concrete(ness): abstractness, 2200; experience, 2216; reasoning abilities, 2227

Conditions, job, 1404

Conduct, classroom, 578

Confidence, 6018: anxiety and, 5490; child management, 2051; information processing, 2907; lack of, 515; occupational perception, 4172; reading, 3276; science and engineering student, 3733; social, 4103; student, 6720

Configurations, part-whole, 13

Conflict(s), 796: adolescent-parent, 6453, 6530; child study, 1466; couples, 6403, 6443; dating, 5742; ethical, 3530; family, 3003; group, 445; handling, 1865, 5810; home-career, 2228; identify, 949; interpersonal, 523, 1950, 2573, 4015, 5769; intragroup, 5783; locus of, 2085; management, 4003, 4480, 5091; marital, 2973; model, 616; mode of handling, 1848; mother-daughter, 6467; non-, 481; parental, 6446, 6471, 6500; personal, 2208; positive choice, 2208; psychodynamic, 5621; resolution, 1857; role, 1687, 2357, 2526, 2641, 3002, 3289, 3290, 3292, 3341, 5617, 6883–6891; spouse, 6447; work-family, 6432, 6433, 6437, 6448, 6523–6528; workplace, 5769

• • •

2176; anomic, 413; dependence, 2199; distance, 50, 56; distress, 35, 2493, 5639, 5641; functioning, 5547, 5555; health, attitude, 1137; help, attitude, 2743; influence, 3324; moods, 1669; needs, 1339, 6630; patient communication, 6350; reactance, 6282, 6329; reports and service, attitude toward, 154; separation, 3040; state, 841; stress, 2517; symptoms, 5554, 5687; testing, 1127; well-being, 2493, 5645, 5646

Psychologist: attitudes, 154; burnout, 3950; career specialization, 7430; perceived, 3265; stress, 2662

Psychology: attitude toward, 1127; knowledge assessment, 5375, 5389; misperceptions about, 6968; occupations in, 142, 903

Psychopath(ic)(y), 855–857: criminal, 2518

Psychopathology, 5468, 5643: child, 6215; dimensions of, 412, 2448, 3346

Psychosexual maturity, 1668

Psychosocial: development, 632, 1941, 2945, 2947, 2955; environment, 1960; stress, 5647

Psychosomatic: complaints, 2480, 2516; symptoms, 3858

Psychotherapists: attitudes, 6155; and patients, 306

Psychotherapy, 1137: check list, 2519; evaluation, 1080, 7319; fear of, 2451; process, 2352, 2616; relationship, 7276

Psychotic symptoms, 773, 853

Psychoticism, 1681

Public exposure to sexual stimuli, 1761

Public policy issues, 1797

Public school(s), 687: teaching, 539

Puerto Ricans, 3967

Pun, 613

Punishment: capital, 1750; direct object, 654; parental intensity, 1949; symbolic love, 654

Punitive-controlling, 652

Punitiveness, attitudes, 2770

Pupil: affect, 1217; attitude, 455, 540; behavior, 574, 578, 6283;

control, 810; control ideology, 1819, 2117, 2771, 3105, 3282, 3283; development, 637; evaluation, 3374; ideal, 1929; information acquisition, 1; interaction, 1027; interest by teacher, 1027; observation by teacher, 1027; opinion, 541, 1820; ratings, 2870; ratings by teachers, 297, 298; responses, 1267; self-esteem, 3276; teacher, 600

• • •

Q sort, 822, 831, 1678

Qualit(ies)(y), 681: class, 3116; classroom, 6592; college departments, 3067; education, 663; hospital, 6593; leadership, 338; of life, 3914, 3915, 5608; of life, diabetes and, 5514; of life, health-related, 5532, 5556; of life, workplace, 4187; mathematics, lecture, 3086; school life, 6599; of services, 6607; of teaching, 7280; work, 7442

Quality circles, 6284

Quantitative, achievement, 1043, 1063; aptitude, 1732

Question(ing)(s): classroom, 1266; skills, 7139

• • •

Races, tolerance of, 1792

Racial: academic predictor, 2684; attitudes, 46, 78, 79, 87, 88, 482, 520, 542, 1147, 1176, 1804, 1812, 1813, 4325, 4327, 5715, 5716, 5717, 5800, 5808, 5831, 6147, 6158, 6161; attitude, first grade, 1813; attitude, preliterate children, 1814; attitude, preschool, 1814; cultural values, 5228; discriminatory behavior, 4451; evaluation, 3448; factors, 386; identity/identification, 2772, 2773, 4315–4317, 4320, 5725–5727, 5802, 5806, 5830, 5892; intermarriage attitudes, 90;

mistrust, 3991; preference, 865, 1459; relations, 76, 99; self-concept, 4929; stereotype, 520, 1154, 4291, 4327; subjective identification, 4818; supervisor-employee relations, 4765; workplace situations, 6007

Radicalism, 280, 529: -conservatism, 1821

Rape, 3684; attitudes, 4246, 4436, 6064, 6077, 6159; empathy, 5202; perceptions, 4931, 4932

Rapport: with students, 33; teacher, 1891

Rating: applicant, 3588; college course, 1024; counseling interviews, 699, 3594; counselor, 35, 72, 3573, 3595; curriculum, 706; managers, 3580; peer, 2556; police, 3577, 3579, 3587; sales person, 3596, 3598; scales, descriptive, 215; students, 24; teacher, 1028, 2395; work trainee, 338

Rational, 2205, 2206: behavior, 1679, 1874, 2774, 2871

Rationality, 1679, 2931

Reaction: counseling, 311; to traumatic events, 5557

Reactive, inhibition, 399

Readers, retarded, 340

Readiness, for first grades: reading, 352, 356, 357, 1118; school, 469; vocational planning, 470; words, 337

Reading, 2, 12, 15, 21, 340, 516, 543, 1048, 3916: achievement, 350, 1035–1037, 1043, 1063, 1598; achievement, first-grade, 602; adult and college, 20; adult attitudes, 4232; aloud, 6151; and spelling ability, perception of, 2147; attitude, 543, 544, 1175, 1787, 1822, 1823, 2741, 2763, 2775, 4313; attitude, elementary school, 1822; beliefs, 6160; Black and White students, 2; comprehension, 14, 20, 1055, 1062, 1609, 2388, 2688, 3669; comprehension, child, 4513; comprehension, college students, 1615; confidence, 3726; consultant, 1334; difficulty, source of, 340; failures, 475; formal, 352; functional skills, 1602;